Principles and Tools for Supply Chain Management

Scott Webster

*Martin J. Whitman School of Management,
Syracuse University*

 **McGraw-Hill
Irwin**

Boston   Burr Ridge, IL   Dubuque, IA   New York   San Francisco   St. Louis
Bangkok   Bogotá   Caracas   Kuala Lumpur   Lisbon   London   Madrid   Mexico City
Milan   Montreal   New Delhi   Santiago   Seoul   Singapore   Sydney   Taipei   Toronto

The McGraw·Hill Companies

McGraw-Hill
Irwin

PRINCIPLES AND TOOLS FOR SUPPLY CHAIN MANAGEMENT

Published by McGraw-Hill/Irwin, a business unit of The McGraw-Hill Companies, Inc., 1221
Avenue of the Americas, New York, NY, 10020. Copyright © 2008 by The McGraw-Hill Companies, Inc.
All rights reserved. No part of this publication may be reproduced or distributed in any form or by any
means, or stored in a database or retrieval system, without the prior written consent of The McGraw-Hill
Companies, Inc., including, but not limited to, in any network or other electronic storage or transmission,
or broadcast for distance learning.

Some ancillaries, including electronic and print components, may not be available to customers outside the United States.

This book is printed on acid-free paper.

1 2 3 4 5 6 7 8 9 0 DOW/DOW 0 9 8 7 6

ISBN 978-0-07-282791-0
MHID 0-07-282791-2

Editorial director: *Stewart Mattson*
Executive editor: *Scott Isenberg*
Developmental editor II: *Christina A. Sanders*
Executive marketing manager: *Rhonda Seelinger*
Lead project manager: *Pat Frederickson*
Manager, New book production: *Heather D. Burbridge*
Senior designer: *Artemio Ortiz Jr.*
Photo research coordinator: *Ira C. Roberts*
Photo researcher: *Keri Johnson*
Lead media project manager: *Cathy L. Tepper*
Cover design: *Dave Seidler*
Typeface: *10/12 Times New Roman*
Compositor: *ICC Macmillan Inc.*
Printer: *R. R. Donnelley*

Library of Congress Cataloging-in-Publication Data

Webster, Scott Taggart, 1958-
    Principles and tools for supply chain management / Scott Webster.
        p. cm.
    Includes index.
    ISBN-13: 978-0-07-282791-0 (alk. paper)
    ISBN-10: 0-07-282791-2 (alk. paper)
      1. Business logistics. 2. Inventory control. 3. Production management. I. Title.

HD38.5.W436 2008
658.5--dc22   2006032471

www.mhhe.com

To Deborah, Jack, and Judy

Brief Contents

Table of Contents

Preface

Sound intuition is important in business, and especially so in the rapidly changing area of supply chain management. It helps one to size up situations quickly by identifying opportunities and assessing the impact of alternative responses. This book emphasizes principles governing human and system behavior and simple analytical tools that promote insight. The purpose is to provide a basis for sound intuition in the context of supply chain management.

AUDIENCE

The book is designed for use in an introductory course on supply chain management, and is also suitable for an introductory operations management course that is taught with a supply chain emphasis and framework. I have used the book in both my undergraduate and my graduate classes, though I have written the book with the undergraduate course in mind.

Throughout the book, there is an emphasis on principles of nature and managerial insights that stem from analysis. These principles and insights are easy to grasp for most students. At the same time, there is a relatively high degree of rigor in the analyses. Chapters that cover analytical models begin with simple analyses and introduce added complexity/realism as the chapter progresses. An instructor is free to pursue the degree of rigor in analysis that is appropriate for his/her course. And, when some analytical models are not covered, the associated managerial insights can still be covered. In summary, the content is structured so that an instructor can choose the level of analysis that fits his/her program and learning objectives. Even if analysis of some issue is not covered or required, the instructor may still require an understanding of the managerial insights that follow from analysis.

OVERVIEW OF THE ORGANIZATION

The book is divided into three major parts—foundation, principles and tools, and synthesis—that are comprised of 12 chapters and three chapter supplements. Four appendices are located at the end of the book.

Part One, "*Foundation*," which contains three chapters, introduces material that is referred to and expanded upon in subsequent chapters. Chapter 1 provides an introductory discussion of what supply chain management is about, how it relates to other functional areas, and why it is important. Chapter 2 introduces information technologies that are relevant for supply chain management. Chapter 3 introduces six drivers of supply chain performance, elements and origins of two management philosophies that are relevant for SCM, and two fundamental approaches for managing material flows.

Part Two, "*Principles and Tools*," which contains eight chapters and three chapter supplements, covers principles and tools for managing supply chains. The content is structured around the five basic supply chain activities of *buy, make, move, store,* and *sell.* These activities represent an organizing framework for Part Two. The framework reinforces how concepts in individual chapters are interrelated and support a larger system governing the movement, transformation, and usage of resources.

While there is discussion that spans multiple activities, each chapter in Part Two largely focuses on concepts in the context of a particular supply chain activity (i.e., buy, make, move, store, or sell). The compartmentalization of content facilitates comprehension, especially in the early stages of learning about a field.

Part Three, "*Synthesis*," which is a single chapter, brings together earlier content by taking a step back to review and consider the entire system. There are three main sections.

The first section covers strategic frameworks that are useful for diagnosing whether a firm's supply chain strategy makes sense for the environment in which it operates. Strategic frameworks could also be presented at the beginning of the book. I positioned this material at the end for two reasons. First, I think students develop a greater appreciation and understanding of strategic issues once operational elements are understood.[1] Second, I think a discussion of strategy complements a summary of the text . . . how ideas from individual chapters support the formulation and execution of a supply chain strategy.

The second section reviews a systematic approach (i.e., SCOR) for identifying performance improvement targets consistent with a supply chain strategy, and for redesigning supply chain processes to achieve performance improvements. The effective application of SCOR requires an understanding of how alternative designs for various supply chain processes influence performance in different environmental and market conditions, which leads to the final section.

The third section reviews how concepts from the first 11 chapters are interrelated, promote a meaningful understanding of supply chain behavior, and ultimately serve as a basis for improving supply chain performance.

Appendix 1 defines and illustrates the principles of nature that appear in the text. Principles of nature are scattered throughout the book and represent an important element of student learning. The purpose of this appendix is to provide a single point of reference for all of the principles.

Appendix 2 covers cryptology. I included this topic for three reasons. First, supply chains increasingly rely on low cost and easy-to-set-up electronic communication links between firms. In addition to the Internet, a critical but lesser-known element that makes this possible is public key encryption and digital signatures. Appendix 2 provides a basic understanding of these technologies. Second, I think it is an interesting topic that can inspire a sense of learning just for the fun of it. Finally, there is a deep result that underlies a managerial insight in Chapter 9 regarding claims by software vendors. Students who are curious to learn more about the result are referred to this appendix.

Appendix 3 lists the notation and formulas that appear in the text.

Appendix 4 contains a normal probability table and a unit normal loss table.

ACKNOWLEDGMENTS

This book, which has taken shape over a number of years, has benefited from the inputs of many individuals. I have many to thank.

- My reviewers for their comments and suggestions:

Jayanta K. Bandyopadhyay
(*Central Michigan University*)

Colin Benjamin
(*Florida A&M University*)

Prashanth N. Bharadwaj
(*Indiana University of Pennsylvania*)

Kimball Bullington
(*Middle Tennessee State University*)

Frank L. Chelko
(*Pennsylvania State University*)

Zhi-Long Chen
(*University of Maryland*)

Eduardo Davila
(*Arizona State University–Tempe*)

Frank Davis
(*University of Tennessee*)

Barbara S. Downey
(*University of Missouri–Columbia*)

Abe Feinberg
(*California State University–Northridge*)

Bruce Fischer
(*Elmhurst College*)

Teresa Friel
(*Butler University*)

---

[1] Similar to why strategies in chess are better understood and appreciated after playing the game for awhile.

Michael Godfrey
(*University of Wisconsin–Oshkosh*)

Johnny C. Ho
(*Columbus State University*)

Frank Hogan
(*University of North Carolina–Charlotte*)

Tony Inman
(*Louisiana Tech University*)

Apurva Jain
(*University of Washington*)

Jonathan Jelen
(*Baruch College*)

Jim Keyes
(*University of Wisconsin–Stout*)

Seung-Lae Kim
(*Drexel University*)

Orsay Kucukemiroglu
(*Penn State University–York*)

Kenneth Lawrence
(*NJIT*)

Ronald Meier
(*Illinois State University*)

Ahmet Ozkul
(*SUNY Oneonta*)

Carl Poch
(*Northern Illinois University*)

William Presutti Jr.
(*Duquesne University*)

Pedro Reyes
(*Baylor University*)

Kaushik Sengupta
(*Hofstra University*)

Andrew M. Stapleton
(*University of Wisconsin–La Crosse*)

Robert Vokurka
(*Texas A&M University–Corpus Christi*).

- My editors Scott Isenberg and Christina Sanders for their encouragement and guidance, and Pat Frederizkson for her help as project manager.
- My students at Queens University, Syracuse University, and Zaragoza Logistics Center for their suggestions and corrections.
- My colleagues in industry, especially Karen Wells (Connected Knowledge Solutions) for her careful reading and comments. I also benefited from the perspectives and experience of Thomas Arenberg (Accenture), Jeff Reinke (American Seating), and Brian Smith (Harley Davidson). Simon Foster (Deloitte Consulting LLP) contributed to Chapter 2 with a segment on large-scale system implementation. Peter Chang (Neversoft) helped me with a case exercise at the end of Chapter 9. Herbert Heinzel (Business Process Training) provided a figure in Chapter 11.
- My colleagues in academia. Rajan Suri (University of Wisconsin–Madison) and Ananth Krishnamurthy (Rensselaer Polytechnic Institute) helped to shape the material on POLCA in Chapter 9 through their comments, figures, and photographs. Andrew M. Stapleton (University of Wisconsin–La Crosse) provided specific suggestions for additional content and six end-of-chapter exercises as well as made contributions to the test bank. Paul Bobrowski (Auburn University), Linus Schrage (University of Chicago), and Charles Wang (SUNY–Buffalo) also contributed exercises, and Jan Van Mieghem (Northwestern University) contributed a case. Prashant Yadav (Zaragoza Logistics Center) read and commented on a draft of Chapter 10. Barbara S. Downey (University of Missouri–Columbia) checked the entire manuscript and solutions manual for accuracy. My colleagues Fred Easton, Gary LaPoint, Pat Penfield, Frances Tucker, and Paul Zinszer at Syracuse University provided helpful comments, and the Robert H. Brethen Operations Management Institute at Syracuse provided financial support. Gary LaPoint deserves special thanks for his extensive feedback and for his insights into the transportation function.

Finally, and most importantly, I thank Deborah for her patience, love, and support.

Scott Webster

Foundation

Chapter **One**

Introduction: Operations and Supply Chain Management

Chapter Outline

1. A Few Words on Terminology
2. Motivation
3. Purpose of This Book
4. Principles and Tools as a Theme
5. Concluding Comments
6. Exercises

Chapter Keys

1. What is operations management?
2. What is a supply chain?
3. What is supply chain management?
4. Why is supply chain management important?

Business is simple . . . you've got to sell the stuff, make the stuff, and collect the money. Naturally, there is a lot involved in these basic business activities, and each is supported by a well-developed discipline. But, when phrased in this way, it helps reinforce the idea that these activities are closely linked and should not be viewed in isolation. This is an idea that is central to supply chain management (SCM).

This book provides an introduction to the field of supply chain management from an operations perspective (shaded area in Figure 1.1). This means that coverage of concepts and tools will draw largely from the discipline of operations management (OM).

In order to set the stage, we will begin in the next section by briefly outlining the scope of SCM and its relationship to other fields of study. Section 2 reviews why SCM is important. The remaining sections of this chapter explain the purpose and organization of the book. In summary, this introductory chapter focuses on what, why, and how . . . what the book is about, why the topic is important, and how the topic is presented.

FIGURE 1.1

SCM spans the overlapping disciplines of marketing, operations, and finance. The shading signifies the operations perspective of SCM that is presented in this book.

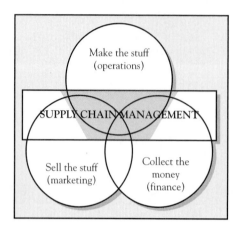

1. A FEW WORDS ON TERMINOLOGY

Broadly stated, **operations management deals with the creation and delivery of goods and/or services,** or "making the stuff." The function involves those on the front line interacting with customers all the way up to the corporate officer level. All organizations deal with operations issues . . . whether we're talking about sports franchises, fraternities/sororities, religious organizations, universities, households, or even organizations within a company. As an area of study, OM is diverse and dynamic.

A **supply chain is two or more parties linked by a flow of resources—typically material, information, and money**—and frequently global in scope (see Figure 1.2).[1] The term *parties* in the definition does not necessarily refer to different firms. It may be appropriate to examine internal or internal/external supply chains where some parties are departments or divisions within a firm.

From the definition of a supply chain, it follows that supply chain management deals with managing flows of resources among departments within a firm, and among independent enterprises. More specifically, **SCM involves the management of activities surrounding the flow of raw materials to the finished product or service enjoyed by end customers, and back, in the case of recycling or returns.** One way to think about activities surrounding flows of resources is in terms of **five basic categories: buy, make, move, store, and sell** (see Figure 1.3). We'll look at each one of these activities in some detail in Part Two of this text.

SCM is related to logistics management, a term with which you may be more familiar and a term that has been around for a long time. Its origins as a defined area of responsibility can be traced to the late 17th century and the creation of the Gran Mareshal de Logis, an officer in the French army charged with providing lodging and support for troops in the field.

There is debate on exactly how SCM and logistics management differ. In 1974 Bowersox (1974, p. 1) defined logistics management as

> the process of managing all activities required to strategically move raw materials, parts, and finished inventory from vendors, between enterprise facilities, and to customers.

---

[1] The essence of this definition was originally proposed in Tsay, Nahmias, and Agrawal (1999).

FIGURE 1.2   An Illustration of a Supply Chain

Material flows are solid lines and information flows are dotted lines. Money flows are generally in the reverse direction of material flows.

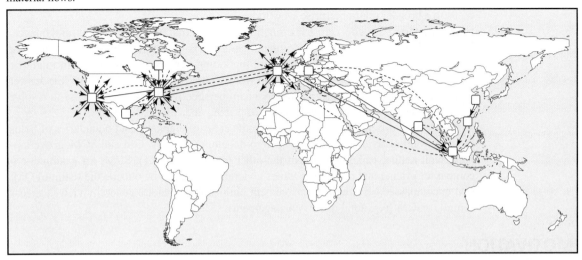

The term *supply chain management* first appeared in a 1982 *Financial Times* article about an approach being developed by Keith Oliver and other consultants at Booz Allen Hamilton (Laseter and Oliver 2003). A few years later, Houlihan (1985), also with Booz-Allen & Hamilton, wrote an article in the *International Journal of Physical Distribution & Inventory Management* that elaborated on SCM. The article draws attention to the changing role of the logistics manager, and the need for a perspective that recognizes the strategic importance of logistics and an integrated systemwide outlook when improving logistics processes. This view is reflected in the Council of Supply Chain Management Professionals' definitions of logistics and supply chain management today (see www.cscmp.org):

> Logistics management is that part of the supply chain management that plans, implements, and controls the efficient, effective forward and reverse flow and storage of goods, services, and related information between the point of origin and the point of consumption in order to meet customers' requirements. Supply Chain Management encompasses the planning and management of all activities involved in sourcing and procurement, conversion, and all Logistics Management activities. Importantly, it also includes coordination and collaboration with channel partners, which can be suppliers, intermediaries, third-party service providers, and customers. In essence, Supply Chain Management integrates supply and demand management within and across companies.

FIGURE 1.3   Major Activities in a Supply Chain

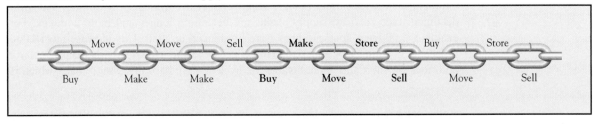

In this book we will not make a distinction between SCM and logistics management. Writings on logistics management have long stressed the importance of a strategic total systems perspective, though there has been a shift of emphasis from a single-enterprise focus to a broader multienterprise view today.

In summary, SCM cuts across the functional areas of marketing, operations, and finance. It is not wholly included in any one functional area. For example, consider an imbalance between supply and demand. From a pure marketing perspective, this problem might be resolved through a change in pricing, and from a pure operations perspective, the answer may be to adjust capacity. From a supply chain perspective, it may make sense to resolve the imbalance through some combination of pricing and capacity changes.

How is OM different from SCM? While the areas of emphasis and boundaries of fields of study continually evolve and are open to debate, many view OM and SCM as overlapping, with neither being a subset of the other (as in Figure 1.1). SCM, for example, encompasses pricing and promotion issues generally viewed to be outside the realm of OM. OM encompasses overarching management philosophies that are generally viewed as less central to SCM (e.g., total quality management).

2. MOTIVATION

There are four reasons why SCM is important.

- **Dollars.** The value of inventory averages around 14 percent of gross domestic product (GDP) and the annual transportation and warehousing expense averages around 9 percent of GDP in the United States (Wilson 2005). Year 2004 U.S. GDP, for example, was almost $12 trillion, which puts the dollar value of U.S. inventory in nearly the same league as the U.S. federal budget. A June 1999 Benchmarking Partners report finds that supply chain management expenses (e.g., inventory holding, transportation, order management, supply chain financing, related information technology) average 25 percent of U.S. corporate budgets.

- **Leverage.** Just as force is amplified by a lever, small supply chain improvements get amplified in measures of interest to top management, for example, profit, stock price, and market share. First, supply chain cost reductions go directly to the bottom line. This is part of what underlies a saying among logisticians that a $12 increase in sales has the same impact on profit as a $1 savings in the supply chain.[2] Second, increased supply chain efficiency is amplified in return on assets (ROA), an influential measure on stock price. For example, if net margin is 5 percent of sales, then a change that reduces assets by 10 percent while generating a 4 percent cost savings will nearly double ROA. There is also evidence that investors are generally sensitive to supply chain problems. Researchers found that stock price drops by nearly 11 percent when a company announces a supply chain problem such as production or shipment delays (Hendricks and Singhal 2003). Third, supply chain improvements have a direct effect on customer perceptions (e.g., improved availability, timely delivery), and thus market share.

- **Challenge.** Product variety is increasing, product life cycles are shrinking, and, with declining trade barriers, supply chains are becoming longer and more complex. For example, 2,000 new food products were introduced in 1980. This increased to 18,000 in 1991, 25,000 in 1997, and 31,000 in 2000. The fashion apparel market is particularly notorious for short and unpredictable life cycles. "'We have this hungry baby which is

---

[2] The other part being that one-twelfth is a reasonable benchmark for average margin before taxes.

the apparel market, and it's constantly screaming for the next new thing,' says Davies-Keller, . . . 'All this baby says is, we want the next best thing! We want innovation!'" (Tilin 2001).

- **Opportunity.** Dollars, leverage, and increasing challenges don't mean much if most supply chains are already well tuned with little opportunity for gains. But this is far from the case. Evidence for opportunity can be seen in two firms that have achieved success through innovative supply chain management: Wal-Mart and Dell.

The Wal-Mart Story

Wal-Mart started with one store in 1962. In 1979 the company set a record for the least amount of time from founding to over $1 billion in sales. In 1990, Wal-Mart became the number one retailer in the world (see www.wal-mart.com → Our Company → The Wal-Mart Story → Timeline for Wal-Mart historical data), and in 2001, Wal-Mart's revenues at $220 billion were higher than at any other company in the world (*Fortune* 2002a, 2002b). The

numbers are impressive but do not fully express the magnitude of Wal-Mart's achievements. Wal-Mart's innovative use of flawless logistics was identified among a select few highlights of 20th-century business (Colvin 1999). Paul Romer, an economist at Stanford University, views Wal-Mart's approach to retail as a more significant innovation than even the transistor (Perkins and Perkins 1999).

What Innovations Account for Wal-Mart's Success?

The answer to this question is a book in itself, and, in fact, we will discuss Wal-Mart and their business practices in subsequent chapters. However, one major theme is *innovative information sharing* across the supply chain.

Wal-Mart essentially started out as a logistics company as a result of Sam Walton's views on logistics shaped by the Berlin Airlift of 1949. In 1985, he invested $700 million in a satellite system so that Wal-Mart could communicate between their stores, distribution centers, home office, and suppliers. The result was improved forecasting, more reliable and faster order processing, and lower inventories at Wal-Mart warehouses (Young 2002).[3] Supply chain costs decreased by about 15 to 20 percent, which in turn led to lower pricing and a significant improvement in the U.S. standard of living (Perkins and Perkins 1999). In a sense, the innovation is akin to getting the dispersed supply chains of Wal-Mart stores, warehouses, and suppliers to behave almost as a single firm with near real-time information on market conditions.

What about Dell?

Dell Inc. was founded in 1984 and is now the global market share leader in the PC industry. The company ranked first in terms of stock price appreciation over the most recent decade;

---

[3] It is interesting that about 50 years after Sam Walton was originally inspired by military logistics, the U.S. Marine Corps was studying Wal-Mart to improve their supply chains (Keenan 2001).

if you invested about $1,200 in Dell stock in January 1990 and sold in December 1999, you would have walked away with over $1 million . . . almost enough to pay for college.

What Innovations Account for Dell's Success?

As with Wal-Mart, there is much to this question, and we will examine Dell's innovative business practices throughout the text. For now we will highlight one key innovation that can be summed up as *trimming the chain*. For Dell, there are no distributors and there are no retailers. These elements, which have been common in PC supply chains, don't exist. Dell PCs are built to order and shipped directly to the end consumer. This innovation goes back to the company's origins when Michael Dell built and sold PCs direct to the consumer from his University of Texas dorm room. Since the year 2000, Dell has averaged more than $50 million per day in sales from its Internet site, where consumers configure a PC to order. (see www.dell.com → About Dell → Company Facts → Dell History for Dell historical data).

Building to order requires rapid response times, and this has been a point of emphasis at Dell. Flows of materials, information, and money move at a fast pace. A PC is typically assembled to specifications, loaded with software, tested, and boxed for shipment within two hours of order receipt (Stewart 1999). This is faster than most companies pick a finished product from a rack in a warehouse, and it helps explain why Dell receives money for the products it sells about 12 days before it pays for the materials (Byrne 2000).

Wal-Mart and Dell use innovative supply chain management as a strategic weapon. In part because of the successes of companies like Wal-Mart and Dell, and in part because of advancing information technology, executives are increasingly viewing SCM as a significant opportunity area (*Harvard Business Review* 2004). A study by Deloitte Consulting found that 91 percent of North American manufacturers rank supply chain management as critical or very important. Only 2 percent rank their supply chains as world class and almost 75 percent rate them as average or below average (*APICS—The Performance Advantage* 1999). And there is evidence of gains. Economists have noted the increasing **focus on supply chains as a reason behind decreasing prices** near the end of the 20th century and that this new model of **retailer–supplier coordination will determine which companies will succeed in the 21st century** (Nelson and Zimmerman 2000).

The Role of the Internet

In 1962, Peter Drucker identified logistics, and distribution in particular, as the last frontier in business—the area where managerial results of great magnitude can still be achieved (Drucker 1962). While the intervening years have witnessed great strides, supply chain management is again an area where managerial results of great magnitude can be achieved. Recall that supply chain management deals with flows of resources within and between companies that are part of supply chains that often span the globe. As a consequence, supply chain performance is particularly sensitive to advances that enhance the accurate and rapid communication and interpretation of data. In short, revolutionary advances in Internet and related technologies are creating revolutionary opportunities for supply chain improvement.

Whirlpool, for example, has implemented an integrated Internet-based supplier management system. Suppliers are electronically linked to factories in order to streamline purchasing and inbound material flows, as well as facilitating auctions for commodities (Holstein 2001). The auto industry is pursuing similar tactics. By using Internet technologies to reduce bureaucracy and streamline logistics, auto companies are projecting cost savings at a level equal to about 25 percent of the retail price of a car (Kerwin, Stepanek, and Welch 2000). Cisco Systems, a leading provider of networking equipment and services, uses Internet technologies to link systems and exchange information throughout its entire supply chain from suppliers to customers (Fonstad 2000). John Chambers, the CEO of Cisco Systems, argues that **highly connected supply chains will be the norm in the future, and that those who understand their significance will have a huge competitive advantage** (Byrne 2000). In summary, SCM is an area of growth and opportunity, and an area undergoing rapid change due to information technology advances.[4]

3. PURPOSE OF THIS BOOK

If we step back and consider the bigger picture for a moment, one of the most meaningful roles of management is to identify opportunities and direction for change. It is true that one can watch and imitate the innovations of others, and that this can sometimes be very effective. One might even be tempted to exclusively pursue a follower strategy for SCM, especially considering that processes supporting the creation and delivery of products and services are complex with many factors interacting in subtle ways to influence performance.

On the other hand, the behaviors of many processes tend to conform to principles of operation that, once understood, become a basis for sound management intuition. Why is this important? The answer is that intuition is a wellspring of innovation. It allows a manager to make quick and educated decisions in response to changing business conditions—identifying problems before they become disasters, identifying opportunities that others do not see, and rapidly assessing the impact of alternative responses.

The purpose of this book is to provide a basis for sound management intuition in the context of supply chain management. The book stresses principles of nature that govern human and system behavior and analytical tools that favor insight over answers to specific questions. By the time you have mastered the material, you will understand (1) what SCM is about and why it is important, (2) relevant existing and emerging information technologies, and (3) the processes and trade-offs associated with managing flows of resources. But, most important, you will understand how your knowledge of principles of nature and your skills with analysis will help you develop innovative solutions to supply chain problems and opportunities.

4. PRINCIPLES AND TOOLS AS A THEME

The great thing about principles of nature is, by definition, they're fundamental. They help us understand phenomena in the world around us. From a practical standpoint, this means they can be applied in lots of creative ways. Take the principle of a lever for instance. An amazing number of mechanical devices take advantage of this principle in all sorts of ingenious ways (e.g., tweezers, hammer, scale, bicycle, crane, and on and on).[5] This book will describe and illustrate 18 principles of nature that are relevant for supply chain management, and, more generally, life (see Table 1.1). Some of these principles appear in multiple chapters, and in multiple sections of a single chapter; in these cases, you'll see a single fundamental idea being applied in different ways in different settings. Appendix 1 contains definitions and examples of all of the principles, and you will find it useful to refer to this from time to time.

---

[4] Read *The World Is Flat* by Thomas Friedman (2006) for a historical perspective on how information technology and supply chain management are behind fundamental changes in the world economy and politics.

[5] At an even more fundamental level, the principle of a lever, as well as the principle of the inclined plane (the basis for screws and plows), is based on the elementary principle of nature that work = force × distance.

TABLE 1.1 18 Principles of Nature That Appear throughout the Text

Appendix 1 contains definitions, implications, and examples of all of the principles of nature.

1. Benford's Law	7. Hockey Stick Effect	13. Pareto Phenomenon
2. Bullwhip Effect	8. It's Hard to Play Catch-Up Ball	14. Recency Effect
3. Central Limit Theorem	9. Khintchine's Limit Theorem	15. Satisfaction = Perception − Expectation
4. Curse of Utilization	10. Law of Large Numbers	16. Time Distortion
5. Curse of Variability	11. Little's Law	17. Trumpet of Doom
6. Fat Head Effect	12. Obligation to Reciprocate	18. Winner's Curse

As with the 18 principles of nature, the process of developing and interpreting simple analytical models is a theme of the text. The results of the process are analytical tools and enhanced skills that can lead to a deeper understanding of the issue at hand. Some of the underlying ideas and insights from our analysis will appear in multiple applications and in multiple chapters.

5. CONCLUDING COMMENTS

This book is organized into three parts: foundation, principles and tools, and synthesis. Part One provides an introduction to basic themes, terms, and concepts that appear throughout the text, and includes two other chapters in addition to this chapter. Chapter 2 outlines information systems and technologies most relevant to supply chain management, and the role of supply chain management in e-commerce. Chapter 3 introduces four core concepts relevant for managing flows of resources in supply chains. These concepts are revisited in subsequent chapters.

Part Two, the heart of the text with eight chapters and three chapter supplements, examines topics surrounding the five basic supply chain activities of buy, make, move, store, and sell. We'll examine the challenges of these activities and we'll study the relevant principles and tools. In most cases, we'll take a building-block approach where we isolate critical factors associated with a particular issue, work through analysis that helps us understand how performance is affected by these factors, and gradually consider the impact of various complications. Throughout this process, we'll emphasize the general insights that come out of the analysis, rather than a specific answer to a specific question. Practice in applying these steps will help you when analyzing new situations that have not previously been considered.

Part Three is a concluding chapter that draws on what you have learned in Parts One and Two. The chapter introduces two strategic frameworks useful for identifying characteristics of a supply chain that make sense for a given product/service and market environment, and then summarizes how knowledge of Parts One and Two is relevant for devising tactics for attaining these characteristics. This summary, which recaps the main ideas in the text, appears in Section 3 of Chapter 12. Periodically reading this section as you work through chapters in Part Two may be useful for developing a deeper understanding of how principles and insights appearing in individual chapters are interrelated and applicable over a wide range of different settings.

Each chapter begins with a list of important questions, or chapter keys. Carefully read and think about these questions. Doing so will help trigger your attention to the most important ideas as you are reading. Also, as you may have noticed in this chapter, text in **bold** is directly related to the chapter keys. After reading a chapter, it is a good idea to test your understanding of the main points by rereading these questions.

Each chapter in Part Two concludes with a list of managerial insights. These insights generally follow from principles of nature and analysis presented in the chapter. This is an important section, and a second area where you should focus your attention. Move beyond memorization to understanding the basis for each insight, which, of course, is key to deepening your intuition.

6. EXERCISES

1. Write a brief answer to each of the chapter keys in your own words. After writing down your answers, review the chapter with a focus on the content in bold to check and clarify your interpretations.

2. Section 2 contained a numerical example illustrating the impact of supply chain improvements on return on assets (ROA), a measure of interest to top management. In the example, the net margin prior to improvements is 5 percent of sales. After implementing supply chain changes, assets decrease by 10 percent and cost decreases by 4 percent. Show how these changes will nearly double ROA. *Hints*: Net margin = Pretax profit = Sales − Cost, and ROA is the ratio of pretax profit to assets.

3. Look at a product that you own and try to imagine the supply chain that eventually got this product to you. Where was it made according to the label, what raw materials went into it, how many different firms may have taken a part, and how many countries were involved? How many days or years may have elapsed between the creation of the raw materials and delivery to you? As you read through the book, you may find it useful to periodically think back to this product and its imagined supply chain, and consider how the ideas being presented might apply.

4. Select an industry or group of firms that are part of a supply chain. Do research (e.g., Internet, annual reports, business press, etc.) to identify how supply chain management practices have changed at these organizations in recent years, and characterize the impact of these changes on firm performance and the market.

Chapter **Two**

Information Technology: ERP Systems, SCA Systems, and E-Commerce

Chapter Outline

1. Enterprise Resource Planning Systems
2. Supply Chain Analytics Systems
3. Caveats
4. How Are ERP and SCA Systems Related to E-Commerce?
5. Emerging Information Technologies and Their Impact on SCM
6. Concluding Comments
7. Exercises

Chapter Keys

1. What do ERP systems do, are these systems easy to implement, and why?
2. What do SCA systems do, are these systems easy to implement, and why?
3. What are the three categories of SCA systems, and what do they involve?
4. What is e-commerce, and what is the difference between e-commerce in its simplest form and e-commerce at a deep level (a.k.a. e-business)?
5. What is the role of ERP/SCA systems in e-commerce, and why?
6. What are the emerging information technologies that affect SCM?

Information technology is advancing . . . and it's creating opportunities for improvement, as well as a minefield of risks. The most important classes of information systems that directly affect supply chain management are (1) enterprise resource planning systems and (2) supply chain analytics systems. As we will see, these systems also play an important role in e-commerce.

Part Two of this book will consider each of the basic supply chain activities—buy, make, move, store, and sell—in detail. Information technology (IT) pertinent to each activity will be discussed. However, prior to Part Two, it is useful to have a broad sense of relevant IT as it relates to one or more of these basic activities. The goal of this chapter is to provide this sense. The content is designed to serve as a foundation that will be referred to and amplified in subsequent chapters.

The chapter is divided into six sections. The first two sections cover enterprise resource planning systems and supply chain analytics systems. We'll focus on the purpose and capabilities of each class of software. Section 3 outlines some of the risks and challenges associated with large system implementation. Section 4 focuses on e-commerce, and, in particular, the role of enterprise resource planning and supply chain analytics systems in buying and selling over the Internet.

Information technologies are rapidly developing and are playing an increasingly dominant role in SCM. Section 5 offers a glimpse into emerging technologies that are most relevant for SCM. Section 6 concludes the chapter by bringing together the main points from earlier sections to explain why the future of IT and SCM should be interesting indeed.

1. ENTERPRISE RESOURCE PLANNING SYSTEMS

Enterprise resource planning (ERP) systems are used to plan, control, and record the day-to-day transactions of running a business and to provide real-time access to information in a consistent manner throughout the organization. This definition is a concise expression of a simple and powerful idea that can be traced back to the early 1970s when five IBM engineers decided to act on an observation. They observed that there are systems that support financial transactions and there are systems that support

material transactions, but they don't tend to communicate very well. This is troublesome because material transactions affect financial transactions and vice versa. They proposed to develop a system for accessing and updating data on company resources through a single enterprisewide database. IBM declined the proposal, so in 1972 the employees founded their own company and developed a product they called System-analyse und Programmentwicklung,[1] or SAP for short. The current flagship product is mySAP ERP, and the company they founded—SAP AG—is the third-largest software provider in the world (www.sap.com, June 2006).

Figure 2.1 presents a high-level view of ERP systems. The vertical axis represents time, ranging from the current period to many periods into the future. The horizontal axis lists resources. The area below the dotted line in Figure 2.1 corresponds to transactions processing, or what is more formally known as *online transaction processing* (OLTP). The area above the dotted line corresponds to analysis in support of planning, which is more formally known as *online analytical processing* (OLAP).

ERP systems support the processing of all types of resource transactions (e.g., money, material, labor, equipment, real estate). Money and material resources are listed in

---

[1] German for "Systems Analysis and Program Development."

FIGURE 2.1

ERP systems initially focused on enterprisewide transaction processing, though analysis and planning capabilities are continuing to improve. Today these capabilities extend beyond the four walls of a company to include suppliers and customers, providing a complete view of source-of-demand through source-of-supply.

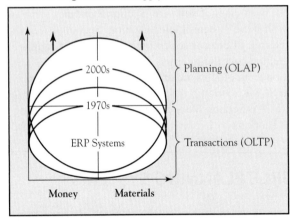

Figure 2.1 in order to simplify the diagram and because these resources are the most dynamic, and consequently receive the most attention. While early generations of ERP systems focused more on transaction processing, the arrows in Figure 2.1 illustrate that planning and analysis capabilities of these systems are continuing to improve.

Toward a Deeper Understanding of ERP

There is obviously quite a lot to a system that is used to **plan, control, and record the day-to-day transactions of running a business.** To help make ERP systems more concrete, begin by thinking about your personal ERP system. The enterprise defined by your life is (hopefully) manageable enough that you essentially have a fairly complete and accurate ERP system running between your ears. You have a good understanding of quantities and locations of your resources, how these levels and locations have been changing over time, and changes you expect in the near future (e.g., payday on Friday and rent due on Saturday). You also have a good understanding of upcoming commitments and you have tentative plans for honoring these commitments (e.g., reserve Saturday morning to complete an assignment due on Monday).

When the enterprise is a firm, the system is more complex and runs on a computer, but the spirit is not too different from your personal ERP system. The database stores past, present, and projected future levels and locations of resources such as money, material, labor, equipment, and real estate. The locations of financial resources (and obligations), for example, are defined by the firm's chart of accounts, and each journal entry transaction posts a change that is recorded in the general ledger. Similarly, future material obligations are recorded (e.g., customer orders added to the system), and location-specific quantities of materials are updated as materials are received, transformed, moved, and shipped.

A record of resource levels and locations is not enough for planning and control. In addition to resource data, an ERP database also contains prescriptions that specify alternative ways resources are used to create products and services. The combination of available resources with detailed descriptions of how resources are used to make money is, in short, a digital representation of the firm; these data are the raw materials for software modules that support planning, control, and early identification of problems and opportunities (see Figure 2.2).

FIGURE 2.2

The ERP database surrounded by example activities supported by ERP and supply chain analytics (SCA) software modules. ERP modules are concentrated more on transactions and control whereas SCA applications (discussed in Section 2) deal more with analysis and alerts.

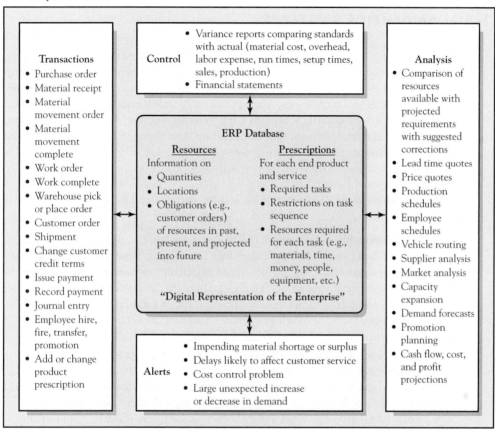

Transactions
- Purchase order
- Material receipt
- Material movement order
- Material movement complete
- Work order
- Work complete
- Warehouse pick or place order
- Customer order
- Shipment
- Change customer credit terms
- Issue payment
- Record payment
- Journal entry
- Employee hire, fire, transfer, promotion
- Add or change product prescription

Control
- Variance reports comparing standards with actual (material cost, overhead, labor expense, run times, setup times, sales, production)
- Financial statements

ERP Database

Resources
Information on
- Quantities
- Locations
- Obligations (e.g., customer orders) of resources in past, present, and projected into future

Prescriptions
For each end product and service
- Required tasks
- Restrictions on task sequence
- Resources required for each task (e.g., materials, time, money, people, equipment, etc.)

"Digital Representation of the Enterprise"

Alerts
- Impending material shortage or surplus
- Delays likely to affect customer service
- Cost control problem
- Large unexpected increase or decrease in demand

Analysis
- Comparison of resources available with projected requirements with suggested corrections
- Lead time quotes
- Price quotes
- Production schedules
- Employee schedules
- Vehicle routing
- Supplier analysis
- Market analysis
- Capacity expansion
- Demand forecasts
- Promotion planning
- Cash flow, cost, and profit projections

The following example illustrates **what ERP systems can do:**

1. A sales rep from International Sneaker Co. takes an order for 1,000 shoes from a Brazilian retailer. From her portable PC, she taps into the R/3 sales module back at headquarters, which checks the price, including any discounts the retailer is eligible for, and looks up the retailer's credit history.

2. Simultaneously, R/3's inventory software checks the stock situation & notifies the sales rep that half the order can be filled immediately from a Brazilian warehouse. The other sneakers will be delivered in 5 days direct from ISC's factory in Taiwan.

3. R/3's manufacturing software schedules the production of the sneakers at the Taiwan factory, meanwhile alerting ISC's warehouse manager in Brazil to ship the 500 purple tennis shoes to the retailer. An invoice gets printed up—in Portuguese.

4. That's when R/3's HR module identifies a shortage of workers to handle the order & alerts the personnel manager of the need for temporary workers.

5. R/3's materials planning module notifies the purchasing manager that it's time to reorder purple dye, rubber, and shoelaces.

6. The customer logs on to ISC's R/3 system through the Internet & sees that 250 of the 500 shoes coming from Taiwan have been made & dyed. He also sees there are 500 orange tennis shoes in stock & places a follow-up order on the Net.

7. On the basis of data from R/3's forecasting & financial modules, the CEO sees that colored sneakers are not only in hot demand but are also highly profitable. He decides to add a line of fluorescent footwear.[2]

2. SUPPLY CHAIN ANALYTICS SYSTEMS

ERP systems have been historically weak in planning functionality or, more specifically, in analysis and decision support tools for planning and coordinating flows through supply chains. Consequently, specialized supply chain analytics (SCA) systems developed by vendors such as i2 Technologies, Manugistics, and Siebel have filled this void.[3] **SCA systems, which are frequently linked to ERP systems, support the detailed planning and control of material, money, and information flow through supply chains**. These systems help managers analyze and interpret massive amounts of ever-changing data. The focus of SCA systems is on decision support activities, which are concentrated in the analysis and alerts boxes in Figure 2.2.

There are three main categories of SCA software (Figure 2.3 illustrates the scope of these categories):

Supplier relationship management (SRM) software helps analyze and manage the "buy" side of the business. Example questions for analysis: How have suppliers been performing in terms of pricing, quality, speed of delivery, on-time delivery, and ability to respond to emergency requests? Which suppliers are candidates for long-term contracts, or for partnering on joint improvement efforts? What products and services are candidates to outsource, or to bring in house? Are there opportunities to consolidate purchasing across divisions, or to reduce the supplier base?

Supply-demand management (SDM)[4] software helps analyze and manage the "make, move, and store" side of the business. Example questions for analysis: What, where, when, and how much should be ordered, produced, and shipped? How should customer orders be loaded onto a truck, and how should trucks be routed? When can an order be delivered? What are the forecasts for future material requirements, and how accurate are these forecasts? When and how should capacity and inventory levels be added or reduced? What is the best response to a late delivery, machine breakdown, or emergency customer order? This last question relates to sense-and-response capabilities, an area that will likely grow in importance as supply chains become leaner. Dell Inc., for example, is known for its efficient supply chain and consequently, with little slack in the system, places a high priority on early detection and resolution of supply chain problems. Immediately after the September 11 disaster, for example, Dell took advantage of its Web-enabled supply chain systems to determine where supplies might be disrupted. It increased overseas production to cover anticipated shortages, while, simultaneously, salespeople checked the Net for configurations that could be assembled quickly and steered customers accordingly (Rocks et al. 2001).

---

[2] Excerpt with permission from G. Edmondson and S. Baker, "Silicon Valley on the Rhine," *BusinessWeek*, November 3, 1997, pp. 162–167.

[3] ERP vendors have since invested heavily in the development of their own planning and analysis capabilities.

[4] Unlike SRM and CRM, there is not a widely accepted term for the category of software dealing with issues between SRM and CRM (e.g., make, move, and store). The acronym SCM has been used in industry, though SDM is used here to reinforce that all three categories of software support analysis of supply chains.

FIGURE 2.3

Three categories of supply chain analytics software.

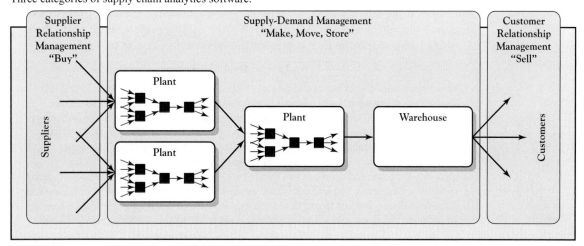

Customer relationship management (CRM) software helps analyze and manage the "sell" side of the business. Example questions for analysis: What do I know about the customer currently on the phone (e.g., lifestyle, past purchases, and other interactions with my company) and are there products and services that might complement or replace the current order (e.g., opportunities for cross-selling and up-selling)? How should product be priced, and how should pricing be changed during periods of shortages or surpluses in supply? Can markets be segmented to expose new product and service opportunities, and to improve the response to targeted promotions? Who are my least and most profitable customers, and which customers have the highest potential to be among the most profitable in the future? Should some channels be expanded or cut back? How have past promotions and campaigns performed, and what lessons from these experiences can be used to improve effectiveness in the future?

Here is an example that illustrates **SCA system capabilities and impact**:

The computer giant's old supply-chain system was relatively inefficient because planning was done manually, with workers breaking down bills of materials into individual orders. IBM had to buy a lot more parts to make sure it could fulfill these orders on time. "Now, i2 allows IBM to automatically plan and notify suppliers when parts need to be delivered to IBM factories," says i2's Wadhwani. The result: IBM's inventory costs have been shaved by 25% to 35%.[5]

3. CAVEATS

ERP and SCA system implementations are risky; they tend to be expensive and affect many people in an organization. The **difficulty of implementing change generally increases exponentially with the number of people affected by the change**. ERP systems can affect the entire organization. **SCA systems tend to be less risky and easier to implement than ERP systems because they affect fewer people in the organization.**

[5] Excerpt with permission from S. E. Ante, "The Second Coming of Software," *Businessweek*, June 19, 2000, pp. 88–90.

It is worth emphasizing that IT is an enabler—when effectively deployed, it enables people to work smarter and more effectively. As illustrated in the following narrative, firms sometimes make the mistake of viewing IT as a solution unto itself with insufficient attention to the human element. More generally, the narrative offers insights into the risks associated with large-scale ERP implementations, as well as keys to success.[6]

Seven Lessons from Experience[7]

I have often started working on a large scale ERP implementation project only to find that some of the decisions taken in advance have hamstrung the project and even planted the seed of its failure. These projects are difficult, not so much because of the newer technology, but because of the impact of the project on the people involved—particularly the end users. Whenever people's jobs change, they instinctively resist. That's why, if you can manage the impact of change on people, the rest is, by comparison, easy. Many corporations have struggled with the scope and approach to ERP projects, only to realize later their mistakes—many of which are common. You will see in this set of example problems that the people issues are a common thread. I would like to have been a fly on the wall of the early meetings where the sub-optimal decisions were made, except that nobody would hear the fly's advice, of course.

1. IT Manager: "We know we have to implement ERP. Let's avoid the analysis to create a business case for implementation." *Fly—but you've also eliminated the opportunity for the business to "buy in" to the project by thinking about competitive advantage and to define in advance what would make it a success for them. Unfulfilled expectations might later lead to disappointment with the results, which, if you think about it, is a pretty good definition of failure.*

   Example: At a large U.S. retailer, the IT department needed to replace systems and wanted to adopt SAP. However, the business leadership was not convinced and did not support it. The project failed to get off the ground because, apart from the CFO, the business did not understand what benefits they could get from the project and were not prepared to invest in resolving the difficulties.

   Recommendation: Take the time to define why you are doing the project and get the business to define the benefits that could result. Does your company suffer from "death from 1,000 initiatives syndrome"? Hold workshops to establish which of the existing initiatives could be boosted, transformed, enabled or cancelled as a result of the ERP project.

2. Supply Chain Manager: "We don't have a project leader, and we don't want to bother the CEO with a staffing issue. Let's ask Joe to lead it part time. He's not doing much since he was ejected from the desktop procurement project." *Fly—but without good leadership that can make things happen, your investment is as good as wasted. These projects are tough. They require persistence, leadership and management muscle to make them succeed.*

   Example: In one food company, one plant manager insisted on being the exception to every standard the ERP project tried to enforce on the grounds that his business was different. He was not being obstructive; he naturally believed he was acting in the best interests of his team, and there was no senior leader who could bring him into line. Result: the project foundered, standards were compromised, and the objective of providing a single transaction support system across the whole business was endangered.

---

[6] The management of large-scale projects is a course in itself. See, for example, Fichman and Moses (1999), Randolph and Posner (1992), and Williams (1996) if you are interested in learning more about this topic. Also, see Slone (2004) for a first-person account of a major IT-based supply chain improvement initiative.

[7] This narrative by Simon Foster draws on his 16 years' experience as a consultant and partner at PricewaterhouseCoopers and IBM Business Consulting Services. During this time, he led nine global ERP system implementations in the pharmaceutical and consumer products industries.

Recommendation: Dedicate a senior individual from the business with a reputation for getting things done and make him/her accountable for delivering results. If you don't have one, hire one. This person should have authority and support directly from the CEO—no lower. If you are ever offered such a job make sure the CEO actively supports it or don't do it.

3. Finance Manager: "Let's go for the highest possible degree of commonality. That way we only invent a process once and everybody re-uses it." Everybody nods. IT Manager: "That makes sense—we'll design once and implement multiple times in a cookie cutter approach." *Fly—yes but be careful—you will necessarily invest large portions of the project design effort in understanding and comparing the intricate details of many processes that are unimportant—which by the way are the majority. Ask yourself if your customers or shareholders care about the details of cash application or materials movement types. If not, try to avoid spending time and energy on them by allowing some diversity.*

   Example: An international food and drinks business spent three years designing the equivalent of a common, global supply chain on a single system when in fact they had country-based supply chains, no global customers, and no global products. In the same time period with half the investment, they could have gone live with separate transaction systems and used a global data warehouse for reporting. Their mistake—they misunderstood the distinction between a global and a multinational business and they thought higher commonality would be simpler.

   Recommendation: Go for commonality where it counts.

4. Operations Manager: "What should be in the scope? I know the ERP supplier has modules for virtually everything, and all our business processes could benefit from this. At this stage let's not rule anything out of scope. We can refine it as we go forward." Sales Manager: "Great idea. Let's use this as an opportunity to re-engineer all our business processes from the ground up. We'll start from first principles to design the business of the future." *Exasperated fly—you risk running a never-ending project that never stabilizes and delivers because it is constantly growing like a snowball. In the midst of one of these it feels as if you are trying to boil the ocean. Everything depends on the design of something else, because all decisions over data, processes, systems, organization or geography are up in the air and are inter-dependent. Coca-Cola's ERP project was named "Project Infinity"—a little too close to the truth if you're not careful.*

   Example: On one project in the confectionery industry, people joked that defining scope was no problem because everything was included. It took a year to define a business process model from scratch before even starting any detailed process or systems design—much too long in the fast-moving consumer goods industry.

   Recommendation: Define a manageable scope that tackles a key need for the business and that delivers concrete business benefits. Manage the scope ruthlessly to deliver what was promised on time and on budget. Once you have set the foundation and achieved a quick win, move to other project phases with equally disciplined scope and project management.

5. Supply Chain Manager: "Our staff are too busy addressing our customer issues and supply chain problems, so we won't be able to put anyone full time on the project." *Fly—if you are not prepared to invest in the future of the business, don't bother doing the project at all. Once a major ERP initiative is launched, people should be clamoring to get on it and business managers should be pushing their best people towards it. The project represents the future and that's where the best people should be focused. (Disney had the right idea when they called their project "Tomorrowland.") And, yes, there will be conflict over the commitment of key resources and sacrifices will be needed.*

   Example: At a steering committee meeting at a cosmetic company, one business leader said, "I don't have anybody to spare. Let the consultants staff the project." This was a major alarm bell. We would be sure to have a sub-standard result if we proceeded because consultants can never understand the intricacies of the business like a team that includes key staff. In this instance, we never reached the critical decision point due to a lack of management commitment.

Recommendation: Only a team approach will yield real results, and the best people must be committed. This often means providing incentives such as bonuses and stock options to talented staff who are co-opted onto the project. Sometimes their full-time jobs need to be back-filled with contractors. In my experience, staffing problems can be resolved with the right combination of top management leadership, money, and expertise.

6. Finance Manager: "Let's lock the time and budget. That's a sure way to prevent over-runs." *Fly—okay, but how do you know the time and cost of the solution before it is defined? On many projects, key, critical deadlines that threaten the quality of the solution turn out to have been nothing more than uninformed guesses in the boardroom. Setting arbitrary budgets in advance can shackle the project and cause frustration over artificial deadlines. It's also a sure way to stifle the possibility of any real step-change resulting from the project.*

Example: At one ERP project at a drinks company, it was shown early on that the business benefits included $200 million/year because the system could provide vital information on potential dilution of the product by co-packers. The question in management's mind went instantly from "how much will it cost?" to "how soon can we get it?"

Recommendation: Time-boxing of open-ended analysis phases can be beneficial in meeting challenging deadlines, but with the completion of these phases, an experienced project leader can accurately determine how much time and effort it will take to deliver the solution.

7. IT Manager: "We won't go with the big consultants because they're too expensive. We can easily find contractors to plug any resource gaps we find we have." *Fly—yes, but have they done it before? And can you hold them accountable? If they prove to be no good, you have no comeback. Getting a real jump on your competition is worth paying for. Time is arguably your most precious commodity.*

Example: On a SAP project at a UK energy company, when rare skills were required, the project manager searched for three weeks for a suitable contract candidate and waited a further two weeks for him to start. On the appointed Monday he did not show up and did not call, and it was a further two days before they found he had accepted a different position and would not be coming. "We finally pulled in a suitable candidate from our 'big 5' consulting organization, but a valuable six weeks had been lost, which ultimately meant this module had to be dropped out of the scope," remarked the frustrated project manager.

Recommendation: Choose the individual consultants carefully and hold the firm accountable for delivery.

4. HOW ARE ERP AND SCA SYSTEMS RELATED TO E-COMMERCE?

What is e-commerce? One simple definition is **the buying and selling of goods and services over the Internet.** In some organizations, e-commerce exists at a relatively superficial level (e.g., Web site displaying product/service information and accepting orders). However, the power of e-commerce exists at a much deeper level where **the buying and selling of goods and services over the Internet is facilitated by dynamic coordination across a supply chain through information and collaboration**, and this is where ERP and SCA systems play a pivotal role.[8]

---

[8] Some refer to e-commerce at a deep level as *e-business* (e.g., linking back-end processes such as purchasing and production with front-end processes such as sales and delivery) and use the term *e-commerce* for firms that have only a Web site with product information and order-taking capability.

How are ERP/SCA systems related to e-commerce? Recall that an **ERP database is a digital representation of the firm.** This digital representation contains information on resources, customer and supplier order histories, as well as alternative ways to purchase, make, and deliver a product/service including estimated costs and times associated with each of the steps. Naturally, this information is a key input to SCA systems that help diagnose problems and identify effective plans for purchasing, production, transportation, and pricing. **SCA systems support the development of an "intelligent" digital representation of an organization into the future.** Together, ERP and SCA systems provide the infrastructure for such e-commerce activities as

- Targeted promotions (e.g., Amazon.com has been known to offer discounts via e-mail for soon-to-be-released music to those customers who have previously purchased music by the artist).
- Customer order tracking and automatic customer notification of changes in delivery times.
- Ability of a customer to configure a product/service and receive near-instantaneous price and lead-time quotes.
- Menus of alternative prices and lead times for standard products/services (dynamically updated in response to changes affecting supply and demand).

In summary, **ERP/SCA systems are the backbone of e-commerce;** these systems provide a digital representation of a firm—historically, in real time, and projected into the future—portions of which can be made available virtually instantly to any person in any location. The combination of the Internet with an accurate digital representation of an entire supply chain provides the foundation for dynamic coordination across a supply chain through information and collaboration and, in turn, raises the buying and selling of goods and services over the Internet to new heights of efficiency and customer satisfaction.

The term *e-gistics* has been coined to emphasize the linkage between e-commerce and supply chain management. Here are two industry examples of how this linkage is played out in practice, the first at a cement company and the second at a company that makes control systems.

Example 1

"Technology allows you to do business in a much different fashion than before," says Zambrano. "We used it not only to deliver a product but to sell a service." For starters, Zambrano linked the company's delivery trucks to a global positioning satellite system so dispatchers could monitor the location, direction, and speed of every vehicle. That means Cemex can quickly send the right truck to pick up and deliver a specific grade of cement, or reroute trucks around congested traffic, or redirect deliveries as last-minute changes occur. It reduced average delivery times from 3 hours to 20 minutes.[9]

Example 2

E-manufacturing has nothing to do with the often frivolous and fast-disappearing dot-coms that tried to sell puppy chow and college-test results over the Internet... For a firsthand look at the payoffs that e-manufacturing can produce, consider Cutler-Hammer... Bid Manager goes far beyond conventional configuration software, which lets a Dell or Compaq customer customize a PC over the Internet... CEO Randy Carson reports that Bid Manager has increased Cutler-Hammer's market share for configured products—motor control centers, control panels, and the like—by 15%.[10]

[9] Excerpt with permission from J. A. Byrne, "Management by Web," *BusinessWeek*, August 28, 2000, pp. 84–96.

[10] Excerpt with permission from G. Bylinsky, "The E-Factory Catches On: Huge Increases in Productivity Result When Customers Can Design the Products They Want and Send Orders Straight to the Plant Floor via the Internet," *Fortune* 144, no. 2 (July 23, 2001), p. 200.

5. EMERGING INFORMATION TECHNOLOGIES AND THEIR IMPACT ON SCM

One of the **main lessons of this chapter is the increasing potential of IT as a means to improve supply chain performance**. Recall that supply chain management is all about managing flows of resources, which of course depends heavily on information. For example, past Federal Reserve Chair Alan Greenspan has noted the significance of these technologies and the associated rapid flow of information for improving performance and dampening economic cycles (Holstein 2001).

While advances in IT have already led to meaningful change in the way supply chains are managed, the magnitude of change will probably increase in the future.[11] This is due to ongoing **technological advances in two areas: (1) broadband communication** (i.e., information transfer at a rate of one megabit per second or more) and **(2) protocols for machine-to-machine communication, both within and among organizations.** Consider a few emerging information technologies:

- The wireless phone communication transfer rate is about 64 kilobits per second (in 2006) and should be about 30 times faster in two years.

- XML has capabilities that will allow automatic business transactions (order placement, quote requests) once an industry agrees on standards. Some view the development of XML to be just below the significance of the Internet itself.

- Business communication protocols are developing. For example, in the not too distant future, a company may post specifications for a new product idea on the Web, and in response, multi-enterprise teams are formed and respond with quotes within a week.[12]

- Jini, a software toolkit developed by Sun, supports networked appliances (e.g., dishwasher automatically submits a repair request to the manufacturer, including information on needed parts).

- Bluetooth wireless technology (i.e., short-range radio that resides on a microchip) transfers data at a rate of two megabits per second over a distance of about 10 meters. A similar technology is known as Wi-Fi (e.g., 802.11g). Wi-Fi transmitters are able to broadcast a broadband Internet connection over a radius of about 100 yards.[13]

- Radio frequency identification (RFID) technology allows wireless tracking of product from small radio transmitter chips that are not much bigger than the size of letters on this page (Want 2004). With the antenna, the total size and thickness of an RFID tag is comparable to a postage stamp. More on RFID below.

Radio Frequency Identification in Practice

RFID can be used to track a wide range of items, from full containers used to transport goods globally to the single prescription bottle of medication at your local pharmacy.

---

[11] See Johnson and Whang (2002) for an overview of research at the intersection of SCM and IT.

[12] Microsoft is pursuing this goal with .Net, which is viewed as the most significant development by the company since the introduction of Windows.

[13] Wi-Fi transmitters have been installed in over 2,000 Starbucks locations (Charny 2002).

Compared to bar codes, RFID tags are attractive because they can be read via wireless radio frequency technology, typically at a distance of about 10 meters.[14] As tagged boxes, crates, and containers pass by an RFID reader at a seaport, airport, warehouse, or loading dock, the reader receives the data and transmits them to company databases.

This technology is being driven primarily by the U.S. government and Wal-Mart Corporation. For example, every cargo container the military sends to the Iraq conflict has a radio tag on it to track its location as it travels from factory to warehouse to battlefield (Nadel 2006). The initiative is a consequence of the Gulf War in the early 1990s, where it is estimated that as much as $10 billion was wasted as thousands of containers were sent to the wrong place. As of 2006, The U.S. military operates the world's largest RFID tracking network, with 2,000 locations in 46 countries.

While the military has been leading the RFID effort in the government sector, Wal-Mart has been pushing the technology in industry. For example, Wal-Mart is requiring many of its vendors to implement RFID on pallets shipped to Wal-Mart locations. A University of Arkansas study of 24 Wal-Mart stores (12 with RFID and 12 without RFID) found a 16 percent drop in out-of-stock merchandise and a threefold reduction in the amount of time that a product remained out of stock in RFID-equipped stores (Rehring 2005).

Take Time to Consider the Implications of Emerging Information Technologies

The growth in use and power of information communication/storage/analysis technology changes will significantly impact supply chain management, and business in general. Hans Peter Brondmo is the founder of Post Communications, a leading provider of customized e-mail marketing solutions (acquired by Netcentives in April 2000). As a recognized authority on the Internet's effect on business, he expects the Internet to be everywhere connecting everyone. Next time you visit San Francisco, look for a purple and yellow taxi with the Yahoo! logo. If you hop in, you'll find an onboard computer with wireless Internet access; you can surf the Web en route at no extra charge.

So what will be the impact on business of an extraordinary networked society? This is a potentially profitable question. As you ponder this question, take a moment to reflect on the thoughts of Chris Burchett, a developer who worked at i2 Technologies:

> Consider the weekly chore of grocery shopping. A wireless PDA with attached barcode scanner and intuitive user interface can effectively eliminate the time spent shopping for regularly replenished consumables. From the convenience of the home, consumers can now scan used items prior to disposing of them and receive delivery at regularly scheduled times. Such an application would be a great boon to those who have difficulty in getting to a store. Furthermore, the wireless device is mobile so groceries may be ordered while at a restaurant, at a friend's house or while walking through the aisle of a grocery store.
>
> As consumers become more comfortable with the device and technology evolves, the device may converge with the TV remote or utilize broadband channels, such as cable TV, into the home. Interactive TV may enable consumers to purchase clothing worn by their favorite actor during the latest episode.
>
> Catalogs delivered to the home may have barcodes beside items to facilitate easy ordering. As technology evolves further, barcodes may be replaced by smart tags or PDF labels, which can carry more detailed information (i.e. real-time price and promotion info) and be reprogrammed remotely based on regional changes in supply and demand.
>
> Consumers will be able to use these devices to make dinner reservations while en route to the restaurant and pay the bill electronically without waiting for the waitress. Location

---

[14] The same technology is used by air traffic control systems to track planes, state highways for automated toll payment (e.g., E-ZPass, Liber-T), and libraries to keep materials from being stolen.

specific and personalized advertising may be delivered to the consumer who is passing by a mall in which a special promotion is being offered for a desired product.

As the number of consumers increases, a variety of very dynamic and special purpose communities will become prevalent. Consumers will be able to join and leave communities such as special interest discussions, neighborhood information/services, office teams, family scheduling, school assignments or homework submission and schedule planning. Many of these communities may form the basis for buying clubs who aggregate demand and negotiate better deals with retailers or manufacturers.

Increasingly, consumers will continue to demand more and more customizable and personalized products. This demand rewards manufacturers who produce more configurable products. As information systems become more knowledgeable of consumer buying patterns and behavior, it will be possible to automatically configure items to consumer needs and tastes. When consumer demand is received by manufacturers or retailers, the final product assembly could be determined based on a combination of automatic and manual product personalization.

Consider the consumer home grocery-shopping example described above. In order to support such a vision, businesses must be able to capture orders, plan and deliver the orders with very high (greater than 90%) accuracy, maintain appropriate inventory and capacity levels to support the home distribution, effectively manage marketing promotions and pricing, and increase consumer loyalty through rewards or incentives—all while making a profit.

This means businesses need to be able to completely integrate virtual and physical operations. As orders are captured across a variety of devices (i.e. PC, webTV, Palm, cell phone, CE PDA, etc.), a real-time promise must be made based on current supply and capacity constraints in order to provide accurate delivery times. To accomplish this feat, supply and capacity profiles will be continuously updated as a normal part of business information flow. When exceptional conditions cause order backlogs, these orders will be handled intelligently and automatically in response to supply and capacity changes, as will unfulfilled current orders.

Cooperative consumer profiles will be maintained and used as a standard part of order processing. Personalized marketing promotions and content will be driven in a collaborative effort between retailers and manufacturers from rule-based campaign management based on the consumer profiles. The profiles will be cooperative in the sense that consumers will give permission for selective use of the information and will indicate how they are willing to be marketed (consumer advocacy groups and consumer fears are already requiring such permission based marketing). Distributors will increasingly be required to merge multiple sub-shipments from various geographically distributed warehouses and factories into a single packaged delivery to the end consumer. This merge-in-transit will be required to take place dynamically as supply, capacity and demand change continuously. To effectively manage this complexity, distributors will be forced to work more closely with both manufacturers and retailers to provide the appropriate level of service.

As consumers demand more personalized products, manufacturers will need to explore new product assembly techniques that enable rapid and easy customization of products. Techniques for delaying key assembly operations will become more and more advanced. Ultimately, manufacturers and distributors may form collaborations in which some products receive final assembly and personalization while in transit. Direct procurement will be consumer demand driven. As orders are received, retailers will communicate demand in real-time to manufacturers where a bill-of-materials explosion will drive supply procurement which may initiate or modify an auction with suppliers or may automatically create a blanket order call-off. Time-phased demand aggregation and fulfillment optimization algorithms will make it possible for manufacturers and retailers to collaboratively determine the most cost-effective way in which to handle a particular order.

Consider another example of pervasive technology in the vending industry. Internet-enabled vending machines will enable vending companies to monitor inventory positions of vending machines in real-time. Automated business rules can control everything from replenishment strategies to real-time pricing of goods (i.e. as the Pepsi inventory in machines in a certain area is depleted the price per can may increase and the replenishment schedule and procurement may automatically be accelerated by 2 days).

Pervasive computing will also allow professionals to receive exception notifications, summary reports, and detailed order status from the above systems anytime, anywhere in real-time via cell-phone, pager, etc. Where manual intervention and response is necessary, professionals will be able to access supplemental information necessary to determine the correct course of action, enter corrective actions and monitor results.[15]

6. CONCLUDING COMMENTS

One of the distinguishing characteristics of the information revolution relative to the industrial revolution is the high financial leverage of a better mousetrap. We are not to the point where this leverage can be exploited to a large degree . . . more work has yet to be done on building up the information infrastructure in industry. You may be wondering where this is going, so let's look at an example. Suppose you have an idea for a great machine. You build a prototype, test it, refine it, decide it truly is great, and work on bringing it to market. You start building and selling these things, and because it is a great machine, it improves our standard of living. The cost to get a copy in the hands of a customer tends to go down as you make more, but this levels off after a certain point. Now, suppose you have an idea for a great piece of software, or a "knowledge machine." As before, you build a prototype, then test, refine, and bring it to market. People that buy your software discover it truly is great and it improves our standard of living. The difference is, if the information infrastructure (e.g., Internet, computer hardware, databases) is largely in place throughout industry, then the cost to get a copy in the hands of a customer is almost zero. While this example is oversimplified, it helps illustrate a key advantage of software over hardware. As software plays a greater role in our society, we may see a period of wealth creation that will surpass the early days of the industrial revolution . . . a revolution that took off in part due to a well-developed transportation infrastructure.[16] So point one is that software has some important advantages over hardware when it comes to copying and disseminating.

Point two: above all else, supply chain planning and control is data intense, and at this point in time, the largest roadblock to widespread productivity gains through software is

inaccurate and incomplete information. However, the capabilities and usage of data collection systems and ERP systems are growing. The roadblock is falling.

Point three: as noted in Chapter 1, society pays a lot of money for logistics—about 9 percent of GDP in the United States—and there is a lot of room for improvement. The total dollar value of inventory in the United States is around 14 percent of GDP, or $1.6 trillion in 2004 (Wilson 2005). This is not small change, and things get even better when you consider that much of the time it takes for material to move through a supply chain is spent lying idle in inventory.

The last point: SCA software is still crude. The development of SCA systems is in an early stage (started in early 1990s for all intents and purposes); there has not been the

---

[15]Excerpt with permission from C. Burchett, "Mobile Virtual Enterprises—The Future of Electronic Business and Consumer Services," *Proceedings from the Academia/Industry Working Conference on Research Challenges,* April 27–29, Buffalo, NY.

[16]Somewhat analogous to the Internet in the information revolution.

Principle of Nature: Recency Effect

DEFINITION
People tend to overreact to recent events.

IMPLICATION
Consider recent events when filtering human judgment.

EXAMPLE
Historically, the U.S. stock market has exhibited sustained periods of growth and sustained periods of stagnation. For example, we have witnessed three long-term bull markets where the Dow has gained a total of approximately 11,000 points. There also have been two long-term bear markets where the Dow lost almost 300 points. The curious thing about the bear markets is that they occurred during periods of economic growth. This raises the question of how the stock market could be stagnant when the economy as a whole is growing. Economists attribute the cause to human psychology, and more specifically, the recency effect—investors are overly influenced by the recent past (Loomis 2001).

benefit of feedback from wide-scale use, and the systems that have been implemented have not been up and running for long.

All four points suggest the potential for a significant effect on our standard of living. While recent economic upheaval in Internet and telecommunications industries may raise questions about future improved living standards, this type of cycle is consistent with history. The introduction of transforming technology, whether railroads and steel in the 1800s or electricity and autos in the early 1900s, follows a pattern of a speculative bubble followed by a crash, and ultimately a sustained improvement in living standards. This boom-bust phenomenon may be partly explained by a tendency for humans to be overly influenced by recent events—a principle of nature that will be discussed further in subsequent chapters.

Finally, there is a biological analogy that builds on the preceding four points and that will help reinforce your understanding of the linkage between ERP/SCA systems and e-commerce. Figure 2.4 presents a view of the e-commerce infrastructure as a collection of digital brains, vocal chords, and languages. In the landscape of business, there are small communities of relatively sophisticated creatures that speak a common digital language and can communicate instantly across great distances with brains capable of rudimentary processing (e.g., Wal-Mart's supply chains). Yet many supply chains and much of commerce span the globe, and there is wide disparity in development of the e-commerce infrastructure. On the whole, the picture is closer to the communication barriers in the biblical city of Babel. However, the power of the best brains is continually advancing and becoming more widely available. Vocal chords are getting stronger with the growth of broadband Internet access, and languages are progressing toward a standard.

FIGURE 2.4
A biological analogy of the e-commerce infrastructure.

E-Commerce Infrastructure		
Brains	**Vocal Chords**	**Languages**
ERP/SCA systems	Transmission technologies	E-commerce protocols
• Digital representation of past, present, future with analysis and decision support capabilities	• Internet	• .Net (MS)
	• Fiber optic lines	• e-Speak (HP)
	• Wireless at broadband speeds	• Java and Jini (Sun)
	• Bluetooth	• XML
	• WiFi	
	• RFID	

Robert Metcalfe, the founder of 3Com, coined a law that says the usefulness of a network increases with the square of the number of users. The e-commerce infrastructure is growing in users and power every day; the "e-commerce network" is approaching critical mass.

7. EXERCISES

1. Write a brief answer to each of the chapter keys in your own words. After writing down your answers, review the chapter with a focus on the content in bold to check and clarify your interpretations.

2. Think about a purchasing or shopping experience you have had in the last year where IT played a role, and more specifically, where some relevant information (e.g., ship date, new product announcement, change in pricing, the product itself, etc.) was made available via e-mail or the Internet. Think about the underlying systems that made this possible. What types of information must be in the company's databases? Does it require that databases be updated in real time (e.g., how time sensitive is the information)? Does it depend on information from other firms (e.g., suppliers, transportation firms)? What role might ERP and/or SCA systems have played in making the information available to you?

3. We live during a time of relatively rapid technological advancement and change—a fertile breeding ground for ideas that will markedly change society. C. West Churchman, a management science philosopher, once said, "The most fruitful reflection of mankind is to think of ways in which he and his age will appear naïve to the next age." As a step towards "fruitful reflection," think of a way in which society seemed naïve in the past when compared to today (e.g., think of an idea or two that changed society for the better within the last 100 years or so). Now put yourself forward in time by about 50 years and think back to the IT developments taking place during the early 21st century (i.e., developments discussed in this chapter). How did these developments lead to significant change in our society?

4. Find examples of three companies that have implemented ERP and/or SCA systems. What were the costs, implementation time, benefits, and lessons learned?

5. Find three recent articles on RFID. Summarize the main points, particularly with respect to the pros and cons.

Chapter **Three**

Supply Chain Foundations: System Slack and Related Concepts

Chapter Outline

Chapter Keys

1. What is system slack?
2. Why does it exist, and should it be eliminated?
3. What do Little's law and the trumpet of doom mean, and how are these principles relevant for system slack?
4. What are the origins, principles, and practices of TQM and JIT (lean production)?
5. How does a pull approach answer the questions of when and how much to order (or produce)?
6. How does a push approach answer the questions of when and how much to order (or produce)?

7. What are the advantages and disadvantages of each approach?
8. How is industry changing in ways that make a pull approach more attractive?
9. How is industry changing in ways that make a push approach more attractive?

This is the last of three chapters dedicated to introducing themes, terms, and concepts that appear throughout the text. Up to this point, you have an understanding of what SCM is about and why it is important. You also have a sense of relevant information technology and its relationship to basic supply chain activities: buy, make, move, store, and sell.

This chapter introduces four concepts that are meaningful for managing flows of resources in supply chains. The first concept is system slack. System slack is almost always present in supply chain activities; it plays a role in how well supply chains are managed and it is central to many SCM improvement initiatives. Before considering each supply chain activity in detail, it is useful to know what system slack is, how it affects supply chain performance, and reasons why it exists. This is the focus of Section 1.

The remaining sections build on Section 1 by reviewing overarching principles and practices that influence how system slack is managed. Section 2 covers the two concepts of total quality management (TQM) and just-in-time (JIT). TQM and JIT are strategic in nature, containing principles and practices that extend to the very top of the organization. The fourth concept, which is operational in nature, is the distinction between two possible approaches for managing material flows on a day-to-day basis, that is, pull versus push. The characteristics of pull and push are reviewed in Section 3.

1. SYSTEM SLACK

Recall that supply chain management is concerned with managing flows of resources, or, at a more detailed level, the movement, storage, usage, and transformation of resources. **System slack is idle, underutilized, or non-value-adding resources.** Examples include inventory, underutilized funds, rework of defective product, and surplus or poorly deployed human capital, materials, building space, and equipment. System slack is widespread in almost any supply chain. Obviously, system slack is expensive and can have a significant bearing on sales, which raises the question: **why does it exist?** This is an important question; an understanding of the basic causes of system slack is a first step toward effective supply chain management. There are at least **six causes of system slack:** quantity uncertainty, time lags, scale economies, changing supply and demand, conflicting objectives, and high market standards for quick response.

1.1. Quantity Uncertainty

Quantity uncertainty stems from three sources: **input, output,** and **demand.** *Input uncertainty refers to the timing and number of inputs to a system.* You are a manager for L.L. Bean. While you project a need for 50 customer service representatives (CSRs) during the weekend after catalogs have been mailed, you schedule 75 CSRs due to the possibility some may call in sick (especially considering that hunting season just opened). Similarly, you arranged for the supplier to ship a new sweater from the catalog more than a month prior to the mailing; you also ordered 10 percent more than you needed. You did this to protect against the possibilities of a late shipment and an uncertain quantity of less than acceptable quality.

Staples' stores experienced input quantity uncertainty in the form of timing and number of units when ordering from 3M. A buyer could place an order for a 3M product and receive a different (smaller) quantity after the scheduled delivery time. 3M has since implemented an online ordering system, and on-time delivery has improved by 20 percent (Little 2000).

The cause-and-effect relationship between input quantity uncertainty and system slack is illustrated by an effect that the September 11, 2001, attacks had on some supply chains. A number of firms experienced material shortages due to transportation delays after September 11. Firms have since increased inventory levels, which is one form of system slack, in order to protect against supply quantity uncertainties due to acts of terrorism (McAuley 2001).

***Output uncertainty* refers to the timing and number of outputs from a process.** You manage a wafer fabrication facility that produces high-quality integrated circuits (ICs) for military applications. The yield rate hovers around 60 percent, but on any given day, ranges from 20 to 90 percent (e.g., 600 acceptable ICs out of a batch of 1,000 corresponds to a yield rate of 60 percent). You need to produce and ship 400 ICs on Monday. Recognizing the high level of output uncertainty, you schedule a production batch of 2,000 ICs.

***Demand uncertainty* refers to the timing and level of demand placed on a system.** As a manager of a small cafe, you arrange to have three employees during lunch hour. You know that three people will not be busy all of the time, but you want to provide reasonably quick service in the face of uncertain demand.

1.2. Time Lags

Your plant in New York produces about $5 million worth of products each week that are sold in West Coast markets. Because it takes about two weeks to ship between coasts, you have $10 million of cash tied up in transit. Eliminate this time lag and you'll generate a one-time inflow of $10 million and, at a 5 percent annual return, add $500,000 per year to your bottom line.

Whirlpool Corporation's Cool Line is a toll-free number that, among other services, can be used to guide minor repairs. It used to take about two years of training before a Cool Line operator became fully proficient, and, consequently, there was always a surplus of operators in training (i.e., to replace those expected to leave within two years). The firm installed an artificial intelligence system that significantly reduced training time and consequently system slack.

There are **two principles of nature** that explain why time lags contribute to system slack. The first is Little's law. Given flow through a system, where a system is defined by an entry and exit point,[1] **Little's law** is the phenomenon that the average amount of stuff in a system is proportional to the time it takes for stuff to flow through the system. More formally,

$$\text{Average inventory} = \text{Throughput rate} \times \text{Average flowtime}$$

[1] In the first example, product enters the system when it is loaded on a truck in New York and exits the system when it is unloaded in Los Angeles. In the second example, the system spans the time between hiring and proficiency.

Principle of Nature: Little's Law

DEFINITION
Average inventory
= Throughput rate × Average flowtime

IMPLICATION
If you can find ways to reduce flowtime, you will benefit from reduced inventory investment, and vice versa.

EXAMPLE
On average, two gallons of milk will last twice as long in your refrigerator as one gallon of milk.

COMMENTS
The name of the law comes from John Little, the person who proved the principle (Little 1961).

In other words, a reduction in time lag leads to a proportional reduction in inventory. Little's law is illustrated in the first example where throughput rate × flowtime = $5 million per week × two weeks = $10 million = average inventory in transit.

The second principle of nature highlights a **connection between quantity uncertainty and time lags.** The **trumpet of doom** is the phenomenon: **as the forecast horizon increases, forecast accuracy decreases,** or, in other words, **as time lags increase, quantity uncertainty increases.** In the first example, eliminating the in-transit time lag would generate a $10 million cash inflow due to Little's law. However, by reducing the delay between placing a replenishment order and receipt of product by two weeks, West Coast markets require less safety stock to protect against uncertainty in demand. The total reduction in inventory slack would be more than $10 million. Similarly, in the second example, the average number of operators in training decreased (due to Little's law), and with reduced uncertainty in trainee turnover, the number of surplus operators decreased as well (due to the trumpet of doom).

Little's law and the trumpet of doom explain why there are powerful incentives to reduce time lags in supply chains, and why time lag reduction efforts are widespread in industry. We have seen a number of examples already; here is another.

> Now Calvin's three-button, $550 crepe suit is blowing out of stores more than twice as fast as the rest of his cK suits … Retailers love the suit too, because it always sells at full price, which keeps margins up. In fact, they've asked Calvin to resupply them via what's known as "quick response," an electronic inventory system that automatically replenishes stock weekly—a common method of ordering staples like white dress shirts, but one that's still relatively new for suits. Quick-response orders now make more than half of cK's total suit business.[2]

1.3. Scale Economies

Why is it that my local grocery store receives replenishments of Ralph's Magic Sauce about once every two weeks even though some of the product is sold almost every day? Why is that when I get a craving for cookies, I bake about four dozen even though I will eat only two dozen right away? Why is it that when your college builds a new building, it is designed to accommodate growth in the foreseeable future instead of expanding every year as needed? Why is it that I buy the super-size box of laundry detergent, or soda by the case? As you probably suspect, the answer is scale economies. **Scale economies refer to the economic benefits of increasing volume—benefits that provide incentive to create/acquire more of a resource than what may be needed at the moment.**

---

[2]Excerpt with permission from L. Goldstein, "Clever Calvin Sells Suits Like Socks," *Fortune*, November 23, 1998, p. 62.

Principle of Nature: Trumpet of Doom

DEFINITION

As the forecast horizon increases, forecast accuracy decreases. This principle gets its name from a "trumpet" showing forecast accuracy decreasing as the time until the forecast event increases.

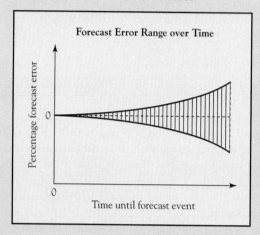

IMPLICATION

Look for ways to reduce flowtimes in a production and delivery system. The other side of this is to reduce the age of the information that is used for forecasting and decision making. For example, traditionally managers make decisions using data that are 20 to 30 days old, whereas newer information technologies are allowing some firms to base decisions on data that are only 24 hours old (Slywotzky 2001).

EXAMPLE

Your friend challenges you to forecast Amazon.com's stock price within plus or minus 10 percent, but she gives you two choices. You may forecast stock price either one week from today or one year from today. Which option would you select? If you go for one week, then you have an intuitive feel for the trumpet of doom.

COMMENTS

Computer Associates, a software company, has used the term "trumpet of doom" when describing the phenomenon. I don't know if CA originated the term.

In the above examples, it's cheaper to ship a case of Ralph's Magic Sauce every few weeks than a few bottles every day; as long as I'm taking the time to make cookies, I might as well make some extra to last a few days; fixed expenses of construction can be reduced through infrequent expansions; and I get a price break by buying detergent and soda in larger quantities.

1.4. Changing Supply and Demand

Even if demand is perfectly predictable, the fact that it changes over time can lead to idle or underutilized resources. For example, the kitchen in a restaurant will be large enough for the dinner crowd even though it may be larger than what is needed for breakfast and lunch. We have all seen incentive schemes designed to help smooth demand over time, for example, early bird specials at a restaurant, reduced price for a movie matinee, reduced phone call cost on weekends and evenings. Of course, the same arguments hold for supply. The quantity and timing of inputs (i.e., supply) may be known but out of synch with demand, for example, harvest season for agricultural products.

1.5. Conflicting Objectives across Departments or Firms

Supply chain activities associated with any end product or service typically span many firms and many departments within a firm, each operating with different reward systems and incentive structures. And what is "best" for an individual firm or department may not represent effective use of resources when viewed from the supply chain as a whole.

A classic example of conflicting interests is the prisoner's dilemma, which you may recall from your economics classes. Two people are picked up at a crime scene, both of whom are guilty. Each is interrogated in a separate room and must make a choice between confessing and remaining silent. If both remain silent, the police have enough evidence to convict both of a lesser crime with a jail term of five years. If both confess, then both will serve 10 years in jail. However, if one confesses and the other does not, the one who confesses is rewarded with a one-year jail term while the other is penalized with a 15-year jail term. Both are better off if both remain silent, yet from an individual self-interest perspective, there is strong incentive to confess.

Variations on the prisoner's dilemma are prevalent in supply chains. For example, each firm in a supply chain may set prices in an attempt to maximize the firm's profit, resulting in a higher price to the end consumer, lower market demand, and lost opportunity for higher total supply chain profit. We will consider this example in more detail in Chapter 5. While boundaries of ownership certainly create challenges to cooperation, conflicting objectives are not limited to the interfirm level. A firm's reward system, for example, may encourage the transportation department to shift more business to a slower and lower-cost transportation mode to the detriment of overall firm performance.

1.6. High Market Standards for Quick Response

Think about something that you bought within the last week. Now estimate how long it took to acquire and transform all of its raw materials (i.e., plants, animals, minerals) into the finished product and get it delivered to the point of purchase. What do you think?

Two weeks, six weeks, a year?[3] Chances are that it is much longer than you'd be willing to wait, and this is a reason for inventory slack along various stages of the supply chain, all the way from the ultimate raw materials to you.

In addition to working on the first five causes to more effectively manage system slack, another alternative is to target a market with lower standards for quick response, that is, quick response is sometimes less important in specialized niche markets. For example, a few years ago, I was in the market for furniture. I was looking for a particular type of wood and style, which I eventually found in a small custom furniture maker from Vermont. Nothing is built ahead of time, and depending upon what is ordered, lead times can range from a few months to a year (i.e., minimal system slack in the form of inventory and labor).

Another example is Levi Strauss & Co.'s move into the custom-fit market. You go into a store, get measured, pick out your style and color, and then wait several weeks for your custom-made pair of jeans. In the meantime, Levi's assembles your jeans from premanufactured components. You pay about $20 more than a pair off the shelf, and with no finished goods inventory costs, the total cost per pair is less than for the premade variety.

[3] A quick and dirty calculation using inventory investment as 15 percent of U.S. GDP with product output value between 50 and 100 percent of GDP suggests an average material flowtime in the United States to be somewhere between 1.8 and 3.6 months.

1.7. Concluding Point

There is **an important point about system slack** that, while possibly obvious, deserves re-inforcement. It would be incorrect to assume that management's goal is to eliminate system slack. Yes, management should always have an eye toward changes and investments that mitigate the causes of system slack. However, while you may be assured that there are always opportunities to do a better job managing system slack, it is also true that **system slack is almost always essential for providing good customer service and value in supply chains.** For any system, there is always a question of balance. It may be that some forms of system slack should be increased, while others should be decreased. That is the challenge.

2. TQM AND JIT

This section introduces **total quality management** and **just-in-time**—two concepts that have a bearing on how system slack is managed. It may be helpful to think about these two phrases as examples of *management mantras*. By definition, a mantra is a commonly repeated phrase. The term, which is Sanskrit in origin, also means a sacred verbal formula containing mystical potentialities that is repeated in prayer or meditation. Drawing on both of these definitions, a management mantra is used here to mean *a phrase that embodies a set of principles and practices for guiding behavior in an organization.*

For some organizations, phrases like these are no more than a buzzword. This means that the phrase receives a lot of management lip service or "buzz" but has no meaningful positive impact on the organization, usually falling out of fashion after a short time. Avoid this buzzword effect when you become CEO—it's like paying lots of money to lower morale in your firm.

Why Should I Learn about Management Mantras in General?

This is a fair question. The short answer is profit potential. Management mantras almost always stem from a few kernels of wisdom, typically in the form of insights into how the world has changed but much of business hasn't, thereby exposing opportunities for many companies. The trick is to draw out these kernels, determine if they make sense for your firm, and, if so, tailor the principles and practices to your environment.[4] And, if there is a good fit, the business press hype that accompanies these mantras may work to your advantage (i.e., hype can be inspiring, and frequent reinforcement of the core ideas aids understanding and acceptance).

Why Should I Learn about Total Quality Management and Just-in-Time in Particular?

It's true that there are a number of management mantras from which to choose, and the list is always expanding. I've selected these two because (1) they are well established and (2) there are significant elements in each that relate to effective management of system slack. Coverage will be brief and focused, highlighting the historical setting that prompted awareness of the underlying insights and identifying key features.[5]

---

[4] General Electric, for example, launched their six sigma quality initiative in 1996, an initiative that draws heavily upon the principles and practices of total quality management (Carley 1997). Six sigma expresses the goal of 3.4 defects per million (see Chapter 11 for additional detail).

[5] The reality is that there is no fixed and universal definition. Interpretations evolve and vary from firm to firm, especially at the level of execution, that is, how principles are put into practice. Coverage here is limited to those features that have been relatively stable and widely accepted over time.

2.1. Brief Historical Perspective[6]

The industrial revolution occurred during the 19th and early 20th centuries. New technologies led to new industries (e.g., rail, electricity, telegraph, telephone, autos) and a shift from a skilled artisan economy to large-scale mass production. Along with these changes came new approaches to management that crystallized in the early 1900s. Two prominent features included a **hierarchical command-and-control style of management and work design that greatly expanded the role of low-skill labor,** that is, standardized tasks that could be mastered quickly with little education or training. The approach proved **particularly successful in the United States,** which emerged from World War II (WWII) as the leading economic power.

Japan, on the other hand, was faced with **rebuilding its economy in an environment of scarce resources and relatively small markets.** This put pressure on finding ways to be extremely efficient through means other than high-volume mass production, and led to openness toward new ideas. Two **sources of influence stand out.** The first is a program called **training within industries** (TWI). TWI was used in the United States during WWII to help improve productivity, essentially through **active employee involvement in the generation and implementation of improvement ideas.** The program was very successful, and consequently was introduced in Japan to help rebuilding efforts. At the height of the effort, there were more than one million Japanese in training, and some credit the program as a major reason for their success.

The second source of influence is the **ideas of two quality pioneers who consulted in Japan after WWII: W. Edwards Deming and Joseph M. Juran.** Both Deming and Juran have written extensively on quality (Deming 1950, 1960, 1982, 1986; Juran 1964, 1988, 1989, 1992). We will limit consideration to two central themes. First, while quality needs to be the concern of all, **responsibility for and control of quality largely rest with management.** Management influences the system (incentives, nature of interaction among employees, work design, etc.), and a critical evaluation of the system is necessary to identify meaningful quality improvement opportunities. The second theme is a set of **techniques for aiding process improvement.**[7] These range from detailed methods such as statistical process control to general principles and procedures to gain and maintain improvements in quality.

In summary, the conditions in Japan after WWII were conducive to critical examination of existing management and production systems, and provided a fertile environment for innovation. This was the backdrop for TQM and JIT.

2.2. Total Quality Management (TQM)

TQM is an organizationwide effort directed toward the continuous improvement of quality. There are **three key ideas** in this definition. First is the notion that quality must be an **organizationwide concern,** not just the purview of those with "quality" in their job title. This idea is put forth strongly in Feigenbaum (1956, 1961), which, at the time, was relatively novel. Second, TQM is not a level to be achieved, but a never-ending effort focused on **continuous improvement.** Third, **quality** in the context of TQM refers to relative **value in the eyes of customers,** whether internal (i.e., "customers" within your firm such as your boss or colleagues in another department) or external. **High quality means**

---

[6] Two sources for an expanded treatment of this topic are Hopp and Spearman (2001) and, for the auto industry in particular, Womack, Jones, and Roos (1991). Also, McKay (2003) offers an illuminating historical perspective on the ideas underlying JIT, product simplification, continuous improvement, focused factories, and integrated information systems.

[7] A number of process improvement techniques are described in Chapter 11.

exceeding customer expectations, which connects right back to the earlier point—high quality raises expectations, thus requiring continual performance increases. In short, this **view of quality dictates a cycle of continuous improvement.**

The above definition identifies three guiding principles—organizationwide, continuously improving, exceeding customer expectations—but offers little in the way of how to put the principles into practice. Three significant elements of TQM practice are (1) **customer focus,** (2) **employee empowerment,** and (3) **data-based decision making.**

The first element reinforces the TQM notion that quality is determined by customer perceptions. While the idea of **customer focus** may appear to be a platitude that goes without saying, it is not always followed in practice, even by TQM adherents. For example, Varian Associates invested heavily in TQM training and boosted on-time delivery from 42 percent to 92 percent while reducing lead times by two weeks. The firm appeared to be on the right track, but the emphasis on hitting production schedules and other performance measures took attention away from the customer (e.g., phone calls not returned, work not explained). Market share plummeted and the company went from a $32 million profit in 1989 to a $4.1 million loss in 1990 (Greising 1994).

Employee empowerment means moving decision-making authority and responsibility to lower levels in the organization. It represents a shift from hierarchical command and control to more of a horizontal organization with fewer levels of management. In some sense, greater employee empowerment is a natural response to an increasingly educated workforce and advancing information systems that make it easier to control and coordinate activities without "over the shoulder" supervision. It also recognizes the potential of novel ideas from those close to the action.

The third element, **data-based decision making,**[8] refers to the use of tools and techniques in combination with appropriate information for problem solving and process improvement. We'll review a number of these tools and techniques in subsequent chapters. Data-based decision making goes hand-in-hand with employee empowerment, that is, provide suitable decision-making support when delegating authority.

2.3. Just-in-Time (JIT) and Lean Production

The principle and practices of JIT were initiated and largely developed at the Toyota Motor Company over a period of more than 20 years. Some inspiration and insights can be traced as far back as 1929 when Kiichiro Toyoda, the founder of Toyota, visited the United States. Here he witnessed the rapid material flow at Ford and the approach of sell-one-then-replace-one for replenishing products on supermarket shelves. Conditions in Japan in the 1930s prevented implementation of these insights (Womack, Jones, and Roos 1991).

Fast forward to 1945. WWII had just ended, Japan was faced with rebuilding its economy, and Toyoda demanded that his company catch up to American automakers in three years (Ohno 1988). This marked the beginning of the development and implementation of JIT, and much of the credit goes to Taichi Ohno, who was chief engineer at the Toyota Motor Company. Ohno originally referred to Toyota's methods as the Toyota Production System (Ohno 1988) and later on as JIT (Ohno and Mito 1988). The significance of JIT is underscored in the title *The Machine That Changed the World*, a best-selling book by Womack, Jones, and Roos (1991) that reported the results of a five-year, $5 million study of Toyota's methods. The authors use the phrase *lean production* to describe the way Toyota operates, and as JIT concepts have been extended and adapted to a wide range of sectors, the approach has come to be more commonly known in industry as simply *lean* (e.g., see Lipin 1993; Womack and Jones 1994, 2003, 2005).

---

[8] Also known as *management by fact.*

The dominant guiding principle of JIT is **produce and deliver material just when needed,** that is, there should be little inventory between stages in a supply chain. Think about the consequences of this principle. First, the **reliability of production and delivery processes must be very high.** With little inventory, late deliveries or more than a few defectives can shut down production. Second, **production and delivery processes must be synchronized with the market,** for example, capable of producing the entire product line at daily rates that approximate market demand.

Reliable processes with minimal inventory require consistent and high quality, and for this reason there is much overlap between JIT and TQM.[9] Major elements of JIT practice include **employee empowerment** and **data-based decision making,** discussed above under TQM. Other major elements are **jidoka, setup reduction,** and the **kanban system.**

Jidoka is a Japanese term[10] that means enhancing a process to make it easy to, not just detect, but *prevent* defects. To the extent possible, machines and processes are augmented to automatically check each part as it is produced, and immediately signal if an abnormality is found. The typical signal is the machine simply stops running, forcing immediate attention and investigation into the cause so that it may be remedied. The goal of jidoka is to identify and resolve quality problems at the source so that each unit produced is a "good" part, which, of course, is important when inventories are lean.

Another example of jidoka is a series of lights displayed along assembly lines.[11] The lights indicate if there is any problem on the line, and, if so, the severity of the problem and where it exists. Operators can turn on lights whenever a problem is observed, and, depending on the severity, others may converge to the area and the line may be shut down so that the problem can be corrected.[12] The magnitude of this change warrants emphasis. Allowing any worker to stop the production line at any time is an extreme form of employee empowerment when viewed in the context of traditional automobile mass production where, due to incentive structures, the attitude was to keep the line running at all costs. The mentality was "move the metal" and if there are quality problems, they can be remedied in the rework area after the car is assembled. Toyota experienced difficulties with frequent stoppages when first experimenting with this new approach, but, in time, root causes of problems were rectified. Toyota's production lines almost never stop and there is almost no rework on assembled vehicles (Womack, Jones, and Roos 1991).

Setup reduction means making setups less costly and time consuming. What is a setup? Setups are typically required when changing production from one type of product or part to another (e.g., cleaning, changing tooling, adjusting settings, making test runs). Production is halted during setup activities, and, consequently, it is economically infeasible to produce small batches when setup times and costs are high. When setup time and cost are small, it becomes possible to produce just what is needed for the day or the next few hours, thus eliminating excess inventory due to large batches. Interestingly, the capability to produce in small batches as needed is in itself a form of jidoka, that is, problems tend to get discovered right away as the parts are used at the next stage.

There are many clever and effective techniques for reducing setups, and setup time reductions of more than 90 percent are not uncommon (Harmon and Peterson 1990; Shingo 1985; Suzaki 1987). As one example, the setup time for a stamping machine in an auto

---

[9] Some view TQM as a subset of JIT.

[10] The corresponding English term is *autonomation*, a word that conveys the essence of the end result: an autonomous system that automatically detects and corrects problems.

[11] The light panel is known as an andon board. *Andon* means lantern in Japanese.

[12] The degree of worker control is similar to that on a U.S. aircraft carrier; any one of the approximately 6,000 crew has authority to shut down the operation at a moment's notice in response to a perceived problem.

plant took a full day and was done by specialists. By the late 1950s, Toyota had reduced this to three minutes while eliminating the need for specialists (Womack, Jones, and Roos 1991).

A **kanban system** is a pull approach for authorizing the production and movement of material. The distinction between pull and push approaches to flow control is outlined in the next section, and we will revisit and expand on these approaches, including details of the kanban system, in subsequent chapters.

3. PULL VERSUS PUSH

Supply chain management is concerned with managing flows of resources, one of which is often material. Naturally, when managing material flows on a day-to-day basis, one must decide **when and how much to order or make** of various products. And the answers to these questions have a bearing on system slack. There are **two opposing approaches that**  **are distinguished by the answer to the question of *when*:** pull and push.

A pull approach is reactive—*actual* inventory (or, equivalently, actual demand) is used to signal when to order or make product. For example, suppose the policy at a bar is to order 12 cases of India Pale Ale (IPA) whenever inventory drops to six cases. An equivalent interpretation of the policy is to order 12 cases of IPA whenever 12 cases have been sold since the last order (i.e., demand is the signal). Another example of a pull approach is a bar that checks inventory every Thursday night and then places an order for Friday delivery. The order quantity is set to bring inventory of IPA up to 18 cases.

An advantage of a pull approach is simplicity. Recall that a pull approach is reactive; it does not use or rely on future expectations or forecasts in order to answer the question of when. Consequently, **a disadvantage of a pull approach arises in situations when demand is not steady and capacity is relatively inflexible.** In these situations, the use of a pull approach while maintaining high levels of service can be expensive (e.g., high inventory investment to protect against periods of high demand relative to capacity). The stability of demand for the cK suit in the Calvin Klein example earlier is the reason a pull approach is viable for this product. Calvin Klein does not use a pull approach for their more fashionable products.

Many companies are becoming more agile and responsive by **reducing setups and time lags in their processes** (e.g., see Lee 2004). These types of change **increase the viability and attractiveness of a reactive, or pull, approach,** that is, there is less need to be proactive when reaction times are short. And the economic benefits can be significant. Caterpillar, for example, invested almost $2 billion to modernize plants and simplify production. As a result, the company was able to reduce the lead time necessary to change production levels from six months to one week, and, with improved market responsiveness, increase operating margins by more than 140 percent (Weimer 1998).

Another example of the economic impact comes from General Electric's appliance division. After investing heavily in methods to reduce setup times and costs, GE now produces every model every day in many of their plants, and has eliminated its long-term forecasting process. Lead times have been cut by more than 80 percent and inventory investment was reduced by about $400 million (Tully 1994).

A push approach is proactive—*projected* inventory (or equivalently, projected demand) combined with projected lead times are used to signal when to order or make product. For example, a caterer has a demand projection in the form of seven engagements over the next five days. For each engagement, the caterer knows what dishes will be served, what ingredients are required, what ingredients need to be purchased, and lead times associated with purchasing and food preparation. On the basis of this information, the caterer plans when and how much to order and make of various ingredients and dishes. Another example of a push approach is a company that plans to assemble 100 gizzards two weeks from now because this is when gizzard inventory is projected to drop below the desired minimum stock levels. Gizzards are assembled from izzards, of which 80 are projected to be in stock after two weeks. Order lead time for izzards is two weeks, so the company orders 200 izzards today (i.e., scale economies dictate full pallet orders of 200 at a time). With the order, 280 izzards are projected to be available in two weeks—more than enough to assemble 100 gizzards.

How would you modify the caterer example to illustrate a pull approach? The key to answering this question is recognizing that actual, not projected, inventory (or demand) will be used to signal when to order or make product. If you focus just on the finished product and not the ingredients, the policy of making 200 double chocolate cakes whenever inventory drops below 50 is an example of a pull approach. Of course, this policy is only workable if there is little chance that more than 50 cakes will be required on any given evening. It also leads to rather stale cake. Alternatively, the policy of not making anything ahead of time, but simply going to the engagement and baking cakes upon request, is also an example of a pull approach. The downside for the cake eater is the long delay between asking for a cake and receiving it.

The advantage of a push approach is that it is proactive. A disadvantage is that it is complex and projections are only as good as the underlying information. As you know from Chapter 2, we are witnessing significant **advances in information technology,** which work to improve the quality and timeliness of market information, and consequently demand and lead-time projections. In addition, there is a **trend toward shorter product life cycles:** the time between the high-growth phase-in of a new product and the steep decline as the product is phased out is shrinking. A very responsive supply chain combined with a pull approach is best for minimizing risk in these settings. However, for many supply chains, the investments required to react quickly to changing demand can be prohibitive. In these settings, it makes sense to be proactive by ordering/producing in advance of the high-growth phase-in of a new product, and reducing order/production quantities in anticipation of the steep decline in demand during phase-out. The trends of advancing information technologies and shorter product life cycles work to **increase the viability and attractiveness of a proactive, or push, approach.**

In practice, many companies combine elements of push and pull.[13] You may have seen examples of this at some fast food restaurants if you wait longer at the register during off-hours than during the mealtime rush. This can happen when a restaurant shifts from a make-to-order policy during slow periods to a make-a-little-ahead policy during busy periods (e.g., make three more items whenever inventory drops below three). Such an approach is proactive in the sense that signals for when to make product are adjusted according to demand projections, but it is purely reactive with respect to a signal in effect at a point in time.

---

[13] We'll examine a hybrid push/pull approach in some detail in Chapter 9.

FIGURE 3.1 **Major Activities in a Supply Chain**

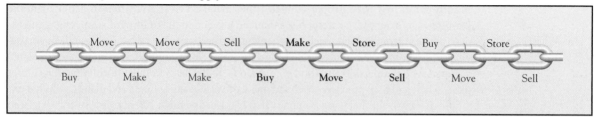

4. CONCLUDING COMMENTS

This chapter completes the coverage of foundation material, and we get to move on to the principles and tools section of the book. Recall that five basic supply chain activities are buy, move, make, store, and sell (see Figure 3.1).

We'll begin with the customer, or the sell side of the business, by examining the topic of demand management in Chapter 4. As you may imagine, the buy side of the business has a fair amount in common with the sell side … sort of looks at the same issue but from the opposite end. Consequently, while this issue is still fresh in our minds, we'll move next to supply management in Chapter 5. From this point, we'll take a look at the make, move, and store activities in the middle—an investigation that will span Chapters 6 through 10. Chapter 11 introduces process improvement tools as well as tips for creative problem solving. The ideas in this chapter are relevant for all five supply chain activities as well as other areas in business and in life. Chapter 12 is where we'll look at the supply chain as a whole and consider how to improve performance. This final chapter requires that you use your understanding of earlier material in combination with several organizing frameworks to (1) identify high-priority supply chain capabilities for a given market and (2) generate ideas for realizing these capabilities. Now, on with the journey.

5. EXERCISES

1. Write a brief answer to each of the chapter keys in your own words. After writing down your answers, review the chapter with a focus on the content in bold to check and clarify your interpretations.

2. Section 1.6 contains the results of a (very rough) calculation that uses Little's law to estimate the average time between creation of raw material and consumption. The estimate is between 1.8 and 3.6 months given that U.S. inventory investment is 15 percent of annual U.S. GDP and that products make up between 50 and 100 percent of U.S. GDP. Show the calculations that led to these results (i.e., 1.8 and 3.6).

3. How much system slack do you have in the form of food where you live? Try to estimate the total dollar value on average, and divide by 20 to get a rough estimate of the cost to you on an annual basis (e.g., you throw away very little food and you are able to invest the money and make a 5 percent return). There are benefits to this system slack in the form of convenience (e.g., good food readily available when hungry) and savings (e.g., less apt to pay higher prices at vending machines or restaurants). After considering costs and benefits, do you think you are doing a reasonable job managing this form of system slack?

Part **Two**

Principles and Tools

Chapter Four

Demand Management: Processing, Influencing, and Anticipating Demand

8. Exercises

Case Exercise: RJ Instruments

Chapter Keys

1. What is the scope of demand management?
2. What does order processing involve; why is it an important area for management attention?
3. What is customer profit potential, and how is it relevant for influencing demand?
4. What are five alternatives for improving forecast accuracy, what do they mean, and how can they be applied?
5. How do the tactics of *part standardization* and *postponement of form or place* help improve forecast accuracy?
6. What is the difference between long-term and short-term forecasting?
7. What are four long-term forecasting methods; what are the risks of salesperson/customer input?
8. What are the components of demand, and which component is not forecasted?
9. How do the moving average, Winters, and focus forecasting methods work?
10. What is the role of the number of periods in the moving average method, and the smoothing parameters in the Winters method?
11. What is the purpose of filtering, and why is it important for computer-based forecasting?
12. What do the following principles of nature mean and how are they relevant for demand management: (1) law of large numbers, (2) trumpet of doom, (3) recency effect, (4) hockey stick effect, (5) Pareto phenomenon?
13. What are the managerial insights from the chapter?

Business is simple . . . you've got to sell the stuff, make the stuff, and collect the money. You may recognize the previous sentence from the first chapter. There is a reason why "sell the stuff" is positioned first in the list of core activities. Much of business is driven by, and relies on, a sound understanding of ever-changing markets . . . an understanding that is a basis for exposing profitable opportunities to "make the stuff" and "collect the money."

This chapter begins Part Two of the text, which builds on the foundation material in the first three chapters and presents a more detailed study of principles and tools for supply chain management. Our first step on this journey is to consider the sell side of the business (see Figure 4.1). More specifically, this chapter deals with *demand management,* or, in the

FIGURE 4.1   A Supply Chain with Emphasis on Demand Management Links

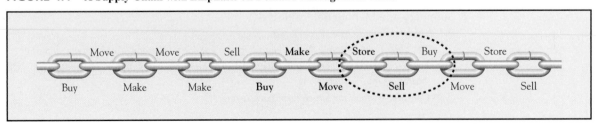

words of the subtitle, processing, influencing, and anticipating demand. We'll begin in Section 1 with a look at processing demand, emphasizing what it is and why it is an important area for management attention.

In Section 2, we shift our focus to influencing demand. There are many levers that can be used to influence demand,[1] and much is written on the topic. Our discussion of influencing demand is limited to three points, the last two of which also relate to anticipating demand.

First, there are growing opportunities to estimate the profit potential of individual customers and to use this information to increase profit. Databases with detailed customer purchase histories and associated demographic information are increasingly available. In response, methods for analyzing large datasets to detect patterns in past behavior and predict future behavior are being developed. Section 2 highlights how estimates of customer profit potential can be used to guide retention efforts, for example, which customers the firm should try hardest to influence.

Second, while it is generally true that the shorter the lead time the better, some customers and markets may be relatively insensitive to lead time. In such cases, it may be profitable to offer incentives for early commitment of future demand as a means to improve forecast accuracy. Section 4.1 reviews the use and benefits of incentives to influence early commitment of future demand.

Third, changes in price and the introduction (or termination) of promotions are often powerful mechanisms for influencing near-term demand, and, as a result, there can be temptations for overuse. Section 4.4 reviews how dynamic pricing and promotion policies (1) may inadvertently work against forecast accuracy and (2) represent a potentially profitable mechanism to better align demand with supply and improve forecast accuracy.

Sections 4.1 and 4.4 address linkages between influencing and anticipating demand (e.g., influencing in a way that improves predictability). The remainder of the chapter concentrates more squarely on anticipating demand, taking policies for influencing demand as a given. We'll look at how various operational aspects of the firm and supply chain impact forecast accuracy in Section 4. Principles of nature play a prominent role in this discussion. Sections 5 covers methods for developing long-term forecasts, and Section 6 covers short-term forecasting methods.

1. PROCESSING DEMAND

There are two things that are important to know about order processing. First you should know what it is, and, second, you should know why it's an important area for management attention.

Order processing[2] is generally viewed to span order booking to order shipment. The specific activities will vary across industries and even companies within an industry, but examples of order processing activities include customer validation, data entry, credit checking, pricing, design changes, availability checks, delivery time estimation, notification of shipment, and notification of delays.

Two things to notice about the definition of order processing are that it (1) is an area of high customer contact and (2) deals almost entirely with information processing. What does this mean for management? First, the order processing function can have a big impact on customer perceptions, so it is especially important that the function be well managed.

---

[1] For examaple, you may recall the "four Ps" from your marketing courses: product, place, price, and promotion.

[2] Also known as *order fulfillment*.

Second, due to ongoing rapid advances in technology, investments in information technology to improve the function could well pay off, especially if it's been years since the area was last scrutinized. Also, like any process, order processing is susceptible to ad hoc modifications that take place over time in response to problems (e.g., an extra credit approval step added in response to an expensive nonpaying customer a few years ago). The result is sometimes a complex and convoluted process that is ripe for streamlining. In addition, advancing technologies are creating opportunities for more dynamic and profitable customer interaction (e.g., moving from a standard price/lead time to a choice of prices/lead times based on current supply conditions and projections on near-term incoming demand from more profitable customers). In summary, **order processing is important because of the impact on customer perceptions and because it can depend so heavily on information technology.**

Here is an example of the importance of accurate and efficient order processing. A number of years ago, Kmart required MasterLock, among other suppliers, to sign a contract. The terms of the contract were simple: the first time MasterLock made an order processing error, the company would pay Kmart $10,000; the second time, $50,000; and if it happened a third time, MasterLock would lose the business. At the time, as many as 1 out of 20 orders were processed incorrectly (e.g., wrong pricing, wrong product, wrong quantity). Needless to say, this was a big deal for MasterLock, and they began to focus attention on the area. The company hired a consulting firm to help design and implement a streamlined and more accurate order processing system. Fortunately, Kmart provided a grace period before the terms of the contract went into effect. Why did Kmart insist on such a contract? One can only speculate, but perhaps part of the reason was a desire to operate with lower inventories, which means supplier reliability has to be high.

2. INFLUENCING DEMAND AND THE ROLE OF UNDERSTANDING CUSTOMER PROFIT POTENTIAL

Some customers are more profitable than others. This is a simple insight that is sometimes ignored, in part because of the difficulty in accurately assessing the profit potential of individual customers and of customer segments. However, advancing information technologies and the availability of extensive data on customers and their interactions with a firm are reducing this roadblock. Some firms are carefully tracking customer attributes, costs, and revenues, and analyzing these data to guide decisions on customer offerings, and ultimately to improve profitability.[3] An understanding of customer profit potential, for example, can be used to influence demand through customer retention policies—some customers receive little attention while extra resources are devoted to other customers in order to discourage them from taking their business elsewhere.

The wireless phone industry experiences wide variations in customer profitability. Monthly *churn rates* in the neighborhood of 2 to 3 percent are typical; a churn rate of 2 to 3 percent means that around 2 to 3 percent of a company's customers stop doing business with the company each month. In other words, a wireless phone company needs to add new customers at a rate of 2 to 3 percent each month just to offset those who leave. Some customers tend to frequently switch providers, going for the best deal whenever a contract expires, while others tend to regularly renew their wireless phone contracts. Couple this

---

[3] The analysis of large datasets to identify patterns that can be useful for decision making is known as data mining. Data mining is an active area of research (e.g., see Gans, Koole, and Mandelbaum 2003; Zheng and Padmanabhan 2006).

with a $200 to $400 gross cost to add a customer (e.g., cost of promotional efforts and incentive packages), and there are powerful incentives to analyze customer profit potential and use this information to guide contract renewal efforts.

One wireless phone company maintains a staff responsible for developing methods and analyzing data to predict the churn potential of each customer. This is no small task. The size of their wireless customer database alone is over five terabytes.[4] In addition, the staff analyzes detailed call records that accumulate at a rate of several gigabytes of data each day on each switch. One result of the staff's analysis is a *churn score* for each customer, that is, a measure of likelihood of switching to a competitor. The information is operationalized in several ways. First, customers with low churn score estimates are part of a proactive retention campaign. These customers are contacted by phone before their contract expires, and, in some cases, are offered special incentives to renew. Second, churn scores influence reactive retention efforts. For example, suppose you call your wireless phone company as your contract is about to expire, you describe the terms of an alternative provider that you are considering, and you ask what the terms of your new contract would be if you renew. The customer service representative has some discretion on renewal contracts to offer, and the lower your churn score, the more likely you will receive a favorable offer. Third, customers with very high churn scores may not even receive a renewal contract in the mail.

In addition to churn scores, the staff at the wireless phone company also estimates the lifetime value of each customer. Lifetime value is an estimate of what each customer will contribute to the company's profits over his/her lifetime. The estimate can be viewed as a composite of two basic components: (1) the length of time the person will be a customer of the company and (2) the profit generated from his/her purchases over time. The company uses these estimates, along with churn scores, to guide customer retention and acquisition effort.

A second example of using customer profit potential to guide customer retention/acquisition effort, and ultimately influence demand, comes from an electronics manufacturer. The manufacturer established a service company in Hong Kong that sells and manages service contracts on the electronics manufacturer's product. Customers that require a lot of service during their contract due to such factors as extraordinarily heavy usage or outside storage in harsh conditions do not receive a renewal offering in the mail.

As a third example, one company found that the cost of sending a sales rep to small dealers offered little return, and consequently small dealers received infrequent visits and relatively little attention. After further analysis of costs and the impact of infrequent sales rep visits on sales, the company eliminated personal sales calls altogether. In its place, the company established a call center expressly for small dealers. The dealers were initially upset, but ended up more satisfied because there was always someone there to help when they called. Prior to this change, dealers would often have to wait a long time before a service rep would get back to them.

The main lesson of this section is that some customers are more profitable than others, and knowledge of customer profit potential is valuable. This has always been true. What is happening today is that advances in information technology are making it more practical and less costly to estimate costs and revenues by individual customer and/or customer segment. Companies that do this well can more efficiently allocate resources to influence demand and increase profits.

---

[4] A terabyte is a trillion bytes. As an example, if the hard drive on your PC has a capacity of 100 gigabytes, then the wireless customer database is 50 times the size of your PC hard drive capacity.

3. MOTIVATION FOR ANTICIPATING DEMAND

Many decisions draw on future expectations . . .

> Did you ever see a bird, in its search for twigs, straw and the like? Hunting these things for fun? Hardly. It is simply planning ahead against the time when a warm comfortable nest will be wanted for the little ones to come. It does not wait until they have arrived—the bird sees to it that the nest is ready before it will be needed, and, as a result, we call it a wise bird (Knoeppel 1911).

. . . so before looking at tools to help us with decision making, we'll begin with the question of how to do a better job predicting the future without a crystal ball.

Why Bother?

One good reason is money. Here are two examples . . . one good and one bad. Sunbeam changed the way they developed monthly demand forecasts. A key aspect of the change was the inclusion of demand estimates developed by their top 200 customers. This information along with other considerations increased forecast accuracy, which in turn led to a 45 percent reduction in inventory investment. The bottom-line impact, as well as impact on stock price, was significant.

With the rapid pace of technological improvement and declining computer component prices, demand forecasting in the PC industry is notorious for creating headaches, and worse. Apple, for example, has had a history of problems with forecasting. Its unfilled orders in the second quarter of 1995 reached $1 billion (Carlton 1995), and poor demand forecasting during the subsequent holiday season contributed to a first quarter loss of $69 million and the firing of its CEO Michael Spindler (Caroll, Carlton, and Rigdon 1996).

4. ALTERNATIVES FOR IMPROVING FORECAST ACCURACY

After your CEO charges you with the task of improving forecast accuracy, it may be natural to begin considering whether better information is available and whether information can be analyzed differently . . . perhaps by buying some new software or setting up focus groups. In other words, **one alternative is to change (and hopefully improve) the forecasting *method*.**

We will consider a variety of forecasting methods shortly. But, before we do, it is important to recognize that forecast accuracy also can be improved by changing the way the firm operates. Four such alternatives are outlined below.

4.1. Introduce Early Warning Mechanisms

Early warning **mechanisms encourage some (or more) customers to provide early commitment of their future demand.** This is a tactic that *influences demand* in a way that improves predictability (i.e., customers commit earlier to demand in the future). There are many ways in which this can be done. Here are four examples. First, a number of years ago, an appliance company began offering a discount off the purchase price for those customers who placed an order 60 days in advance. This option was particularly attractive in the builder market where contractors of large apartment complexes know a good deal ahead of time when units will be ready for appliances. Prior to this program, builders rarely placed orders much in advance of the appliance company's standard two-week lead time.

Second, a light bulb manufacturer instituted a similar program offering a 3 percent discount on contractor orders placed more than five weeks in advance. The savings due to smoother and more predictable production are in excess of $1 million per year (Mentzer and Moon 2004).

Third, if you are a snowboarder or skier, you may know that some resorts offer "early bird specials." Ski areas, for example, will sometimes offer a discount if you buy a package of multiple lift tickets before the season begins. In addition to cash flow benefits, the practice provides early warning of future demand.

Fourth, customers of steel distributors expect very short lead times, often placing an order the day before the steel is needed. The result is that the distributor faces a great deal of demand uncertainty and invests heavily to provide quick response in the face of this uncertainty. Analysis of the supply chain has shown that both the steel distributor and customers can save money when the distributor offers price reductions for advance orders (Ballou, Gilbert, and Mukherjee 1999).

4.2. Take Advantage of the Law of Large Numbers

The **law of large numbers** is the phenomenon: **as volume increases, relative variability decreases.** This is a particularly powerful principle of nature in the sense that it can be applied in many ways to exact benefits, and not just in the area of forecasting. For example, this principle plays a role in

- Why you can be protected against catastrophic loss while paying relatively nominal insurance premiums.
- Why, given a suitable sample size, results from surveys and polls are trustworthy.
- Why investment firms recommend diversification of financial portfolios.
- Why, in spite of randomness at the atomic level, we can accurately predict the movement of planets.[5]

So how is the law of large numbers relevant for improving the accuracy of forecasts? The idea is to change operations so as to increase the level of aggregation in units being forecast. The notion is perhaps best understood through examples. As you know, Dell operates on a make-to-order basis. This means that you can get on their Web site, select the options you would like for your PC, and submit your order; then your PC is assembled and shipped. Dell does not need to forecast demand for each of the many thousands of possible PCs that could be ordered.[6] Rather, Dell and their suppliers forecast demand for the relatively small number of basic components that can be combined in many different ways according to customer preference (e.g., the 12 components of four chips, five hard drive capacities, and three CD-ROMs can be combined in 60 different ways).

Reflect.com LLC was a cosmetics spin-off of Procter & Gamble that borrows from the Dell model. Customers custom-design their own cosmetics and perfumes. Reflect.com's demand forecasting is limited to the stable demand of relatively few raw materials (due to the law of large numbers) that can be mixed and matched in more than 50,000 different ways to suit an individual customer.

An $8 billion electronics company sells similar products under several brands. The manufacturing process at this firm was redesigned so brand differences are added at the very end of the process rather than early. With the change, production planning is based on

---

[5] In the early 20th century, physicists had difficulty reconciling Newtonian physics with the randomness prescribed by quantum mechanics. As observed by Max Born, reconciliation hinged on the law of large numbers, that is, randomness at the quantum level is accepted and the effectiveness of classical physics for larger objects can be explained by the law of large numbers (Rao 1989, p. 13).

[6] Dell custom-assembled more than 25,000 different computer configurations for buyers in 1999 (Kerwin, Stepanek, and Welch 2000).

Principle of Nature: Law of Large Numbers

DEFINITION
As volume increases, relative variability decreases.

IMPLICATION
Look for ways to change operations so that planning can be done at a more aggregate unit.

EXAMPLE
Hewlett-Packard used to customize printers for foreign markets at the factory, which is cheaper than customizing in the field. But there were significant mismatches between demand and supply, for example, not enough printers configured for the

British market and too many for the French market. HP changed operations so that generic printers were shipped to a European warehouse and configured in response to customer orders (Feitzinger and Lee 1997). This change increased production costs, but by more effectively matching supply and demand, HP saved more than $3 million per month (Coy 1999).

COMMENTS
There are more precise ways to state the law of large numbers (e.g., see Ross 1988). The definition above is most convenient for our purposes.

demand forecasts for all brands of a product. The allocation of this total quantity to brand quantities is done at a later point according to current market conditions.

Another example comes from my experience with a network design study. One question concerned the reduction in inventory when reducing the number of U.S. warehouses from 54 to 11 (i.e., 11 warehouses serving U.S. demand rather than 54). On the basis of a theoretical reduction that would occur if inventories were optimally managed and what had been observed in practice in other networks, we estimated a percentage reduction between 33 and 50 percent. Why the reduction? The short answer is the law of large numbers. With a reduction in the number of warehouses, volume per warehouse increases, and relative variability decreases.[7] With lower relative volatility, the inventory investment to provide a target level of customer service is less.

The preceding four examples illustrate a tactic called *postponement* (also known as *delayed differentiation*), that is, changing operations so that the **form or place of the product is postponed.** Form is postponed in the first three examples, whereas place is postponed in the last example. Dell and Reflect.com postpone the creation of the end product until an order is received, and the electronics company postpones the brand identities of products (i.e., form is postponed). In the last example, suppose that the Northwest markets are served out of Sacramento instead of Sacramento, Portland, and Seattle when the number of warehouses is reduced. With this change, the movement of product to the Portland and Seattle markets is postponed until a customer order is received (i.e., place is postponed).

Part standardization is a related tactic that takes advantage of the law of large numbers. For example, take a look at the sandwich wrapper next time you go to Arby's. A single wrapper is used for different sandwiches (i.e., a standardized part) but can be folded in different ways so that the outside properly identifies the sandwich. Arby's is able to use combined sandwich volume when estimating demand for sandwich wrappers rather than worry about wrappers for each sandwich.[8]

4.3. Reduce Information Delays and Replenishment Lead Times

The **trumpet of doom** is the phenomenon: **as the forecast horizon increases, forecast accuracy decreases.** From this principle of nature, we know that if we can find ways to

[7] See Eppen (1979) for additional detail.
[8] See Baldwin and Clark (1997) for other examples of how firms gain advantage through standardization.

Principle of Nature: Trumpet of Doom

DEFINITION
As the forecast horizon increases, forecast accuracy decreases. This principle gets its name from a "trumpet" showing forecast accuracy decreasing as the time until the forecast event increases.

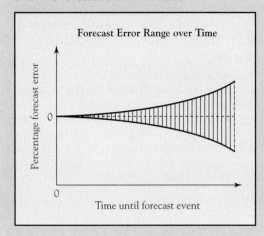

IMPLICATION
Look for ways to reduce flowtimes in a production and delivery system. The other side of this is to reduce the age of the information that is used for forecasting and decision making.

EXAMPLE
Wal-Mart electronically sends their sales data of P&G product to P&G every evening. P&G uses this information to adjust their expectations of demand. Prior to this new way of doing business, P&G may have updated demand forecasts on a monthly basis, potentially using sales information at least a week out of date. Forecast accuracy improved through more up-to-date information.

change the way we operate so that we don't need to forecast demand as far into the future, or if we base our plans on more up-to-date information, then our CEO will be happy. Here are a few examples from industry.

Dell Inc. is known for exploiting this principle by continuing to pull time out of their processes. First, as noted earlier, Dell builds PCs to order and ships direct to the end consumer. There are no resellers, retailers, or even a Dell-owned warehouse storing finished goods in their supply chain. To put this into perspective, after a traditional PC manufacturer assembles a PC, it stays in their warehouse for several weeks before being shipped to a reseller or retailer, where it sits for several more weeks before being purchased by the consumer. In order

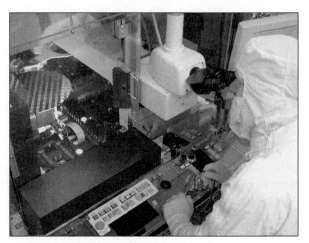

to plan how many PCs to make of a given model, the company needs to forecast demand for at least a couple of months into the future—pretty tricky in the volatile PC industry. It is also very risky when you consider that component prices have historically decreased at a rate of nearly 1 percent per week. For Dell, a customer's computer is typically assembled to specifications, loaded with the requested software, and ready to ship within two hours of

Principle of Nature: Hockey Stick Effect

DEFINITION
Volume and activity increase near the end of a reporting period.

IMPLICATION
Be aware and plan for the effect and, since the periods of mad rush are usually relatively inefficient, look for ways to reduce the magnitude of the effect.

EXAMPLE 1
If you graph the number of hours spent studying for this class each week, you'll probably see an upward spike (i.e., the blade of the hockey stick) near exam time. This example highlights a major cause of the hockey stick effect—procrastination.

EXAMPLE 2
Compaq has used channel stuffing to hit revenue targets, and has suffered the consequences. First quarter 1998 was particularly disastrous. After shoving excess product into its distribution channels to hit 1997 revenue targets, IBM announced steep price cuts in February. Compaq sales plummeted and the firm was stuck with 8 to 10 weeks of inventory—a very expensive proposition when PC component prices are dropping by about 1 to 2 percent per week (Schonfeld 1998).

COMMENTS
You may hear the phrase "end of period push," which is the same thing as the hockey stick effect. You also may hear the term *channel stuffing* or *trade loading*, which is an activity that contributes to the hockey stick effect. Channel stuffing occurs when a company encourages their customers to load up on inventory, usually by offering a limited term discount (e.g., example 2 above).

receipt of the order—faster than some companies can get finished goods out of a warehouse (Stewart 1999).

Second, Dell also has reduced the time it takes to keep suppliers abreast of their component needs. For example, Intel is able to view the mix of Dell PC sales on a real-time basis via the Internet; Intel uses this information to more quickly respond to Dell's needs for Intel chips. Not only does time reduction benefit forecasting, but the flow of material through the supply chain is so fast that Dell gets money from a PC customer weeks before they need to pay the suppliers for the components inside the PC—not a bad deal.

Lantech is a company that makes complex shrink-wrap machinery for customers such as Procter & Gamble. In the early 1990s, it took about five weeks to make the machine; now it takes about 10 hours. Lantech has changed their operations to cut lead times and, as a consequence, Lantech no longer builds to a forecast. Instead of relying on inaccurate demand forecasts, the company produces in response to customer orders (Ansberry 2002).

4.4. Reduce Demand Volatility

Company behaviors and policies influence demand volatility, or, in other words, one way to improve forecast accuracy is to change behaviors and policies to reduce demand volatility. Like early warning, such changes **influence demand** in a way that improves predictability.

Tame the Hockey Stick Effect

One example of company behavior that amplifies demand volatility is exhibited in a **principle of nature** called the **hockey stick effect.** The hockey stick effect is the phenomenon of **volume and activity increasing near the end of a reporting period.** After all, why do today what you can put off until tomorrow, and there is no tomorrow near the end of a reporting period.

FIGURE 4.2

The hockey stick effect exhibited in a surge of demand near the end of the month.

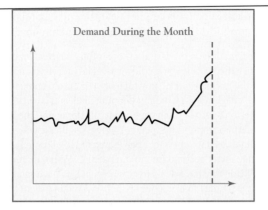

In terms of demand, it is not unusual to see a "hockey stick" when plotting demand during a month (or a quarter or a year; see Figure 4.2). For example, I know of a medical supply manufacturer that ships an average of 21 percent of their monthly orders on the last shipping day of each month. To put this in perspective, there are roughly 22 working days in a month. This means that about 3.8 percent of monthly demand is shipped each day until the end of the month, when demand jumps by a factor of five. The shipping manager lists numerous reasons—had letter-of-credit problems, wanted to ship the order complete, didn't have the paperwork, was out of boxes—but the truth of the matter is that they dragged their feet and got behind.

What Does the Hockey Stick Effect Mean to You as a Manager?

Check if the hockey stick effect is significant at your firm, and, if so, look for ways to reduce it. There are at least two good reasons for doing this. First, as indicated above, behaviors that contribute to the hockey stick effect tend to exacerbate demand volatility and, thus, work against forecast accuracy. Second, the hockey stick effect usually contributes to inefficiency. The blade of the hockey stick corresponds to the mad rush of activity near the end of a reporting period, and times of mad rush are usually inefficient. For example, Gillette conducted business in a manner that contributed to the hockey stick effect through a practice known as channel stuffing or trade loading. In order to hit their numbers, Gillette's salespeople would do whatever it took to make a sale, including cut-rate deals near the end of a reporting period. This practice is common in many industries, and in many cases it does not make good business sense. Gillette has recognized this and has instituted changes to reduce trade loading (Brooker 2002).

Why Does the Hockey Stick Effect Occur?

It's true, if you are going to work on reducing the hockey stick effect, it helps to have an idea of why it exists. One cause, as illustrated in the medical supply company above, is procrastination. There are potentially many effective ways to help reduce the tendency for procrastination. For example, C.R. England, a transportation firm, operates on a weekly reporting cycle with performance continually monitored—there is little opportunity to get behind.

Sometimes the pressure on top management or salespeople to hit revenue targets leads to channel stuffing or trade loading, which contributes to the hockey stick effect. As illustrated in the Gillette example above, channel stuffing occurs when a firm offers price discounts or other incentives in order to book lots of sales near the end of a reporting period. The following example from a novel illustrates a particular pay structure that helps mitigate the effect.

> I popped in on Pete Cittadini on the last afternoon of the quarter, June 30, a day that finds most VPs of sales in Silicon Valley in a cold sweat. The industry is notorious for a sales pattern nicknamed the "hockey stick," in which up to half of a company's quarterly sales close on the very last day. I found Cittadini hopping mad, and he was letting someone have it over the phone. "I don't care if you have to do it all over again," he was saying, "you get it done right." An underperforming sales person? Nope. On the last day of the quarter, Pete Cittadini was, of all things, moving into a new home in Hillsborough. "The contractor cut the marble countertops wrong. I told him to do it again." Wait a minute. Moving, on the last day of the quarter? Didn't he have deals to close? Didn't he have salespeople to motivate? "I had a garage sale yesterday to clean out my house. Couldn't seem to move the queen mattress." Besides, he explained, it wouldn't make any difference if he rushed to close deals. In order to prevent the last-minute desperate price-cuttings that only undermine a company's revenue structure, Actuate doesn't pay sales commissions when contracts are signed, only when the cash is collected. Dan Gaudreau, the CFO, refuses to play hockey.[9]

Critically Assess the Value Added from Temporary Price Reductions and Promotions

Another example of company behavior that can amplify demand volatility is frequent price changes and/or promotions. There are good reasons for temporary price markdowns and promotions (e.g., respond to a competitor price reduction), but there are also risks, especially when price reductions become frequent and predictable by the market. The result can be a perverse cycle where customers defer purchases in anticipation of the next price decrease and a firm is forced to discount prices because few are buying. An additional consequence of this cycle is volatile and difficult-to-predict demand. Procter & Gamble has made a concerted and successful effort to reduce the number of price changes over time with their *every day low pricing* (EDLP) program. EDLP has helped P&G to smooth out demand, reduce inventory, and improve efficiency.

One message from the previous paragraph is that variable pricing and promotions can make demand more volatile than it would otherwise be with stable pricing and no promotions (i.e., frequent discounts/promotions can create artificial demand volatility). One can take this message a step further by noting that the tools of pricing and promotion also can be used to

make demand less volatile than it might otherwise be. Copacino (1999), for example, describes a study where the prices of selected PC models were recorded at the end of each week over a period of time. As expected in the deflationary PC industry, he found that price was generally either the same as in the prior week or lower. There was one exception, however. A PC sold by Dell occasionally increased in price. We do not know Dell's reasoning for the occasional

[9] Excerpt with permission from P. Bronson, *The Nudist on the Late Shift* (New York: Random House, 1999).

FIGURE 4.3

A plot of cumulative percent of the product line versus cumulative percent of volume for a firm that sells stethoscopes. The curve illustrates the Pareto phenomenon.

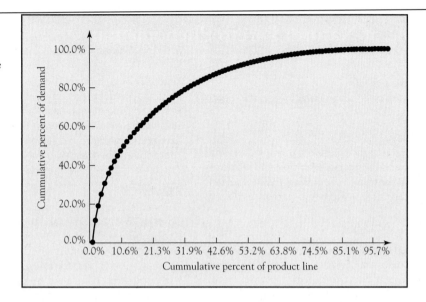

price increase, but the practice raises the possibility that Dell may have been using price changes to help align supply with demand.

Beware of Product Proliferation

There is almost always pressure on a firm to increase sales revenue, and one tried-and-true means towards this end is to expand the product line, for example, new colors, features, and so on.[10] When taken to the extreme, this tactic can result in significant cannibalization[11] and thus little increase in total sales. In addition, with total volume spread over more products, demand for each product becomes more volatile. (Which principle of nature explains this phenomenon?)

Length of Line Analysis and the Pareto Phenomenon

Periodic length of line analysis helps ensure that product proliferation does not detract from the bottom line. And, when low-volume products can be eliminated with minimal or no reduction in total volume, average demand per product increases and demand volatility tends to decrease (due to the **law of large numbers**). The purpose of length of line analysis is to assess whether the length of the product line within each product category makes good business sense. In practice, the analysis focuses more often on identifying candidate products for elimination, but could just as well identify opportunities for expansion.

Length of line analysis is an example of a widely applied form of analysis that is more generally known as Pareto analysis. In order to explain Pareto analysis (and length of line analysis), we first need to understand the principle of nature on which it is based, that is, the **Pareto phenomenon.** The Pareto phenomenon says that **the lion's share[12] of an**

[10] Interestingly, increasing the number of options available to consumers can have negative psychological effects (Schwartz 2004).

[11] Demand for the new product is offset by a reduction in demand for the firm's other products.

[12] One of Aesop's fables concerns a lion, fox, and ass who must divide the kill after a joint hunt. The ass divides the kill into three equal parts and invites the others to choose. The lion is incensed and eats the ass, and, afterwards, asks the fox to make the division. The fox divides into one huge heap and one tiny morsel. "Who has taught you, my excellent fellow, the art of division," says the lion. The fox replies, "I learned it from the ass, by witnessing his fate," proving once again that the party with the power gets the "lion's share."

Principle of Nature: Pareto Phenomenon

DEFINITION
The lion's share of an aggregate measure is determined by relatively few factors.

IMPLICATION
Invest time and energy to identify a few factors that drive performance and focus attention and resources on these. The process of separating the "important few" from the "trivial many" is known as *Pareto analysis*.

EXAMPLE
Sunbeam changed their approach to developing demand forecasts a while back. One major element of their approach was the use of customer input, though they first conducted Pareto analysis to rank their customers by volume, and then focused on a small set of customers that contributed most of the volume. Each month, their 200 largest customers would provide demand estimates for Sunbeam products in their market. Sunbeam found demand forecast accuracy improved significantly, which allowed them to reduce their inventory by nearly 50 percent. The impact of this change was significant.

COMMENTS
The name comes from the person who formally recognized the phenomenon, though it was no doubt known before this time. Vilfredo Pareto was a 19th-century Italian economist who studied the distribution of wealth. He found, for example, that 15 percent of the population controlled 85 percent of the wealth in Milan, Italy. At a more fundamental level, the phenomenon stems from diversity in the environment.

aggregate measure is determined by relatively few factors, or, in other words, the important are few and the trivial are many. Pareto analysis is the process of separating the important few from the trivial many. Figure 4.3 illustrates the Pareto phenomenon at a firm that sells stethoscopes. The firm sells 94 different models of stethoscopes. The top 20 models in terms of volume make up 21.3 percent (= 20/94) of the product line and 68.5 percent of the volume.

Here are two examples illustrating Pareto analysis of the length of a product line and the resulting impact on demand volatility and costs. First, I know of a firm that offered over 500 products within four product categories. Analysis of historical volumes showed that 110 products contributed less than 5 percent of the corresponding product category volume. In this example, the relevant aggregate measure is total sales and the 110 low-volume products qualify as the "trivial many." Further analysis suggested minimal impact on sales volume if the 110 low-volume products were eliminated and, due to reduced demand volatil-

ity, a 10-percentage-point improvement in product availability with no change in inventory investment. To put this in perspective, the increase in inventory investment required to achieve a 10 percent increase in service level with no reduction in the product line was approximately $4 million. The firm cut their product line by more than 25 percent over a five-year period.

Second, studies have shown that nearly 25 percent of products in a supermarket experience average demand of less than one unit per month and 7.6 percent of personal-care and household products account for 84.5 percent of sales (Schiller, Burns, and Miller 1996). P&G evaluated their product line for low-value-added products and, over a period of years, trimmed their product line by one-third. The number of varieties of Head & Shoulders, for example, was reduced from 31 to 15, and volume per hair care product more than doubled after trimming the line. Pareto analysis of their product line was one element of a broader simplification strategy that helped the company cut its annual production and distribution costs by $1.6 billion (Schiller, Burns, and Miller 1996).

4.5. Two Comments

In addition to a basic understanding of alternatives for improving forecast accuracy, the **main lesson of this section** is that it is important to step back and consider a range of different alternatives before jumping into specific solutions. Of the **five alternatives— method, early warning, law of large numbers, trumpet of doom, reduce demand volatility**—solutions relating to changes in the forecasting method may come to mind first, but there may be many **creative and effective approaches for improving forecast accuracy that have nothing to do with the forecasting method.**

In a moment, we shall consider long-term and short-term forecasting methods, but before we do, it is worth emphasizing a point that is sometimes lost when it comes to forecasting. The high costs of poor forecasts and the pervasive interest in forecast accuracy sometimes whither the skepticism that should accompany investments to improve forecasting. As with any investment, investments to improve forecast accuracy should be critically evaluated. More generally, current, as well as proposed, steps of a forecasting process in an organization may not all add value. A $2 billion consumer packaged goods company, for example, decided to require all sales reps to submit weekly demand forecasts (Gilliland 2002). The company evaluated the impact of this change and found no improvement in forecast accuracy. The requirement was dropped, thus allowing the sales reps to spend more time on value-adding activities. The company took their analysis further and discovered that 60 percent of management overrides to the computer-generated forecast actually made the forecast worse. The discovery led to new guidelines for manually overriding a forecast.

5. LONG-TERM FORECASTING

First, here is a quick characterization of what is meant by "long term." In general, this pertains to forecasts that have an impact on decisions that take a long time to implement, cost a lot of money, and are typically costly to reverse. Examples include whether or not to buy a $100 million press, expand into the Asian market, or build a new facility in Ireland. Typically, long-term demand forecasts specify demand by month and/or year for a year or more in the future. In addition, the forecasts are for categories of products (or services), rather than specific models.

The situation is this. You are looking for ways to do a better job with long-term forecasting. You are considering alternatives that relate to **early warning, law of large numbers, trumpet of doom, and reducing demand volatility,** but you also want to entertain the possibility of using a different **method** for long-term forecasting. One thing that we can notice is that there is a lot of diversity in the way organizations go about developing long-term forecasts. We'll sketch a few of the more popular long-term forecasting methods here.

5.1. Judgment

Effective long-term forecasts require an in-depth understanding of the product (or service) and its market, e.g., knowledge of historical company volumes and trends, historical competitor volumes and trends, shifts in consumer tastes, and plans for design changes, pricing, and promotions. This knowledge provides a foundation for judgment, which almost always

Principle of Nature: Recency Effect

DEFINITION
People tend to overreact to recent events.

IMPLICATION
Consider recent events when filtering human judgment.

EXAMPLE
Hughes Electronics Corp. developed an artificial intelligence-based financial trading system. The developers did this by encoding the wisdom of Christine Downton, a successful portfolio manager. One motivation for creating the system is that it is immune to the recency effect, that is, humans tend to get overly fixated on the most recent information (Davidson 1996).

plays a role in long-term forecasting. The consequences of error tend to be high and, from the **trumpet of doom** (see Section 4.3), we know that what happened yesterday is a poor indicator of what will happen in the distant future.

My industry experience included forecasting freight expense by year for five years out. Accuracy was important, so simply inflating prior year numbers by some standard percentage was not viable. Judgment played a large role; I used past history, demand projections, my judgment, and the judgment of experts on such factors as future fuel costs, transportation deregulation, demographic shifts, and expansion to new markets.

5.2. Salesperson and Customer Input

Salesperson input and customer input can be excellent sources of information for demand forecasts (see the Sunbeam example in Section 3 above). After all, this is where the action is.

A Few Caveats

There are a couple of **caveats that go along with using human input for forecasting.** First, **beware of the potential for bias.** Salespeople, for example, are sometimes paid in part according to how well they do relative to a quota (e.g., selling a lot more than the quota can be a little like winning the lottery . . . a nice bonus and a free trip to Hawaii). The incentive structure may encourage salespeople to "lowball" their demand estimates (in some situations, it could go the other way as well). Similarly, it is common for customers to have an incentive to overestimate demand (can you guess why?).

Second, people have a tendency to be **overly influenced by recent events.** This is a **principle of nature known as the recency effect.** For example, a salesperson who has had several very good months in a row, other things being equal, will tend to overestimate demand in the future. The recency effect should be considered when filtering human judgment.

5.3. Outside Services

Outside services in this context refer to firms that develop and sell forecasts. For example, in established industries, there frequently exist organizations that forecast industrywide demand by product and service category. There are also companies that develop forecasts of economic indicators such as housing starts, GDP growth, interest rates, and so forth. These sources of information can be useful for arriving at industrywide demand projections that in turn can be combined with company-developed market share projections to generate demand forecasts.

5.4. Causal Methods

Causal methods attempt to identify a cause-and-effect relationship, and use the relationship to predict the future. The determination of an accurate cause-and-effect relationship can be time consuming, but is cost-effective in some settings. One example of a causal method is the statistical tool *regression*—a tool that you may have seen in other courses.[13]

Causal methods tend to be used in connection with promotions and other events that both influence demand and can be predicted. For example, the number of housing starts in December, January, and February is a good indicator of second-quarter appliance sales in the builder market. As another example, I once worked on a project where the problem was to accurately forecast monthly natural gas and electricity usage over a year's time at a plant. We found regression-derived formulas based on weather forecasts to work quite well.

In the context of promotion planning, causal methods based on regression analysis of past promotions can be used to predict how promotion choices (e.g., duration, discount, and media) affect demand. Firms use this information to incorporate the effects of a promotion plan into the demand forecast. The benefits of such analysis extend beyond forecasting, yielding insight into how effective promotions should be designed.

6. SHORT-TERM FORECASTING

The meaning of "short term" is the flip-side of long term: the time horizon tends to be weeks or months instead of a year or more, the *time bucket* tends to be days or weeks (i.e., demand forecast is reported by day or week) instead of months or years, and demand tends to be forecasted for individual models (or specific services) rather than product categories.

Do you think long-term forecasts tend to be more accurate than short-term forecasts, or vice versa? The reason for posing this question has little to do with a specific answer, and, in fact, there is no single answer. The reason is to reinforce your understanding of the difference between long- and short-term forecasts, and, more importantly, two principles of nature. Let's see how.

According to the **law of large numbers,** long-term forecasts should be more accurate than short-term forecasts. The unit being forecast is aggregated over a segment of the product line and over time. Volume is higher, relative variability is lower, and, therefore, forecast accuracy is better.

According to the **trumpet of doom,** short-term forecasts should be more accurate than long-term forecasts. Last week's demand is a better indicator of next week's demand than demand 53 weeks from now, and, therefore, accuracy of short-term forecasts is better. The two principles work in opposite directions, and the answer to the question could go either way in practice depending on product, industry, and forecasting methods.[14]

6.1. Components of Demand

One nice thing about short-term forecasts is that they can often be developed almost automatically with little human intervention. There are two reasons for this. One is the **trumpet**

---

[13] Strictly speaking, regression can be used to specify a *correlation* between a dependent variable (e.g., demand) and various independent variables (e.g., price, advertising). A correlation may not reflect a true cause-and-effect relationship.

[14] I found long-term demand forecasts to generally be more accurate than short-term demand forecasts in my industry experience; that is, the law of large numbers more than offset the trumpet of doom.

of doom—what happened in the recent past is generally a pretty good indicator of what will happen in the near future. A second reason is that the consequences of error don't tend to be that significant, at least relative to long-term forecasts. It's not a big deal if you overestimate demand on July 15 for 12-packs of Pepsi at Wegmans by 70 percent. Overestimating annual demand for Pepsi product in the North American market by 70 percent is another story. The bottom line is that it is a lot easier to get away with simple mechanical methods for forecasting short-term demand than long-term demand. Fortunately, there are also fairly simple and effective short-term forecasting methods. In order to understand these tools, we need to first understand the components of demand.

Demand in a period can be divided into **four components: (1) mean, (2) trend, (3) seasonality, and (4) randomness.** Randomness is the variation in demand over time that cannot be explained by the other three components. Seasonality refers to one or more patterns in demand that repeat on a cyclic basis (e.g., demand on Saturday tends to be about 20 percent higher than the average demand per day). A given product or service may exhibit multiple cycles over which a seasonal pattern is apparent (e.g., weekly cycle, monthly cycle, annual cycle). Trend refers to the rate of increase or decrease in demand over time after seasonality effects are removed. The mean component refers to the average demand in a period after trend and seasonality effects are removed. For example, the fact that our forecast was 600 and actual demand came in at 720 may be due to some combination of a one-time upward shift in the average demand, an increase in the upward trend, an increase in the seasonality effect, and pure randomness. The challenge is to **estimate the mean, trend, and seasonality components.** We'll begin with the simplest starting point where our only concern is estimating the mean demand (i.e., assume no trend or seasonality is present).

6.2. Moving Average

The mechanics of the moving average method are largely apparent in the name: the average of demand per period during the recent past is the forecast. As each period ends, the average is updated (i.e., moves through time) to yield an updated forecast.

Notation for Moving Average Method

x_t = actual in period t (could be demand, sales, interest rate, etc.)

ma_t = moving average calculated at the end of period t

m = number of periods used in the average calculation

$F_{t,j}$ = forecast calculated at the end of period t for period $t + j$

Mechanics

An m-period moving average is calculated as the average of the m most recent periods. This means that a moving average calculated at the end of period t is the average of demand in period t, period $t - 1$, and so on back to period $t - m + 1$. This number is used to forecast period $t + 1$, and as many periods into the future as needed.

Formulas for the Moving Average Method

$$ma_t = \frac{\sum_{i=1}^{m} x_{t-m+i}}{m} = (x_{t-m+1} + x_{t-m+2} + \cdots + x_{t-1} + x_t)/m$$

$$F_{t,j} = ma_t$$

Example

Suppose $t = 20$, so time period 20 just ended. Demand for the last 10 periods was $x_{11} = 450$, $x_{12} = 320$, $x_{13} = 411$, $x_{14} = 452$, $x_{15} = 799$, $x_{16} = 286$, $x_{17} = 360$, $x_{18} = 422$, $x_{19} = 530$, $x_{20} = 490$. What is the forecast for periods 21, 22, and 23 using a four-period moving average? We need to first calculate the most up-to-date moving average, which is ma_{20}, the average calculated at the end of period 20. Since $m = 4$,

$$ma_{20} = (x_{17} + x_{18} + x_{19} + x_{20})/4 = (360 + 422 + 530 + 490)/4 = 450.5$$

As of the end of period 20, the forecast for periods 21, 22, and 23 is 450.5, or in terms of the notation

$$F_{20,1} = F_{20,2} = F_{20,3} = ma_{20} = 450.5$$

Remember that with the moving average method, we are assuming there is no trend or seasonality; the challenge is to estimate the mean demand. This estimate is the forecast for the next period (e.g., period 21) and for as many periods we need to forecast into the future (e.g., periods 22 and 23). Of course, our forecast for future periods will be updated over time as we update our estimate of mean demand, which leads to the next part of the example.

Suppose time period 21 just ended, so $t = 21$. Observed demand was $x_{21} = 605$. What is the updated forecast for periods 22 and 23? The answer is ma_{21}, which works out to

$$ma_{21} = (x_{18} + x_{19} + x_{20} + x_{21})/4 = (422 + 530 + 490 + 605)/4 = 511.8$$

and

$$F_{21,1} = F_{21,2} = ma_{21} = 511.8$$

In this example, we see the forecast for periods 22 and 23 increased from 450.5 to 511.8 as we move through time (due to the high demand of 605 in period 21 replacing the low demand of 360 in period 17 in the average calculation).

Example Summary

Period (t)	Actual Demand (x_t)	4-Period Moving Average (ma_t)	Next Period Forecast ($F_{t,1}$)	Period $t + 2$ Forecast ($F_{t,2}$)
17	360			
18	422			
19	530			
20	490	450.5	450.5	450.5
21	605	511.8	511.8	511.8

450.5 is calculated at the end of period 20 as the average of the four most recent demands and is an estimate of mean demand in period 20; it is the forecast for periods 21 and 22.

511.8 is calculated at the end of period 21 as the average of the four most recent demands and is an estimate of mean demand in period 21; it is the updated forecast for period 22 and the new forecast for period 23.

The Role of m

As the **number of periods in a moving average increase, the method becomes less responsive to changes in the market.** To make this statement more concrete, consider the example above except $m = 10$. At $t = 20$, the 10-period moving average is $ma_{20} = (x_{11} + x_{12} + \cdots + x_{20})/10 = 452.0$. One period later, at $t = 21$, the 10-period moving average is $ma_{21} = (x_{12} + x_{13} + \cdots + x_{21})/10 = 467.5$. With $m = 4$, the moving average changed from 450.5 to 511.8, which compares to a shift from 452.0 to 467.5 with $m = 10$. This is actually another example of the **law of large numbers** at work; the average becomes more stable as the sample size increases.

What Does This Mean for the Choice of m?

Remember that we are assuming that there is no trend or seasonality to worry about; we are using the moving average method to estimate the mean demand, which may shift over time. If the moving average is overreacting to randomness in the market, then increase m. On the other hand, if the moving average is not picking up on shifts in the mean over time, then decrease m.

The moving average method is simple, and can be reasonable in settings where there is no trend or seasonality. However, there is something better—a method that is generally more effective for estimating the mean and that is easily adapted to incorporate trend and seasonality. Let me introduce you to Mr. Winters (Winters 1960).

6.3. Winters Method and Exponential Smoothing

Suppose you're interested in a hassle-free method for short-term forecasting—something that is simple, requires little data, adapts automatically to changes in the environment, and, most important, requires little personal involvement. You're gladly willing to give up a little accuracy just so you don't have to bother with trying to come up with the numbers. You're also able to accept the fact that the method will be dumb, using only the past to project the future. What is it that you want? Exponential smoothing, which is probably the most popular computer-based method in industry.

Let's first take a look at the end result. Here we're going to be forecasting weekday demand (except for Friday when we close up shop to study SCM). I'm going to make up some wild data; things will start off pretty stable, then I'll introduce increasing trend, throw in some daily "seasonality," then reverse the trend, then stabilize but leave the seasonality—quite a brew. With the above in mind, I generated a plot for demand over time using the random number generator in Excel. Then I overlaid the one-period-ahead forecast using the method (known as the **Winters method** after its originator; see Figure 4.4).

Now let's get into the details on how to make it happen. Our goal is to understand the

Winters method, a forecasting tool that accommodates the possibilities of trend and one or more patterns (e.g., seasonal cycles). We'll begin with the simplest form of the Winters method known as basic exponential smoothing. For this method, the only component of demand to forecast is the mean (i.e., no trend or seasonality). Then we'll incrementally consider trend, seasonality, and, finally, both trend and seasonality together. But first, some notation.

Notation for the Winters Method

x_t = actual in period t (could be demand, sales, interest rate, etc.)

s_t = smoothed estimate of the mean demand in period t, calculated at the end of period t

FIGURE 4.4

The Winters method used to forecast demand one period into the future. The plot illustrates how the method picks up on a cyclic pattern and upward/downward trends in highly erratic data.

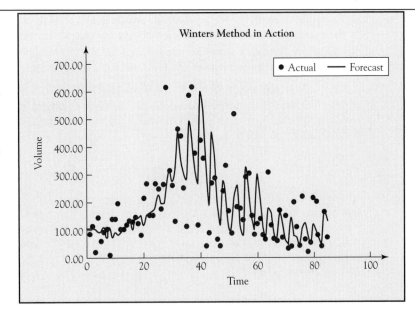

α = smoothing parameter for s_t, $\alpha \in [0, 1]$

b_t = smoothed estimate of the trend component in period t, calculated at the end of period t; the value of b_t is an estimate for the amount of increase or decrease per period after seasonality effects are removed

β = smoothing parameter for b_t, $\beta \in [0, 1]$

M_t = smoothed estimate of the seasonal index for the season of period t, calculated at the end of period t; the seasonal index for a particular season is a measure of (mean demand in the season) ÷ (mean demand over all seasons); for example, if the seasonal index for the month of January is 1.20, then we expect demand in January to be 20 percent higher than the average monthly demand

γ = smoothing parameter for M_t, $\gamma \in [0, 1]$

L = number of seasons in a cycle

$F_{t,j}$ = forecast calculated at the end of period t for period $t + j$

Basic Exponential Smoothing

Basic exponential smoothing, which is the Winters method without trend or seasonality, is appropriate if you don't believe there is any trend or seasonality present. The value of s_t represents the smoothed estimate of mean demand calculated at the end of time period t; that is, it's an estimate of the mean demand as of the end of period t (just like ma_t is an estimate of mean demand at the end of period t for the moving average method). The estimate of the mean, s_t, is updated at the end of each period.

Formulas for the Basic Exponential Smoothing Method

$$s_t = \alpha x_t + (1 - \alpha)s_{t-1} = s_{t-1} + \alpha(x_t - s_{t-1}) = \text{old estimate} + \alpha(\text{error})$$

$$F_{t,j} = s_t$$

From these formulas we see that all we need to calculate a new *smoothed estimate* of the mean (s_t) is our old smoothed estimate (s_{t-1}) and the most recent actual demand (x_t). Once we have s_t, it becomes our forecast for any period into the future ($F_{t,j} = s_t$), at least until the next period passes and our forecasts can be updated.

Example

Period 5 just ended, that is, $t = 5$. Given $s_5 = 31.2$ and $\alpha = 0.2$, what are the forecasts for periods 6, 7, and 8? In terms of the notation, we need $F_{t,j}$ where $t = 5$ and $j = 1$, 2, and 3. From the formula, $F_{t,j} = s_t$, the best estimate of the mean as of the end of period 5; therefore, the forecast for periods 6, 7, and 8 is

$$F_{5,1} = F_{5,2} = F_{5,3} = s_5 = 31.2$$

While it can take some time to get used to the notation, this question was easy in the sense that no calculation was required. This is about to change. Suppose period 6 just ended, that is, $t = 6$. Actual demand in period 6 was $x_6 = 35.0$. What are the updated forecasts for periods 7 and 8, and what is the new forecast for period 9? We'll use the same approach as above and begin with the end. We need $F_{t,j}$ where $t = 6$ and $j = 1$, 2, and 3. Since $F_{t,j} = s_t$, all we need is s_6. From the formula,

$$s_t = s_{t-1} + \alpha(x_t - s_{t-1})$$
$$t = 6$$

$$s_6 = s_5 + \alpha(x_6 - s_5) = 31.2 + 0.2(35.0 - 31.2) = 32.0$$

$$F_{6,1} = F_{6,2} = F_{6,3} = s_6 = 32.0$$

Example Summary

Period (t)	Actual Demand (x_t)	$\alpha = 0.2$ Smoothed Estimate (s_t)	Next Period Forecast ($F_{t,1}$)	Period $t + 2$ Forecast ($F_{t,2}$)	Period $t + 3$ Forecast ($F_{t,3}$)
5		31.2	31.2	31.2	31.2
6	35.0	32.0	32.0	32.0	32.0

31.2 is calculated at the end of period 5 and is an estimate of mean demand in period 5 (which is given in the example); it is the forecast for periods 6, 7, and 8.
  32.0 = 31.2 + 0.2(35.0 – 31.2) is calculated at the end of period 6 and is an estimate of mean demand in period 6; it is the updated forecast for periods 7 and 8, and the new forecast for period 9.

Do the Updated Forecasts for Periods 7 and 8 Make Sense?   As of the end of period 5, our best guess of mean demand was 31.2, so this was our forecast for periods 6, 7, and 8. Demand in period 6 came in higher than our forecast at a value of 35.0, so it is not surprising that our new updated forecast of periods 7 and 8 (at a value of 32.0) is larger. The method appears rational, though we can break down the logic at a more detailed level to see if it makes sense. The method interprets the period 6 forecast error of 3.8 = 35.0 − 31.2 as partially due to randomness and partially indicative that the mean demand rate has increased. More specifically, with $\alpha = 0.2$, 20 percent of the error is assumed to

FIGURE 4.5

The new estimate used to forecast demand in period 7 is updated according to the error in period 6. With a smoothing parameter $\alpha = 0.2$, new estimate = old estimate + 20% of the error, or 32.0 = 31.2 + 0.2 × 3.8.

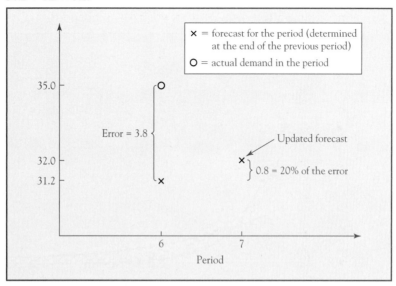

be indicative of a change in the mean, that is, new estimate = old estimate + 0.2(error) = 31.2 + 0.2(35.0 − 31.2) = 32.0 (see Figure 4.5). This leads to the role of α.

The Role of α Just like the value of m in the moving average method, the value of α controls the responsiveness of the method. The **larger the value of α, the more responsive the method is to changes in the market.** This makes intuitive sense in light of the formula $s_t = s_{t-1} + \alpha(x_t - s_{t-1})$, or new estimate = old estimate + α(error). As α gets larger, the adjustment gets larger and the method is more responsive. Forecasting software will often include a feature for determining an effective value of α based on past history. In practice, $\alpha \in [0.1, 0.3]$ usually works well.

Exponential Smoothing and the Trumpet of Doom   In Section 6.2 we saw how the moving average forecasting method estimates the mean demand as the average of recently observed demand. The method recognizes that the mean demand can shift over time, and uses the most recent information to estimate the mean at a given point in time. In this sense, the moving average method accounts for the **trumpet of doom**—the principle of nature that the recent past is a better indicator of the near future than what happened a long time ago. However, exponential smoothing exploits the trumpet of doom in a more refined and more complete manner, and this may partially explain the method's popularity and effectiveness. Figure 4.6 shows the weights applied to historical demand with the exponential smoothing method. The figure illustrates how weights gradually decrease as demand data become more out of date; in contrast, the moving average method weights each of the most recent m periods equally. The figure also shows why the method is known as *exponential* smoothing—the weight decreases exponentially in time.[15]

---

[15] Specifically, the weight applied to x_{t-i} is $\alpha(1 - \alpha)^i$.

FIGURE 4.6

A plot of the weights applied to historical demand according to exponential smoothing for three different values of α. Formulas for the weights can be obtained by repeated substitution of $s_{t-i} = \alpha x_{t-i} + (1 - \alpha)s_{t-i-1}$ into $s_t = \alpha x_t + (1 - \alpha)s_{t-1}$; for example, $s_t = \alpha x_t + (1 - \alpha)s_{t-1} = \alpha x_t + \alpha(1 - \alpha)x_{t-1} + (1 - \alpha)^2 s_{t-2} = \alpha x_t + \alpha(1 - \alpha)x_{t-1} + \alpha(1 - \alpha)^2 x_{t-2} + (1 - \alpha)^3 s_{t-3}$, and so on.

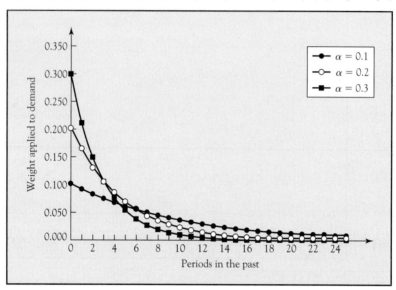

Exponential Smoothing with Trend

Exponential smoothing with trend, which is the Winters method without seasonality, is based on an estimate of the mean demand in period t (s_t) and an estimate of the change in demand per period (b_t). At the end of the current period t, we compute a smoothed estimate of the mean (s_t) and a smoothed estimate of the rate of change, or trend (b_t). From these two estimates, it is possible to compute a forecast for any period in the future. For example, the forecast for demand three periods from now is the latest estimate of the mean plus three times the latest estimate of the change per period (i.e., $F_{t,3} = s_t + 3b_t$).

Formulas for the Exponential Smoothing with Trend Method

$$s_t = \alpha x_t + (1 - \alpha)(s_{t-1} + b_{t-1}) = s_{t-1} + b_{t-1} + \alpha[x_t - (s_{t-1} + b_{t-1})]$$
$$= \text{old estimate} + \alpha(\text{error})$$

$$b_t = \beta(s_t - s_{t-1}) + (1 - \beta)b_{t-1} = b_{t-1} + \beta[(s_t - s_{t-1}) - b_{t-1}] = \text{old estimate} + \beta(\text{error})$$

$$F_{i,j} = s_i + jb_t$$

Example

Period 5 just ended, that is, $t = 5$. Given $s_5 = 31.2$, $\alpha = 0.2$, $b_5 = 9.1$, and $\beta = 0.2$, what are the forecasts for periods 6, 7, and 8? In terms of the notation, we need $F_{t,j}$ where $t = 5$ and $j = 1, 2,$ and 3. From the formula $F_{t,j} = s_t + jb_t$,

$$F_{5,1} = s_5 + b_5 = 31.2 + 9.1 = 40.3$$
$$F_{5,2} = s_5 + 2b_5 = 31.2 + 2(9.1) = 49.4$$
$$F_{5,3} = s_5 + 3b_5 = 31.2 + 3(9.1) = 58.5$$

Suppose period 6 just ended, that is, $t = 6$. Actual demand in period 6 was $x_6 = 35.0$. What are the updated forecasts for periods 7 and 8, and what is the new forecast for period 9? We'll use the same approach as above and begin with the end. We need $F_{t,j}$ where $t = 6$ and $j = 1, 2$, and 3; that is, $F_{6,1} = s_6 + b_6$, $F_{6,2} = s_6 + 2b_6$, and $F_{6,3} = s_6 + 3b_6$. So, all we need are s_6 and b_6.

$$s_t = s_{t-1} + b_{t-1} + \alpha[x_t - (s_{t-1} + b_{t-1})]$$

$$t = 6$$

$$s_6 = s_5 + b_5 + \alpha[x_6 - (s_5 + b_5)] = 40.3 + 0.2(35.0 - 40.3) = 39.2$$

$$b_t = b_{t-1} + \beta[(s_t - s_{t-1}) - b_{t-1}]$$

$$t = 6$$

$$b_6 = b_5 + \beta[(s_6 - s_5) - b_5] = 9.1 + 0.2[(39.2 - 31.2) - 9.1] = 8.9$$

$$F_{6,1} = s_6 + b_6 = 39.2 + 8.9 = 48.1$$

$$F_{6,2} = s_6 + 2b_6 = 39.2 + 2(8.9) = 57.0$$

$$F_{6,3} = s_6 + 3b_6 = 39.2 + 3(8.9) = 65.9$$

Example Summary

Period (t)	Actual Demand (x_t)	$\alpha = 0.2$ Smoothed Mean Estimate (s_t)	$\beta = 0.2$ Smoothed Trend Estimate (b_t)	Next Period Forecast $(F_{t,1})$	Period $t + 2$ Forecast $(F_{t,2})$	Period $t + 3$ Forecast $(F_{t,3})$
5		31.2	9.1	40.3	49.4	58.5
6	35.0	39.2	8.9	48.1	57.0	65.9

31.2 is calculated at the end of period 5 and is an estimate of mean demand in period 5; 9.1 is calculated at the end of period 5 and is an estimate of trend in period 5 (both values are given in the example).

40.3, 49.4, and 58.5 are forecasts for periods 6, 7, and 8.

39.2 is calculated at the end of period 6 and is an estimate of mean demand in period 6; 8.9 is calculated at the end of period 6 and is an estimate of trend in period 6.

48.1 and 57.0 are the updated forecasts for periods 7 and 8, and 65.9 is the new forecast for period 9.

Do the Updated Forecasts for Periods 7 and 8 Make Sense? As of the end of period 5, our forecast for period 6 was 40.3, and for periods 7 and 8, 49.4 and 58.5. Actual demand in period 6 was 35, or below our forecast. Consequently, our updated forecasts for periods 7 and 8 are lowered somewhat to 48.1 and 57.0. The method squares with intuition—a good sign.

The Role of α and β α is the smoothing parameter for s_t (smoothed estimate of mean demand) and β is the smoothing parameter for b_t (smoothed estimate of the trend). The **larger the smoothing parameters, the more responsive the smoothed estimates will be to the changes in the market.**

Exponential Smoothing with Seasonality

Exponential smoothing with seasonality, which is the Winters method without trend, is based on an estimate of the mean demand and estimates of the seasonal indices for each of the seasons in a cycle. At the end of each period, we update the estimate of the mean (s_t) and an estimate of the seasonal index that corresponds to the season of the period that just ended. From these estimates, it is possible to compute a forecast for any period in the future.

Formulas for the Exponential Smoothing with Seasonality Method

$$s_t = \alpha(x_t/M_{t-L}) + (1 - \alpha)s_{t-1} = s_{t-1} + \alpha[(x_t/M_{t-L}) - s_{t-1}] = \text{old estimate} + \alpha(\text{error})$$

$$M_t = \gamma(x_t/s_t) + (1 - \gamma)M_{t-L} = M_{t-L} + \gamma[(x_t/s_t) - M_{t-L}] = \text{old estimate} + \gamma(\text{error})^{16}$$

$$F_{t,j} = s_t M_{t-L+j}$$

Note: While relatively simple, the preceding formula for $F_{t,j}$ is incorrect when forecasting more than L periods into the future (i.e., when $j > L$). Recall from the notation that L is the number of periods in a cycle. For example, there may be seasonality in daily demand over the course of a week at a restaurant, in which case the length of the cycle is seven days, or $L = 7$. The following formula holds for any number of periods into the future.

$$F_{t,j} = \begin{cases} s_t M_{t-L+j \bmod L} & \text{if } j \bmod L > 0 \\ s_t M_t & \text{if } j \bmod L = 0 \end{cases}$$

The term $j \bmod L$ is a function that returns the remainder after dividing j by L. For example, $4 \bmod 5 = 4$, $15 \bmod 5 = 0$, and $18 \bmod 5 = 3$. I recommend ignoring the subscripts on M when manually updating a forecast (this subscript notation is presented in order to precisely define the method and to facilitate implementation of the method in spreadsheet or database software). Rather, select the appropriate seasonal index according to your knowledge of the current season (e.g., for the case of updating M) or the season you're forecasting. Both approaches will be illustrated in the example below.

Example

Suppose that quarter 3 just ended. The first step is to update the estimate of the mean (i.e., compute s_t). In the formula for s_t above, x_t corresponds to the third quarter actual demand and M_{t-L} corresponds to the seasonal index for quarter 3 (since quarter 3 is the season that just ended). After computing s_t, the next step is to compute M_t, which is our updated estimate of the quarter 3 seasonal index. We see in the formula that to update our estimate of the quarter 3 seasonal index, we need actual (x_t), our latest estimate of the mean (s_t), and our current estimate of the quarter 3 seasonal index (M_{t-L}). Given s_t and the seasonal indices, we compute a forecast for demand in period $t + j$ by multiplying the mean (s_t) by the seasonal index that corresponds to the season of period $t + j$ (e.g., to forecast demand in quarter 4 we would multiply the mean by the quarter 4 seasonal index). Now let's try an example with some numbers.

Period 5 just ended, that is, $t = 5$. Given $s_5 = 31.2$, $\alpha = 0.2$, two seasons per cycle with $M_4 = 1.10$, $M_5 = 0.90$, $\gamma = 0.4$, what are the forecasts for periods 6, 7, and 8? In terms of the notation, we need $F_{t,j}$ where $t = 5$ and $j = 1$, 2, and 3. From the formula,

---

[16] Theoretically, the average value of the seasonal indices should equal 1. For example, if there are two seasons and demand in the high season is projected at 20 percent above the mean demand (index = 1.2), then demand in the low season should be projected at 20 percent below the mean demand (index = 0.8, and average index = 1.0). The formula for updating the seasonal index does not necessarily maintain this average. Consequently, it is common in practice to periodically renormalize the indices to an average of 1.

$$F_{5,1} = s_5 M_4 = 31.2(1.10) = 34.3$$
$$F_{5,2} = s_5 M_5 = 31.2(0.90) = 28.1$$
$$F_{5,3} = s_5 M_{5-2+3\bmod 2} = s_5 M_{5-1} = s_5 M_4 = 31.2(1.10) = 34.3$$

Alternatively, the most up-to-date estimate of the seasonal index for the even period was calculated at the end of period 4 with value $M_{even} = 1.10$. Similarly, the most up-to-date estimate of the seasonal index for the odd period was calculated at the end of period 5 with value $M_{odd} = 0.90$. The forecast for any even period in the future is our estimate of the mean $\times M_{even}$, and for any odd period is mean $\times M_{odd}$, that is,

$$F_{5,1} = s_5 M_{even} = 31.2(1.10) = 34.3$$
$$F_{5,2} = s_5 M_{odd} = 31.2(0.90) = 28.1$$
$$F_{5,3} = s_5 M_{even} = 31.2(1.10) = 34.3$$

Suppose period 6 just ended, that is, $t = 6$. Actual demand in period 6 was $x_6 = 35.0$. What are the updated forecasts for periods 7 and 8, and what is the new forecast for period 9? We need $F_{t,j}$ where $t = 6$ and $j = 1$ and 2; that is, $F_{6,1} = s_6 M_5 = s_6 M_{odd}$, $F_{6,2} = s_6 M_6 = s_6 M_{even}$, and $F_{6,3} = s_6 M_5 = s_6 M_{odd}$. So, all we need are s_6 and an updated even period seasonal index, or M_6.

$$s_6 = s_5 + \alpha[(x_6/M_4) - s_5] = s_5 + \alpha[(x_6/M_{even}) - s_5] = 31.2 + 0.2[(35.0/1.10) - 31.2] = 31.3$$
$$M_6 = M_4 + \gamma[(x_6/s_6) - M_4] = 1.10 + 0.4[(35.0/31.3) - 1.10] = 1.11$$

or, in alternative notation,

$$M_{even}^{new} = M_{even}^{old} + \gamma[(x_6/s_6) - M_{even}^{old}] = 1.10 + 0.4[(35.0/31.3) - 1.10] = 1.11$$
$$F_{6,1} = s_6 M_5 = s_6 M_{odd} = 31.3(0.90) = 28.2$$
$$F_{6,2} = s_6 M_6 = s_6 M_{even} = 31.3(1.11) = 34.7$$
$$F_{6,3} = s_6 M_5 = s_6 M_{odd} = 31.3(0.90) = 28.2$$

Example Summary

Period (t)	Actual Demand (x_t)	$\alpha = 0.2$ Smoothed Mean Estimate (s_t)	$\gamma = 0.4$ Smoothed Odd Season Index (M_t)	$\gamma = 0.4$ Smoothed Even Season Index (M_t)	Next Period Forecast ($F_{t,1}$)	Period $t + 2$ Forecast ($F_{t,2}$)	Period $t + 3$ Forecast ($F_{t,3}$)
4				1.10			
5		31.2	0.90		34.3	28.1	34.3
6	35.0	31.3		1.11	28.2	34.7	28.2

1.10 is calculated at the end of period 4 and is an estimate of the even season index (which is given in the example).

31.2 is calculated at the end of period 5 and is an estimate of mean demand in period 5; 0.90 is calculated at the end of period 5 and is an estimate of the odd season index (both values are given in the example).

34.3, 28.1, and 34.3 are forecasts for periods 6, 7, and 8.

31.3 is calculated at the end of period 6 and is an estimate of mean demand in period 6; 1.11 is calculated at the end of period 6 and is an estimate of the even season index

28.2 and 34.7 are the updated forecasts for periods 7 and 8, and 28.2 is the new forecast for period 9.

Do the Updated Forecasts for Periods 7 and 8 Make Sense? Our original forecasts for periods 7 and 8 were 28.1 and 34.3. Actual in period 6 came in slightly above the forecast (35 versus 34.3), and consequently the revised forecasts are slightly higher. Notice also that our revised estimates of the mean and even period seasonal index slightly increased—31.2 to 31.3 and 1.10 to 1.11. Note that with an increase in the seasonal index, the average value of the seasonal indices is now a little larger than 1.0, that is, $\frac{1}{2}(M_{odd} + M_{even}) = \frac{1}{2}(0.90 + 1.11) = 1.005$. In practice, seasonal indices are periodically normalized to an average value of 1.0.

The Role of α and γ By now you know the role of smoothing parameters well: the **larger the smoothing parameters, the more responsive the smoothed estimates will be to changes in the market.**

Exponential Smoothing with Trend and Seasonality

Exponential smoothing with trend and seasonality, which is the Winters method, combines the ideas present in the previous methods.

Formulas for the Exponential Smoothing with Trend and Seasonality

$$s_t = \alpha(x_t/M_{t-L}) + (1 - \alpha)(s_{t-1} + b_{t-}) = s_{t-1} + b_{t-1} + \alpha[(x_t/M_{t-L}) - (s_{t-1} + b_{t-1})]$$
$$= \text{old estimate} + \alpha(\text{error})$$

$$b_t = \beta(s_t - s_{t-1}) + (1 - \beta)b_{t-1} = b_{t-1} + \beta[(s_t - s_{t-1}) - b_{t-1}] = \text{old estimate} + \beta(\text{error})$$

$$M_t = \gamma(x_t/s_t) + (1 - \gamma)M_{t-L} = M_{t-L} + \gamma[(x_t/s_t) - M_{t-L}] = \text{old estimate} + \gamma(\text{error})$$

$$F_{t,j} = (s_t + jb_t)M_{t-L+j}, \text{ or if } j > L, \text{ then}$$

$$F_{t,j} = \begin{cases} (s_t + jb_t)M_{t-L+j \bmod L} & \text{if } j \bmod L > 0 \\ (s_t + jb_t)M_t & \text{if } j \bmod L = 0 \end{cases}$$

The Winters method can be adapted to accommodate multiple seasonal cycles (e.g., weekly, monthly, annually) and different types of trend (e.g., stock prices might be better modeled with trend as a percentage increase rather than a unit increase).

Example

Period 5 just ended, that is, $t = 5$. Given $s_5 = 31.2$, $\alpha = 0.2$, $b_5 = 9.1$, $\beta = 0.2$, two seasons per cycle with $M_4 = 1.10$, $M_5 = 0.90$, $\gamma = 0.4$, what are the forecasts for periods 6, 7, and 8? In terms of the notation, we need $F_{t,j}$ where $t = 5$ and $j = 1, 2,$ and 3. From the formula,

$$F_{5,1} = (s_5 + b_5)M_4 = (31.2 + 9.1)1.10 = 44.3$$
$$F_{5,2} = (s_5 + 2b_5)M_5 = [31.2 + 2(9.1)].90 = 44.5$$
$$F_{5,3} = (s_5 + 3b_5)M_4 = [31.2 + 3(9.1)]1.10 = 64.4$$

Suppose period 6 just ended, that is, $t = 6$. Actual demand in period 6 was $x_6 = 35.0$. What are the updated forecasts for periods 7 and 8, and what is the new forecast for period 9? We need $F_{t,j}$ where $t = 6$ and $j = 1, 2,$ and 3. So, all we need are s_6, b_6, and an updated even period seasonal index, or M_6.

$$s_6 = s_5 + b_5 + \alpha[(x_6/M_4) - (s_5 + b_5)] = 40.3 + 0.2[(35.0/1.10) - 40.3] = 38.6$$
$$b_6 = b_5 + \beta[(s_6 - s_5) - b_5] = 9.1 + 0.2[(38.6 - 31.2) - 9.1] = 8.8$$
$$M_6 = M_4 + \gamma[(x_6/s_6) - M_4] = 1.10 + 0.4[(35.0/38.6) - 1.10] = 1.02$$
$$F_{6,1} = (s_6 + b_6)M_5 = (38.6 + 8.8)(0.90) = 42.7$$
$$F_{6,2} = (s_6 + 2b_6)M_6 = [38.6 + 2(8.8)](1.02) = 57.3$$
$$F_{6,3} = (s_6 + 3b_6)M_5 = [38.6 + 3(8.8)](0.90) = 58.5$$

Example Summary

Period (t)	Actual Demand (x_t)	$\alpha = 0.2$ Smoothed Mean Estimate (s_t)	$\beta = 0.2$ Smoothed Trend Estimate (b_t)	$\gamma = 0.4$ Smoothed Odd Season Index (M_t)	$\gamma = 0.4$ Smoothed Even Season Index (M_t)	Next Period Forecast $(F_{t,1})$	Period $t + 2$ Forecast $(F_{t,2})$	Period $t + 3$ Forecast $(F_{t,3})$
4					1.10			
5		31.2	9.1	0.90		44.3	44.5	64.4
6	35.0	38.6	8.8		1.02	42.7	57.3	58.5

1.10 is calculated at the end of period 4 and is an estimate of the even season index (which is given in the example).

31.2 is calculated at the end of period 5 and is an estimate of mean demand in period 5 (which is given in the example); 9.1 is calculated at the end of period 5 and is an estimate of trend in period 5; 0.90 is calculated at the end of period 5 and is an estimate of the odd season index (all three values are given in the example). 44.3, 44.5, and 64.4 are forecasts for periods 6, 7, and 8.

38.6 is calculated at the end of period 6 and is an estimate of mean demand in period 6; 8.8 is calculated at the end of period 6 and is an estimate of trend in period 6; 1.02 is calculated at the end of period 6 and is an estimate of the even season index.

42.7 and 57.3 are the updated forecasts for periods 7 and 8, and 58.5 is the new forecast for period 9.

Do the Updated Forecasts for Periods 7 and 8 Make Sense?   Our forecast for period 6 was high (forecast of 44.3 versus actual of 35.0). Consequently our updated forecasts for periods 7 and 8 are lower, which makes intuitive sense.

The Role of α, β, ***and*** γ The **larger the smoothing parameters, the more responsive the smoothed estimates will be to the changes in the market.**

6.4. Focus Forecasting

Focus forecasting is an intuitive and flexible approach that tends to work well in practice. Here's the basic idea. Take a bunch of your favorite forecasting methods (e.g., Winters, moving average, etc.), let them compete with one another, and use the winner (i.e., most accurate) to generate your forecasts. You can set this up yourself using Visual Basic and Excel, or you can purchase a focus forecasting software package.

Focus forecasting was the brainchild of Bernie Smith when he was an inventory manager at American Hardware Supply (AHS). He was responsible for 21 buyers who each had responsibility for a portion of the 100,000 stock keeping units (SKUs)[17] sold at AHS. Buyers routinely ignored a computer-generated report with recommended purchase quantities. One reason: buyers didn't trust the demand forecast, in part because it was not clear how the numbers were derived. Buyers tended to manually develop their own forecasts

---

[17] A *stock keeping unit*, which is usually pronounced as *skew* for its acronym, is a product identifier used by merchants for tracking purposes. A six-pack of Coke, for example, will have a different SKU (or product identifier) than a 12-pack of Coke. Today, a product's SKU is commonly encoded in a bar code located on the product label, and scanners at the checkout register read the SKU to determine the proper price and to update sales and inventory records in the store's database. In the future, it may be commonplace that the SKU and other product information are encoded in an RFID chip that is used in place of a bar code.

and use these to determine purchase quantities. This problem with the existing system led to focus forecasting. Seven forecasting methods, including some of the buyer methods, generate forecasts, with the most accurate method used for the official forecasts. Buyers accepted the new approach—after all, their methods were being used. Recommended purchase quantities on the report were more widely accepted, inventory went down, and the level of service went up. Bernie eventually left AHS to start his own firm that develops and implements focus forecasting software.

If there is competition, how is the winner determined and when does the official forecast method change? First, the current champ is not easily dethroned. Focus forecasting uses various stabilizing rules to help keep the official method from changing too frequently (e.g., it could cause wild swings in plans as forecasts are updated if the method is always changing). Second, there are a number of ways to measure historical forecast accuracy. One of the more common measures is mean absolute deviation—more on this in the next section.

6.5. Filtering

Most computer-based forecasting systems in practice are used for thousands of different items, with forecasts updated on a daily or weekly basis. **Filtering is used in these systems to help identify problems.** For example, if the difference between actual demand and forecasted demand for a product is beyond a prespecified limit, then the product will appear on an exception report. Limits are set high enough so that it is unlikely for a product to get caught by the filter unless there has been some sort of data collection error. So, we see **one purpose of filtering is to catch data errors.**

A **second purpose of filtering is to catch products with consistently poor forecasts** so that alternative methods or parameter values may be considered. One common way to do this is through a *tracking signal* that is computed for each product. A tracking signal, which is described in more detail below, measures the degree to which a forecast is consistently low or high. Products with a tracking signal value that is outside of a prespecified range appear on an exception report. This type of filtering allows one to manage forecasts by exception, spending more time on products where the benefit is likely to be greatest, that is, filtering is an example of Pareto analysis.

Two common measures of forecast accuracy are mean absolute deviation (MAD)[18] and mean forecast error (MFE). These error measures may be updated at the end of each period using exponential smoothing, or as a straight average over some number of periods. For example, using the straight average over the most recent n periods, the mean absolute deviation at the end of period t is

$$\text{MAD} = \frac{\sum_{i=1}^{n} \left| x_{t-n+i} - F_{t-1-n+i,1} \right|}{n}$$

The mean forecast error is the same except the absolute value signs are removed:

$$\text{MFE} = \frac{\sum_{i=1}^{n} (x_{t-n+i} - F_{t-1-n+i,1})}{n}$$

MFE is also known as bias; it gives an indication of whether a forecast method is consistently high or consistently low. For example, a value of MFE = 30 indicates that the forecast is lower than actual by an average of 30 units. An alternative measure of bias is

---

[18] Other error measures include the mean squared error and mean absolute percentage error; see the RJ Instruments case exercise at the end of the chapter.

the cumulative forecast error (CFE), which is the sum of forecast errors over time, for example,

$$\text{CFE} = n \times \text{MFE} = \sum_{i=0}^{n}\left(x_{t-n+i} - F_{t-1-n+i,1}\right)$$

CFE is commonly used in combination with MAD to yield a standardized measure of bias known as a *tracking signal*. In particular, tracking signal = CFE/MAD measures the total bias (CFE) as a percent of the average absolute forecast error (MAD). The tracking signal is updated at the end of each period, and thus *tracks* the degree of bias in the forecasting method; a value above or below a prespecified range *signals* the need for management attention.

7. SUMMARY AND MANAGERIAL INSIGHTS

This chapter has covered a lot of ground. We focused on three main areas related to demand management: processing, influencing, and anticipating demand.

Processing Demand

We looked at the scope and importance of order processing, a process that is often a major point of contact with a firm's customers. One consequence is that, relative to other processes, mistakes and problems in this area can have a disproportionate effect on customer perceptions. We also learned that order processing is largely about information processing. The rapid rate at which information technologies are advancing and opening new opportunities to improve the area is another reason why order processing is an important area for management attention.

Influencing Demand

We saw how advancing data collection and analysis technologies are opening new opportunities to measure customer profit potential, a measure that is relevant for identifying customer segments that warrant the most attention. Such information can play a role in tactics and strategies for influencing demand, for example, by guiding customer retention efforts.

Anticipating Demand

As noted in Chapter 3, one cause of system slack is quantity uncertainty. In this chapter, we considered a variety of approaches for reducing quantity uncertainty by improving forecast accuracy. There are many methods that are used for long-term forecasting in practice, and we learned about the basic features of some of the more popular methods: judgment, salesperson input, customer input, outside services, and causal methods. We examined the details of the moving average and the Winters method, which are widely used for short-term forecasting. We also learned about focus forecasting and various measures of forecast accuracy.

In addition to alternative forecasting methods, we learned how changes in a firm's operations and reward systems can be a powerful, and sometimes neglected, lever for improving forecast accuracy. In particular, we learned about four tactics—early warning, forecast aggregation, reduce delays, and reduce volatility—and we saw many examples of how these tactics are used in practice. The chapter also covered five principles of nature—law of large numbers, trumpet of doom, hockey stick effect, Pareto phenomenon, recency effect—and illustrated the relevance of these principles for improving forecast accuracy. Key managerial insights from the chapter are summarized below.

7.1. Pay Attention to Order Processing

Order processing is a primary area of customer contact and consequently it can have a big impact on customer perceptions. Order processing is almost entirely the processing of information, and information technology is advancing so fast that there could well be opportunities to profitably improve the area.

Dell Inc. has used order processing to its advantage. More than 50 percent of Dell's orders are placed online, which is faster and less labor-intense compared to the alternative of phone orders. In addition, Dell has created more than 60,000 custom Web sites for corporate customers, and the order processing cycle from receipt of the order to the shipment of a built-to-order PC typically completes within a few days (Park and Burrows 2001).

7.2. The Most Cost-Effective Approach to Improve Forecast Accuracy May Involve Changing Your Operations Rather Than Collecting More Data or Using Different Techniques for Analyzing Information

Beyond changing the forecasting method, four other alternatives for improving forecast accuracy are to take advantage of (1) early warning, (2) law of large numbers, (3) trumpet of doom, and (4) reducing demand volatility. These alternatives are potentially quite powerful and will likely continue to be applied in new and creative ways. Bakos and Brynjolfsson (1999), for example, study the impact of bundling digital products (e.g., selling a group of software applications as a package). They find that bundling a large number of unrelated information goods can be quite profitable, and the reason is the **law of large numbers. It is much easier to predict a consumer's valuation of a bundle of goods than the individual valuations of each good.** As a result, a firm can price more effectively and achieve greater sales and profits.

7.3. Consider Winters for Short-Term Forecasting

The Winters method is a practical, powerful, and easy-to-implement (e.g., using Excel) tool for *casting for*ward the past to predict the future. You will likely come across this tool in one of two possible ways. First, if you work for a large company, then the Winters method or some other exponential smoothing variant will be included in software that is in use or under consideration for purchase. If you're involved in forecasting at all, it's important to understand the underlying mechanics. Forecasting, even when supported by software, requires judgment . . . and sound judgment requires knowledge of how the numbers are generated and available options for influencing the forecast method. Second, if you work for a small company or start your own business, this chapter gives enough information to implement the Winters method using spreadsheet or database software.

8. EXERCISES

Carry seasonal index calculations to two decimal places; carry other components of a forecast to one decimal place.

1. Write a brief answer to each of the chapter keys in your own words. After writing down your answers, review the chapter with a focus on the content in bold to check and clarify your interpretations.

2.

t	x_t	s_t
1	12	13.0
2	14	12.8
3	14	
4	10	
5	16	
6	17	

a. s_t was calculated using the basic exponential smoothing method with $\alpha = 0.2$. Calculate the forecasts one period ahead through period 6.

b. Calculate forecasts one period ahead through period 6 using the two-period moving average method.

c. Which method is more accurate in this instance?

d. How does focus forecasting work? If the methods in the answers to questions (a) and (b) were used in a focus forecasting system with accuracy measured by average absolute error over the most recent four periods, then what would be the forecast for period 7?

e. Suppose a different value of α was used in the calculation of s_2. **Regardless of the value of α, there is an error somewhere in the calculation of s_2.** How is this known?

3.

t	x_t	$s1_t$	$s2_t$
1	25	25.0	25.0
2	30	25.5	29.5
3	32	26.2	31.8
4	40	27.6	39.2

a. $s1_t$ and $s2_t$ are generated using the basic exponential smoothing method. Is $s1_t$ calculated using a larger or smaller value of α than $s2_t$?

b. What alpha values were used for $s1_t$ and $s2_t$?

4.

t	x_t	$F_{t,1}$	s_t	b_t
0			20.0	5.0
1	25			
2	30			
3	32			
4	40			

a. Complete the table using $\alpha = 0.2$ and $\beta = 0.4$.

b. In retrospect, will forecasting accuracy improve over periods 1 through 4 using $\alpha = 0.8$ and $\beta = 0.8$?

c. What is your most up-to-date forecast for period 10?

5.

Sales by Quarter ($000)							
Year 1				Year 2			
1	2	3	4	1	2	3	4
271	120	89	344	300	125	95	390

      a. What seasonal indices would you suggest for the four quarters?

      b. Can you think of any potential problems with using the above data for generating forecasts?

6. Using the data from the previous problem with the following initial values and smoothing parameters, calculate quarterly forecasts for years 1 through 4 (forecast one period ahead): $M_{Q1} = 1.22$, $M_{Q2} = 0.63$, $M_{Q3} = 0.43$, $M_{Q4} = 1.72$, $s_0 = 220.0$, $\alpha = 0.2$, $\gamma = 0.5$.

7.

t	x_t	$F_{t,1}$	s_t
0			21.5
1	25		
2	14		
3	30		
4	16		

Complete the above table using $M_{odd\ period} = 1.50$, $M_{even\ period} = 0.5$, $\alpha = 0.1$, $\gamma = 0.5$.

8. Use the following information and complete the table (the first period is quarter 1): $M_{Q1} = 1.20$, $M_{Q2} = 0.75$, $M_{Q3} = 0.75$, $M_{Q4} = 1.30$, $\alpha = 0.2$, $\beta = 0.2$, $\gamma = 0.4$.

t	x_t	$F_{t,1}$	s_t	b_t
0			20.0	1.0
1	25			
2	14			
3	30			
4	16			
5	30			
6	18			
7	32			
8	21			
9	45			
10	27			
11	43			
12	22			

9. Illustrate how the Winters method with trend and seasonality is a generalization of any one of the models that exclude trend and/or seasonality (i.e., determine the parameter values for trend and seasonality that result in a method that ignores trend and/or seasonality). Notice an implication is that you only need to learn one method (i.e., Winters in full).

10. Use the basic exponential smoothing method with $\alpha = 0.2$ and the two-period moving average method to complete the table below:

t	x_t	s_t	ma_t
0		41.00	
1	42		
2	47		
3	51		
4	53		
5	55		
6	58		

Which method seems more accurate? Why?

11. The data in the previous question suggest a trend. Complete the table using basic exponential smoothing with trend, given $\alpha = 0.2, \beta = 0.3$.

t	x_t	s_t	$F_{t,1}$	$F_{t,2}$	b_t
0		39.0			4.0
1	42				
2	47				
3	51				
4	53				
5	55				
6	58				

12. Perry wants to incorporate seasonal effects into his forecasts to account for the differences between sales rates when students are and aren't in session. He wants you to do the work. $M_7 = 1.00, M_8 = 1.40, M_9 = 1.40, \alpha = 0.2, \beta = 0.3, \gamma = 0.4$.

t	x_t	s_t	$F_{t,1}$	b_t	M_t
10		10.0		2.0	.20
11 (school)	11				
12 (school)	13				
13 (school)	12				
14 (summer)	4				
15	12				
16	15				
17	12				
18	5				

13. A file containing subscription levels and forecasts for your self-published newsletter has become corrupted, and there is no backup. You find an old hard copy of a report, but some of the numbers are not legible. Fill in the missing pieces in the following worksheet given $\alpha = 0.2, \gamma = 0.4$. (An electronic spreadsheet will be helpful here; you may assume that the average value of M_7 through M_{10} is 1.0.)

M_7	M_8	M_9	M_{10}
	1.35	1.45	

t	x_t	s_t	$F_{t,1}$	M_t
10		441.9	331.4	
11			603.3	
12			643.6	
13		442.0		
14		454.0		
15		448.1		
16			643.8	
17			206.9	
18			322.1	

14. Suppose you want to forecast the number of students who will sign up for a class. Information for the previous years' registration is year 1 = 41, year 2 = 44, year 3 = 50, year 4 = 57, year 5 = 59. Furthermore, $s_0 = 39$, $b_0 = 2.0$, $\alpha = 0.25$, and $\beta = 0.5$. Answer the following questions:

    a. At the end of year 5, what is your forecast for enrollment in year 6?

    b. What would be your most up-to-date forecast for year 12?

15. VoiceStream offers a family plan wireless phone package. The package includes four phones, 800 weekend minutes per month, and 240 weekday minutes per month for a monthly fee of $119.95. Extra minutes cost $0.20 per minute.

    There are two possible ways to determine when the extra minutes charged at $0.20 accrue. One way is when usage on any particular phone goes beyond a 200-minute weekend limit or a 60-minute weekday limit. The other way is when total usage on all four phones goes beyond an 800-minute weekend limit or a 240-minute weekday limit. In other words, the limits can be defined by individual phones at 200 and 60 per phone, or by the group of four phones at 800 and 240.

    Which principle of nature explains why one of these two options will be cheaper for you in the long run (other things being equal), and why? Your explanation also should identify which option is the better bargain.

16. Your company stocks a full line of product at 15 distribution centers (DCs) serving the U.S., Canada, and Mexico markets. The DCs are strategically located; you are able to deliver to 96 percent of your customers within 24 hours, assuming product is in stock. The fill rate (i.e., percentage of orders shipped from stock within 24 hours) averages around 80 percent. Inventory investment averages $200 million and last year the annual cost of goods sold to these markets was $2.4 billion.

    a. These data suggest that DCs maintain about 30 days of supply in inventory. Explain how this is so. (*Hint*: Two helpful figures are $200 million worth of inventory and cost of goods sold at $2.4 billion.) What happens to the value of the days of supply if inventory investment doubles to $400 million, and how is this related to Little's law?

    b. Over 50 percent of the product line is assembled in Mexico, with the remainder manufactured overseas. Next to the plant in Mexico is a 600,000-square-foot DC. Products are assembled and boxed in the plant, then are moved via conveyer to the DC. In addition, all overseas product destined for North American markets is shipped to the DC in Mexico, and from there, product is shipped to the remaining 14 DCs as needed. Due to the distribution network structure, the Mexico DC has come to be called the *super DC*, whereas the other 14 DCs are known as regional DCs. Transit time from the super DC to the regional DCs is about 6 days to the most distant regional DC, and averages 3.5 days over all DCs. The entire product line is comprised of 21 product categories and 821 different stock keeping units (SKUs). One product category, for example, is "compact DVD systems," and there are 35 SKUs in this category (i.e., different colors, speeds, case designs, and variations on features). After carefully analyzing SKU volumes, you find that the top-selling two or three SKUs in a category (a total of 13 percent of all SKUs) contribute 90 percent or more of the total volume in the category. What principle of nature explains this phenomenon and what is a name for this type of analysis?

    c. The results of your analysis suggest that there may be an opportunity to save your company millions per year in inventory costs while improving the fill rate and customer satisfaction. The idea is to stock only the top-selling two or three SKUs in each product category at the regional DCs. This means that 13 percent of your product line, making up 90 percent of the volume, will be stocked at regional DCs and the full product line is stocked only at the super DC. Analysis of demand variability indicates that maintaining a 30-day supply of these selected high-volume SKUs at the regional DCs will increase the fill rate from the current 80 percent to an almost perfect 98 percent. Better yet, by consolidating North American market demand for the low-volume SKUs at the super DC, you find that maintaining a 10-day supply of these SKUs should be sufficient to achieve a 98 percent fill rate. The change is expected to reduce overall inventory investment by $5 million. How will customers perceive such a change? Transit time for low-volume SKU orders will increase by several days, but the level of product availability will significantly improve (i.e., from 80 percent to 98 percent). The data suggest a win-win opportunity (and a promotion?). What principle of nature explains the economic and service improvement benefits of the idea, and why?

Case Exercise: *RJ Instruments*

RJ Instruments produces a line of pens targeted at architects and graphic artists. This market is served primarily through small retailers. However, two years ago, RJ began selling product through a mail/Internet-order firm with a large customer base (e.g., see www.levenger.com). The combination of design quality, functionality, and moderate pricing has made RJ's products popular with general consumers, who primarily purchase through the mail/Internet-order channel.

RJ currently produces and sells five models of pens. Manufacturing is done at a single plant located in Indianapolis, Indiana. A distribution center (DC) located next to the plant serves North American markets. The DC also ships RJ pens to independent distributors—one in Dublin and another in Hong Kong—that serve retailers in Europe and Asia.

RJ develops demand forecasts by month and model. Historically, this has been done manually. The challenge for this case exercise is to recommend and implement a computer-based forecasting method for each model of RJ pen using spreadsheet software such as Excel. The method will be used to forecast one month into the future. Twenty months of historical shipment data are available (see Table 1). The first 12 months are used to calibrate your method, with the remaining 8 months used to evaluate your method for each pen model according to five measures of accuracy.

BACKGROUND ON FIVE MEASURES OF FORECAST ACCURACY

The five measures are mean absolute deviation (MAD), mean forecast error (MFE), and tracking signal (TS), which are described in the chapter, and two other measures that

are used in practice: mean squared error (MSE) and mean absolute percentage error (MAPE). In practice, error measures are commonly updated at the end of each period using exponential smoothing, or as a straight average over some number of periods. For example, using the straight average over the most recent n periods, the formulas for MSE and MAPE are

$$MSE = \frac{\sum_{i=1}^{n}(x_{t-n+i} - F_{t-1-n+i,1})^2}{n}$$

$$MAPE = \frac{1}{n}\left[\sum_{i=1}^{n}\frac{|x_{t-n+i} - F_{t-1-n+i,1}|}{x_{t-n+i}}\right] \times 100$$

Questions

1. Which of the short-term forecasting methods from the chapter would you recommend RJ use? Provide the rationale for your recommendation. (*Hint*: You may find it useful to plot the shipment data.)

2. Implement and evaluate the method recommended in your answer to question 1. This involves three basic tasks. First, use actual shipments in periods 1 through 12 to establish the initial parameter values for your method; the parameter values need not be the same for each model of pen. Explain the logic that you used to determine the initial parameter values. Second, enter the formulas for calculating the shipment forecast for one month into the future for periods 13 through 21. On the basis of your initial parameter values (and appropriate logic for updating parameter values), calculate the forecasts for periods 13 through 20 (i.e., $F_{12,1}$, $F_{13,1}, \ldots, F_{19,1}$). Third, compute the MAD, MFE, TS,

TABLE 1 Unit Shipments by Month for Each RJ Pen

Period	Month	Model RJ1	RJ2	RJ3	RJ4	RJ5	Total
1	Jan	103,261	33,375	612,415	30,612	4,061	783,724
2	Feb	98,316	28,289	743,751	42,843	2,441	915,640
3	Mar	153,655	30,988	962,413	80,148	7,547	1,234,751
4	Apr	106,576	109,884	915,407	76,259	15,197	1,223,323
5	May	103,569	43,482	1,033,109	82,403	4,182	1,266,745
6	Jun	159,363	13,862	1,159,238	84,721	15,748	1,432,932
7	Jul	159,173	45,413	655,494	77,154	1,337	938,571
8	Aug	91,774	55,917	687,275	44,814	5,031	884,811
9	Sep	249,231	54,672	859,699	60,159	5,682	1,229,443
10	Oct	178,474	38,681	535,204	34,492	53,426	840,277
11	Nov	158,982	38,289	586,090	50,384	6,107	839,852
12	Dec	261,182	11,737	1,186,844	60,864	6,826	1,527,453
13	Jan	78,362	42,550	988,804	136,668	5,252	1,251,636
14	Feb	176,840	51,895	1,533,203	37,056	2,273	1,801,267
15	Mar	225,600	34,268	1,549,970	57,939	24,333	1,892,110
16	Apr	106,261	16,130	1,352,460	44,835	3,404	1,523,090
17	May	156,914	34,805	1,266,730	73,394	4,868	1,536,711
18	Jun	83,417	27,546	1,467,067	62,532	9,346	1,649,908
19	Jul	90,627	15,152	757,364	49,140	2,945	915,228
20	Aug	80,438	103,195	680,794	44,946	2,560	911,933
	Average	141,101	41,507	976,667	61,568	9,128	1,229,970

MSE, and MAPE at the end of periods 13 through 20. For each period 13 through 20, calculate a straight average since period 13 for the computations. For example, the MAD calculated at the end of period 13 is $|x_{13} - F_{12,1}|$, and at the end of period 14 is $\frac{1}{2}[|x_{13} - F_{12,1}| + |x_{14} - F_{13,1}|]$, and so on.

3. Comment on the accuracy of your method for the five pens by answering the following questions.

   a. Which measure(s) of accuracy do you find most useful for evaluating forecast accuracy, and why?

   b. For which pen does your method appear to be most biased?

   c. What might explain the relatively high bias, and what adjustment to your method could be considered to reduce bias for the "problem" pen, and why?

   d. Test out your proposed adjustment on the pen in question. What is the impact on measures of bias as well as other measures of forecast accuracy?

Chapter **Five**

Supply Management: Trends, Technologies, and Tactics

Chapter Outline

Chapter Keys

1. Why is supply management a high-impact area for management attention?
2. What two trends explain why the importance of supply management is increasing?
3. What is XML, how does it differ from HTML, and what are the ramifications for supply management if XML becomes widely used?

4. What is EDI and how is XML relevant for EDI?

5. What is VMI, what is CPFR, and how do these tactics help mitigate the bullwhip effect?

6. What are trade exchanges, reverse auctions, and shopbots?

7. What are the pros and cons of supplier/buyer partnerships and arm's-length agreements?

8. How do a total value perspective and volume buying influence sourcing decisions?

9. What are the features and pros/cons of the six types of contracts discussed in the chapter?

10. How is the Robinson-Patman Act relevant for supply management?

11. What are four insights into effective negotiation?

12. What are the bullwhip effect, recency effect, winner's curse, Pareto phenomenon, Benford's law, and obligation to reciprocate, and how are these principles of nature relevant for supply management?

13. What are the managerial insights from the chapter?

The previous chapter focused on the outputs of an organization. This chapter reverses the perspective and focuses on the inputs to an organization, or supply management (see Figure 5.1).[1] The material complements the content in the previous chapter because, while the emphasis is on supply management, many of the concepts are equally relevant for demand management.

The content is organized around trends, technologies, and tactics. We will begin in Section 1 by reviewing two trends that are raising the importance of supply management in many organizations.

Section 2 covers current and emerging information technologies that facilitate buying (and selling). The objective of the section is not to gain an in-depth understanding of how the technologies work, but to develop a sense of capabilities and impact. By the end of Section 2, you should be in a position to identify information technologies worthy of further investigation in response to a particular supply management problem or opportunity.

Section 3 describes the range of relationships that may exist between a buyer and seller. The content is closely related to Section 2 because (1) emerging technologies are introducing new alternatives for buyer/supplier relationships and (2) the desired relationship with a supplier influences the amount and types of investments in information technology. The nature of the relationship with a supplier also has a bearing on buyer tactics—the topic of Section 4. In particular, Section 4 covers four categories of tactical considerations that are relevant for supply management: total value perspective, volume buying, contract design, and negotiation.

FIGURE 5.1 A supply chain with emphasis on supply management links.

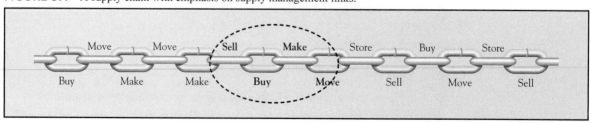

---

[1] Other terms for the supply management function in an organization are *sourcing*, *purchasing*, and *procurement*.

1. TRENDS

Supply management has historically been a fruitful area for management attention. Why the historical importance? The answer lies in the **dominant impact of purchased items on the bottom line**, through quality (e.g., input quality affects output quality), delivery reliability (e.g., input delays contribute to output delays), and cost. For example, purchased item costs typically comprise **70 to 90 percent of total expenses in wholesaling and retailing**, and in manufacturing, purchased materials are commonly **over half of a product's cost**. However, while the high cost and revenue impact of supply management have long served to focus management attention on sourcing, there are two trends that underlie a growing interest in the area.

First, the growing adoption and advances in information technology (IT) are introducing new opportunities (as well as pitfalls) in the way sourcing is managed. The U.S. Department of Commerce reports that almost 20 percent of U.S. manufacturers' shipments—worth $725 billion—relied on computer exchange of shipping and purchasing data in 2001, and that online buying increased 28 percent from second quarter 2002 to second quarter 2003 (U.S. Dept. of Commerce 2003). The impact of the trend is not limited to large firms. Small and medium-sized firms that formerly communicated by fax or phone are able to do business electronically with minimal investment. Online marketplaces exist that require only an Internet connection and a browser to participate.

DuPont, for example, has moved all aspects of purchasing to the Net and is expecting to save $400 million per year (*BusinessWeek* 2001). A division of Fisher Scientific International that distributes laboratory equipment is investing in an online network linking into accounting systems of suppliers and customers allowing invoices to be transferred electronically. The project is expected to pay for itself within six months and should cut bill processing expense by 80 percent for an annual savings of approximately $300,000 (Reinhardt 2001).

The **second trend** that is raising the level of management attention on the sourcing function is a **growth in outsourcing.** Outsourcing means moving work done within a firm to an outside provider. A survey by PricewaterhouseCoopers found an increasing number of companies are contracting business processes to an outside provider as a means to improve performance. In another survey, 50 percent of executives viewed outsourcing of noncore functions as critical to improving supply chain performance (Chabrow 2002). As more work is outsourced, improvements in the way the sourcing function is managed become increasingly significant for overall firm performance.

These two trends are related; the growth in outsourcing is being facilitated in part by IT advances that are making it easier and less expensive to tightly coordinate supplier and buyer operations. In essence, the technology is allowing interfirm interactions to approach, if not match, the quality of intrafirm interactions. For example, Cisco Systems, the market share leader in routers and other network hardware, focuses on research, development, and marketing while outsourcing much of the production and distribution functions (Elmaghraby 2000). Cisco maintains an electronic hub accessible to their suppliers, manufacturers, and distributors as a means to coordinate and plan supply chain activities.

2. E-COMMERCE TECHNOLOGIES RELATED TO SUPPLY MANAGEMENT

As illustrated in examples from the preceding section of this chapter and earlier in this book, technological advances have opened up opportunities for increased collaboration and real-time information sharing between buyers and sellers in a supply chain. Why is this meaningful? The beginnings of an answer to this question can be traced to the discussion of system slack in Chapter 3. Access to and exchange of up-to-date information throughout the supply chain helps to reduce time lags, quantity uncertainty, scale economies, and misalignment of objectives—four causes of system slack. And changes that mitigate causes of system slack translate into a combination of lower cost, higher service, and ultimately higher profit. We will build on this insight into system slack and its causes by learning about a principle of nature called the bullwhip effect. But first, a motivating example.

The Largest Inventory Write-Down in History

Consider the events that led to a $2.2 billion inventory write-down by Cisco Systems in May 2001 (Kaihla 2002; Narayanan and Raman 2004). Cisco develops and markets routers, which are devices that essentially serve as traffic cops for the Internet. Cisco relies on

contract manufacturers for final assembly (i.e., tier-one suppliers). Contract manufacturers are supplied by component producers (i.e., tier-two suppliers), who in turn are supplied by commodity suppliers (i.e., tier-three suppliers). Cisco's supply chain is electronically linked, but in May 2001, these linkages were limited to adjacent levels so that visibility of end consumer demand was limited.

Around the beginning of the 21st century, the Internet surge was booming and routers were in short supply. Customers would place duplicate orders with Cisco and Cisco's competitors, with the idea that once an order was received, the remaining orders would be canceled. From Cisco's perspective, demand appeared much greater than it actually was, and this perception became further distorted at higher tiers in the supply chain. The reason was that contract manufacturers, who were competing for business from Cicso and other router firms, were placing large orders with component providers in an attempt to lock in a supply of scarce components. In short, an imbalance between supply and demand caused router customers to overorder, which caused Cisco and other router firms to overorder, which created a greater sense of scarce supply and further overordering at higher tiers in the supply chain. By the time Cisco discovered that actual demand was much lower, it was too late. The firm was left with $2.2 billion of overvalued inventory.

The Bullwhip Effect

The Cisco example illustrates a case where demand became increasingly distorted as it propagated up through the supply chain. This phenomenon, which is prevalent in industry, is known as the **bullwhip effect: demand variability is higher at upstream stages (e.g., factory) than downstream stages (e.g., retailer) in a supply chain** (see Figure 5.2).[2]

---

[2] The term *bullwhip effect* was coined by Procter & Gamble. The firm observed highly variable demand from wholesalers and retailers for disposable diapers on the one hand, yet, on the other, knew that end consumer demand for diapers was stable. Further investigation revealed that demand volatility increased when moving upstream from retailer to wholesaler to manufacturer, and so on—analogous to a small distortion propagating through a bullwhip, eventually culminating with a crack as the tip moves faster than the speed of sound.

Principle of Nature: Bullwhip Effect

DEFINITION
Variability in observed demand increases with higher stages in a supply chain; for example, consumer demand on a retailer is less volatile than factory orders.

IMPLICATION
The bullwhip effect contributes to high cost and poor service in supply chains. Understand the causes of the bullwhip effect, and look for ways to limit the effect by controlling the causes.

EXAMPLE
Robert Grove, a regional marketing director for Viewlocity, has experience with the bullwhip effect. He observes how business reactions to a change in the market get more exaggerated as the firm gets further away from the source of the change. Information becomes more distorted, which contributes to poor forecasting, poor customer service, and higher costs (Ng 2001).

Four major causes of the bullwhip effect are (1) demand forecast updating, (2) order batching, (3) price fluctuation, and (4) rationing and shortage gaming (Lee, Padmanabhan, and Whang 1997a, 1997b). Demand forecast updating refers to how an increase or decrease in a demand forecast by a firm tends to get amplified in an order to a supplier. Two reasons for this are time lags and quantity uncertainty. For example, suppose that the current demand forecast is 100 units per day and the supplier lead time is 10 days. The firm routinely orders 100 units at the end of each day to bring the inbound pipeline inventory (i.e., the number of replenishment units in transit) up to 1,000 units (= 10 days × 100 units/day). Due to perceived changes in the market, the firm increases its demand forecast by 2 percent to 102 units per day. This means that pipeline inventory should increase to 1,020 in order to cover the next 10 days of demand. Consequently, the firm orders 120 units from the supplier. Here we see that a 2 percent increase in the demand forecast gets translated into a 20 percent increase in the next order. The amplification will likely be even greater than 20 percent because the amount of inventory to protect against demand uncertainty during the replenishment lead time also will increase. This example illustrates how time lags and quantity uncertainty contribute to amplification in demand volatility when a forecast is updated. In addition, forecasts that are manually developed are susceptible to the recency effect—an effect that further amplifies volatility when forecasts are updated. **In the context of demand forecasting, the recency effect is the human tendency to overadjust a forecast in response to signals of changing market conditions.**

FIGURE 5.2   HP printer demand at the warehouse (orders) is more volatile than customer demand (sales), which is an example of the bullwhip effect.

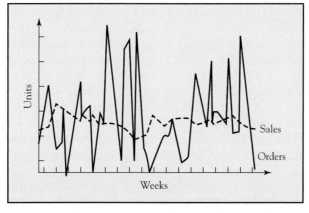

Source: Used with permission from Callioni and Billington (2001).

Principle of Nature: Recency Effect

DEFINITION
People tend to overreact to recent events.

IMPLICATION
Consider recent events when filtering human judgment.

EXAMPLE
Aggregate planning (AP) is the process of planning output and employment levels, usually by month over a period of one year or more. In 1963, E. H. Bowman proposed a tool for AP that is based on an insight into human behavior. He observed that planners would respond to negative feedback by overcompensating in the next plan (e.g., a plan with insufficient inventory is followed by a plan with excessive inventory). Bowman's idea was to collect data on past demand levels, relevant costs, and AP decisions, then perform statistical analysis (i.e., regression analysis) of the data. The analysis results in guidelines that provide more consistency in future decisions.

Order batching, a second major cause of the bullwhip effect, refers to ordering more than just what is needed for the immediate future. As a result, relatively steady demand observed by a firm is translated into sporadic demand on a supplier. For example, a retailer may sell some of a particular product every day, but replenishment orders may be placed once every several weeks in order to save money in transportation and order processing. By consolidating demand over several weeks, the retailer qualifies for full truckload shipments, which are less costly per unit than less-than-truckload shipments. In addition, as we will see in the next chapter, the fixed cost of processing a replenishment order can be significant. This example illustrates how scale economies in transportation and order processing costs contribute to order batching.

Price fluctuation, a third major cause of the bullwhip effect, refers to how supplier price changes can lead to forward buying and a distorted demand pattern observed by a supplier. For example, it may make good economic sense for a firm to more than double its order quantity from a supplier in response to a temporary 5 percent price reduction. The supplier observes a spike in demand followed by a lull as the buyer sells off excess inventory. In effect, the temporary price reduction introduces short-term economies of scale in the order size.

The fourth major cause of the bullwhip effect is rationing and shortage gaming, which refers to self-interested behavior directed at "beating the system" during shortages. For example, a retailer may order twice as much as needed, reckoning that only 50 percent of the order will be filled in the near future, and the rest of the order can be canceled once a partial shipment is received. Shortage gaming was a major factor behind the demand distortion that led to Cisco's $2.2 billion inventory write-off discussed above. At a fundamental level, shortage gaming is a consequence of misalignment of objectives that can exist among firms in a supply chain.

In summary, the bullwhip effect is very pronounced and detrimental to performance in some supply chains. Major causes include demand forecast updating, order batching, price fluctuation, and shortage gaming, which in turn can be traced to causes of system slack discussed in Chapter 3: time lags, quantity uncertainty, scale economies, and misalignment of objectives. In what follows we will examine a number of information technologies that can help mitigate these causes.[3] One lesson from the bullwhip effect is that, while a primary motivation for implementation of new technology may be narrowly focused on a particular area (e.g., supply management), it is important to be aware of potential broader supply chain implications.

---

[3] See Croson and Donohue (2003) and Sahin and Robinson (2002) for detail on the impacts of electronic exchange of point-of-sale data, as well as other forms of information sharing, on the bullwhip effect.

2.1. XML

It is prudent to have a basic understanding of XML because it has potential to significantly change the way sourcing and other aspects of business are conducted. The technology is relatively new and its ultimate impact is uncertain—a little like a wild card, though worth understanding how it may be played.

XML is an acronym that stands for eXtensible Markup Language. More substantively, **XML is an Internet-based technology that facilitates intelligent purchasing and replenishment decisions.** To see why this is so, we'll begin with **an example that exposes a weakness of HTML**. HTML, which stands for hypertext markup language, is the dominant language of the Web today.

Let's say you want to write a program that will search the Web for the book *A Proven Alternative to MRPII for Optimizing Supply Chain Performance*. If it finds this book and it is under a price that you specify, then it should save the relevant vendor information for you. It sounds like a simple task, but see Table 5.1 for the HTML code that your program will need to interpret when it gets to Amazon's Web site.

We see the title of the book and two prices (indicated in bold). The challenge in this case is determining which, if any, of the numbers is the price that Amazon will charge. We might be able to write a program to do this based on Amazon's particular format for listing the price (e.g., scan for "our price" followed by a number beginning with "$"), but Amazon may change their format and other online book vendors may not follow this same format.

XML gets around this difficulty by using tags that identify pertinent information on a Web site (e.g., what are the title, price, and other terms and conditions of sale?). Of course, each industry has to come to an agreement on the set of "tag words" to be used and their specific meaning—not a trivial task and one that is currently the biggest roadblock to wide use of XML. However, XML does provide an infrastructure that allows tag definitions to be somewhat dynamic (i.e., through industry- or field-specific XML dictionaries that are embedded in XML and that can be updated over time). JP Morgan and Pricewaterhouse-Coopers, for example, have proposed a dictionary for foreign exchange currency and other financial transactions called FpML (Roche 2000).

In summary, **HTML is a language that tells your HTML browser how to display information on your computer screen**. This is largely done through tag words in brackets, such as SCM, for example, which tell your browser to display SCM in bold. **XML, on the other hand, is used for defining languages that tell your "XML browser" what the information means**. It's a little like an alphabet and grammar rules. The vocabulary of a particular XML language (e.g., FpML) is defined through the set of tag words.

TABLE 5.1   **HTML Code from Amazon.com's Web Site**

```
<td VALIGN=TOP WIDTH="83%"><b><font size=-1><a href= "/exec/obidos/ASIN/ 1574442716/qid =
997823743/sr=1-2/ref=sc_b_2/104-6240622-9900712">3C: A Proven Alternative to MRPII for Optimiz-
ing Supply Chain Performance</a></font></b><br><font size=-1><font face="verdana,arial,helvetica">by
Miguel Fernandez-Ranada (Editor), et al</font>(Hardcover - August 1999) </font><br><font size=-1>Aver-
age Customer Review: </font><img SRC="http://g-images.amazon.com/ images/G/01/detail/stars-4-0.gif"
ALT="4.0 out of 5 stars" BORDER =0 height=12 width=64><br><font color= "#990000"><font size=-1>In
stock</font></font></td></tr></table><table BORDER=0 WIDTH="100%" > <tr VALIGN=TOP><td VALIGN =TOP
WIDTH="50%"><span class="small"><font face="verdana,arial,helvetica"> <font size=-1><b>List Price:<span
class=listprice></b>$54.95</font></font> </span><br><b><font face="verdana,arial, helvetica"><font size=
-1>Our Price:<font color="#990000">$38.46</font></font></font></b>
```

Source: www.amazon.com, extracted on August 14, 2001.

TABLE 5.2 **Example of XML Code**

```
<?xml version "1.0"?>
<product>
    <!-- root element -->
    <name>book</name>
    <!-- elements -->
    <title>A Proven Alternative to MRPII for Optimizing Supply Chain Performance</title>
    <author1>
        <last_name>Fernandez-Ranada</last_name>
        <first_name>Miguel</first_name>
    </author1>
    <author_type>editor</author_type>
    <product_detail>
        <binding>hard back</binding>
        <isbn>1574442716</isbn>
        <pages>304</pages>
        <copyright>August 1999</copyright>
        <dimensions unit="inch">.8 × 9.29 × 6.28</dimensions>
        <ship_wgt unit="lb">.72</ship_wgt>
        <description>List price is USD $54.95</description>
        <price currency="usd">38.46</price>
    </product_detail>
    <product_detail>
        <binding>paper back</binding>
        <!-- the rest of the product detail on the paper back version of the book would be comparable to above -->
    </product_detail>
</product>
```

For contrast, Table 5.2 gives an example of an XML document containing information on the book by Fernandez-Ranada shown in the HTML example of Table 5.1.

The particular tag words in this example (e.g., <isbn>) are not necessarily accurate because, to my knowledge, a vocabulary has not yet been specified for the publishing industry. Nevertheless, the example illustrates how XML describes the meaning of data in a document.

Jon Bosak and Tim Bray, two of the developers of XML, discuss the role and importance of standardized documents in commerce (Bosak and Bray 1999). If history is any gauge, widespread **electronic commerce will rely heavily on document exchange—a task for which HTML is ill suited and for which XML is designed.**

As a final note, it is worth emphasizing that XML is not a replacement for HTML. Rather, XML and HTML are complementary, with HTML describing how information should be displayed and XML providing a foundation for languages that describe what the information means.

2.2. Electronic Data Interchange

The previous chapters contain industry examples illustrating the use of information technology in sourcing. Electronic data interchange (EDI) is present in all of these examples.

A simple definition of **EDI is computer-to-computer communication.**[4] EDI has historically been achieved by leasing dedicated high-speed communication lines (e.g., T1

---

[4] Some authors define EDI as computer-to-computer communication via private communication lines because this is how EDI was originally implemented. We use the generic definition of computer-to-computer communication, meaning that EDI can be implemented over either private lines or the Internet.

lines) between the computers of two or more companies, often relying on an industry-specific communication protocol. This is not a minor investment,[5] but it is secure, fast, and reliable. These days there is a move toward wider use of public communication lines (e.g., the Internet) for computer-to-computer communication, and this is where **XML will likely play a large role.**

Large companies can average in excess of 1,000 purchase transactions per day with a supplier base numbering in the thousands. Compared to phone/fax/mail, computer-to-computer communication between buyer and supplier (i.e., EDI) can increase purchasing efficiency through time savings, fewer errors, and automatic early detection of potential supply problems. Dell, for example, has EDI links with about 60 of its parts suppliers. Updated schedules are sent to suppliers every 15 minutes. The system has helped Dell cut raw material inventory by more than 50 percent (Young 2002).

EDI is necessary for a range of industry-specific initiatives that rely on sharing point-of-sale data with upstream suppliers to increase efficiency. For example, *quick response* is an initiative that started in the apparel industry as a means for North American firms to compete against low-wage overseas firms. Suppliers use daily point-of-sale data transmitted via EDI to help coordinate their production schedules with the market. The food industry introduced a similar initiative called *efficient consumer response* (ECR). ECR strives for efficient and responsive replenishments with computer-to-computer exchange of point-of-sale data, but also includes efforts to increase efficiency in promotion, new product introductions, and store assortment (additional detail on ECR can be found at the Food Marketing Institute site, www.fmi.org).

In summary, EDI is playing a growing role in supplier/buyer relationships, and it is pivotal for two technology-based tactics that can be characterized as raising the decision-making perspective from the level of the firm to the level of a supply chain: *vendor-managed inventory* and *collaborative planning, forecasting, and replenishment.*

2.3. Vendor-Managed Inventory

EDI capability is often an element of **vendor-managed inventory (VMI), a sourcing tactic where the responsibility for replenishing stock falls on the supplier.** Depending on the terms of the VMI contract, ownership may transfer to the buyer either upon receipt of product or when the buyer sells the product (i.e., consignment). In return, the buyer provides detailed information on sales and inventory of the vendor's products (e.g., via EDI).[6] In the Dell example above, we see that EDI is used for transmitting orders, but since Dell maintains responsibility for releasing orders to its suppliers, it is not an example of VMI.[7] VMI is practiced between Kimberly-Clark and Costco. Kimberly-Clark tracks inventory and sales information on diaper products at the many Costco locations

---

[5] The cost to set up a private link can run $100,000 and the maintenance cost can run about $1,000 per month (Young 2002).

[6] EDI is not necessary nor is it always used for VMI. For example, the replenishment of vending machines can be viewed as a form of VMI where, with some exceptions (e.g., vending machines capable of transmitting inventory and sales data over the Internet), there is no EDI. Similarly, VMI had been used for replenishing potato chips and other snack products long before EDI existed; for example, a Frito-Lay delivery truck visits a number of grocery stores each day and restocks shelves according to available space.

[7] The statement that Dell does not use VMI does not give the complete picture. For example, Dell contracts with distributors (referred to as *revolvers* by Dell) located near Dell's assembly plant in Austin. One distributor stocks components that go inside a PC while another distributor stocks outside products such as printers, speakers, and so forth. These distributors deliver about two hours' worth of material at a time in response to Dell's requests. The distributors, however, have VMI relationships with some of their vendors. Wal-Mart is experimenting with a similar approach in an effort to cut inventory by $6.5 billion (LaGesse 2006). Nearby distributors are responsible for replenishing Wal-Mart stores on short notice, essentially eliminating the need for Wal-Mart to carry safety stock for some of its products.

via EDI and uses this information to plan and release replenishment shipments (Nelson and Zimmerman 2000). As of 2006, more than 60 percent of Wal-Mart's product line is replenished using VMI.

Recall that four causes of the bullwhip effect, and consequently supply chain inefficiency, are (1) demand forecast updating, (2) order batching, (3) price fluctuation, and (4) rationing and shortage gaming. The implementation of VMI can mitigate each of these causes. First, the responsibility for forecasting shifts from buyer to vendor, or is a joint effort, which reduces distortions from a change in the buyer's forecast on the buyer's order quantity. Second, the order batching effect is reduced because the buyer no longer incurs the fixed cost of preparing and submitting a purchase order. Third, without VMI, a seller may offer periodic price reductions to encourage larger order quantities from the buyer. With VMI, the buyer no longer has responsibility for ordering, and pricing remains relatively stable (e.g., pricing established in a VMI contract that is renewed/renegotiated on a periodic basis). Finally, shortage gaming by the buyer is eliminated when the vendor has responsibility for replenishments. While VMI has potential to significantly improve supply chain performance, there can be considerable implementation challenges.

Here's a problem. You're in the process of implementing VMI with vendor X. EDI is already in place. Within two months, you will no longer place orders for vendor X's products; vendor X will have this responsibility. This seems attractive from a supply chain view. Vendor X now has flexibility on the timing and quantity of replenishment shipments to you, and thus can better coordinate these decisions with production and with shipments to other customers. But what happens if vendor X messes up? Arriving at a reasonable answer to this question can be a hurdle when implementing VMI. Supplier and buyer must carefully think through and come to an agreement on such potentially thorny issues as what performance measures are appropriate, what defines acceptable versus unacceptable performance, and what are the consequences of poor performance.

2.4. Collaborative Planning, Forecasting, and Replenishment

Collaborative planning, forecasting, and replenishment (CPFR) is a technology-based sourcing tactic that goes beyond VMI to include computer-supported collaborative planning and forecasting, as well as replenishment. In addition, CPFR may link multiple parties in a supply chain rather than a single supplier/buyer pair.

CPFR is supported by the Voluntary Interindustry Commerce Standards (VICS) Association (see www.vics.org). The CPFR Committee, which includes representatives from over 120 firms and is under the auspices of VICS, has developed CPFR guidelines and a process model to facilitate CPFR in industry. The CPFR process model specifies nine suggested steps grouped into the three levels of planning (e.g., developing rules for cooperation and a joint business plan), forecasting (e.g., creating and monitoring sales and replenishment order forecasts), and replenishment (e.g., generating and releasing replenishment orders). Details on the CPFR guidelines and process model are available at www.cpfr.org.

There are a number of CPFR software packages on the market, all of which include EDI capability. Figure 5.3 is a screenshot from Logility's CPFR software.

One can view forecasts, inventory levels, scheduled promotions, sales history, and other relevant information for managing the supply chain. One also can enter and edit these data. A variety of automated transactions can occur. For example, the software may generate recommended replenishment transactions, and even initiate these transactions. Alternatively, if a buyer updates a demand forecast and this new forecast is significantly different from the corresponding supplier forecast, then an e-mail message to this effect is automatically sent to buyer and seller so that some consistency in expectations can be worked out. In short, the

FIGURE 5.3

Screenshot of Logility's CPFR application.

level of information sharing and joint decision making in CPFR can approach that of suppliers and buyers working in different departments of the same firm.

Some firms have gained significant advantages through CPFR. For example, the energy producer Ashland Inc. has established links with its suppliers using software from i2 Technologies. Purchases that were made independently by individuals at its 100 facilities are now done through a single online catalog. In the process, tens of thousands of suppliers have been reduced to about 1,000, buying power is greater, and Ashland has cut annual costs by about $30 million. And closer collaborative relationships have been formed with the remaining suppliers; for example, suppliers use information in the system to make product recommendations that better fit Ashland's needs (Hamm 2001). Industry surveys suggest that a growing number of firms are viewing supplier collaboration via Internet-based collaborative software as a critical factor to their success (Whyte 2001).[8]

2.5. Trade Exchanges

Trade exchanges are Internet portals that facilitate commerce. Other names for trade exchanges include trading networks, electronic marketplaces, and electronic hubs. Buyers and sellers accessing a trade exchange Web site can engage in a host of information and financial exchange activities related to business transactions; for example, auction off goods or services, post design specifications with a request for quote, obtain letters of credit, arrange for logistics services, monitor inventory and price levels at customer or supplier sites, perform electronic funds transfer. Some see strong potential in the concept. Doug Smith, the managing director for investment banking firm ChaseH&Q, observes that supply chains could become so efficient as buyers/sellers synchronize operations through trade exchanges that build-to-order product may become the norm in the future (Henig 2000).

Some trade exchanges are open to the public, whereas others are restricted. Sun, for example, established a private trade exchange that links Sun with 35 suppliers. Hewlett-Packard

---

[8] A general word of warning—beware of any idea receiving a lot of hype. While heavy hype may point to a legitimate opportunity (i.e., suggests an in-depth understanding of the idea is worthwhile), if it sounds too good to be true, it probably is.

along with 11 other companies announced the formation of a trade exchange in September 2000. Other trade exchanges that you may have read about include Covisint (auto industry), Hightechmatrix (computer industry), and Exostar (aerospace industry).

2.6. Reverse Auctions

An auction is where multiple buyers bid on a product or service offered by a seller (e.g., eBay). A **reverse auction is where multiple sellers quote a price for a product or service wanted by a buyer.** There are a number of companies in the business of setting up reverse auctions over the Internet, typically for commodity-type products and services, including logistics services. The retail giant The Limited Inc., for example, ran a reverse auction for transportation services and realized a savings of about $1.2 million (Leibs 2001).

Figure 5.4 illustrates the bidding history of an electronic reverse auction for transportation services. A manufacturer with a projected need of about $4.8 million worth of transportation services (based on the current carrier) worked with FreeMarkets, a company that provides reverse auction software and helps identify qualified vendors and manage the reverse auction process. The reverse auction took place over approximately 30 minutes with carriers submitting bids over the Internet. Fifty-seven bids were submitted with the low bid yielding a savings of approximately $1.3 million, which translates into more than a 25 percent reduction in freight cost.

A reverse auction can benefit the buyer by increasing competition among sellers of a product or service. However, there is also a subtler phenomenon that can play a role that is known as the winner's curse. The **winner's curse is the tendency for the winner of an auction to quote a money-losing price.** It is most likely to be apparent in auctions where the unit cost of a product or service is difficult to estimate. In this case, the bidder who makes a mistake by underestimating costs and quoting a money-losing price is more likely to win. For example, suppose you want to sign a contract with a distributor to provide 1,000 tons of wheat during the upcoming year. While distributors can estimate their cost of acquiring wheat over the year, no one knows exactly how the commodity price will fluctuate over the duration of the contract. With enough distributors bidding for your business, there will likely be some that significantly underestimate the cost and submit a money-losing bid.

FIGURE 5.4

Screenshot of a reverse auction for a year's worth of domestic air freight.

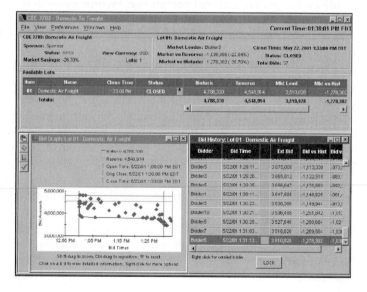

Principle of Nature: Winner's Curse

DEFINITION
The probability of unfavorable bidding error in an auction is highest for the winner. In other words, the winner of a reverse auction is likely to lose money.

IMPLICATION
Cost uncertainty makes the winner's curse more pronounced. A seller should (1) consider investments to reduce cost estimation errors prior to quoting and (2) bear in mind that it is not necessarily a good thing to win every auction. In addition, there are bidding strategies that a seller can employ to mitigate the winner's curse (see, e.g., Kagel and Levin 2002). A buyer may consider the potential significance of the winner's curse when considering whether to set up a reverse auction.

EXAMPLE
The phenomenon of the winner's curse was originally proposed by three petroleum engineers who wondered why oil companies experienced consistent and unexpectedly low rates of return on oil leases (Capen, Clapp, and Campbell 1971). They suggested that the cause was the winner's curse—the winning bidder of a mineral rights lease tended to overpay.

In summary, characteristics conducive to reverse auctions (from the buyer's perspective) include a high-cost item, many potential suppliers, and a standardized product or service. From the winner's curse, it also follows that another characteristic is a product or service with an obscure cost structure.

2.7. Shopbots

A *bot* is a software agent or, more specifically, an autonomous computer program that operates on your behalf. For example, though it is not widely available today, before long you may have your own personalized *infobot* that will learn your interests and tendencies over time. You'll activate the bot and specify the information you want, and the bot will begin scouring the Web and interacting with search engines to gather this information.

A **shopbot is a software agent that shops for you, perhaps even negotiating with other bots and making purchases.** You might ponder this for a moment. The preceding statements portend a possible future where your computer program negotiates with other computer programs and spends your money. Is this disturbing?

There are consumer sites that use shopbot technology today (e.g., mySimon.com, DealTime.com, PriceGrabber.com), but the real power of these tools will not be unleashed until pricing, availability, and other terms and conditions of sale can be easily and automatically gleaned from the Web (e.g., via XML). As an aside, bots and XML are a curious combination that may lead to upheaval in many aspects of business, not just sourcing.[9]

3. BUYER/SELLER RELATIONSHIPS

A common thread through VMI and CPFR is a long-term **supplier/buyer partnership**. This is necessary to justify the investment (e.g., software and hardware technology; negotiating the division of responsibilities, penalties, and rewards) and to gain the trust to share information. One example of a strong supplier/buyer partnership is the relationship

---

[9] Will the person with the smartest bots be the next Bill Gates? Some thoughts on a future with bots can be found in Kephart and Greenwald (2000).

between Procter & Gamble and Wal-Mart; P&G stations about 250 people near Wal-Mart's headquarters in Arkansas (Nelson and Zimmerman 2000).[10]

At the opposite end of a supplier/buyer partnership is an **arm's-length agreement.** An arm's-length agreement between a supplier and buyer is potentially short term in nature. It means that, as a buyer, I am retaining the flexibility to switch to a different supplier with my next purchase.

A supplier/buyer partnership and an arm's-length agreement can be viewed as two ends of a continuum. The differences between these tactics are a little like the differences between marriage and dating. From the buyer's perspective, a **supplier/buyer partnership offers the advantages of low search costs and tight coordination, but typically requires significant investment to initiate and maintain** (e.g., marriage). On the flip side, an **arm's-length agreement offers sourcing flexibility with the drawbacks of higher search and coordination costs** (e.g., dating). Thus, at the most basic level, the choice along the continuum largely boils down to finding a good balance between the value of sourcing flexibility and the value of tight supply chain coordination.

Suppose that you are VP of logistics at a firm. You sense that there may be high payoff opportunities through stronger relationships with select suppliers, but there is a question of where to start. An early step is to identify promising candidates that warrant study and/or engagement to sort out possible investments and associated returns. Pareto analysis, which is a simple and systematic approach for separating the important few from the trivial many, may be useful during this step. Once a meaningful measure is identified (e.g., raw material expense over the last 12 months), Pareto analysis involves collecting data and ranking suppliers according to the measure.

The power and relevance of Pareto analysis come from a principle of nature called the Pareto phenomenon. Take any aggregate measure, that is, some statistic where the value is determined by the aggregation of many elements or factors. If you analyze the contribution of the individual elements, you'll likely see evidence of the **Pareto phenomenon: the lion's share of the statistic's value is determined by relatively few elements.** For example, the total personal wealth of the U.S. population is an aggregate measure. The richest 1 percent of the population owns about 40 percent of the wealth. The implications of the Pareto phenomenon and Pareto analysis extend well beyond supply management. As a manager you will be charged with setting direction and identifying opportunities for investment. You know from the Pareto phenomenon that attention should be focused on a relatively small number of elements. The challenge is identifying these elements, and this is where Pareto analysis can play a role.

It is worth noting that the choice along the continuum of arm's length to supplier/buyer partnership is more one-sided for the supplier; a long-term and close relationship with a buyer is generally positive, though it must be balanced against investments to initiate and maintain. Intel, for example, established an Internet-based private trade exchange for ordering and information sharing, but until year 2000, access to the exchange was limited to its 20 largest customers. The system reduced order-entry errors by 75 percent, and access has since been extended to thousands of customers with about 95 percent of Intel's orders placed though the exchange (Young 2002).

As evidenced by the examples in this and earlier chapters, there is a trend in supply management away from many suppliers and arm's-length agreements toward fewer suppliers and supplier/buyer partnerships. This trend may soften in the future if XML and shopbots become widespread. A shopbot, in conjunction with XML tags on supplier Web sites, has

---

[10] See Lambert and Knemeyer (2004), Liker and Choi (2004), and Stuart and McCutcheon (2000) for other examples of supplier partnerships.

Principle of Nature: Pareto Phenomenon

DEFINITION
The lion's share of an aggregate measure is determined by relatively few factors.

IMPLICATION
Invest time and energy to identify a few factors that drive performance and focus attention and resources on these. The process of separating the

"important few" from the "trivial many" is known as *Pareto analysis*.

EXAMPLE
There are thousands of magazine titles sold through nearly a quarter of a million retail outlets in the United States, but the top 100 titles account for over 80 percent of all unit sales.

the potential to significantly lower search and coordination costs while maintaining sourcing flexibility.

4. TACTICAL CONSIDERATIONS

Beyond an awareness of alternative information technologies and supplier relationships, there are a number of tactical considerations that are relevant for guiding day-to-day behavior and improving the supply management function. The list is arguably long, but in this section we will focus on four that stand out: (1) maintain a total value perspective, (2) look for volume buying opportunities, (3) recognize the importance of contract design, and (4) be aware of negotiating tactics.

4.1. Total Value Perspective

Suppose that, after careful analysis, the decision has been made to outsource a particular product or service to one of a handful of candidate suppliers. The question now is which supplier. The decision should be based on **which supplier is likely to provide the highest total value to the firm,** a simple idea that follows from the total systems view that underlies supply chain management. The **value of a product or service from a supplier is determined by the impact on profit** of the end product or service sold to the firm's customers. Differences in total cost among suppliers tend to be the biggest determinant of relative value, but for some inputs, the impact on the "top line"[11] can be meaningful and should be considered. For example, a PC maker may be able to charge a higher price and achieve higher market share by selecting an Intel processor over a less-well-known alternative with comparable specs. Similarly, the choice of a very responsive supplier may translate into fewer lost sales and consequently higher revenues when compared with alternative suppliers.

There are many factors that can influence the relative value of a supplier offering, and performance data on these factors for all current suppliers should be collected for periodic review, for example:

- Purchase price.
- Transportation cost, including tariffs, duties, and so forth, if applicable.
- Quality (e.g., scrap rate, manufacturing problems, contribution to warranty expenses).
- Supplier reliability (e.g., on-time performance).

---

[11] "Top line" refers to the revenue, which appears at the top of an income statement. Revenue is influenced by price and volume, two factors that in turn can be influenced by the choice of supplier.

- Supplier flexibility and responsiveness (e.g., can respond quickly to a large unplanned order).
- Supplier viability (e.g., likelihood of avoiding bankruptcy).
- Replenishment lead time.
- Administrative cost (e.g., ability to easily and cost efficiently share information, place orders, and coordinate replenishments).
- Opportunity for joint improvement efforts (e.g., collaborative design, investments in shared technology).

Some of the factors listed above may not be worth estimating, either because the time and cost to develop estimates is too high or because the degree of precision of the estimate is too poor. Identifying relevant factors to be estimated, selecting an appropriate time horizon for analysis (e.g., likely length of relationship), and estimating the impact of factors on profit can be challenging. There is no single recipe. Naturally, the care and attention to the supplier selection decision should be consistent with the potential impact on the firm. From the Pareto phenomenon, we know that there will likely be many supplier decisions of relatively minor consequence that can be handled in a routine manner. There also will be significant decisions, and for these, the use of a multidisciplinary team that spans all affected areas may be justified (e.g., engineering, manufacturing, marketing, sourcing).

The main point of this section is that a total value perspective should be maintained and should be executed at a level of detail that makes good business sense. While this may seem obvious, it is not always followed in practice. Some firms make the mistake of using reward systems that emphasize low purchase price (e.g., a buyer's bonus tied to a favorable purchase price variance). While easy to measure, the consequence can be a focus on low price to the detriment of firm performance.

4.2. Volume Buying

One way for a firm to increase profit through sourcing is to examine total purchasing volume (units and dollars) by supplier, and by item broken down by supplier. Materials and services that are similar should be identified. The idea is to **look for consolidation opportunities, either by shifting more volume to a primary supplier or by part standardization, which can be used as leverage to gain more favorable terms** (e.g., as noted in Section 2.4 of this chapter, Ashland saved $30 million annually using this approach). It is not uncommon in large organizations for similar, if not identical, materials and services to be purchased by multiple individuals from multiple suppliers. This tends to be especially pronounced with indirect materials such as maintenance, repair, and operations items (MROs). In contrast with direct materials that get transformed, assembled, and ultimately move on to the customer, indirect materials do not go into products sold to the firm's customers (e.g., stationery, PCs, lubricants, tools). MROs traditionally receive little attention, are often purchased by employees in many different departments (e.g., no central point of control), and thus may be ripe for consolidation opportunities.

It is important to recognize that moving to the extreme of purchasing an item from a single supplier, or sole sourcing, can be a risky proposition. A less risky alternative is a small set of complementary suppliers, for example, a fast but expensive supplier used for periodic emergency replenishments as a complement to a slow but cheap primary supplier.[12] This type of complementary sourcing tactic can be especially valuable in markets with highly volatile demand (e.g., fashion products).

---

[12] See Elmaghraby (2000) and Ferguson (2003) for additional discussion of this issue.

4.3. Contract Design

A contract between a buyer and seller defines the terms and conditions of sale. Consequently, the choice of contract has far-reaching ramifications, influencing total buyer-seller profit, how profit is divided, and the allocation of risk. In this section, we will first examine how self-interested behavior under the terms of a contract is not necessarily best for the system as a whole. We'll then look at how different contract terms influence total profit and the allocation of risk and reward between buyer and seller. The contracts and terms are summarized in Table 5.4.

Double Marginalization

Over 50 years ago, Joseph Spengler was investigating antitrust law and considered the following question: how does performance of a supply chain change if a manufacturer buys a distributor of their product? What he observed was a phenomenon known as **double**

marginalization—the manufacturer and distributor each sets its margin to maximize its own profit with the result being a higher market price, lower market demand, and lower total profit when compared with an integrated manufacturer/distributor firm.

Here is an example.[13] The cost to manufacture and ship the product to the distributor is $20 per unit and the cost for the distributor to handle and ship to the customer is $20 per unit. Market demand per week decreases by two units for every $1 increase in price and goes to zero once price reaches $90. The distributor sets his selling price to maximize his profit, and, knowing this, the manufacturer maximizes her profit by charging the distributor $45 per unit. At a purchase price of $45 per unit, the distributor maximizes profit by selling 25 units per week at $77.50 per unit. The manufacturer makes $25(45 − 20) = $625 per week, the distributor makes $25(77.5 − 45 − 20) = $312.50 per week, and total supply chain profit is $625 + $312.50 = $937.50 per week. What if the manufacturer owned the distributor? Given the manufacturing and distribution cost of $40 per unit, the integrated firm maximizes profit by charging a price of $65 per unit. The demand per week is higher

---

[13] This example is based on an example in Spengler (1950).

> ## Example Summary
>
> Manufacturing and shipping cost = $20/unit
> Distributor handling cost = $20/unit
> If manufacturer and distributor are independent, then
> - Manufacturer charges the distributor $45/unit.
> - Distributor charges the customer $77.50/unit.
> - Total supply chain profit is $937.50/week.
>
> If manufacturer and distributor are one firm, then
> - The firm charges the customer $65/unit.
> - Total supply chain profit is $1,250/week.

at 50 units per week because the price is lower, and the total supply chain profit increases by 33 percent to $50(65 - 20 - 20) = \$1,250$ per week. Customers benefit through lower-priced product and the supply chain benefits through higher profits.[14]

The **main lesson from Spengler's paper** is that there can be significant degradation in overall supply chain performance due to self-interested behavior of independent firms,[15] or, stated another way, there can be **significant opportunity to improve supply chain performance and customer satisfaction through contracts that align independent interests with overall supply chain performance.** In the next two sections, we'll look at features of several basic contracts. Uncertainty is a major consideration in most real-world supply chains, so we'll look at how the choice of contract influences the allocation of risk between buyer and seller. We'll also consider the extent to which various features of a contract can help align individual interests with overall supply chain performance.

Cost Uncertainty

Suppliers do not normally know the exact cost to provide a product or service to a buyer ahead of time. Cost uncertainty introduces the risk of lower-than-anticipated profit, perhaps to the point of a loss (e.g., recall the winner's curse from Section 2.6).

The example in the last section illustrated a **fixed-price contract.** The buyer, which was the independent distributor in the example, paid a fixed price of $45 per unit. **All of the risk associated with the possibility of higher-than-anticipated seller costs was borne by the seller.**

At the other extreme is a **cost plus fixed fee contract.** Here the buyer reimburses the seller for costs incurred and, in addition, pays a fixed fee. The seller profit, which is the fixed fee, is known and **all the risk due to cost uncertainty is borne by the buyer.** This type of contract is more common when there is a high degree of cost uncertainty (e.g., developing a new weapon system); the alternative of a fixed price contract would likely require a very high price to compensate the seller for bearing all of the risk.[16]

We have looked at two basic contracts—fixed price and cost plus fixed fee—where all the risk due to uncertainty in the cost of providing the product or service is borne by either the buyer or the seller. **Various risk-sharing contracts can be devised that fall between these two extremes.** One example is a **fixed price incentive contract, which associates a**

---

[14] See Lee (2004) and Narayanan and Raman (2004) for additional discussion and examples on the impacts of conflicting objectives on supply chain performance.

[15] Recall that conflicting objectives is one of the six causes of system slack identified in Chapter 3.

[16] The positive correlation between risk and return underlies the capital asset pricing model (CAPM), which you may have seen in your finance classes.

price with a cost target (Corbett and DeCroix 2001). If cost turns out to be less than the target, then savings are split according to contract terms (e.g., a $50 reduction in price to the buyer if cost is $100 below target). Similarly, if cost turns out to be more than the target, then price is increased to cover a portion of the loss up to some predetermined maximum price (e.g., price to the buyer is increased by $50 if cost is $100 above target). A buyer who seeks to understand a seller's attitude toward risk can be in a position to negotiate a mutually beneficial contract; for example, by accepting a small chance of higher price, a buyer may gain a high probability of a lower price and be better off overall.

What about Double Marginalization?

In the previous section, we saw that one drawback of a fixed price contract is a higher market price and lower supply chain profit when compared with an integrated supply chain (i.e., due to double marginalization). Interestingly, the **double marginalization effect disappears with a cost plus fixed fee contract.** From a buyer's perspective, the fixed fee is a sunk cost, so the **variable cost underlying the buyer's decisions is the same variable cost of an integrated firm.**

Building on the example in the last section, suppose that instead of charging $45 per unit (fixed price contract), the manufacturer charges a fixed fee and sets price at cost, which is $20 per unit (cost plus fixed fee contract). As we saw in the example, a distributor paying a total of $40 per unit (purchase price of $20 plus handling cost of $20) can maximize profit by buying 50 units per week and selling for $65 per unit, which generates gross profit of $1,250 per week. The negotiated fixed fee is subtracted from distributor gross profit and paid to the manufacturer. The total supply chain profit is $1,250 per week, which is the same as for the integrated firm and 33 percent more than the supply chain profit under the fixed price contract.[17]

A **cost plus fixed fee contract** also has two notable disadvantages, one of which will be discussed in the section on other considerations. The other **disadvantage is the seller's profit is guaranteed so there is no direct financial incentive for a seller to control costs.** One can expect less seller effort on cost control when compared with a fixed price contract, and other contracts where the seller faces some penalty for higher-than-anticipated cost. Thus, while a **cost plus fixed fee contract aligns quantity and market pricing decisions with that of an integrated firm, it also reduces the incentives for cost control.**

Demand Uncertainty

Another form of uncertainty stems from unknown market demand. Demand uncertainty can create considerable risk in a supply chain, especially when replenishment lead times are long and the selling season is short (Petruzzi and Monahan 2003). For example, suppose you are a buyer for the summer swimsuit line. You need to place an order in November for shipments that will arrive in late March and early April. While there may be some opportunity to place replenishment orders during the selling season, the selection is limited. For many styles and sizes, if you don't order enough, you will not be able to get more, which translates into unhappy customers and lost sales opportunities. On the other hand, ordering too much means leftover suits that will likely have to be marked down and sold at a loss.

The contracts considered up to this point place the risk due to uncertain market demand on the buyer. The buyer assesses market potential, sizes up the risks associated with ordering too much and too little, and places an order. The seller receives orders from buyers and

---

[17] A cost plus fixed fee contract is an example of a quantity discount schedule because the average price is decreasing in the order quantity (i.e., average price = cost + fixed fee ÷ quantity). Some have argued that the lack of double marginalization with a cost plus fixed fee contract explains, in part, why firms use quantity discount price schedules in practice (Jeuland and Shuugan 1983).

produces and delivers the product before the selling season; with the exception of some replenishment orders during the selling season, the seller's profit is largely set. Uncertainty in market demand is reflected in uncertainty in buyer profit.

Both buyer and seller may benefit from a contract that shares the risk due to demand uncertainty, especially in cases where the seller is much larger and therefore in a better position to accommodate risk. **Buyback contracts, quantity flexibility contracts, and revenue sharing contracts** are three examples of contracts that **shift some (or all) of the risk due to the uncertainty in market demand to the seller**. Each of these three contracts **can be used in combination with a fixed price contract, a cost plus fixed fee contract, or a contract that shares the risk of cost uncertainty (e.g., fixed price incentive contract).**

A **seller offering a buyback contract agrees to pay the buyer for leftover units at the end of the selling season.** The payment may be for the full price paid by the buyer, or some fraction of the price, and there may be an upper limit on the number of units that qualify for a rebate. Depending on the terms of the contract, the buyer may or may not be required to return leftover units to the seller. Buyback contracts are used in the publishing and music industries. In the apparel industry, the credit for leftover product is commonly referred to as markdown money (Tsay 2001).

A **quantity flexibility contract requires that a buyer place an order for the total quantity to be delivered over the duration of the selling season.** However, the buyer has the **flexibility to adjust this quantity up or down within some range up to some point in time.** For example, a swimsuit buyer may place an order for 100 suits of a particular size and style in November, 50 of which may be delivered at the end of March. The buyer has until the end of April, when there is better information on market demand, to increase or decrease the size of the original order by 50 percent (i.e., a second shipment between 0 and 100 units). The seller takes on some risk of holding unwanted product at the end of the season if demand is low and buyer order quantities are reduced. Quantity flexibility contracts are used in the electronics industry (Tsay 1999). This type of contract also is used in the fashion apparel industry, where it is more commonly known as a backup agreement (Eppen and Iyer 1997).

A **revenue sharing contract sets a low price to the buyer (e.g., at seller cost) and, in return, the seller receives a percentage of the buyer's sales revenue from the product.** A low buyer purchase price means more room for the buyer to mark down product without a loss, which decreases the buyer's cost of leftover product. And lower-than-expected demand means lower-than-expected profit for both buyer and seller. Blockbuster, for example, has revenue-sharing contracts with movie studios, which, compared to the traditional contracts in years past, have resulted in more videos on the shelves, happier customers, and higher profits for Blockbuster and the studios (Cachon and Lariviere 2001, 2005).

Buyback, quantity flexibility, and revenue-sharing contracts are similar in that each reduces the negative impact of low demand on buyer profit, thereby shifting some risk to the seller. One consequence is that order quantities are larger, which also helps to reduce the double marginalization effect present in a fixed price contract. Like a cost plus fixed fee contract, these three types of contracts help to align quantity and market pricing decisions with that of an integrated firm. However, as is the case with a cost plus fixed fee contract, this benefit may come at a cost of reduced effort, that is, **a reduction in the buyer's cost of leftover product also means less financial incentive to work hard selling the product.**

Other Considerations

Trust, But Verify A **fixed price contract has an important advantage—it's simple.** By the nature of sharing risk of cost uncertainty, **cost plus fixed fee contracts** and

Principle of Nature: Benford's Law

DEFINITION

Numbers starting with 1 appear about six times more frequently than numbers starting with 9, or, more specifically, the predicted frequencies by starting digit are 1—30.1 percent, 2—17.6 percent, 3—12.5 percent, 4—9.7 percent, 5—7.9 percent, 6—6.7 percent, 7—5.8 percent, 8—5.1 percent, and 9—4.6 percent.

IMPLICATIONS

Humans commonly view the likelihood of each starting digit to be approximately equal, meaning that data with roughly equal starting digits may be concocted numbers, or potentially evidence of fraud.

EXAMPLE

About 30 percent of the constants in physics (gravitation, speed of light, Planck, Avogadro, etc.) begin with 1 (Knuth 1969), and, more generally, the first digit frequencies are approximated by the Benford frequencies. This result hints at a fundamental property that was shown to hold by Pinkham (1961) and Hill (1995): a random variable with sample space $(0, \infty)$ is scale invariant if and only if the probability distribution of first digits is the Benford distribution. Loosely speaking, scale invariance means that the unit of measure does not affect the probability distribution. In light of this property, it is not surprising that the first digit frequencies of constants in physics are close to Benford frequencies.

fixed price incentive contracts require that seller cost be determined and agreed upon before final payment is made. The seller knows that the higher the cost, the higher the payment, which **raises the question of how a buyer can verify cost data provided by the seller.** While a buyer may want full access to detailed cost data (e.g., material invoices, routing and scrap data, hours worked, wage rates), sellers are naturally reluctant to share this information. While some access may be granted, a full and thorough verification of costs is usually not possible, nor economically justified due to time and effort required. Consequently there is always an element of trust, usually supported by some combination of aggregate reasonability tests (e.g., are itemized costs in line with expectations) and spot checks of detailed cost data to the extent that the right to inspect such information is allowed under the terms of the contract.

Aggregate reasonability tests rely on a good understanding of the seller's business and business processes in the seller's industry, but **fraudulent data sometimes exhibit telltale signs** that can be detected without such knowledge. One example comes from a counterintuitive principle of nature that has been used to detect fraudulent income tax returns (Hill 1998). The **principle of nature is Benford's law**, after Frank Benford, a physicist at General Electric. He noticed a **pattern in the first digit of lists of numbers.** His formula to predict this pattern has become known as Benford's law. Table 5.3 compares predictions from Benford's law with observed first digit frequencies appearing in river basin areas, population figures, baseball statistics, and numbers appearing in ***Reader's Digest*** articles (Benford 1938).

TABLE 5.3 A **Comparison of First Digit Frequencies Predicted by Benford's Law with Various Datasets**

First Digit	1	2	3	4	5	6	7	8	9
Benford's law	30.1%	17.6%	12.5%	9.7%	7.9%	6.7%	5.8%	5.1%	4.6%
River basin areas	31.0	16.4	10.7	11.3	7.2	8.6	5.5	4.2	5.1
Population	33.9	20.4	14.2	8.1	7.2	6.2	4.1	3.7	2.2
American League	32.7	17.6	12.6	9.8	7.4	6.4	4.9	5.6	3.0
Reader's Digest	33.4	18.5	12.4	7.5	7.1	6.5	5.5	4.9	4.2

Here is a hypothetical example of Benford's law applied to analysis of seller costs. Your firm has been helping a key supplier reduce their costs for the past several years with the arrangement that any cost savings are split. As you're viewing the monthly unit cost reports from the supplier, a name suddenly pops into your head, "Benford." Thinking back to college days, you recall a couple of benchmarks for first digit Benford frequencies: 30 percent for a first digit of 1 and 70 percent for the first digits of 1 through 4. The data in the reports don't match up, you become suspicious, and you do a little investigation. It's now six months later. Your firm just received a $250,000 check from the supplier due to an "accounting error" in costing, and your boss is still talking about your uncanny sense of something amiss in the supplier cost reports.

While less of a concern to the buyer, **verification of buyer sales can be an issue when negotiating contracts that share demand uncertainty risk with the seller**. A seller negotiating a revenue-sharing contract, for example, will want verification of sales revenue. This can be less of an issue when EDI linkages are already in place (e.g., daily transmission of point-of-sale data). Some buyback contracts require that leftover product be returned to the seller for a credit. This is not always economically practical, and other forms of verification are used. For example, in some cases, retail outlets for newspapers get credit by cutting out the corner of the front page of leftover newspapers and sending them to the supplier. The verification system is not perfect—I've seen newspapers for sale with the corner already cut out.

A Law to Help Level the Playing Field   From the above discussion, it may seem like contract negotiations are like horse trading—anything is possible as long as both parties agree. This is not necessarily the case. In the United States, the **Robinson-Patman Act prohibits a seller from charging buyers different prices for the same product**. This means, for example, that Procter & Gamble must offer the same price schedule for Pampers to Wal-Mart and a small independent grocery store. In practice, Wal-Mart will likely pay lower prices because price schedules normally show lower prices for higher volumes. A quantity discount pricing schedule is legal as long as the lower prices are not a form of price discrimination, but are due to cost savings that accrue at higher shipping volumes.

A Tricky Design Problem   Finally, a word of warning that **devising incentives to achieve certain behaviors is not as simple as it may seem**. Enough hard-won lessons have been learned in government and industry to elevate this point to a law . . . the so-called law of unintended consequences. Chopra and Meindl (2004) share an example involving a DaimlerChrysler contract designed to increase dealer sales effort. The contract established an overall sales target and four sales ranges (i.e., 0 to 75 percent of target, 75 to 100 percent of target, 100 to 110 percent of target, more than 110 percent of target). A per-car bonus to be paid to the dealer was set for each sales range with the higher the range, the higher the bonus (e.g., $0, $150, $250, $500). The contract provides incentives to reach

higher sales levels, but it also can increase demand variation. In fact, sales went down in the first month of the new contract. Given the incentive scheme, a dealer can benefit by delaying sales contracts near the end of one month to get a jump in sales in the next month and having a good chance of hitting a high sales range.

A similar effect is seen among salespeople where rewards are traditionally tied to performance relative to a sales quota. Here is a familiar pattern. A star salesperson

TABLE 5.4
Characteristics of Some Types of Contracts Used in Practice

Contract Features	Risk Characteristics	Pros and Cons
Fixed price Buyer pays a fixed price per unit.	Risk due to seller cost uncertainty borne by seller	Pros: simple Cons: higher market price and lower volume than integrated firm—double marginalization
Cost plus fixed fee Buyer pays a fixed fee plus a unit price equal to seller's cost.	Risk due to seller cost uncertainty borne by buyer	Pros: eliminates double marginalization Cons: (1) may require buyer to verify seller cost; (2) may reduce seller cost-control effort; (3) since the fixed fee is independent of volume, it can be challenging to negotiate a "fair" value
Fixed price incentive Buyer pays a fixed price per unit that is adjusted by some percentage of the difference between the seller's cost and a cost target.	Risk due to seller cost uncertainty is shared by buyer and seller	Pros: compared to fixed price, sharing of cost risk generally means lower price to buyer, higher volume, and lower double-marginalization effect Cons: (1) may require buyer to verify seller cost; (2) may reduce seller cost-control effort
Buyback Buyer receives a credit from seller on units left over at the end of the selling season. Units may or may not be returned to the seller.	Risk due to demand uncertainty is shared by buyer and seller	Pros: encourages higher buyer order quantities, which lowers double-marginalization effect Cons: (1) may require seller to verify left-over units; (2) may reduce buyer selling effort
Quantity flexibility Buyer receives a portion of total order quantity prior to selling season.	Risk due to demand uncertainty is shared by buyer and seller	Pros: encourages higher buyer order quantities, which lowers double-marginalization effect
Can adjust total quantity up or down within prespecified limits during the selling season.		Cons: may reduce buyer selling effort
Revenue sharing In addition to other payment terms, buyer pays seller some percentage of sales revenue.	Risk due to demand uncertainty is shared by buyer and seller	Pros: encourages higher buyer order quantities, which lowers double-marginalization effect Cons: (1) may require seller to verify sales revenue; (2) may reduce buyer selling effort

has five great years garnering sales awards and consistently exceeding quota. The sixth year is a disaster. Why is this? The year started off a little slow and the salesperson got the sense it would be tough to hit quota. A rational response is to write the year off by taking it easy, getting a reduction in quota for the next year, and coming out charging in year seven. Seasoned sales managers are well aware of this effect and try to manage around it.

4.4. Negotiating Tactics

Negotiation plays a large role in supply management. Even in cases where competitive bidding is used to identify a promising supplier, a buyer and seller may still need to negotiate nonprice terms and conditions of sale (e.g., payment terms, delivery schedules, transportation modes, nonperformance penalties). Negotiation skills can be developed through practice. There is also an extensive body of knowledge on how to negotiate effectively (e.g., Fuller 1991; Lynch 1998; Sebenius 2001; Thompson 2001). This section presents selected highlights from this literature in the form of four insights.

Know the Seller

If a buyer knows the lower limit of what a seller will accept, then the negotiation process will be relatively brief and terms will be as favorable as possible for the buyer. In reality, this information will not be known (and may even be fluid), but the observation reinforces the **importance of knowledge about the firm and the firm's negotiator when entering negotiations.** A buyer should strive for a good sense of how important the contract is to the selling firm. Does the firm have excess capacity, have sales revenues been flat or declining, are there any extra pressures for the firm to book sales revenue (e.g., near the end of the fiscal year—recall the hockey stick effect from Chapter 4[18])? Answers to questions like these are sometimes available in public documents such as annual reports and newspapers. Naturally, information about the firm's cost structure is helpful, though usually hard to ascertain, as well as insight into the opposing negotiator's tendencies and time limits for concluding the negotiation. It is nice to know, for example, the date and time of departure of a seller who is flying in to negotiate a contract. Concessions are more likely as the negotiating deadline approaches.

On the flip side, it is **similarly important to protect against information leaks that give the seller an advantage.** Technical departments of a buying firm may inadvertently give signs on the importance of the pending contract to the seller, and a firm may consider a policy of limiting discussions with the seller to only those associated with the negotiations. Information leaks can be costly, though U.S. law offers some protection against purposeful leaks—a firm can hold an employee personally liable for sharing confidential information that gives advantage to a seller, customer, or competitor (Burt, Dobler, and Starling 2003).

Develop a Best Alternative to a Negotiated Agreement

What are the consequences if an agreement with a seller cannot be reached? Is there another viable supplier, can an alternative material or service be substituted, can the funds freed from terminating the project be productively invested elsewhere? The **consequence of terminating negotiations without an agreement is called the best alternative to a negotiated agreement, or BATNA.** There may be many alternatives to an agreement, and time invested in identifying the most attractive alternative can **save the buyer from making undue concessions to reach a settlement.** In a similar vein, efforts to get a sense of the seller's BATNA can be worthwhile.

Draft Agreements

After you learn as much as time and budgets allow about the seller and after you develop the BATNA, a useful step prior to negotiation is to **develop one or more detailed drafts specifying possible terms and conditions of the purchase agreement.** This step serves two purposes. Most important, the process forces the buying team to think through the details and merits of possible contract terms, thus reducing the chance of unpleasant surprises discovered after a contract has been signed. Second, having thought through the details, the buying team will be in a position to more readily reach closure once the framework of a settlement has been established.

---

[18] Savvy buyers of large software packages tend to defer decisions to the end of a quarter when salespeople feel the greatest pressure to close deals and consequently are most likely to offer the best terms to gain the sale.

Principle of Nature: Obligation to Reciprocate

DEFINITION
Individuals feel some obligation to repay in kind.

IMPLICATION
Reciprocity can be a basis for tactics to persuade others, or for others to persuade you.

EXAMPLE
Random pedestrians were asked if they would be willing to chaperone juvenile detention center inmates for a day trip to the zoo. Seventeen percent said yes. In another trial, pedestrians were asked is they would be willing to serve as an unpaid counselor at the center for two hours per week for the next two years. Everyone said no. They were then asked, "if you can't do that, would you chaperone a group of juvenile detention center inmates on a day trip to the zoo?" The percentage of those who agreed nearly tripled to 50 percent. In this example, the requester offered a concession from a two-year request to a few hours, which in turn created some pressure on the person to repay with a concession of her own (Cialdini 2001).

COMMENTS
In addition to reciprocation, five other psychological principles of persuasion are consistency, social validation, liking, authority, and scarcity (see Appendix 1).

Cultivate Obligation to Reciprocate

There is a branch of social psychology that attempts to understand why and how people are influenced to say yes. The principle of **obligation to reciprocate** is a behavioral pattern that can play a role; the principle is **humans feel motivated to repay what another person has provided them.** In recognition of this, negotiators should take time to **prepare a list of "throwaways," or concessions of relatively little cost, but of value to the other side.** These concessions can be offered at opportune moments, always with something expected in return, to move the negotiation process along in a favorable manner. Similarly, a negotiator can benefit by taking an extreme opening position. The tactic leaves lots of room for concessions and opportunities for the seller to reciprocate. Of course, tactics based on this principle also can be used by sellers, which is a reason why some firms have policies that restrict those with buying responsibility from accepting gifts from sellers.

5. SUMMARY AND MANAGERIAL INSIGHTS

In this chapter, we learned about a particularly rich business function, both in terms of opportunity for a firm and as an area of study. With respect to a rich opportunity, we learned that the "buying side of the business" has long been a high priority for top management in many firms and we learned about long-term trends that are increasing its importance. With respect to a rich area of study, we learned that effective supply management relies on ideas and concepts from a diverse set of disciplines including information technology, economics, law, and psychology. At a more detailed level, the chapter covered five main points.

First, supply management is a prime target for management attention in many industries, and is becoming even more prominent due to the interrelated trends of advancing information technologies and a growth in outsourcing.

Second, there are number of e-commerce technologies relevant to supply management (i.e., XML, EDI, VMI, CPFR, trade exchanges, reverse auctions, shopbots). We learned how some of these technologies can help attenuate a potentially costly supply chain phenomenon known as the bullwhip effect. Firms are embracing EDI, in part because it reduces information delays and order processing cost, and consequently the bullwhip effect. VMI and CPFR help smooth out the bullwhip effect even further by reducing price fluctuation and shortage gaming. Price fluctuation and gaming are less of an issue because the supplier is responsible for replenishing customer inventory.

Third, a buyer's relationship with a particular supplier lies somewhere between a long-term commitment with a high degree of collaboration and information sharing (i.e., partnership) and a single transaction with little assurance of future transactions (i.e., arm's length). E-commerce technologies play a role in the choice and specific nature of a relationship with a supplier.

Fourth, four tactical considerations relevant for supply management are to (1) maintain a total value perspective, (2) look for volume-buying opportunities through part standardization and reduction of the supplier base, (3) be aware of the range and impact of alternative features in a buyer/seller contract, (4) recognize that negotiation is a skill that benefits from focused front-end preparation (e.g., know the seller, develop a BATNA, and draft agreements) and an understanding of psychology (e.g., obligation to reciprocate).

Finally, we saw throughout the chapter how an awareness of six principles of nature (i.e., bullwhip effect, recency effect, winner's curse, Pareto phenomenon, Benford's law, and obligation to reciprocate) not only help to understand phenomena that impact supply management, but also can lead to new ways to improve performance. Key managerial insights from the chapter are summarized below.

5.1. Keep Current on the Growth and Development of XML and XML-Based Tools in Your Industry

There are some who rank the importance of XML just below the creation of the Internet itself due to its potential influence on processes that span entire supply chains (Kerstetter 2001). While it is too early to accurately gauge the impact of XML and related technologies on sourcing (as well as business in general), there is potential for great change. Of course, with great change, giants will fall and new leaders will emerge. Hopefully you'll be in position to be a leader.

5.2. Tame the Bullwhip

To what degree are the causes of the bullwhip effect present in my supply chain? Is there a significant bullwhip effect today, and if not, how about in the future as economic conditions change? It is worth spending time on these questions because (1) the bullwhip effect can be very expensive in terms of cost and lost market share and (2) it is becoming increasingly viable to control the causes (i.e., Internet technologies are decreasing EDI implementation and maintenance costs).

5.3. Use Pareto Analysis—a Simple and Widely Applicable Tool

A major role of management is to identify opportunities and allocate resources toward areas of high payoff. Pareto analysis is a useful, simple, and commonsense tool that can support this task when, as in the case of sourcing, meaningful measures of importance can be quantified.

5.4. Work to Align Interests throughout the Supply Chain

Be aware that the behavior and decisions of independent firms (and even departments within a firm) are often suboptimal for the supply chain as a whole. Double marginalization, for example, is evident in high prices, lower demand, and lower total supply chain profit. Maintain a systems view, and assess the degree to which performance can be improved through better integration and aligned incentives. Close working relationships and creative contractual terms can sometimes significantly reduce this effect to the benefit of all supply chain parties, including the end consumer. The one caveat is that the design of incentive systems is usually more difficult than expected; therefore, beware the law of unintended consequences.

6. EXERCISES

1. Write a brief answer to each of the chapter keys in your own words. After writing down your answers, review the chapter with a focus on the content in bold to check and clarify your interpretations.

2. "Direct procurement will be consumer demand driven. As orders are received, retailers will communicate demand in real-time to manufacturers where a bill-of-materials explosion will drive supply procurement which may initiate or modify an auction with suppliers . . ." (Burchett 2000). When viewed in its entirety, a supply chain for a consumer product includes all the firms between creation/extraction of raw materials and the end consumers—a vast network spanning many countries and firms from a one-person business to a Fortune 200 company. XML is arguably a requirement if large portions of a supply chain are to become interconnected to the degree envisioned in the preceding quote. Why?

3. Section 2 of this chapter contained some of the reasons for Cisco's $2.2 billion inventory write-down. As noted in the section, Cisco is now moving toward an XML-based private trade exchange where all levels in the supply chain will have access to end-market demand information. Why should this help to reduce the chance of a similar problem in the future?

4. In the late 1990s, the Bios Group and Stu Kauffman of the Santa Fe Institute developed and studied models of P&G's supply chain. They found irregular disruptive flow even though end consumer demand was relatively smooth. P&G had a requirement that all shipments occur in full truckload quantities. This saves transportation cost, but when this requirement was relaxed, flows became smooth and out-of-stocks decreased. The project demonstrated the bullwhip effect in P&G's supply chain, which was due to one of the four causes listed in this chapter. Which one, and why?

5. You decide to put a big clear jug of quarters in the middle of campus. Everyone can see, but no one can touch. People submit sealed bids for how much they will pay for the jug. Over 10,000 individuals submit bids, and you award the jug to the highest bidder. What principle of nature explains why you are likely to make money on this deal, and why?

6. It's been one week since you started your position as business manager for the campus newspaper. There's been a history of problems with payables, though not much other information is available. As a first step toward diagnosis, you'd like to identify a small group of suppliers for initial investigation. The total charges by supplier for last year are available:

Supplier	Amount Billed
1	$342.80
2	167.25
3	1,200.00
4	87.61
5	4,512.46
6	214.58
7	7,456.23
8	412.00
9	897.66
10	341.74
11	55.60
12	1,922.35
13	145.21
14	197.88
15	244.99
16	602.00
	$18,800.36

Use Pareto analysis to stratify the total amount billed by supplier (e.g., using Excel). Which are the largest suppliers that make up about 80 percent of the total amount billed, and what percentage are these suppliers of the total supply base?

7. Are the first digit frequencies in the amount billed by the 16 suppliers in the previous question approximately consistent with Benford frequencies?

8. Consider the example in the section on double marginalization that shows supply chain profit is 33 percent higher when the manufacturer owns the distributor. Verify that an independent distributor maximizes profit by setting price equal to $77.50, a manufacturer/distributor firm maximizes profit by setting price equal to $65, and supply chain profit increases by 33 percent with the price reduction.

Case Exercise: *KB Plumbing*

Your firm, KB Plumbing, is a major U.S. distributor of plumbing supplies. In the past year, an overseas plumbing supply manufacturer (ACTCO) has been buying small U.S. distributors. ACTCO's strategy is to increase U.S. market share through acquisition of a distribution network and aggressive pricing. The strategy is working. Demand for plumbing supplies, which are close to commodity status, is highly price sensitive. Your customers are shifting more of their volume to ACTCO. In many cases, matching ACTCO's price would mean selling below your firm's cost.

The purchase contracts with all of your suppliers are the same basic form: a fixed price contract with occasional incentive programs (e.g., a bonus for surpassing a quarterly volume target). You decide to approach your major supplier with a proposal for a new type of contract—a contract that will allow your supply chain (i.e., manufacturer → your distribution firm → customers) to compete on a more equal footing with ACTCO.

Questions

1. Estimate the percentage increase in supply chain volume and profit due to a cost plus fixed fee contract (i.e., supplier sells product at variable cost and receives a fixed monthly fee).

2. Develop (with rationale) a proposal for a new type of contract between your firm and the supplier. This proposal must specify the percentage reduction in the supplier's price and the size of the fixed fee to be offered to the supplier. As part of your answer to these questions, (a) develop the projected impact of your proposal on profit for your supplier and for your firm and (b) identify costs (e.g., risks) of your proposal, from the perspective of both your firm and your supplier. You may initially focus your analysis by concentrating on a representative product, say, product X, which is 1 of 30 products purchased from the supplier.

The following cost and demand rate estimates have been developed for product X:

- Purchase cost = $11.60 per unit
- Handling and transportation cost = $3 per unit (paid by your firm)
- Selling price = $15.80 per unit (i.e., contribution margin = $1.20)
- Demand rate = 2,400 units per month

The product X demand rate decreases by 2,000 units per month for every $1 increase in price and increases by 2,000 units per month for every $1 decrease in price.

You estimate the supplier's contribution margin (price less variable cost) as a percent of selling price at 33 percent (i.e., product X variable cost = 0.67 × 11.60 = $7.77).

Chapter **Six**

Inventory Management I: Deterministic Analysis

Chapter Outline

Chapter Keys

1. What are the roles of inventory?
2. What are the costs of holding inventory?
3. Why do estimates of inventory holding cost rates tend to be low?
4. What is the basic cost trade-off in the economics of quantity?

5. How prevalent is this type of cost trade-off?
6. How can the various order quantity models be applied (e.g., EOQ, EOQ with backorders, EPQ, EOQ with quantity discounts, EOQ prior to a price increase)?
7. What are the managerial insights from the chapter?

This chapter introduces the topic of inventory management, a topic that links material in the previous two chapters (see Figure 6.1). Day-to-day execution and periodic modification of inventory policies are highly dependent on demand forecasts and ways in which demand is managed (Chapter 4), and ultimately must be translated into replenishment orders from suppliers (Chapter 5).

Two recurring questions when managing inventory are *when* to order and *how much* to order. As we saw in Chapter 3, pull and push represent alternative approaches for answering the question of when to order. The question of how much to order is addressed in this chapter. In particular, we will assume that demand is constant—the term *deterministic* in the chapter title means determined, or known with certainty—and concentrate on the economics of quantity. The next chapter will introduce the complication of uncertainty, and the scope will be expanded to include not only the question of how much to order, but when to order according to a pull approach. A push approach for answering when and how much will be discussed in Chapter 9.

A study of how to manage inventory begins with an understanding of why it exists and how much it costs. We will see in Section 1, where the roles and costs of inventory are covered, that reasons for holding inventory are rooted in causes of system slack discussed in Chapter 3.

Section 2 can be viewed as a warm-up to the main content of the chapter. Here we'll see the potential for wide application of analysis and insights surrounding quantity decisions, through discussion and a motivating example.

Section 3 is the heart of the chapter. The objectives of this section are to develop (1) analytical skills in the context of a fundamental trade-off that, among other applications, is present in ordering decisions and (2) intuition into the trade-off. For the first objective, we'll begin with the simplest of settings, and then gradually expand our analysis by considering a series of complications. In each case, we'll start with an example and work through the analysis from scratch. The examples all revolve around situations that you are facing as the new CFO of a growing venture. For the second objective, we'll look at general properties that can be deduced from the analysis and interpret what these mean for guiding management decisions.

1. INVENTORY ROLES AND COSTS

The level and cost of inventory are substantial. In the United States, for instance, inventory investment averages about 14 percent of GDP, or $1.6 trillion (Wilson 2005). So, before we get into the economics of quantity, it is first worth considering why this inventory exists

FIGURE 6.1   A supply chain with emphasis on inventory management links.

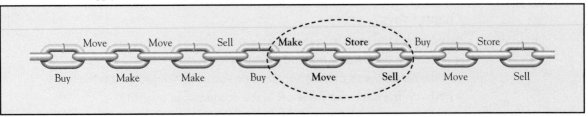

and what the costs are. **Inventory serves a number of roles** that stem from the causes of system slack discussed in Chapter 3 (the related causes of system slack from Chapter 3 are identified in *italics*):

Inventory Roles

1. **Cycle stock** is excess inventory due to order batching (e.g., order a truckload once per month); *scale economies.*
2. **Speculative stock** is excess inventory acquired prior to an anticipated price increase (e.g., limited-time coupon); *scale economies.*
3. **In-transit/in-process stock** is inventory undergoing transformation in either place (e.g., product on trucks, trains, ships, and planes) or form (e.g., material in production); *time lags.*
4. **Safety stock** is inventory to protect against uncertainty (e.g., uncertain demand, lead time, losses due to pilferage or decay); *quantity uncertainty.*[1]
5. **Seasonal stock** is inventory built up prior to a selling season due to insufficient capacity (e.g., skis manufactured during the off-season); *changing supply and demand.*

This chapter concentrates on cycle stock. In particular, we'll look at factors that influence appropriate batch sizes, which in turn determine the level of cycle stock in a firm. We'll also briefly consider the economics of speculative stock.

There are many costs of holding inventory, some that are relatively objective and measurable and some that aren't. Doug Lambert (1975) investigated the costs of holding inventory in his Ph.D. dissertation. He identified the following **four cost categories:**

Inventory Holding Costs

1. **Capital costs**
   - Inventory investment (e.g., cost to finance the inventory, or, alternatively, the opportunity cost of funds tied up in inventory).
   - Investment in assets required by inventory (e.g., material-handling equipment, information systems for inventory tracking).

2. **Inventory service costs**
   - Insurance.
   - Taxes.

3. **Storage space costs**
   - Plant warehouses.
   - Public warehouses (e.g., storage fees assessed by an outside warehousing firm).
   - Rented warehouses.
   - Company-owned warehouses.

4. **Inventory risk costs**
   - Obsolescence (e.g., price markdowns for out-of-style or obsolete product).
   - Damage.
   - Pilferage.
   - Relocation costs (e.g., transferring product to a different warehouse due to shortages).

---

[1] Safety stock is also known as buffer stock.

An estimate of the variable cost of holding inventory and insight into the estimate's likely accuracy are important for planning and decision making. Investments in supporting assets (e.g., material-handling equipment, information technology, building space) may or may not change much as inventory levels vary, and this can make for a tricky cost estimation problem. In addition, there are subjective inventory costs (not explicitly noted above) related to **delays in the discovery of quality problems, which in turn inhibit problem-solving effectiveness.** Inventories mask problems that negatively affect quality, delivery, customer service, and production scheduling. The higher the inventory, the longer the time to discovery, which makes identification and correction of root causes more difficult. The costs of delays in problem discovery due to increases in inventory are difficult to measure. Consequently, cost estimates of this effect, if captured at all, tend to be subjective.

The **wide scope of contributing factors and the difficulty in estimating the cost impact of some of these factors are reasons why holding costs tend to be underestimated in practice,** which can negatively affect analysis and ultimately management decisions. Simple awareness of the types of costs listed above can help guard against this possibility. In addition, models and analyses in this chapter are useful for gaining some intuition into the impact of incorrect parameter estimates (e.g., cost and demand rates) . . . intuition that has two very practical benefits: (1) a sense of when it can be worth the time and cost to develop more accurate parameter estimates and (2) insight into the direction to slant a decision if you suspect that an estimate may be low or high. Smart managers understand the limits of their knowledge and will make decisions that judiciously hedge against their ignorance. They will deviate from the "best decision" under the scenario where assumptions and estimates are perfect as a hedge against the possibility that they aren't. Of course, a key to doing this well is having enough sense of the impact of errors to deviate in the right direction.

2. TRANSACTION COSTS AND ECONOMIES OF SCALE

Recall from Chapter 3 that economies of scale refer to economic benefits of increasing volume—benefits that provide incentive to create/acquire more of a resource than what may be needed at the moment. The analysis we are about to explore captures a **fundamental trade-off between transaction costs that exert pressure for large production or order quantities and the various costs that work against large batches.** Our first step in the analysis will be to consider the economic order quantity (EOQ) model.

Before we get into details, a reasonable question is—what does all this mean and how critical is it in today's world of quick-change flexibility and an environment that seems to be increasingly chaotic, fast-paced, and unpredictable? The EOQ model has little value when viewed narrowly (i.e., at the level of plugging numbers into a formula with little understanding). That said, the analysis that underlies the EOQ model is important, in part for the very changes in the environment noted above. Let me explain. Economies of scale are widespread in society and business. We see these economies in ordering, advertising, hiring/firing, teaching, eating, warehousing, and on and on. We'll look at some simple back-of-the-envelope analysis that gets at balancing the benefits of increasing volume with the associated drawbacks. The value of this type of analysis is in speed (can be done on the back of an envelope or using a spreadsheet within minutes) and in insights that come from viewing a problem without excessive detail. It is most appropriate when used to provide a sense of whether there is high payback potential in changing a policy or system (i.e., diagnostic analysis), or to give an indication of how one might adapt a policy in the face of change in the environment. Let's look at an example.

Example.[2]

As a newly appointed CFO, you discover that your company maintains two cash accounts. As cash becomes available, it is deposited into a high-yield account with an annual interest rate of 8 percent and is periodically transferred to a low-yield account with an interest rate of 3 percent. The high-yield account is analogous to a personal savings account and the low-yield account is analogous to a personal checking account, that is, payments are made out of the low-yield account. There is no charge for electronic funds transfers or checks written out of the low-yield account. However, the bank charges a $25 transaction fee for each electronic funds transfer out of the high-yield account. The current policy is to transfer an amount of $1 million to the low-yield account when the account balance is close to zero. Annual payments out of the low-yield account total about $10 million, which means there is an average of 10 transfers over the course of the year. Why not transfer money every day, or why not transfer funds once per year? What is the trade-off, and can money be saved by changing the policy? As you consider these questions, you might consider what factors influence how frequently you withdraw cash from your bank account.

Example Summary

Annual cash requirement paid out of low-yield account = $10 million
Annual high-yield account interest = 8%
Annual low-yield account interest = 3%
Transfer fee = $25
Current transfer quantity = $1 million
Alternative transfer quantity = $100,000
Annual savings through reduced lost interest and transfer fees ≈ $20,000

If you find yourself in this situation, there are at least a couple of ways you can save your company money—one easy way and another way that may take some time but will have a bigger impact. First, the easy option. You can generate about $20,000 annually to the bottom line by transferring $100,000 at a time. **Here's the trade-off—on one hand you want to transfer a large amount to save transaction fees while on the other hand you want to transfer a small amount to keep a low average balance in the low-yield account.** You lose 5 percent interest on cash in the low-yield account; this is the difference between the high-yield interest rate of 8 percent and the low-yield interest rate of 3 percent. Therefore, transferring $1 million at a time means 10 transactions at $25 each for a total of $250 per year. The balance in the low-yield account will range between $0 and $1 million with an

---

[2] This example helps illustrate the broad applications of EOQ analysis. Later in the chapter we will look at more traditional supply chain examples where product is ordered from a supplier or produced in-house.

average balance of $500,000 and a lost interest cost of $(0.05)(500,000) = \$25,000$ per year. So the current policy costs $25,250 per year. The total cost of transferring $100,000 at a time is $5,000 per year (see if you can verify this), and this is the optimal transfer quantity.[3]

Now for the second option. We can see that **the root of the problem is the transaction fee.** If this is eliminated, then payments can essentially be made directly from the high-yield account, eliminating all lost interest and transaction costs. This is an important general insight because management usually has some control over the cost per transaction, whether associated with funds transfers, deliveries to customers, purchase orders, or other transactions. There are usually fewer opportunities to significantly influence the inventory holding cost rate (5 percent in this example), the other side of the EOQ trade-off. The bottom line: **look for ways to reduce the cost per transaction in all areas of your organization.**

3. ORDER AND PRODUCTION QUANTITY DECISIONS

The focus of this section is on developing basic cost analysis skills in the context of order and production quantity decisions. We will formalize the analysis of the cash management example in the previous section by developing a model that predicts how cost changes with quantity, and then we'll consider how to extend our analysis when various complications are introduced.

The development of cost (or profit) models that capture the essence of reality is usually the hardest part of analysis. Once this is done, the real fun begins—playing with the model (e.g., using a spreadsheet or "back of an envelope") to (1) get a feel for a decision that makes good business sense and, more substantively, (2) develop some intuition into a less-than-obvious relationship between changing environmental conditions and sound policies. For most of the cost models, we will also look at formulas for the optimal quantity and the optimal cost. And we'll see how these formulas provide a shortcut to developing intuition . . . intuition that will be summarized in the form of five managerial insights in Section 4.

Our analyses rest on six assumptions:

A1. Demand is constant and known with certainty.

A2. When a unit is being produced, the production rate is constant and known with certainty.

A3. The lead time between when an order is placed and when the order arrives is constant and known with certainty.

A4. The cost to place an order or to begin production is independent of the quantity, that is, a pure transaction cost.

A5. Inventory holding cost is proportional to average inventory.

A6. Backorder cost, if applicable, is proportional to the average number of units on backorder.

Notation for Order and Production Quantity Models

$D =$ demand rate in units per period

$P =$ production capacity in units per period

$c =$ purchase (or production) cost per unit

$h =$ inventory holding cost per $-period

$c_e =$ inventory holding cost per unit-period (excess cost rate), for example, $c_e = h \times c$

---

[3] We ignored the impact of the lost interest associated with annual transaction cost. We ignored this complication in the interest of clarity, and because the bottom-line impact is minimal (i.e., accounting for the complication is equivalent to increasing the cost per transaction from $25 to $25.04).

c_s = backorder cost per unit-period (shortage cost rate)

A = cost per transaction (cost to place order or begin production)

Q = amount to order (or produce) at a time, or units per transaction

b = number of units on backorder when replenishment order arrives (or production begins)

Some of the notation can be illustrated using numbers from the preceding example. Many of the terms defined above refer to a rate, or number per period, and for the purposes of illustration we'll use annual rates (i.e., length of the period is one year). A transaction in the example refers to the transfer of funds from the high-yield account to the low-yield account, and the cost per transaction = A = $25. The firm loses 5 percent annual interest on dollars in the low-yield account; that is, $1 in the low-yield account is earning 3 percent interest when it could be earning 8 percent if in the high-yield account. This means that h = inventory holding cost per $-period = $0.05 per $-year. The way we express the annual demand and excess cost rates depends on our choice of unit. If we define one unit as $1 million, then D = demand rate in units per period = 10 units per year and c_e = inventory holding cost per unit-period = $0.05 \times \$1,000,000$ = $50,000 per unit-year. In words, c_e = $50,000 per unit-year means that it costs $50,000 to have a "unit" of $1,000,000 in the low-yield account for one year. The more natural choice is to define a unit as $1, in which case D = 10,000,000 units per year and c_e = $0.05 per unit-year.

3.1. Economic Order Quantity

A relatively simple cost structure, and a nice starting point for cost analysis, is evident in the example of Section 2. Given that demand is stable and predictable, and the order lead time is constant, orders will be placed so that inventory will be down to zero when the order arrives. The average number of units ordered over the course of a year will match total demand, so the major question is how frequently orders should be placed or, equivalently, how much should be ordered at a time. As the order size increases, annual transaction cost declines because there are fewer orders per year, and annual inventory holding cost increases because average inventory increases. From an understanding of the general cost trade-off, the next step is to determine specifically how cost varies with quantity.

It is often useful to work with a concrete example when working through analysis. Recall the example in Section 2 where surplus cash, as it arrives, is deposited in a high-yield account. Payments are made out of a low-yield account. As the balance in the low-yield account approaches zero, money is transferred from the high-yield account to the low-yield account. Transfers are not done every day because a transaction fee is charged for each withdrawal from the high-yield account. We know that A = cost per transaction = $25, D = demand rate in units per period = 10,000,000 units per year, and c_e = inventory holding cost per unit-period = $0.05 per unit-year. If the policy is to transfer Q = $1,000,000 at a time, then since we know we'll need a total of $10,000,000 over the course of the year, there will be 10 transactions per year at a cost of $25 per transaction. This means that the total transaction cost per year is $25(10) = $250. More generally,

$TC(Q)$ = average transaction cost per period as function of the order quantity Q

= (cost per transaction)(# of transactions per period)

= $(A)(D/Q)$

Testing this out for A = $25, D = 10,000,000 units per year, and Q = 1,000,000 units,

$$TC(1,000,000) = \$25(10,000,000/1,000,000) = \$250$$

as expected.

FIGURE 6.2

Inventory over time when $Q = 1,000,000$ and $D = 10,000,000$. The average balance is 500,000. There are 10 transactions per year, and time between transactions is $1/10$ year = 36.5 days.

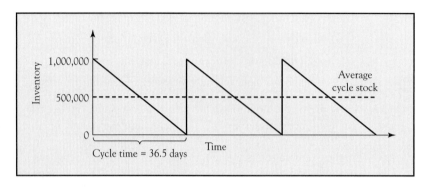

FIGURE 6.3

Transaction, holding, and total cost per period as a function of the order quantity Q. $C(Q) = TC(Q) + HC(Q)$ is minimized at the quantity Q^*, where the transaction and inventory holding cost curves intersect.

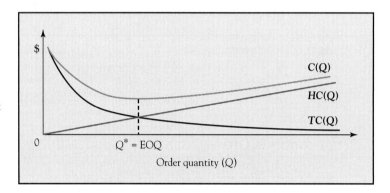

The formula for inventory cost may be less obvious, which brings to mind a saying for back-of-the-envelope analysis: when in doubt, run in circles, scream, and shout . . . and draw a picture. Figure 6.2 portrays inventory (i.e., balance in the low-yield account) over time.

The balance starts off at $1,000,000, and since the demand rate is constant, the balance decreases at a steady rate until it hits zero, and the next transfer of $1,000,000 arrives. It makes economic sense to drain the low-yield balance all the way to zero before replenishing; that is, there is no uncertainty in demand or lead time, so any positive balance when the $1,000,000 arrives is unnecessary and costly. From the picture, it is apparent that the average balance during a cycle is $(\$1,000,000 + \$0)/2 = \$500,000$, and that cycles repeat so $500,000 is the overall average balance, or average cycle stock. Since 5 percent interest is lost on cash in the low-yield account, the annual inventory holding cost is $500,000(0.05) = \$25,000$. More generally,

$HC(Q)$ = average inventory holding cost per period as a function of the order quantity Q

$\quad$ = (average inventory)c_e

$\quad$ = $(Q/2)c_e$

Testing this out for $Q = 1,000,000$ units and $c_e = \$0.05$/unit-year,

$$HC(1,000,000) = (1,000,000/2)\$0.05 = \$25,000$$

as expected.

There are no other costs that depend on the order quantity Q, which means that an expression for total relevant cost per period is (see Figure 6.3)

$$C(Q) = TC(Q) + HC(Q) = AD/Q + (Q/2)c_e$$

Example Summary

D = demand rate = 10 million dollars/year
A = cost/transfer transaction = $25
c_e = excess cost rate = $0.05/unit-year
If transfer $1,000,000 at a time, then Q = 1,000,000 and
$TC(Q)$ = $25/transaction × 10 transactions/year = $250/year
$HC(Q)$ = average of 500,000 "units" in inventory × $0.05/unit-year = $25,000/year
If transfer $100,000 at a time, then Q = 100,000 and
$TC(Q)$ = $25/transaction × 100 transactions/year = $2,500/year
$HC(Q)$ = average of 50,000 "units" in inventory × $0.05/unit-year = $2,500/year

After computing $C(Q)$ with a few trial values for Q, one can quickly determine that the optimal order quantity is $Q^* = 100,000$. Thus, as we saw in Section 2, the annual savings associated with changing from $Q = 1,000,000$ to $Q = 100,000$ is significant: $C(1,000,000) - C(100,000) = [25(10,000,000/1,000,000) + (1,000,000/2).05] - [25(10,000,000/100,000) + (100,000/2).05] = 25,250 - 5,000 = \$20,250$. The EOQ formulas are summarized below.

Formulas for the Economic Order Quantity Model

D/Q = average number of orders per period
   = (demand per period)/(quantity per order)

Q/D = number of periods between placement of orders
   = $1/$(number of orders per period)

$Q/2$ = average inventory, or, more precisely, average cycle stock

$TC(Q)$ = average transaction cost per period
   = (cost per transaction)(transactions per period) = AD/Q

$HC(Q)$ = average inventory holding cost per period = (average inventory)c_e
   = $(Q/2)c_e$

$C(Q)$ = average transaction and holding cost per period
   = $AD/Q + (Q/2)c_e$

Q^* = economic order quantity (order size with lowest average transaction plus inventory holding cost) = $(2AD/c_e)^{1/2}$

$TC(Q^*)$ = average transaction cost per period if the order quantity is Q^*
   = $AD/Q^* = (ADc_e/2)^{1/2}$

$HC(Q^*)$ = average inventory holding cost per period if the order quantity is Q^*
   = $(Q^*/2)c_e = (ADc_e/2)^{1/2}$

$C(Q^*)$ = average transaction and holding cost per period if the order quantity is Q^*
   = $(2ADc_e)^{1/2}$

Example

Your firm has just purchased the rights to take over as the exclusive distributor of Kalina products in North America. Kalina is a leading Russian manufacturer of cosmetics and other personal-care products. The four brands are Chiorny Zhemchug (Black), Zolotaya Linia (Golden), Serebryannaya Linia (Silver), and Chistaya Liniya (Clean). Products are purchased from Kalina in palletized lots. The historical North America demand rates are 60,000 pallets per year for Black

products, 25,000 pallets per year for Golden products, 5,000 pallets per year for Silver products, and 10,000 pallets per year for Clean products. Your firm incurs an annual inventory holding cost rate of 45 percent of product value (i.e., h = $0.45/\$-year). There are a variety of fixed fees associated with processing and receiving each order: $3,126 for customs clearance and export/import document preparation fees[4] and $80 for purchase order preparation (i.e., $A = 3126 + 80 = $3,206). Kalina pays transportation to port of entry and sets prices in US$ (Kalina bears the risk of a fluctuating currency exchange rate). The specific charges depend on the product mix, but based on demand history, the variable purchase and transportation costs by brand are estimated at $42 per pallet of Black products, $105 per pallet of Golden products, $81 per pallet of Silver products, and $15 per pallet of Clean products. How many pallets of aggregated Kalina product should be ordered at a time, what is the length of time between orders, and what is the annual transaction plus inventory holding cost?

The aggregated annual demand rate is 100,000 pallets per year, with percentage contribution by brand of 60 percent Black, 25 percent Golden, 5 percent Silver, and 10 percent Clean. This means that the average variable cost for a pallet is c = 60%(42) + 25%(105) + 5%(81) + 10%(15) = $57 per pallet. The holding cost per pallet-year = c_e = hc = ($0.45/\$-year)($57/pallet) = $25.65 per pallet-year. In summary,

D = demand rate = 100,000 pallets/year

A = fixed fees for placing an order = $3,206

c_e = inventory holding cost rate = $25.65/pallet-year

Annual transaction and holding cost can be computed for various trial values of Q to find the economic order quantity, or the EOQ formula can be used.

$$Q^* = \text{EOQ} = [2AD/(hc)]^{1/2} = (2AD/c_e)^{1/2} = (2 \times 3,206 \times 100,000/25.65)^{1/2}$$
$$\approx 5,000 \text{ pallets}$$

$$Q/D = \text{time between orders} = (5,000 \text{ pallets})/(100,000 \text{ pallets/year}) = 0.05 \text{ year}$$
$$= (0.05 \text{ year})(365 \text{ days/year}) \approx 18 \text{ days}$$

$$C(Q) = \text{transaction and holding cost} = AD/Q + (Q/2)c_e$$
$$= 3,206 \times 100,000/5,000 + (5,000/2)25.65$$
$$= \$64,120 + \$64,125 = \$128,245/\text{year}$$

The most economical ordering policy is to order about 5,000 pallets at a time. Of these 5,000 pallets, the specific brand and product mix will be based on market demand; for example, 60 percent Black brand, 25 percent Golden brand, 5 percent Silver brand, and 10 percent Clean brand. The time between when orders are placed (or, equivalently, between when orders are received) is about 18 days. The total transaction and inventory holding cost per year is projected to be $128,245, or $128,245/100,000 ≈ $1.28 per pallet.

---

[4] The fixed fees associated with export/import can be substantial due to the many laws and regulations (e.g., see Chapter 10, Supplement B). For example, the May 26, 2003, issue of *Traffic World* notes that a typical cross-border transaction involves filing 35 documents, interfacing with 25 parties, and complying with more than 600 laws and 500 trade agreements.

Example Summary

D = demand rate = 100,000 pallets/year
A = cost/order transaction = \$3,206
c_e = excess cost rate = \$25.65/pallet-year
Q^* = economic order quantity = $(2AD/c_e)^{1/2} \approx$ 5,000 pallets

---

3.2. Economic Order Quantity with Planned Backorders

Consider the cash management example, and suppose the bank offers the option of over-draft protection. This means that the bank will loan money to cover any negative balance in the low-yield account, say, at an annual interest rate of 18 percent. A negative balance in the low-yield account is analogous to a firm with no inventory of a product and some demand on backorder. In the case of the bank account, when cash is transferred into the low-yield account, the loan is paid off and the remainder is available for future payments. In the case of the product, when a shipment arrives from a supplier, the backorders are shipped and the remainder is available for future demand.

Given the new overdraft protection option, can money be saved by allowing the balance in the low-yield account to go negative before a transfer is received, can money be saved by changing the transfer quantity from Q = 100,000, and, if so, would the transfer quantity increase or decrease? Try to guess the answers to these questions.[5]

Taking cost analysis a step at a time, we'll begin with transaction cost. Working with our example where D = 10,000,000 units per year and letting Q = 100,000, we see that there will be 100 transactions per year at a cost per transaction of A = \$25. In other words, the expression for transaction cost is unchanged from the basic EOQ model, that is,

$$TC(Q) = \text{average transaction cost per period as function of the order quantity } Q$$
$$= (\text{cost per transaction})(\# \text{ of transactions per period})$$
$$= (A)(D/Q)$$

Testing this out for A = \$25, D = 10,000,000 units per year, and Q = 100,000 units,

$$TC(100,000) = \$25(10,000,000/100,000) = \$2,500$$

as expected.

The effect of overdraft protection becomes evident in the expression for holding cost and in a requirement for an additional expression that captures the cost of a negative bal-ance (i.e., shortage cost). We lose 5 percent interest on excess dollars in the low-yield account. In terms of our notation, c_e = inventory holding cost per unit-period = \$0.05 per unit-year, which is the same as saying that \$1 sitting in the low-yield account for one year costs \$0.05. But how much do we lose if the balance in the low-yield account is $-\$1$ for one year? The answer to this question gives the shortage cost rate. To conclude that c_e = \$0.05 per unit-year, we observed that, relative to a zero balance, a low-yield balance

---

[5] One way to develop your intuition is to take some time to answer less-than-obvious questions with your "gut." Then, after completing analysis and presumably understanding the answers, reconsider your initial gut response. What was the basis for this response, and why was it different from what you eventually discovered? As you consider these questions, you'll either gain a deeper understanding of the issue by exposing earlier erroneous assumptions and biases, or perhaps, just as likely, discover potential flaws in your analysis, which in turn spurs a new take on analysis and a richer understanding.

FIGURE 6.4

Inventory over time when $Q = 100,000$ and $b = 20,000$. The value of $T = T_1 + T_2$ is the length of the cycle where T_1 is the length of time that the balance is positive and T_2 is the length of time that the balance is negative.

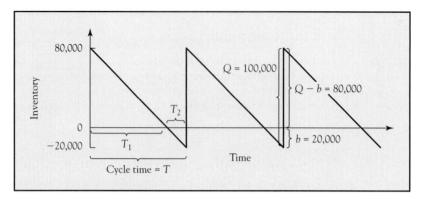

of $1 means one less dollar in the high-yield account earning 5 percent more than the low-yield account. Similarly, relative to a zero balance, a balance of −$1 in the low-yield account means one additional dollar in the high-yield account earning 8 percent that is offsetting the loan interest of 18 percent. Consequently, c_s = shortage (or backorder) cost per unit-period = 0.18 − 0.08 = $0.10 per unit-year.

What remains is to determine the average positive and negative balance in the low-yield account. Suppose we transfer $Q = 100,000$ when the balance in the low-yield account is −20,000. In terms of our notation, this means that b = number of units on backorder when replenishment order arrives = 20,000 (see Figure 6.4).

Figure 6.4 gives some clues into how holding and shortage cost depend on Q and b. We see that the average positive balance during T_1 is $80,000/2 = 40,000$ and there is no positive balance during T_2. In other words, the average positive balance during the cycle is

$$(T_1/T)(Q - b)/2 + (T_2/T)0 = (T_1/T)(80,000/2)$$

Similarly, the average negative balance during the cycle is

$$(T_1/T)0 + (T_2/T)(b/2) = (T_2/T)(20,000/2)$$

Finally, here is a remnant from high school geometry: the triangles in Figure 6.4 are all similar, and the ratios of corresponding sides of similar triangles are equal. This means that

$$Q/T = (Q - b)/T_1 = b/T_2$$

or

$$T_1/T = (Q - b)/Q \quad \text{and} \quad T_2/T = b/Q$$

Since $c_e = 0.05 per unit-year and $(Q - b)/Q = 80,000/100,000 = 0.8$, the average positive balance is $0.8(80,000/2) = 32,000$ and the annual inventory holding cost is $32,000(0.05) = $1,600$. More generally,

$HC(Q,b)$ = average inventory holding cost per period as a function of Q and b

= (average inventory)c_e

= $[(Q - b)^2/2Q]c_e$

Testing this out for $Q = 100,000$ units, $b = 20,000$ units, and $c_e = $0.05 per unit-year,

$$HC(100,000, 20,000) = [80,000^2/(2 \times 100,000)]\$0.05 = \$1,600$$

as expected.

Since $c_s = \$0.10$ per unit-year and $b/Q = 20{,}000/100{,}000 = 0.2$, the average loan balance is $0.2(20{,}000/2) = 2{,}000$ and the annual "backorder" cost is $2{,}000(0.10) = \$200$. More generally,

$SC(Q,b)$ = average backorder cost per period as a function of Q and b

$$= [b^2/2Q]c_s$$

Testing this out for $Q = 100{,}000$ units, $b = 20{,}000$ units, and $c_s = \$0.10$ per unit-year,

$$SC(100{,}000, 20{,}000) = [20{,}000^2/(2 \times 100{,}000)]\$0.10 = \$200$$

as expected.

Example Summary

D = demand rate = \$10 million/year
A = cost/transfer transaction = \$25
c_e = excess cost rate = \$0.05/unit-year
c_s = shortage cost rate = \$0.10/unit-year
If transfer \$100,000 at a time, which arrives when low-yield balance is −\$20,000, then
Q = 100,000, b = 20,000, and
$TC(Q)$ = \$25/transaction × 100 transactions/year = \$2,500/year
$HC(Q, b)$ = average of 32,000 "units" in inventory × \$0.05/unit-year = \$1,600/year
$SC(Q, b)$ = average of 2,000 "backordered units" × \$0.10/unit-year = \$200/year

---

There are no other costs that depend on the order quantity Q and backorder quantity b, which means that an expression for total relevant cost per period is

$$C(Q,b) = TC(Q) + HC(Q,b) + SC(Q,b)$$

$$= AD/Q + [(Q - b)^2/2Q]c_e + [b^2/2Q]c_s$$

For this example, $C(100{,}000, 20{,}000) = TC(100{,}000) + HC(100{,}000, 20{,}000) + SC(100{,}000, 20{,}000) = \$2{,}500 + \$1{,}600 + \$200 = \$4{,}300$. As we saw in Section 3.1, the optimal cost without overdraft protection (e.g., $Q^* = 100{,}000$, $b = 0$) is $C(100000, 0) = \$5{,}000$. We reduce cost by 14 percent, or \$700 per year, by transferring \$100,000 into the low-yield account when the balance is −\$20,000 instead of \$0.

After computing $C(Q,b)$ with a few trial values for Q and b, one can quickly determine that the optimal order and backorder quantities are $Q^* \approx 122{,}475$ and $b^* \approx 40{,}825$. The option of overdraft protection essentially makes it cheaper to transfer a larger quantity, and, consequently, the optimal order quantity increases from 100,000 to 122,475. The cost at $Q = 122{,}475$ and $b = 40{,}825$ is $C(122{,}475, 40{,}825) = TC(122{,}475) + HC(122{,}475, 40{,}825) + SC(122{,}475, 40{,}825) = 2{,}041.23 + 1{,}360.83 + 680.42 = \$4{,}082.48$, for an annual savings of more than \$900 per year when compared to the alternative of $Q = 100{,}000$ and $b = 0$. The EOQ with planned backorders formulas are summarized below.

Formulas for the Economic Order Quantity Model with Planned Backorders

$$D/Q = \text{average number of orders per period}$$

$$Q/D = \text{number of periods between placement of orders}$$

$$(Q - b)^2/2Q = \text{average inventory, or, more precisely, average cycle stock}$$

$$b^2/2Q = \text{average number of units backordered}$$

$$TC(Q) = \text{average transaction cost per period} = AD/Q$$

$$HC(Q,b) = \text{average inventory holding cost per period} = [(Q - b)^2/2Q]c_e$$

$$SC(Q,b) = \text{average backorder cost per period} = [b^2/2Q]c_s$$

$$C(Q,b) = \text{average transaction, holding, and backorder cost per period}$$
$$= AD/Q + [(Q - b)^2/2Q]c_e + [b^2/2Q]c_s$$

$$Q^* = \text{economic order quantity} = [2AD/c_e]^{1/2}[(c_e + c_s)/c_s]^{1/2}$$

$$b^* = \text{optimal backorder quantity when order arrives} = Q^* c_e/(c_e + c_s)$$

$$TC(Q^*) = \text{average transaction cost per period if the order quantity is } Q^*$$
$$= AD/Q^* = (ADc_e/2)^{1/2}[c_s/(c_e + c_s)]^{1/2}$$

$$HC(Q^*,b^*) = \text{average inventory holding cost per period if the order quantity is}$$
$$Q^* \text{ and } b^* \text{ units are backordered when the order arrives}$$
$$= [(Q^* - b^*)^2/2Q^*]c_e = (ADc_e/2)^{1/2}[c_s/(c_e + c_s)]^{1/2}[c_s/(c_e + c_s)]$$

$$SC(Q^*,b^*) = \text{average backorder cost per period if the order quantity is } Q^* \text{ and } b^*$$
$$\text{units are backordered when the order arrives}$$
$$= [b^{*2}/2Q^*]c_s = (ADc_e/2)^{1/2}[c_s/(c_e + c_s)]^{1/2}[c_e/(c_e + c_s)]$$

$$C(Q^*,b^*) = \text{average transaction, holding, and backorder cost per period if the}$$
$$\text{order quantity } Q^* \text{ and } b^* \text{ units are backordered when the order arrives}$$
$$= AD/Q^* + [(Q^* - b^*)^2/2Q^*]c_e + [b^{*2}/2Q^*]c_s$$
$$= (2ADc_e)^{1/2}[c_s/(c_e + c_s)]^{1/2}$$

Notice that $Q^* \approx [2AD/c_e]^{1/2}$ if the shortage cost rate c_s is very high (i.e., $c_s \approx \infty$), which is the same formula as when backorders are not allowed. This makes sense in retrospect—if it's very expensive to backorder product, you probably don't want to plan to have backorders.

Example

Recall that your firm recently purchased the rights to distribute Kalina product in North America. Demand averages $D = 100{,}000$ pallets per year, the cost per order transaction is \$3,206, and the inventory holding cost rate is \$25.65 per pallet-year. The current policy is to order 5,000 pallets at a time, with each order arriving as inventory reaches zero. There are no backorders (i.e., always enough inventory to satisfy demand) and product is shipped to customers 24 hours after an order is placed.

Drawing on your intuition, you get an idea that you call a "pay-for-delay" program—customers get a 1 percent reduction in price for each week of delay beyond the standard 24-hour order-to-shipment cycle. You pitch the program to your customers and discover that the response is overwhelmingly positive. How much money does your pay-for-delay program save over the current policy, how much should be ordered at a time, what is the time between orders, and how many pallets' worth of demand should be backordered when a replenishment shipment arrives?

The only missing piece of information to develop answers to these questions is the backorder cost rate. The average variable cost of Kalina product is $c = \$57$ per pallet and your markup averages 50 percent. This means that a pallet of products purchased for \$57 will be sold for $\$57(1.5) = \$85.50$. This price is discounted at a rate of 1 percent per week of delay; that is, $c_s =$ backorder cost per unit-period $= 0.01(85.50) = \$0.855/\text{pallet-week} = (52 \text{ weeks/year})(\$0.855/\text{pallet-week}) = \$44.46$ per pallet-year. In summary,

D = demand rate = 100,000 pallets/year

A = fixed fees for placing an order = \$3,206

c_e = inventory holding cost rate = \$25.65/pallet-year

c_s = backorder cost rate = \$44.46/pallet-year

Annual transaction, holding, and backorder cost can be computed for various trial values of Q and b to find the optimal quantities, or the EOQ with planned backorders formulas can be used.

$$Q^* = \text{EOQ} = [2AD/c_e]^{1/2}[(c_e + c_s)/c_s]^{1/2}$$

$$= (2 \times 3{,}206 \times 100{,}000/25.65)^{1/2} \times [(25.65 + 44.46)/44.46)]^{1/2}$$

$$\approx 6{,}280 \text{ pallets}$$

$$b^* = Q^*c_e/(c_e + c_s) = 6{,}280[25.65/(25.65 + 44.46)] \approx 2{,}300 \text{ pallets}$$

$$Q/D = \text{time between orders} = (6{,}280 \text{ pallets})/(100{,}000 \text{ pallets/year}) = 0.0628 \text{ year}$$

$$= (0.0628 \text{ year})(365 \text{ days/year}) \approx 23 \text{ days}$$

$$C(Q,b) = \text{transaction, holding, and backorder cost} = AD/Q + [(Q - b)^2/2Q]c_e + [b^2/2Q]c_s$$

$$= 3{,}206 \times 100{,}000/6{,}280 + [(6{,}280 - 2{,}300)^2/(2 \times 6{,}280)]25.65 + [2{,}300^2/(2 \times 6{,}280)]44.46$$

$$= \$51{,}050.96 + \$32{,}349.22 + \$18{,}725.59 = 102{,}126$$

The most economical ordering policy is to order about 6,280 pallets at a time, with each order placed so that there are 2,300 pallets' worth of product backordered when the replenishment order arrives. The time between when orders are placed (or, equivalently, between when orders are received) is about 23 days. The total transaction, inventory holding, and backorder cost per year is projected to be \$102,126, or $\$102{,}126/100{,}000 \approx \$1.02$ per pallet. Compared to the optimal policy with no backorders in Section 3.1, your pay-for-delay program saves $C(5{,}000, 0) - C(6{,}280, 2{,}300) = \$128{,}245 - \$102{,}126 = \$26{,}119$ per year. Given the early favorable customer response to the program, there is also potential for a sales revenue increase. Looks like a winner.

Example Summary

D = demand rate = 100,000 pallets/year
A = cost/order transaction = \$3,206
c_e = excess cost rate = \$25.65/pallet-year
c_s = shortage cost rate = \$44.46/pallet-year
Q^* = economic order quantity = $(2AD/c_e)^{1/2} \approx 6{,}280$ pallets
b^* = optimal number of backorders when replenishment shipment arrives = $Q^*c_e/(c_e + c_s) \approx 2{,}300$ pallets

---

3.3. Economic Production Quantity

It's 6:35 a.m. Monday morning and, as usual, you're starting your day with a quick read of the *Financial Times*. Your heart momentarily stops as you turn to page 2, "CXW Bank Hacked for \$500m." Apparently someone hacked into the bank's system and got away with \$500,000,000 by executing a nontraceable electronic funds transfer (EFT). Your firm's high- and low-yield accounts are with CXW Bank, and you're wondering if there will be any implications for your business. Sure enough, the phone rings a few hours later and you're informed of a change in policy to go into effect next week: among other safeguards imposed by CXW Bank's insurance company, CXW Bank EFTs will be limited to a rate of $50,000 per day. You wonder what this means for you, and suddenly it hits you—this is good news. Let's see why.

To keep things simple (and to leave some fun for an end-of-chapter exercise), we'll ignore the possibility of overdraft protection. You will arrange for funds to begin arriving in the low-yield account at a rate of $50,000 per day at the point in time when the balance in the low-yield account hits zero. Earlier analysis in Section 3.1 found an EOQ of 100,000 with an annual transaction and holding cost of $5,000. Does the annual transaction and holding cost with $Q = 100,000$ change when the transfer amount arrives gradually over two days at a rate of 50,000 per day instead of a single instantaneous transfer as in Section 3.1? And can money be saved by changing the transfer quantity from $Q = 100,000$, and, if so, would the transfer quantity increase or decrease?

As before, we'll begin with transaction cost. Given $D = 10,000,000$ units per year and letting $Q = 100,000$, we see that there will be 100 transactions per year at a cost per transaction of $A = \$25$. In other words, the expression for transaction cost is unchanged from the basic EOQ model, that is,

$$TC(Q) = \text{average transaction cost per period as function of the order quantity } Q$$

$$= (\text{cost per transaction})(\# \text{ of transactions per period})$$

$$= (A)(D/Q)$$

Testing this out for $A = \$25$, $D = 10,000,000$ units per year, and $Q = 100,000$ units,

$$TC(100,000) = \$25(10,000,000/100,000) = \$2,500$$

as expected.

The effect of gradual replenishment at rate $P = 50,000$ units per day becomes evident in the expression for holding cost. The daily demand rate for cash in the low-yield account is $D = (10,000,000 \text{ units per year})/(365 \text{ days per year}) = 27,397.26$ units per day. The timing of transfers will be such that money will begin arriving in the low-yield account as soon as the balance hits zero (see Figure 6.5).

Figure 6.5 shows that it takes $Q/P = (100,000 \text{ units})/(50,000 \text{ units/day}) = 2$ days to transfer 100,000 into the low-yield account at a rate of 50,000 units per day. Once the transfer begins, the balance in the low-yield account builds up at a rate of $P - D = 50,000 - 27,397.26 = 22,602.74$ units per day, hits a maximum of $I_{max} = 2(22,602.74) = 45,205.48$ after two days, then decreases at a rate of $D = 27,397.26$ per day until the balance is zero and

FIGURE 6.5

Inventory over time when $Q = 100,000$, $P = 50,000$ per day, and $D = 10,000,000$ per year $\approx 27,397$ per day. The maximum inventory is $I_{max} \approx 45,205$.

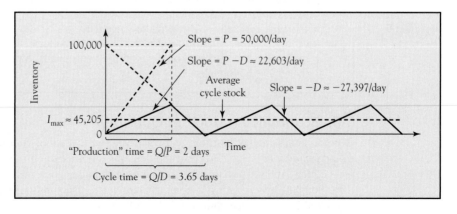

the cycle repeats. The average balance in the low-yield account is $I_{max}/2 = 45{,}205.48/2 = 22{,}604.74$, and given $c_e =$ inventory holding cost per unit-period $= \$0.05$ per unit-year, the annual inventory holding cost is $22{,}604.74(0.05) = \$1{,}130.14$. More generally,

$$I_{max}(Q) = (Q/P)(P - D)$$

$HC(Q) =$ average inventory holding cost per period as a function of the order quantity Q

$$= \text{(average inventory)} c_e$$

$$= [I_{max}(Q)/2] c_e$$

$$= [Q(P - D)/(2P)] c_e$$

Testing this out for $Q = 100{,}000$ units and $c_e = \$0.05$ per unit-year,

$$HC(100{,}000) = 100{,}000[(50{,}000 - 27{,}397.26)/(2 \times 50{,}000)].05 = \$1{,}130.14$$

as expected.

There are no other costs that depend on the order quantity Q, which means that an expression for total relevant cost per period is

$$C(Q) = TC(Q) + HC(Q) = AD/Q + [Q(P - D)/(2P)] c_e$$

For this example, $C(100{,}000) = TC(100{,}000) + HC(100{,}000) \approx \$2{,}500 + \$1{,}130 = \$3{,}630$. As we saw in Section 3.1, the optimal cost with instantaneous transfer is $\$5{,}000$. Perhaps surprisingly, the transfer rate limit imposed by the insurance company as a safeguard actually reduces the cost to your firm by about 27 percent, or almost $\$1{,}400$ per year.

Example Summary

$D =$ demand rate $= \$10$ million/year
$P =$ "production" rate $= \$50{,}000$/day
$A =$ cost/transfer transaction $= \$25$
$c_e =$ excess cost rate $= \$0.05$/unit-year
If transfer $\$100{,}000$ at a time, then $Q = 100{,}000$ and
$TC(Q) = \$25$/transaction $\times$ 100 transactions/year $= \$2{,}500$/year
$HC(Q) =$ average of 22,605 "units" in inventory $\times$ $\$0.05$/unit-year $= \$1{,}130$/year

---

After computing $C(Q)$ with a few trial values for Q, one can quickly determine that the optimal order quantity is $Q^* \approx 148{,}732$. The transfer rate limit causes the low-yield account balance to build up gradually rather than instantaneously. Consequently, it becomes cheaper to transfer a larger quantity and the optimal order quantity increases from 100,000 to 148,732. The cost at $Q = 148{,}732$ is $C(148{,}732) = TC(148{,}732) + HC(148{,}732) = 1{,}680.88 + 1{,}680.87 = \$3{,}361.75$.

The preceding analysis is based on the economic production quantity (EPQ) model. Compared to the EOQ model where an order arrives as a single shipment at some time instant, inventory builds up gradually in the EPQ model. A classic example of gradual replenishment is a production environment. If the capacity of the production equipment (P) is higher than the demand rate (D), then the system must be periodically turned on and off. There is often a cost associated with setting up equipment to begin production; for example, there is a fixed cost associated with each setup "transaction." The economic production quantity (Q^*) minimizes the sum of setup cost (TC) and inventory holding cost (HC) per period. The economic production quantity formulas are summarized below.

Formulas for the Economic Production Quantity Model

D/Q = average number of production setups per period

Q/D = number of periods between production setups

Q/P = number of periods to produce Q units

$I_{max}(Q)$ = maximum inventory level given production quantity $Q = Q(P - D)/P$

$I_{max}(Q)/2$ = average inventory, or, more precisely, average cycle stock

$TC(Q)$ = average transaction cost per period = AD/Q

$HC(Q)$ = average inventory holding cost per period = $c_e Q(P - D)/2P$

$C(Q)$ = average transaction and holding cost per period
    = $AD/Q + [Q(P - D)/2P]c_e$

Q^* = economic production quantity (EPQ) = $[2AD/c_e)]^{1/2}[P/(P - D)]^{1/2}$

$TC(Q^*)$ = average transaction cost per period if the production quantity is Q^*
    = $AD/Q^* = (ADc_e/2)^{1/2}[(P - D)/P]^{1/2}$

$HC(Q^*)$ = average inventory holding cost per period if the production quantity is Q^*
    = $c_e Q^*(P - D)/2P = (ADc_e/2)^{1/2}[(P - D)/P]^{1/2}$

$C(Q^*)$ = average transaction and holding cost per period if the production quantity is Q^*
    = $(2ADc_e)^{1/2}[(P - D)/P]^{1/2}$

Notice that $Q^* \approx [2AD/c_e]^{1/2}$ if the production rate is very high (i.e., $P \approx \infty$), which is the same formula as when product is not produced but ordered. This makes sense in retrospect—if the production rate is very high, Q units can be produced almost instantly and the quantity arrives in one single large batch just like a replenishment order from a supplier.

Example

The last several years as CFO have been great for your career, and lately you've been hearing rumors that you're in line for the top job. Why is this? First, your ideas for a new policy governing the periodic transfer of funds between high- and low-yield accounts while taking advantage of overdraft protection were implemented and are saving the firm money. The CEO is especially pleased that the changes took no more than a few days to implement and required no capital investment. Second, your pay-for-delay program has succeeded beyond expectations. It has been expanded to other products that your firm distributes, and you're even seeing some of your competitors implementing similar programs. Customers are happy, market share is increasing, and savings are being realized. Third, you identified a new money-making opportunity for mixing and packaging the Golden line of Kalina perfumes, and, through about eight months of hard work, it is about to come to fruition.

It was eight months ago when you became aware that some of the mixing and packaging equipment at the Nikolaev, Ukraine, perfume plant was being replaced. You know that perfume is mostly water, and that more than 80 percent of the transportation cost would be eliminated if the water was eliminated. In the ensuing eight months, you have negotiated the terms of a business venture where Kalina Golden brand perfumes will be mixed and packaged at your U.S. location using the old equipment from the Nikolaev plant. You've run the numbers; the investment should pay back within six months of startup, and profits from the Golden line should more than triple. The equipment is in the process of being installed and tested, and there is the question of how much perfume to produce at a time.

The demand rate for the Golden line of perfume is $D = 400,000$ liters per year and the capacity of the mixing and packaging equipment is $P = 550,000$ liters per year. Fragrance compounds are supplied in powdered form from Russia. The cost to mix and package the perfume is $c = \$300$ per liter. The annual inventory holding cost rate is 45 percent of product value (i.e., $h = \$0.45$ per \$-year), and, consequently, the holding cost per liter-year $= c_e = hc = (\$0.45/\$\text{-year})(\$300/\text{liter}) = \$135$ per liter-year. Once production has stopped, it takes about eight hours to get the mixing and packaging equipment set up and running smoothly, which costs your firm \$775.

In summary,

D = demand rate = 400,000 liters/year

P = production capacity = 550,000 liters/year

A = fixed fees for setting up the production equipment = \$775

c_e = inventory holding cost rate = \$135/liter-year

Annual transaction and holding cost can be computed for various trial values of Q to find the economic production quantity, or the EPQ formula can be used.

$$Q^* = EPQ = [(2AD/c_e)]^{1/2}[P/(P - D)]^{1/2}$$

$$= (2 \times 775 \times 100{,}000/135)^{1/2} \times [550{,}000/(550{,}000 - 400{,}000)]^{1/2}$$

$$\approx 4{,}104 \text{ liters}$$

$$Q/D = \text{time between production setups} = (4{,}104 \text{ liters})/(400{,}000 \text{ liters/year})$$

$$= 0.0103 \text{ year} = (0.0103 \text{ year})(365 \text{ days/year}) \approx 3.75 \text{ days}$$

$$Q/P = \text{number of periods to produce } Q \text{ units} = (4{,}104 \text{ liters})/(550{,}000 \text{ liters/year})$$

$$= 0.0075 \text{ year} = (0.0075 \text{ year})(365 \text{ days/year}) \approx 2.72 \text{ days}$$

$$C(Q) = \text{transaction and holding cost} = AD/Q + c_e Q(P - D)/2P$$

$$= 775 \times 400{,}000/4{,}104 + 135(4{,}104)(550{,}000 - 400{,}000)/(2 \times 550{,}000)$$

$$\approx \$75{,}536 + \$75{,}551 = \$151{,}087/\text{year}$$

The most economical production policy is to produce 4,104 liters at a time with production to begin when perfume inventory hits zero. The time between production setups is about 3.75 days, and it takes about 2.72 days to produce 4,104 liters. The total transaction and inventory holding cost per year is projected to be \$151,087, or $\$151{,}087/400{,}000 \approx \$0.38$ per liter.

Example Summary

D = demand rate = 400,000 liters/year
P = production rate = 550,000 liters/year
A = cost/setup transaction = \$775
c_e = excess cost rate = \$135/liter-year
Q^* = economic order quantity = $[2AD/c_e)]^{1/2}[P/(P - D)]^{1/2} \approx 4{,}104$ liters

---

3.4. Economic Order Quantity with Quantity Discounts

You may have noticed that unit price often decreases with quantity (e.g., the 128-ounce container of laundry detergent is cheaper per ounce than the 16-ounce container). Quantity discounts also arise in supplier pricing. Economic analysis of order quantity in the presence of quantity discounts follows the basic EOQ cost analysis of Section 3.1, *but includes consideration of purchase cost.* The supplier pricing structure determines how the unit cost function $c(Q)$ depends on the order quantity Q. Recall that $h =$ inventory holding cost per $-period and the inventory holding cost per unit-period is $c_e = hc(Q)$. Thus, the total relevant cost per period is comprised of three terms: transaction cost, inventory holding cost, and purchase cost. With the exception of the purchase cost per period, which is the product of the demand rate and purchase price, the expressions from earlier sections apply. The formulas are summarized below.

Formulas for the Economic Order Quantity with Quantity Discounts Model

$$c(Q) = \text{average unit price as a function of the order quantity } Q$$

$$h = \text{inventory holding cost per \$-period}$$

$$c_e = \text{inventory holding cost per unit-period} = hc(Q)$$

$$TC(Q) = \text{average transaction cost per period}$$
$$= (\text{cost per transaction})(\text{average \# of transactions per period}) = (A)(D/Q)$$

$$HC(Q) = \text{average inventory holding cost per period}$$
$$= (\text{average inventory})c_e = (Q/2)hc(Q)$$

$$PC(Q) = \text{average purchase cost per period}$$
$$= (\text{demand per period})(\text{average purchase cost per unit}) = Dc(Q)$$

$$C(Q) = \text{average transaction, holding, and purchase cost per period}$$
$$= TC(Q) + HC(Q) + PC(Q)$$

The optimal order quantity can be quickly found by calculating $C(Q) = TC(Q) + HC(Q) + PC(Q)$ for a few trial values of Q.[6]

Two common quantity discount pricing structures in practice are an *all-units* discount and an *incremental-units* discount. These discount pricing structures basically govern how the average unit purchase cost $c(Q)$ changes as Q gets larger. We'll begin by illustrating analysis of an all-units discount structure. Then we'll briefly outline how an incremental-units discount structure works, and how the analysis would differ.

All-Units Discount Example

Fragrance compounds need to be ordered for the mixing and packaging of the Golden line of perfumes. The compounds are purchased from a Russian supplier in powdered form according to the following price schedule:[7]

- If $Q < 10,000$, then the unit price is $c(Q) = \$75$ per pound.
- If $10,000 \le Q < 20,000$, then the unit price is $c(Q) = \$70$ per pound.
- If $Q \ge 20,000$, then the unit price is $c(Q) = \$65$ per pound.

Annual demand for fragrance compounds is $D = 80,000$ pounds per year, the total transaction fees for placing an order are $A = \$3,206$, and your firm incurs an annual inventory holding cost rate of 45 percent of product value (i.e., $h = \$0.45$ per $-year). Consequently, the

---

[6] You'll be asked to propose a more systematic approach for finding the optimal order quantity in exercise 13.

[7] In addition to material cost, the price schedule includes all variable transportation and handling charges associated with delivery.

FIGURE 6.6   Total transaction, holding, and purchase cost per year for different values of Q. Cost is minimized at the break-point quantity of $Q = 20,000$ pounds.

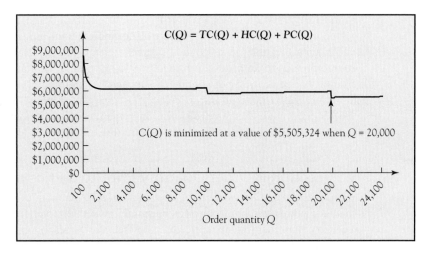

total relevant cost per year is

$$C(Q) = TC(Q) + HC(Q) + PC(Q)$$

$$= AD/Q + (Q/2)hc(Q) + Dc(Q)$$

$$= \begin{cases} (3{,}206 \times 80{,}000)/Q + (Q/2)(0.45 \times 75) + 80{,}000 \times 75, & \text{if } Q < 10{,}000 \\ (3{,}206 \times 80{,}000)/Q + (Q/2)(0.45 \times 70) + 80{,}000 \times 70, & \text{if } 10{,}000 < Q < 20{,}000 \\ (3{,}206 \times 80{,}000)/Q + (Q/2)(0.45 \times 65) + 80{,}000 \times 65, & \text{if } Q > 20{,}000 \end{cases}$$

(see Figure 6.6 where $C(Q)$ is calculated for many values of Q).

The optimal order quantity is 20,000 pounds and the total cost per year is

$$C(20{,}000) = TC(20{,}000) + HC(20{,}000) + PC(20{,}000)$$

$$= (3{,}206 \times 80{,}000)/20{,}000 + (20{,}000/2)(0.45 \times 65) + 80{,}000 \times 65$$

$$= \$12{,}824 + \$292{,}500 + \$5{,}200{,}000 = \$5{,}505{,}324$$

All-Units Example Summary

D = demand rate = 80,000 lbs/year
A = cost/order transaction = \$3,206
h = holding cost rate as a percent of product cost = \$0.45/\$-year
If order 20,000 at a time, then Q = 20,000, purchase cost = \$65/lb, and
c_e = excess cost rate = \$0.45/\$-year × \$65/lb = \$29.25/lb-year
$TC(Q)$ = \$3,206/transaction × 4 transactions/year = \$12,824/year
$HC(Q)$ = average of 10,000 "units" in inventory × \$29.25/lb-year = \$292,500/year
$PC(Q)$ = 80,000 lbs/year × \$65/lb = \$5,200,000/year

An Incremental-Units Discount Structure

The above illustration is based on an all-units discount structure. An incremental-units discount structure applies a lower price to only the incremental units beyond a break point. Consider the unit prices and quantity breaks from the above example: \$75 per pound for 9,999 pounds or less, $70 for between 10,000 and 19,999 pounds, and $65 per pound for 20,000 pounds or more. If an incremental-units discount structure is in effect, then the first 9,999 pounds of an order are priced at $75 per pound, the next 10,000 pounds of an order are priced at $70 per pound, and any additional units of an order are priced at $65 per pound. This means, for example, that the average unit price for an order of 15,000 pounds is $c(15{,}000) = (\$75 \times 9{,}999 + \$70 \times 5{,}001)/15000 \approx$ $73.33 per pound. Cost analysis of an incremental-units discount structure follows the approach of the all-units discount structure illustrated above, except the way that $c(Q)$ is determined is different.

3.5. Economic Order Quantity Prior to a Price Increase

What if a supplier announces a future price increase? Economic analysis of a quantity discount structure often boils down to determining whether the price savings from increasing the size of an order to gain a price break offsets the corresponding increase in transaction and inventory holding cost. A similar issue arises when you have knowledge of a future price increase. The question is how much extra to order before the price increase goes into effect considering the offsetting effects of lower price and higher transaction and holding cost. Any extra units ordered as a consequence of an expected future price increase (or a temporary price reduction) are considered speculative stock, which is one of the roles of inventory noted at the beginning of this chapter. Prior to this point in the chapter, we have only considered cycle stock (i.e., inventory due to order batching).

On the basis of the current price, you would normally order Q^* units. However, when placing the last order before a price increase, you'd like to know how many extra units to order to save the most money. Finding an approach to attack this question is not too difficult if we step back to consider what we know. We know that it is worth adding an extra unit to the last order before a price increase if the cost of this unit is not more than the average cost per unit under the new higher price structure. We also know how to determine the average unit cost under the new higher price structure (e.g., earlier analysis dealt with determining the optimal order quantity and the corresponding cost). The key, then, is to find a formula for the cost of the last unit of the last order before the price increase (see Figure 6.7).

FIGURE 6.7 **Inventory over Time**

Q^* is the optimal order quantity at the current price and Q^*_{new} is the optimal order quantity at the new higher price. Δ extra units are included with the last order prior to the price increase, and the last unit of the order remains in inventory for $(Q^* + \Delta)/D$ periods.

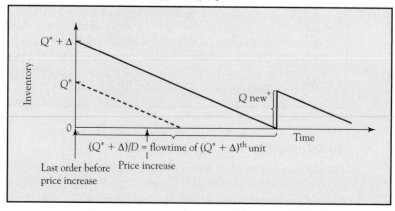

The cost of the last extra unit ordered prior to the price increase is the sum of the purchase price c and the cost to hold the unit in inventory for $(Q^* + \Delta)/D$ periods (i.e., $c + [(Q^* + \Delta)/D]hc$).[8] The average cost per unit at the new higher price is the sum of the purchase price c_{new} and the average transaction and holding cost per unit (i.e., $c_{new} + [TC(Q^*_{new}) + HC(Q^*_{new})]/D$). Thus, we can save money by continuing to increase Δ until $c + [(Q^* + \Delta)/D]hc = c_{new} + [TC(Q^*_{new}) + HC(Q^*_{new})]/D$. Solving for Δ yields the optimal number of extra units:

$$\Delta^* = (c_{new} - c)D/(hc) + [TC(Q^*_{new}) + HC(Q^*_{new}) - Q^*hc]/(hc)$$

If Q^* and Q^*_{new} are set according to the basic EOQ formula (e.g., no quantity discounts), then the lost savings from ignoring the second term are generally small, and it can be reasonable to use

$$\Delta^* \approx (c_{new} - c)D/(hc)$$

as a rule of thumb. The rule of thumb is to order an extra $(c_{new} - c)/(hc)$ periods' worth of demand, or, equivalently, pick a value of Δ so that the cost to hold one unit in inventory for Δ/D periods is equal to the price increase (i.e., $(\Delta/D)hc = c_{new} - c$). The formulas are summarized below.

Formulas for Economic Order Quantity Prior to a Price Increase

h = inventory holding cost per \$-period

c = current price per unit

c_{new} = higher price per unit to go into effect in the near future

Q^* = current optimal order quantity (at price c)

Q^*_{new} = optimal order quantity at price c_{new}

$TC(Q^*_{new})$ = average transaction cost per period at price c_{new} if the order quantity is Q^*_{new}

$HC(Q^*_{new})$ = average holding cost per period at price c_{new} if the order quantity is Q^*_{new}

Δ^* = optimal number of extra units in the last order before a price increase

$$= (c_{new} - c)D/(hc) + [TC(Q^*_{new}) + HC(Q^*_{new}) - Q^*hc]/(hc)$$

If Q^* and Q^*_{new} are set according to the basic EOQ formula (e.g., no quantity discounts), then

$$Q^* = [2AD/hc]^{1/2}$$

$$TC(Q^*_{new}) = [ADhc_{new}/2]^{1/2}$$

$$HC(Q^*_{new}) = [ADhc_{new}/2]^{1/2}$$

$$\Delta^* = \{(c_{new} - c)D + (c_{new}^{1/2} - c^{1/2})[2ADh]^{1/2}\}/hc \approx (c_{new} - c)D/hc$$

---

[8] For simplicity, we have ignored the possibility of placing an order for Δ units just before the higher price goes into effect. A more complete analysis would compare this cost with the cost of including Δ units in the last order and select the cheapest (e.g., an extra order is worthwhile if the transaction cost is less than the cost of holding Δ units between receipt of the last order and the point in time an order of Δ units would arrive if placed just prior to the price increase).

Example

The end of the year is approaching and you are aware of two price increases that will go into effect at the beginning of next year. Kalina has announced a 10 percent price increase and the supplier of fragrance compounds has announced a $5.00 price increase.

We'll look at Kalina product first. Your firm's demand rate for Kalina product is now up to $D = 112,000$ pallets per year, total transaction fees associated with placing an order are $A = \$3,206$, the annual inventory holding cost is 45 percent of product value (i.e., $h = \$0.45$ per \$-year), the current purchase price is $c = \$60$ per pallet, and the price after the beginning of the year will be $c_{new} = 1.1(60) = \$66$ per pallet. The current economic order quantity is

$$Q^* = [2AD/(hc)]^{1/2} = [2 \times 3,206 \times 112,000/(0.45 \times 60)]^{1/2} \approx 5,157 \text{ pallets}$$

According to the rule of thumb, since $(c_{new} - c)/(hc) = (66 - 60)/(0.45 \times 60) \approx 0.22$ year, you'd like to order enough extra pallets to last about 0.22 year, or 81 days, that is,

$$\Delta^* \approx (c_{new} - c)D/(hc) = (66 - 60) \times 112,000/(0.45 \times 60) \approx 112000 \times 0.22 \approx 24,889 \text{ pallets}$$

which means the last order of the current year will be for

$$Q^* + \Delta^* = 5,157 + 24,889 = 30,046 \text{ pallets}$$

How much is saved by ordering 24,889 extra pallets before the price increase? After January 1, the price will increase to $c_{new} = \$66$ per pallet and the optimal order quantity will decrease slightly to

$$Q^*_{new} = [2AD/(hc_{new})]^{1/2} = [2 \times 3,206 \times 112,000/(0.45 \times 60)]^{1/2} \approx 4,917 \text{ pallets}$$

At the higher price, the average unit cost is

$$C(4,917)/D = [TC(4,917) + HC(4,917) + PC(4,917)]/D$$
$$= [3,206 \times 112,000/4917 + 4,917 \times 0.45 \times 66/2 + 112,000 \times 66]/112,000$$
$$= \$67.30/\text{pallet}$$

The average unit cost of the extra 24,889 pallets in the last order of the year is the sum of the purchase cost and the average cost to hold the extra Δ pallets in inventory. All of the extra pallets are in inventory for Q^*/D periods, the first extra pallet is sold right after this point in time, and the last pallet is sold Δ/D periods later. Thus, on average, the extra pallets are in inventory for $Q^*/D + (1/2)(0 + \Delta/D)$ periods, and the average unit cost is

$$c + [(Q^* + \Delta/2)/D]hc = \$60 + [(5,157 + 24,889/2)/112,000] \times 0.45 \times 60 = \$64.24/\text{pallet}$$

This means that, on average, an extra pallet in the last order of the year saves $67.30 - 64.24 = \$3.06$, for a total savings of ($\$3.06$/pallet) $\times$ (24,889 pallets) $\approx \$76,160$. Not bad.

If we use the more precise expression of

$$\Delta^* = (c_{new} - c)D/(hc) + [TC(Q^*_{new}) + HC(Q^*_{new}) - Q^*hc]/(hc),$$

then $\Delta^* = 25,141$ extra pallets would be ordered instead of 24,889. The impact of the extra precision is minor; the total savings increase by less than $8.

Kalina Product Example Summary

D = demand rate = 112,000 pallets/year
A = cost/order transaction = $3,206
h = holding cost rate as a percent of product cost = $0.45/\$-year
c = purchase cost = $60/pallet
c_{new} = purchase cost in the near future = $66/pallet
Δ^* = extra units in the last order before the price increase $\approx (c_{new} - c)D/(hc)$
$\approx$ 24,889 pallets

The case of the fragrance compounds supplier is a little different because the quantity discount structure influences the optimal order quantity. The main lesson is that causal use of simple rules of thumb can be risky. Let's see why.

Your firm's current demand rate for fragrance compounds is $D = 100,000$ pounds per year, total transactions fees associated with placing an order are $A = \$3,206$, the annual inventory holding cost is 45 percent of product value (i.e., $h = \$0.45$ per \$-year), the current purchase price is $c = \$65$ per pound, and the price after the beginning of the year will increase by \$5 to $c_{new} = \$70$ per pound. The current optimal order quantity is $Q^* = 20,000$, which is sufficient to qualify for the lowest possible price and is much larger than the quantity that minimizes transaction and holding costs. According to the rule of thumb,

$$\Delta^* \approx (c_{new} - c)D/(hc) = (70 - 65) \times 100,000/(0.45 \times 65) \approx 17,094 \text{ pounds}$$

which means the last order of the current year will be for

$$Q^* + \Delta^* = 20,000 + 17,094 = 37,094 \text{ pounds}$$

Does this plan save money? A few quick calculations show that the optimal order quantity does not change with the price increase, that is, $Q^*_{new} = 20,000$ pounds. At the higher price, the average unit cost is

$$C(20,000)/D = [TC(20,000) + HC(20,000) + PC(20,000)]/D$$
$$= [3,206 \times 100,000/20,000 + 20,000 \times 0.45 \times 70/2 + 100,000 \times 70]/100,000$$
$$= \$73.31 \text{ per pound}$$

The average unit cost of the extra 17,094 pounds in the last order of the year is

$$c + [(Q^* + \Delta/2)/D]hc = \$65 + [(20,000 + 17,094/2)/100,000] \times 0.45 \times 65$$
$$= \$73.35 \text{ per pound}$$

and we would actually lose about $17,094 \times (73.35 - 73.31) \approx \$700$ compared to the alternative of ordering no extra pounds. The ramifications of misapplying the rule of thumb are even more significant in light of the lost opportunity to save money. Applying the more precise expression of

$$\Delta^* = (c_{new} - c)D/(hc) + [TC(Q^*_{new}) + HC(Q^*_{new}) - Q^*hc]/(hc)$$

yields $\Delta^* \approx 8,411$ pounds, which results in savings of over \$10,000. In this case, the rule of thumb broke down because of the quantity discount pricing structure, and the example illustrates some of the risks of simple approximations.

Fragrance Compound Example Summary

D = demand rate = 100,000 lbs/year
A = cost/order transaction = \$3,206
h = holding cost rate as a percent of product cost = \$0.45/\$-year
c = purchase cost = \$65/lb
c_{new} = purchase cost in the near future = \$70/lb
Δ^* = extra units in the last order before a price increase
= $(c_{new} - c)D/(hc) + [TC(Q^*_{new}) + HC(Q^*_{new}) - Q^*hc]/(hc) \approx 8,411$ lbs

---

3.6. Recap

This section focused on order and production quantity decisions. The cost structure underlying these types of decisions often exhibits a fundamental trade-off between costs that decrease with quantity and the various costs that work against large batches.

We began with the question of how much to order to minimize transaction and inventory holding costs. Then we considered the complications of planned backorders, gradual replenishment, and quantity discounts. We also considered the related question of how many additional units to order before a price increase. In all cases, our analyses were based on simplified idealizations of the real world. Such an approach can be powerful because it captures the essence of an issue with minimal data, thereby allowing a deeper understanding than might otherwise be possible. But it is worth emphasizing that there are risks (e.g., misapplication of the rule of thumb in the fragrance compound example from Section 3.5). As with any quick and approximate analysis, the sensible interpretation of insights or conclusions requires a keen awareness and scrutiny of underlying assumptions.

The content of this section and the associated exercises are designed to help develop your back-of-the-envelope analysis skills while fostering a systemwide perspective through consideration of all relevant costs/revenues that are affected by a decision. These skills, which allow one to quickly gain insight into how to approach a new situation (e.g., for which there is minimal guidance in available books or journals), are becoming increasingly valuable as the pace of business change is increasing.[9]

4. SUMMARY AND MANAGERIAL INSIGHTS

This chapter is the first of several on the question of how to manage inventory. We learned that this question carries significant ramifications for profit in retail, wholesale, and manufacturing firms—a consequence of the magnitude of investment (e.g., about $1.6 trillion worth of inventory in the United States) and the impact on sales (e.g., customer purchasing from a competitor when a firm's product is unavailable). We also learned about the various costs associated with holding inventory, the challenges of inventory cost estimation that underlie a tendency for these costs to be underestimated, and the consequent implications for interpreting and using inventory cost estimates to support management decisions.

We then focused on the economics of a fundamental trade-off that arises in a host of application areas, including inventory management—a trade-off that stems from the prevalence of transaction costs in the economy. We studied this cost structure in the context of how much to order or produce (the question of when to order or produce is left for other chapters). In particular, we considered how much to order (EOQ), how much to produce (EPQ), and how to extend analysis to accommodate complications such as planned backorders, quantity discounts, and future price increases. The emphasis was on developing skill in the formulation and analysis of simple models and on translating the results of analysis into managerial insights. The examples throughout the chapter illustrated how back-of-the-envelope analysis supports the development of insight, and ultimately ideas for increasing profit. Key managerial insights from the chapter are summarized below.

4.1. For a System with an EOQ-Type Cost Structure, Operating Cost Increases with the Square Root of Volume When Operating at Maximum Efficiency (e.g., see expressions for $C(Q^*)$)

Example 1

(Adapted from an example prepared by Linus Schrage.) Suppose you've just been hired as the Southwest Region Director of Marketing and Operations at Target (a Wal-Mart competitor). Your knowledge of Target's business is pretty superficial at this point, so your focus is on understanding their business and performing diagnoses to identify possible opportunities for

---

[9] Exercises 17 through 21, for example, require you to either modify analysis in the chapter to accommodate a slightly different setting or apply some of the concepts to analyze a problem in a new setting.

improvement. It's Saturday morning and you're scanning the financial statements of the two distribution centers in your region.

	Annual Volume (000s)	Annual Transaction and Cycle Stock Holding Cost (000s)
DC #1	100,000	$400,000
DC #2	400,000	$1,500,000

The question you're considering is whether one DC is performing notably better than the other. If this was the case, then there could be opportunities in information sharing to improve operations at the weaker DC. What do you think? The cost per unit is about the same (DC #2 cost per unit is slightly lower), so it may be natural to conclude that performance is comparable and move on to diagnosing other elements of the business. Upon consideration of insight 4.1, and recognizing that the typical DC operating cost structure approximately conforms to the EOQ model, you conclude that DC #1, in fact, may be performing significantly better than DC #2. DC #2 volume is four times DC #1 volume; if DC #2 is operating efficiently, operating cost at DC #2 should be closer to the square root of four, or twice the cost of DC #1 (i.e., $C(Q^*) = [2ADc_e]^{1/2}$).

Example 2

Diebold (1952, pp. 43–45) shares an example that illustrates how standardization can lead to scale economies, as well as opportunities to gain market share. An appliance manufacturer produced 16 variations of home ranges within two major price lines (e.g., low end and high end). Product was produced in batches using labor-intensive machinery. The company redesigned the product line so that all 16 models used the same basic body style, with variations achieved by changing the control panel and position of the heating element. With the new design, it became economical to replace a highly manual process with a semiautomatic press that could produce all 16 models and be operated continuously. However, shortly after installation, the company decided to introduce a new price line to respond to a competitor. This was done in two days by varying the control panel and a few other features. The standardization program not only lowered costs and brought product to people who had not previously been able to afford it, but also improved the company's ability to respond to competition.

4.2. When a System with an EOQ-Type Cost Structure Is Operating at Maximum Efficiency, Transaction Cost per Period = Excess/Shortage Cost per Period (e.g., compare AD/Q^* with $(Q^*/2)c_e$)

Example 1

Consider Example 1 above, where you are trying to get a sense of whether there are easy ways to improve operations at either of the warehouses. From managerial insight 4.2, you have a quick diagnostic indicator for efficiency. If annual transaction (e.g., ordering) costs in the income statement are nowhere near annual inventory holding cost (excluding safety stock), then there is a fair chance that the ordering policies at the warehouse are inefficient. This indicator on its own is likely not enough to conclude that operations are out of whack, but it's probably enough to justify further investigation.

Example 2

As a new brand manager, you notice that your predecessor had a policy of updating the advertising campaign (new slogan, jingle, etc.) every 18 months. You're considering the reasonableness of this policy and you begin by noticing a similarity with the EOQ cost structure. In particular,

- The cost to develop a new campaign is essentially a fixed constant (in today's dollars) that does not depend on the length of time before the campaign is revised.
- The effect of a new campaign on buyers (with respect to generating sales) diminishes in proportion to the age of the campaign.

The cost of developing a new campaign is $9 million. What does this imply about the annual opportunity cost of lost profits due to a "stale" (i.e., outdated and less effective) advertising campaign if this policy is effective? From insight 4.2, the annual opportunity cost—if the policy is effective—is about $6 million (i.e., $9 million per 18 months = $6 million per year). If this number is highly suspect based on your intuition, then it may be worthwhile to investigate the reasonableness of this policy further (i.e., if the opportunity cost of $6 million seems unbelievable, then you've just completed some quick diagnosis that suggests the "patient" may require an "operation").

Example 3

The spirit of the managerial insight is also evident in the question of how much extra to order prior to a price increase. We saw that a rule of thumb for answering this question is based on balancing holding cost with the price increase; that is, the inventory holding cost of the last "extra" unit ordered should equal the price increase.

4.3. The EOQ-Type Cost Structure Is Robust with Respect to Errors in Parameter Estimates (e.g., A, D, P, c_e, c_s)

Example 1

If you calculate and implement an EOQ based on an estimate for the cost per transaction (A) that is 30 percent too high, then annual transaction plus holding costs will only be 1 percent higher than costs with an EOQ based on an accurate estimate of A.[10]

Example 2

As the new operations manager for the Princeton, New Jersey, plant of Rhone Poulenc, you're assessing the reasonability of production batch-size policies for various products. Your plant produces strains of bacteria used in the dairy industry. It costs about $8,000 to set up the system each time a new batch of bacteria is brewed (i.e., $8,000 to thoroughly clean the tanks). You aren't quite sure what it costs the company to carry finished product in inventory; according to your rough estimate, current batch sizes are close to numbers calculated using EPQ analysis. One of your colleagues suggests putting a junior accounting person on the task of gathering data for the purposes of developing a more precise estimate of the holding cost rate. You nix the idea—you know that even if your estimate of the holding cost rate is a little off, it's not going to make much difference on the bottom line.

4.4. Reduce Cost per Transaction and You Shall Be Rewarded

Example 1

Look what happens to annual optimal transaction and excess/shortage cost (i.e., $C(Q^*, b^*) = (2ADc_e)^{1/2}[c_s/(c_e + c_s)]^{1/2}$) when A goes to zero. $C(Q^*, b^*)$ goes to zero because there is no need for cycle stock. The great thing about this is the impact that information technology can have on transaction costs. "Working together, Moore's law[11] and Metcalfe's law[12] are blowing the economic status quo into smithereens. They are **dramatically cutting into what Nobel**

---

[10] For those who are curious about where these numbers came from, suppose the actual cost per transaction is A and your estimate is $A_1 = xA$. From above, we know that substituting $Q^* = (2AD/c_e)$ into $C(Q) = A(D/Q) + c_e(Q/2)$ yields the optimal transaction plus holding cost per period of $C(Q^*) = (2ADc_e)^{1/2}$. Suppose we order $Q_1 = (2A_1D/c_e)^{1/2} = (2xAD/c_e)^{1/2}$ at a time. Then substituting Q_1 into $C(Q)$ yields a transaction cost plus holding cost per period of $C(Q_1) = 0.5[(1/x)^{1/2} + x^{1/2}](2ADc_e)^{1/2} = 0.5[(1/x)^{1/2} + x^{1/2}]C(Q^*)$. If our estimate of A is 30 percent too high, then $A_1 = 1.3A$ and $x = 1.3$. For these numbers, $C(Q) \approx 1.01C(Q^*)$, which says that transaction plus holding cost is about 1 percent higher than the optimum.

[11] Gordon Moore, the founder of Intel, proposed Moore's law: computing power will double about every 18 months while cost remains constant.

[12] Robert Metcalfe, the founder of 3Com, proposed Metcalfe's law: the power of a network grows with the square of the number of participants.

laureate Ronald H. Coase dubbed 'transaction costs'—intangibles such as the time people must spend on finding, negotiating for, and deciding on a product or service" (Downes and Chunka 1998).

Example 2

Remember the bullwhip effect from Chapter 5? The **bullwhip effect is the phenomenon of demand volatility increasing as you move up a supply chain.** One cause of the bullwhip effect is order batching, and one cause of order batching is the "transaction cost" of transportation; for example, on a per-unit basis, transportation cost is lower when you ship a full truckload instead of multiple partial truckloads. One result is the common practice of accumulating demand over time until an order for a full truckload quantity can be placed. This cause-and-effect relationship was apparent, for example, in a 1998 project for P&G by the Bios Group and Stu Kauffman of the Santa Fe Institute. The team developed and studied a number of models of P&G's supply chain. The models consistently showed an irregular disruptive flow even though end consumer demand was relatively smooth. The main cause was a requirement that all shipments occur in full truckload quantities. This saves transportation cost, but when this requirement was relaxed, flows became smooth and out-of-stocks decreased (Regis 2000).

Example 3

Investment bank Bear, Stearns estimates that full supply chain integration within an exchange could enable the average company to reduce supply chain management costs by 25 percent. Where is this savings coming from? One major area is reduced ordering transactions costs, which in turn means more frequent ordering and less inventory investment. Mary Meeker, an analyst with Morgan Stanley Dean Witter, estimates that the cost of processing a purchase order manually ranges from $125 to $175, and that this can drop to about $10 to $15 with online procurement . . . over a 90 percent reduction in A (Henig 2000).

Example 4

Dell Inc. uses the Internet to reduce ordering transaction costs, which in turn helps smooth and speed the flow over their supply chain. Over 90 percent of their purchases are made online. Dell's Austin plant works on a two-hour replenishment cycle; near the end of each cycle, Dell electronically orders what they will produce during the next two hours (Rocks 2000).

Example 5

Some firms use blanket purchase orders (BPOs) as a means to reduce the cost of placing an order. A BPO commits a buyer to purchase a total quantity, usually within some range, over a specified period of time (e.g., one year). Price and other terms and conditions of sale are defined in the BPO agreement. This simplifies order processing because, as product is needed, orders are released against the BPO. There is no need to resolve price and other terms and conditions of sale prior to placing each order.

4.5. Increases in the Excess Cost Rate and the Shortage Cost Rate, and Decreases in the Cost per Transaction, Mean That You Should Order More Frequently in Smaller Quantities

Example

You are a member of Procter & Gamble's logistics support group at Wal-Mart.[13] Suppose that the current policy for replenishing Wal-Mart's Atlanta warehouse is to place an order for a month's worth of P&G product at the beginning of each month. This policy has been cost-effective. It's now the middle of the month and, as a result of the Federal Reserve's tightening of the money supply, the prime rate has jumped two percentage points. Do you think this should have any impact on your policy, and if so, how? The first step to answering this question is realizing that the prime rate tends to influence the inventory holding cost rate c_e—as the cost to borrow money goes up, the cost to tie up money in inventory goes up. Managerial insight 4.5, which follows from $Q^* = [2AD/c_e]^{1/2}$, says that Q^* gets smaller as c_e gets larger. You should consider ordering smaller quantities more frequently.

---

[13] P&G maintains a logistics support staff near Wal-Mart's headquarters in Arkansas.

5. EXERCISES

1. Write a brief answer to each of the chapter keys in your own words. After writing down your answers, review the chapter with a focus on the content in bold to check and clarify your interpretations.

2. Order cost is $31 for material that costs $12.50 per pound. The annual holding cost rate is estimated at 18 percent of material cost, and monthly requirements are fairly stable at 15,000 pounds. Backorders should not be considered, as shortage costs are very high. Orders must be in whole pounds.

   a. How many pounds should be ordered at a time?
   b. What is the average number of orders per year, and what is the average number of days between orders?
   c. What is the average annual ordering cost; what is the average annual holding cost (given your recommendation)?
   d. Suppose you currently order material once per month. Determine the annual savings under your plan.
   e. Suppose that you have bad information on order cost and that the "true" order cost is $15.50. What is the percentage cost premium associated with pursuing your original recommendation instead of the true best policy?

3. Consider the previous problem but with the modification that planned backorders may be considered as an option. Each unit backordered is estimated to cost the company $0.45 per pound for each month it is backordered.

   a. Suppose the optimal order quantity is updated using this new information. Will this new policy have a lower or higher cost than the policy you recommended in the previous problem? (*Hint:* This can be answered without calculation.)
   b. How many pounds should be ordered at a time and how many backorders should be outstanding when the order arrives?
   c. What is the average number of orders per year?
   d. What is the average annual ordering cost, what is the average annual holding cost, and what is the average backorder cost?
   e. What is the percent of time that the company is operating with backorders?

4. Mill 7 at the Gary Steel Works is capable of producing 3,000 tons per month of one particular grade of steel. Unfortunately, monthly demand is averaging 1,750 tons with no change in sight. The cost of shutting down and restarting the mill is estimated at $1,200 and the annual holding cost per ton is estimated at $70.

   a. How long should the production runs be and how much should be produced at a time (to the nearest ton)?
   b. What is the length of time between production runs?
   c. How does the annual cost of your policy compare with the annual cost of the best policy for the same problem except Mill 7 has a monthly production rate of 5,000 tons instead of 3,000 tons?

5. A retailer uses a point-of-sale system to maintain inventory records. A particular item has an average annual demand of 40,000 units. It costs $25 to place an order and the item has a value of $10 per unit. Annual inventory holding cost is 20 percent of unit value. Determine how many units should be ordered at a time to minimize order processing and inventory holding costs.

6. You are purchasing manager at Perot's Men's Shop. You must make sure the store is fully stocked. You sell only one item—a blue shirt. It costs $25 to place each order and

each shirt costs $47.50. Your annual holding cost is 22 percent of the purchase price per shirt. The demand currently is 500 shirts per month. Do not consider backorders because Perot hates backorders. Round calculations to the nearest whole shirt.

a. How many shirts should you order each time?
b. What will be your average number of orders per year?
c. What will be your average annual holding cost and your average annual order cost?

7. Perot's business is booming. He believes he can now sell three times as many shirts and can get a 35 percent discount in purchase price by wielding his new power. He suggests ordering 3,000 shirts every other month. Do you agree with him? What numbers would you show him to support your answer? If he promises to pay you one-half of any savings you can create, how much money will you make?

8. Consider the setting in the previous problem and suppose you know that the annual backorder cost is $5.50 per shirt. Would you suggest that Perot allow backorders? What would be your backorder level by the time you place the next order? Given the same promise by Perot, would you make any more money? If so, how much?

9. Pretend you are the "sole" producer of sandals for the Caribbean market. You have a facility capable of producing 150,000 pairs of cork-soled sandals per year. There are 80,000 feet that need sandals twice a year. The cost to start up/shut down the plant is $2,000, and storage cost is $3 per pair per year. Assume no backorders.

a. What is the optimal number of pairs to produce each run?
b. How often will you start up the factory?
c. What is the total cost given your Q^*?
d. What will be your maximum level of inventory?
e. Now assume your sandals wear out very fast and people must buy a new pair every three months. What is the new optimal production level?
f. If consumers need only one pair per year, what is Q^*? Does total inventory cost go up or down? By how much (percent)?

10. How does the model from problem 2 differ from the model used in problem 3? What is the difference in the patterns of inventory buildup and rundown?

11. The Bureau of Water Testing uses a chemical reagent that costs $500 per gallon. Use is regular at one-third gallon per week. The holding cost rate is 12 percent per year and the cost of an order is $125.

a. What is the optimal order quantity?
b. The Department of Maintenance could make this reagent at the rate of one-eighth gallon per day, at a cost of $300 per gallon. The setup cost is $150. How much should be produced at a time? Which course of action do you recommend (buy or make)?

12. Observe that for the basic EOQ model, $C(Q^*)/D$ = average optimal transaction and inventory holding cost per unit-period = $[TC(Q^*) + HC(Q^*)]/D = (2ADc_e)^{1/2}/D = c_e(2AD/c_e)^{1/2}/D = c_eQ^*/D$. Recognition of this can provide a means to quickly estimate per-unit transaction and holding cost at Q^*. For example, if Q^* is equal to one month's worth of demand, then the per-unit transaction and holding cost is equal to the monthly inventory holding cost rate.

a. Why is it that the per-unit optimal transaction plus holding cost per period should equal the cost to hold one unit in inventory for Q^*/D periods? (Here are two hints: first, think about managerial insight 4.2; second, recall that average inventory is $Q/2$.)

b. Observe that for the basic EOQ model, $C(Q^*)/D$ = average optimal transaction and inventory holding cost per unit-period = $[TC(Q^*) + HC(Q^*)]/D = (2ADc_e)^{1/2}/D = (2Ac_e/D)^{1/2} = 2A/Q^*$. Recognition of this can provide a means to quickly estimate per-unit transaction and holding cost at Q^*. For example, if $A = 100$ and $Q^* = 50$, then the per-unit transaction and holding cost is equal to $2(100/50) = \$4$. Why is it that the per-unit optimal transaction plus holding cost per period should be equal to twice the optimal transaction cost per unit?

13. Section 3.4 developed analysis of the economic order quantity with quantity discounts. As noted in the section, the optimal order quantity can be determined by calculating $C(Q) = TC(Q) + HC(Q) + PC(Q)$ for various trial values of Q until the optimal quantity becomes apparent. There is a slightly more efficient approach that takes advantage of the EOQ formula from Section 3.1; that is, the quantity that minimizes transaction and holding cost is $Q = [2AD/(hc)]^{1/2}$. Propose an approach for an all-units quantity discount structure where, given a schedule with n different prices (and $n - 1$ quantity breakpoints), $C(Q)$ is calculated for no more than n different values of Q.

14. Suppose the demand rate is $D = 1,000$ units per year, annual inventory holding cost is 25 percent of product value (i.e., $h = \$0.25$ per \$-year), and the cost to place an order is $A = \$30$. If 1,000 or more units are ordered, then the purchase price is \$9 per unit. If $Q < 1,000$ units, then the purchase price is \$10 per unit. How many units should be ordered at a time, and what is the length of time between orders?

15. Section 3.5 developed analysis for determining how many extra units to order prior to an announced price increase. A rule of thumb is to order an extra $(c_{new} - c)/(hc)$ periods' worth of demand. Strictly speaking, more money can be saved by ordering an additional $q = [TC(Q_{new}^*) + HC(Q_{new}^*) - Q^*hc]/(hc)$ units. However, the argument was made that the rule of thumb can be reasonable when quantity discounts do not apply, presumably because the lost savings from ignoring the value of q is generally small. Develop the formal basis for this argument by showing that the lost savings from the rule of thumb are equal to the cost to hold q units in inventory for $\frac{1}{2}(q/D)$ periods, and that the value of q is $Q^*[(c_{new}/c)^{1/2} - 1]$.

16. Maintaining accurate records on the quantity and location of stock keeping units (SKUs) in a warehouse is often challenging. Some firms employ *cycle counting* as a means to verify and correct inventory records in a database. Cycle counting means that someone counts the inventory of an SKU, a group of SKUs, or SKUs located in a section of the warehouse on a cyclic basis. For example, high-volume SKUs might be counted every two weeks, with the product line divided up so that some units are counted every day, whereas lower-volume SKUs might be counted once every four weeks.

You are the manager of a warehouse with a cycle counting program. With each count, there are frequently "corrections" to the numbers in the system. You are disturbed by the frequency and magnitude of corrections, and you decide to examine the data for 10 SKUs. Table 6.1 reports the number of units counted in inventory over the last 40 cycles (sorted by initial digit).

Review of the data leads you to suspect that the errors stem from inventory figures that are being made up, rather than due to counting mistakes. What is the basis for this suspicion? (*Hint:* A relevant principle of nature was introduced in the previous chapter.)

17. Consider the cash management example given in Section 3.1. In this example, the optimal amount to transfer between high- and low-yield accounts at a time is \$100,000 (i.e., $Q^* = 100,000$), and the transfer arrives when the balance in the low-yield account

TABLE 6.1
Inventory counts over time

17	22	31	44	5	6	7	80	9
17	22	31	44	5	6	7	80	9
18	24	306	46	50	61	73	82	90
100	24	309	46	51	65	79	83	93
106	24	314	402	53	67	702	84	94
110	200	316	402	59	69	703	85	94
119	203	324	403	503	602	703	88	97
119	205	324	404	508	608	705	800	900
123	205	326	404	511	609	706	804	902
126	206	327	409	511	610	707	805	904
129	213	329	420	514	613	707	806	905
131	214	330	421	515	618	708	812	907
132	217	332	422	520	622	709	817	910
133	232	333	423	522	622	712	824	913
134	235	335	424	522	623	713	824	915
140	236	341	425	525	625	714	826	918
140	236	342	425	526	626	718	831	919
142	239	346	426	531	627	722	833	919
147	242	347	428	533	628	722	836	924
150	248	352	430	538	632	725	836	924
150	254	354	438	545	636	726	837	924
153	255	356	440	549	644	732	838	926
154	264	357	440	552	649	732	839	927
156	264	360	442	556	650	732	839	929
157	268	360	447	557	651	733	840	932
162	270	363	449	560	653	733	840	935
163	271	367	450	561	654	739	841	938
171	273	373	455	564	654	739	843	940
173	278	374	456	565	656	739	845	947
174	278	374	456	570	662	741	847	949
175	285	378	457	570	662	741	857	949
179	287	379	462	578	663	758	857	950
181	294	380	475	578	668	759	857	954
184	299	380	475	580	672	761	861	955
184		381	486	583	675	761	861	960
185		384	487	589	676	762	862	961
187		386	488	596	676	773	865	964
190		388	488	598	678	776	874	966
191		391	490	598	679	778	875	967
191		391	492		680	780	875	969
194		394	495		684	781	876	974
195		394			688	783	876	977
196		394			689	784	877	979
197		398			693	785	878	981
198		399			697	788	881	982
198					697	794	882	983
1000					698	796	884	983
							892	984
							896	984
								984
								988
								990
								990
								991
								992
								994
								994
								995
								996
								996

reaches zero. This example was revisited in Section 3.2, but with the allowance for overdraft protection in the low-yield account; with this feature, the bank covers the shortfall (at interest) when the low-yield account is overdrawn. Considering overdraft protection, the optimal amount to transfer between high- and low-yield accounts at a time is $122,475 (i.e., $Q^* = 122,475$) and the transfer arrives when the low-yield account is overdrawn by $40,825 (i.e., $b^* = 40,825$). In addition, the introduction of the overdraft protection feature reduces transaction and holding cost by almost 20 percent. In summary, overdraft protection is a good deal for the firm. But, other things being equal, how is the bank's revenue affected by the introduction of overdraft protection? Evaluate the change in revenue for the bank when overdraft protection is introduced. You may initially work out the analysis using the figures in the example, but go beyond this to develop the change in bank revenue as a function of the parameters A, D, c_e, and c_s.

18. Section 3.2 develops cost formulas that apply when product is ordered and backorders are planned (EOQ with backorders). Section 3.3 develops cost formulas when product is produced instead of ordered (EPQ). For this question, you will need to combine these two models to develop and analyze a model of production with backorders (EPQ with backorders).

    a. Develop expressions for transaction cost per period as a function of Q, holding cost per period as a function of Q and b, and shortage cost per period as a function of Q and b.

    b. What are the formulas for the optimal values of Q and b? (*Hint:* Look at the optimal expressions in Sections 3.2 and 3.3.)

    c. Suppose the demand rate is $D = 1,000$ units per year, the excess cost rate is $c_e = \$3$ per unit-year, the shortage cost rate is $c_s = \$20$ per unit-year, the transaction cost to set up production is $A = \$30$, and the production rate is $P = 2,000$ units per year. What is the EPQ, what is the optimal number of units backordered when production begins, what is the average time between production setups, and what is the length of time of a production run?

19. Section 3.5 contains analysis for how many extra units to order prior to a price increase, that is,

$$\Delta_1^* = (c_{new} - c)D/(hc) + [TC(Q_{new}^*) + HC(Q_{new}^*) - Q^*hc]/(hc)$$

$$= (c_{new} - c)D/(hc) + \{[2ADhc_{new}]^{1/2} - [2ADhc]^{1/2}\}/(hc)$$

This formula is based on the assumption that Δ_1^* extra units are included in the last order prior to the announced price increase (i.e., the last order prior to the price increase is for $Q^* + \Delta_1^*$ units). An alternative is to order only Q^* units, then place a new order for Δ_2^* units just prior to the price increase. This question requires that you analyze this alternative. For the purposes of this question, you may assume that the replenishment lead time is negligible, or, equivalently, the price per unit is based on when units are received rather than when the order is placed (there is no substantive change in the results of analysis when positive lead times are considered, though the explanation of the analysis would be a little more involved).

To facilitate analysis, let δ = number of periods between when the order for $Q^* + \Delta_1^*$ units is placed (and arrives) and the price increase. Since the Δ_1^* extra units are included in the last order prior to the announced price increase, we know that $Q^*/D > \delta$ (i.e., otherwise the order would be for Q^* units and a future order would be for

$Q^* + \Delta_1^*$ units). In summary, Chapter 6 gave analysis for a single large order for $Q^* + \Delta_1^*$ units that is placed $\delta < Q^*/D$ periods prior to the unit price increase from c to c_{new}. An alternative is to order Q^* units that arrive $\delta < Q^*/D$ periods prior to the unit price increase from c to c_{new}, and then place an extra order for Δ_2^* units at the instant before the price increase.

a. Derive the formula for Δ_2^* as a function of the relevant parameters (the complete list of parameters is A, c, c_{new}, D, δ, and h). Make sure to clearly explain how you arrived at your function for Δ_2^*.

b. Consider the example in Section 3.5 where $c = \$60$ per pallet, $c_{new} = \$66$ per pallet, $D = 112{,}000$ pallets per year, $A = \$3{,}206$, and $h = 45$ percent per year. In this example, $\Delta_1^* = 25{,}141$ and the savings due to including $\Delta_1 = 25{,}141$ units in the last regular order is \$76,187. Suppose $\delta = 10/365$ year, or 10 days. Compute Δ_2^* and determine the savings from ordering Δ_2^* units right before the price increase.

20. When selecting the mode of transportation for inbound materials, a manager must take into consideration all relevant cost elements, for example, the transportation cost, and in the case where ownership is transferred to the buyer when the product leaves the seller's plant, the in-transit inventory carrying cost. These carrying costs consist primarily of the cost of capital tied up when items are purchased at the vendor's plant but are not available for use until they arrive at the firm's plant. For example, suppose that a firm located in Amherst, New York, has agreed to purchase raw materials from a vendor in Vancouver, British Columbia, Canada. The purchasing agent in Amherst, Guy Turner, has identified two alternatives for shipping the materials: truck and cargo ship. If the items are shipped by truck, it will take 14 days at a cost of \$3 per unit to cross the continent and clear customs. A cargo ship will take 45 days through the Panama Canal, but the transportation cost is \$1.50 per unit. The firm expects to procure 2,000 units per year at a cost of \$150 per unit. The annual carrying cost rate of in-transit inventory is estimated to be 20 percent of the product value. Which mode of transportation should the agent select?

21. Sometimes a firm is asked to expedite a shipment to a customer, which costs more than normal delivery. If it is an important customer, the firm may choose to expedite with no questions asked. But if not, the firm will want to understand the difference in total cost before making a decision. For example, suppose that a firm is shipping a single unit that sells for \$15,000 from Onalaska, Wisconsin, to Tempe, Arizona. The firm can ship by FedEx at a cost of \$475, and the transit time is two days. Alternatively, the firm can use a slower transit option that costs \$390 and takes five days to deliver. The annual carrying cost associated with in-transit inventory of outbound shipments is estimated to be 20 percent of unit price. What is the total cost per unit for each of these alternatives?

22. According to the EOQ model, the annual transaction cost is equal to the annual cost of carrying cycle stock when the order quantity is optimal, that is, $TC(Q^*)/HC(Q^*) = 1$. A ratio of transaction-to-holding cost that is significantly different from 1.0 is a signal of a potential money-saving opportunity. At your firm, the ratio is about 0.50, yet results of analysis show that order quantities are optimal. What differences in assumptions can explain an optimal ratio of less than 1? In order to answer this question, first identify the assumptions of the EOQ model. Then identify a change in at least one of the assumptions that would lead to an optimal ratio less than 1.0.

Case Exercise: *JNG Foods*

JNG Foods owns and operates 31 grocery stores in Ontario, Canada. You joined JNG 12 months ago. Since then, you've worked at three different stores doing everything from stocking to checkout, staffing, and store manager. For the last several weeks, you've been on temporary assignment in the Sourcing Department at corporate headquarters in Ottawa, and, beginning next week, you will start work in a new position as a product manager for private-label beverages. Product managers at JNG are charged with overseeing the entire supply chain process for a group of products, which spans activities from product acquisition (e.g., vendor selection, negotiation of purchase contracts, inbound transportation) to final sale (e.g., pricing, promotion, display).

You are brimming with ideas for improving the business, some of which will require significant investment and also offer the potential for large profit gains. From your experience in the field, you know that a history of small successes can be critical when it comes to gaining support for more substantive changes. Accordingly, your strategy going into your new position is to initially focus on implementing a series of "quick and easy" improvements, while at the same time gathering information that you can use to refine your ideas on major improvement initiatives. A candidate for a potential quick and easy improvement involves the ordering policy. You've gathered some data, blocked out some time during the weekend, and plan to pitch a proposal to your boss on Monday.

BACKGROUND ON GROCERY STORE REPLENISHMENTS

JNG owns and operates four distribution centers (DCs). A DC in Ottawa, for example, supplies eight grocery stores located in and around Ottawa. The DCs are used for *break-bulk* and *mixing*.[14] Vendor product is shipped to the DC, sometimes in large quantities, and company-owned vehicles make daily deliveries from the DC to the grocery stores. Approximately 95 percent of the product line is stocked at DCs; the other 5 percent is comprised of highly perishable items such as breads and some dairy products, which are delivered to grocery stores direct from suppliers.

You've learned from experience to favor small-scale tests of your ideas in the field prior to full-scale rollout. Accordingly, you've targeted the Ottawa DC as the pilot site, and this is where you will focus your analysis.

BACKGROUND ON PRIVATE-LABEL BEVERAGES AND THE OTTAWA MARKET

JNG sells cans of soda under its own label. These products are supplied by AR Beverage, located in London, Ontario, and are shipped *F.O.B. origin, freight collect*[15] to the Ottawa DC. The policy is to order 300 12-packs at a time.[16]

There are a number of elements associated with this policy that have led you to suspect that money can be saved by making some changes to the ordering policy. First, you know that economic order quantities often depend on levels of demand. Second, you know the policy has not changed or been evaluated in years, yet volumes in this product line have been increasing by nearly 15 percent per year over the last five years. Third, demand within a year is highly seasonal. Fourth, from a quick inspection of accounting data, the annual cost of carrying cycle stock of private-label beverages is notably less than the annual transaction cost associated with placing orders.

A BASIS FOR A PROPOSAL

The challenge is to create an Excel spreadsheet that computes economic order sizes for alternative demand rates, and computes annual savings over the current policy of ordering 300 12-packs at a time. Such a spreadsheet can be updated over time to reflect changing cost rates, and can be used as a guide for determining order quantities over the course of the year as demand rates change (e.g., due to seasonal effects).

---

[14] Break-bulk refers to the activity of transforming large inbound quantities into small outbound quantities; for example, products from a few distant suppliers are shipped in large quantities to a warehouse and the warehouse ships in small quantities to many nearby customers. Mixing refers to the activity of transforming inbound shipments that each contains a limited variety of different products into outbound shipments that each contains a wide variety of different products; for example, truckloads containing a single type of product coming from different sources arrive at a warehouse and the warehouse ships truckloads of mixed product to customers.

[15] *F.O.B. origin, freight collect* means that ownership (and responsibility for freight claims associated with damages in-transit) is transferred from AR Beverage to JNG Foods when it is loaded on the truck (i.e., at the origin) and that JNG Foods is responsible for paying the transportation costs.

[16] A 12-pack holds 12 cans, each containing 355 ml of soda (i.e., about 12 ounces).

Questions

1. Why is a low cycle stock carrying cost relative to order transaction cost an indicator of a potential savings opportunity? Consider that transportation cost rates decrease as the order quantity increases. How does a quantity discount cost structure affect the "benchmark" ratio of cycle stock holding cost to order transaction cost?[17]

2. Prepare a spreadsheet that uses the costs below to compute the optimal order quantity as well as the savings over the current policy for the following average demand rates in 12-packs per week: 10, 20, . . . , 350. The range of demand from 10 to 350 more than covers what has been observed in recent years. For example, the average demand for 12-packs per week last year was 122; during the slow season, the average was 50 (i.e., midwinter), and during the high season (i.e., August) the average was nearly 200. Order quantities are limited to increments of 100 12-packs (e.g., the order quantity can be 100, 200, 300, etc.).[18]

   The annual inventory holding cost as a percentage of product cost is estimated at 25 percent. The purchase cost per 12-pack is $4.80, and the cost to place and process each purchase order is estimated to be $15. A pallet of 100 12-packs weighs 939.15 pounds (and 426.00 kilograms). The cost per cwt[19] to transport from AR's facility in London to JNG's DC in Ottawa is given in the following table.

Weight	$/cwt	Minimum Charge	Full Truckload Cost
0–499 lbs	$11.23	$31.45	
500–999 lbs	$8.98		
1,000–1,999 lbs	$7.44		
2,000–4,999 lbs	$6.60		
5,000–9,999 lbs	$5.26		
10,000–19,999 lbs	$4.74		
20,000–45,000 lbs			$984.40

The spreadsheet should be structured so that one can change the cost and/or demand rates and the calculations are automatically updated (i.e., it is not necessary to make any manual adjustments to formulas). Also, create a graph that concisely displays the results of your analysis. Finally, create a one-page proposal that consists of the graph, an explanation of what the graph is showing, and how the graph could be used as a quick reference for determining how much to order during different times of the year.

---

[17] A benchmark ratio is the value one would expect to see when costs are minimized.

[18] AR ships in shrink-wrapped soda pallets of 100 12-packs (i.e., four levels at 25 per level). The soda comprising a pallet does not have to be a single type; JNG can order any mix of 12-pack sodas desired, which are then palletized for shipment.

[19] The letters *cwt* stand for "hundredweight" (C is the roman numeral for 100). In certain instances, it is less expensive to ship at a higher-weight breakpoint. For example, the cost to ship one pallet that weighs 9.3915 cwt (or 939.15 pounds) is the smaller of two possibilities: 9.3915 × $8.98 = $84.34 and 10 × $7.44 = $74.40. In this example, the transportation cost would be based on the cost of shipping 1,000 pounds (i.e., 60.85 pounds of *deficit weight*), which is $74.40. It is less expensive to ship 1,000 pounds at the 1,000-pound rate and pay for the additional 60 pounds than it is to ship 939 pounds at the 500-pound rate.

Chapter **Seven**

Inventory Management II: Stochastic Analysis

Chapter Outline

Chapter Keys

1. What is the cost trade-off captured by the single-period model (SPM)?
2. In what settings is SPM analysis appropriate and how can an order quantity be determined?
3. What is the definition of base stock level, and how does a base stock policy answer the questions of when and how much to order?
4. In what settings is a base stock policy reasonable and how can the base stock level be determined?
5. How do (Q, R) and (I, S) policies answer the questions of when and how much to order, when is each policy appropriate, and how can the values of policy parameters be determined?

6. What is the difference between fill rate and service level, and how do these performance measures depend on policy parameters?

7. How can the return on investments to reduce demand uncertainty be estimated, and how are the Pareto phenomenon and the central limit theorem relevant for this question?

8. What are the managerial insights from the chapter?

This chapter extends the previous chapter by introducing the element of uncertainty (the term *stochastic* in the chapter title means random, or not known with certainty). The focus is on understanding the impact of demand uncertainty on decisions and policies for managing inventory (see Figure 7.1).

After examining the costs of demand uncertainty in Section 1, we'll consider order quantity decisions in Section 2. Section 3 will extend this discussion to consider not only how much to order but also when to order. In particular, we will learn about three pull policies for answering the questions of when and how much to order; later in Chapter 9, a push approach for answering the same questions will be described.

Finally, we will see how the content in Section 3 enriches our understanding of an issue raised in Chapter 4 on demand management. Chapter 4 covered a number of approaches and concepts for reducing demand uncertainty, but the question of how to estimate the return (i.e., cost savings and/or profit increase) from lower demand uncertainty was largely left unanswered. In Section 4, we'll consider how the concepts of Section 3 can be applied to help answer this question.

1. COSTS OF DEMAND UNCERTAINTY

What is the impact on profit or cost when demand during some period of time is different from expected? The answer to this question will depend on the responsiveness of the supply chain and on the market characteristics. We'll consider two possibilities.

One possibility involves a product that drastically declines in value after a selling season that is shorter than the replenishment lead time (e.g., newspapers for a corner newsstand, doughnuts at a grocery store, t-shirts for a one-time event, fashion products, Christmas trees). The main consequence is that product must be ordered before the selling season begins, and there are costs of ordering too much (e.g., leftover products sold at a loss) and for ordering too little (e.g., lost profit margin and goodwill). Shortage and excess costs stem from the uncertainty of demand during the selling season. This setting is considered in Section 2.

The second possibility involves a product with a selling season, or life cycle, that is much longer than the replenishment lead time. If demand during the replenishment lead time is higher than available inventory when the replenishment order is placed, then

FIGURE 7.1

A supply chain with emphasis on inventory management links.

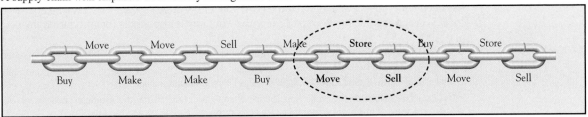

unsatisfied demand is backordered (or lost), which, in turn, can negatively affect profit through unhappy customers and lower future demand. If demand during the replenishment lead time is lower than available inventory when the replenishment order is placed, then the result is more inventory than necessary, which can negatively affect profit through higher inventory holding cost. Shortage and excess costs stem from the uncertainty of demand during the replenishment lead time. This setting is considered in Section 3.

Sections 2 and 3 address two variations of a fundamental economic question—that of "guessing" a number in the face of uncertainty when there are costs for guessing high and for guessing low.[1] Intuition gained from our analysis extends well beyond questions of inventory, and decisions that draw upon such analysis can save money. For example, airlines often sell more tickets than available seats on a flight—a practice known as overbooking. Airlines overbook because approximately 10−15 percent of airline passengers don't show up for their reservation (Rosato 1998), and an empty seat due to a no-show is a lost opportunity to make money. The question is how many extra tickets to sell when the number of no-shows is uncertain. Guessing low means empty seats and lost opportunity for additional ticket revenue. Guessing high means some passengers will be bumped, which requires payments or travel vouchers to volunteers who give up their seats. The question of how much to overbook a flight is one element of a more comprehensive approach for maximizing the revenue from available capacity (e.g., seats on a plane) via forecasting, pricing, and overbooking that is known as *revenue management.*[2] American Airlines estimates that revenue management generates about $1 billion in annual incremental revenue, an amount that is higher than total profit in most years (Cook 1998). The case of American Airlines illustrates the potential economic importance of the analysis in this chapter. The next example illustrates the types of questions considered in Sections 2 and 3.

Example

It's been an amazing ride. You are now CEO of what was once a small North American personal-care products distributor when you joined the firm 10 years ago. The spark for change can be traced back to acquiring the rights to distribute Kalina product in North America, and your innovations played a large role in the success of this initiative. Your firm is now a growing distributor of personal-care products in Europe and Asia, and is involved in some manufacturing as well as development and introduction of new products.

There are two pressing issues to be addressed in tomorrow's meeting. The first involves the introduction of a new drug and the second involves an anticipated jump in the level of working capital necessary to support operations.

Here is issue one for tomorrow's meeting.[3] Two years ago, researchers at Kalina were investigating compounds for teeth whitening and discovered a promising antidepressant. The drug has been undergoing evaluations by the FDA, and it now appears likely that it will be approved for U.S. distribution within the next 12 months. Your firm is responsible for introducing the new

---

[1] The term *guessing* is used here to emphasize the uncertainty surrounding the problem, not the manner in which a number is selected.

[2] See Talluri and Van Ryzin (2004) for more detail on revenue management.

[3] This issue helps illustrate the broad applications of analysis in this chapter; for example, capacity can be viewed as a form of inventory where there are costs of having too much and too little.

drug to the market, beginning in the United States. You have identified the company that will produce the drug (pending FDA approval), but due to the industrywide undersupply of capacity, it is necessary to pay for the right to keep capacity available for your firm's use 12 months from now. The question is how much capacity to reserve. The cost to reserve production capacity is $100 per milliliter (ml), with a minimum of a three-month reservation at 5,000 ml per month (that is, one must reserve at least 15,000 ml at a cost of $1,500,000). The contribution margin per ml is estimated at $900; this means that you expect to make about $900 on each ml sold (one ml of the purified drug is used to produce many pills). Demand is highly uncertain at this point; research suggests that anything within the range of 0 ml per month to 20,000 ml per month is equally likely. The current proposal is to reserve the midpoint of this range, or 10,000 ml per month for three months. Your intuition suggests that more capacity should be reserved, and that reconsideration could be worth millions in profit.

Here is issue two for tomorrow's meeting. About 75 percent of perfume product sales occur during September through the first week of February, and September is only six months away. The inventory investment in perfume products during this critical time last year was about $10 million. Due to a number of factors, including the bankruptcy of a competing firm, volume during the upcoming holiday/Valentine season is expected to be about 50 percent higher than last year. The question is how much additional inventory investment is appropriate to support the increased business. The current proposal is to increase inventory investment by 50 percent, or $5 million. You're skeptical.

We'll work through analysis to get a handle on answers to these two questions in Sections 2 and 3. But, as we saw in Chapter 6, it is also important to consider whether root causes of the problem can be reduced or eliminated. In Section 4, we'll look at how results from the earlier sections can be useful for estimating the return on investments that reduce the primary root cause—demand uncertainty.

2. HOW MUCH TO ORDER BEFORE A SHORT SELLING SEASON

Here's a common problem.[4] An **order must be placed before we know exactly how much we can use, and we lose money if we order more or less than the actual realized quantity.** In the Kalina example from the previous section, the quantity of capacity to reserve must be "ordered" when market demand is highly uncertain. For another, rather close-to-home example, consider a college bookstore selecting the number of textbooks to order based on enrollment estimates. Guess low and incur the wrath of students and professors, potentially losing future business. Guess high and incur return fees. College bookstores return about 40 percent of all new textbooks, and packing and shipping costs about $0.35 on every dollar's worth of textbooks at the end of the term (Padmanabhan and Png 1995).

An early step in analysis is to identify assumptions that will be the basis for estimating costs and profits:

A1. Demand during the selling season is unknown, though the probability distribution of demand during the selling season is known.

A2. An order must be placed before the selling season begins, and there are no replenishment shipments during the selling season.

A3. The cost of ordering too few (i.e., shortage cost) is proportional to the error.

A4. The cost of ordering too many (i.e., excess cost) is proportional to the error.

These four assumptions define a simplified and approximate model of reality known as the **single-period model.**

[4] Edgeworth (1888) presents perhaps the first formal analysis of this problem. The context for his study is the banking industry. Petruzzi and Dada (1999) review the extensive body of knowledge on the problem.

Notation for the Single-Period Model

D = demand during the period, which is uncertain (i.e., D is a random variable)

p = selling price per unit

c = cost per unit

s = salvage value per unit (i.e., selling price per unit for units left over at the end of the period)

g = goodwill cost per unit (e.g., lost future profit due to unsatisfied demand, or, alternatively, cost to reimburse a customer for inconvenience due to unsatisfied demand)

c_e = cost per unit excess (e.g., purchase cost less salvage value, or $c - s$)

c_s = cost per unit short (e.g., lost profit plus goodwill cost, or $p - c + g$)

Q = order quantity

$P[D \leq x]$ = probability that demand during the period is x units or less; $P[D \leq x]$ defines the probability distribution of demand in the period as a function of possible realized demand x, and $P[D \leq Q]$ is the anticipated "service level" (SL) during the period if Q units are ordered

$E[D]$ = expected (or mean) value of D

Recall the example from Section 1 and the question of how much capacity to reserve. If 10,000 ml of capacity per month is reserved at a cost of $100 per ml, but only 9,999 ml are needed, then the loss of picking one ml too high is $100. In terms of the notation,

c_e = cost per unit excess = $100 per ml

If 10,000 ml of capacity per month is reserved, but 10,001 ml are needed, then this means that 1 ml of demand is unsatisfied and the loss of picking 1 ml too low is the contribution margin of $900 (assuming loss of goodwill is insignificant). In terms of the notation,

g = goodwill cost per unit = $0

$p - c$ = contribution margin per unit (i.e., price less cost) = $900 per ml

c_s = cost per unit short = $p - c + g$ = $900 per ml

Research suggests that demand (D) may be anywhere between 0 ml per month and 20,000 ml per month, and each possibility within this range is equally likely. This means that demand is *uniformly* distributed between 0 and 20,000; for example, there is a 50 percent probability that demand will be 10,000 ml per month or less and a 75 percent probability that demand will be 15,000 ml per month or less. In terms of the notation, $P[D \leq 10,000]$ = 50 percent, $P[D \leq 15,000]$ = 75 percent, and more generally,

$$P[D \leq x] = x/20,000 \quad \text{for } 0 \leq x \leq 20,000$$

The current proposal is to reserve 10,000 ml per month for three months,[5] which corresponds to the expected (or average) demand rate. Is this reasonable? A good start to answering this question is to think through some possible scenarios. For instance, suppose capacity is 10,000 ml per month and demand is 20,000 ml per month. In this case, 10,000 ml of demand are unsatisfied and the opportunity to make an additional profit of $900 \times (20,000 - 10,000) = $9,000,000 per month is lost. At the opposite extreme, suppose

[5] Three months of capacity will buy enough time to judge market potential and make the necessary investments for long-term production capacity if the drug is approved.

TABLE 7.1   **Expected Impact of Increasing the Order Quantity for Various Trial Values of Q**

The probability distribution of demand (D) is uniform between 0 and 20,000. The cost per unit excess is c_e = $100 and the cost per unit short is c_s = $900. The optimal order quantity in this example is Q^* = 18,000.

| | | Expected Change if Q Is Increased by 1 Unit | | |
| | | Increase in Excess | Decrease in Shortage | |
Q	$P[D \leq Q]$ = $Q/20,000$	Cost, $c_e P[D \leq Q]$	Cost, $c_s(1 - P[D \leq Q])$	Change in Profit
5,000	25%	$ 25	$675	Increase
10,000	50	50	450	Increase
15,000	75	75	225	Increase
18,000	90	90	90	No change
19,000	95	95	45	Decrease
20,000	100	100	0	Decrease

capacity is 10,000 ml per month and demand is 0 ml per month (e.g., a nasty side effect is discovered during FDA tests). The capacity is not used and your firm spent $100 × 10,000 = $1,000,000 per month more than necessary. The large difference in impact—$9 million versus $1 million—hints that the reservation quantity of 10,000 ml per month may be low.

Extending the analysis from here is not too difficult if we step back to consider what we know. We know that increasing Q increases the probability of leftover units and decreases the probability of a shortage of units, or, in other words, an increase in Q causes the expected excess cost to increase and the expected shortage cost to decrease. We also know that it makes economic sense to increase Q if the increase in expected excess cost is less than the decrease in expected shortage cost. The only remaining piece is estimating how expected excess and shortage costs change when Q is increased.

Increase in Expected Excess Cost from a Small Increase in Q   If $D \leq Q$, then an increase in Q will cause an increase in excess cost at rate c_e. If $D > Q$, then increasing Q by a small amount will have no impact on excess cost (because no units are left over). This means that if Q is increased by a small amount, then expected excess cost increases at rate

$$c_e P[D \leq Q] + 0 P[D > Q] = c_e P[D \leq Q].$$

Decrease in Expected Shortage Cost from a Small Increase in Q   If $D \leq Q$, then increasing Q will have no impact on shortage cost (because Q is sufficient to cover all demand). If $D > Q$, then a small increase in Q will cause a decrease in shortage cost at rate c_s. This means that if Q is increased by a small amount, then expected shortage cost decreases at rate

$$0 P[D \leq Q] + c_s P[D > Q] = c_s P[D > Q] = c_s(1 - P[D \leq Q])$$

The rates of change in excess and shortage costs can be computed for various trial values of Q to determine an optimal quantity. From Table 7.1 it is apparent that expected change in profit from increasing Q is positive when $Q < 18,000$ ml and negative when $Q > 18,000$ ml, and that the optimal quantity is $Q^* = 18,000$. By increasing the reservation quantity from 10,000 ml per month to 18,000 ml per month for three months, expected firm profit increases by almost $5 million.[6]

[6] We will not take the space to go through the derivation of expected profit as a function of Q. In general, expected profit is expected demand × margin less expected losses due to excess and shortage. In this example with uniformly distributed demand between 0 and 20,000, expected profit per month = $E[D] \times (p - c) - 1/2\{c_e(Q - 0)P[D \leq Q] + c_s(20,000 - Q)P[D > Q]\}$ = $10,000 \times 900 - 1/2\{100QP[D \leq Q] + 900(20,000 - Q)P[D > Q]\}$.

Example Summary

How much production capacity to reserve? The unknown demand is estimated to be uniformly distributed between 0 and 20,000 ml per month, that is,

D = demand per month $\sim U[0, 20000]$

The excess and shortage cost rates are

c_e = cost per unit excess = \$100/ml (i.e., idle capacity)

c_s = cost per unit short = \$900/ml (i.e., lost profit)

Continue to increase the reserved capacity quantity Q as long as the expected marginal savings in shortage cost are more than the expected marginal increase in excess cost, that is,

Marginal excess cost = $c_e P[D \leq Q]$

Marginal shortage cost savings = $c_s(1 - P[D \leq Q])$

Reserve $Q^* = 18,000$ ml per month because

$100P[D \leq 18,000] = 900(1 - P[D \leq 18,000])$

In general, it makes economic sense to increase Q as long as $c_e P[D \leq Q] < c_s(1 - P[D \leq Q])$, which means that the optimal order quantity Q^* is the point where $c_e P[D \leq Q^*] = c_s(1 - P[D \leq Q^*])$, or, equivalently,

$$P[D \leq Q^*] = c_s/(c_s + c_e)$$

This formula is intuitive; $c_e P[D \leq Q]$ is the expected marginal cost from increasing Q and $c_s(1 - P[D \leq Q])$ is the expected marginal savings from increasing Q, and the optimal order quantity sets marginal cost equal to marginal savings.

Depending on the probability distribution of demand, it may not be possible to find a value of Q^* satisfying $P[D \leq Q^*] = c_s/(c_s + c_e)$. In these cases, Q^* is the smallest value satisfying $c_e P[D \leq Q^*] > c_s(1 - P[D \leq Q^*])$, or, equivalently, the smallest value satisfying $P[D \leq Q^*] > c_s/(c_s + c_e)$ (i.e., continue to increase Q as long as the marginal cost is not more than the marginal savings). For example, suppose that demand is either 5 or 10, each with a 50 percent probability. Then $P[D \leq 5] = P[D \leq 6] = \cdots = P[D \leq 9] = 50$ percent and $P[D \leq 10] = 100$ percent. If $c_s/(c_s + c_e) = 75$ percent, then no quantity satisfies $P[D \leq Q^*] = 75$ percent, and the optimal order quantity is $Q^* = 10$. The **single period model formulas are summarized below.**

Formulas for the Single-Period Model

Q^* = optimal order quantity

SL^* = optimal service level = $c_s/(c_s + c_e)$

Finding the Value of Q^* in General

Select the quantity Q^* that satisfies

$$P[D \leq Q^*] = SL^*$$

If there is no quantity satisfying $P[D \leq Q^*] = SL^*$, then Q^* is the smallest value satisfying

$$P[D \leq Q^*] > SL^*$$

Finding the Value of Q^* If Unknown Demand Is Approximated by a Uniform Distribution between a and b; That Is, $D \sim U(a, b)$ and $E[D] = (a + b)/2$

$$Q^* = a + SL^*(b - a) \quad \text{(because } P[D \le Q] = (Q - a)/(b - a))$$

Finding the Value of Q^* If Unknown Demand Is Approximated by a Normal Distribution with Mean μ_D and Variance σ_D^2; That Is, $D \sim N(\mu_D, \sigma_D^2)$

$$Q^* = \mu_D + z_{SL}^* \sigma_D \quad \text{(because } P[D \le Q = \mu_D + z_{SL}\sigma_D] = SL)$$

Example

Your firm recently completed successful negotiations with DreamWorks SKG. The plan is to introduce a new perfume called Ovid that will be prominently featured in a movie of the same name. Market introduction will coincide with the movie release, which is scheduled for six months from now. The question is how many liters of the perfume to produce and have placed in the market when the movie is released. The question is tricky because the success of the new perfume will likely be tied to the success of the movie. If the movie is a flop, then the perfume will probably do poorly in the market and excess supply will have to be liquidated at a loss. If the movie is a hit, then the demand for Ovid perfume will likely be high. And sales and profit will be lost if the initial production batch is not enough to satisfy demand during the first several weeks following the movie's release.

The contribution margin of Ovid perfume is estimated at $500 per liter (i.e., $p - c = $500 per liter). The cost for production, packaging, and delivery is estimated at $750 per liter (i.e., $c = $750 per liter). The cost of lost goodwill from a stockout is estimated to be negligible (i.e., $g = $0 per liter). The salvage value of excess perfume is estimated at $500 per liter (i.e., $s = $500 per liter). Based on the above information,

$$c_e = \text{cost per unit excess} = c - s = \$750 - \$500 = \$250 \text{ per liter}$$
$$c_s = \text{cost per unit short} = p - c + g = \$500 + \$0 = \$500 \text{ per liter}$$

and the optimal service level is

$$SL^* = \text{optimal service level} = c_s/(c_s + c_e) = 500/(500 + 250) = 2/3 \approx 66.7 \text{ percent}$$

The optimal service level can be viewed as the point that balances the excess and shortage cost rates (see Figure 7.2).

Given SL^*, the next step is to determine Q^*, the optimal size of the initial production batch of Ovid perfume. This will depend on the probability distribution of demand during the first several weeks following the movie's release.[7] We'll consider three possibilities.

FIGURE 7.2

A balance scale illustrating that the optimal service level corresponds to the placement of a fulcrum that balances the weights of c_e and c_s.

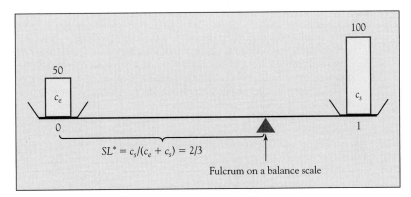

[7] Additional perfume can be produced and placed in the market after the movie's release if necessary, but the lead time is several weeks. This means that the initial production batch should ideally match the first several weeks of demand.

1. *What is Q^* if demand is uniformly distributed between 100 and 1,000 liters?* In terms of our notation, $a = 100$, $b = 1,000$, and

$$Q^* = a + SL^*(b - a) = 100 + 2/3(1,000 - 100) = 700 \text{ liters}[8]$$

2. *What is Q^* if demand is normally distributed with a mean of 550 liters and a standard deviation of 150 liters?* In terms of our notation, $\mu_D = 550$ and $\sigma_D = 150$. However, the formula for Q^* also requires the value of z associated with a probability of $SL^* \approx 66.7$ percent. This value can be found by examining a standard normal probability table (see Appendix 4).[9] From Appendix 4, the value of z associated with a probability of 66.64 percent is 0.43, or $z_{.6664} = 0.43$. Similarly, the value of z associated with a probability of 67.003 percent is 0.44, or $z_{.67003} = 0.44$. Either of these z values is fine:

$$Q^* = \mu_D + z^*_{SL}\,\sigma_D \approx 550 + (z_{.6664})150 = 550 + 0.43(150) = 614.5 \text{ liters}$$

or

$$Q^* = \mu_D + z^*_{SL}\,\sigma_D \approx 550 + (z_{.67003})150 = 550 + 0.44(150) = 616 \text{ liters}.$$

3. *What is Q* if the probability distribution of demand is given by Figure 7.3?* The optimal service level is $SL^* = 2/3 \approx 66.7$ percent, which does not appear in the probability table. According to the table in Figure 7.3, $P[D \leq 610] = 65.2$ percent and $P[D \leq 620] = 67.65$ percent. The smallest quantity satisfying $P[D \leq Q^*] > SL^*$ is

$$Q^* = 620 \text{ liters}.$$

Example Summary

How many liters of Ovid perfume to produce?
c_e = cost per unit excess = \$250/liter (i.e., loss due to markdown)
c_s = cost per unit short = \$500/ml (i.e., lost profit)
SL^* = optimal service level = $c_s/(c_s + c_e) = 2/3 \approx 0.667$
Select production quantity Q^* so that $P[D \leq Q^*] = SL^*$.
    If D = demand $\sim U[100, 1000]$, then

$$Q^* = a + SL^*(b - a) = 100 + 2/3(1,000 - 100) = 700 \text{ liters}$$

If D = demand $\sim N[550, 150^2]$, then

$$Q^* = \mu_D + z^*_{SL}\sigma_D = 550 + z_{.667}(150) \approx 616 \text{ liters}$$

---

[8] The result that $Q^* = a + SL^*(b - a)$ is deeper than it may appear at first glance. It is interesting, for example, that the formula is also optimal when the only thing known about the probability distribution of demand is that the random variable can be no smaller than a and no larger than b, and the decision maker wishes to select an order quantity that will minimize the maximum possible expected loss in profit due to ignorance of the probability distribution (Perakis and Roels 2006). In other words, if there is no information to suggest what the probability distribution of demand could be, other than it has lower and upper limits of a and b, then it makes reasonable economic sense to use the prescribed formula. It is also optimal if all that is known about the probability distribution is that it is nonnegative and symmetric and has mean μ, in which case $a = 0$ and $b = 2\mu$ in the formula (Perakis and Roels 2006). We also see evidence of the fundamental nature of the uniform distribution in other bodies of knowledge. One example is information theory and the notion of entropy (Shannon 1948). The entropy of a probability distribution measures the amount of uncertainty (or information content) associated with the distribution. The uniform probability distribution is the maximum entropy distribution among all distributions that are supported by the interval $[a, b]$ (e.g., to assume any other distribution is to assume additional information is known about the distribution). Another example is the *principle of insufficient reason* put forward by Pierre Laplace in the 1700s: with no information available, all outcomes should be considered equally likely (e.g., as in the uniform distribution).

[9] Alternatively, the function in Excel that returns the value of z associated with probability SL is $z_{SL} = $ NORMSINV(SL).

FIGURE 7.3 A plot of the cumulative probability distribution of demand, and an excerpt of the probability table.

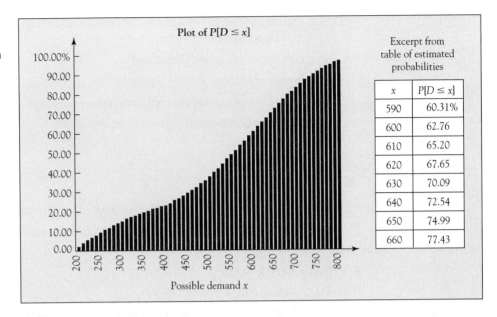

Plot of $P[D \leq x]$

Excerpt from table of estimated probabilities

x	$P[D \leq x]$
590	60.31%
600	62.76
610	65.20
620	67.65
630	70.09
640	72.54
650	74.99
660	77.43

Possible demand x

3. POLICIES FOR WHEN AND HOW MUCH TO ORDER

Up to this point, we have only considered the question of how much to order. In Chapter 6, we considered how much to order in the context of balancing order transaction cost with inventory holding and shortage costs. In the **previous section, we considered how much to order prior to a short selling season when there is demand uncertainty and costs of ordering too much and too little.**

In this section, we'll look at three policies for answering the questions of when and how much to order on a routine basis. Each of these policies is an example of a pull approach because the answer to the question of when to order is based on actual demand (or, equivalently, actual inventory).

The first policy, known as a base stock policy, is very simple but often economically impractical. The remaining two policies are slight variations on a base stock policy and are more common in practice. The assumptions and notation for these three policies follow:

A1. Demand during the lead time (or the lead time plus order interval) is unknown, though the probability distribution is known.

A2. Inventory holding cost is proportional to average inventory.

A3. Demand that cannot be satisfied from inventory is backordered.

A4. Backorder cost per period is proportional to the average number of units on backorder.

Notation for Policies of When and How Much to Order

LD = demand during the replenishment lead time, which is uncertain (i.e., LD is a random variable)

ILD = demand during the order interval plus replenishment lead time, which is uncertain (i.e., ILD is a random variable)

$P[X \leq x]$ = probability that random variable X is x units or less; for example, $P[LD \leq x]$ defines the probability distribution of LD and $P[ILD \leq x]$ defines the probability distribution of ILD

$E[X]$ = expected (or mean) value of X; for example, $E[LD]$ is the mean of LD and $E[ILD]$ is the mean of ILD

c = cost per unit (e.g., purchase cost)

h = inventory holding cost per \$-period

c_e = inventory holding cost per unit-period (excess cost rate), for example, $c_e = h \times c$

c_s = backorder cost per unit-period (shortage cost rate)

Q = order quantity

S = base stock level

R = reorder point

SL = service level = probability of no backorders during some period of time

FR = fill rate = proportion of demand shipped from inventory (e.g., proportion shipped on time)

3.1 Base Stock Policy

How Does a Base Stock Policy Work?

First, a definition: *inventory position* is the number of units on hand[10] plus the number of units on order.[11] A base stock policy is a very simple policy for answering when and how much to order. The inventory position doesn't change over time and is referred to as the level of *base stock* in the system.

In a **base stock policy, the answer to *when to order* is *whenever demand occurs*, and the answer to *how much to order* is the *demand amount*.** For example, as soon as a customer buys 10 units, an order for 10 units is placed with the supplier. With this pair of transactions, on-hand dropped by 10 and on-order increased by 10, so the base stock level (and inventory position) is unchanged. The linkage between demand and replenishment orders is why a base stock policy is also known as a *one-for-one replenishment policy*. The dynamics of inventory over time are illustrated for the simple case of constant demand and lead time in Figure 7.4.

The frequency of replenishment orders in a base stock policy matches the occurrence of demands. For this reason, a base stock policy doesn't make economic sense unless the fixed cost of placing an order is very low relative to other system costs, or demand occurs infrequently. Nevertheless, an understanding of a base stock policy is a useful starting point for understanding two alternative policies that are more common in practice.

How Should the Base Stock Level Be Set?

Figure 7.4 illustrates inventory over time when there is no uncertainty. Base stock = 3 units, lead time = 2 days, demand rate = 1 unit per day, demand during the lead time = (2 days) × (1 unit/day) = 2 units, and, after the first two days, average inventory = 1 unit. In general, average inventory is equal to base stock minus average demand during the lead time. Testing this out with the numbers from Figure 7.4,

$$\text{Average inventory} = \text{base stock} - \text{average demand during the lead time}$$
$$= 3 - 2 = 1$$

as expected. In summary, when there is no uncertainty, setting base stock to average demand during the lead time results in no inventory (or backorders) and low cost.

---

[10] We'll use the convention where on-hand inventory includes backorders; for example, if on-hand inventory = −5, then there is no inventory in stock and five units are on backorder.

[11] The number of units *on order* is the number of units that have been ordered from the supplier(s) but have not yet been received.

FIGURE 7.4
Inventory and Base Stock over Time according to a Base Stock Policy
Demand is one unit per day, the replenishment lead time is two days, base stock is three units, and the initial on-hand inventory is three units with no inventory on order. The base stock level remains constant at three units, and after the first two days, on-hand inventory is constant at one unit.

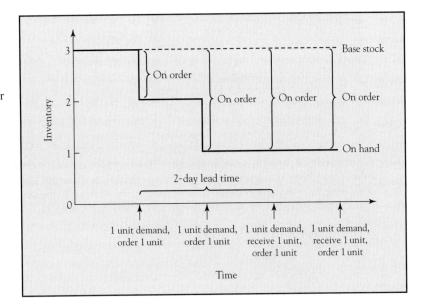

A cost-effective level of base stock when demand is uncertain may be less clear, at least at first glance. As it turns out, the analysis and results from the previous section also can be used to find a base stock level that minimizes average inventory and backorder costs. Let's see how.

Example

Your company maintains two cash accounts: a high-yield account that earns 8 percent annual interest and a low-yield account that earns 3 percent annual interest. The high-yield account is analogous to a personal savings account and the low-yield account is analogous to a personal checking account; that is, payments are made out of the low-yield account. The bank provides overdraft protection by offering a loan at an 18 percent annual interest rate if the balance in the low-yield account goes negative. Due to your negotiating persistence and threats to take your business elsewhere, a change is on the horizon. Beginning next month, the bank will no longer charge $25 to transfer money between high- and low-yield accounts. This is a big deal that will save your firm a lot of money, as long as you can devise an effective policy for managing the movement of cash between accounts.

Example Summary

Data for managing transfers between a high-yield and low-yield account:

High-yield interest rate = 8%
Low-yield interest rate = 3%
Loan interest for overdraft protection = 18%
Transaction fee for funds transfers between high- and low-yield accounts = $0
Average cash requirements = $30,000 per day

The current policy, which is based on analysis from Chapter 6, is to periodically transfer funds between accounts so that transaction, holding, and shortage costs are minimized. The elimination of the $25 transaction fee means that the high-yield account can essentially be used as a checking account, as funds can be transferred between accounts whenever there is a payment from the low-yield account. In other words, the new cash management policy will be a one-for-one replenishment policy, that is, a base stock policy. It takes two days for the bank to process an electronic funds transfer between accounts (that is, the replenishment lead time is two days) and the demand for funds averages $30,000 per day, or almost $11 million per year. If the demand for funds is constant at $30,000 per day, then the base stock level in the low-yield account can be set to the average demand during the lead time ($2 \times \$30,000 = \$60,000$), and the average balance will remain constant at zero.

But what if demand for funds during the two-day lead time is not constant? The cost of an excess dollar in the low-yield account is the difference between high and low yields, or $c_e = 0.08 - 0.03 = \$0.05$ per $-year. The cost of a dollar short in the low-yield account is the difference between the loan rate and the high yield, or $c_s = 0.18 - 0.08 = \$0.10$ per $-year. The cost structure is identical to the single-period model of Section 2. The only difference is that **Section 2 dealt with selecting a quantity to cover *demand during the selling season* whereas here we are concerned with selecting a quantity (i.e., base stock) to cover *demand during the replenishment lead time*. Many of the same formulas apply,** and are listed below.

Formulas for the Base Stock Policy

$$S = \text{base stock level}$$

$$E[LD] = \text{expected (or mean) demand during the replenishment lead time}$$

$$S - E[LD] = \text{safety stock inventory}$$

$$S^* = \text{optimal base stock level}$$

$$SL^* = \text{optimal service level} = c_s/(c_s + c_e)$$

Finding the Value of S^* in General

Select the quantity S^* that satisfies

$$P[LD \leq S^*] = SL^*$$

If there is no quantity satisfying $P[LD \leq S^*] = SL^*$, then S^* is the smallest value satisfying

$$P[LD \leq S^*] > SL^*$$

Finding the Value of S^* If Unknown Demand Is Approximated by a Uniform Distribution between a and b; That Is, $LD \sim U(a, b)$ and $E[LD] = (a + b)/2$

$$S^* = a + SL^*(b - a) \quad (\text{because } P[LD \leq S] = (S - a)/(b - a))$$

Finding the Value of S^* If Unknown Demand Is Approximated by a Normal Distribution with Mean μ_{LD} and Variance σ_{LD}^2; That Is, $LD \sim N(\mu_{LD}, \sigma_{LD}^2)$

$$S^* = \mu_{LD} + z_{SL^*}\,\sigma_{LD} \quad (\text{because } P[LD \leq S = \mu_{LD} + z_{SL}\sigma_{LD}] = SL)$$

The optimal service level in the cash management example is $SL^* = c_s/(c_s + c_e) = 0.10/(0.10 + 0.05) = 2/3 \approx 66.7$ percent. $SL^* = 2/3$ means that expected excess and shortage costs are minimized when there is a 66.7 percent probability that demand during the lead time is not more than the base stock quantity. Following the approach from Section 2, the determination of base stock consistent with a 66.7 percent service level requires an estimate of the probability distribution of demand during the lead time. For example, if past experience suggests that demand for funds during the lead time of two days is approximately normally distributed with a mean of $\mu_{LD} = 60,000$ and a standard deviation of $\sigma_{LD} = 20,000$, then

$$S^* = \text{optimal base stock} = \mu_{LD} + z^*_{SL}\,\sigma_{LD} = 60,000 + z_{.667} \times 20,000$$

The value of z corresponding to the probability of 66.7 percent can be found in a standard normal probability table (see Appendix 4). As we saw in Section 2, $z_{.6664} = 0.43$ and $z_{.67003} = 0.44$, either of which is fine for the purposes of computing S^*. Using $z_{.6664} = 0.43$,

$$S^* = \mu_{LD} + z^*_{SL}\,\sigma_{LD} \approx 60,000 + 0.43 \times 20,000 = \$68,600$$

FIGURE 7.5
Inventory in the Low-Yield Account over Time with Base Stock Set to \$68,600
Due to demand uncertainty during the lead time, the balance in the low-yield account will sometimes go negative, though the long-run average balance is \$8,600.

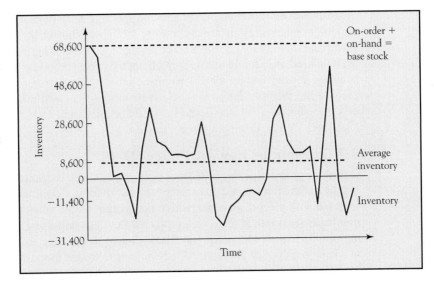

In summary, the optimal base stock level in the low-yield account is \$68,600. Anytime a payment is made out of the low-yield account, a request for a funds transfer from high- to low-yield account in the amount of the payment is simultaneously initiated. The electronic funds transfer takes two days to process, during which an average of \$60,000 will be paid out of the low-yield account (i.e., average demand during the replenishment lead time is $E[LD] = \mu_{LD} = 60,000$). The average balance in the low-yield account is

$$S^* = E[LD] = \text{safety stock} = \text{average inventory} = 68,600 - 60,000 = \$8,600$$

The average balance of \$8,600 is the "safety stock," which is used to protect against the uncertainty of demand during the replenishment lead time (see Figure 7.5).

If instead of a normal distribution, demand during the lead time is more accurately approximated by a uniform distribution between $a = 15,000$ and $b = 105,000$, then

$$S^* = a + SL^*(b - a) = 15,000 + 2/3(105,000 - 15,000) = \$75,000$$

$$E[LD] = \text{expected demand during the lead time}$$

$$= (a + b)/2 = (15,000 + 105,000)/2 = \$60,000$$

$$S^* - E[LD] = \text{safety stock} = \text{average inventory} = 75,000 - 60,000 = \$15,000$$

Example Summary

What should be the base stock level in the low-yield account?
c_e = excess cost rate = \$0.05/\$-yr (i.e., lost interest income)
c_s = shortage cost rate = \$0.10/\$-yr (i.e., net cost of loan interest)
SL^* = optimal service level = $c_s/(c_s + c_e)$ = 2/3 ≈ 0.667
Select base stock quantity S^* so that $P[LD \le S^*] = SL^*$.
   If LD = demand during lead time ~ $N[60,000, 20,000^2]$, then
$S^* = \mu_{LD} + z^*_{SL}\sigma_{LD} = 550 + z_{.667}(150) \approx \$68,600$
If LD = demand during lead time ~ $U[15,000, 105,000]$, then
$S^* = a + SL^*(b - a) = 15,000 + 2/3(105,000 - 15,000) = \$75,000$

It is worth emphasizing that excess and shortage costs of an optimal base stock policy are due to uncertainty in demand during the replenishment lead time. Eliminate uncertainty, and these costs go to zero. For example, consider what happens when there is no delay in electronic funds transfers. With each payment from the low-yield account, there is also a transfer request for the payment amount. The transfer from high- to low-yield account and the payment occur at the same instant (i.e., lead time = 0). There is never a need to maintain a balance in the low-yield account, and all excess cash remains in the high-yield account earning 8 percent interest.

3.2 Continuous Review Policy (Q, R)

One of the problems with a base stock policy is that, unless demand is infrequent, it results in high transaction volume. In many situations, **there is a significant transaction cost associated with placing an order, which means that a base stock policy will often be economically impractical** (e.g., very costly for Levi's to ship a single pair of jeans to a store in response to each individual purchase). Consequently, there are two common variations of a base stock policy in practice. One option is to review inventory every fixed interval of time (e.g., order interval of day, week, or month) and place an order for whatever was sold since the previous order. This is an example of a periodic review policy, which is the topic of Section 3.3. If the length of the order interval is very small (e.g., a few minutes), then the periodic review policy is essentially a base stock policy.

A second option, which provides tighter control of inventory, is known as a **(Q, R) policy; when inventory reaches the reorder point R, an order is placed for Q units.** Thus, the **policy for specifying** *when and how much* **is defined through the two values Q and R, that is, the value of Q answers the question of how much to order and the value of R answers the question of when to order.** A (Q, R) policy also can be interpreted as **ordering Q units whenever a total of Q units of demand has accrued since the last order,** which will bring the inventory position up to Q + R. A (Q, R) policy is a **continuous review policy** because inventory must be continually tracked in order to know when the reorder point is reached. If the value of Q is very small (e.g., Q = 1), then the (Q, R) policy is essentially a base stock policy.

How Can the Values of Q and R Be Set to Minimize Cost?

One simple and **approximate approach for setting the values for Q and R is to treat the selection of Q and R as two independent questions.** Accordingly, the methods of Chapter 6 are used to identify an economic order quantity Q that minimizes the sum of purchase cost, transaction cost, and the average holding cost of cycle stock. And the methods of the previous section are used to identify a reorder point R that results in a service level of $SL^* = c_s/(c_s + c_e)$. While this approach is not optimal, it generally results in a close to optimal solution.[12] The **formulas are listed below.**

Formulas for the Reorder Point Given Q

$$Q = \text{order quantity}$$

$$R = \text{reorder point}$$

$$E[LD] = \text{expected (or mean) demand during the replenishment lead time}$$

$$Q/2 = \text{average cycle stock inventory}$$

$$R - E[LD] = \text{safety stock inventory}$$

$$SL^* = \text{optimal service level} = c_s/(c_s + c_e)$$

[12] Compared to the values of Q and R found using this approach, the optimal Q will be somewhat larger and the optimal R will be somewhat smaller (Zipkin 2000, p. 218)

Finding the Value of *R* in General

Select the quantity *R* that satisfies

$$P[LD \leq R] = SL^*$$

If there is no quantity satisfying $P[LD \leq R] = SL^*$, then *R* is the smallest value satisfying

$$P[LD \leq R] > SL^*$$

Finding the Value of *R* If Unknown Demand Is Approximated by a Uniform Distribution between *a* and *b*; That Is, $LD \sim U(a, b)$ and $E[LD] = (a + b)/2$

$$R = a + SL^*(b - a) \quad (\text{because } P[LD \leq R] = (R - a)/(b - a))$$

Finding the Value of *R* If Unknown Demand Is Approximated by a Normal Distribution with Mean μ_{LD} and Variance σ_{LD}^2; That Is, $LD \sim N(\mu_{LD}, \sigma_{LD}^2)$

$$R = \mu_{LD} + z_{SL}^* \sigma_{LD} \quad (\text{because } P[LD \leq R = \mu_{LD} + z_{SL}\sigma_{LD}] = SL)$$

What Is Fill Rate, and What Is the Relationship between Q, R, and Fill Rate?

The **fill rate** is the proportion of demand shipped on time, or, in the setting of this chapter, the **proportion of demand shipped from inventory**.[13] The concept of a service level was introduced earlier, and sometimes it is difficult to see the **difference between service level and fill rate.** One way to help separate the two in your mind is to think of **service level as a probability** (i.e., service level is the probability of satisfying *all* demand from inventory during some time interval) and **fill rate as a proportion** (i.e., fill rate is the average proportion of demand shipped from inventory).

Here is a numerical example to help clarify the difference. Over the last five years, you've shipped 5 million units, 100,000 of which were backordered. This means that 4,900,000 out of 5,000,000 units were shipped from inventory, and that the fill rate over the last five years is 49/50 = 98 percent. Suppose also that a total of 500 replenishment orders, each for about 10,000 units, were placed during the last five years, and in 400 instances, there were no backorders by the time the replenishment order was received. On the basis of these numbers, we can conclude that there was a 400/500 = 80 percent probability of satisfying all demand during the replenishment lead time and that the service level during the replenishment lead time is 80 percent.

In practice, a shortage cost rate is often difficult to estimate (e.g., imagine estimating the cost if a customer order is backordered for five days, and how this estimate changes if the delay doubles or triples). It usually does not make a lot of sense to optimize the reorder point when using cost rate estimates that could be highly inaccurate. This is one reason why a target fill rate[14] can be more relevant for setting safety stock and reorder point levels than an "optimal" service level. In addition, customers are not particularly concerned with the probability that your firm can satisfy all demand from inventory during the replenishment lead time. Customers are more interested in your firm's overall record of on-time delivery,

---

[13] Different fill rate measures are tracked in industry. For example, the *order fill rate* refers to the proportion of orders shipped on time, whereas the *line item fill rate* is the proportion of line items within orders that are shipped on time.

[14] The particular choice of a target fill rate represents management's judgment on an appropriate balance between concerns for high customer service and low inventory holding costs.

Example Summary

What are the fill rate and service level given that a (Q, R) policy is in effect with Q = 10,000 units?

Demand = 5,000,000 over last five years

Backorders = 100,000 units over last five years

Fill rate = percent of demand shipped on time (not backordered) = 1 − 100,000/5,000,000 = 98 percent

Number of replenishment orders = 500 over last five years

Instances of no backorders during the replenishment lead time = 400 over the last five years

Service level per replenishment cycle = probability of no backorders during replenishment lead time = 400/500 = 80 percent

or fill rate. In short, fill rate is a meaningful and commonly used measure of customer service in practice, which raises the question of how the choices of Q and R influence the fill rate. Let's begin with an example.

Example

Suppose that your firm uses a (Q, R) policy to order cases of shampoo with Q = 50 and R = 10. This means that 50 cases are ordered when there are 10 cases left in inventory. An examination of demand during the replenishment lead time over the last 18 months suggests the following probability distribution:

x	P[LD = x]	P[LD ≤ x]	Number of Units Backordered if LD = x and R = 10
6	8%	8%	0
7	10	18	0
8	12	30	0
9	22	52	0
10	12	64	0
11	14	78	1
12	12	90	2
13	10	100	3

According to the probability table, we can expect a long-run fill rate of 98.6 percent when $Q = 50$ and $R = 10$. Why is this? To answer this question, we'll first determine the expected number of cases backordered when an order of 50 cases arrives. From the probability table, we see that there is a 64 percent chance that demand during the lead time will be 10 cases or less. In other words, if the reorder point is 10 cases, then there is a 64 percent chance that there will be no backorders when the replenishment shipment of 50 cases arrives. However, there is a 14 percent chance that demand will be 11, which means that there is a 14 percent chance that one case will be backordered (i.e., if we start with 10 cases and demand is for 11 cases, then 1 case is backordered). There is also a 12 percent chance that demand will be 12, which means that there is a 12 percent chance that two cases will be backordered (i.e., if we start with 10 cases and demand is for 12 cases, then 2 cases are backordered). Similarly, there is a 10 percent chance that three cases will be backordered. A 64 percent chance of zero backorders, combined with a 14 percent chance of one backorder, a 12 percent chance of two backorders, and a 10 percent chance of three backorders means that the expected (or average) number of cases backordered when the replenishment shipment arrives is

$$E[(LD - 10)^+]^{15} = 0.64(0) + 0.14(1) + 0.12(2) + 0.10(3) = 0.68 \text{ case}$$

Since $R + Q = 10 + 50 = 60 \geq$ maximum possible demand during the lead time, there is no possibility of backorders carrying over to the next replenishment cycle, that is, $E[(LD - 60)^+] = 0$. Thus, the expected number of backorders accumulated during the current replenishment cycle is $E[(LD - 10)^+] - E[(LD - 60)^+] = 0.68$ case. Finally, recall that one interpretation of how a (Q, R) policy answers the questions of when and how much to order is to order Q units whenever a total of Q units of demand has accrued since the last order. When a (Q, R) policy is viewed in this way, it becomes clear that the average demand between placement of orders is Q. Similarly, **the average demand between receipt of orders is Q,** which for this policy is 50. Therefore, for every 50 cases of demand, an average of 0.68 case is backordered. So, the percent of demand backordered is $0.68/50 \approx 1.4$ percent, which means that the fill rate (percent of demand not backordered) is $FR = 1 - 0.68/50 \approx 98.6$ percent.

Example Summary

What is the fill rate given that a (Q, R) policy is in effect with $Q = 50$ cases and $R = 10$ cases?

Average number of units backordered when replenishment shipment of 50 cases arrives = $64\%(0) + 14\%(11 - 10) + 12\%(12 - 10) + 10\%(13 - 10) = 0.68$ case

Average demand between receipt of replenishments = $Q = 50$ cases (i.e., an average of 0.68 case backordered for every 50 cases of demand)

Fill rate = percent of demand shipped on time (not backordered) = $1 - 0.68/50 = 98.6$ percent

---

To recap, we determined the fill rate (FR) from the order quantity (Q), the reorder point (R), and the probability distribution of demand during the lead time ($P[LD \leq x]$). We first computed the expected number of units on backorder when a replenishment shipment arrived ($E[(LD - R)^+]$), then we subtracted the expected number of units on backorder left over from the previous replenishment cycle ($E[(LD - (R + Q))^+]$). The result is the expected number of backorders accumulated during the current replenishment cycle, and since the average demand per replenishment cycle is Q, the average backorder rate is $\{E[(LD - R)^+] - E[(LD - (R + Q))^+]\}/Q$ and the fill rate is $FR = 1 - \{E[(LD - R)^+] - E[(LD - (R + Q))^+]\}/Q$. The **fill rate formulas** are listed below.

Formulas for Fill Rate

Q = order quantity = expected demand between receipt of orders

R = reorder point

FR = fill rate

$E[LD]$ = expected (or mean) demand during the replenishment lead time

$Q/2$ = average cycle stock inventory

$R - E[LD]$ = safety stock inventory

---

[15] $E[(LD - 10)^+]$ refers to the expected value of max $\{0, LD - 10\}$.

$$E[(LD - R)^+] = \text{expected number of units backordered when a replenishment order arrives}$$

$$E[(LD - (R + Q))^+] = \text{expected number of units left over on backorder from the previous replenishment cycle}$$

$$E[(LD - R)^+] - E[(LD - (R + Q))^+] = \text{expected number of units backordered from demand during the current replenishment cycle when a replenishment order arrives}$$

Finding the Value of *FR* in General

$$FR = 1 - \{E[(LD - R)^+] - E[(LD - (R + Q))^+]\}/Q$$

Finding the Value of *FR* If Unknown Demand Is Approximated by a Uniform Distribution between *a* and *b*; That Is, $LD \sim U(a, b)$ and $E[LD] = (a + b)/2$

$$FR = P[LD \leq R + Q/2] = (R + Q/2 - a)/(b - a) \quad \text{if } R + Q \leq b$$

$$FR = 1 - P[LD > R](b - R)/2Q = 1 - (b - R)^2/[2Q(b - a)] \quad \text{if } R + Q \geq b$$
$$\text{(because } E[(LD - x)^+] = 1/2(b - x)^2/(b - a))$$

Finding the Value of *FR* If Unknown Demand Is Approximated by a Normal Distribution with Mean μ_{LD} and Variance σ_{LD}^2; That Is, $LD \sim N(\mu_{LD}, \sigma_{LD}^2)$

$$FR = 1 - [G(z_1) - G(z_2)]\sigma LD/Q^{16}$$

where

$z_1 = (R - \mu_{LD})/\sigma_{LD}$

$z_2 = (R + Q - \mu_{LD})/\sigma_{LD}$

(because $E[(LD - x)^+] = \sigma_{LD}G[(x - \mu_{LD})/\sigma_{LD}]$)

$G(z)$ *is the right linear loss integral of a standard normal distribution* (a.k.a. unit normal loss function; a table of $G(z)$ values can be found in Appendix 4). Linear loss integrals arise in a variety of applications, and we'll look at a couple of quick examples to help make the meaning more concrete. Suppose that the probability distribution of the random variable X is the standard normal distribution (i.e., X is normally distributed with $\mu_X = 0$, $\sigma_X = 1$). Then $G(2) = E[(X - 2)^+]$ is the expected value of max$\{0, X - 2\}$. This means that the average number of backorders at the end of a day is $G(2) = 0.0085$ if I began the day with two units in stock and demand followed a standard normal distribution. Alternatively, for those who have been exposed to option pricing, suppose it's September and you believe the stock price of a firm in early October is normally distributed[17] with a mean of 79 and a standard deviation of 10 (note that $85 = 79 + 0.6 \times 10$). Then, ignoring transaction costs and dividend announcements, the future value of an October call option with a strike price of 85 is $G(0.6) \times 10 \approx \$1.69$.

Example

It's Saturday morning and you are working through some quick analysis in preparation for Monday's meeting. One of the agenda items is a discussion of the appropriate increase in inventory investment for the upcoming holiday/Valentine season—a length of time spanning September through the first part of February when most perfume sales occur. A decision needs to be made soon so that alternatives for raising capital can be evaluated and pursued. The inventory investment in perfume products during this critical time last year was about $10 million. Due to a number of factors, including the bankruptcy of a competing firm, perfume volume during the upcoming holiday/Valentine season is expected to be about 50 percent higher than last year. The current proposal is to increase inventory investment by 50 percent, or $5 million.

[16] A common approximation given in texts is $FR = 1 - G(z_1)\sigma_{LD}/Q$. The approximation is usually quite good, especially when Q is large relative to the demand during the lead time.

[17] A lognormal distribution is the more typical assumption.

The 3.4-ounce bottle of Angelica Varum (AV) perfume comes to mind as a representative product for analysis. This product has demand and replenishment lead time characteristics in the mid-range of the over 5,000 different perfume products that your firm distributes, and, consequently, the percentage increase in inventory for this product should be roughly representative of the overall increase in perfume product inventory.

You are able to access information on this and other products from your firm's ERP database via the Internet. AV is shipped in boxes containing 24 bottles from the Kalina plant in Nikolaev, Ukraine. Replenishment lead time is four weeks and the average demand rate during last year's holiday/Valentine season was 250 boxes per week. While orders for this product were often combined with other Kalina products from the Nikolaev plant, the data show that each order included 750 boxes of AV ($Q = 750$) and AV inventory at the time of order was consistently close to 1,050 boxes ($R = 1,050$). The fill rate for AV, as well as for all perfumes combined, averaged about 80 percent during last year's holiday season, which is 10 points below your firm's fill rate target of 90 percent.

You begin by assessing the increase in inventory necessary to raise the fill rate to 90 percent assuming no increase in demand. The impact of a higher demand rate will be considered later. Examination of the data suggests that demand during the replenishment lead time is approximately normally distributed with mean $\mu_{LD} = 1,000$ and $\sigma_{LD} = 440$. Plugging the numbers into the fill rate formula yields

$$z_1 = (R - \mu_{LD})/\sigma_{LD} = (1,050 - 1,000)/440 \approx 0.11$$

$$z_2 = (R + Q - \mu_{LD})/\sigma_{LD} = (1,050 + 750 - 1,000)/440 \approx 1.82$$

$$FR = 1 - [G(z_1) - G(z_2)]\sigma_{LD}/Q \approx 1 - [G(0.11) - G(1.82)](440)/750$$

The value of $G(z) = E[(LD - z)^+]$ is the expected number of backorders with a reorder point of z when the probability distribution of demand during the lead time is a standard normal distribution. Appendix 4 contains a table of $G(z)$ values.[18] According to Appendix 4, $G(0.11) = 0.34635$ and $G(1.82) = 0.01357$, so

$$FR \approx 1 - [G(0.11) - G(1.82)](440)/750 = 1 - [0.34635 - 0.01357](440)/750 \approx 80.5 \text{ percent}$$

This is a good sign—the fill rate predicted by the model for AV is close to last year's actual fill rate of 80 percent. While not conclusive, it is an indicator that the model may be reasonable for estimating the percentage increase in inventory to bring the fill rate up to 90 percent, and to accommodate the projected increase in volume.

The fill rate can be computed for a few trial values to find a reorder point associated with a fill rate close to 90 percent. For example, at $R = 1,250$,

$$FR = 1 - [G(z_1) - G(z_2)]\sigma_{LD}/Q \approx 1 - [G(0.57) - G(2.27)](440)/750 \approx 89.9 \text{ percent}$$

Average inventory is the sum of average cycle stock and safety stock, or $Q/2 + (R - E[LD])$.[19] According to the model, at $R = 1,050$,

$$\text{Average inventory} = Q/2 + (R - E[LD]) = 750/2 + (1,050 - 1,000) = 425$$

---

[18] $G(z)$ also can be computed using the NORMDIST function in Excel; that is, $G(z) = \text{NORMDIST}(z,0,1,0) - z \times [1 - \text{NORMDIST}(z,0,1,1)]$.

[19] Technically, average inventory understates inventory investment because of our convention of treating backorders as negative inventory in the average inventory calculation. A more precise analysis requires computing the average nonnegative inventory, which is $Q/2 + (R - E[LD])$ + average number of units on backorder. This level of detail is not critical for our purposes of quick analysis to gauge the required increase in inventory investment.

which is close to the actual average inventory as reported in the database. At $R = 1,250$,

$$\text{Average inventory} = Q/2 + (R - E[LD]) = 750/2 + (1,250 - 1,000) = 625$$

which is about 47 percent more than the average inventory at $R = 1,050$. In other words, analysis suggests that inventory investment would need to increase by nearly 50 percent to raise the fill rate from 80 percent to 90 percent, and this is with no increase in volume!

Example Summary

How much should inventory increase in order to raise the fill rate from 80 to 90 percent?

μ_{LD} = mean demand during lead time = 1,000 cases

σ_{LD} = standard deviation in demand during lead time = 440 cases

FILL RATE WITH $(Q, R) = $ (750 CASES, 1,050 CASES)

$z_1 = (R - \mu_{LD})/\sigma_{LD} = (1,050 - 1,000)/440 \approx 0.11$

$z_2 = (R + Q - \mu_{LD})/\sigma_{LD} = (1,050 + 750 - 1,000)/440 \approx 1.82$

$FR = 1 - [G(z_1) - G(z_2)] \; \sigma_{LD}/Q \approx 80.5 \, \text{percent}$

Average inventory $\approx Q/2 + (R - E[LD]) = 750/2 + (1,050 - 1,000) = 425$

FILL RATE WITH $(Q, R) = $ (750 CASES, 1,250 CASES)

$z_1 = (R - \mu_{LD})/\sigma_{LD} = (1,250 - 1,000)/440 \approx 0.57$

$z_2 = (R + Q - \mu_{LD})/\sigma_{LD} = (1,250 + 750 - 1,000)/440 \approx 2.27$

$FR = 1 - [G(z_1) - G(z_2)] = \sigma_{LD}/Q \approx 89.9 \, \text{percent}$

Average inventory $\approx Q/2 + (R - E[LD]) = 750/2 + (1,250 - 1,000) = 625$

Inventory increase = $625/425 - 1 \approx 47$ percent

Accounting for the 50 percent increase in volume will push the percentage increase in inventory investment higher. If demand during the lead time is normally distributed, then

$$\text{Average inventory} = Q/2 + (R - E[LD]) = Q/2 + z_1\sigma_{LD}$$

In Chapter 6 we saw that the economic order quantity increases with the square root of the demand rate; this means that Q (and $Q/2$) should increase by $1.5^{1/2} - 1 \approx 22$ percent. Two observations are relevant for assessing the percentage increase in safety stock $z_1\sigma_{LD}$.

1. Under appropriate assumptions relating to independent random demands, the increase in the standard deviation σ_{LD} is proportional to the square root of the increase in the mean demand rate; that is, σ_{LD} increases by $1.5^{1/2} - 1 \approx 22$ percent. In this case, the ratio σ_{LD}/Q stays constant as the demand rate increases, and since the backorder rate[20] $\approx G(z_1)\sigma_{LD}/Q$ should remain fixed at 10 percent as volume increases, the value of $G(z_1)$, and thus the value of z_1, should remain approximately unchanged. If z_1 is unchanged and σ_{LD} increases by about 22 percent, then safety stock $z_1\sigma_{LD}$ increases by about 22 percent.

2. If independence assumptions don't hold, then the standard deviation σ_{LD} will increase by at least 22 percent, though not more than 50 percent. In turn, the value σ_{LD}/Q gets larger as demand increases, and in order to keep the backorder rate fixed at 10 percent $\approx$ $G(z_1)\sigma_{LD}/Q$, the value of z_1 also gets larger (to make $G(z_1)$ smaller). As a result, safety stock $z_1\sigma_{LD}$ increases by more than 22 percent.

---

[20] The expression $G(z_1)\sigma_{LD}/Q$ is generally a close approximation to the exact expression for the backorder rate given by $[G(z_1) - G(z_2)]\sigma_{LD}/Q$.

From 1 and 2, we see that in order to maintain a stable fill rate as demand increases, safety stock needs to increase by at least the square root of the increase in demand. The bottom line: (1) average inventory will need to increase by at least 22 percent to accommodate a 50 percent increase in volume with no change in fill rate. (2) A 47 percent increase in inventory is necessary to raise the fill rate from 80 percent to 90 percent with no increase in volume. (3) The targeted increase in inventory investment for the upcoming year should be at least $1.47(1.22) - 1 \approx 80$ percent, or $8 million. This analysis alone may not be enough to finalize the decision on capital requirements, but probably is enough to be wary of the recommended 50 percent increase.

Example Summary

How much should inventory increase if demand increases by 50%?

CHANGE IN CYCLE STOCK WHEN Q IS BASED ON EOQ-ANALYSIS

Average cycle stock = $Q/2$

EOQ is proportional to the square root of volume (see Chapter 6) $\Rightarrow (1.5)^{1/2} \approx 1.22 \Rightarrow$ order quantity and cycle stock increase by about 22 percent

CHANGE IN SAFETY STOCK

Safety stock = $R - E[LD] = z_1\sigma_{LD}$ (from $z_1 = (R - \mu_{LD})/\sigma_{LD}$ and $E[LD] = \mu_{LD}$)

σ_{LD} is approximately proportional to the square root of volume (this is an example of the law of large numbers; the relationship is described in detail in Chapter 11) $\Rightarrow (1.5)^{1/2} \approx 1.22 \Rightarrow \sigma_{LD}$ increases by about 22 percent

CHANGE IN INVENTORY

Average inventory = average cycle stock + safety stock

Average inventory should increase by about 22 percent when demand increases by 50 percent

To accommodate the 10-point increase in fill rate and the 50 percent increase in volume, average inventory should increase by about $1.47(1.22) - 1 \approx 80$ percent

---

The underlying question of the previous example is not hypothetical. A number of years ago, Lands' End faced a similar question. About 70 percent of Lands' End sales occur during the holiday season. The firm was considering how much additional inventory investment should be authorized for the upcoming holiday season given a target fill rate of 90 percent. The decision was not inconsequential because each 10 percent increase in inventory required a $20 million investment and the holiday season largely determines annual performance.

What Can Be Said about the Relationship between Fill Rate and Safety Stock?

Perhaps the single most important idea concerns the **increasingly high investment in safety stock required to increase fill rate by one percentage point as the fill rate gets high** (see Figure 7.6). We saw some evidence of this in the example where a fivefold increase in safety stock ($50 \rightarrow 250$) was required to increase fill rate from 80 percent to 90 percent. This insight **tends to hold true in general** (i.e., is not limited to (Q, R) policies), and it is a reason why firms typically do not set a target fill rate at 100 percent.

3.3 Periodic Review Policy (I, S)

A **periodic review policy may be used when inventory is not continuously monitored, or when multiple products from a single supplier are ordered together.** One common

FIGURE 7.6
**Illustration of
Required Level of
Safety Stock for
Various Fill Rates**
The plot is based on
a (Q, R) policy with
$Q = 750$. The demand
during lead time is
normally distributed
with a mean of 1,000
and a standard deviation
of 440.

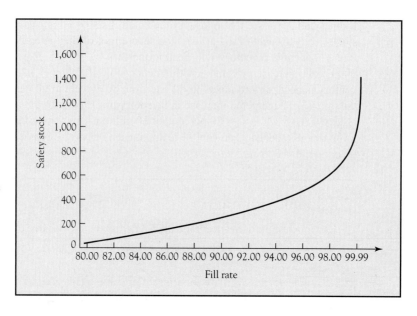

type of periodic review policy is defined by the choices for an *order interval I* and an
order-up-to quantity *S*. Inventory is checked every *I* periods, and the difference between
S and the current inventory position is ordered. For example, consider a vending machine
where all products are stocked to capacity every Monday; for each product, $I = 7$ days and
S = number of units that can fit in the machine.

For an (I, S) policy, the **value of *I* answers the question of when to order** and the **value
of *S* is used to answer the question of how much to order.** If the order interval is very
small (e.g., $I = 1$ minute), then an (I, S) policy is essentially a base stock policy where the
value of *S* is the base stock level.

In addition to understanding how an (I, S) policy works, there are two other lessons of
this section. First, the analysis of the previous section applies to an (I, S) policy with minor
modifications. We will see that the expressions governing the relationships between policy
parameters, service level, and fill rate are similar to those in Section 3.2. Second, other
things being equal, an (I, S) policy requires more inventory than a (Q, R) policy.

How Can the Values of I and S Be Set to Minimize Cost?

One simple and **approximate approach for setting the values for *I* and *S* is to treat the
selection of *I* and *S* as two independent questions.** Accordingly, the methods of Chapter
6 are used to identify an economic order quantity Q that minimizes the sum of purchase
cost, transaction cost, and the average holding cost of cycle stock. The order interval can
be set so that the average demand between orders is equal to the economic order quantity;
that is, $I = Q/\mu_D$ where μ_D = mean demand per period. The methods of the previous two
sections are used to identify an order-up-to quantity *S* that results in a service level of
$SL^* = c_s/(c_s + c_e)$. **The formulas are listed below.**

Formulas for the Order-up-to Quantity Given I

$$I = \text{order interval}$$
$$S = \text{order-up-to quantity}$$
$$E[ILD] = \text{expected (or mean) demand during the replenishment lead time plus}$$
$$\text{order interval}$$

$$Q/2 = \text{average cycle stock inventory}$$
$$S - E[ILD] = \text{safety stock inventory}$$
$$SL^* = \text{optimal service level} = c_s/(c_s + c_e)$$

Finding the Value of S in General

Select the quantity S that satisfies

$$P[ILD \leq S] = SL^*$$

If there is no quantity satisfying $P[ILD \leq S] = SL^*$, then S is the smallest value satisfying

$$P[ILD \leq S] > SL^*$$

Finding the Value of S If Unknown Demand Is Approximated by a Uniform Distribution between *a* and *b*; That Is, *ILD* ~ *U*(*a*, *b*) and *E*[*ILD*] = (*a* + *b*)/2

$$S = a + SL^*(b - a) \quad (\text{because } P[ILD \leq S] = (S - a)/(b - a))$$

Finding the Value of S If Unknown Demand Is Approximated by a Normal Distribution with Mean μ_{ILD} and Variance σ^2_{ILD}; That Is, *ILD* ~ $N(\mu_{ILD}, \sigma^2_{ILD})$

$$S = \mu_{ILD} + z^*_{SL}\sigma_{ILD} \quad (\text{because } P[ILD \leq S = \mu_{ILD} + z_{SL}\sigma_{ILD}] = SL)$$

What Is the Relationship between I, S, and Fill Rate?

The **formulas are similar to the formulas for the (Q, R) policy, and are listed below.**

Formulas for Fill Rate

$$I = \text{order interval}$$
$$S = \text{order-up-to quantity}$$
$$\mu_D = \text{mean demand per period}$$
$$I \times \mu_D = \text{average order quantity}$$
$$FR = \text{fill rate}$$

$E[LD] =$ expected (or mean) demand during the replenishment lead time

$E[ILD] =$ expected (or mean) demand during the replenishment lead time plus order interval

$$I \times \mu_D/2 = \text{average cycle stock inventory}$$
$$S - E[ILD] = \text{safety stock inventory}$$

$E[(ILD - S)^+] =$ expected number of units backordered when a replenishment order arrives

$E[(LD - S)^+] =$ expected number of units left over on backorder from the previous replenishment cycle

$E[(ILD - S)^+] - E[(LD - S)^+] =$ expected number of units backordered from demand during the current replenishment cycle when a replenishment order arrives

Finding the Value of FR in General

$$FR = 1 - \{E[(ILD - S)^+] - E[(LD - S)^+]\}/(I \times \mu_D)$$

Finding the Value of *FR* If Unknown Demand Is Approximated by Normal Distributions; That Is, *ILD* ~ $N(\mu_{ILD}, \sigma^2_{ILD})$ and *LD* ~ $N(\mu_{LD}, \sigma^2_{LD})$

$$FR = 1 - [G(z_1) - G(z_2)]\sigma_{ILD}/(I \times \mu_D)^{21}$$

where

$z_1 = (S - \mu_{ILD})/\sigma_{ILD}$

$z_2 = (S - \mu_{LD})/\sigma_{LD}$

Why Does an (I, S) Policy Require a Larger Inventory Investment Than a (Q, R) Policy, Other Things Being Equal?

A (Q, R) policy continuously monitors inventory. An order is triggered at the instant that inventory hits the reorder point R. A stockout occurs if the demand during the lead time is more than the reorder point. The level of safety stock in a (Q, R) policy protects against uncertainty in demand during the lead time.

An (I, S) policy only considers the possibility of placing a replenishment order every I periods. Each order brings the inventory position up to S, and associated with each order is the possibility of a stockout. In particular, a stockout occurs if the demand during the lead time plus the order interval is more than S. The level of safety stock in an (I, S) policy protects against uncertainty in demand during the lead time plus the order interval.

Intuitively, a continuous review policy is more responsive than a periodic review policy, and so it is not surprising that a (Q, R) policy can provide tighter inventory control than an (I, S) policy. The difference boils down to the length of time that each policy is exposed to uncertainty in demand. **While an (I, S) policy requires more inventory than a (Q, R) policy, this disadvantage may be offset by the advantages of a routine schedule for delivery of orders** (e.g., multiple products being ordered from a single supplier and shipped together).

4. REDUCING DEMAND UNCERTAINTY

The costs of inventory in the form of expenses and poor customer service are significant for many organizations. Step one is to make sure that the choice of policy is appropriate for your firm's supply chain environment and that the choices for policy parameters are sensible. This step, which is the focus of the previous sections, requires relatively little time and dollar investment to execute, and consequently is an attractive starting point for improvement. Assuming effective policies are in place and periodically tuned as necessary, the challenge is to continually identify, select, and implement new ways of doing business that affect more fundamental improvements, for example, lower uncertainty in demand. This challenge is the focus of this section. In particular, we'll review first a simple tool discussed in earlier chapters that stems from a principle of nature called the **Pareto phenomenon: the lion's share of the statistic's value is determined by relatively few elements.** Second, we'll consider how to estimate the impact on inventory and fill rate from an investment that reduces demand uncertainty.

What Lessons Does the Pareto Phenomenon Have for Investments to Reduce Demand Uncertainty?

As a manager you will be charged with setting direction and identifying opportunities for investment. In the context of investments to reduce uncertainty in demand, you know from the Pareto phenomenon that investments in certain suppliers and/or products will be more

---

[21] A common approximation given in texts is $FR = 1 - G(z_1)\sigma_{LD}/(I \times \mu_D)$. The approximation is usually quite good, especially when I is large relative to the replenishment lead time.

Principle of Nature: Pareto Phenomenon

DEFINITION

The lion's share of an aggregate measure is determined by relatively few factors.

IMPLICATION

Invest time and energy to identify a few factors that drive performance and focus attention and resources on these. The process of separating the "important few" from the "trivial many" is known as *Pareto analysis*.

EXAMPLE

Amana, an appliance maker, has used a tactic they call ABC scheduling that works like this. First the product line is stratified according to importance. "A" items are the high-volume products; they tend to be the most popular models at each price point. "B" items are of moderate volume and "C" items are the dogs. "A" items are produced every month, "B" items are produced about once per quarter, and "C" items are produced once every six months. In this example, "A" items are most critical for the business and thus warrant close synchronization with the market.

profitable than others. **Pareto analysis, which is the process of separating the "important few" from the "trivial many,"** is a simple tool that can be useful for quickly identifying promising candidates for consideration. For example, Dataram, a company that produces computer memory devices, conducted Pareto analysis of their raw materials. First, management collected data on average weekly purchase cost of all purchased materials. Next, they identified those materials with average weekly purchase cost of more than $40 and deemed these to be the critical parts (i.e., the A items). Dataram then invested money and effort to reduce demand uncertainty of the A items.

In the Dataram example, the aggregate measure of total raw material cost per period was stratified by the contribution of each purchased part (i.e., in order to identify those parts warranting more management attention). Alternatively, as discussed in Chapter 5, Pareto analysis could be used to stratify total material expense by supplier and stratify profit contribution by customer, typically to identify the most promising candidates for closer collaboration.

How Can the Impact of Reduced Demand Uncertainty on Inventory and/or Fill Rate Be Estimated?

The main source of high inventory cost and/or poor customer service discussed in this chapter is demand uncertainty, and there are a host of investments in tactics and technologies that reduce demand uncertainty (e.g., postponement, leadtime reduction, VMI, CPFR). Evaluating the attractiveness of alternative investments requires estimates of the reduction of demand uncertainty and the subsequent impact on inventory and customer service. We'll look at some **quick analysis for gauging the impact of reducing demand uncertainty on safety stock and customer service.** The analysis largely draws on the results in the previous sections, and relies on three assumptions.

A1. The probability distribution of demand during a period (D) is reasonably approximated by a normal distribution with mean μ_D and standard deviation σ_D, that is, $D \sim N(\mu_D, \sigma_D)$.

A2. The probability distribution of the replenishment leadtime (L) is reasonably approximated by a normal distribution with mean μ_L and standard deviation σ_L, that is, $L \sim N(\mu_L, \sigma_L)$.

Principle of Nature: Central Limit Theorem

DEFINITION
As the number of independent random variables increases, the probability distribution of the sum approaches the normal distribution.

IMPLICATION
Random measures of interest are often comprised of many approximately independent random components. In such cases, analysis of uncertainty based on the normal distribution is a good approximation.

EXAMPLE
Cineval LLC is a media-consulting firm that develops valuations of film investments. Their data on profits from 28 live-action films shows a wide range of performance with a sizable percentage of the films incurring losses or miniscule profits, and a random scattering of increasingly profitable films up to a single extraordinarily successful film. But a different picture, in the shape of a bell curve, appears when the distribution of average profit from multiple randomly selected films is plotted. As predicted by the central limit theorem, the distribution of profit approaches normal as one diversifies across additional films, and this phenomenon is incorporated into Cineval's valuation methods. Interestingly, Cineval also finds evidence of another principle of nature. Their data suggest that "the chance of losing your shirt drops from about 20% with a single film to about 1% with four films" (Savage 2003). Why is this? It's because of the law of large numbers; the uncertainty in the valuation per film is lower with a group of four films than for a single film. According to the president of Cineval, it requires decades of experience for some people to learn that.

A3. The random variables D and L are independent of each other, and demand in a period is independent of demand in the previous period.

The first two assumptions tend to be reasonable in practice due to a principle of nature known as the **central limit theorem** (CLT); that is, **as more independent random elements are added together, the probability distribution of the resulting sum approaches a normal distribution.** Both demand and lead time are typically a composite of many random variables, which provides some evidence that the CLT will play a role. Demand in a period can be viewed as the sum of the random demands of individual customers. Replenishment lead time can be viewed as the sum of multiple elementary random tasks (e.g., load into truck, drive to port, load on ship, transport by ocean, etc.). The independence of demand over time (or across customers), while perhaps less tenable, simplifies the analysis and interpretation of results, and is suitable for our purposes of quickly gauging impact and promoting insight.

The forecast for demand per period is the mean demand rate μ_D. The standard deviation is a measure of the uncertainty in the forecast. The following **formulas show how changes in μ_D, $\sigma_D, \mu_L, \sigma_L$, and policy parameters affect forecast uncertainty, safety stock, and fill rate.**

Formulas for the Impact of Reducing Demand Uncertainty

D = demand during a period (e.g., one day), which is uncertain (i.e., D is a random variable)

L = replenishment lead time

LD = demand during the replenishment lead time

ILD = demand during the order interval plus replenishment lead time

$D \sim N(\mu_D, \sigma_D)$

$$L \sim N(\mu_L, \sigma_L)$$

$$LD \sim N(\mu_{LD}, \sigma_{LD}), \text{ where } \mu_{LD} = \mu_L\mu_D \text{ and } \sigma_{LD} = [\mu_L\sigma_D^2 + \mu_D^2\sigma_L^2]^{1/2}$$

$$I + L \sim N(\mu_{IL}, \sigma_{IL}), \text{ where } \mu_{IL} = I + \mu_L \text{ and } \sigma_{IL} = \sigma_L$$

$$ILD \sim N(\mu_{ILD}, \sigma_{ILD}), \text{ where } \mu_{ILD} = (I + \mu_L)\mu_D \text{ and } \sigma_{ILD} = [(I + \mu_L)\sigma_D^2 + \mu_D^2\sigma_L^2]^{1/2}$$

For a (Q, R) Policy

$$\text{Safety stock} = z_1\sigma_{LD}$$

$$\text{Backorder rate} = [G(z_1) - G(z_2)]\sigma_{LD}/Q$$

$$\approx G(z_1)\sigma_{LD}/Q$$

where

$$z_1 = (R - \mu_{LD})/\sigma_{LD}$$
$$z_2 = (R + Q - \mu_{LD})/\sigma_{LD}$$

$$FR = 1 - \text{backorder rate}$$

For an (I, S) Policy

$$\text{Safety stock} = z_1\sigma_{ILD}$$

$$\text{Backorder rate} = [G(z_1) - G(z_2)]\sigma_{ILD}/(I \times \mu_D)$$

$$\approx G(z_1)\sigma_{ILD}/(I \times \mu_D)$$

where

$$z_1 = (S - \mu_{ILD})/\sigma_{ILD}$$
$$z_2 = (S - \mu_{LD})/\sigma_{LD}$$

$$FR = 1 - \text{backorder rate}$$

The formulas show how a reduction in demand uncertainty translates into lower safety stock and/or a lower backorder rate. For example, if z_1 remains unchanged as σ_{LD} (or σ_{ILD}) is reduced, then the percentage reduction in σ_{LD} (or σ_{ILD}) is also the percentage reduction in safety stock $z_1\sigma_{LD}$ (or $z_1\sigma_{ILD}$) and the approximate percentage reduction in the backorder rate $G(z_1)\sigma_{LD}/Q$ (or $G(z_1)\sigma_{ILD}/(I \times \mu_D)$). More generally, the formulas can be used to evaluate the impact of specific improvement initiatives.

Example

Suppose that a (Q, R) policy is in effect with $Q = 750$ units, $R = 1{,}250$ units, $\mu_D = 250$ units per week, $\sigma_D = 220$ units per week, $\mu_L = 4$ weeks, and $\sigma_L = 0$ weeks. The value of $\sigma_L = 0$ weeks means that the replenishment lead time is constant at $\mu_L = 4$ weeks. Your firm is considering an investment opportunity that is expected to cut the replenishment lead time in half. The current value of σ_{LD} is $\sigma_{LD} = [\mu_L\sigma_D^2 + \mu_D^2\sigma_L^2]^{1/2} = [\mu_L\sigma_D^2 + \mu_D^2 \times 0]^{1/2} = (\mu_L)^{1/2}\sigma_D$. If μ_L is cut in half, then the new value of σ_{LD} is $\sigma_{LD} = (\mu_L/2)^{1/2}\sigma_D$, or about $1 - 1/2^{1/2} \approx 29$ percent lower than the current value. If z_1 is unchanged, then the reduction in lead time results in about a 29 percent reduction in safety stock and backorder rate; that is, lower inventory holding cost and better customer service. The formulas can be used to evaluate other possibilities for impact on safety stock and fill rate. For example, if the safety stock remains at the current level of 250, then cutting the lead time in half causes the fill rate to increase from about 90 percent to about 95 percent. Alternatively, if the fill rate remains at the current level of about 90 percent, then cutting the lead time in half causes safety stock to reduce by about 54 percent from 250 to 115.

Example Summary

Impact of 50 percent reduction in replenishment lead time? When a $(Q, R) = (750, 1,250)$ policy is in effect,

μ_D = average demand = 250 units per week

σ_D = standard deviation in demand = 220 units per week

μ_L = current average lead time = 4 weeks

σ_L = standard deviation in lead time = 0 weeks

σ_{LD} = standard deviation in demand during the lead time = $[\mu_L \sigma_D^2 + \mu_D^2 \sigma_L^2]^{1/2}$
    $= (4)^{1/2}(220)$

If μ_L is reduced by 50 percent, then $\sigma_{LD} = (2)^{1/2}(220)$ and is reduced by $1 - (1/2)^{1/2} \approx$ 29 percent.

If σ_{LD} is reduced by 29 percent, then

(a) leaving inventory investment unchanged, fill rate increases from 90 percent to 95 percent, or

(b) leaving fill rate unchanged, safety stock is reduced by 54 percent.

5. SUMMARY AND MANAGERIAL INSIGHTS

Chapter 6 dealt with a fundamental economic trade-off that stems from transaction costs. This chapter builds on Chapter 6 by considering a second fundamental economic trade-off, but one that stems from uncertainty. Both of these trade-offs are central to managing inventories and are widespread in other application areas.

In this chapter, we have seen how basic marginal analysis led to a simple ratio for balancing shortage and excess costs in the face of uncertainty, and we saw applications of this ratio in order quantity decisions and in safety stock levels. We learned about different pull policies for answering when and how much to order, and how choices for policy parameters impact measures of performance. Finally, we studied the relationship between measures of performance and environmental characteristics such as lead time and demand uncertainty—a relationship that supports analysis of alternative improvement initiatives. Key managerial insights from the chapter are summarized below.

5.1. The Optimal Service Level Is the Shortage Cost Rate Divided by the Sum of the Shortage and Excess Cost Rates

Example 1

When returning home after a summer vacation, I was offered $200 if I would give up my seat (if necessary) and fly on a later flight.[22] US Airways had sold 11 more plane tickets than they had seats. Suppose US Airways plans to overbook their flights so that 67 percent of the time there are enough no-shows that they don't need to get volunteers to give up their seats. If this is the case, we can deduce that the company considers it to be less expensive to fly with an empty seat

[22] As a side note, we can thank Ralph Nader for the inducements that airlines offer passengers to surrender their seats. A gate agent refused to let Nader board a flight from Washington to Connecticut. His subsequent 1972 lawsuit prompted a ruling that airlines must seek volunteers to give up their seats before bumping anyone.

("shortage cost") than to reimburse someone for the hassle of giving up their seat ("excess cost"). More precisely, US Airways is estimating shortage cost to be twice excess cost (i.e., $2x/(1x + 2x)$ = 67 percent). (For the curious, I did volunteer to get bumped, and even made plans on how to spend the money. In the end, I didn't collect $200 because there were plenty of no-shows.)

Example 2 (Fisher et al. 1994.) The contribution margin for a Sport Obermeyer Pandora Parka is $14.50 and any unsold jackets left over at the end of the season are sold for $5.00 less than cost. Accordingly, Sport Obermeyer estimates excess and shortage costs for their Pandora Parka to be $5.00 and $14.50, respectively. For this reason, they attempt to make enough Pandora Parkas for the upcoming season so there is a 74 percent chance they will have enough to satisfy all demand (i.e., $14.50/(14.50 + 5.00) \approx 74$ percent).

Example 3 Insight 5.1 is based on a fundamental property. From a civil engineering perspective, SL^* is the percentage of the way through a horizontal beam that you would want to place a vertical support so that the sum of the left and right moments of force are as small as possible (c_e and c_s are density measures). From a financial perspective, the formula can be used to deduce the market-perceived probability distribution of a stock price 30 days from now using only prices of put and call options. I suspect there are creative and profitable applications of this insight that have yet to be discovered.

Example 4 While both the property and analysis underlying insight 5.1 have wide application, it is important to not focus so intensely on technical analysis as to ignore psychological considerations, especially when human perceptions play a role. For example, suppose you own a large restaurant with the costly problem of customers not showing up for their reservation. One option is to apply principles of the single-period model to develop guidelines for how much to overbook when accepting reservations. However, another way to look at the problem is how to get customers to honor their reservation. Gordan Sinclair is an owner of a Chicago restaurant that was suffering from the common problem of no-shows. He solved the problem with one minor change in the conversation with a customer reserving a table. The request "Please call if you have to change your plans" was replaced with a question, "Will you please call if you have to change your plans?" followed by a pause to wait for an answer. The pause was critical because it forced the customer to make a public commitment, and public commitments have a notable effect on future action (Cialdini 2001).

Example 5 If you purchase fresh bread (or other perishable product) from a retailer who always seems to be in-stock, even when you arrive late in the day, then you are probably paying a high markup over cost. For example, if the retailer purchases at cost c and sells at price p and the product has no value at the end of the period, then $1 - SL^* = 1 - (p - c)/p = c/p$ = probability of stockout. In other words, if the probability of stockout (c/p) is low, then cost (c) is low relative to selling price (p).

5.2. Reducing Demand Uncertainty Leads to Reduced Inventory Investment and Better Customer Service

Example 1 For normally distributed demand: (1) In the single-period model, the expected loss in profit due to excess and shortage costs is proportional to σ_D, and the expected lost sales due to insufficient supply is proportional to σ_D. (2) For a (Q, R) policy, safety stock and the backorder rate are proportional to σ_{LD}. (3) For an (I, S) policy, safety stock and the backorder rate are proportional to σ_{ILD}.

Example 2 One of the drivers of growth in SCM software is that it can help provide a clearer view of what's going on in the market and consequently lead to reduced market uncertainty. Reduced inventory holding costs typically make up the largest line item in the savings used to justify the investment in SCM software.

5.3. Each Percentage Point Increase in Fill Rate Requires an Increasing Incremental Investment in Inventory

Example An order placed at Lands' End is viewed to be on time if it is shipped within 24 hours of when the order is placed. In the interest of great customer service, Lands' End would naturally like to maintain a fill rate of 100 percent (i.e., 100 percent of all orders shipped within one day), yet the firm uses a lower fill rate target as a matter of policy. They recognize that a 100 percent fill rate would be prohibitively expensive, and the target fill rate is set to strike a reasonable balance between inventory costs and the cost of delayed shipments.

6. EXERCISES

1. Write a brief answer to each of the chapter keys in your own words. After writing down your answers, review the chapter with a focus on the content in bold to check and clarify your interpretations.

2. Suppose you want to sell pumpkins as a fundraiser. You buy pumpkins from a local farmer for $0.85 each and sell them for $2. The extra pumpkins can only be smashed in celebration and therefore have no salvage value. Determine the optimal service level and order quantity if demand is uniformly distributed between 250 and 400 pumpkins, and if demand is normally distributed with mean of 300 and variance of 25.

3. As luck would have it, the American Medical Association publishes a study that finds pumpkin bread reduces cholesterol 60 percent more than oat bran. You decide to go into the pumpkin business permanently and apply a base stock policy for managing your inventory. You maintain the same deal with the local farmer, but you now incur a 30 percent annual holding cost and are charged a $0.10 premium per week for each pumpkin back-ordered. Finally, demand during lead time for your pumpkins is 40 to 55 units. In contrast with the previous problem where no sale could be made if you didn't have a pumpkin, people will place an order with you and come back later when you have pumpkins available (the customer is reasonably understanding because of your policy of marking down the cost of the pumpkin by $0.10 for each week the customer had to wait). Calculate your base stock level given that demand during lead time is approximated by a discrete uniform distribution (i.e., each of the values 40, 41, 42, . . . , 55 is equally likely).

4. An independent wholesaler uses a base stock policy for ordering switching devices. Once an order is placed, an average of 140 units (uniformly distributed in integer quantities between 100 and 180) are shipped before the order arrives. The cost is $120 per switch and the annual holding cost rate is estimated at 30 percent. In addition, the wholesaler estimates the per-month shortage cost for a backordered unit to be $12.50.

   a. Suggest a base stock level for this item.

   b. Suppose that an (I, S) policy is used. The order interval I is one week and the replenishment lead time is one week. Demand during the order interval plus lead time (ILD) is normally distributed with mean $\mu_{ILD} = 280$ and standard deviation $\sigma_{ILD} = 65$. Demand during the lead time (LD) is normally distributed with mean $\mu_{LD} = 140$ and standard deviation $\sigma_{LD} = 45$. What is the fill rate if the order-up-to quantity is $S = 300$? What is the service level if the order-up-to quantity is $S = 300$ (i.e., the probability that demand during $I + L$ is not more than 300)?

5. Demand during the lead time is estimated to follow a normal distribution with mean 450 and standard deviation 120. A (Q, R) policy is used, and the order quantity Q is 1,000.

   a. What is the fill rate and what is the service level (i.e., $P[LD \leq R]$) if the reorder point $R = 475$?

   b. What reorder point is consistent with a fill rate of 98 percent? The approximation $FR = 1 - G(z_1)\sigma_{LD}/Q$ may be used to answer this question.

6. HG's Clothes sells a large number of white dress shirts. The shirts, which bear the store label, are shipped from a manufacturer in New York City. Hi, the proprietor, says:

"I want to be sure that I never run out of dress shirts. I always try to keep at least two months' supply in stock. When my inventory drops below that level, I order another two-month supply. I've been using that method for 20 years and it works!" The shirts cost $8.00 each and sell for $25 each. The cost of processing an order and receiving new goods amounts to $80 and the replenishment lead time is one month. Monthly demand is approximately normally distributed with mean 120 and standard deviation 60. Assume a 15 percent annual holding cost rate.

a. What values of Q and R is Hi using to control the inventory of white dress shirts?

b. What fill rate is being achieved with the current policy?

c. Determine an alternative economic (Q, R) policy based on the 99 percent fill rate criterion. The approximation $FR = 1 - G(z_1)\sigma_{LD}/Q$ may be used to answer this question.

d. Determine the difference in annual holding and ordering costs between the policies in a and c.

e. Estimate how much time would be required to pay for a $25,000 inventory control system, assuming that dress shirts represent 5 percent of Hi's business and similar savings could be realized on other items as well.

7. This and the following three problems are identical or are variations of problems developed by Linus Schrage. All Sinners Hospital Pharmacy stocks a highly unstable serum that is used to treat a certain illness. At the beginning of each week, the pharmacy must decide how much serum to order for the week. Assume the pharmacy cannot reorder during the week. A vial of serum costs $1.50. Because the serum is not stable, it is unusable after one week. Since it is potentially dangerous at this time (if someone tried to use it), state law requires careful disposal. This costs the pharmacy $0.10 a vial. Finally, the director of the pharmacy feels that the illness is serious enough that there should be a cost of $7.50 per unit assigned to being out of the serum when a patient needs it. Pharmacy records show that on the average, the distribution of demand is

Number of vials	Probability
0	0.03
1	0.14
2	0.36
3	0.19
4	0.11
5	0.09
6	0.06
7	0.02

How many vials should the pharmacy stock?

8. GorillaHardware produces semiconductors for a variety of applications. A photoreactive polymer (a photoresist) is first applied to the wafer's surface and exposed, and then the circuits are etched. Later, the excess photoresist is removed by dipping the wafer in sulfuric acid and rinsing in water. (GorillaHardware goes through about six million gallons of water each day.) To speed drying, wafers are then bathed in isopropyl alcohol. The sulfuric acid has a shelf life of only three months. GorillaHardware estimates that they will need between 100,000 and 300,000 gallons of acid for the next three-month period and assumes that all values in this interval are equally likely. The acid costs $150 per gallon when purchased in bulk from an overseas supplier. The company assumes a 20 percent annual interest rate for the money it has invested in inventory, and the acid costs the company $35 per gallon to store for three months. (Assume that all inventory costs are assessed on acid that remains after the three-month period.)

Acid left over must be disposed at a cost of $75 per gallon. If the company runs out of acid, they can quickly purchase emergency supplies for $600 per gallon.

a. How many gallons of nitric acid should GorillaHardware purchase?

b. It is discovered that acid demand is closer to a normal distribution with mean 280,000 and standard deviation 48,000. How many gallons of nitric acid should GorillaHardware purchase?

c. After review of the previous results, it is determined that a 94 percent fill rate criterion be used (i.e., on average, 94 percent of the acid requirements should be met from the original order). How many gallons of nitric acid should GorillaHardware purchase?

9. The Hewart Howes Tool Company (HHTC) of Tripoli stocks drill bits for supply to local well-drilling companies. The demand for bits is somewhat random; however, over a year, the total demand is a fairly predictable 2,000 bits. The fixed cost of placing an order for a shipment from the manufacturer in Texas is $160. The holding cost per year of a drill bit is $4. HHTC will not intentionally stock out because, in that case, the buyer will immediately go elsewhere. What HHTC does in this case is quickly buy an extra bit from a local supplier at an excess cost of $16 per bit. The reason that stockouts may occur is that delivery lead time is nontrivial and demand during the lead time is random. In fact, past records show that the average demand that occurs after an order is placed to Texas but before it is received is 80 bits with a standard deviation of 10 (assume distribution of demand is approximately normal). Specify a (Q, R) policy satisfying a 98 percent fill rate. The approximation $FR = 1 - G(z_1)\sigma_{LD}/Q$ may be used to answer this question.

10. The Glen Ford automobile agency has the opportunity to place one more order for this season's autos before next year's models are introduced. The cost per car is $7,000 and the selling price is $10,000. Any autos not sold before the introduction of the new models are sold at a loss for $6,800. The demand for the current cars between now and the introduction of the new models is judged to be uniformly distributed over the interval [11, 20]. Cars sold now will not affect demand for next year's models. Glenn currently has several cars in stock. How many cars should be ordered? Suppose that there is a fixed cost of $1,725 to place an order. How will this affect your decision (e.g., order any and, if so, how many)?

11. Average annual demand for a new product is forecasted to be 5,000 units. It costs $57 to replenish inventory, 25 percent of unit cost to carry the inventory, and $300 to purchase each unit. The demand during lead time is estimated to follow a normal distribution with a mean of 50 units and a standard deviation of 12. The reorder point is 54.

a. How would you define fill rate?

b. What is an estimate of fill rate in this situation? (*Hint:* You first must determine the order quantity.)

c. What is an estimate of the fill rate if the order quantity is tripled, and why does it increase?

12. Demand is 1,200 units per year. Whenever an order is placed, it is for 100 units. Based on historical performance, a reorder point of 80 units results in an average of 3.2 units backordered by the time the order arrives and a reorder point of 200 units results in an average of 0.8 unit backordered by the time the order arrives. Select the reorder point (80 or 200) that is most compatible with a target fill rate of 99 percent.

13. Demand in a period is equally likely to be 10, 15, or 20. Each unit costs $1.00, is sold for $1.80, and has a salvage value of −$0.20 (i.e., it costs $0.20 to dispose of each excess unit).

    a. How many units should be ordered?

    b. What is the range of salvage values if the optimal order quantity is 20?

14. This question was prepared by Paul Bobrowski. A large automobile service center specializes in selling oil by the quart to customers who change their automobile's oil at home. The manager orders 850 quarts per order from the distributor; the oil distributor requires a one-week lead time for deliveries to the service center. Demand during the week follows a normal distribution with a mean of 400 quarts of motor oil and a standard deviation of 100 quarts. The service center prides itself on customer service so the manager desires to maintain a 99 percent fill rate. The manager is utilizing a (Q, R) policy for stocking this item. What reorder point is consistent with a 99 percent fill rate? The approximation $FR = 1 - G(z_1)\sigma_{LD}/Q$ may be used to answer this question.

15. Determine the fill rate given an order quantity of 25,000, and reorder point of 12,000, and the following probability distribution of demand during the lead time (LD):

x	$P[LD = x]$
10,000	10%
11,000	12
12,000	33
13,000	28
14,000	17

16. It's late Saturday night in Las Vegas and you're pumped because the NCAA men's basketball championship will take place this Monday evening. During a walk around town a few hours earlier, you came across an opportunity to bet on total points scored, though the odds for betting high are different from the odds of betting low. The bookie has set the line at 180.5 total points with a 2-to-1 payoff for betting high and a 1-to-2 payoff for betting low. For example, if you bet $100 high and 181 or more points are scored, then you win $200, and if 180 or fewer points are scored, then you lose $100. Alternatively, if you bet $100 low and 180 or fewer points are scored, then you win $50, and if 181 or more points are scored, then you lose $100. If the high and low odds were even, then the decision of how to bet would be simple: bet high if you feel more than 180 points will be scored and bet low otherwise. In this case, it may be smart to bet high even if you think that 180 or fewer will be scored. As an expert on the two teams, you estimate that there is an 80 percent chance that 180 or fewer points will be scored.

    a. Determine whether it is better to bet high or low, and provide analysis to justify your decision.

    b. Generalize your analysis in part (a) to develop a simple rule of thumb for how to bet in these types of games where the odds for betting high are H-to-L and the odds for betting low are L-to-H. Your rule of thumb should allow you to almost instantly determine whether it is better to bet high or low given H, L, and the line.

17. Consider a (Q, R) policy when demand during lead time is uniformly distributed between a and b, that is, $LD \sim U(a, b)$. Show that

$$FR = P[LD \leq R + Q/2] = (R + Q/2 - a)/(b - a) \quad \text{if } R + Q \leq b$$

$$FR = 1 - P[LD > R](b - R)/2Q = 1 - (b - R)^2/[2Q(b - a)] \quad \text{if } R + Q \geq b$$

    Hints: $FR = 1 - \{E[(LD - R)^+] - E[(LD - (R + Q))^+]\}/Q$ and $E[(LD - x)^+]$
    $= 1/2(b - x)^2/(b - a)$.

18. VF and County Seat use a continuous replenishment system where VF is responsible for managing the inventory of VF product at County Seat. Every evening, County Seat sends VF the number of items sold of VF product during the day. At the end of the week, VF uses this sales information to determine the appropriate replenishment amount. The shipment is sent out Saturday morning and arrives at County Seat on the following Tuesday morning. VF and County Seat management use a target fill rate of 95 percent for the mainstream VF products (i.e., type A products) and VF is considering the appropriate increase in safety stock levels in County Seat stores for the upcoming holiday season.

    Focus on one SKU that is considered to be a mainstream product—the size 32/32 Wrangler jean. Average weekly demand during the holiday season for this product at a representative store is expected to double from 11.5 to 23 pairs, and the uncertainty in demand over a 10-day period (as measured by standard deviation) is expected to increase by 60 percent from the currently level of 8.05. Assuming no change in the 95 percent target fill rate, what is the estimated percentage increase in safety stock for the upcoming holiday season? Assume that demand is normally distributed and use the approximate fill rate expression.

19. The future is now. A massive fusion reactor located outside of New York City generates the country's power supply. A single link network creates a powerful, yet harmless, *superelectro* field that provides electrical power without wires (e.g., no more plugs). A tunnel connecting New York City to Los Angeles contains a massive cable that acts as a field generator. Ten pickup stations are located above the 3,000-mile tunnel (see diagram below). These pickup stations receive power from the reactor via a satellite transmission, amplify it, then circulate it along the cable 100 miles in the easterly direction and 200 miles in the westerly direction. The field is sustained by circulating about 400 gigawatts per linear mile on an annual basis. Annual fixed operating cost of a pickup station is $2 billion. The cost to circulate power increases with distance from the pickup station; in particular, annual cost is $1,000 per gigawatt-mile in the easterly direction and, due to unfavorable effects associated with earth's rotation, $8,700 per gigawatt-mile in the westerly direction.

    As noted above, each pickup station currently circulates power over a 300-mile distance and is located 100 miles from its eastern boundary. You suspect that this may not be particularly cost-effective. At what mile mark from the eastern boundary should the pickup station be located to minimize circulation cost? What is the annual savings associated with your recommendation?

    Hints: This cost structure is identical to the shortage and excess cost trade-off that we saw in the EOQ model with backorders, the single-period model, the base stock model, and the (Q, R) and (I, S) policies.

Case Exercise: *KKY Clothiers*[23]

As long as she can remember, KK Yuen has been interested in the clothing industry. This interest led to a business opportunity, sparked by a chance when, at age 19, she and Pojjaman Soorangura were assigned as roommates at National University of Singapore. Pojjaman's family owns and operates

Pha Thai Textile in Chiang Mai, Thailand, which produces garments for Benetton and Gap, among others. KK's business started on a small scale, with weekend trips to purchase from garment manufacturers for resale to university students. By the time she had graduated, KK had developed business

[23] This case exercise has benefited from the experience and comments of Amanda Nicholson.

relationships with seven suppliers and made enough money to open her own clothing shop in downtown Singapore. That was three years ago. Today she owns and operates four stores in Singapore.

KK faces many business challenges, not the least of which is ordering and pricing of fashion products. The peach-colored silk evening dress is a good example. Fashion news suggests that peach may be a hot color in the upcoming season, but there is a lot of uncertainty. KK must order the dress before the season begins, and it is unlikely that she will be able to order more during the season. Of course, the size of the order will be influenced by how she decides to price the product.

Questions

1. The purchase cost per dress is $c = \$79.95$ (in Singapore dollars). KK is considering two different selling price points: $99.95 and $119.95. She has a policy of sticking with the initial selling price throughout the selling season, after which time she sells the leftover product to a liquidator.[24] At selling price $p = \$99.95$, she estimates expected demand during the selling season to be 150. In order to account for uncertainty, she estimates that demand $D_{99.95}$ could be anywhere between 60 and 240, with each value equally likely; that is, $D_{99.95} \sim U[60, 240]$ and $E[D_{99.95}] = 150$. Alternatively, at selling price $p = \$119.95$, she estimates that demand $D_{119.95}$ is uniformly distributed between 10 and 190, which means that expected demand at $p = \$119.95$ is 100; that is, $D_{119.95} \sim U[10, 190]$ and $E[D_{119.95}] = (10 + 190)/2 = 100$. KK can sell unsold dresses at the end of the selling season to a liquidator for $s = \$19.95$ per dress. Given a choice of pricing at either $99.95 or $119.95, what price do you recommend and how many dresses should be ordered? Would your recommendation change if price could be any value in the range of $99.95 to $119.95?[25]

   Hints: (1) The expected profit when $D_p \sim U(a_p, b_p)$ is

   $$E[D_p] \times (p - c) - 1/2\{(c - s)(Q - a_p)P[D_p \leq Q] + (p - c)(b_p - Q)P[D_p > Q]\}$$

   (2) For the purposes of estimating demand at other prices, you may assume a linear price-expected demand relationship and a range of 180. For example, since $E[D_{99.95}] = 150$ and $E[D_{119.95}] = 100$, a price increase of $20 causes expected demand to decrease by 50, and since the relationship is linear, a price increase of $10 causes expected demand to decrease by 25; that is, $E[D_{109.95}] = 125$. The

range is 180, or 90 below and above the expected value, so $D_{109.95} \sim U[35, 215]$.

2. KK is familiar with the practice of markdown money in the apparel industry. Markdown money refers to a payment from seller to buyer to cover part of the loss when merchandise has to be marked down in order to sell. In 2004, for example, the department store Nordstrom received almost $48 million in markdown money, or more than 12 percent of net income (Kratz 2005).

   A contract that includes a provision for markdown money is an example of a buyback contract (see Chapter 5). The practice can potentially benefit all parties, including the consumer; the availability of markdown money encourages the retailer to place larger orders, which leads to higher sales (and fewer out-of-stocks) and potentially higher profit for the retailer and supplier.

   KK's business is relatively small, and she is not in a strong position to demand markdown money from her suppliers. On the other hand, she may be able to convince a supplier to offer markdown money if she can show that the supplier should benefit. Consider the impact of a markdown money contract where the supplier pays a fixed percentage of the markdown, and consider two possible percentages—15 percent and 30 percent (e.g., at 15 percent, the supplier pays KK 15 percent of the difference between start-of-the-season selling price and the liquidator price for each leftover garment). For each of these two possibilities, what is the percentage increase in order volume (which is also the increase in supplier sales revenue) and what is the percentage increase in expected retailer profit relative to the alternative of no markdown money? Suppose that the supplier's contribution margin is 50 percent. For each markdown money percentage (i.e., 15 percent and 30 percent), what is the percentage change in expected supplier profit? Why might a supplier be wary of a markdown money contract even if calculations show that the supplier should be better off in the long run?[26] You may use the data on the peach dress for the purpose of answering these questions.

   Hints: (1) From KK's perspective, the effect of markdown money is equivalent to increasing the price she gets from the liquidator (e.g., if she gets $10 in markdown money per leftover unit, then her expected profit is the same as receiving no markdown money and selling to the liquidator at $19.95 + $10 = $29.95 instead of $19.95). (2) The expected supplier profit is the product of units sold to KK and the profit per dress, less

---

[24] Her past experiments of periodically lowering the price of slow-moving product during the selling season led her to suspect that shoppers were holding off on purchases until she lowered her price. This is why she no longer lowers the price during the season, but one consequence is that the initial pricing decision is quite important (i.e., can significantly impact profit).

[25] For psychological reasons, KK always sets prices as $__.95. Accordingly, throughout your analysis of this case exercise, you may limit consideration to prices that end in 0.95, for example, 99.95, 100.95, and so forth.

[26] At least one good reason can be found in Kratz (2005).

the expected markdown money payment to KK. There are a number of approaches that could be used to compute the expected markdown money payment. One option is to compute KK's expected profit with the markdown money, then compute KK's expected profit (given no change in the order quantity) without the markdown money. The difference is the expected markdown money payment. Alternatively, $E[\text{markdown money payment}] = 1/2m(p - s)(Q - a_p)P[D_p \le Q]$, where m = markdown money as a percentage of the markdown and s = markdown selling price (i.e., s is the liquidator price in this case).

3. KK is beginning to have second thoughts about selling her leftover product to a liquidator. She originally chose to use a liquidator because of simplicity and market separation. The use of a liquidator is a simpler option because KK doesn't have to sell the leftover product herself and she is able to dispose of all leftover product (and receive the cash) immediately after the selling season. Market separation refers to the distinct market segments served by KK and the liquidator; there is little risk of a KK customer realizing that a product he/she wants could possibly be purchased at a lower price by delaying the purchase until a later time. On the other hand, she believes that the average price for leftover product will be significantly higher if she sells it herself.

Just as it happened seven years ago, the genesis for a potential new business opportunity can be traced to Pojjaman Soorangura. Pojjaman recently left a consulting firm to join her family's business. Pha Thai Textile is one of KK's largest suppliers, and she regularly makes trips to Chiang Mai. During her last visit, she and Pojjaman talked about the possibility of opening a clothing store in Chiang Mai. The store would sell KK's leftover product, as well as other products.

KK would like to estimate her increase in profits if she sells leftovers at a store in Chiang Mai instead of selling to the liquidator. If leftover product remains unsold after six weeks, she can sell it to a liquidator at that time, though at a lower price than what she could get if she sold to a liquidator immediately after the selling season.

One key to estimating the increase in expected profit from selling leftovers in Chiang Mai is to determine how leftover product will be priced, and, ultimately, her expected revenue per leftover product as it depends on the leftover quantity.[27] In general, the larger the quantity of leftovers, the lower the price in the Chiang Mai store (e.g., with a lot of product, it takes a lower price to move it).

The data on the peach-colored silk dress can be used as a basis for estimating the profit impact associated with opening a "clearance store" in Chiang Mai. At price $p2 = \$29.95$, KK estimates expected Chiang Mai demand

$D2_{29.95}$ to be 150. And she estimates that demand $D2_{29.95}$ could be anywhere between 100 and 200, with each value equally likely; that is, $D2_{29.95} \sim U[100, 200]$ and $E[D2_{29.95}] = 150$. Alternatively, at selling price $p2 = \$49.95$, she estimates that demand $D2_{49.95}$ is uniformly distributed between 50 and 150, which means that expected demand at $p2 = \$49.95$ is 100; that is, $D2_{49.95} \sim U[50, 150]$ and $E[D2_{49.95}] = (50 + 150)/2 = 100$. KK thinks she can sell unsold dresses at the Chiang Mai store to a liquidator for a price of $s2 = \$9.95$ (i.e., \$10 less than if she sold to a liquidator immediately after removing the product from her Singapore stores).

What price do you recommend for the peach-colored silk dress in the Chiang Mai store if there are $Q2 = 10$ dresses to be sold (i.e., 10 unsold dresses from the Singapore stores), and what is the expected revenue per dress? What price do you recommend for the peach-colored silk dress in the Chiang Mai store if there are $Q2 = 60$ dresses to be sold (i.e., 60 unsold dresses from the Singapore stores), and what is the expected revenue per dress? What is the percentage increase in expected gross profit if KK sells leftovers at a store in Chiang Mai, relative to current practice of selling unsold Singapore merchandise through a liquidator? Even if the estimated percentage increase in expected gross profit is positive and significant, what other factors should KK consider before going forward with the option?

Hints: (1) The expected Chiang Mai revenue when $D2_{p2} \sim U(a2_{p2}, b2_{p2})$ and $Q2$ dresses are available for sale is

$$Q2 \times \left\{ p2\left(1 - \frac{E[(Q2 - D2_{p2})^+]}{Q2}\right) + s2\left(\frac{E[(Q2 - D2_{p2})^+]}{Q2}\right)\right\}$$

$$= Q2 \times s(Q2)$$

where

$$E[(Q2 - D2_{p2})^+] = \begin{cases} \dfrac{(Q2 - a2_{p2})^2}{2d2}, & Q2 \ge a2_{p2} \\ 0, & Q2 \le a2_{p2} \end{cases}$$

= expected number of leftover dresses at the Chiang Mai store that are sold to a liquidator at price $s2$, $d2 = b2_p - a2_p$ = the range of demand (i.e., $d2 = 100$ is used for the above figures). The term in brackets is the expected Chiang Mai revenue per unit (i.e., salvage value function), which is denoted above by the function $s(Q2)$. The value of $\left(1 - \dfrac{E[(Q2 - D2_{p2})^+]}{Q2}\right)$ is the expected fraction of units sold in the Chiang Mai store at price p2; the value of $\dfrac{E[(Q2 - D2_{p2})^+]}{Q2}$ is the expected fraction of units sold to the

---

[27] KK plans to follow the same pricing policy that she uses in her Singapore stores—the price will remain fixed for about six weeks, and anything left over at that time will be sold to a liquidator.

liquidator at price $s2$. The above expressions can be used to find a selling price $p2$ that maximizes expected revenue for any given value of $Q2$. (2) You may use the optimal expected revenue per unit at two quantities, say, $Q2 = 10$ and $Q2 = 60$, as a basis for a linear approximation of the expected salvage value function; for example,

Optimal expected Chiang Mai revenue per unit = $s(Q2) \approx AQ2 + B$

where

$$A = \frac{s(60) - s(10)}{50}$$

$$B = s(10) - 10A^{28}$$

(3) The expected profit when $D_p \sim U(a_p, b_p)$ and $s(Q2)$ is approximated by $AQ2 + B$ is

$E[D_p] \times (p - c) - 1/2\{(c - B)(Q - a_p)P[D_p \leq Q] + (p - c)(b_p - Q)P[D_p > Q]\} + 1/3 A(Q - a_p)^2 P[D_p \leq Q].$

4. Pojjaman's consulting experience took her all over the world, and included engagements with Harrod's in London and Nordstrom in Seattle. During KK's visit to Chiang Mai, Pojjaman described how these stores, among others, run brief end-of-season clearance sales a few times per year. While there are risks of some consumers holding off purchases near the end of a season in anticipation of impending markdowns, the practice also offers a number of benefits in the form of increased consumer loyalty, access to a different market segment, and increased sales of the new full-priced line. For example, the store may initially run a special one- or two-day "silent sale" during off-hours for which the best customers receive invitations. Clearance pricing is significant (e.g., 50 percent off). The combination of significant savings and the first opportunity to buy helps build customer loyalty among the store's most profitable customers. The clearance sale is then widely publicized, and can attract more cost-conscious consumers who do not normally shop at the store. Full-priced product sales get a boost because the clearance sale, which generates a lot of in-store traffic, is timed to coincide with the start of a new season when the new product line is prominently on display.

KK would like to get a sense of the profit impact of running a one-week end-of-season 50-percent-off clearance sale,[29] and, more specifically, whether the percentage increase in profit should be significantly more or less than the Chiang Mai option. While she could always run an end-of-season clearance sale before shipping leftovers to Chiang Mai (i.e., both options in effect), for the purposes of this question, you may assume that any leftover product will be sold to a liquidator.

What is the projected percentage change in profit with the clearance sale option relative to KK's current practice? Discuss the advantages and disadvantages of the three end-of-season options (i.e., current, Chiang Mai, Singapore clearance sale). Which of these three options do you recommend, and why? Should KK consider another alternative or alternatives, and, if so, what and why?

The percentage increase in profit associated with the peach-colored silk dress should be approximately representative of KK's overall profit increase. The relationships between clearance demand and clearance price from question 3 can be used here. As in question 1, you may assume that KK can sell unsold dresses at the end of the clearance sale to a liquidator for $19.95 per dress. Note that the end-of-season clearance price in Singapore is 50 percent of the full price.

---

[28] By evaluating the expected revenue per unit at other quantities, you will see that the function is close to linear over a fairly wide range of $Q2$ values.

[29] KK would run the clearance sale at the largest of her four stores, which is located near the university.

Chapter **Eight**

Capacity Management: Analysis and Psychology

Chapter Outline

1. Analysis
   - *1.1. Deterministic Capacity Analysis*
   - *1.2. Queueing Model Analysis*
   - *1.3. Computer Simulation Analysis*

2. Psychology

3. A Word on Block Scheduling

4. Summary and Managerial Insights
   - *4.1. Average Inventory = Throughput Rate × Average Flowtime*
   - *4.2. Average Flowtime Skyrockets As Resource Utilization Gets Close to 100 Percent*
   - *4.3. Variance Causes Congestion; As Variance in Interarrival Times and/or Processing Times Increases, Average Flowtime Increases*
   - *4.4. Reduce Congestion and Improve Efficiency by Taking Advantage of the Law of Large Numbers, for Example, through Cross-Training and Other Tactics*
   - *4.5. Customer Satisfaction Depends Both on Perceptions and Expectations, Both of Which Can Be Influenced by Management*
   - *4.6. People Are More Sensitive to Small Losses Than Small Gains; Work Hard to Avoid a Negative First Impression*
   - *4.7. Perceived Time Slows to a Crawl When People Are Bored; Look for Ways to Engage, Entertain, and, More Generally, Reduce Awareness of Time by Your Customers While They Wait*

5. Exercises
   Case Exercise: EPR Scientific A
   Case Exercise: EPR Scientific B

Chapter Keys

1. What are three areas to consider when improving flowtime performance?

2. What are three options for capacity analysis, and their pros and cons?

3. How does deterministic capacity analysis work?

4. What are the assumptions of the $M/M/1$ and $M/D/1$ models, and how are these models applied?

5. How are principles from the psychology of capacity management related to prospect theory?

6. How does block scheduling work, and when is it appropriate?

7. What do the following principles of nature mean and how are they relevant for capacity management: Little's law, Khintchine limit theorem, curse of variability, curse of utilization, law of large numbers, satisfaction = perception − expectation, it's hard to play catch-up ball, time distortion.
8. What are the managerial insights from the chapter?

We have recently passed the midpoint of tools and principles that make up Part Two of this book, so it is a good time to step back to briefly consider where we have been and what remains. Figure 8.1 illustrates five basic supply chain activities—buy, make, move, store, and sell. We began with *sell,* or demand management (Chapter 4), an activity that drives other supply chain activities and thus is a natural place to start. We followed this up by reversing the perspective, from sell to *buy,* with Chapter 5 on supply management. The focus then shifted to *store* with two chapters on inventory management.

Two supply chain activities remain. This chapter on capacity management is the first of two chapters that center on *make.* Whether "making" a service or a product, there are questions of how to (1) determine appropriate capacity levels and (2) effectively use available capacity. Section 1 of this chapter addresses the first question, and Sections 2 and 3 focus on the effective use of available capacity in a service environment. Chapter 9 continues this theme of how to effectively use available capacity, but in production environment. We'll see that some concepts in Chapter 9 are relevant in a wide variety of "production" settings including, for example, the processing of insurance quotes or bank deposits.

Chapter 10 on transportation management covers the last remaining activity—*move.* Chapter 11 covers quality management, which is a topic that is relevant for all five supply chain activities. Chapter 11 completes Part Two of this book. Part Three shifts to synthesis and takes a strategic orientation. Just as in chess, it can be difficult to evaluate, appreciate, and execute alternative strategies when new to the game. The material in Parts Two and Three provides a foundation for supply chain strategy, which is the topic of the final chapter of the book. In addition to coverage of strategic frameworks, Chapter 12 recaps the role of tools and principles in devising and executing supply chain improvement. Now for the topic at hand.

Here's the Challenge

You would like to decide whether or how to change a system where flowtime is an important consideration. For example, maybe you're thinking about

- How many tollbooths should be built at a toll stop on a new highway.
- Whether to purchase a low-speed stamping machine or the more expensive faster machine.
- How to reduce complaints about delays in baggage claim at an airport.
- How many maitre'd's to employ at the local pub.

FIGURE 8.1

A supply chain with emphasis on capacity management links.

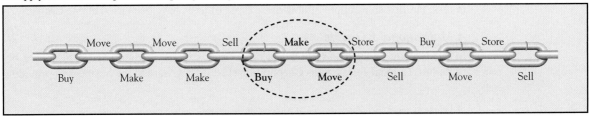

Basic Areas for Improvement

Before considering specifics, let's step back and consider basic areas for change. You could make changes to the **service process** (e.g., add more workers or machines, cross-train the workforce, install RFID readers at the checkout registers), the **arrival process** (e.g., implement a reservation system at your restaurant, offer discounts during periods of slow demand), or the **waiting process.** The last area is sometimes overlooked, yet it can be the area of highest payback. Changes to the waiting process often involve influencing perceptions, and this is where an understanding of psychology comes into play.

We'll begin in Section 1 by examining tools for analyzing and assessing the impact of changes to the arrival and/or service processes. The emphasis is on tools that are (1) simple and easy to apply and (2) useful for gaining insight into how environmental factors and design choices impact performance. The main objective is to lay a foundation for understanding the complex interplay between demand rate, level of capacity, variation in demand, variation in the service/production process, and measures of performance such as flowtime and congestion. While the tools will be largely discussed in the context of simple single-stage service/production systems, the tools and concepts can be applied to understand the behavior of more complicated multistage systems.[1]

Whereas Section 1 pursues insight for managing capacity through analysis methods, Section 2 pursues insight for managing capacity through an understanding of psychology. We'll examine several psychological principles, and, in so doing, we'll see how an understanding of human nature is useful for managing capacity in a service environment. Finally, in Section 3, we'll briefly look at the pros and cons of a particular type of appointment system.

1. ANALYSIS

Suppose you have some ideas for change in the service and/or arrival process. In some cases, especially if you have lots of experience or the changes are simple and cheap to implement, there is no need for any analysis—simply try it out and see how it works. In other cases, it's worthwhile to get a sense of the impact ahead of time. A steel company, for example, was considering whether or not to build a third unloading dock at a port they owned and operated. With a new plant coming on line within six months, they expected their requirements of 250 shiploads of iron ore per year to double to about 500. It takes 24 hours to unload ore from a ship, and a new dock will cost about $12 million. On the other hand, if the docks are full, the company has to pay a daily charter rate of $3,000 while a ship is anchored in the bay waiting for an open dock. The question is, will the reduced charter fees due to reduced wait time be sufficient to justify a $12 million investment in a new dock?

There are **three basic options for analyzing the impact of design ideas. Deterministic capacity analysis** is very simple and quick but is also very limited in the types of questions it can answer and in the restrictive assumptions upon which it is based. **Queueing models** take a little more time but can answer more questions and are based on less restrictive assumptions. **Computer simulation** is an analysis tool that tends to be the most time consuming but is also the most flexible and comprehensive. We'll consider each analysis tool in turn, but first an example of how these types of tools have been used at one company.

A Motivational Example

In 1983, Doug Samuelson (1999) and three friends founded Micro Zeit, which later became International Telesystems Corporation (ITC). They were in the business of providing

---

[1] For example, see the case exercises at the end of the chapter.

outbound call services, and a computer-based outbound dialing system invented by Samuelson was a key competitive advantage. These systems, which are used in telemarketing, debt collection, and fund-raising, automatically dial and connect those who answer to a live sales representative. Sometimes someone answers when no representative is available, in which case, the system will hang up.[2] Here's the basic problem as outlined by Samuelson:

> If all we wanted was to keep the representatives as busy as possible, we could simply dial every available line all the time. This, however, would result in larger numbers of abandoned calls. Most call-center managers want to keep abandoned calls under 5% of completed calls; some insist that they want no abandoned calls at all. We could ensure no abandoned calls by dialing one line per idle representative, and only for idle representatives, but this typically results in keeping representatives busy less than 40 minutes per hour. Most call-center managers insist on 50 minutes per hour and would prefer more than 55.

Samuelson's invention is a method that accurately determines when a new call could be made. The method uses a queueing model that is tuned using computer simulation. Here are the results:

- Traditional computer-based outbound dialing systems generally kept representatives busy about 35 to 40 minutes per hour and generated between 5 and 10 percent abandoned calls. ITC's system, which was called Smart-Pace, kept representatives busy between 50 and 55 minutes per hour with fewer than 2 percent abandoned calls.

- Smart-Pace became the most talked-about development in the industry for about a year after its introduction.

- A few large competitors who didn't adopt the new system weren't able to keep up and went out of business.

- Legal council estimates the value of Samuelson's invention (which has been patented) to be between $1 million and $2 million, just as intellectual property.

- In terms of the effect on business, ITC estimates the value of Smart-Pace could be as high as $20 million.

- EIS International, a major player in the market and an ITC competitor, bought ITC in 1993 for $12 million.

The example illustrates how an understanding of the types of tools in Sections 1.2 and 1.3 led to an effective automatic dialing system. In addition to relating to the topic at hand, the example is noteworthy because it illustrates how money can be made without a lot of capital, but from simply being smarter about the way things are done. In this same vein, automatic dialing systems can be beat with a little cleverness and minimal capital. The following suggestion appeared in McManus (2002), and the key is knowing that these systems automatically hang up when detecting the three-note tone before the message "we're sorry, the number you have reached has been disconnected." How can you take advantage of this knowledge? One

[2] If you ever received a call between 5 p.m. and 7 p.m. on a weekday, picked up the phone, and no one was on the line, then there's a fair chance the call was dialed by a computer-based telephone dialing system at a call center. The proportion of call attempts answered typically quadruples around dinnertime on weekdays—call centers know this is the prime time to call if they want to get hold of you.

alternative is to search for the file sit.wav on the Internet, which is an audio file containing the three tones. You can edit out the second and third tones using an application such as Microsoft Sound Recorder, then record the tone at the start of your answering machine's message. If an automatic dialing system calls and gets your answering machine, it will detect the tone, perceive your number as invalid, hang up, and drop your number from the telemarketer's database. On the other hand, if you're into verbal jousting, you may wish to use telemarketer tactics to take control of the conversation; see www.xs4all.nl/~egbg/counterscript.html for one suggestion on how to do this.

1.1 Deterministic Capacity Analysis

Deterministic capacity analysis is a simple tool for quickly getting a rough idea on the amount of resources necessary to support a given level of demand. It is best explained through examples.

Example 1

Suppose you are trying to decide how many tollbooths should be built at a toll stop on a new highway. About 300 cars per hour should be passing through the tolls during the busy times, and it takes an average of 20 seconds to exchange money at a booth. What do you think? According to deterministic capacity analysis, you'll need at least two booths. Let's see how. The **main idea is to compare the capacity of a server with the demand rate.** If it takes 20 seconds for a car to pull into the booth area, exchange money, and take off, then a tollbooth can handle three cars per minute (60 seconds per minute ÷ 20 seconds per car = 3 cars per minute). A capacity of the three cars per minute can be restated as a capacity of 180 cars per hour (60 minutes per hour × 3 cars per minute = 180 cars per hour). Since demand is 300 cars per hour, one tollbooth is not sufficient. Two tollbooths can handle 360 (2 × 180) cars per hour, so two tollbooths are sufficient.

Example 2

You are in charge of organizing an overnight trip to the city. You've hired 15 buses for transporting the 750 people who have already purchased tickets. The question is how much time to allow for loading so that the last bus departs by 8:00 a.m. There is room for only three buses in the loading area, which means that three buses can be loaded simultaneously and, when full, can depart, leaving room for an empty bus to pull in. You estimate it will take about six seconds to check each person in as he/she boards the bus, and 30 seconds for the full bus to depart and an empty bus to pull up for loading. Each bus will be loaded with 50 people. Given this information, loading should begin by about 7:30: 5.5 minutes for loading and departure of each bus (i.e., 6 seconds per person × 50 people + 30 seconds = 330 seconds = 5.5 minutes) and five rounds of buses to load makes 5.5 × 5 = 27.5 minutes.

Example Summaries

EXAMPLE 1. HOW MANY TOLLBOOTHS?
Demand rate = 300 cars per hour
Service time at booth = 20 secs/car = 1/180 hour per car
Service rate = 180 cars per booth-hr
Number of tollbooths = demand rate/service rate = 300 cars/hr ÷ 180 cars/booth-hr = 1.67 ⇒ 2 tollbooths

EXAMPLE 2. HOW MUCH TIME FOR BUS LOADING?
Total demand = 750 people = 15 busloads = 5 rounds of buses to load (loading 3 buses at a time)
Service time per bus = 6 secs/person × 50 people/bus + 30 secs = 330 secs/bus = 5.5 minutes per bus
Total loading time = 5 rounds × 5.5 min/round = 27.5 minutes

The question in example 1 was how much capacity, whereas the question in example 2 was how much time. However, both examples illustrate the same basic approach of comparing demand with capacity, though the choice of units is slightly different. In example 1, demand per period (300) ÷ capacity per server-period (180) = number of servers. And in example 2, total demand (750) ÷ total capacity per period (150 every 5.5 minutes) = number of periods.

The major **weakness of deterministic capacity analysis is that it ignores variability** by assuming that the demand rate and the service rate are perfectly constant. Another way of saying this is that it assumes that the arrival and service rates are completely *determined,* or *deterministic.* The introduction of variability creates congestion. For this reason, results from deterministic capacity analysis tend to be optimistic; for example, to avoid long waiting lines, you will likely need more than two tollbooths in example 1 above. The next option for analysis accommodates variability.

1.2 Queueing Model Analysis

There are many queueing models that can be used to analyze many different types of systems. We will look at only two simple single-server models because they show how queueing models can be used to answer meaningful questions and, more important, these two models expose insights related to two principles of nature: *curse of utilization* and *curse of variability.*[3] The difference between the two models is that one assumes service time is variable and the other assumes service time is constant. We'll begin with assumptions and notation.

A1. The system is in *steady state.*

A2. The mean arrival rate is constant.

A3. The mean service rate (i.e., capacity) is constant.

Notation for Queueing Models

Parameters

λ = mean arrival rate = average number of units arriving at the system per period

$1/\lambda$ = mean interarrival time, or time between arrivals (i.e., the inverse of a *rate* is *time,* and vice versa)

μ = mean service rate per server = average number of units that a server can process per period

$1/\mu$ = mean service time (i.e., the inverse of a *rate* is *time,* and vice versa)

m = number of servers

Performance Measures

ρ = system utilization = proportion of the time that a server is busy

W_s = mean time that a unit spends in the system (i.e., in queue or in service)

W_q = mean time that a unit spends waiting for service (i.e., in queue)

L_s = mean number of units in the system (i.e., in queue or in service)

---

[3] The end-of-chapter case exercises show how these simple models can be applied in more complex multistage settings. Useful references covering a range of systems modeled using queueing theory are Gross and Harris (1998) and Hall (1997).

L_q = mean number of units in line for service (i.e., in queue)

p_n = probability of *n* units in the system (i.e., in queue or in service)

A Few Words on Assumptions and Notation

Assumption A1 says that the system is in *steady state,* which, loosely speaking, means that the mean arrival rate is equal to the mean departure rate. For example, McDonald's is probably not in steady state between 11 a.m. and noon because the lunchtime surge is occurring. The mean arrival rate tends to stabilize somewhat during lunchtime, so McDonald's is probably close to a steady-state operation between noon and 1 p.m. Assumption A2 says that the mean arrival rate is a constant that is independent of the number in the system (e.g., customers do not leave the system when lines get long). Similarly, assumption A3 says that the mean service time is a constant that is independent of the number in the system (e.g., servers do not speed up when lines get long).

The notation for parameters can be illustrated using the tollbooth example from Section 1.1. An average of 300 cars passing through the tolls each hour means that

$$\lambda = \text{mean arrival rate} = 300 \text{ cars per hour}$$

It takes an average of 20 seconds to exchange money at a booth. In general, rate is the multiplicative inverse of time per unit, so a time of 20 seconds per car corresponds to a rate of

$$\mu = \text{mean service rate} = 1/20 \text{ car/second} = 60 \text{ seconds/minute} \times 1/20 \text{ car/second}$$
$$= 3 \text{ cars/minute} = 60 \text{ minutes/hour} \times 3 \text{ cars/minute} = 180 \text{ cars per hour}$$

In the example, we decided that two tollbooths would be needed; we essentially looked at the ratio $\lambda/\mu = 300/180 \approx 1.67$ and rounded up to 2.

The notation includes performance measures for the average time and number in the system, and the average time and number in the queue. Figure 8.2 illustrates the distinction between *the system* and *the queue*; a unit in the system is either in service (i.e., being processed) or in the queue (i.e., waiting for service).

FIGURE 8.2

A Picture of a Barbershop System
There is one person in the queue, one person in service, and two customers in the system.

In service   In queue

System

Principle of Nature: Little's Law

DEFINITION
Average inventory = throughput rate × average flowtime

IMPLICATION
If you can find ways to reduce flowtime, you will benefit from reduced inventory investment, and vice versa.

EXAMPLE
Little's law can also be written as average inventory ÷ throughput rate = average flowtime. Suppose, for example, that the average demand rate is 20 units per day and average inventory is 100 units. With these numbers, it makes sense that inventory can cover an average of five days' worth of demand (i.e., five days of supply) and so the average length of time a unit is in inventory is five days (i.e., average flowtime is five days). In terms of the numbers in the example, 100 units ÷ 20 units/day = 5 days, or, more generally, average inventory ÷ throughput rate = average flowtime.

The following formulas show how various performance measures are related for a system operating in steady state.

Formulas for Performance Measures

$m\mu$ = total service rate = number of servers × service rate of each server

ρ = system utilization = arrival rate ÷ total service rate = $\lambda/(m\mu)$

W_s = average time in system = average time in queue + average service time
$= W_q + 1/\mu$

L_s = average number in system = average number in queue + average number in service = $L_q + m\rho$

L_s = average number in system = arrival rate × average time in system = λW_s (and $W_s = L_s/\lambda$)

L_q = average number in queue = arrival rate × average time in queue = λW_q (and $W_q = L_q/\lambda$)

The preceding formulas, while a consequence of the assumptions, appeal to common sense. In fact, you may have seen a variation on $L_s = \lambda W_s$ (or $L_q = \lambda W_q$) in your accounting or finance classes. Inventory turnover is one measure of performance that can be calculated from a firm's balance sheet; that is, inventory turnover rate = sales/inventory.[4] In terms of our notation, average inventory = L_s, sales = λ, so inventory turnover rate = λ/L_s and $L_s =$ $\lambda(1/\text{inventory turnover rate}) = \lambda(\text{average time in inventory}) = \lambda W_s$.

The expression $L_s = \lambda W_s$ is a formal statement of a principle of nature known as Little's law: the average amount of stuff in a system (L_s) is proportional to the time it takes for stuff to flow through the system (W_s).

Given an estimate for any one of W_s, W_q, L_s, L_q, the remaining three performance measures can be calculated from the formulas. The question then becomes how to determine the value of one of these measures from the mean arrival rate (λ), the mean service rate (μ), and the number of servers (m). The answer to this question will depend on the nature of the variation in the timing of arrivals and the service times. The assumptions and formulas for two queueing models are listed in Table 8.1.

---

[4] The alternative of inventory turnover rate = (cost of goods sold)/inventory also is used.

TABLE 8.1 **Assumptions and Formulas for Two Queueing Models**

M/M/1 Model	*M/D/1* Model
Assumptions	**Assumptions**
• **M**: Exponentially distributed interarrival times, or, equivalently, the number of arrivals per period follows a Poisson distribution, that is, a "**M**arkov" arrival process • **M**: Exponentially distributed service times, or, equivalently, the number of units that can be processed per period follows a Poisson distribution, that is, a "**M**arkov" service process • **1**: There is a single server, that is, $m = $ **1**	• **M**: Exponentially distributed interarrival times, or, equivalently, the number of arrivals per period follows a Poisson distribution, that is, a "**M**arkov" arrival process • **D**: Constant service times, or, equivalently, the number of units that can be processed per period is constant, that is, a "**d**eterministic" service process • **1**: There is a single server, that is, $m = $ **1**
Formulas	**Formulas**
$\rho = $ system utilization $= \lambda/\mu$ $L_q = $ average number in queue $= \rho^2/(1 - \rho)$ $L_s = $ average number in system $= \rho/(1 - \rho)$ $W_q = $ average time in queue $= L_q/\lambda$ $W_s = $ average time in system $= L_s/\lambda$ $p_0 = $ probability of 0 in system $= 1 - \rho$ $p_n = $ probability of n in system $= p_0\rho^n = (1 - \rho)\rho^n$	$\rho = $ system utilization $= \lambda/\mu$ $L_q = $ average number in queue $= (1/2)\rho^2/(1 - \rho)$ $L_s = $ average number in system $= \rho/(1 - \rho) - (1/2)\rho^2/(1 - \rho)$ $W_q = $ average time in queue $= L_q/\lambda$ $W_s = $ average time in system $= L_s/\lambda$ $p_0 = $ probability of 0 in system $= 1 - \rho$

Example 1

You've developed a new system that allows you to cut hair fast—it takes an average of 10 minutes to cut someone's hair and exchange money. Your shop, SpeedCuts, has been open for two weeks and demand has been slow. You hope this will change with an article about your business that will appear in Sunday's paper. You suspect that average demand will triple from one to three per hour, and you'd like to get a handle on what this may mean for various performance measures such as (1) the average time that a customer waits in line (W_q), (2) the average number of people in the shop (L_s), (3) the proportion of the time that the shop is empty (p_0), and (4) the probability of one or more people in line. In general, estimates of only three values are needed to calculate all of the performance measures; these three values are the mean arrival rate (λ), the mean service rate (μ), and the number of servers (m).

What do we know? The mean arrival rate $= \lambda = 3$ people per hour and the mean service time $= 1/\mu = 10$ minutes per person. Since the mean service time is 10 minutes per person, the mean service rate is $\mu = 1/10$ person per minute, or $\mu = 6$ people per hour (60 minutes/hour $\times$ 1/10 person/minute). Also, since you're a single server, $m = 1$. Accordingly, the system utilization is $\rho = \lambda/(m\mu) = 3/6 = 0.5$. This makes sense in hindsight; if people arrive, on average, 20 minutes apart (i.e., three per hour), and it takes an average of 10 minutes to cut hair, then you'll be busy 50 percent of the time.

Now for the performance measures according to the *M/M/1* model. The average time that a customer waits in line is

$$W_q = L_q/\lambda = [\rho^2/(1 - \rho)]/\lambda = [0.5^2/0.5]/3 = 0.5/3 \text{ hours} = 0.5(60)/3 \text{ minutes} = 10 \text{ minutes}$$

The average number of people in the shop is

$$L_s = L_q + m\rho = 0.5 + 0.5 = 1 \text{ person}$$

The proportion of the time that the shop is empty is

$$p_0 = 1 - \rho = 1 - 0.5 = 50 \text{ percent}$$

The probability of one or more people in line is the same as the probability of two or more people in the system (e.g., two in the system means one person in service and one person in line), which is

$$p_2 + p_3 + p_4 + \cdots = 1 - (p_0 + p_1) = 1 - [(1 - \rho) + (1 - \rho)\rho]$$
$$= 1 - [0.5 + 0.5(0.5)] = 1/4^5$$

Example Summary

Performance when service time is exponentially distributed (*M/M/1*)?
λ = average arrival rate = 3 people per hour
μ = average service rate = 6 people per hour
ρ = system utilization = λ/μ = 1/2
L_q = average number in line = $\rho^2/(1 - \rho)$ = 0.5 person
W_q = average time in line = L_q/λ = 1/6 hour = 10 minutes
L_s = average number in the system = $L_q + \rho$ = 1 person
p_0 = probability of zero in the system = $1 - \rho$ = 1/2
$1 - (p_0 + p_1)$ = probability of two or more in the system = probability of one or more in line = $1 - [(1 - \rho) + (1 - \rho)\rho]$ = 1/4

The preceding results are based on an assumption that service time averages 10 minutes but is variable (more precisely, service time is exponentially distributed). If service time is always 10 minutes—never more, never less—then the *M/D/1* model applies. In this case, the average time that a customer waits in line is

$$W_q = L_q/\lambda = [(1/2)\rho^2/(1 - \rho)]/\lambda = [0.5^3/0.5]/3 = 0.25/3 \text{ hours} = 5 \text{ minutes}$$

The average number of people in the shop is

$$L_s = L_q + m\rho = 0.25 + 0.5 = 0.75 \text{ person}$$

The proportion of the time that the shop is empty is

$$p_0 = 1 - \rho = 1 - 0.5 = 0.5$$

---

[5] An alternative approach is to take advantage of the following identity that holds when $0 < \rho < 1$: $1 + \rho + \rho^2 + \cdots = 1/(1 - \rho)$. From the formula $p_n = (1 - \rho)\rho^n$, $p_2 + p_3 + \cdots = (1 - \rho)[\rho^2 + \rho^3 + \cdots] = (1 - \rho)\rho^2[1 + \rho + \rho^2 + \cdots] = (1 - \rho)\rho^2/(1 - \rho) = \rho^2$. Thus, in general, the probability of n or more in the system is ρ^n. In this case, $n = 2$ and $\rho^2 = 0.5^2 = 25$ percent.

> ## Example Summary
>
> Performance when service time is deterministic (*M/D*/1)?
> λ = average arrival rate = 3 people per hour
> μ = service rate = 6 people per hour
> ρ = system utilization = λ/μ = 1/2
> L_q = average number in line = $(1/2)\rho^2/(1 - \rho)$ = 0.25 person
> W_q = average time in line = L_q/λ = 1/12 hour = 5 minutes
> L_s = average number in the system = $L_q + \rho$ = 0.75 person
> p_0 = probability of zero in the system = $1 - \rho$ = 1/2

For the *M/D*/1 model, there are no formulas for p_1, p_2, p_3, and so forth.

Example 2

Wal-Mart is working on staffing plans in preparation for the opening of a new distribution center (DC) and the realignment of DC service territories. One question is whether a skeleton crew, which includes only one person for unloading inbound shipments, is viable during the slow period of the day. Management anticipates that inbound containers will arrive at a rate of 4.2 per hour during the slow period. It takes an average of 12 minutes for a crew member to unload a container, though there is considerable variability in the service time and the interarrival time. What is the degree of inbound congestion that can be expected at this minimal staffing level? More specifically, what are the values of (1) the probability that an arriving container has to wait for service, (2) the average number of containers waiting for service, (3) the average time that a container waits for service, and (4) the probability that there are no containers in the loading dock when a container arrives?

Due to the variation in arrivals and service times, the *M/M*/1 is most appropriate. The mean arrival rate = λ = 4.2 containers per hour and the mean service time = $1/\mu$ = 12 minutes per container. Accordingly, the mean service rate is μ = 1/12 container per minute = 5 containers per hour (60 minutes/hour × 1/12 container/minute), and the system utilization is $\rho = \lambda/(m\mu)$ = 4.2/(1 × 5) = 0.84.

The system utilization is the percent of time that the system is busy, or, in other words, the probability that an arriving container has to wait for service is ρ = 84 percent. The average number of containers in line is

$$L_q = \rho^2/(1 - \rho) = 0.84^2/0.16 \approx 4.4$$

The average time in line is

$$W_q = L_q/\lambda = [0.84^2/0.16]/4.2 \approx 1.1 \text{ hours}$$

The probability that there are no containers in the loading dock when a container arrives is

$$p_0 = 1 - \rho = 1 - 0.84 = 16 \text{ percent}$$

> ## Example Summary
>
> Inbound congestion at a Wal-Mart DC?
> λ = average arrival rate = 4.2 containers per hour
> μ = average service rate = 5 containers per hour
> ρ = system utilization = λ/μ = 0.84
> L_q = average number in line = $\rho^2/(1 - \rho) \approx$ 4.4 containers
> W_q = average time in line = $L_q/\lambda \approx$ 1.1 hours
> p_0 = probability of zero in the system = $1 - \rho$ = 0.16

Principle of Nature: Khintchine Limit Theorem

DEFINITION
As the number of independent random arrival processes increases, the probability distribution of the time between arrivals of the aggregate process is more closely approximated by an exponential distribution.

IMPLICATION
If a random process is an aggregation of many independent processes, then it is likely to be well approximated by a Poisson process.

EXAMPLE
Poisson processes are observed in a diverse range of phenomena, including radioactive decay (Kendall 1943), the number of raisins in a slice of raisin bread (Feller 1965), the number of new wars in the world during a year (Richardson 1956), the number of tornado touchdowns, and the number of Web server hits (Hayes 2002).

The Exponential Probability Distribution and a Principle of Nature

The $M/M/1$ and $M/D/1$ **models assume that the time between arrivals is exponentially distributed.** You're probably familiar with the shape of the probability density function of the normal distribution (looks like a bell curve). The probability density function for the exponential distribution is illustrated in Figure 8.3.

When interpreted for an arrival process, the basic character of the exponential distribution is "feast or famine"—there are periods of mad rush followed by idleness. This can be seen from the curve where there is a relatively high chance that the time between arrivals is very small and, while the odds are low, it can be a very long time between arrivals. This feast-or-famine character is fairly realistic for many businesses that experience walk-in traffic (e.g., retail shops, restaurants that don't take reservations), and there is a principle of nature called the Khintchine limit theorem that helps explain why this is so.

Loosely speaking, the **Khintchine limit theorem states that if you have a lot of individual customers that periodically visit your store, then the time between consecutive arrivals of customers will be approximately exponentially distributed.** In other words, regardless of how particular individuals arrive at your store, the aggregate

FIGURE 8.3 **The Probability Density Function of an Exponential Distribution**

The mean arrival rate is $\lambda = 5$ units per period and the mean interarrival time is $1/\lambda = 0.2$ period per unit.

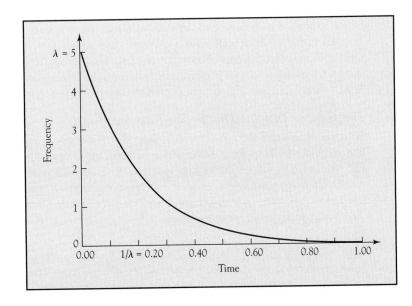

FIGURE 8.4 The Average Number in Queue (L_q) as Utilization (ρ) Increases, as Predicted by the *M/M*/1 and *M/D*/1 Models

The sharp increase in the slope as utilization approaches 100 percent illustrates the curse of utilization. The upward arrows show that the system becomes more congested as service time changes from being deterministic (as in *M/D*/1) to stochastic (as in *M/M*/1). This illustrates the curse of variability.

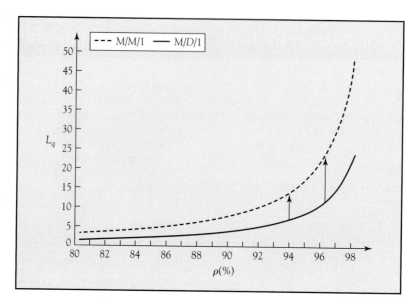

of all customer arrivals tends to behave as a Poisson process.[6] The Khintchine limit theorem is one of three fundamental results that help explain the prevalence of certain types of probability distributions in the world around us. The other two, which have been noted in earlier chapters, are the central limit theorem and Benford's law. While it is prudent to examine historical data to assess the reasonableness of assumptions, the Khintchine limit theorem provides some assurance that the assumption of exponential interarrival times is reasonable for purposes of quick initial analysis, or when historical data are not available.

A Few Words on the Service Time Assumptions

The *M/M*/1 model assumes that **service time is exponentially distributed while the *M/D*/1 model assumes that service time is constant.** These service time assumptions represent two extremes of what one is likely to observe in practice. The exponential distribution exhibits a high degree of variability; in fact, the standard deviation of service time is equal to the mean service time. Of course, the assumption of constant service times represents the other extreme of no variation at all. Thus, given that the other model assumptions are reasonable, actual performance is likely to be better than what is predicted by the *M/M*/1 model and worse than what is predicted by the *M/D*/1 model.

Two General Insights That Follow from the Models

Both the *M/M*/1 and the *M/D*/1 models show that performance rapidly degrades as utilization gets close to 100 percent. For example, consider the formula for the average length of the line for the *M/D*/1 model (the formula is similar for the *M/M*/1 model): $L_q = (1/2)\rho^2/(1 - \rho)$. As utilization ($\rho$) gets close to one, the denominator gets close to zero and L_q gets very large (see Figure 8.4). And, since we know that time is proportional to number (i.e., Little's law), very long queues mean very long queue times.

---

[6] More formally, under fairly general conditions, the superposition of a large number of independent renewal processes is close to a Poisson process (see Khintchine 1960 or Feller 1965). A Poisson process is another way of saying that the number of arrivals per period follows a Poisson distribution and that the interarrival times are exponentially distributed.

Principle of Nature: Curse of Utilization

DEFINITION
Average flowtime skyrockets as resource utilization gets close to 100 percent.

IMPLICATION
Utilization of a system or resource is the percent of time that the system or resource is busy. Unless there is very little variability in a process, resources will have to be underutilized to provide responsive service.

EXAMPLE
Ananth is registered for 9 credit hours in the fall semester while Vernon has an 18-hour credit load and is also a member of the football team. Vernon, whose utilization with respect to scholastic and athletic time commitments is very high, will probably have more difficulty completing assignments on time.

Figure 8.4 illustrates a principle of nature called **the curse of utilization.** One hundred percent utilization may sound good from the standpoint that resources are used to the maximum degree possible, but there is also the curse of poor service; that is, **average flowtime skyrockets as resource utilization gets close to 100 percent.** Managers facing uncertain and time-sensitive markets typically will plan for less than 100 percent utilization of resources so that the system can quickly respond to unexpected surges in demand. Of course, there is the question of how much extra capacity (a.k.a. surge capacity) is appropriate, and queueing models as well as simulation are helpful in this regard;[7] these tools can be used to gain insight into the relationship between investment in excess capacity, investment in excess inventory, and level of service (e.g., see Aviv and Federgruen 2001, exercise 15, and the two case exercises at the end of the chapter).

The **curse of variability** is a related principle that is evident by comparing the performance of $M/M/1$ with $M/D/1$. For example, $L_q = \rho^2/(1 - \rho)$ for $M/M/1$ and $L_q = (1/2)\rho^2/(1 - \rho)$ for $M/D/1$ (see Figure 8.4). We see that the **average length of the line is cut in half when the variance in the service time is removed.** We could take this a step further by considering what happens when the variance in interarrival times also is removed. In short, wait times disappear completely. For example, suppose that the mean time between arrivals is 10 minutes and the mean service time is 8 minutes. If there is **no variability,** then customers arrive exactly 10 minutes apart and finish service exactly 8 minutes after arriving. **Average wait time is zero.** For contrast, the average wait time is $W_q = [\rho^2/(1 - \rho)](1/\lambda) = [0.8^2/0.2]$ (10 minutes) = 32 minutes for the $M/M/1$ model.

In summary, **the curse of variability is the phenomenon that congestion and wait times increase as variability increases. The sensitivity of system performance to changes in variability increases with utilization.** This observation on the linkage between the two principles has meaningful managerial implications: (1) **Efforts to reduce variance are most likely to pay off if resources are highly utilized.** (2) **To provide comparable service, systems with high variability should operate at lower levels of resource utilization than systems with lower variability.**

Flowtime Efficiency and an Alternative View of the Curse of Utilization and the Curse of Variability

Suppose it takes an average of 30 minutes of work to process a personal loan application, but a customer waits an average of four days. For comparison, a commercial loan requires an average of five hours of work and a customer waits an average of five days. Which

---

[7] See Raman and Kim (2002) for an example of the impact of surplus capacity in apparel manufacturing. For additional detail on the use of strategic surplus capacity, see Netessine, Dobson, and Shumsky (2002) and Van Mieghem (2003).

Principle of Nature: Curse of Variability

DEFINITION
Variability causes congestion.

IMPLICATION
Look for ways to reduce variance in processes.

EXAMPLE
A common way to reduce variance in service time, as well as service time, is to simplify the process of providing the service. Next time you go to McDonald's, look behind the cash register. In some markets, McDonald's uses registers that have pictures of food items rather than numbers on the buttons. One advantage of this design is that it helps reduce variance in checkout time by making it harder to make a mistake when pricing an order.

process is more responsive? The personal loan application process has a shorter average flowtime, but its performance is worse when accounting for the work content. Flowtime efficiency is the ratio of average value-added time to average flowtime. It is a standardized measure that can be useful for comparing the relative responsiveness of different systems or processes. For example,

$$\text{Flowtime efficiency of the personal loan process} = 0.5 \text{ hour} \div 96 \text{ hours} \approx 0.5 \text{ percent}$$
$$\text{Flowtime efficiency of the commercial loan process} = 5 \text{ hours} \div 120 \text{ hours} \approx 4 \text{ percent}$$

Figure 8.5 plots flowtime efficiency as a function of utilization for the $M/M/1$ and $M/D/1$ models. As in Figure 8.4, each curve in isolation illustrates the curse of utilization; that is, flowtime efficiency decreases as utilization increases. And the curves in combination illustrate the curse of variability; that is, flowtime efficiency decreases when variability in service time is introduced.

The earlier SpeedCuts and Wal-Mart examples illustrated the straightforward application of queueing formulas. The next example reinforces how this tool can be used, but in a richer setting.

FIGURE 8.5
Flowtime Efficiency as a Function of Utilization for the $M/M/1$ and $M/D/1$ Models
For $M/M/1$, flowtime efficiency = average service time ÷ average time in the system = $(1/\mu) \div W_s = 1 - \rho$. For $M/D/1$, flowtime efficiency = average service time ÷ average time in the system = $(1/\mu) \div W_s = 1 - \rho/(2 - \rho)$.

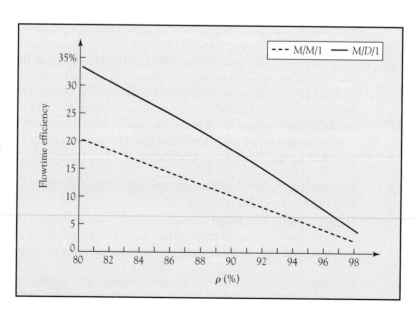

Example

Due to a family connection in the music industry, you were able to purchase a special licensing arrangement that allows you to copy and sell music by a wide range of artists. Over the past year, you've been preparing and selling custom mixes with 5 to 20 gigabytes of music to friends and acquaintances.

You have a talent for translating a basic knowledge of a person's taste in music into a mix that he or she really enjoys. In fact, you are about to take the step from a profitable hobby to a full-fledged business. You purchased the rights to the domain name custom-mix.com, you've created a Web site, and you've placed an ad in two music magazines that will appear next month.

The buying process is simple. A customer completes an online survey about music preferences on your Web site, selects the amount of music in five-gigabyte increments, pays by credit card, and waits for the mix to be loaded onto his or her account on the custom-mix.com server. You are savvy—you know that it is especially important for a new business to avoid a negative first impression caused by a long wait.[8] The challenge is to get a sense of the average flowtime between when a customer places an order and the mix is completed and loaded onto the server. If flowtimes are likely to be long, then you'll make arrangements to hire and train some helpers before the ads appear in print.

Here are the data. It takes about two hours to interpret the results from the survey, create a five-gigabyte mix, and load onto the server (at which time an e-mail is automatically sent to the customer). From past experience, you know that you can easily put in 10 hours of work in each 24-hour period, that is,

Moderate service rate = μ = 10 hours/day ÷ 2 hours/mix = 5 mixes per day

If necessary, you can produce mixes for up to 14 hours per day. However, this capacity level is not sustainable for a long time; for example, it is acceptable for the amount of time it takes to hire and train helpers. At 14 hours per day,

High service rate = μ = 14 hours/day ÷ 2 hours/mix = 7 mixes per day

While demand is unknown, a plot of average flowtime over a range of possible demand rates can be useful. There is relatively high variation in the amount of time to prepare a mix, which suggests that the *M/M/1* model is more appropriate than the *M/D/1* model. Accordingly, the average flowtime is

$$W_s = L_s / \lambda = \rho / [(1 - \rho)\lambda] = (\lambda/\mu) / [(1 - (\lambda/\mu))\mu] = 1/(\mu - \lambda)$$

which is plotted in Figure 8.6.

Example Summary

Hire and train helpers before the ads appear in print?

$1/\mu$ = mean work time per order = 2 hours per mix

μ = mean service rate = 1/2 mix per hour

At 10 hours per day:

μ = 1/2 mix/hour × 10 hours/day = 5 mixes per day

At 14 hours per day:

μ = 1/2 mix/hour × 14 hours/day = 7 mixes per day

Finally,

W_s = order flowtime = $1/(\mu - \lambda)$

which is plotted in Figure 8.6.

---

[8] This insight is based on a principle of nature that is discussed in Section 2; that is, "it's hard to play catch-up ball."

FIGURE 8.6 A plot of average flowtime (W_s) by average demand rate (λ) for two possible capacities—a 10-hour workday ($\mu = 5$ mixes per day) and a 14-hour workday ($\mu = 7$ mixes per day). At a 10-hour workday, average flowtime becomes very large as the average demand rate approaches five, which is another example of the curse of utilization. The average flowtime curve shifts to the right as capacity increases.

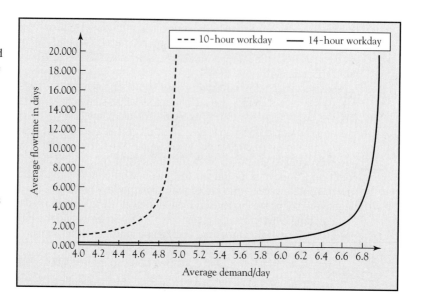

How Can the Results in Figure 8.6 Be Used to Help Decide Whether or Not to Hire Helpers Right Away?

Suppose, for example, that an average flowtime of two or fewer days is consistent with market perceptions of good service.[9] Figure 8.6 shows that the average flowtime is within two days if the average demand rate is not more than about 4.5 mixes per day, at least when capacity is based on a 10-hour workday. There is probably no need to hire helpers right away, unless market evidence suggests there is a chance that the average demand could be more than 6.5 mixes per day (i.e., at $\lambda = 6.5$ and a 14-hour workday, the average flowtime is within two days).

Queueing, Cross-Training, the Law of Large Numbers, and the Curse of Variability

Before introducing the third alternative for analyzing the impact of changes to service or arrival processes, we'll briefly look at how queueing models can be used to predict some of the benefits of cross-training. At the same time, we'll see another manifestation of the law of large numbers, a principle we have seen in many of the earlier chapters. The **law of large numbers** is the phenomenon of **decreasing relative variability as volume increases.** You already may have a good intuitive feel for why cross-training leads to more stable workloads on employees. However, we can now reinforce this intuition using queueing theory.

Yasodha and Xiaoqiang work at a travel agency. Yasodha handles only retail customers (e.g., family vacations) and Xiaoqiang handles only commercial customers (e.g., work-related travel). Their workload is about the same and each tends to have an average of about 20 customer requests in process. What if Yasodha and Xiaoqiang are cross-trained so that each can work on both retail and commercial requests? Perhaps surprisingly, the average number of customer requests in process will probably be cut in half and, by Little's law, customers will get their travel arrangements finalized in about half the time.

---

[9] Remember that an average flowtime of two days means some customers may wait considerably longer than two days (and many will wait less than two days). Other measures, such as the percentage of customers who wait less than two days, also may be of interest.

Principle of Nature: Law of Large Numbers

DEFINITION
As volume increases, relative variability decreases.

IMPLICATION
Look for ways to change operations so that planning can be done at a more aggregate unit.

EXAMPLE
The order processing department at a small company had two people—one person was responsible for order entry and the other person was responsible for credit checking. The company decided to train both workers to perform both tasks. They found that the workload on each person became much smoother.

You may be wondering where these numbers came from. In the current situation we have a case where Yasodha and Xiaoqiang are like two separate $M/M/1$ systems. If each keeps busy about 95.2 percent of his or her working day (i.e., $\rho = 0.952$), then each has about 20 customers in process on average; that is, $L_s = \rho/(1 - \rho) = 0.952/(1 - 0.952) \approx 20$, for a total of about $2L_s = 2\rho/(1 - \rho) = 2[0.952/(1 - 0.952)] \approx 40$ retail and commercial customers in process. With cross-training, Yasodha and Xiaoqiang appear as a single $M/M/2$ system; that is, two people serving a single line of retail and commercial customers.[10] Plugging the numbers into the $M/M/2$ formula for L_s yields an average of 20 retail and commercial customers in process.[11] From Yasodha's and Xiaoqiang's perspective, the volume of potential customers that each can service doubles after cross-training. The combined retail and commercial arrival process has **less relative variability than a pure retail or a pure commercial arrival process (due to the law of large numbers). And, with less relative variability, there is less congestion (due to the curse of variance).**

Example Summary

Yasodha is trained for retail customers only and maintains an average of 20 customer requests in process.

Xiaoqiang is trained for commercial customers only and maintains an average of 20 customer requests in process.

An average of 40 customer requests are in process, but sometimes Xiaoqiang is busy and Yasodha is idle, and vice versa.

If Yasodha and Xiaoqiang are cross-trained so that both can work on both customer types, then queueing theory predicts that the average number of outstanding requests will be cut in half.

Why? Because of the law of large numbers.

---

[10] If the retail customer arrival process is Poisson and the commercial customer arrival process is Poisson, then the combined retail and commercial customer arrival process is also Poisson. This property allows the formulas for the $M/M/2$ model to be used.

[11] We won't take the space to introduce all of the formulas for the $M/M/2$ model, but for the curious, $L_s = 2\rho/(1 - \rho^2) = 2[0.952/(1 - 0.952^2)] \approx 20$. See Hopp, Tekin, and Van Oyen (2004) for an example of the impact of cross-training at a company that produces lighting products.

1.3 Computer Simulation Analysis

Computer simulation is a very flexible tool for assessing the impact of change. The idea is to write a computer program that simulates the behavior of the system over time. The software to do this is becoming increasingly easy to use, even allowing visualization (e.g., like watching Sim City). Almost any type of performance information of interest can be captured (e.g., percentage of customers that have to wait more than 10 minutes, average wait times, etc.). The **main drawback is that the analysis is more time consuming than the preceding two options,** where results can be developed in a matter of minutes. Assuming proficiency in simulation coding and analysis, the time required to write and validate a simulation program, run the simulations, and analyze the results is measured in hours for simple systems, and potentially weeks for complex systems.

Caveat. It is important to bear in mind that performance measures from a computer simulation are random variables; performance is based on a "sampling" of the system. For example, you might compare two alternative designs using simulation and find that the average profits are higher for design A than for design B. However, if the simulation is run again, average profits will be different and design B might come out on top. The main point of the caveat is that **statistical analysis of computer simulation results is important** (e.g., to assess the degree of confidence in inferences from analysis).

2. PSYCHOLOGY

In this and the following section, we'll consider how to effectively use available capacity in a service setting with walk-in customers. The next chapter continues this theme in a production environment.

Your perception of time spent in line is based only in part on the actual clock time. This is what the psychology of waiting is all about. There are three principles of nature that deal with waiting psychology:

1. Satisfaction = perception − expectation.
2. It's hard to play catch-up ball.
3. Time distortion.

Satisfaction = perception − expectation is the phenomenon that **how good you feel about an experience depends on the difference between what you perceived and what you expected** (Maister 1984). As a manager, look for opportunities to influence both customer expectations and customer perceptions. For example, an airline at a new airport was receiving many complaints about the long waits at baggage claim. Their solution—they moved the terminal farther from baggage claim; people had to walk a longer distance, but, by the time they got to the baggage claim area, there was very little wait. Actual time from arrival to receipt of baggage remained virtually unchanged, but the perception of this time changed for the better and complaints were significantly reduced (Evans 1991). Similarly, it is known among passenger train conductors that it is better to travel a few miles at a slow speed than to temporarily stop when there is a delay ahead. Passengers have no difficulty perceiving a speed of 0, but the difference between 10 and 20 miles per hour is not so easy to detect.

The Walt Disney Company is well known for their attention to the psychology of waiting lines in their amusement parks. For example, lines zigzag through a series of rooms, which not only hides the total length of the line, but also fosters camaraderie and social interaction as guests come to recognize one another and exchange comments when passing back and forth in the line. Wait time estimates are posted at multiple points, and the estimates are slightly inflated to promote satisfaction as the line moves faster than expected.

Principle of Nature: Satisfaction = Perception − Expectation

DEFINITION
How good you feel about an experience depends on the gap between what you experienced and what you expected.

IMPLICATION
Look for opportunities to influence both customer expectations and customer perceptions.

EXAMPLE
A tactic in the hospitality and restaurant industry that is based on this principle of nature is the *unexpected extra*. The idea is to try to surprise your customer with something extra that he or she didn't expect. For example, I went to a restaurant for breakfast. After breakfast, we were served a small scoop of ice cream. This unexpected extra, which cost relatively little, stood out in my mind.

And there is often in-line entertainment that complements the theme of the ride to relieve boredom and build anticipation (e.g., you can play video games while you're waiting for a tour of Nickelodeon Studios). These tactics don't change the length of time that you wait, but they do influence your perception of the wait.

It's hard to play catch-up ball is the phenomenon that **negative impressions are often difficult to reverse** (Maister 1984). As a manager, invest extra attention and resources in the front-end of a service to avoid a negative first impression. The preceding principle included an example about my experience at a breakfast restaurant in Chicago, and the use of the unexpected extra. Something else happened during my visit. The owner appeared as I was waiting in line for a table. He did two things: first, he engaged in small talk with waiting customers and, second, he passed out bananas and Milk Duds. Another example concerns a bread-making shop that opened for business. They operated for two weeks before their grand opening promotion. The owners reduced the likelihood of a negative first impression by waiting until things were running smoothly before spurring demand with a promotion. The principle is also evident in a tactic used at some restaurants where wait time estimates are slightly inflated. If you're willing to wait, and you get seated earlier than the estimate, the experience begins on a positive note. On the other hand, if you're told a table should be ready in 15 minutes and you end up waiting 30 minutes, it may be difficult for the restaurant to turn your attitude around.

The managerial implication of this principle is: invest extra attention and resources in the front-end of a service to avoid getting behind. This deserves some qualification in light of the previous principle: getting behind in the eyes of a customer may not be so bad as long as you can recover very quickly relative to expectations. For example, a global hotel chain discovered that guests who experienced a problem that was quickly resolved rated the hotel service higher than those guests who experienced no problems (Schrage 2001). In this case, investments in recovery management may be more profitable than investments in problem prevention. Of course, a key to the success of this tactic is the preponderance of poor service with minimal resolution in everyday life; customers are so surprised by the

Principle of Nature: It's Hard to Play Catch-Up Ball

DEFINITION
Once behind in the eyes of your customer, it's difficult to turn the situation around. Another way of saying this is people tend to be more sensitive to losses than gains.

IMPLICATION
Invest extra attention and resources in the front-end of a service to avoid getting behind.

EXAMPLE
Awareness of the insight can be traced back at least 2,000 years to Plutarch, who observed that "bad news travels fast."

---

rapid and polite resolution of their problem that the experience stands out in a positive way, or, in other words, satisfaction = perception − expectation.

Time distortion is the phenomenon that **perceived time slows to a crawl when bored.** As a manager, look for ways to engage and entertain customers in line. For example, I walked into a grocery store, and, while in line, I saw how something had changed since my last visit—the store had installed TVs above the checkout registers that were broadcasting CNN. Russ Ackoff (1991) describes a problem of a gas station firm experiencing low demand. After months of market analysis directed at identifying key determinants of demand (e.g., their price, competitor's price, location of competitors, appearance of the station, layout of the station, etc.), "in-and-out time" was found to be the most important factor. The realization came from studying the rates at which cars stopped for gas for each of 16 ways to get in and out of an intersection (the company almost always located gas stations on a street corner). The highest stop rate was for cars turning right at an intersection where the station was located at the near-right corner (on average, this pattern also takes the least amount of time to get in and out of the station). The rate at which cars stopped decreased roughly in proportion with the square of the time to get in and out of the station (e.g., a route that took twice as much time had one-fourth of the stop rate). The insight influenced the firm's process for selecting the corner to locate a new station and led to new tactics to speed up service time.

David Maister (1984) shares a number of related observations about the perception of time when waiting. If you look around different businesses, you'll likely see creative ways

Principle of Nature: Time Distortion

DEFINITION
Perceived time increases approximately with the square of actual time when there is something else you'd much rather be doing.

IMPLICATION
There is a tendency to underestimate the negative effect of making a customer wait, especially when the customer is bored. Be aware of this principle when considering investments either that result in reduced wait time or that make wait time more tolerable.

EXAMPLE
"A watched pot never boils."

FIGURE 8.7
Individual Utility as a Function of Gains and Losses according to Prospect Theory

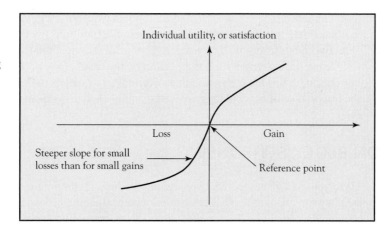

in which these observations are put into practice, as well as instances where they probably should, but aren't.

- Unoccupied time feels longer than occupied time.
- Preprocess waits feel longer than in-process waits.
- Anxiety makes waits seem longer.
- Uncertain waits are longer than known, finite waits.
- Unexplained waits are longer than explained waits.
- Unfair waits are longer than equitable waits.
- The more valuable the service, the longer the customer will wait.
- Solo waits feel longer than group waits.

Prospect Theory and the Psychology of Perception

Prospect theory is a branch of contemporary psychology initiated by Daniel Kahneman and Amos Tversky (e.g., see Kahneman, Slovic, and Tversky 1982; Kahneman and Tversky 1979; Tversky and Kahneman 1992). Prospect theory **explains biases in the way people perceive information, or assess prospects.** The theory is supported by the results of many experiments and is well accepted.[12]

    Figure 8.7, which reflects the essence of prospect theory, illustrates two of the three psychological principles of this section. First, whether an **individual perceives something as a loss or gain depends, in part, on an individual's reference point** (e.g., what he or she expected), or, in other words, **satisfaction = perception − expectation.** Retailers, for example, try to influence a shopper's reference point by prominently displaying the full price when marking down a product. Second, the **steeper slope of the curve for small losses indicates that people tend to be more sensitive to small losses than to small gains** (i.e., losing $5 feels worse than finding $5 feels good). This heightened sensitivity to loss is a reason why **it's hard to play catch-up ball.** It also explains the power of negative campaign strategies in elections and the effectiveness of appealing to fears in advertising (e.g., common in advertising for insurance and safety products).

    As an aside, notice that the curve in Figure 8.7 is not a straight line. The thrill of finding $10 is less than twice the thrill of finding $5, or, alternatively, the sorrow of losing $10 is

---

[12] Kahneman received the Nobel Prize in Economics in 2002 "for having integrated insights from psychological research into economic science, especially concerning human judgment and decision-making under uncertainty."

less than twice the sorrow of losing $5. This is why, other things being equal, it is better to consolidate losses and split gains; for example, multiple small unexpected bonuses are perceived more favorably than one large bonus of the same total value.

The overriding lesson from this section on the psychology of the waiting process is that options under this area are sometimes overlooked as means to improvement. Recognizing the importance of psychology may lead to simple and easy-to-implement ideas that have a high payback.

3. A WORD ON BLOCK SCHEDULING

Have you ever wondered why you end up waiting a long time in a doctor's office, even if you have an appointment? There is a fair chance that the office is using a type of appointment system known as *block scheduling*. By understanding the basics of how block scheduling works and why it is used, you will be able to determine if it can be helpful when you start your company and, if so, design and implement your own variation on the scheme. You also will get some insight into how to reduce your wait time during your next visit to a medical clinic.

You just opened up a medical practice, and patient appointments are to be scheduled for each doctor beginning at 8 a.m. A doctor spends an average of 10 minutes with each patient, which means that six patients per hour could be scheduled to see each doctor. If block scheduling is used, then *blocks* of patients are given the same appointment time. For example, six patients are scheduled for an 8 a.m. appointment, six patients are scheduled for a 9 a.m. appointment, and so on. Of course, if all six patients arrive at 8 a.m. and the doctor spends about 10 minutes per person, then one person will be waiting about 50 minutes before being seen by the doctor. In other words, if block scheduling is used, then people will tend to wait. So **why use it?** A hint for this answer comes from characteristics of a medical practice: (1) the **resource is expensive,** (2) **people don't always show up on time,** or at all, for their appointment, and (3) the **time a doctor needs to spend with a patient is not always predictable.** With block scheduling, it is unlikely that a doctor will be idle, even if some patients don't arrive at their scheduled time or diagnosis takes less time than expected. In other words, **block scheduling tends to keep the resource busy even with uncertainty in arrivals and service times, but at a cost of long waits.**

The preceding description is a simplified variation of what is actually used in practice, but it captures the basic idea.[13] So how can you beat the system? You probably won't be able to eliminate waiting, but you can help keep it to a minimum by first figuring out the length of the appointment interval (i.e., the time between appointments), then arriving 10 minutes before your appointment or 10 minutes before the next appointment. For example, if the appointment interval is 45 minutes, then you might plan to arrive at 7:50 or 8:35 for an 8 a.m. appointment. This works because patients are normally seen in first-come-first-serve order based on when you signed in, or, in other words, the trick is to arrive when other people aren't.

4. SUMMARY AND MANAGERIAL INSIGHTS

This chapter introduced three basic methods for estimating measures of system performance related to flowtime and congestion: deterministic capacity analysis, queueing model analysis, and simulation analysis. The methods are useful for determining capacity levels

---

[13] See Cayirli and Veral (2003) and Fries and Marathe (1981) for more detail.

(e.g., how much surplus capacity to accommodate uncertainty and variation), and, more specifically, gauging the impact of changes in capacity and/or demand on system performance. The methods are also useful for gaining insight into the behavior of complex dynamic systems, in part by contributing to the theory underlying such principles of nature as Little's law, curse of variability, curse of utilization, and the law of large numbers.

In the second part of the chapter, we shifted our focus to more subjective considerations relating to how humans perceive delays and congestion. The material draws on human psychology and identifies principles of nature that contain lessons for managers: satisfaction = perception − expectation, it's hard to play catch-up ball, and time distortion. The content is particularly relevant for service systems where walk-in clientele and waits are common. We concluded with an overview of block scheduling—a tactic that can be useful for managing capacity in service settings where idle resources are costly and there is uncertainty in arrivals/service times. Key managerial insights from the chapter are summarized below.

4.1. Average Inventory = Throughput Rate × Average Flowtime

This insight, which is the principle of Little's law, is evident in the expressions $L_s = \lambda W_s$ and $L_q = \lambda W_q$. Reducing flowtime yields proportional reductions in inventory. The effect can be powerful, simultaneously affecting the top line (e.g., shorter flowtime → faster market response → higher sales) and the bottom line (e.g., lower inventory → lower cost of goods sold → higher margin).

4.2. Average Flowtime Skyrockets as Resource Utilization Gets Close to 100 Percent

This insight is based on the principle of nature called the curse of utilization. The result holds whenever there is any variability in the system, which is almost always the case in the real world. The insight is evident in the following expressions for the average number in line according the $M/M/1$ and $M/D/1$ models: $L_q = \rho^2/(1 - \rho)$ and $L_q = (1/2)\rho^2/(1 - \rho)$. As resource utilization gets close to 100 percent, the denominator gets close to zero, and the value of L_q gets very large.

4.3. Variance Causes Congestion; As Variance in Interarrival Times and/or Processing Times Increases, Average Flowtime Increases

This insight is based on the principle of nature called the curse of variance. Consider the L_q expressions for $M/M/1$ and $M/D/1$: $L_q = \rho^2/(1 - \rho)$ and $L_q = (1/2)\rho^2/(1 - \rho)$. The average number waiting in line is cut in half if the variance in service time is eliminated. If we go a step further and also eliminate variability in the time between arrivals, congestion is eliminated altogether (i.e., $L_q = 0$). For example, if the time between arrivals is exactly 20 minutes and the service time is exactly 10 minutes, then no one is ever waiting in line. This means there is no waiting time when there is no variability; compare this with the situations where $W_q = L_q(1/\lambda) = [\rho^2/(1 - \rho)](1/\lambda) = [0.5^2/(1 - 0.5)](20) = 10$ minutes for $M/M/1$ and $W_q = L_q(1/\lambda) = (1/2)[\rho^2/(1 - \rho)](1/\lambda) = (1/2)[0.5^2/(1 - 0.5)](20) = 5$ minutes for $M/D/1$.

This insight and the previous insight can be combined to yield two additional two lessons: (1) Efforts to reduce variance are most likely to pay off if resources are highly utilized. (2) To provide comparable service, systems with high variability should operate at lower levels of resource utilization than systems with lower variability. The fashion industry, for example, tends to plan for more surplus capacity (e.g., to respond to surges in demand) than less volatile industries such as paper goods. We will revisit this point in Chapter 12.

4.4. Reduce Congestion and Improve Efficiency by Taking Advantage of the Law of Large Numbers, for Example, through Cross-Training and Other Tactics

The law of large numbers is a principle of nature that says as volume increases, relative variability decreases. Cross-training increases the volume of incoming tasks that a worker can perform, which leads to more stable workloads on employees, and consequently reduced congestion. Essentially, instances where one worker trained in skill A is overloaded while another worker trained in skill B is idle are eliminated—a cross-trained worker can help reduce the overload of tasks requiring skill A. Of course, advantages due to cross-training must be considered in light of training time and costs, and any other costs (e.g., higher wages).

An example in Section 1.2 illustrates the effect on average flowtime of cross-training two workers—Yasodha and Xiaoqiang—at a travel agency. This effect, in combination with the decreasing cost of communications technology, helps explain why McDonald's is experimenting with remote order-takers for their drive-through business. Employees at a call center in California and others who are working out of their homes in North Dakota take drive-through orders for about 100 McDonald's restaurants around the country (Richtel 2006). After a drive-through order is taken, it is transmitted instantaneously over the Internet to the restaurant. The benefits of such an approach are not due to lower wages of order-takers, which are comparable to other McDonald's employees. Rather, a key advantage stems from the law of large numbers. With the high order volume, the workload of incoming orders to the group of remote order-takers is relatively steady—there are few gaps in time between taking orders and, thus, worker productivity increases.

In order to relate the usage of remote order-takers at McDonald's to the travel agency example, imagine that Yasodha and Xiaoqiang are order-takers for a drive-through line at two different restaurants. The switch to remote order-taking is similar to cross-training; as remote order-takers, Yasodha and Xiaoqiang can serve customers at both restaurants. The calculations in the travel agency example illustrate how increasing the volume that each worker can handle leads to a reduction in average flowtime. Of course, an alternative way to gain from the law of large numbers is, instead of keeping the workforce fixed and reducing flowtime, keep average flowtime fixed and reduce the workforce.

4.5. Customer Satisfaction Depends Both on Perceptions and Expectations, Both of Which Can Be Influenced by Management

This insight follows from the psychological principle: satisfaction = perception − expectation. The hospitality industry recognizes this principle in a tactic called the *unexpected extra*. The idea is to pleasantly surprise a customer without spending a lot of money—a small investment that can pay dividends in the form of customer loyalty and word-of-mouth advertising. Examples include mints left in a hotel room and out-of-the-ordinary service. The tactic leaves lots of room for creativity, as an unexpected extra today will likely lose its novelty over time.

4.6. People Are More Sensitive to Small Losses Than Small Gains; Work Hard to Avoid a Negative First Impression

This insight follows from the psychological principle: it's hard to play catch-up ball. In 1967, a successful book was published with the title *How to Dress for Success,* and, since that time, a number of books have followed on the same theme. In essence, the book and its relatives are based on the power of a first impression, with respect to both the lasting effects of a positive first impression and the difficulty of reversing a negative first impression.

4.7. Perceived Time Slows to a Crawl When People Are Bored; Look for Ways to Engage, Entertain, and, More Generally, Reduce Awareness of Time by Your Customers While They Wait

This insight follows from the psychological principle of time distortion. This insight is well understood (e.g., we have all experienced the slow passing of time while waiting), but not always acted on by management. This is in spite of the fact that there may be simple and inexpensive ways to occupy those who are waiting.

When generating ideas for mitigating waiting time distortion, it can be useful to keep in mind the eight observations by Maister (1984) noted in Section 2: (1) unoccupied time feels longer than occupied time; (2) preprocess waits feel longer than in-process waits; (3) anxiety makes waits seem longer; (4) uncertain waits are longer than known, finite waits; (5) unexplained waits are longer than explained waits; (6) unfair waits are longer than equitable waits; (7) the more valuable the service, the longer the customer will wait; and (8) solo waits feel longer than group waits.

5. EXERCISES

1. Write a brief answer to each of the chapter keys in your own words. After writing down your answers, review the chapter with a focus on the content in bold to check and clarify your interpretations.

2. Schneider Logistics has a mean overall arrival rate of 0.69 truckload per hour and a mean service rate of 1 truckload per hour. Neither the arrival rate nor the service time is constant.
   a. What is the probability that no truckloads are in the system?
   b. What is the average number of truckloads in the waiting line?
   c. What is the average number of truckloads in the system?
   d. What is the average time that a truck spends in the waiting line?
   e. What is the average time a truck spends in the system?
   f. What is the probability that an arriving truck has to wait for service?

3. There is one computerized stationary bicycle in the basement of Marion Hall. During peak periods, students arrive at an average rate of three per hour with the time between arrivals exponentially distributed (this means that the number of arrivals per hour follows a Poisson distribution or, stated another way, the arrival process is Poisson). Each person rides for an average of 15 minutes and riding time is exponentially distributed.
   a. How many students should be waiting to ride on the average?
   b. What is the probability that the bike will be available if you arrive during a peak period?
   c. What is the probability that two or more people will be waiting in line?
   d. What is the average amount of time spent waiting in line?
   e. The results of a six-month multimillion-dollar study of the Marion Hall stationary bicycle are in; during peak periods, average wait times and the average number of people waiting in line were found to be less than what you predicted. Why might this be so?

4. Answer parts a, b, and d of the previous question under the assumption that each person rides for exactly 15 minutes.

5. A vending machine dispenses hot chocolate, cider, and coffee. It takes 30 seconds from the time money is deposited to the time when the cup can be removed. Customers arrive according to a Poisson process with a mean of 80 per hour.
   a. What is average number of customers waiting in line?
   b. What is the system utilization?
   c. What is the average amount of time spent in the system?

6. Consider a bank that operates with multiple tellers. Why is it common to find ropes forcing a single line feeding all tellers instead of a separate line for each teller? Why does McDonald's have a separate line for each order-taker instead of a single line like Wendy's?

7. Trucks using a loading dock arrive at a rate of 12 per day. The loading/unloading rate is 18 per day. Both the arrival and service processes are Poisson.
   a. What is the probability that the dock will be idle?
   b. What is the average number of trucks waiting for service?
   c. What is the average time that a truck waits?
   d. What is the probability that a truck will have to wait?
   e. Answer parts (a) through (d) under the assumption that the service process is deterministic.

8. There is one voting booth at the student center for the presidential election. Voters arrive at a rate of 25 per hour and the arrival process is Poisson. Each voter requires an average of 90 seconds in the booth, and voting time is exponentially distributed.
   a. On average, how many voters will be waiting to vote?
   b. What is the probability the booth is empty?
   c. If you get claustrophobic around a line of three or more, what is the probability that you won't vote?
   d. If you get grumpy waiting five minutes or more, on average, will you be grouchy by the time you reach the booth?

9. If each voter needed exactly 90 seconds to vote, what are the answers to (a), (b), and (d) in the previous question? What is the average time you would spend in the system?

10. If there were 45 voters per hour arriving, what are the answers to 8(a)−(d)? Arrival and voting processes are Poisson.

11. You are charged with doing a system utilization survey at Ale and Skittles Emporium. In looking at the beer service operation, you note there are four bartenders, who need exactly 30 seconds to pour a fresh beer. The customers' arrival process is Poisson with an average of 200 arriving each hour.
   a. What is the system utilization?
   b. What is the average time a customer spends waiting for a beer? (*Hint*: In line and in service.)
   c. If, during the Monster Truck Extravaganza, peak customer flow increases to 400 beer guzzlers per hour, and the only bartender is the Great Gus, who can draw as many beers per minute as the other four bartenders combined, what is the average number of people waiting in the system?

12. As an employee of HB Consulting, you have been hired by a Coca-Cola distributor to analyze their bottling process. After studying the situation, you learn that Liam

can fill a bottle, on average, in six seconds. Samson requires two seconds to cap the bottle. The filling and capping processes are Poisson. The bottles arrive in the system at the rate of 400 per hour with the time between arrivals exponentially distributed.

    a. What is the average time it takes Liam and Samson to fill and cap a case of Coke (1 case = 24 bottles)?

    b. How long does a bottle remain in the entire system, on average?

    c. What is the probability that Samson has nothing to do?

    d. Liam is bored so he puts his glove on a bottle of Coke he has just filled. How long will the bottle with the glove remain in queue before Samson finds the glove and yells at Liam for being silly?

    e. If Liam and Samson were to drink all the Cokes in the system at any moment, how many would each guy have, on average?

13. A barber has customers arrive at a rate of 2.5 per hour according to a Poisson process. It takes him an average of 20 minutes per head with a standard deviation of 2 minutes. He remains open for eight hours per day.

    a. How much time during the day does he have for reading his Danielle Steele novels?

    b. Give a range on an estimate for the average number of people waiting in line.

14. Connie would like to be prepared to handle 150 customers per hour during the grand opening extravaganza of Connie's TechLine. Each customer requires about five minutes of time by a server.

    a. Use deterministic capacity analysis to estimate the number of servers to have on duty.

    b. Why is it that deterministic capacity analysis tends to give optimistic results (i.e., will likely need more servers to provide a reasonable level of service)?

15. You've invented, patented, and built a machine for creating a diamond from raw carbon that is comparable in quality to natural diamonds. The machine requires enormous amounts of energy to run. Your factory is your garage, where you keep the machine, raw materials, and your server that hosts your Web site. The machine can create one diamond at a time, requiring 220 hours on average. While the average is 220 hours, the "cooking" time per diamond varies significantly for a variety of reasons (e.g., variation in voltage, changes in raw materials, humidity, ambient temperature). The final step in the process, which is handled within 24 hours by a local firm, is cutting, mounting, and shipping. The demand rate has been averaging one diamond every 10 days.

    You began this business on the side, but there are signs demand is about to pick up. With the potential for future problems in responding quickly to customer orders, you are beginning to mull over two options: (1) increasing your investment in diamond inventory and (2) spending time and money to improve your machine in a way that will reduce the average cooking time. You currently manage inventory and production by means of a base stock policy, with the base stock level set at 10 diamonds (recall the base stock policy from Chapter 7). This means, for example, that a new diamond begins production immediately after a diamond is sold. However, if the machine is currently running, then the production request waits in line until the machine is available. You track the percentage of orders shipped "on time" (i.e., fill rate), which you define as shipping within 24 hours of the order. Historically, your fill rate has been running at about 60 percent, which means that 40 percent of the orders are placed when there are no diamonds in inventory. Remember that for a base stock policy, no diamonds in inventory means 10 or more diamonds on order (i.e., one in process in the machine and nine or more orders waiting). This is a key observation that will allow you to get a quick sense of the merits of each option using the $M/M/1$ queueing model.

   a. What assumptions are required for the $M/M/1$ model, and what evidence is there on the reasonability of the assumptions in this setting?

   b. What is the current fill rate according to the $M/M/1$ model?[14] Does the answer to this question have any implications for the question in part (a)?

   c. How much will the fill rate increase if the base stock level is increased to 20 diamonds? How much will the fill rate increase if the base stock level remains at 10 diamonds, but the machine is modified so that average processing time is 180 hours instead of 220?

[14] Here are some hints. First, the fill rate corresponds to the probability that there are nine or fewer orders in the system. This probability also can be interpreted as the percentage of the time that there are nine or fewer orders in the system. Since the arrival of orders is completely random (at least under the Poisson arrival process assumed by the $M/M/1$ model), the percentage of time there are nine or fewer orders in the system is also the fraction of demand that can be shipped from inventory given a base stock level of 10. Second, there is a way to simplify the expression for probability of 10 or more orders in the system, which also leads to a simple expression for nine or fewer orders in the system. The simplified expression comes from the following identity that holds when $0 < \rho < 1 : 1 + \rho + \rho^2 + \cdots = 1/(1 - \rho)$.

Case Exercise: *EPR Scientific A*

EPR Scientific recently acquired a firm that develops and manufactures voltmeters. Customer service as measured by fill rate has traditionally been poor at the firm, and EPR's management team is considering where and how much to invest in order to improve performance.

BACKGROUND ON CASE CONTENT AND RELATIONSHIP TO CONCEPTS IN THE TEXT

This case draws on concepts in Chapters 7 and 8. It extends exercise 15 in Chapter 8 to consider the impact of investments in lead-time reduction and inventory on performance in a multistage supply chain. A base stock policy is used to answer production and ordering decisions at each stage. We'll look at the theory that underlies an approximation method that is generally quite accurate in this setting. You will be asked to set up a spreadsheet that uses the approximation method to compute fill rate (i.e., percent of demand shipped from inven-

tory) as a function of lead time and base stock level at each stage. The analysis illuminates the nature of trade-offs that arise when considering how to manage inventories and lead times throughout a supply chain.

THE SETTING AND NOTATION

There are two stages in the supply chain (see diagram below). Both stages manage inventory according to a base stock policy; the base stock levels by stage are denoted S_1 and S_2. Transportation and production times are constant. It takes L_1 periods to replenish stage 1 inventory and, given that a unit is available in stage 1 inventory, it takes L_2 periods to replenish stage 2 inventory. If stage 2 orders a unit from stage 1 when there is no stage 1 inventory, then the order is backlogged and transferred to stage 2 for processing when available. Customers order product from stage 2 at rate λ. The demand process is Poisson, and any unsatisfied demand is backordered. A demand process that is Poisson means that the time between unit demands is an exponential random variable with mean $1/\lambda$.

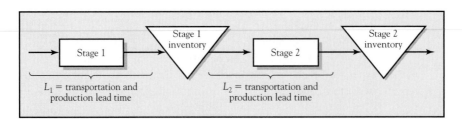

THE THEORY

Imagine the system with no orders, S_1 units in stage 1 inventory, and S_2 units in stage 2 inventory. Now, a customer places an order for one unit. Stage 2 immediately places an order on stage 1 to bring its inventory position back up to the base stock level of S_2. In response to the order, stage 1 similarly places a replenishment order to bring its inventory position up to S_1. In other words, in a supply chain operating under base stock policies, customer demands at the end of the supply chain are immediately propagated upstream to the beginning of the supply chain. Consequently, the demand at stage $j \in \{1, 2\}$ during time L_j is a Poisson random variable (denoted LD_j) with mean λL_j.

We are interested in characterizing the random variable for the net inventory (i.e., on-hand less backorders; denoted IN_j). For example, if there are five units backordered, which means there is no on-hand inventory, then net inventory is -5. Similarly, if there are seven units in inventory, which means there are no backorders, then net inventory is seven.

Since unit demands arrive randomly at stage 2 and a backorder is registered when demand occurs at a point in time when $IN_2 \leq 0$, the fill rate for the supply chain is

$$FR = 1 - P[IN_2 \leq 0] = P[IN_2 > 0]$$

So, in order to estimate the fill rate, we need to understand the random variable IN_2. We can take a step toward understanding this random variable from several recursive relationships. We'll look at these relationships for the two-stage supply chain, but the same logic can be repeated to incorporate any number of stages. Intuitive arguments for the relationships will be given (see Zipkin 2000 for additional detail including proofs).

The time to replenish stage 1 inventory is fixed at L_1 (i.e., supply is 100 percent reliable), and, consequently, the demand between when a unit is ordered and when it is received is a Poisson random variable LD_1 with mean λL_1, that is,

$$E[LD_1] = \lambda L_1$$

From the base stock analysis in Chapter 7, it follows that

$$IN_1 = S_1 - LD_1$$

Since S_1 is a constant (i.e., the base stock level) and LD_1 is a Poisson random variable, it follows that IN_1 is a Poisson random variable with mean $S_1 - \lambda L_1$. An order received by stage 1 (from stage 2) generates a replenishment order. Backorders at stage 1 accumulate L_1 periods later if demand during the lead time is greater than the base stock level. In other words, when the system is in steady state, the random variable for backorders at stage 1 (denoted B_1) is

$$B_1 = (LD_1 - S_1)^+ = (-IN_1)^+$$

(recall that $(x)^+ = \max\{0, x\}$).

Now for a key insight. The two stages in series can be viewed as two independent stages where the replenishment lead time at the second stage is random due to the possibility of insufficient inventory at stage 1. When stage 1 has backorders (i.e., when $B_1 > 0$), it means that some orders placed by stage 2 have not been shipped. In this sense, B_1 can be viewed as pent-up demand at stage 2, and, in fact, the random variable for demand during the replenishment lead time at stage 2 (denoted LD_2') is exactly

$$LD_2' = B_1 + LD_2$$

Recall LD_2 is a Poisson random variable with mean λL_2, which is the average demand during L_2 periods. Net inventory is the difference between base stock and demand during the lead time, that is,

$$IN_2 = S_2 - LD_2' = S_2 - B_1 - LD_2$$

In general, we know that a low base stock at stage 1 will contribute to poor service at stage 2, though this can be offset by a high base stock at stage 2. Reduction in lead times also will improve service. This general directional insight into the effects of lead times and base stock levels is a starting point for understanding supply chains, but it is not enough to formulate policies that guide where to invest to get the most benefit. The expressions above provide a basis for more detailed analysis, though the presence of truncated random variables (e.g., $B_1 = (LD_1 - S_1)^+$) complicates matters. However, the independence between B_1 and LD_2 leads to an accurate approximation method that is described below.

THE APPROXIMATION METHOD

The key relationships for computing fill rate $FR = 1 - P[IN_2 \leq 0] = P[IN_2 > 0]$ are

$$B_1 = (LD_1 - S_1)^+$$
$$IN_2 = S_2 - B_1 - LD_2$$

The random variable $B_1 + LD_2$ (which is the sum of two independent random variables) can be approximated as a negative-binomial distribution using its mean $E[B_1] + \lambda L_2$ and variance $V[B_1] + V[LD_2] = V[B_1] + \lambda L_2$ (i.e., the variance of a Poisson random variable is equal to its mean). $E[B_1]$ and $V[B_1]$ can be determined by noting that LD_1 is a Poisson random variable with mean λL_1. Putting it all together:

$$E[B_1] = (\lambda L_1 - S_1)P[LD_1 > S_1] + \lambda L_1 P[LD_1 = S_1]$$

$$V[B_1] = [(S_1 - \lambda L_1)^2 + S_1]P[LD_1 > S_1] - \lambda L_1(S_1 - \lambda L_1)P[LD_1 = S_1] - E[B_1](E[B_1] - 1)$$

where the probability mass function of a Poisson random variable is

$$P[LD_1 = x] = \frac{(\lambda L_1)^x e^{-\lambda L_1}}{x!} \quad \text{and}$$

$$P[LD_1 > S_1] = 1 - P[LD_1 \leq S_1]$$

The random variable $B_1 + LD_2$ is approximated as a negative-binomial distribution with parameters

$$p = 1 - \frac{E[B_1] + \lambda L_2}{V[B_1] + \lambda L_2}$$

$$n \approx \frac{(1 - p)(E[B_1] + \lambda L_2)}{p}$$

(the parameter n is integer, so the value of $[(1 - p)(E[B_1] + \lambda L_2)]/p$ should be rounded accordingly). There is a useful recursive relationship that can be used to compute the probability mass function of a negative-binomial random variable, that is,

$$f(0) = (1 - p)^n$$

$$f(x) = \left(\frac{n - 1 + x}{x}\right)pf(x - 1) \quad \text{for } x \geq 1$$

Using the above, the fill rate can be approximated as

$$FR = P[IN_2 > 0] = P[B_1 + LD_2 < S_2] \approx \sum_{i=0}^{S_2-1} f(i)$$

Questions

The average demand rate is $\lambda = 10$ units per period, and current lead times and base stock levels are $L_1 = L_2 = 10$, $S_1 = S_2 = 100$. The fill rate has been averaging less than 36 percent. As a first step toward evaluating where and how much to invest to improve the fill rate, evaluate the impact of a 10 percent reduction in lead time and/or 10 percent increase in base stock. Specifically, compute the fill rate for the following 16 combinations of lead time and base stock levels: $L_1 \in \{9, 10\}$, $L_2 \in \{9, 10\}$, $S_1 \in \{100, 110\}$, $S_2 \in \{100, 110\}$, and address the following questions:

1. Given a fixed total lead time of $L_1 + L_2 = 19$, where does the short lead time provide the most value in terms of fill rate (i.e., $L_1 = 9$ or $L_2 = 9$)? Also, given a fixed total base stock level $S_1 + S_2 = 210$, where does the high base stock level provide the most value in terms of fill rate (i.e., $S_1 = 110$ or $S_2 = 110$)? What might explain the reason for your answers (i.e., offer intuitive arguments for the answer that are supported by an analogy)?

2. Suppose that relative to the current values of $L_1 = L_2 = 10$, $S_1 = S_2 = 100$, the annual cost for a 10 percent reduction in lead time and a 10 percent increase in base stock are as follows.

	Approximate Annual Cost
10% reduction in L_1	$1.10 million
10% increase in S_1	$1.00 million
10% reduction in L_2	$1.65 million
10% increase in S_2	$1.50 million

What is the least-cost combination of inventory and lead-time investments to achieve a target fill rate of about 80 percent or more? (For this question, you may limit consideration to the 16 combinations computed above.)

3. Speculate on conditions (e.g., range of parameter values) where a 10 percent increase in the base stock level at a stage is likely to yield a larger increase in fill rate than a 10 percent reduction in lead time at the same stage. Explain the rationale underlying your speculation. For this question you will need to investigate other parameter combinations (i.e., beyond the 16 used in analysis for questions 1 and 2).

   Hints: For computing $E[B_1]$ and $V[B_1]$, note that Excel contains functions for Poisson probabilities (e.g., $P[LD_1 = x] = \text{POISSON}(x, E[LD_1], 0)$ and $P[LD_1 > x] = 1 - \text{POISSON}(x, E[LD_1], 1)$). From the Poisson probability function, an array formula in Excel is one way to rather easily compute $\sum_{i=0}^{S_1-1} P[LD_1 > i]$. For computing $P[B_1 + LD_2 = x]$ (and ultimately $P[B_1 + LD_2 < S_2]$), note that Excel contains a function for computing negative-binomial probabilities (e.g., $P[B_1 + LD_2 = x] = \text{NEGBINOMDIST}(x, n, 1 - p)$. As a cautionary note, probabilities in Excel functions are not always computed correctly when probabilities are small (Knüsel 2005).

4. For this question, you will investigate the relationship between average inventory levels and fill rate, and how changes in lead time and/or base stock affect average inventory. Specifically, you will plot the average inventory – fill rate relationship and answer six questions. But first, some background.

   Recall that IN_1 and IN_2 are net inventory random variables at stages 1 and 2, respectively, that is,

   $$IN_1 = S_1 - LD_1 \quad \text{and} \quad IN_2 = S_2 - B_1 - LD_2$$

   In the above formulas, S_1 denotes the base stock level at stage 1, S_2 denotes the base stock level at stage 2, LD_1 is the random variable for demand during the stage 1 lead time, LD_2 is the random variable for demand during the stage 2 lead time, and B_1 is the random variable for backorders at stage 1 (i.e., $B_1 = (LD_1 - S_1)^+ = (-IN_1)^+$). Inventory only exists at a stage when IN_1 (for stage 1) and IN_2 (for stage 2) are positive. In other words, the inventory random variable and average (or mean) inventory at each stage are

   $$(IN_1)^+ = (S_1 - LD_1)^+$$

   $$E[(IN_1)^+] = E[(S_1 - LD_1)^+]$$

   $$(IN_2)^+ = (S_2 - B_1 - LD_2)^+$$

   $$E[(IN_2)^+] = E[(S_2 - B_1 - LD_2)^+]$$

   (recall that $(x)^+ = \max\{0, x\}$). Prepare a scatter diagram with average inventory on the x-axis and fill rate on the y-axis. The scatter diagram will plot the following four series:

   - Series 1—fill rate as a function of average inventory (i.e., $E[(IN_1)^+] + E[(IN_2)^+]$) over $L_1 \in \{6, 6.5, 7, 7.5,$

8, 8.5, 9, 9.5, 10, 10.5, 11, 11.5, 12, 12.5, 13, 13.5},
with $L_2 = 10$, $S_1 = 100$, $S_2 = 100$.

- Series 2—fill rate as a function of average inventory over $L_2 \in \{6, 6.5, 7, 7.5, 8, 8.5, 9, 9.5, 10, 10.5, 11, 11.5, 12, 12.5, 13, 13.5\}$, with $L_1 = 10$, $S_1 = 100$, $S_2 = 100$.

- Series 3—fill rate as a function of average inventory over $S_1 \in \{65, 70, 75, 80, 85, 90, 95, 100, 105, 110, 115, 120, 125, 130, 135, 140\}$, with $L_1 = 10$, $L_2 = 10$, $S_2 = 100$.

- Series 4—fill rate as a function of average inventory over $S_2 \in \{65, 70, 75, 80, 85, 90, 95, 100, 105, 110, 115, 120, 125, 130, 135, 140\}$, with $L_1 = 10$, $L_2 = 10$, $S_1 = 100$.

    Hints: $E[(IN_1)^+] = E[IN_1] + E[B_1]$ and $E[(IN_2)^+] =$
    $$\sum_{x=0}^{S_2-1} P[B_1 + LD_2 = x](S_2 - x).$$

a. Why does average inventory increase as lead time decreases?

b. At the base case of $L_1 = L_2 = 10$, $S_1 = S_2 = 100$, why is it that average inventory at stage 1 is higher than average inventory at stage 2?

c. What conclusions can you draw from the scatter diagram with respect to the impact of changes in L_1, S_1,

L_2, and S_2 on average inventory, and with respect to the impact of increasing inventory at stage 1 (e.g., due to changes in L_1 and S_1) and at stage 2 (e.g., due to changes in L_2 and S_2) on fill rate?

d. Each unit in stage 1 inventory requires an investment of $1,000 and each unit in stage 2 inventory requires an investment of $1,500. Suppose that management is willing to commit to maintaining a target total average inventory investment of about $20,000. If there are no changes in lead time (i.e., $L_1 = L_2 = 10$), then what base stock levels would you recommend,[15] what are the average inventories at each stage, and what is the projected fill rate?

e. If lead times are 50 percent lower (i.e., $L_1 = L_2 = 5$), then what base stock levels would you recommend, what are the average inventories at each stage, and what is the projected fill rate?

f. Why is it that the fill rate is higher for the same (approximate) level of inventory investment at lower replenishment lead times (e.g., how do you explain the difference in fill rates in the previous two questions)? (*Hint:* Think of a principle of nature.)

---

[15] Base stock levels should be in integer quantities because demand is in integer quantities.

Case Exercise: *EPR Scientific B*

EPR Scientific recently acquired a firm that develops and manufactures voltmeters. Customer service as measured by fill rate has traditionally been poor at the firm, and EPR's management team is considering where and how much to invest in order to improve performance.

HOW THIS CASE DIFFERS FROM EPR SCIENTIFIC A

The companion case, EPR Scientific A, assumes that each stage has infinite capacity; that is, the lead time for a unit at stage *j* is always L_j regardless of how many orders are placed during the period. The two-stage supply chain in this case differs in two ways. First, each stage can process only one unit at a time (i.e., finite capacity). Second, the processing time at a stage is random instead of constant. As in EPR Scientific A, a base stock policy is used to answer production and ordering decisions at each stage. You will be asked to set up a spreadsheet to compute fill rate (i.e., percent of demand shipped

from inventory) as a function of capacity and base stock level at each stage. The analysis illuminates the nature of trade-offs that arise when considering how to manage inventories and capacities throughout a supply chain.

THE SETTING AND NOTATION

There are two stages in the supply chain (see diagram below). Both stages manage inventory according to a base stock policy; the base stock levels by stage are denoted S_1 and S_2. Processing times at each stage are exponentially distributed with mean $1/\mu_1$ and $1/\mu_2$. If stage 2 orders a unit from stage 1 when there is no stage 1 inventory, then the order is backlogged at stage 1 (i.e., put in the queue for processing). A unit that completes processing at stage 1 goes into stage 1 inventory if there are no backlogged orders; otherwise the completed unit goes directly to either the stage 2 input queue (if the stage 2 processor is busy) or the stage 2 processor. Raw material is always available for processing at stage 1.

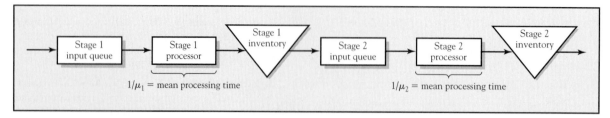

Customers order product from stage 2 at rate λ. The demand process is Poisson, and any unsatisfied demand is backordered. A demand process that is Poisson means that the time between unit demands is an exponential random variable with mean $1/\lambda$.

THE THEORY

If $S_1 = 0$ (i.e., stage 1 does not build to inventory), then we can use a powerful result proved by Jackson (1957); he showed that the steady-state performance of the system can be analyzed as two independent $M/M/1$ queues in series. Such an approach is not exact when $S_1 > 0$, but analysis under the assumption of two independent $M/M/1$ queues in series generally provides a good approximation.

This case requires the application of the above approximation method, that is, computing the fill rate as a function of base stock levels (S_1, S_2), capacities (μ_1, μ_2), and demand rate (λ) using formulas from the $M/M/1$ model. In order to outline the computation approach, we'll use much of the notation from EPR Scientific A. Let IN_j denote the random variable for net inventory at stage j, B_j is the number of units on back order at stage j, and N_j is the number of orders in the stage j "system" (i.e., in queue and in process at stage j). The role of N_j is analogous to LD_j in EPR Scientific A.

The fill rate for the supply chain is the probability that net inventory at stage 2 is positive, that is,

$$FR = 1 - P[IN_2 \le 0] = P[IN_2 > 0]$$

The following relationships hold among random variables and parameters.

$$IN_1 = S_1 - N_1$$

$$B_1 = (N_1 - S_1)^+ = (-IN_1)^+$$

$$IN_2 = S_2 - B_1 - N_2$$

Consequently,

$$FR = P[IN_2 > 0] = P[B_1 + N_2 < S_2]$$

$$= P[N_1 \le S_1 \;\&\; N_2 < S_2] + P[N_1 = S_1 + 1 \;\&\; N_2 < S_2 - 1]$$
$$+ \cdots + P[N_1 = S_1 + S_2 - 1 \;\&\; N_2 < 1]^{[16]}$$

Recall that for an $M/M/1$ queue,

$$P[N_j = n] = (1 - \lambda/\mu_j)(\lambda/\mu_j)^n$$

Due to the result by Jackson (1957), when $S_1 = 0$, then N_1 and N_2 are independent and the above formula can be used to compute the exact steady-state fill rate.[17] When $S_1 > 0$, the same approach can be used to approximate the steady-state fill rate.

Questions

The following questions require you to analyze the impact of changes in capacity and base stock in the two-stage supply chain, and to sort out the managerial implications from your analysis. The average demand rate is $\lambda = 10$ units per period.

1. Limit consideration to cases where the utilization at stage 1 is the same as at stage 2 (i.e., stages 1 and 2 have the same capacity). By testing alternative parameter values, verify that a 10 percent increase in capacity (at both stages) generally provides a greater increase in fill rate than a 10 percent increase in base stock (at both stages). Identify a rule of thumb for indicators (i.e., in terms of utilization and fill rate) for when the difference in impact of a 10 percent increase in capacity (μ_1 and μ_2) versus a 10 percent increase in base stock (S_1 and S_2) is likely to be greatest. How do these indicators change when the mean demand rate is 100 units per period instead of 10 units per period, and what do you think are the reasons for the results that you observe when you answer this question?

2. Limit consideration to cases where the utilization at stage 1 is the same as at stage 2 (i.e., stages 1 and 2 have the same capacity). What conclusion can you draw about the difference in impact on fill rate from a 10 percent increase in capacity at stage 1 versus stage 2? What conclusion can you draw about the difference in impact on fill rate from a 10 percent increase in base stock at stage 1 versus stage 2?

3. Identify conditions where the conclusions in the previous question regarding the impact of stage 1 changes versus stage 2 changes are reversed. That is, under what conditions is fill rate likely to be more sensitive to investments in the stage other than the one identified as more significant in question 2?

[16] Note that when μ_1 is very large relative to λ and/or when S_1 is large, $P[N_1 < S_1] \approx 1$, and the analysis essentiallly becomes identical to the analysis of the single-stage supply chain in exercise 15 of Chapter 8.

[17] Note that for independent random variables N_1 and N_2, $P[N_1 = a \;\&\; N_2 < b] = P[N_1 = a] \times P[N_2 < b]$.

Chapter **Nine**

Production Management:
Flow Control and
Scheduling

Chapter Outline

1. Production Framework
2. When and How Much to Produce
   2.1. *Pull Systems*
   2.2. *Push Systems*
   2.3. *Combining Pull and Push*
3. Sequencing and Scheduling
   3.1. *Single-Machine Sequencing Rules*
   3.2. *Two Machines in Series*
   3.3. *Scheduling Problems Are Hard*
4. Summary and Managerial Insights
   4.1. *Sequencing Jobs at a Resource in Increasing Order of Time per Dollar Value Minimizes the Average Value of Unprocessed Jobs*
   4.2. *If an EDD Sequence Results in One or More Late Jobs, Then It Is Impossible to Find a Different Sequence Where All Jobs Are Completed on Time*
   4.3. *Most Real-World Scheduling Problems Are Intractable*
5. Exercises
   Case Exercise: MA Life Happenings

Chapter Keys

1. What are the differences between MTS, ATO, MTO, and ETO product, and what is the role of the law of large numbers?
2. What are the differences between pull and push systems?
3. What are the pros/cons of pull systems such as (Q, R) or kanban systems?
4. What is the difference between dependent and independent demand?
5. What are the three main inputs to MRP, what is the output, and how does it work?
6. When is MRP appropriate, what is a weakness, and what are two major extensions?
7. How does POLCA combine elements of pull and push, when is POLCA appropriate, and how do POLCA cards differ from kanban cards?

8. How are the sequencing rules applied to construct a schedule?
9. For each rule, what are the properties of the resulting sequence?
10. What are the managerial insights from the chapter?

Chapter 8 dealt with determining appropriate capacity levels for a system that "makes" a service or product. Chapter 8 also introduced principles and methods for managing capacity in settings where customers wait for service. This chapter shifts the focus to managing capacity in production settings, an amazingly rich area of study (see Figure 9.1). Think of all the different things that are made in the world. As you can imagine, there is great diversity in product and market characteristics, and, correspondingly, a wide variety of production systems. Section 1 presents a framework for structuring the diversity by grouping product production into four basic categories.

Section 2 describes pull and push approaches for managing the flow of materials through a production system. In addition to the mechanics of how each approach answers the questions of when and how much to produce, we'll examine pros/cons and environments suited to each approach. We'll also consider a hybrid approach that contains elements of pull and push.

Section 3 takes the choreography of production to a deeper level through consideration of three related questions: (1) Out of the list of jobs waiting to be processed at a workcenter, what should be done first? (2) What jobs, if any, are behind schedule? (3) What delivery date should be quoted on a new customer order? Section 3 also highlights a significant computational challenge associated with these questions and sheds some light on assessing the validity of claims by software vendors.

1. PRODUCTION FRAMEWORK

One way to **classify production characteristics of a product** is according to the following categories: **make-to-stock (MTS), assemble-to-order (ATO), make-to-order (MTO), engineer-to-order (ETO).** As the name implies, **finished goods inventory is maintained for MTS product,** which is produced in anticipation of future demand. **MTO product, on the other hand, is not made ahead of time.** Raw materials may be stored in inventory, but the end product is only produced in response to a specific customer order. **ATO product occupies a middle ground between MTS and MTO; the firm builds and stores some components in inventory based on demand projections,** but end product is produced in response to a specific customer order. **ETO product is quite distinct from the other three categories. An ETO product is designed, developed, and produced in response to a customer request.** The categories are summarized in Table 9.1. We'll make use of this framework when reviewing different approaches for managing production in the next two sections.

FIGURE 9.1

A supply chain with emphasis on production management links.

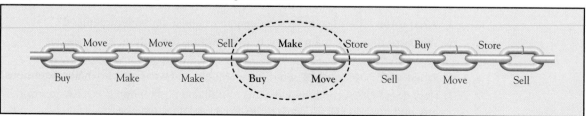

TABLE 9.1 **Characteristics of Four Basic Types of Production Systems**
The four types are listed in order of increasing market response time and capability for customization. Firms may make use of two or more the basic production systems, for example, low-volume product via MTO and high-volume product via MTS.

Make-to-stock (MTS)	Finished product is produced prior to a customer order, typically in consideration of forecasted demand. Customer demand is satisfied primarily through finished goods inventory.
	An MTS production system is responsive to the market (e.g., demand satisfied immediately from inventory, given sufficient stock) but can be expensive due to high inventory requirements when demand is volatile and difficult to predict. MTS is popular for high-volume standardized product with relatively stable demand (e.g., refrigerators).
Assemble-to-order (ATO)	Finished product is assembled in response to a specific customer order from prebuilt and purchased components. Finished goods inventory is not maintained. Some components are produced in-house prior to a customer order, typically in consideration of forecasted demand.
	An ATO production system is less responsive than MTS due to the additional lead time required for assembly. ATO is popular when a large number of end products can be quickly assembled from different combinations of common components (e.g., power tools).
Make-to-order (MTO)	Finished product is produced in response to a specific customer order from purchased components. Finished goods inventory is not maintained and product is not partially built prior to a customer order. Inventory of purchased materials is typically maintained with planned purchases developed in accordance with demand forecasts or material usage.
	An MTO production system is less responsive than ATO due to the additional lead time required for fabricating parts and subassemblies. As is the case with ATO, MTO is popular for customized end product (e.g., furniture).
Engineer-to-order (ETO)	Finished product is designed, developed, and produced in response to a specific customer request.
	An ETO production system is the least responsive of the four due to the lead time for design and development. ETO is popular for highly customized, even one-of-kind, product (e.g., custom nameplates).

The Role of a Principle of Nature in Production System Alternatives

Management decisions on the length of the firm's product line in each product category are influenced by a trade-off between the opportunity to increase sales by increasing the number of options available to customers and the challenges associated with higher volatility in demand for each end item. Demand volatility increases because the average demand per end item generally decreases as the number of options expands (e.g., cannibalization occurs as some demand for an existing product is shifted to a product with a new option/feature). And, by the **law of large numbers, as volume decreases, relative demand variability increases.**

Some firms are investing in agile and fast production systems, and moving away from MTS toward ATO and MTO (e.g., postponement of form) because doing so can make it possible to **increase the range of end-product choices available to customers without the negative effects of increased demand volatility.** Why is this? High market volatility can be very expensive when inventory is used to respond quickly to market demand (e.g., need enough inventory to cover the possibility of a hot market, which means lots of excess inventory when the market is not so hot). Under ATO and MTO, end items are not built ahead of time. This can allow a firm to offer a wide range of customer choice while

Principle of Nature: Law of Large Numbers

DEFINITION
As volume increases, relative variability decreases.

IMPLICATION
Look for ways to change operations so that planning can be done at a more aggregate unit.

EXAMPLE
Sherwin-Williams used to stock different colors of paints in their stores. Today, stores basically carry only white paint and an inventory of dyes. The company has installed precise mixing machines. A customer selects the color of paint from a template of options, and the dyes are mixed with white paint to create the desired color (i.e., an MTO production system). Customized colors are also possible; a customer can bring in a sample of a desired color, and paint is mixed to match it. The result is a wide array of color choices, high availability of colors "in stock," and relatively low inventory investment.

experiencing relatively high average volumes (and steady demand) on materials maintained in inventory. For example, five choices for processor speed, five choices for hard-drive capacity, and five choices for type of CD/DVD-ROM lead to 125 different PCs that can be sold to a customer. The average volume per item maintained in inventory is about 25 times more than the average volume per end item (given that each PC includes a processor, hard drive, and CD/DVD-ROM).

2. WHEN AND HOW MUCH TO PRODUCE

Chapter 3 introduced the difference between pull and push approaches for managing flows. A **pull approach is reactive—actual inventory (or, equivalently, actual demand) is used to signal when to order or make product.** The use of pull approaches in a production setting is the topic of Section 2.1. A **push approach is proactive—projected inventory (or, equivalently, projected demand) combined with projected lead times are used to signal when to order or make product.** A common push approach in industry is material requirements planning, the topic of Section 2.2. Section 2.3 outlines a hybrid pull/push approach.

2.1 Pull Systems

Chapter 7 covered three types of inventory management policies: a **base stock policy, a continuous review policy known as (Q, R), and a periodic review policy known as (I, S).** All of these policies are **examples of pull** approaches to answer the questions of when and how much. We considered these policies in the context of ordering from a supplier, but the policies also can be used to control the production and movement of materials in a factory.

For example, imagine a sequence of workcenters in a production system—say, grinding, polishing, priming, and painting—that produces two types of parts (see Figure 9.2). Parts are produced and placed in bins for use at the next workcenter. There are three bins of part type 1 and two bins of part type 2 between each pair of workcenters, and each bin holds 100 parts. Figure 9.2 illustrates the use of what is essentially **a (Q, R) policy to control production and material flow.** Each workcenter produces in response to orders from its "customer" (i.e., downstream workcenter) and orders raw materials from its "supplier" (i.e., upstream workcenter) in response to its usage. For example, the polishing workcenter

FIGURE 9.2   Two Workcenters in a System That Produces Two Types of Parts—1 and 2

The polishing workcenter transforms an A1 part into a B1 part and transforms an A2 part into a B2 part. Similarly, the priming workcenter transforms part B1 into C1 and part B2 into C2. There are three bins for part type 1 and two bins of part type 2 between each pair of workcenters. The bin of B1 parts in the priming workcenter has just emptied, which triggers an order for new production of B1. The inventory position of part B1 just prior to the order is two bins, with one bin on order (and in production at the polishing workcenter) and one bin on hand.

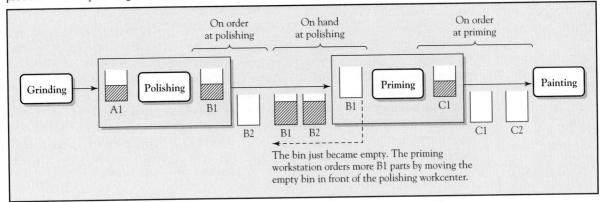

receives a signal to produce part B1 whenever the inventory position of part B1 reaches two bins (i.e., $R = 2$ bins $= 200$ parts). The order quantity is one bin (i.e., $Q = 1$ bin $= 100$ parts).

Figure 9.2 shows an empty bin for B1 parts next to the priming workcenter. This means that the priming workcenter has just completed production of 100 C1 parts and that the reorder point of two B1 bins has just been reached. The priming workstation will order the polishing workstation to produce 100 B1 parts by moving the empty B1 bin to the polishing workstation. There is an empty C1 bin and an empty C2 bin after the priming workstation. This means that both parts are on order from the painting workcenter. Section 3 of this chapter addresses the question of which of the two parts to produce next.

The pull production system illustrated in Figure 9.2 is **sometimes referred to as a *kanban system* after the type of signaling mechanism.** *Kanban* means card or action plate in Japanese. A kanban typically fits in a slot on each bin. A kanban at a workcenter signals that production can begin (i.e., production cannot begin without a kanban), and information on the card specifies the part and the quantity to be produced.[1] While kanbans are common in pull production systems, there are a variety of alternative ways to signal production. A Kawasaki motorcycle plant, for example, has used colored golf balls. When an engine is placed on the assembly line, a golf ball is placed in a trough and rolls down to the engine assembly area. The color of the ball indicates what type of engine to make.

Figure 9.2 illustrates the pull process over successive workcenters but doesn't answer the question of what triggers the flow at the last workcenter. The answer for most pull production systems is end-item production, which is determined by the master production schedule. The **master production schedule is the planned production of the end items** at the plant. Ideally, this schedule should be set so that some of every product is produced

---

[1] In some pull production systems (e.g., especially when workcenters are far apart or the movement of containers requires special equipment), there are two types of kanban cards—*production kanbans* are used to signal production and *move kanbans* are used to signal the movement of parts between workcenters.

every day at rates that approximate average demand per day. In addition, the master production schedule is typically frozen[2] for a period of time into the future. The repetition of a constant daily schedule promotes smooth and efficient flow through the factory.

A main **advantage of a pull system is simplicity.** Production and material movement occur in response to demand, or, in other words, downstream stages "pull" material from upstream stages. An additional **advantage is that a pull system, and the kanban system in particular, limits the amount of inventory between stages.**[3] For instance, the amount of inventory between two workcenters in Figure 9.2 is limited to five bins. This not only allows tight control of inventory investment, but also facilitates a cycle of improvement. Inventory can be gradually lowered until problems become obvious (e.g., at low inventories, periodic breakdowns at polishing cause idleness at priming). Inventory can be raised while efforts focus on eliminating problems, and, after attempts to correct, inventory can be lowered again.

A **disadvantage of a pull system arises in situations when capacity is relatively inflexible and demand is fluctuating.** In these situations, the use of a pull approach while maintaining high levels of service can be expensive (e.g., high investment in excess inventory and/or capacity to protect against periods of surging demand).

2.2 Push Systems

Dependent and Independent Demand

The first step to understanding a common push system in industry known as material requirements planning (MRP) is to understand the difference between dependent and independent demand items. The **demand for a dependent demand item depends upon something else the firm makes,** whereas this condition does not hold for an independent demand item. In other words, **independent demand items are the products sold to customers and dependent demand items are the parts that go into the firm's end products.** Sometimes a part can have both dependent and independent demand (e.g., a pump that goes into a product and that is sold to repair shops).

Why Understand the Difference?   Because (1) the **requirements of dependent demand items are more predictable** and (2) **push systems such as MRP are only as good as the inputs**—this is **why MRP is widely used to plan dependent demand items.**

MRP Mechanics

So how does MRP work? Think back to the caterer example in Chapter 3. Given a number of scheduled engagements during the upcoming weeks, the caterer knows the types and quantities of foods to be served at each engagement. She also knows what ingredients go into the end items as well as preparation and ordering lead times. Putting this together, she plans when and how much to make. This is the essence of MRP.

As illustrated in Figure 9.3, there are three main input files to MRP. As noted above, the **master production schedule is the planned production of the end items,** or, in other words, the independent demand items. In the caterer example, the master schedule corresponds to the schedule of engagements. The **bill of materials is the list of parts that go into each end item.** This corresponds to the list of ingredients in each dish for the caterer. The **item master contains the inventory levels and lead times of each item** in the bill of material. If you think of a caterer developing meal preparation plans, the logic of MRP is intuitive. **Beginning with the master production schedule, determine what and how**

---

[2] A schedule that is frozen for a month, for example, means that the schedule cannot be changed for a month into the future. Changes to the schedule beyond this point would be allowed.

[3] Technically, a (Q, R) policy implemented at each stage in Figure 9.2, which is an example of a pull system, does not limit inventory between stages in certain circumstances. This point is considered further as an end-of-chapter exercise.

FIGURE 9.3 **The Main Inputs and Output of Material Requirements Planning**

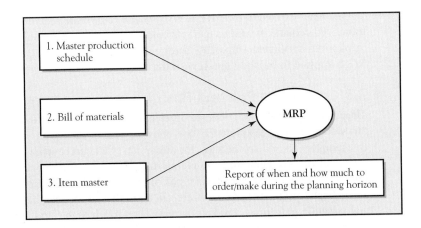

many parts are needed (bill of materials), then check inventories (item master), and, for those parts with insufficient inventory, use the lead times (item master) to determine when work should begin or orders should be placed. The result is a *material requirements plan;* that is, when and how much to make/order of materials that go into end items.

A Little History

While the logic of MRP may be intuitive, the execution typically involves massive amounts of data. The number of different parts in a bill of materials file can easily be in the hundreds of thousands. For this reason, MRP did not become widely used until computers began to appear in industry (in the 1970s). Today MRP is probably the most widely implemented manufacturing planning and control system, and MRP modules are offered in ERP systems.

When Is MRP Appropriate?

If a firm produces very simple products (e.g., toothpicks), then it doesn't make a lot of sense to invest in a computer system to help plan material requirements. If demand for a firm's product line is very stable and the production system is flexible enough to make some of every product every day, then again, it doesn't make a lot of sense to invest in a computer system to help plan production. Production planning follows a routine where there is little change day-to-day. Key **requirements for the viability of MRP are (1) a complex product and (2) a master production schedule that is both predictable and dynamic** (i.e., not the same every week).

Weaknesses and Extensions

MRP uses **fixed lead times, and this can create problems for a couple of reasons.** First, there is **no explicit consideration of capacity.** For example, suppose the lead time to make an engine is set at two weeks in the item master. This lead time is used for planning purposes regardless of whether two million engines or two engines are needed. Consequently, MRP is susceptible to generating plans that are infeasible due to insufficient capacity. *Manufacturing resource planning* **(a.k.a. MRP II) is an extension of MRP that includes a module to compute the capacity requirements of a materials plan.** If a problem is observed, then adjustments are made.

A second problem with fixed lead times is that **lead times tend to get inflated over time.** There are natural pressures for this to occur (e.g., two years ago, the lead time for engines was doubled because they weren't made in time). The consequences are bad. Product that gets ordered and made earlier and earlier leads to a lot of excess product lying around—a costly proposition.

One other **extension of MRP is *distribution requirements planning* (DRP).** DRP uses forecasted demand in various markets combined with inventory and lead-time information to plan replenishment shipments throughout the distribution network. In short, **DRP is MRP applied to finished goods distribution.**

2.3 Combining Pull and Push

The preceding two sections outlined the elements of pull and push for managing production. In this section, we'll first explore the roots and pros/cons of each approach in more detail through an example. This will set the stage for discussion of a hybrid approach known as POLCA.

I know of a GE plant that makes four different sizes of refrigerators. The manufacturing process is a good example of the types of environments that inspired the development of MRP. Each refrigerator size is offered in a number of models that reflect different colors and variation in features. Product demand is relatively stable and finished goods inventory is maintained to provide short replenishment lead times to customers (i.e., an MTS production system). The plant has an assembly line for the production of finished product, though the vast majority of the space is dedicated to operations prior to final assembly (e.g., cutting, stamping, injection molding, painting, subassembly).

A key characteristic of the manufacturing process is the presence of significant scale economies that drive the batching of production. The master production schedule cycles through the four refrigerator sizes on a monthly basis, with three of the four sizes produced once per month and one size produced twice per month (e.g., size A produced for five days followed by size B for three days, and so on). Naturally, there is demand for every size every day. The reason for the batching in final assembly is scale economies induced by learning effects. Whenever the assembly line switches over to production of a different size, the assembly rate slows down and it takes some time to get back up to speed. The batching of production extends to many of the operations prior to final assembly due to significant setup times and costs.

Here we have a case where there are meaningful advantages to being proactive through a push approach. The knowledge that only a particular size refrigerator will be assembled for a week at a time can be translated into the requisite material requirements. In addition, the changing requirements over time can be considered in the determination of appropriate batch sizes at the various operations leading up to final assembly.

How Would a Pull Approach Work at the Plant?

The plant sets the master production schedule, and the execution of this schedule could be used to pull material through the plant and trigger orders from suppliers. A pure pull approach is reactive; replenishments are triggered by actual demand without the visibility of when future demand is likely to occur. One difficulty is that, in order to be responsive in this setting, there should be available inventory of all parts produced at a workcenter—a potentially expensive option when a particular part is used for only a few days each month. As we saw earlier, a way to get around this problem is to find ways to reduce setup costs to the point where it becomes economically viable to produce some of every product and every part every day in accordance with average market demand.[4]

In summary, the roots of both push and pull production are in an MTS environment. Material flows are driven by a master production schedule that typically remains frozen for a number of periods into the future. In the case of push, material is pushed through the production system by following a material requirements plan specifying when and how much to make/order over time. In the case of pull, material is pulled through the production system by the execution of the master production schedule.

Many manufacturers operate in environments where a repetitive and stable master production schedule is not viable. Characteristics of such settings include **markets with short product life cycles, frequent new product introductions, a wide range of varying product features with highly varying demand (e.g., ATO or MTO product), and custom-engineered or one-of-a-kind product (i.e., ETO product). A pure pull approach tends to break down in these settings,** requiring significant investment in excess capacity and/or inventory in order to respond quickly to varying demand. **POLCA is an approach designed for products with highly varying demands that combines elements of pull and push.**

What Is POLCA?

POLCA stands for paired-cell overlapping loops of cards with authorization, and is due to Rajan Suri and his colleagues in conjunction with the Center for Quick Response Manufacturing at the University of Wisconsin–Madison. The system has helped a number of factories reduce lead time and inventory, increase on-time delivery, and boost employee satisfaction (Suri and Krishnamurthy 2003).

The remainder of this section gives a high-level overview of POLCA that is directed at two objectives. The first objective is to provide a reasonable basis from which to assess whether POLCA may warrant consideration at your firm. More significantly, the second objective is to lay groundwork for future innovations. Exposure to how the elements of pull and push are creatively combined in POLCA leads to a richer understanding of the two elements—an understanding that is useful when thinking about alternative approaches or modifications suited to a particular environment. Additional details on POLCA may be found in Suri (1998, 2003).

Let's begin with a picture. Figure 9.4 is a schematic of a factory that produces customized faceplates that are mounted on a range of products. The plates are made from a variety of materials, come in different sizes, contain printed information, and have features to assist mounting (e.g., holes, notches). The factory floor contains 10 cells that are organized according to basic functions. For example, P1 contains equipment used for screen printing while P2 contains equipment used for lithographic printing. Due to the high degree of customization, there is much variation in routings across orders. Figure 9.4 illustrates the routing for an order with operations at cells P1, F2, A4, and S1.

How Does POLCA Answer the Questions of When and How Much?

In summary, POLCA combines the power of MRP to specify precise material requirements with a card-based control mechanism oriented toward fast flow through the system. The richness of information in the MRP database also is used to coordinate orders from suppliers and to generate high-level timing guideposts. These guideposts protect against favoring fast flow at the expense of some orders being late. We'll look at each of the two elements in turn, beginning with the role of MRP.

---

[4] The GE plant has moved in this direction, reducing setup costs to the point where MRP is used to plan replenishment orders from suppliers while a pull approach is used for material flow in the plant.

FIGURE 9.4 **A Schematic of a Factory with Four Types of Cells**

The boxes inside each cell depict different workcenters. The figure shows POLCA loops for a customer order that requires processing at cells P1, F2, A4, and S1. The large arrows show the flow of the order and the small arrows show the circulation of POLCA cards between pairs of cells, that is, P1/F2, F2/A4, and A4/S1.

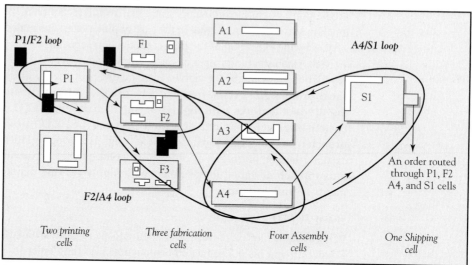

Source: Reprinted with permission from Suri and Krishnamurthy (2003).

Given an end-item plan (e.g., a set of customer orders with due dates), **MRP software generates the timing and quantity of materials to be ordered from suppliers.** In addition, shop orders are generated for each cell. The **MRP system** contains lead times for each cell that, via standard MRP back-scheduling logic, are used to **specify the start time for each order at each cell. The start times can be viewed as guideposts that regulate the timing of work at a high level.** Work on a particular order at a cell is not *authorized* to begin until the start time has been reached. This is the extent to which MRP, or push, is used in the system. The remaining element is the **POLCA card, which is used to pull work through the cells within the confines of the timing guideposts generated by MRP.**

POLCA cards exist for each from-to pair of cells through which an order could flow. P1/F2 POLCA cards, for example, cycle between cells P1 and F2. Imagine an order corresponding to the routing in Figure 9.4 (i.e., P1 → F2 → A4 → S1) that is waiting in front of cell P1. Work on the order can only begin if it is authorized by the MRP system and if a P1/F2 POLCA card is available at cell P1. When the order completes processing at cell P1, the P1/F2 POLCA card moves with the order to cell F2. The same checks must be satisfied for the order to begin processing at cell F2 (i.e., MRP authorization for the order at cell F2 and availability of an F2/A4 POLCA card), and any subsequent cell. Once the order completes processing at cell F2, it is moved along with an F2/A4 card to cell A4, and the P1/F2 card is returned to cell P1.

On the surface, the role of POLCA cards may appear similar to the role of kanban cards illustrated in Figure 9.2, but there are **three significant differences.** First, a **kanban card controls movement between a pair of workcenters whereas a POLCA card controls movement between a pair of cells.**[5] Second, **each kanban card is associated with a**

[5] There are some exceptions where firms have not established cells and use POLCA cards to control flow between workcenters.

specific product or part. A POLCA card is associated with a pair of cells and thus can be used with any product that flows between the cells. This leads to the most significant difference between the roles of kanban and POLCA cards: a **kanban card signals that material is needed** whereas a **POLCA card signals that capacity is available.**[6] This is how POLCA favors getting work through the system quickly. For example, if there is no P1/F2 card available at cell P1, it means that all of the P1/F2 cards are at cell F2, or, in other words, cell F2 is backed up with a lot of work. It doesn't make a lot of sense to start the order at cell P1 if the next cell is overloaded with work; doing so will only add to work-in-process. Furthermore, if a P1/F1 card is available, cell P1 might be able to use its capacity to work on another order that is destined for cell F1, and since the P1/F1 card is available, it means cell F1 will soon be needing work.[7] Without the feedback from the POLCA control cards, cell P1 might begin work on something that cell F2 couldn't use, while delaying work on something that cell F1 needs. In this way POLCA helps to ensure that upstream cells work on orders that will most likely be needed by downstream cells in the near future.

[6] This difference is also reflected in the unit of work specified by a card. A kanban card specifies work as the number of a particular part to be produced at a workcenter. A POLCA card specifies work as the amount of capacity to be used at a cell. The capacity required by the order at the next cell determines the number of POLCA cards that travel with the order. Just as there are trade-offs to be considered when determining the number of parts associated with a kanban card, there are trade-offs to be considered when selecting the unit of capacity of a POLCA card. The question of how to set the unit of capacity is discussed in Suri and Krishnamurthy (2003).

[7] Formally, the availability of many P1/F1 cards at cell P1 doesn't give a full picture of whether or not cell F1 will soon run out of work because cell P2 also may send orders to cell F1. Nevertheless, it is an indicator that capacity will soon be available at cell F1, and it has the advantage of being simple (i.e., not dependent on a centralized information system)

An Illustration of POLCA at the Alexandria Extrusion Company[8]

COMPANY AND PRODUCTS
Alexandria Extrusion Company (AEC), based in Alexandria, MN, is a manufacturer of aluminum extrusions. The firm specializes in providing customized extrusions with short lead times. A few of their products are displayed here.

PROCESS FLOW
Products start as aluminum logs and undergo primary operations at one of three extrusion presses, secondary operations (e.g., sawing), and finishing operations (e.g., milling). The jobs flow between workcenters in baskets (shown in the photograph at right).

[8] All photographs in this illustration are reprinted with permission from the Alexandria Extrusion Company. The content of this illustration was prepared with the help of Rajan Suri.

POLCA AT AEC

In an effort to reduce work in process between operations and improve the coordination between workcenters, AEC implemented POLCA in 2005. There are 35 POLCA loops between the workcenters, as illustrated below.

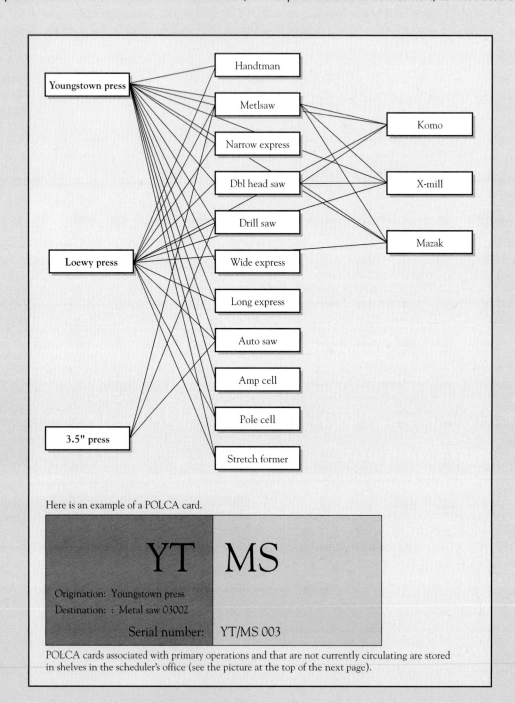

Here is an example of a POLCA card.

YT	MS
Origination: Youngstown press	
Destination: : Metal saw 03002	
Serial number:	YT/MS 003

POLCA cards associated with primary operations and that are not currently circulating are stored in shelves in the scheduler's office (see the picture at the top of the next page).

The process starts with the scheduler reviewing the dispatch list from the MRP system showing the jobs that are authorized to begin. If a POLCA card is available for the next job, he takes the card and job work order down to the press for its primary operation.

The picture below shows a press operator, and a slot containing work orders and POLCA cards.

As cards circulate between workcenters, they are returned to bulletin boards near the workcenters where operators can check to see if a particular card is available.

The picture below shows jobs (baskets of extrusions) with work orders and POLCA cards.

AEC observed significant results within six months of implementing POLCA, including

- Sixty percent reduction in work-in-process inventory within the POLCA loop.
- Reduction in lead times for jobs, and less effort in expediting.
- On-time delivery actually better, although there is less inventory in the system.
- Simplification in shop floor personnel's tasks by making it clear which job should be run next at each workcenter.

In summary, **POLCA is a production management approach designed for customized products with highly varying demands.** Elements of push and pull are combined in a way that is conducive to fast flows and on-time delivery. **MRP provides visibility into changing material and timing requirements that are a consequence of varying demand. POLCA cards facilitate the rational use of capacity in the face of workloads at cells that can vary significantly over time.**

At this point, we have considered several alternatives for answering the question of when and how much to order/make at various stages in a supply chain. If we consider what happens after these questions are answered, we'll find that, in many production environments, new questions arise. In particular, out of the number of things waiting to be processed at a workcenter or cell, what should be processed next? This and related questions are the topic of the next section.

3. SEQUENCING AND SCHEDULING

We are about to touch on the field of number theory as we briefly tour the topic of scheduling. Number theory is one of the older branches of mathematics that deals with properties of numbers. In addition to scheduling theory, some of its applications include cryptology (the study of secret codes), valuing of derivatives such as collateralized mortgage obligations, and design of experiments. One characteristic of the field is that it often deals with simple, easy-to-state questions that can be real skull-poppers to answer. For the sake of curiosity, here are three examples:

1. How many people does it take to form a group that always contains either four mutual acquaintances or four mutual strangers?[9]
2. There are 60 VIPs coming together for a several-day conference. Meal tables hold six people. What is the minimum number of "seatings" to ensure that everyone gets to sit at a table with every other person at the conference at least once?[10]
3. Vita Plus, a health care company, makes daily deliveries to area customers. Each truck holds 12 units, they do not split orders across trucks, and they're interested in minimizing the number of trucks making deliveries. One way to assign orders to trucks is to first arrange orders from largest to smallest, then assign to trucks with a new truck added only if the order won't fit anywhere else. This has the advantage of being simple, but it raises the question of just how bad are the solutions; for example, what is the worst that it can do relative to the optimum?[11]

Enough background on the range and types of questions that draw on number theory; let's consider the question of what to produce next, or, more generally, sequencing and scheduling.

A customer calls and wants to know when you can make and deliver an order. Your ability to evaluate your current schedule, adjust as necessary, and respond with a lead-time promise that you can keep is becoming increasingly important. Problems in this area are significant. One study found that stock price drops by nearly 11 percent after a company announces a supply chain problem such as production or shipment delays (Hendricks and Singhal 2003).

---

[9] The answer is 18. This question comes from Ramsey theory, a theory that is relevant for designing communications networks as well as information transmission and retrieval systems.

[10] The answer is 12. This question arose when I worked in industry.

[11] The answer is 11/9, or no more than 22 percent worse than the best (Johnson 1973). Vita Plus uses spreadsheet software to attack this problem.

Problems in this area are also challenging. As noted in Chapter 2, some firms deploy supply chain analytics software to help sort through millions of scheduling alternatives. Other firms leave the analytics—the process of identifying and evaluating viable alternatives—largely to individuals who have honed their skills through years in the business. This section is devoted to the properties of simple rules that provide some insight into the question of what to do next. Elements of these rules and their properties are often incorporated into more complex algorithms embedded in scheduling software.

A Few Words on Terminology

A *job* is work to be done for a customer. A job in a silkscreen shop, for example, could be 50 shirts with a two-color sorority logo that are due on Thursday. The work to complete a

job is divided into *operations* that are separable by time and resource (e.g., logo design, application of color 1, application of color 2, packaging). A *sequence* is an ordered list, and the action of selecting the operation to process next is called *dispatching* (e.g., the dispatcher at a taxi company decides who will be picked up next by an open cab). A *schedule* is a timing plan for resources and operations. A *Gantt chart* is a picture of a schedule, usually with resources along the vertical axis and time along the horizontal axis (see Figure 9.5). The name comes from Henry Gantt, who is known for popularizing the format.

We'll begin with the simplest possible scheduling situation—that of developing a schedule for a single machine. Jobs with known process times are available to be scheduled. Examining every possible sequence in order to select the "best" is prohibitive even for

FIGURE 9.5   A Gantt Chart Showing a Schedule for 11 out of Hundreds of Resources
The vertical axis lists workcenters and the horizontal axis is time. The horizontal bars correspond to operations, some of which are scheduled downtime. A right mouse click exposes the schedule details of an operation (illustrated in the lower center of the chart).

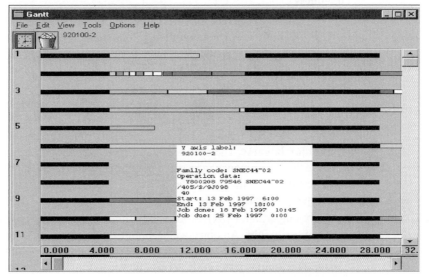

moderately sized problems (e.g., there are about 3.5 million different ways to sequence 10 jobs). However, there are a variety of simple rules for sequencing that perform optimally with respect to particular measures of performance. Some selected sequencing rules and properties of the resulting schedule are described in Section 3.1. In Section 3.2, we'll consider a multistage production system comprised of two consecutive workcenters and the problem of completing all jobs as soon as possible.

3.1. Single-Machine Sequencing Rules

We'll look at six sequencing rules organized according to performance criteria—fairness, efficiency, and timeliness.

Fairness

1. First-come-first-served (FCFS). Jobs are **sequenced in order of arrival.** The resulting sequence is perceived as **fair,** and, consequently, the rule is common when jobs are customers waiting for service (e.g., deli counter).

Efficiency

2. Shortest processing time (SPT). Jobs are **sequenced in order of smallest to largest processing time.** This rule **minimizes the average number of jobs in the system,** or, equivalently, since time is proportional to number (due to Little's law), the **average job completion time.** Perhaps you use this rule when you are opening your mail or when doing homework assignments; for example, process the short ones first and gain the satisfaction of quickly clearing your desk.

3. Weighted shortest processing time (WSPT). Each job j has a weight w_j, which is the per-period cost assessed against the job while in the system. The weight, for example, could be the inventory holding cost rate for the job. Jobs are **sequenced in order of smallest to largest processing time to weight ratio.** This rule **minimizes the weighted average number of jobs in the system,** which, if weights correspond to inventory holding cost rates, is the same as minimizing inventory holding cost. Also, due to Little's law, the rule **minimizes the weighted average job completion time.** If the job weights are all the same value, then the WSPT rule is the same as the SPT rule.

Timeliness

4. Earliest due date (EDD). Jobs are **sequenced in due date order** (from earliest to latest). This rule **minimizes the maximum job lateness.** One important implication—if a job is late using the EDD rule, then there is no sequence where all jobs are completed on time. In other words, the EDD rule can be used to quickly determine if it is possible to get everything done on time.

5. Least slack (LS). The slack for a job j is the difference between its due date d_j and its processing time p_j; that is, the slack for job j is $d_j - p_j$. Jobs are **sequenced in order of smallest to largest slack.** This rule has the unusual property of **maximizing the minimum job lateness.** The rule essentially keeps any one job from completing very early. While this performance measure is not normally a priority in practice, empirical results suggest that the rule tends to be effective for getting work done on time when there are multiple production stages.

6. Moore's algorithm (MA). Moore's algorithm is a procedure for **minimizing the number of tardy jobs.** An objective of minimizing the number of tardy jobs is the same as **maximizing the fill rate** (i.e., percent of jobs completed on time)—a common performance measure in practice. The basic idea is to initially sequence jobs in due date order

(i.e., EDD rule). Then, if there is more than one tardy job, adjustments are made in a way that favors jobs with small processing times. Think about why this basic idea makes sense by using what you know about the properties of EDD and SPT sequences. We will not take the space to present the detailed steps of the algorithm here.[12] The main point of inclusion is to reinforce how insight gained from an understanding of very simple rules (e.g., EDD and SPT) can be useful in more complicated situations. In addition, fill rate performance measures are often important in practice, and so it is worth knowing that there is a simple and efficient optimization algorithm available.

Examples

Job	A	B	C	D
Process time (p_j)	12	5	9	2
Periods until due (d_j)	17	10	18	11
Weight (w_j)	6	1	1	1
Slack ($d_j - p_j$)	5	5	9	9
Time/Weight (p_j/w_j)	2	5	9	2

SPT

SPT sequence	D	B	C	A				
					Performance Measures			
Processing time	2	5	9	12				
					Total	**Average**	**Max**	**Min**
Start time	0	2	7	16				
Completion time (c_j)	2	7	16	28	53	53/3 = 13.3	28	2
Lateness ($c_j - d_j$)	−9	−3	−2	11	−3	−3/4 = −0.8	11	−9
Tardiness (max{0, $c_j - d_j$})	0	0	0	11	11	11/4 = 2.8	11	0
Weighted completion time ($w_j c_j$)	2	7	16	168	193	193/4 = 48.3	168	2

WSPT

WSPT sequence	A	D	B	C				
					Performance Measures			
Processing time	12	2	5	9				
					Total	**Average**	**Max**	**Min**
Start time	0	12	14	19				
Completion time	12	14	19	28	73	73/4 = 18.3	28	12
Lateness	−5	3	9	10	17	17/4 = 4.3	10	−5
Tardiness	0	3	9	10	22	22/4 = 5.5	10	0
Weighted completion time	72	14	19	28	133	133/4 = 33.3	72	14

WSPT sequence	D	A	B	C				
					Performance Measures			
Processing time	2	12	5	9				
					Total	**Average**	**Max**	**Min**
Start time	0	2	14	19				
Completion time	2	14	19	28	63	63/4 = 15.8	28	2
Lateness	−9	−3	9	10	7	7/4 = 1.8	10	−9
Tardiness	0	0	9	10	19	19/4 = 4.8	10	0
Weighted completion time	2	84	19	28	133	133/4 = 33.3	84	2

---

[12] See Baker (2005) or Pinedo (2001) for details.

EDD

EDD sequence	B	D	A	C	Performance Measures			
					Total	Average	Max	Min
Processing time	5	2	12	9				
Start time	0	5	7	19				
Completion time	5	7	19	28	59	59/4 = 14.8	28	5
Lateness	−5	−4	2	10	3	3/4 = 0.8	10	−5
Tardiness	0	0	2	10	12	12/4 = 3.0	10	0
Weighted completion time	5	7	114	28	154	154/4 = 38.5	114	5

Least Slack Sequence[13]

Least slack sequence	A	B	D	C	Performance Measures			
					Total	Average	Max	Min
Processing time	12	5	2	9				
Start time	0	12	17	19				
Completion time	12	17	19	28	76	76/4 = 19.0	28	12
Lateness	−5	7	8	10	20	20/4 = 5.0	10	−5
Tardiness	0	7	8	10	25	25/4 = 6.3	10	0
Weighted completion time	72	17	19	28	136	136/4 = 34.0	72	17

Lease slack sequence	B	A	D	C	Performance Measures			
					Total	Average	Max	Min
Processing time	5	12	2	9				
Start time	0	5	17	19				
Completion time	5	17	19	28	69	69/4 = 17.3	28	5
Lateness	−5	0	8	10	13	13/4 = 3.3	10	−5
Tardiness	0	0	8	10	18	18/4 = 4.5	10	0
Weighted completion time	5	102	19	28	154	154/4 = 38.5	102	5

Ties can be broken arbitrarily when applying a sequencing rule. For example, jobs A and D both have a time-to-weight ratio of 2, so either can go first in a WSPT sequence. The weighted-average completion time is 33.3 for both sequences, and since the WSPT minimizes weighted-average completion time, no sequence out of the 4 × 3 × 2 × 1 = 24 possibilities will result in a lower value.

The start times and completion times associated with a sequence define a machine schedule, which also can be portrayed as a Gantt chart, for example,

Period	1	2	3	4	5	6	7	8	9	10	11	12	13	14	15	16	17	18	19	20	21	22	23	24	25	26	27	28
Job	B					A												D	C									

3.2. Two Machines in Series

This section extends the previous section by adding a **second operation.** The first operation of each job is processed at machine 1 and the second operation is processed at machine 2. A job cannot begin processing on machine 2 until it is completed on machine 1. For example, if jobs are loads of laundry, then machine 1 is a washer and machine 2 is a dryer.

[13] Other least slack sequences are A-B-C-D and B-A-C-D.

Johnson's rule is a sequencing procedure that **minimizes the time it takes to complete all jobs; it also minimizes machine idle time.** The rule may be relevant from time to time in your personal life; for example, in situations where you and a partner have a number of jobs to get done during the day. Johnson's rule can be used to identify a sequence that maximizes your free time for other activities. The mechanics are listed below.

Johnson's Rule

1. Select the job with the shortest processing time at a machine considering both machines.

2. If the shortest processing time corresponds to machine 1, then schedule the job as far toward the beginning of the sequence as possible; if the shortest processing time corresponds to machine 2, then schedule the job as far toward the end of the sequence as possible. Jobs are assigned to positions in the sequence from the outside to the inside (see example).

3. Continue with steps 1 and 2 until all jobs have been assigned.

Example

Job	A	B	C	D
Machine 1 process time	12	5	9	2
Machine 2 process time	8	18	12	3

The positions in the sequence are 1, 2, 3, and 4. The shortest process time is 2, which corresponds to job D and machine 1. Job D is selected and assigned to position 1 (instead of 4) because the process time of 2 is for machine 1. Of the remaining jobs (i.e., jobs A, B, and C), the shortest process time is 5, which corresponds to job B and machine 1. Therefore, job B is selected and assigned to position 2. Now the shortest process time of the remaining jobs is 8 for job A and machine 2. The process time of 8 is associated with machine 2, so the job is scheduled as far toward the end of the sequence as possible, that is, position 4. Job C is the only job left and is assigned to position 3. The schedule is illustrated below.

Johnson's rule sequence	D	B	C	A
Machine 1 start time	0	2	7	16
Machine 1 completion time	2	7	16	28
Machine 2 start time	2	7	25	37
Machine 2 completion time	5	25	37	45

3.3 Scheduling Problems Are Hard

One of the great outstanding questions of mathematics will be answered if you can find an efficient method to solve the following "simple problem" (alternatively, you may wish to prove that no efficient method will ever be discovered): Partition n positive integers, a_1, $a_2, \ldots, a_n$, into two sets—A and B—so that $(\Sigma_{i \in A} a_i)^2 + (\Sigma_{i \in B} a_i)^2$ is as small as possible. When you are done, be sure to schedule a press conference, and be prepared because you will be on the front page of *The New York Times* the next day. The implications of your achievement are deceptively far-reaching, touching areas such as cryptology, optimal constitution of financial portfolios, clinical detection of glaucoma, and a host of business planning and scheduling problems. The other good thing is that you will acquire some spending money—you will have solved one of the Millennium Prize problems, each of which carries a reward of $1 million (see www.claymath.org/millennium).

Most real-world scheduling problems are computationally related to the problem posed above, which explains why scheduling problems are hard, and why there is good reason to be skeptical when a vendor claims their software can optimize your supply chain. We will not take the space here, but for the curious, Section 2 of Appendix 2 reviews the theoretical underpinnings of this claim.

4. SUMMARY AND MANAGERIAL INSIGHTS

In this chapter, we studied how production systems can be classified into four broad categories (MTS, ATO, MTO, ETO), each suited to certain market characteristics and production capabilities. In fact, a given firm may deploy multiple categories of production systems to fit the range of products produced and markets served.

We built on this broad framework by considering how market characteristics and production capabilities are related to the design of a system for planning and execution. We learned about the kanban system (pull) and about material requirements planning (push), two relatively common approaches in practice. We then explored the distinction between pull and push in greater detail through our study of POLCA, a system that combines reactive elements of pull with proactive elements of push in a manner suited to environments with highly varying, yet predictable, demands.

Lastly, we considered the detailed choreography of production and material flow, or scheduling. We learned that effective management of this area can have a large bearing on customer perceptions, particularly in make-to-order environments, for example, central to such issues as

- Quoting an accurate lead time for a customer order.
- Developing an effective response to a request to expedite an order (or order cancellation).
- Determining which orders are affected in the event of a mechanical breakdown or delayed delivery from a supplier, and developing a suitable response.

As a step toward understanding how these issues can be addressed, we studied a number of simple scheduling rules and their properties, and we learned of computational challenges in the area. Key managerial insights from the chapter are summarized below.

4.1. Sequencing Jobs at a Resource in Increasing Order of Time per Dollar Value Minimizes the Average Value of Unprocessed Jobs

Example 1

Large banks typically have back-office operations that input information on checks deposited in customer accounts. Naturally, it is in the bank's interest to get checks processed as quickly as possible—this reduces "float time" and allows the dollars to be working for the bank and its customers. One bank followed a policy of selecting bags of checks to process according to a first-come-first-served rule. The firm began experimenting with alternative sequencing rules and found, depending on the rule, float could be reduced anywhere from 50 percent to 90 percent. Needless to say, the bank changed their sequencing rule for processing checks. The result was powerful for two reasons. First, the change was very easy and cheap to implement (e.g., required no capital—just a simple instruction on how to select the next bag of checks to process). Second, the cost to the bank of float time was high. This company averaged receipts of $30 million worth of checks per day. On average, they were running about three days behind, or an average of nearly $100 million in unprocessed checks. As an example of impact, cutting the float balance by 80 percent brings in $80 million worth of cash that, if the bank is able to make 10 percent on their assets, generates $8 million annually to the bottom line. Not too bad for a change in operations that can be implemented in a day with virtually no investment. How does this story relate to insight 4.1? We know that the WSPT rules will minimize the average value of unprocessed checks—since the time to process the check is the same regardless of its dollar value, the rule in this context is to select the bag suspected of having the highest average dollar value per check. One can't do better than this rule if the objective is to minimize the average unprocessed check balance.

Example 2

If you get lots of mail, then there's a fair chance that you process it according to the following approximate rule: scan the return addresses of all the envelopes, open the envelopes that can be processed very quickly while saving the long and involved letters for later. In other words, mail is processed according to the SPT rule. Intuitively, this clears your desk as fast as possible (i.e., the average number of unprocessed letters is minimized) and tends to increase satisfaction.

4.2. If an EDD Sequence Results in One or More Late Jobs, Then It Is Impossible to Find a Different Sequence Where All Jobs Are Completed on Time

Alternatively, if it is possible to sequence jobs at a resource so that all are completed on time, the EDD rule will return such a sequence.

Example

It's near the end of the semester and you have 10 projects to complete. If you were to focus on one project at a time, there are about 3.5 million sequences. A quick way to check whether you may have some problems hitting the due dates is to estimate when each project will be completed if you follow an EDD sequence.

4.3. Most Real-World Scheduling Problems Are Intractable

One interpretation of this insight is software that is guaranteed to generate the "best" schedule in a reasonable amount of time cannot be developed, at least in the foreseeable future.[14]

Example

If a supply chain management software vendor states that their software will generate an optimal schedule for your supply chain, then they're lying.

5. EXERCISES

1. Write a brief answer to each of the chapter keys in your own words. After writing down your answers, review the chapter with a focus on the content in bold to check and clarify your interpretations.

2. This question requires you to think through and develop the logic that is used to generate a material requirements plan. There are two end items—A and B. The bill of materials for each end item is illustrated on the next page.

---

[14] This insight may have to be modified if research on quantum computing or DNA computing leads to a practical alternative to the silicon-based computer. Quantum computers use states of subatomic particles to encode information (for an overview, see Gershenfeld and Chuang 1998). A quantum computer, if ever developed, will likely be able to factor a 400-digit number in about one year (factoring is important for "cracking" an encrypted message). This compares with a supercomputer that would take much more than the estimated age of the universe to perform the same task. DNA computers use DNA to encode information. The DNA molecules are manipulated using biotechnology tools. In 1993, Leonard Aldeman of the University of Southern California tested the concept by solving a form of a traveling salesperson problem (i.e., find a route visiting a bunch of cities with the minimum total distance). The experiment took seven days in a laboratory (for an overview, see Aldeman 1998).

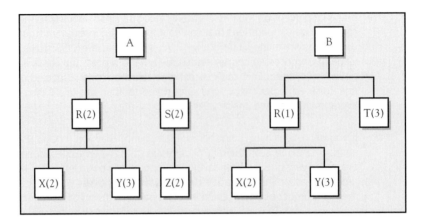

The bill of materials diagrams show that there are two X's and three Y's in each R, two Z's in each S, two R's and two S's in each A, and one R and three T's in each B.

   a. There is no inventory available. How many T's, X's, Y's, and Z's are required to make 200 A's and 70 B's? How many R's and S's are required to make 200 As and 70 Bs?

   b. There are 200 R's, 120 S's, and 100 Y's in inventory. How many T's, X's, Y's, and Z's must be ordered to make 200 A's and 70 B's?

   c. It is 8:00 a.m. on March 3rd. According to the item master, the lead time to make an R is three days, and it takes 10 days for the vendor to deliver an order of X's. When should an order for X's be placed if 200 A's are scheduled to begin assembly at 8:00 a.m. on March 20th?

3. A footnote in Section 2.1 referred to a distinction between a kanban pull system and a (Q, R) pull system. This question describes the difference and asks you to identify pros and cons of each approach. To keep things simple, imagine a two-stage production system that produces one product (see schematic below). We'll look at the case where each bin contains one part, so there will be one kanban card per part, and $Q = 1$ in the (Q, R) policy.[15] This will simplify the comparison, though the distinction between the two systems extends to cases where parts are produced in batches.

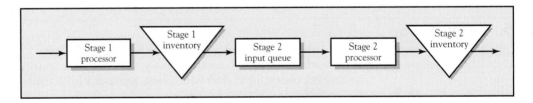

First, consider a kanban system for answering the question of when and how much to produce at each stage.[16] Suppose there are four stage 1 kanban cards and four stage 2 kanban cards. Each card is attached to a bin that contains one part. When a part is removed from stage 2 inventory, the stage 2 kanban card is removed from the bin, which in turn signals that stage 2 needs to produce a new part. If there is a part in stage 1 inventory, then (1) the stage 1 kanban card is removed from a bin signaling production of a new part at stage 1, (2) the stage 2 kanban card is attached to the bin, and (3) the bin is moved from

---

[15] Note that the (Q, R) policy with $Q = 1$ reduces to a base stock policy with the base stock level set to $R + 1$.

[16] There are variations in the details of how kanban pull systems are implemented in practice. The description here is one variation.

stage 1 inventory to either the stage 2 input queue (if the stage 2 processor is busy) or the stage 2 processor (if the stage 2 processor is idle). If there is no part in stage 1 inventory, which means that there are four parts on order at stage 1 (because there are four stage 1 kanban cards), then the stage 2 kanban card is held until a part becomes available, at which time the events described in the previous sentence take place.

Now consider a (Q, R) system for answering the question of when and how much to produce at each stage. To be comparable to the kanban system, the reorder point at each stage is three and the order quantity is one (i.e., this is a base stock pull system with the base stock level set to four at each stage). This means that, just as with the kanban system, there can never be more than four parts in inventory after each stage. Also, just as with the kanban system, production is triggered at stage 2 when a part is removed from stage 2 inventory. In fact, the base stock pull system will behave identically to the kanban system above whenever there is inventory at each of the stages. A difference between the two systems appears when there is no inventory. For kanban, production is signaled whenever demand is *filled* (i.e., a part removed from stage *i* inventory signals production of a new part at stage *i*). This means that if there is customer demand at stage 2, but there are already four units on order to be produced at stage 2 and consequently no inventory (and demand cannot be filled), then there is no signal that stage 2 should produce another part. Once stage 2 completes production of a part, the demand is filled, which in turn signals production of a new part at stage 2.

For base stock, production is signaled whenever demand *occurs*, regardless of whether it is filled. So suppose, for example, that there are four units on order at stage 2, which means there is no stage 2 inventory. There is one unit in process at stage 2, and three production requests in the queue. The current inventory position is four (four units on order and zero units in inventory) and demand occurs. A backorder is registered, causing the inventory position to drop to three (i.e., on-hand = -1 due to the backorder, so on order + on hand = $4 - 1 = 3$), and a production request for one unit at stage 2 is generated to bring the inventory position back up to the base stock level of four. At the same instant, the order for production at stage 2 triggers a demand for a unit from stage 1. In summary, demand that occurs at the last stage in a base stock pull system is instantly propagated back through the upstream stages. The same is true for kanban only if there is inventory at each stage, because demand for new production occurs only when demand is filled.

On the basis of the preceding description, discuss the advantages and disadvantages of kanban and base stock pull systems.

4. Imagine a factory with the workcenters illustrated in Figure 9.2. The four workcenters are used to produce a part that is used in final assembly of all products. Accordingly, the material flow for the part flow looks like this: raw material → grinding workcenter (GR) → polishing workcenter (PO) → priming workcenter (PR) → painting workcenter (PA) → final assembly → finished product. The firm specifies an end-item plan, or master production schedule. Demand for the product is relatively stable and the master production schedule is set to a constant daily production rate that is updated every 20 days. This is a prototypical setting for a kanban pull system. Nevertheless, in order to probe your understanding of pull, push, and POLCA, suppose that a POLCA system is used. Each workcenter is defined as a cell. Since there are four cells, there must be three different types of POLCA cards. There are five GR/PO cards, five PO/PR cards, and five PR/PA cards. The unit of work on each POLCA card corresponds to the amount of capacity needed for one part (i.e., one POLCA card will be attached to a part). The lead time specified in the MRP system for each cell is two hours. The current end-item plan is fixed at one unit every two hours, or four units each eight-hour day.

Describe how the operation of the POLCA system differs, if at all, from a kanban pull system with the same master production schedule, five kanban cards after each cell, and each kanban card corresponding to one unit of the product.

5. It's 10:00 in morning at Carl's Auto Service and the following repairs need to be done.

Job in order of arrival	A	B	C	D	E
Estimated time for repair (hours)	2.0	0.5	1.5	2.5	1.0
Promised completion time	11 a.m.	2 p.m.	3 p.m.	5 p.m.	5 p.m.

a. What method could Carl use if he wanted to minimize the maximum job lateness? Develop a schedule using this method. Identify job start and completion times, average completion time, the number of late jobs, and the maximum lateness.

b. Develop a schedule that minimizes average completion time. Generate the information requested in part (a) for this schedule.

c. Develop a schedule with information requested in part (a) that minimizes the maximum completion time.

d. All jobs have a weight of one except job D, which has a weight of five. Find at least two schedules that minimize weighted completion time. What is the weighted completion time and what are the average completion times for the two schedules? Are there any other schedules that minimize weighted completion time?

e. What method could Carl use if he wanted to minimize the number of late jobs?

6. Why is the first-come-first-served rule commonly used in stores?

7. The SPT rule has a weakness that can arise in an environment where new jobs are periodically arriving. This weakness has led to a rule termed the "truncated SPT rule" that could well be used to some degree in your own day-to-day sequencing decisions. What is this weakness and how might it be offset?

8. A distribution center uses a two-step process to fill orders. Develop a schedule that minimizes the time to fill the following orders and illustrate the schedule in Gantt chart format.

Order	A	B	C	D	E	F	G
Step 1 time	1.20	0.90	2.00	1.70	1.60	2.20	1.30
Step 2 time	1.40	1.30	0.80	1.50	1.80	1.70	1.40

9. Could the schedule identified in the previous problem be improved if the two people working performed both steps for the orders they processed (i.e., instead of having one person perform step 1 for all orders and the other person perform step 2 for all orders)? What reasons might explain the approach to processing used in the previous problem?

10. Explain why a good strategy for minimizing the number of late jobs is to initially sequence in due-date order and discriminate against long jobs when problems arise.

11. You are working at Dud & Suds. You are standing in front of a washing machine at 10:00 a.m. looking at five loads of laundry.

Load	A	B	C	D	E
Wash time (minutes)	45	60	70	55	60
Due at	11:30	11:00	12:30	14:00	13:00
Weight	3	1	2	1	2

a. Sequence the jobs according to SPT, EDD, and WSPT methods. Provide figures for average completion time, average lateness, number of late jobs, and weighted-average completion time for each method. Which schedule would you choose?

b. Now you also must dry all the loads. Forgetting about the due time, sequence the jobs so as to minimize the time it takes to wash and dry all jobs.

Load	A	B	C	D	E
Dry time (minutes)	60	30	45	50	60

12. Priya has put all of her homework off until Sunday night. It is 6:00 pm, and Priya needs eight hours of sleep. Her homework consists of the following:

Homework	Marketing	Statistics	Supply Chain	Finance
Estimated time	45 minutes	1.5 hours	1 hour	2.5 hours
Due Sunday at	7 p.m.	10 p.m.	11 p.m.	9 p.m.

a. If Priya wanted to minimize average homework completion time, what scheduling method would she use? What would be the value of average completion time, number of late jobs, and the maximum lateness?

b. Assume Priya is penalized for project lateness. How would she schedule her projects now? What would be the values of average completion time, number of late jobs, and maximum lateness? What exactly is she minimizing/maximizing?

c. What is the earliest time Priya could get up Monday morning to meet you for coffee?

13. You and your partner must complete a series of papers. You are doing the research and analysis, and your partner will do the writing. The time needed for each is

Paper	1	2	3	4	5	6
Research time (hours)	2.2	0.8	1.2	2.0	4.6	3.8
Writing time (hours)	1.0	0.6	2.0	2.0	3.0	1.4

a. How would you and your partner schedule the papers to minimize the time it takes to complete all the papers? Use Gantt chart format to display the schedule.

b. If you and your partner perform both research and writing functions, could the schedule from part (a) be improved? If so, by how much?

c. What are advantages/disadvantages of the schedules in parts (a) and (b)?

Case Exercise: *MA Life Happenings*

It's been three years since M.A. graduated college, and cash is tight. Most of the income from her full-time job goes to paying off her college loan, car loan, apartment rent, and groceries. She also does occasional evening work for a caterer—a job she's been doing on and off for the last 10 years. The arrangement with the caterer is flexible. M.A. puts her name in for evenings when she wants to work, and she usually (but not always) gets put on the schedule. Her mode of operation is to request catering work when she is running low on cash, or, more specifically, whenever her combined checking/savings account balance dips below $1,000.

Questions

1. The situation described above can be viewed in terms of a "production policy"; that is, M.A. currently uses a simple rule for deciding when and how much supplemental cash to produce via catering. Explain why this approach corresponds to a pull production system.

2. Due to the high cost of maintaining an unpaid balance, M.A. generally pays her credit card bill in full each month.

Recently, the credit card company informed her that there will soon be an annual fee of $40 for credit card use. She had been paying nothing. After shopping around, the best alternative is a credit card with no annual fee, but there is a hitch. To avoid an interest charge, the bill must be paid within five days of receipt instead of the 20 days allowed with the current card. Consider how M.A.'s production policy will be affected by the switch to the new credit card. Specifically, explain why a shift to a push production policy may be appropriate, and how such a policy would work.

3. M.A.'s approach to deciding when to request work with the caterer can be viewed as a production policy—the topic of Section 2 in the chapter. The question of when and what bill to pay next can be viewed as a sequencing and scheduling problem—the topic of Section 3 in the chapter. M.A. pays each bill a few days before the due date as long as she has sufficient cash, and in situations when she is short, she pays past-due bills in due-date order. Why is M.A. using this approach to pay her bills? More specifically, identify a property of M.A.'s sequencing and scheduling

rule that helps explain why it can be a popular approach in practice.[17] Make sure to clearly justify the property that you identify (i.e., provide arguments that verify that the property holds in general). Also, illustrate and explain the property that you identify through an example. In order to do this, you need to first make up some data: (1) an initial account balance, (2) a time schedule of cash inflows (e.g., income from her work), and (3) a list of bills with due dates over the same period of time. Next, construct and compare at least two schedules,[18] one of which corresponds to M.A.'s approach; for example, by viewing the schedules, we should see that your proposed property holds.

4. M.A. works as an associate producer at a leading video game development studio.[19] This question introduces you to some of the challenges faced by M.A. But first, some background.

Video Game Industry and Terminology Video games are developed and brought to market by *development studios* and *publishers*. Publishers are firms that are ultimately responsible for bringing a new video game to market; responsibilities include distribution, marketing, and advertising. In addition to product managers and staff who work in the areas of marketing and finance, publishers typically have a department responsible for quality assurance (e.g., game testers) and maintain a small development staff of programmers, artists, and designers. For example, a publisher will use the development staff to make last-minute changes to lines of code or other elements of content when preparing to present a prerelease demo to media outlets.

Development studios are firms that are responsible for creating the games. Development studios typically have a production department and a testing department. The production department, as implied by the name, is responsible for everything from game concept (typically with guidance from a publisher) to implementation. Producers, associate producers, and assistant producers are responsible for overseeing the development of a game, which involves planning and coordinating the activities of programmers, designers, and artists. The testing department is responsible for verifying the quality of a game. Production testers identify problems and feed this information back to the production department for correction.

In summary, publishers focus on the business side of bringing new video games to market in consideration of market and competitive conditions, whereas development studios focus on making the games. It is not uncommon for a publisher to own one or more development studios. For example, Neversoft Entertainment is one of the development studios owned by Activision, a leading publisher in the industry. Neversoft creates the Tony Hawk Skateboarding games, among other titles.

The New Game Development Cycle and the Differences between Game Testers and Production Testers Game testers in a publisher's quality assurance (QA) department play a different role than production testers at the development studio. Production testers typically have more experience and expertise, and it is not uncommon for a tester to start in QA before moving into production.[20]

Here is an example scenario that illustrates the new game development cycle and the roles of production testers and game testers. Work on the game in progress adheres to a weekly cycle. A Wednesday deadline is set at the development studio to complete the latest build for QA. By Wednesday eve, the production testers make sure that all of the basic menus are working as they should and that the game can be played through sufficiently to a set standard. They also can be responsible for meeting the console manufacturer's technical certification requirements. These requirements range from having a certain color gamut available for all TVs, decreased violence and gore for the German market, animations on loading screens, and warning messages when memory cards and controllers are disconnected. In addition, while production testers generally take care of the big problems at the source of creation, they also may find bugs and work as an on-site QA tester. The main purpose of this small team of production testers (e.g., 8–12 people) is to make sure there is a strong enough foundation for the QA department to test the product further.

The QA department is then responsible for going through the latest build and finding every minute detail that is "wrong." The QA department has many more testers on staff. This allows them to focus on segments of the product and pick it apart for minor bugs such as color choice, use of language in dialogue, as well as the important long-winded bugs. Here's an example: The game crashes when a player presses the pause button 179 times on level 3 after completing levels 1 and 2 in less than five minutes and waiting at the start of level 3 for 10^+ hours (10^+ hours is

---

[17] A *property* is simply a characterization of a performance measure associated with the resulting schedule; for example, the average job completion time of a schedule developed using the shortest processing time rule is as small as or smaller than any other schedule.

[18] A schedule in this setting shows the payments with corresponding cash balance over time and, in the case that bills are paid late, the number of days that each bill is late.

[19] I would like to acknowledge the helpful insights and contributions of Peter Chang in the creation of this question. Peter has firsthand experience working for both a video game development studio and a publisher.

[20] Check out www.gamespot.com/gamespot/features/all/gamespotting/032303/2.html for Alex Navarro's take on "The Lowly Life of a Game Tester."

Video Game Industry Terminology

build (n) an in-work version of the product used for testing and evaluation.

build (v) building to a build (e.g., updating the game to another version).

latest short for the latest build. (As an aside, animators have learned to be wary of working on the latest—it tends to crash. If an animator builds to the latest, and wishes to test the work, there is a risk that the game will crash, possibly causing loss of work or significant delay.)

prototype working build that is pre-alpha with some working components.

pre-alpha any working build that is before alpha—anywhere from the prototype to a more refined version of the prototype.

alpha an alpha-test version of a game. There are several conflicting definitions of alpha. One is the first complete integration of all major code components. The other is an in-house product, not released to the public even in a limited way; also known as IR, for internal release.

beta a beta-test version of a game, which is an incomplete or incompletely debugged version of a game that is released to the public (either in a limited release beta or a full public beta) for the purpose of large-scale debugging as well as exposure of the game.

gold when a game has successfully passed through beta testing and is ready to duplicate, it is considered to have gone gold.

E3 Electronic Entertainment Expo, an annual event in May where future releases of video games among other forms of electronic entertainment are demonstrated.

---

an overnight soak—leaving the game on all night). The QA department is also a useful group to use for focus testing; that is, a sample of testers can be used to predict and forecast the success of an upcoming game or game idea.

M.A.'s Challenges As an associate producer, M.A.'s emotions are surging with a strange mix of elation and anxiety—elation because one of her products went gold on schedule and budget two days ago and anxious because she is responsible for ensuring that the alpha of *Spiñal Tap* is ready for its prerelease demo at E3. Today is Saturday, February 3rd, which leaves only 81 days (or 58 weekdays) until E3.

Spiñal Tap lets gamers create music via a virtual band that competes with other virtual bands, with the possibility of becoming rich and famous.[21] M.A.'s development studio is owned by a publisher, which in turn is owned by a major music label. The firm has arrangements with a cable TV channel that will devote one hour per week to music and videos from *Spiñal Tap* virtual bands. The firm also has deals in the works for periodic release of *Spiñal Tap* CDs, regular air time on an affiliate cable radio station, and a possible weekly TV show called *Battle of the Bands*. The product is scheduled to go gold at the end of October of this year.[22] However, E3 will be the first public viewing of the concept and is the critical opening play in a carefully sequenced series of media events designed to build the *Spiñal Tap* buzz to a peak just before release at the end of October.

The lead programmer for *Spiñal Tap* is Peter Chang, who is one of the most experienced programmers at M.A.'s firm. Peter recently finished the system design. He and M.A. have identified nearly 200 tasks that need to be complete before the initial alpha (i.e., first "complete" version of the game). The test department will be continually testing various elements of *Spiñal Tap* up until E3, but it is imperative that the initial alpha be ready at least 30 days before E3. Both M.A. and Peter believe from experience that 30 days should be sufficient for the inevitable production/test cycles (i.e., production gives the latest to test, test discovers problems, production updates the build, and the cycle repeats). There are two issues on M.A.'s mind.

Issue 1. Near-Term Problem of Assessing the Likelihood of Delays Due to Concept Art The making of a video game can be divided into five basic activities with associated expertise:

1. Concept art of the environment and characters—concept artists.
2. Modeling the concept art in 3D—character designers/artists.

---

[21] The game includes powerful tools for creating music (e.g., via muses that are shaped and controlled by the gamer), music videos, and all the elements of a real band—the collection of musicians and instruments, personalities, logo, and so forth. The tools are designed to tap into and harness the creative musical energy of individuals and groups, even those who are not proficient with a musical instrument.

[22] The game itself will be available for download at no cost, but there will be charges for various types of participation activities (e.g., band formation, recording, music video prep, distribution, etc.).

TABLE 1   **Stella's Tasks with Estimated Work Content**

The due dates indicate when the various concept art requirements must be completed and provided to the character designers/artists if the project is to remain on schedule.

Task	Work Content in Hours	Due at 8 a.m. on	Task	Work Content in Hours	Due at 8 a.m. on	Task	Work Content in Hours	Due at 8 a.m. on
1A-01	4.0	6-Feb	2C-01	4.0	16-Feb	1F-02	12.5	26-Feb
1B-01	8.5	7-Feb	3A-01	3.0	19-Feb	1F-03	9.5	26-Feb
1B-02	1.5	7-Feb	3A-02	3.0	19-Feb	1F-04	8.0	26-Feb
2A-01	2.5	8-Feb	3A-03	3.5	19-Feb	1F-05	3.0	26-Feb
2A-02	7.0	8-Feb	3A-04	2.0	19-Feb	1F-06	2.5	26-Feb
1C-01	6.5	9-Feb	3A-05	2.5	19-Feb	4A-01	2.0	27-Feb
2B-01	0.5	12-Feb	3A-06	1.0	19-Feb	1X-01	2.0	28-Feb
2B-02	1.5	12-Feb	3C-01	1.5	21-Feb	1X-02	1.0	28-Feb
2B-01	2.0	12-Feb	3C-02	3.5	21-Feb	1X-03	2.0	28-Feb
2B-03	3.5	12-Feb	1D-01	12.5	23-Feb	1X-04	1.0	28-Feb
2B-04	2.0	12-Feb	1F-01	15.0	26-Feb	1X-05	1.0	28-Feb

3. Programming the AI (environment and enemy)—programmers.

4. Scripting the actions (runs the programs)—designers.

5. Testing the game—testers, designers, programmers.

The *Spiñal Tap* team has been assigned one concept artist, Stella, who was pulled off assignment during the push to complete the game that went gold two days ago. M.A. is concerned about the possibility that concept art will hold up other tasks, and whether she needs to press her boss for an additional concept artist. Stella's tasks, with estimated work content and due dates, are listed in Table 1.

M.A. would like to develop a sense of whether Stella has sufficient time to complete all of her tasks on time, assuming that the time estimates are accurate and that she doesn't work on weekends. M.A. would like the answer in two forms if necessary—first assuming Stella works eight hours per day and, second, if tasks cannot be completed on time when Stella works eight hours per day, whether there are still delays if Stella works 12 hours per day.

Issue 2. Longer-Term Challenge of Reducing the New Game Development Cycle Time and Uncertainty   M.A. and Peter are well aware of the importance of completing a game by its release date. This release date (i.e., when the product is scheduled to gold) must be met because of the significant investments in marketing and advertising that are arranged months in advance. In fact, marketing and advertising costs are generally larger than the cost to develop a game.

In M.A.'s and Peter's experience, there are two main challenges to hitting the release date with an error-free high-quality game within budget. One challenge has to do with the trap of extensive production/test cycles as new problems seem to increase with each new build. This trap has become more prevalent in recent years as the complexity of video games has increased with the advancing capabilities of technology. A sound and robust design is critical for avoiding this trap. Peter has read about some of the new analysis tools that are available for evaluating software designs. While the focus of these tools has been on large-scale commercial applications (e.g., banking, communications, airliner flight control), Peter has suggested to M.A. that a small team research the applicability of these tools for video game designs.

A second challenge has to do with coordinating and maintaining up-to-date information on individuals and tasks during a project. The significance of this challenge is increasing as supply chains are lengthening and project teams are becoming more dispersed geographically (e.g., spanning multiple countries), institutionally (e.g., spanning multiple firms), and professionally (e.g., spanning multiple disciplines, each with specialized terminology and expertise). The game producer and the product manager must continually have their hands on the "pulse of the project" to detect potential delays early, which is essential to resolving problems before they become hugely expensive. M.A. has heard of a competitor that uses a tool for defect and project tracking called DevTrack. She would like to know more about DevTrack and similar tools, as well as software design checking tools as suggested by Peter.

Hints for addressing issue 2: Information on software design checkers can be found in D. Jackson, "Dependable Software by Design," *Scientific American* 294, no. 6 (June 2006), pp. 68–75. Information on DevTrack can be found at the company's Web site: www.techexcel.com.

Chapter **Ten**

Transportation Management: Elements and Insights

Chapter Outline

1. Elements of Transportation
   1.1. Modes
   1.2. Pricing
   1.3. Other Services and Service Providers

2. Tactical Decisions
   2.1. Delivery Frequency
   2.2. Multiple Stops

3. Strategic Decisions
   3.1. Estimating Delivery Distance and Cost
   3.2. Network Design

4. Summary and Managerial Insights
   4.1 Delivery Frequency to a Warehouse: Indicators That a Warehouse Should Receive Frequent Replenishment Deliveries Are High Volume, Close Proximity to Source of Supply, and High Inventory Holding Cost Rate; the Increase in Cost Due to Moderate Deviations from the Optimal Frequency Is Minor
   4.2. Use of Stop-Offs for Warehouse Replenishment: Look for Stop-Off Locations That Are Nearly on the Way and in Close Proximity to the More Distant Location
   4.3. Transportation Distance, Cost, and the Market Area Served by a Warehouse: Average Distance to Customers and Outbound Transportation Cost Are Approximately Proportional to the Square Root of the Market Area
   4.4. Network Design Diagnostic and Robustness: If the Number of Warehouses Is Cost-Effective, Then Annual Warehousing Overhead Cost Is About One-half of the Annual Outbound Transportation Cost; the Increase in Cost Due to Moderate Deviations from the Optimal Number of Warehouses Is Minor

5. Exercises
   Case Exercise: GL Electric

Chapter Keys

1. What are the transportation modes and characteristics?
2. How are product classes and class rates relevant for negotiations with carriers?

3. What are the roles of freight forwarders and transportation brokers?
4. What is the tariff of accessorial services, and what are the following services: diversion, reconsignment, detention, demurrage, stop-off privileges?
5. What factors influence delivery frequency?
6. What factors influence the use of stop-offs?
7. What is the relationship between the size of the market served by a warehouse and transportation cost/distance?
8. What factors influence the size of the market served by a warehouse?
9. What are cross-docking and drop-shipping?
10. What are the managerial insights from the chapter?

The topic of this chapter focuses on moving stuff, or transportation management (see Figure 10.1). Transportation plays an important role in the world economy. Historically it often has been a factor in the location and economic development of cities, and annual transportation costs are significant. In 2004, for example, U.S. firms spent over \$600 billion transporting product, or about 5.5 percent of U.S. GDP (Wilson 2005).

This chapter takes the perspective of a firm that purchases transportation services, though some of the content is also relevant for managing a company-owned fleet. We'll begin in Section 1 by reviewing the elements of transportation—the various resources and alternatives available for getting product to market.

The elements of transportation can be combined and deployed in many ways. In Sections 2 and 3, we will consider how this can be done effectively, but in a manner that favors the development of transportation intuition over detailed analysis. We will look at back-of-the-envelope analyses related to tactical decisions in Section 2, and to strategic decisions in Section 3. As noted in earlier chapters, back-of-the-envelope analysis attempts to capture the essential elements of a question with minimal data. The purpose is to gain insight into the most important trade-offs influencing a decision—insight that is the foundation for making quick and educated decisions in response to changing business conditions and, when time allows, for guiding more data-intensive and detailed analysis of an issue.

This chapter is followed by two supplements. The first supplement is a case that illustrates the practical application of analysis and insights discussed in Section 3. The second supplement is a primer on moving product across international borders.

1. ELEMENTS OF TRANSPORTATION

This section reviews various transportation modes, pricing structures, and services. To begin, however, it is important to be familiar with the terms *shipper, carrier,* and *consignee*. The

FIGURE 10.1

A supply chain with emphasis on transportation management links

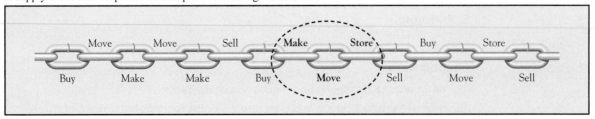

TABLE 10.1
2001 U.S. Freight
Expenditure and
Ton-Miles by Mode

Mode	$ (billions)	Percent	Ton-Miles (billions)	Percent	Average ¢/ton-mile
Truck	$467	82%	1,051	28%	44.5
Rail	37	6	1,558	42	2.4
Air	26[1]	5	15	<1	121.5
Water	28[2]	5	494	13	0.9
Pipeline	9	2	616	16	1.5

Source: Wilson 2002.

[1] About $7 out of $26 billion is associated with international shipments.

[2] About $23 out of $28 billion is associated with international shipments. Ton-miles is the product of tons of freight and miles moved, and is reported for domestic shipments only. The average ¢/ton-mile is estimated by dividing the fourth column into the second column after removing international air and water freight expenses. Year 2004 U.S. freight expenditure is about 9 percent above year 2001, and the percentage contribution of each mode is virtually unchanged (Wilson 2005).

shipper is the party that hires another firm to transport its product. The carrier is the firm that does the transporting. The consignee is the party receiving the product.

1.1. Modes

A transportation *mode* refers to the means of transport. There are **five basic transportation modes: truck, rail, air, water, and pipeline.** Table 10.1, while limited to firms in the United States, sheds some light on the relative usage and cost of each mode.

Table 10.2 provides a qualitative characterization of each mode that is expanded upon in the following discussion. The costs in the table refer to the cost structure of the mode, which in turn influences carrier pricing.

Truck

Today, truck is the **dominant transportation mode for moving a wide variety of freight.** It occupies a **middle ground between the extremes of high prices and short lead times of air and low prices and long lead times of rail or water.** However, a key **advantage of trucking stems from the vast road networks throughout the world,** allowing pickup and delivery to locations not accessible by other modes.

TABLE 10.2
Qualitative Characteristics of Alternative Transportation Modes

	Truck	Rail	Air	Water	Pipeline
Capacity	Moderate	High	Moderate	Very high	High
Variable cost	Moderate	Low	High	Low	Very low
Fixed cost	Low	High	Low	Moderate	High
Lead time	Moderate	Long	Short	Long	Moderate
Lead time reliability	Moderate	Low	High	Moderate	Very high
Availability of service	High	Moderate	Moderate	Moderate	Low
Typical products and shipment distances	Wide variety of products shipped over a wide range of distances	Raw materials, autos, machinery shipped over long distances (e.g., > 500 miles)	Small, high-value, perishable, or time-sensitive product shipped over long distances (e.g., > 500 miles)	Inland: raw materials shipped over long distances (e.g., > 300 miles) Ocean: wide variety shipped over long distances	Liquids and gasses shipped over a range of distances

Truck trailers range in size, and may be enclosed, open, tank, refrigerated, or flatbed. A common trailer size in the United States is 8.5'W × 9'H × 48'L. Fifty-three-foot-long trailers are also quite common. Weight capacity is generally 22.5 to 30 tons. Carriers will sometimes link two or three trailers together (e.g., two 48-foot or three 28-foot) in order to increase capacity, though these doubles and triples are not allowed on some roads.

The U.S. trucking industry is segmented into truckload (TL) carriers and less-than-truckload (LTL) carriers. TL shipments are "full" truckloads (e.g., > 15,000 pounds) that generally travel from a single origin to a single destination. An LTL shipment consumes a fraction of a truck's capacity. Consequently, LTL carriers consolidate multiple LTL shipments on a single truck. Compared to TL, an LTL shipment is more expensive per pound, takes longer to deliver, and is more susceptible to damage because product is routed through various consolidation centers, where loads are exchanged among trucks en route to their destination.

Variable trucking costs include fuel, labor, usage taxes, and tolls. Fixed costs are low compared to other modes—primarily associated with investment in terminals and trucks. It is not uncommon to find an individual in business as the owner and operator of a single truck.

As a rough rule of thumb, trucks can cover about 500 miles in a day. Loading and unloading times tend to be short, so particularly for TL shipments, most of the delivery lead time is due to travel time. And, while susceptible to environmental variability (e.g., bad weather and road congestion), delivery lead times are more reliable than for rail or water.

Rail

Rail is a **relatively low-cost transportation mode that is attractive for long-distance shipping of large and heavy loads when short and reliable lead times are not important.** Availability of service is limited by available track (e.g., about 100,000 miles of

track versus about one million miles of highway for trucks in the United States). Raw materials such as coal, grain, lumber, and paper, as well as autos and heavy machinery, are typical of products shipped via rail.

Railcars share similarities to the length and width of truck trailers, and, like truck trailers, railcars can be enclosed, open, tank, refrigerated, or flatbed. However, railcars can be taller than truck trailers and can carry more weight. For example, while waiting at a railroad crossing, you may see three levels of autos on a railcar (a truck will have no more than two levels) or two 40-foot containers stacked on top of one another on a flatbed.[1]

[1] Called a *double stack*.

Variable costs are lower for rail than for truck, but fixed costs are higher. In addition to the fixed costs associated with equipment and terminals, rail companies are responsible for track maintenance. In contrast, road networks are publicly maintained and largely financed through user fees (e.g., fuel taxes, tolls) that trucking firms incur as variable cost.

Freight trains travel at about 20 miles per hour, but travel time can be less than half of the delivery lead time. There are economic incentives to run trains with many railcars (e.g., 50 or more), and a load may spend time in a railyard waiting for a suitable number of railcars before departing. Also, it is unusual to have a full train's worth of material traveling between a single origin and destination;[2] as with LTL shipments in trucking, time is spent in railyards as railcars are moved between trains en route to their destination. Compared to TL, rail delivery lead times are longer and more variable.

Air

The **main advantage of air is short delivery lead times over long distances; the main drawback is high cost.** Accordingly, air is most commonly used for high-value, time-sensitive product shipped overseas or over inland distances of 500 miles or more.[3] Availability

of service is limited by the location of airports, and, consequently, air is often used in combination with truck as product is moved to and from an airport.

Cargo capacity varies with the plane but can range up to about 130 tons (e.g., Lockheed 500). Most air freight today is shipped in the cargo holds of passenger aircraft. Variable costs are very high and fixed costs are relatively low. Airports and terminals are generally publicly maintained with fees charged according to usage.

The cruising speed of a jet is typically between 500 and 600 miles per hour. While air is susceptible to delays due to weather conditions, the impact is mitigated by the high travel speed, and delivery lead times over long distances are short and reliable. For example, a typical international shipment takes about 8 to 12 days, though the vast majority of this time is spent on the ground awaiting required documents and customs clearance (Hart 2005).

Water

Water transportation is via inland waterway and ocean. **Barges are common for river and canal traffic. Capacity is very high;** a barge can tow up to about 40,000 tons. Average travel speeds are generally less than 10 miles per hour (depending on the current), and the cost structure exhibits **low variable and moderate fixed costs** as waterways are often publicly maintained. A main drawback of river/canal water transport by barge is limited waterway accessibility, and this is not easily offset by combining with truck due to large differences in capacity. Barges are **mostly used for low-value commodities when short lead time is not a priority.**

---

[2] An exception is a *unit train;* many railcars of a commodity such as coal are moved as a single train from origin to destination.

[3] Truck delivery lead times can be shorter than air over inland routes of several hundred miles.

Large **cargo ships are used for ocean freight and, in some cases, on inland waterways** (e.g., the Saint Lawrence Seaway and Great Lakes in North America). As with barges, **capacity is very high.** A large oil tanker can hold 500,000 gallons. Many ocean freightliners are designed to hold containers. A typical container is 8'W × 8'H × 40'L, and ship capacity ranges from a few thousand up to around 12,000 containers.[4] Cruising speeds are generally between 20 and 30 miles per hour. Delivery lead times of international shipments overseas are long and susceptible to variability from weather and delays in loading/unloading and customs clearance. Also, carrier liability for loss and damages at sea is limited to $500 per package under the Carriage of Goods by Sea Act. The main consequence is that, relative to other modes, the shipper generally faces greater exposure to costs from loss

or damage in-transit.[5] However, overseas transit by water is much less expensive than by air and is used for a wide variety of product.

Pipeline

Pipeline is a distinctive mode because it is limited in what it can transport. Pipelines are used to **transport liquids such as petroleum products as well as natural gas.** Solids are sometimes mixed in a liquid to create slurry for transport via pipeline. Pipeline as a mode of transport has very low variable cost but requires a large fixed investment to build. Material typically moves at a rate of about three miles per hour, though its slow speed is offset somewhat by the fact that material is continually moving. Pipeline capacity is high. For example, the capacity of a 12-inch-diameter pipe moving material at three miles per hour is in the neighborhood of 70,000 gallons per hour.[6]

Intermodal

Intermodal transportation refers to the use of multiple modes between origin and destination. This raises the potentially time-consuming and costly proposition of moving product between modes. An important innovation that eased this problem and facilitated

---

[4] 8'W × 8'H × 20'L containers are also relatively common and these dimensions are used to specify container capacity of a ship (i.e., capacity stated in TEUs, which are 20-foot equivalent units). Since truck trailers are usually either 48 or 53 feet long, it is possible that one of these lengths will emerge as a standard container length in the future.

[5] This point is explored further in Chapter 10, Supplement B.

[6] Theoretical capacity is (3 miles/hour) × (63,360 inches/mile) × 3.14159 × (6-inch radius)^2/(231 cubic inches/gallon) ≈ 93,000 gallons per hour, but material will not fill the entire volume of the pipe.

intermodal transportation was the introduction of containerized freight in 1956 (*The Wall Street Journal* 1989).[7] **Once a container is sealed, it can remain unopened and moved as a unit to the customer. With the exception of pipeline, each transportation mode includes capability to transport containers, and a number of carriers offer services that combine two or more of these modes.** Well-known examples of carriers that employ intermodal transportation include DHL, FedEx, and UPS, which specialize in small-package delivery. Examples of intermodal carriers capable of transporting containers are CSX, Hub Group, Maersk Sealand, and Schneider National. The availability of economical intermodal transportation allows shippers to combine advantages of different modes and leads to a richer array of choices for getting product to market.

Terms that are specific to intermodal transportation are *trailer on a flatcar* (TOFC), *container on a flatcar* (COFC), *fishyback,* and *birdyback,* which are known generically as *piggyback.* As the name suggests, TOFC refers to a truck trailer that is placed on a flatbed railcar. Space and weight can be saved by removing the chassis from a truck trailer before it is placed on a railcar, which is known as COFC.[8] COFC also refers to ship containers placed on a railcar. Fishyback refers to trailers or containers on a ship, and birdyback refers to trailers or containers in a plane.

1.2. Pricing

Transportation pricing is commonly negotiated between shipper and carrier. However, pricing benchmarks exist and consequently play a role in negotiations. In the United States, for example, *class rates* effectively represent the upper limit of what a shipper will pay a carrier. Negotiated discounts of 30 to 70 percent below class rates through volume commitments are not uncommon.

This section briefly explains U.S. class rates for LTL truck shipments and identifies sources for further information. The trucking industry classifies all products according to shipping characteristics; making sure that each product is properly classified can mean significant savings for a shipper. However, there is a broader point to the coverage of this material. The details of transportation pricing evolve over time and vary by mode and country. The objective here is not to master these time/location-sensitive details.[9] Rather, the exposure to freight classes and prices serves to illustrate an important lesson of this section—that transportation pricing can be complex and that a good understanding of the underlying drivers can be crucial to effective transportation management.

The single most important reference for shipping by truck in the United States is the *National Motor Freight Classification* (NMFC). NMFC is regularly updated and is available through SMC[3] at www.smc3.com under an agreement with the American Trucking Associations and the National Motor Freight Traffic Association, Inc. Major sections of NMFC are

1. A list of participating carriers.
2. Indexes to assist in locating specific commodities.
3. An index providing rules governing the use of the NMFC.
4. Rules relating to the movement of commodities, including specific shipping, packaging, and transportation requirements to which the shipper and carrier must adhere.

---

[7] Insurance costs are also significantly lower for containers (e.g., relative to the alternative of boxes/pallets).

[8] This is limited to trucks that are designed to use a container as the truck trailer.

[9] More detail on transportation pricing, as well as other aspects of transportation, can be found in Boyer (1997) and Coyle, Bardi, and Novak (2006).

5. Examples of the Uniform Domestic Bill of Lading, with its terms and conditions.

6. Descriptions and classifications for every commodity.

7. Specifications for required packaging.

8. Rules for overcharge, loss, and damage claims.

What Is the Meaning of Product Classification, or Item Six in the Preceding List?
Consider the shipping characteristics of sand, TVs, and picnic baskets. One ton of picnic baskets requires more space in a trailer than one ton of sand, with the space requirements for one ton of TVs somewhere in between. On the other hand, a shipment of TVs has greater liability exposure (e.g., damage, pilferage) than sand or picnic baskets. These product differences affect transportation cost. This is particularly so for the case of LTL shipments. For full truckload shipments, the shipper essentially pays for the space of a full trailer at a per-mile rate; what is shipped in this space usually has little effect on pricing.

NMFC classifies products that could be shipped by truck into 18 classes ranging from 50 to 500.[10] **Products in the same class exhibit similar cost per hundred-weight (cwt) to transport. LTL trucking firms establish transport rates per cwt based on the origin-destination of the shipment and the class of the freight. The lower the class, the lower the rate.** The NMFC classification scheme in combination with class rates greatly simplifies pricing for carriers; for example, relative to the alternative of maintaining rates by individual product.

The primary factors that determine the class of a product are (1) density, (2) value, (3) stowability and handling, and (4) susceptibility to damage, and, of these, density generally plays the largest role. As an example, for the three products considered above, sand is class 50, TVs are class 125, and picnic baskets are class 200.

How Do NMFC Classification and Class Rates Enter into Negotiations with LTL Carriers?   To answer this question, we need to take a brief look at the history of transportation regulation in the United States. Prior to 1980, each carrier belonged to a *motor carrier conference* based on the carrier's regional location. Representatives from each carrier in a conference met annually to set point-to-point transportation rates in ¢/cwt by class and shipment weight, which in turn were filed with the Interstate Commerce Commission for approval. Once approved, the class rates were published in a document called a conference tariff. The conference tariffs specified rates for shipping through different parts of the country. For a shipper, this meant that the point-to-point transportation cost for a particular class and shipment size was determined by the applicable tariff(s), and carriers were differentiated solely by service.[11] The Motor Carrier Act in 1980 opened the door to negotiated pricing between carrier and shipper.[12] However, the legacy of class rates and published tariffs remains to this day. SMC[3], for example, is an organization that is an outgrowth of the Southern Motor Conference. Among other resources, SMC[3] maintains a tariff of class rates for Canada, the United States, and Mexico. Now, back to the question of how NMFC classification and class rates enter into negotiations with LTL carriers.

---

[10] The specific classes are 50, 55, 60, 65, 70, 77.5, 85, 92.5, 100, 110, 125, 150, 175, 200, 250, 300, 400, and 500.

[11] Formally, the above requirements applied to *common carriers*, which handled the vast majority of freight. *Exempt carriers and contract carriers,* which are alternative legal forms of transportation, had greater pricing latitude.

[12] The Staggers Rail Act of 1980 played a similar role in the railroad industry.

Suppose you have an LTL quantity of product that you want shipped between two points in North America. One of the first things to do is identify the freight class. Many carriers will provide assistance with this step. The cost per cwt rate, or class rate, can then be determined and used as a starting point for shipper/carrier negotiations. The class rate may be provided by the carrier or obtained from a conference tariff (e.g., purchase a license for access to the SMC³ tariff). As a shipper, you also should be aware of the Truth in Rates (TIR) initiative established in 2003 by the Surface Transportation Board. TIR requires that carriers participating in bureau rates (such as the SMC³ tariff) notify their customers of the range of discounts provided on these rates. The **class rate and discount range are useful benchmarks to be considered along with volume commitments and other factors during negotiations.** In addition, it is important to keep in mind that NMFC classes are, by necessity, rather coarse and should not be viewed as absolute. **By understanding how the transport cost drivers of your unique product differ from other products in the class, you may be in a position to make a case for a class reduction, and therefore a rate reduction.** This knowledge also can pay dividends when negotiating rates for mixed loads of product. Some shippers will regularly ship multiple products on a single truck. But a mixed load of products from different classes means that the effective class of the load can be open to discussion with the carrier. A wise shipper will want to bring a thorough knowledge of cost drivers and the basis for product classification to this discussion.[13]

We have only considered truck shipments to this point in the section. For rail, there is a book somewhat analogous to NMFC called the *Uniform Freight Classification* (UFC). UFC groups products into 31 classes ranging from 35 to 400. However, rail carriers today rarely use these classes to quote freight rates. UFC classes have been largely replaced by codes published in the *Standard Transportation Commodity Code* (STCC). STCC classifies products into 38 commodity codes, and products with the same commodity code have similar transport cost characteristics. Today UFC is used primarily as a reference for rules and regulations. As with NMFC for truck, UFC codifies the rules and regulations for moving freight by rail (e.g., packaging, documentation, claims procedures).[14]

1.3. Other Services and Service Providers

This section reviews some of the other transportation services available to a shipper. Some of these services are offered by firms that operate little or no transportation equipment. In particular, we will consider the services available from freight forwarders, transportation brokers, and reverse auction providers. Other services, such as diversion and reconsignment, detention and demurrage, and stop-off privileges, are available through carriers.

Freight Forwarders and Transportation Brokers

Freight forwarders specialize in consolidating small shipments from various shippers into a large shipment. The consolidated shipment is later divided into the original smaller shipments for local delivery. By aggregating demand from multiple shippers, freight forwarders can qualify for volume discounts. In addition, due to the law of large numbers, demand is relatively stable compared to that of an individual shipper. Freight forwarders take advantage of this by buying cargo space for many months into the future at the most attractive prices. Some of the savings from the reduced transport rate are passed on to the shipper, with the balance accruing as revenue for the freight forwarder. The shipper benefits from lower transport pricing and, in some cases, shorter delivery lead times.

---

[13] In addition to a rate, one outcome of this discussion is a "freight all kinds" (FAK) class designation, with guidelines on what constitutes a mixed product shipment that qualifies for the FAK rate.

[14] More information on UFC and STCC can be found at the American Association of Railroads (www.aar.org) and RAILINC (www.railinc.com).

Principle of Nature: Law of Large Numbers

DEFINITION
As volume increases, relative variability decreases.

EXAMPLE
Years ago I worked on a project related to new product introductions. We had demand rate projections but no information on demand volatility, which, among other uses, is important for planning inventory buildup prior to market introduction. In the end, we used the projected demand rate to estimate demand volatility. From regression analysis, we found that the standard deviation of demand per week was proportional to the demand rate raised to the 0.63 power. This means, for example, that a 100 percent increase in the demand rate is associated with only a 55 percent increase in the standard deviation, or, in other words, as volume increases, relative variability decreases.

Transportation brokers coordinate and manage the transportation requirements for a shipper through such services as carrier selection, rate negotiation, document preparation, shipment tracing, and bill processing. The service can be especially useful for small firms that are less able to justify the investment necessary to perform the services in-house. Other transportation brokers act as agents for a carrier by finding shipments for available equipment.

Shipping across international borders introduces a host of requirements not associated with domestic freight. A number of shippers rely on the import/export expertise of freight forwarders and brokers. This is discussed further in Supplement B of this chapter.

In summary, freight forwarders and transportation brokers provide useful services and, particularly for small, low-volume shippers, it is important to be aware that these services are available. Their economic impact is significant. In 2004, for example, U.S. firms spent $18 billion on freight forwarding services (Wilson 2005). However, our discussion of these service providers also reinforces a more fundamental message. Freight forwarders and transportation brokers are intermediaries that profit and add value from a combination of transportation expertise and a network of shipper/carrier contacts. The significance of their role underscores both the richness and complexity of the area and the rewards due to those who master it.

Reverse Auction Providers

Reverse auctions are covered in Chapter 5, "Supply Management." That chapter includes an example of a reverse auction for transportation service. The reverse auction was facilitated by FreeMarkets, a firm that provides reverse auction software and helps identify qualified vendors and manage the reverse auction process.

Our coverage of reverse auctions here will be brief. We'll review what a reverse auction is and how it is relevant for purchasing transportation services. Readers interested in additional detail may refer to Section 2.6 of Chapter 5.

An auction is where multiple buyers bid on a product or service offered by a seller. A reverse auction is where multiple sellers quote a price for a product or service wanted by a buyer. A large-volume shipper may use a reverse auction to purchase transportation service for annual shipping volume. Transportation savings can accrue from increasing the competition among carriers, and the benefit may be amplified by the winner's curse.[15] The

---

[15] For example, The Limited Inc. reported transportation savings of over $1 million after running a reverse auction (Leibs 2001). Sheffi (2004) reports shipper savings of 3 to 15 percent of transportation cost with no decrease in the level of service.

Principle of Nature: Winner's Curse

DEFINITION
The probability of unfavorable bidding error in an auction is highest for the winner.

EXAMPLE
Bazerman and Samuelson (1983) report an experiment where MBA students placed sealed bids on jars of pennies, nickels, and paper clips. The winner would receive the jar and the right to sell it for its true value, which, unknown to the subjects, was $8.00. The average winning bid was $10.01, resulting in an average loss of $2.01. The winner lost money in over half of the auctions.

winner's curse is the tendency for the winner of an auction to lose money. In the context of a reverse auction, for example, a firm that makes the mistake of underestimating cost and quoting a money-losing price is more likely to win. The winner's curse is most apparent in auctions where cost is challenging to estimate. It is probably less evident today in the transportation industry than it would have been 10 years ago. Carriers have greatly improved capabilities to accurately track and estimate costs since deregulation in 1980 (e.g., those who were not able to do this found out the hard way and went out of business). In addition, carriers commonly protect against fuel price volatility through a provision in their quote that allows their price to increase if fuel price increases beyond a certain level.[16]

Other Services

Carriers offer a number of services beyond simple point-to-point delivery. Some of the more widely used of these are *diversion and reconsignment, detention and demurrage,* and *stop-off privileges.* As an aside, the fees and charges for various accessorial services are generally spelled out in the shipper/carrier contract, but not necessarily for all services the shipper may use. **Each carrier regularly publishes a tariff of accessorial services with fees, and shipper/carrier contracts typically contain a clause referring to the tariff publication for services/fees not listed in the contract. Service charges can add up quickly and shippers will want to be familiar with this publication.**

Diversion and reconsignment are two options that provide flexibility to the shipper after a shipment has departed. **Diversion refers to changing the destination of a shipment while en route and reconsignment refers to changing the consignee, sometimes after the shipment has reached its original destination.** These options provide reactive flexibility (e.g., shipment rerouted to an alternative plant in the event of a strike) and also can be used strategically. For example, a firm may send a shipment to a distant market area, and later identify specific delivery locations as demand develops.

Detention and demurrage can be viewed as a form of timing flexibility at a source or destination. Carriers usually specify a time limit, known as *free time,* for loading and unloading. For example, if a motor carrier sets free time at one hour, then a shipper will have one hour to load the truck after it arrives. Similarly, the consignee will have one hour to unload the truck after it arrives. The time limit can be exceeded, but at a cost that increases with the delay. These charges are referred to as detention in the trucking industry and demurrage in the rail industry.

---

[16] One example is a shipper/carrier contract that includes a fuel surcharge schedule specifying an *x* percent surcharge for every $*y* increase in fuel above an established base. The contract may identify the average weekly fuel price published by the Department of Energy as the source for gauging how fuel prices are moving.

Stop-off privileges allow for partial loading and unloading at various points between an origin and destination. For example, a truck may pick up product at several different plants on its way to a customer. Alternatively, several customer orders may be combined on a single truck with a drop-off at each point. A route composed of multiple pickups and/or drop-offs is referred to as a milk run. The transportation rate is generally based on the presumption that the entire load moves between a single origin and destination, with additional fees charged for stop-offs. Milk runs have the potential to save money over multiple independent shipments because transportation pricing exhibits economies of volume (e.g., $/cwt-mile gets smaller as the shipment size gets larger). We'll explore the economics of milk runs and other delivery tactics in the next section.

2. TACTICAL DECISIONS

This and the next section consider different types of decisions involving transportation. In this section, we'll look at tactical decisions such as shipment frequency and whether or not to combine multiple customer orders on a single truck. We'll see that the analysis underlying these decisions is very similar to what we saw in Chapter 6 on economic order quantities. Section 3 addresses strategic decisions related to the design of a distribution network.

Throughout both sections, we will periodically revisit an industry setting from Chapters 6 and 7 to illustrate the main ideas. You are the CEO of a rapidly growing firm with exclusive rights to distribute Kalina products in North America, Europe, and Asia. Your firm also produces a few Kalina products. Kalina is a leading Russian manufacturer of cosmetics and other personal-care products.

Last year you became a board member of Inditex, one of the world's largest fashion distributors with Zara as its flagship brand. Inditex is known for fresh designs, good value, and innovative supply chain management. You are on a long flight home after an invigorating board meeting in Barcelona, and your mind is alive with a number of issues.

First, you were struck by the frequency of deliveries to Zara stores—twice per week in Europe and once per week in North America. The policy at your firm is to ship to warehouses using a truckload carrier, which, depending on the warehouse, corresponds to a shipment frequency somewhere between once every 1.5 to 9 weeks. You are questioning whether this policy makes good sense.

Second, like your firm, Inditex is expanding at a rapid pace as new stores are opening around the world. Inditex regularly evaluates and modifies their distribution network so that

it remains effective under changing market conditions. In contrast, your firm has never undertaken such a review. The question of an appropriate network design is all the more pressing because there are plans to expand distribution to India at the start of next year. The first issue is considered in this section; the second issue is addressed in Section 3.

2.1. Delivery Frequency

An emphasis on minimizing transportation cost can lead to large infrequent shipments that may not make good economic sense when total costs are considered. In this section, we will consider costs that are affected by delivery frequency.

Frequent, small replenishment shipments to a warehouse or retailer offer the advantages of low inventory and an input stream that can be tuned to closely match demand. On the other hand, the unit transportation cost decreases as the shipment quantity increases. The goal of this section is to develop quick and approximate analysis that lends insight into factors that influence the frequency of replenishment deliveries to a warehouse. While we use trucking as a basis for illustration, the analysis extends to other modes of transportation.

The first task is to identify simple expressions that approximate transportation and inventory cost. In general, transportation cost is approximately proportional to distance.[17] For reasons that will become clearer after you read Section 3, it is typically not cost-effective to replenish warehouses using LTL. For truckload replenishments, the transportation cost expression is straightforward because cost is customarily based on the use of the entire truck, regardless of whether or not it is filled to capacity.

The frequency of deliveries, or, equivalently, the average replenishment quantity, affects the average cycle stock at the receiving location. Cycle stock is excess inventory due to order batching, and the larger the replenishment quantity, the larger the average cycle stock. In order to formalize how costs depend on the replenishment quantity, we need to identify assumptions and notation.

A1. Demand is constant.

A2. Truckload transportation cost is proportional to distance.

A3. Inventory holding cost at the receiving location is proportional to average inventory.

Notation for Truckload Shipment Quantity Analysis

D = demand rate in units per period

A = fixed cost per shipment transaction; for example, order processing and
other costs that are independent of distance and shipment quantity

δ = shipping distance in miles

A_{TL} = truckload cost per mile

c_e = inventory holding cost per unit-period

Q_{max} = truckload capacity

Q = shipment quantity

The cost per period to ship Q units at a time to a location δ miles away via truckload is

$$C(Q) = (A + A_{TL}\delta)D/Q + (Q/2)c_e$$

The first term is the cost per shipment $(A + A_{TL}\delta)$ multiplied by the number of shipments per period (D/Q). The second term is the inventory holding cost of the average cycle stock at the receiving location. In Chapter 6, we saw a similar cost expression for the ordering and inventory cost per period, that is, $C(Q) = AD/Q + (Q/2)c_e$, which is minimized at the economic order quantity $Q^* = (2AD/c_e)^{1/2}$ with cost $C(Q^*) = (2ADc_e)^{1/2}$. Accordingly, the cost minimizing truckload shipping quantity is

$$Q^* = [2(A + A_{TL}\delta)D/c_e]^{1/2}$$

with cost $C(Q^*) = [2(A + A_{TL}\delta)Dc_e]^{1/2}$.[18]

---

[17] The possibility of economies of distance is considered in Section 3.

[18] These expressions are valid as long as $[2(A + A_{TL}\delta)D/c_e]^{1/2}$ doesn't exceed the capacity of a truck; that is, as long as $[2(A + A_{TL}\delta)D/c_e]^{1/2} \leq Q_{max}$. If $[2(A + A_{TL}\delta)D/c_e]^{1/2} > Q_{max}$, then $Q^* = Q_{max}$ and cost can be expressed as $C(Q^*) = (A + A_{TL}\delta)D/Q_{max} + (Q_{max}/2)c_e = 0.5(y^{-1} + y)[2(A + A_{TL}\delta)Dc_e]^{1/2}$, where y is the truckload capacity as a fraction of the "natural" economic shipment quantity; that is, $y = Q_{max}/[2(A + A_{TL}\delta)D/c_e]^{1/2}$. The modification of the cost expression is considered in an end-of-chapter exercise.

The formulas are summarized below.

Formulas for Truckload Shipment Quantity and Frequency Analysis

D/Q = average number of replenishment shipments per period to a location with demand rate D

Q/D = average time between replenishment shipments, or replenishment cycle time

$Q/2$ = average cycle stock

$C(Q)$ = cost per period; includes transportation cost, transaction cost (e.g., order processing), and inventory holding cost at the receiving location

$$= (A + A_{TL}\delta)D/Q + (Q/2)c_e$$

Q^* = economic shipment quantity = $\min\left\{Q_{max}, \left(\dfrac{2(A + A_{TL}\delta)D}{c_e}\right)^{1/2}\right\}$

D/Q^* = economic delivery frequency = $\max\left\{\dfrac{D}{Q_{max}}, \left(\dfrac{Dc_e}{2(A + A_{TL}\delta)}\right)^{1/2}\right\}$

$y(D)$ = truck capacity as a fraction of the "natural" economic shipment quantity at demand rate $D = Q_{max}/[2(A + A_{TL}\delta)D/c_e]^{1/2}$

$C(Q^*)$ = optimal transportation and inventory cost per period

$$= \begin{cases} [2(A + A_{TL}\delta)Dc_e]^{1/2}, & \text{if}[2(A + A_{TL}\delta)D/c_e]^{1/2} \leq Q_{max} \\ 0.5[y(D)^{-1} + y(D)][2(A + A_{TL}\delta)Dc_e]^{1/2}, & \text{otherwise} \end{cases}$$

Example

Your firm, which distributes and produces Kalina products, has a large distribution center (DC) and manufacturing facility in a free-trade zone outside of Boston. The DC serves 30 of your firm's warehouses located throughout North America, as well as some overseas facilities. Customers in the Northeast region and large accounts in other regions are served directly from the DC. Replenishment shipments to the 30 warehouses are via a truckload carrier, with delivery frequencies ranging from once every 10 to 60 days depending on the warehouse. The contrast with Zara's high delivery frequency has motivated you to understand the factors that drive this tactical decision, and ultimately to assess whether your firm's current policy should be changed. Several hours into the flight out of Barcelona, you've worked out the formulas above, and you now turn your attention to making sense out of it by considering a series of questions.

1. *What are the economic shipment quantities for the Chicago and San Francisco warehouses?* A reasonable early step toward understanding the trade-offs underlying the economic shipment quantity is to work through a few example calculations. Two of the 30 warehouses replenished by the Boston DC are in Chicago and San Francisco. Table 10.3 illustrates the calculations for the economic shipment quantity and length of the replenishment cycle. Truckload capacity is $Q_{max} = 45,000$ pounds.

TABLE 10.3
Calculation of the Economic Shipment Quantity and Replenishment Cycle for the Chicago and San Francisco Warehouses

	Chicago	San Francisco
Demand rate (D)	625 pounds/day	2,250 pounds/day
Fixed cost/shipment ($A + A_{TL}\delta$)	$1,800	$4,800
Inventory cost rate (c_e)	$0.0036/pound-day	$0.0036/pound-day
Economic shipment quantity (Q^*)	min{45,000, [2 × 1,800 × 625/0.0036]$^{1/2}$} = 25,000 pounds	min{45,000, [2 × 4,800 × 2,250/0.0036]$^{1/2}$} = 45,000 pounds
Economic replenishment cycle (Q^*/D)	25,000/625 = 40 days	45,000/2250 = 20 days

Example Summary

Economic shipment quantity to Chicago:
Q_{max} = truck capacity = 45,000 pounds
D = demand rate = 625 pounds per day
$A + A_{TL}\delta$ = cost/shipment = \$1,800
c_e = holding cost rate = \$0.0036 per pound-day
Q^* = economic shipment quantity = $\min\{Q_{max}, [2(A + A_{TL}\delta)D/c_e]^{1/2}\}$ = 25,000 pounds

Example Summary

Economic shipment quantity to San Francisco:
Q_{max} = truck capacity = 45,000 pounds
D = demand rate = 2,250 pounds per day
$A + A_{TL}\delta$ = cost/shipment = \$4,800
c_e = holding cost rate = \$0.0036 per pound-day
Q^* = economic shipment quantity = $\min\{Q_{max}, [2(A + A_{TL}\delta)D/c_e]^{1/2}\}$ = 45,000 pounds

2. *What patterns should be present in the delivery frequencies to the 30 warehouses?* The expression for the optimal delivery frequency is $\left(\dfrac{Dc_e}{2(A + A_{TL}\delta)}\right)^{1/2}$ if truckload capacity is sufficient; otherwise a replenishment shipment will occur whenever there is enough demand to fill a truck, and the delivery frequency is D/Q_{max}. Fixed shipment transaction cost (A), cost per truck-mile (A_{TL}), and the inventory holding cost rate (c_e) are comparable across the 30 warehouses. The expression indicates that delivery frequency is proportional to the square root of the demand rate, and approximately inversely proportional to the square root of the distance from the Boston DC. Alternatively, if truckload capacity is dictating the frequency, then distance plays no role and delivery frequency is proportional to demand.

The expression for the economic shipment quantity provides an indication of when delivery frequency is likely to be determined by truckload capacity. The economic shipment quantity is $\min\left\{Q_{max}, \left(\dfrac{2(A + A_{TL}\delta)D}{c_e}\right)^{1/2}\right\}$, which is limited by truckload capacity whenever

$$Q_{max} < \left(\frac{2(A + A_{TL}\delta)D}{c_e}\right)^{1/2}$$

It may be obvious that truckload capacity is less likely to be restrictive when demand (D) is low. What may be less obvious is the role of distance (δ). The above inequality is less likely to hold when shipping over short distances (e.g., compare Chicago with San Francisco in Table 10.3). The reason is that transportation cost plays a smaller role and inventory holding cost plays a larger role for nearby warehouses than for distant warehouses. The relative dominance of inventory on total cost amplifies the benefit of frequent and small replenishment shipments.

Finally, the relationship between the average cycle stock holding cost and the shipping cost may be useful for diagnosis. For example, if truckload capacity is not binding, then the average cycle stock holding cost per period is equal to the shipping cost per period, that is,

$$(Q^*/2)c_e = (A + A_{TL}\delta)D/Q^*$$

Alternatively, if truckload capacity is binding, then

$$(Q^*/2)c_e < (A + A_{TL}\delta)D/Q^{*19}$$

A case where cycle stock holding cost is more than replenishment shipping cost signals a potential opportunity to save money by increasing the replenishment frequency.

Summary of Insights into Delivery Frequency

For **moderate levels of demand, delivery frequency is decreasing in distance and increasing in demand, and cycle stock holding cost is equal to shipping cost. For high-volume warehouses or relatively distant warehouses, delivery frequency is based on truckload capacity and is proportional to demand, and cycle stock holding cost is less than shipping cost.** Significant deviations from these patterns suggest that a closer look at delivery policies could be profitable.

What Is the Impact of Deviating from the Economic Delivery Frequency?

Today, each truck is filled to capacity before being dispatched from the Boston DC to a warehouse. You suspect this may be a consequence of reward systems that emphasize low transportation cost. If true, then there could be opportunities to reduce total cost by modifying the policy (and reward systems). From the answer to the previous question, savings opportunities, if they exist, are most likely to be with low-volume warehouses in the East and Midwest. While you expect to raise this topic as an issue for investigation, its priority will be influenced by the potential impact on the bottom line. An indication of priority can be found in the expression for $C(Q^*)$.

The formula for $C(Q^*)$ specifies the optimal transportation and inventory cost per period as one of two possibilities. If truckload capacity is binding, then

$$C(Q^*) = 0.5[y(D)^{-1} + y(D)][2(A + A_{TL}\delta)Dc_e]^{1/2}$$

which is the cost of shipping Q_{max} at a time instead of the natural economic shipment quantity. The value of $y(D)$ is truck capacity as a fraction of the natural economic shipment quantity. This formula also has meaning when capacity is not binding. If $Q^* = [2(A + A_{TL}\delta)D/c_e]^{1/2} < Q_{max}$, then trucks should not be filled to capacity and $0.5[Q^*/Q_{max} + Q_{max}/Q^*][2(A + A_{TL}\delta)Dc_e]^{1/2}$ is the cost of shipping Q_{max} instead of the smaller optimal quantity Q^*. This compares with the optimal transportation and inventory cost per period of $[2(A + A_{TL}\delta)Dc_e]^{1/2}$, so the percentage increase in cost from shipping full trucks instead of the smaller optimal quantity in a truck is

$$0.5[Q^*/Q_{max} + Q_{max}/Q^*] - 1$$

Table 10.4 reports the percentage increase in transportation and inventory cost over a range of values for Q_{max}/Q^*. It shows that **the cost impact is relatively minor for moderate deviations from the optimal shipment quantity.**

TABLE 10.4 Percentage Increase in Cost If Trucks Are Filled to Capacity instead of the Optimal Quantity over Different Values of Truck Capacity as a Fraction of the Optimal Quantity

Q_{max}/Q^*	1.0	1.1	1.2	1.3	1.4	1.5	1.6	1.7	1.8	1.9
Percent cost increase	0.0%	0.5%	1.7%	3.5%	5.7%	8.3%	11.3%	14.4%	17.8%	21.3%

---

[19] Verifying the relationships among holding and shipping cost is left as an end-of-chapter exercise.

Although you don't have the data to run the calculations, you suspect that there are some warehouses where it is worthwhile to increase delivery frequency by not filling trucks to capacity. At the same time, the data in Table 10.4 suggest that the savings potential could be limited. It occurs to you that the use of stop-offs may be an effective alternative. While this option is not currently offered by your carrier, it may be open to negotiation, and there are other carriers. The first step is to get a sense of the value.

2.2. Multiple Stops

As noted in Section 1.3, a stop-off refers to the partial unloading or loading of a shipment between an origin and destination. In this section, we will limit discussion to the use of stop-offs for deliveries, though the ideas also apply to pickups and delivery/pickup combinations.

The objective is to illuminate why and when stop-offs can add value. The answer to *why* requires a general understanding of how material flows and costs are affected by the use of stop-offs. We will focus on two main sources of value—one that is probably obvious and another that may be less obvious. The answer to *when* takes the answer to why to a deeper level. We'll seek to understand the role of such fundamental elements as volume levels, shipping distance, and various cost rates in whether or not stop-offs add value. We'll build on the results in Section 2.1 and reinforce how skills in back-of-the-envelope analysis are useful for developing a sense of when particular tactics are likely to pay off. We will not go through detailed cost analysis of stop-off options, a data-intensive step that could be carried out if pay-off potential is perceived to be high.

To understand why stop-offs can add value, it is important to know how stop-off charges are determined. The transportation rate is generally based on the presumption that the entire load moves between a single origin and destination, with additional fees for stop-offs. The more the intermediate locations are out of the way to the final destination, the higher the stop-off fees. For example, a Boston-to-Chicago shipment with a stop-off in Cleveland may have a $144 stop-off fee. The carrier will travel through Cleveland en route to Chicago. On the other hand, a stop-off in Cincinnati instead of Cleveland will require that the carrier travel about 400 miles out of the way. Accordingly, the cost for the Boston–Cincinnati–Chicago shipment will be notably higher, and may even be billed as two separate shipments—one to Cincinnati and one to Chicago (i.e., stop-off option is not offered).

The above example highlights one source of potential savings from stop-offs, that is, transportation cost. The charge for a stop-off at a location is less than the cost of a separate shipment to the location. A second source of potential savings is inventory holding cost. Stop-offs can be used to economically achieve smaller, more frequent deliveries, which in turn lead to lower inventories and inventory holding cost.

Let us now turn our attention to the details underlying transportation and inventory savings due to stop-offs, or, more generally, how this tactic can be effectively deployed. We'll do this through examples that draw on cost analysis from Section 2.1. But, first, it is worth reiterating that stop-off charges are influenced by the incremental distance and time over a single direct shipment. Consequently, it makes sense to initially look for stop-off locations that are (nearly) on the way to another location.

Example
It must have been the glass of wine. What else could explain a dream about a grocery shopping trip that would never end? Awake, somewhat refreshed, and now four hours into your flight from Barcelona to Boston, you reflect on how grocery shopping has become less of a burden since Sainsbury opened a large store between home and office. The thought hangs in your head as you begin to focus attention on the tactic of stop-offs. Two illustrations come to mind.

1. *An illustration of transportation cost savings.*   There is a warehouse in Cleveland and a warehouse in Chicago supplied by the Boston DC. Each warehouse receives a truckload shipment every 40 days, though the replenishment quantities and truckload costs differ—15,000 pounds at $1,080 for Cleveland and 25,000 pounds at $1,800 for Chicago.[20] The average transportation cost is (1,800 + 1,080)/40 = $72 per day. An alternative is to ship 40,000 pounds to Chicago every 40 days with a stop-off in Cleveland to unload 15,000 pounds, in which case the transportation cost is $1,800 plus a stop-off fee of $144, or (1,800 + 144)/40 = $48.60 per day. Compared to the option of no stop-offs, transportation cost is 1 − 48.6/72 = 32.5 percent lower. There is no difference in the average inventory at each warehouse.

Example Summary

Transportation cost savings with a Cleveland stop-off:
Boston to Cleveland—15,000 pounds every 40 days at a cost of $1,080
Boston to Chicago—25,000 pounds every 40 days at a cost of $1,800
Transportation cost = (1,080 + 1,800)/40 = $72 per day
Boston to Chicago with stop-off in Cleveland—40,000 every 40 days at a cost of (1,800 + 144)/40 = $48.60 per day
Percentage transportation cost reduction = 1 − 48.6/72 = 32.5 percent

---

2. *An illustration of inventory holding cost savings.* Since the combined Cleveland and Chicago demand rate is 1,000 pounds per day, a second alternative is to ship 27,000 pounds to Chicago every 27 days with a stop-off in Cleveland to unload 10,125 pounds. The transportation cost is $1,800 plus a stop-off fee of $144, and since there is a shipment every 27 days, the transportation cost is (1,800 + 144)/27 = $72 per day. Compared to the option of no stop-offs, there is no difference in transportation cost. But, since the time between replenishment shipments is 27 days instead of 40 days, the average cycle stock holding cost at each warehouse is 1 − 27/40 = 32.5 percent lower.

Example Summary

Inventory cost savings with a Cleveland stop-off:
  Ship a total of 40,000 pounds to Cleveland and Chicago every 40 days with no stop-off
⇒ Average transportation cost per day = $72
⇒ Average cycle stock = 40,000/2 = 20,000 pounds
  Ship a total of 27,000 pounds to Chicago every 27 days with a stop-off in Cleveland
⇒ Average transportation cost per day = $72
⇒ Average cycle stock = 27,000/2 = 13,500 pounds
Percentage cycle stock holding cost reduction = 1 − 13,500/20,000 = 32.5 percent

---

Similarity with Sainsbury

In all likelihood, savings would be greater with an alternative between the two extremes considered above. Nevertheless, the illustrations are useful for gaining a sense of the details underlying how stop-offs can add value. The effect is comparable to the new Sainsbury

---

[20] The cost of a shipment in this and subsequent examples includes all relevant costs associated with the shipment transaction.

store opening between home and work. Prior to that point, you made about two shopping trips per week, one to a store with very good fruits and vegetables, and another to a different store for other foods. Today you do all your shopping at Sainsbury where you can easily stop off for groceries on your way home, saving both time and gas. Also, with two trips to Sainsbury per week, you pick up just what is needed for the next few days, food is fresher, and there is less waste.

Generalizing the Two Illustrations

While devising stop-off plans in practice will likely require detailed cost analysis of alternatives using a spreadsheet or some other software, there are general indicators for when such detailed analysis is likely to be of value and where to find promising routes for investigation. These indicators follow from consideration of two cases.

Case 1. Two Independent Truckload Shipments Can Be Combined without Violating Truckload Capacity   With few exceptions, the use of **a stop-off in this case will save money over two independent shipments.** In order to see why this is so, note first that the stop-off fee is less than a separate shipment to the intermediate location (otherwise a stop-off would not be offered). Second, the only possible economic downside of using stop-offs is it requires that the replenishment cycle time of one of the two locations be a multiple of the other. This is necessary so that shipments to the two locations, at least periodically, can be combined. However, even when you begin with an optimal policy without stop-offs, the cost of enforcing such a requirement is minimal.[21] Finally, consider the option of independent shipments with replenishment cycle times satisfying the integer multiple requirement. The cost of a truckload to the intermediate location, for at least some if not all replenishment shipments, can be replaced with a stop-off at a lower cost. There is no change in inventory cost, and transportation cost is lower.

Let's revisit the Boston–Cleveland–Chicago illustration. Suppose the inventory holding cost rate is $0.0036 per pound-day. The demand rates at the Cleveland and Chicago warehouses are 375 pounds per day and 625 pounds per day, respectively. The cost per shipment to Cleveland is $1,080 and to Chicago is $1,800. According to the cost expressions in Section 2.1, the optimal replenishment cycles and costs are

Cleveland:

$$Q^*/D = \left(\frac{2 \times 1,080}{0.0036 \times 375}\right)^{1/2} = 40 \text{ days}$$

$$C(Q^*) = \$54 \text{ per day}$$

Chicago:

$$Q^*/D = \left(\frac{2 \times 1,800}{0.0036 \times 625}\right)^{1/2} = 40 \text{ days}$$

$$C(Q^*) = \$90 \text{ per day}$$

In this example, the replenishment cycles are "naturally" synchronized at 40 days. Leaving the cycle at 40 days and combining the two locations into a single shipment with a $144 stop-off fee reduces transportation cost by 32.5 percent (as noted in the illustration above), and total cost is reduced by 16.25 percent.[22]

---

[21] The cost increase will be no more than $0.5(0.5^{-0.5} + 0.5^{0.5}) - 1 \approx 6$ percent (Roundy 1985).

[22] Transportation cost and inventory cost are equal at Q^* when the quantity is not limited by truckload capacity.

Additional savings are possible by reducing the replenishment cycle time. The cost per shipment to Chicago with a stop-off in Cleveland is $1,800 + 144 = \$1,944$. Consequently, the optimal stop-off replenishment cycle and cost are

Cleveland and Chicago:

$$Q^*/D = \left(\frac{2 \times 1,944}{0.0036 \times (375 + 625)}\right)^{1/2} = 33 \text{ days}$$

$$C(Q^*) = \$118 \text{ per day}$$

The percentage reduction in cost is $(90 + 54 - 118)/(90 + 54) \approx 18$ percent, a slight improvement over the 16.25 percent savings associated with the 40-day replenishment cycle.

Example Summary

Cost savings with a Cleveland stop-off:
Inventory holding cost rate = \$0.0036 per pound-day
  Ship a total of 40,000 lbs to Cleveland and Chicago every 40 days with no stop-off
⇒ Average transportation cost per day = \$72
⇒ Average inventory cost per day = 20,000 lbs × \$0.0036/lb-day = \$72
⇒ Total cost per day = 72 + 72 = \$144
  Ship a total of 33,000 pounds to Chicago every 33 days with a stop-off in Cleveland
⇒ Average transportation cost per day = (1,800 + 144)/33 ≈ \$59
⇒ Average inventory cost per day = 16,500 lbs × \$0.0036/lb-day ≈ \$59
⇒ Total cost per day = 59 + 59 = \$118
Percentage cost reduction = 1 − 118/144 ≈ 18 percent

In summary, if two independent shipments can be combined on a truck without violating capacity, then a stop-off at the intermediate location, if available, will likely save money. The **guideline extends to any number of shipments; that is, look to consolidate shipments by using stop-offs as long as there is space in the truck.** The benefit of stop-offs becomes less one-sided when truckload capacity is a limiting constraint. One such case is considered next.

Case 2. Two Independent Shipments with Trucks Filled to Capacity   The **viability of stop-offs for this case depends to large degree on two factors. One factor, as noted above, is the out-of-the-way distance of the intermediate location. A second, perhaps less obvious, factor is the proximity of the intermediate location to the final destination. A stop-off is more likely to be viable when the intermediate location is much closer** to the final destination than to the origin. This is because full truckloads without a stop-off can be replaced by full truckloads with a stop-off at the intermediate location. Inventory levels and costs at both receiving locations are lower, but transportation costs are higher. The total number of full truckload shipments is unchanged, but each shipment incurs a stop-off charge, and the cost of a separate shipment to the intermediate location is replaced by the higher cost to ship to the final destination. These effects are illustrated in Tables 10.5 and 10.6 for two warehouses on the West Coast that are replenished by the Boston DC. Truckload capacity is $Q_{max} = 45,000$ pounds.

According to the formula in Section 2.1, the economic truckload shipment quantity to Sacramento is

$$\min\left\{Q_{max}, \left(\frac{2 \times 4,500 \times 1,500}{0.0036}\right)^{1/2}\right\} = \min\{45,000, 61,327\} = 45,000$$

TABLE 10.5 **Full Truckload Replenishment Shipments from Boston to Sacramento and from Boston to San Francisco**
Cost is minimized with the above shipping schedule, given that a stop-off is not considered.

	Sacramento	San Francisco	Total
Delivery quantity	Q_{max} = 45,000 pounds	Q_{max} = 45,000 pounds	
Demand rate	D_1 = 1,500 pounds/day	D_2 = 2,250 pounds/day	3,750 pounds/day
Replenishment cycle	Q_{max}/D_1 = 30 days	Q_{max}/D_2 = 20 days	
Average cycle stock	$Q_{max}/2$ = 22,500 pounds	$Q_{max}/2$ = 22,500 pounds	45,000 pounds
Transportation cost per shipment	A_1 = $4,500	A_2 = $4,800	
Inventory cost rate	c_e = $0.0036 per pound-day	c_e = $0.0036 per pound-day	
Transportation cost	$A_1/30$ = $150 per day	$A_2/20$ = $240 per day	$390 per day
Inventory cost	$(Q_{max}/2)c_e$ = $81 per day	$(Q_{max}/2)c_e$ = $81 per day	$162 per day
Total cost	$231 per day	$321 per day	$552 per day

which shows that truckload capacity is a binding constraint. The same is true for San Francisco. Table 10.6 breaks down the alternative of shipping full truckloads to San Francisco with a stop-off in Sacramento. The use of a stop-off lowers cost from $552 per day to $493 per day, or by about 11 percent.

Example Summary

Cost savings with a Sacramento stop-off:

Ship 45,000 pounds to Sacramento every 30 days and 45,000 pounds to San Francisco every 20 days (no stop-off)

⇒ Average transportation cost per day = $390
⇒ Average inventory cost per day = $162
⇒ Total cost per day = 390 + 162 = $552

Ship a total of 45,000 pounds to San Francisco every 12 days with a stop-off in Sacramento

⇒ Average transportation cost per day = $412
⇒ Average inventory cost per day = $81
⇒ Total cost per day = 412 + 81 = $493
Percentage cost reduction = 1 − 493/552 ≈ 11 percent%

TABLE 10.6 **Full Truckload Replenishment Shipments from Boston to San Francisco with a Stop-Off in Sacramento**
Cost is minimized with the above shipping schedule, given that a stop-off is considered.

	Sacramento	San Francisco	Total
Delivery quantity	Q_1 = 18,000 pounds	Q_2 = 27,000 pounds	45,000 pounds = Q_{max}
Demand rate	D_1 = 1,500 pounds per day	D_2 = 2,250 pounds per day	3,750 pounds per day
Replenishment cycle	Q_1/D_1 = 12 days	Q_2/D_2 = 12 days	
Average cycle stock	$Q_1/2$ = 9,000 pounds	$Q_2/2$ = 13,500 pounds	22,500 pounds
Transportation cost per shipment	A_s = $144 per stop-off	A_2 = $4,800 per shipment	
Inventory cost rate	c_e = $0.0036 per pound-day	c_e = $0.0036 per pound-day	
Transportation cost	$A_s/12$ = $12 per day	$A_2/12$ = $400 per day	$412 per day
Inventory cost	$(Q_1/2)c_e$ = $32.40 per day	$(Q_2/2)c_e$ = $48.60 per day	$81 per day
Total cost	$44.40 per day	$448.60 per day	$493 per day

In general, the inventory cost savings due to a stop-off is $(Q_{max}/2)c_e$, which is offset against an increase in transportation cost of $A_s(D_1 + D_2)/Q_{max} + (A_2 - A_1)D_1/Q_{max}$, yielding a net savings (or loss) per period of

$$(Q_{max}/2)c_e - [A_s(D_1 + D_2)/Q_{max} + (A_2 - A_1)D_1/Q_{max}]$$

Consequently, a stop-off at an intermediate location saves money over full truckload shipments to each location whenever

$$A_s(D_1 + D_2)/Q_{max} + (A_2 - A_1)D_1/Q_{max} < (Q_{max}/2)c_e$$

If the condition is satisfied and a stop-off is added (e.g., shipment to San Francisco with a stop-off in Sacramento), then the same condition can be repeatedly evaluated to assess whether it is economical to add another stop-off (e.g., in Denver). In this case, the values of A_1, A_s, and D_1 correspond to the rates for the candidate stop-off location (e.g., Denver), A_2 is the cost per shipment to the final destination (e.g., San Francisco), and D_2 is the demand rate on the existing route to the final destination (e.g., combined demand of Sacramento and San Francisco).

The above analysis supports three indicators for when and where to look for stop-off opportunities among locations currently being served by trucks operating at capacity. First, **look for an intermediate location with minimal out-of-the-way distance to a more distant location.** The option of a stop-off is more likely to be offered by the carrier and the quoted stop-off fee is more likely to be low, that is, small A_s.[23]

Second, **look for an intermediate location that is much closer to the final destination than to the origin.** This reduces the impact of replacing the truckload cost to the intermediate location with the truckload cost to the more distant location, that is, small $A_2 - A_1$.

Finally, the analysis sheds light on economics of routes with more than one stop-off. In contrast with the uncapacitated scenario of Case 1, there are **diminishing marginal returns from adding stop-offs when capacity is binding.** For Case 1, money is saved by using all stop-off opportunities that are available en route to some destination. For Case 2, **it pays to be selective.** The basic reason for this is that each additional stop-off moves the shipment size of Q_{max} farther away from the unconstrained economic truckload shipment quantity; this effect is not present in the uncapacitated Case 1. At a more detailed level, the total cycle stock among a set of locations is cut in half whenever a new stop-off is added, so the inventory savings rate is constant. But transportation cost increases at an increasing rate as stop-off locations are added, and could well surpass the inventory savings. When not all locations can be economically accommodated by stop-offs, the judicious selection of stop-off locations can mean greater savings.

The numerical example in Tables 10.5 and 10.6 also **reinforces the importance of a systemwide view,** and, in particular, how **a narrow focus on minimizing transportation cost can translate into lower profit.** Here we see that a stop-off in Sacramento increases transportation cost by 5.6 percent, yet the combined transportation and inventory cost drops by 11 percent.

The preceding illustrations made use of the formulas given in Section 2.1, though notation was slightly augmented to account for two shipments and a stop-off fee. The augmented notation and formulas for stop-off analysis are summarized below.

Notation for Truckload Stop-Off Analysis

D_i = demand rate in units per period at location i

A = fixed cost per shipment transaction; for example, order processing and other costs that are independent of distance and shipment quantity

δ_i = shipping distance in miles to location i

---

[23] In the words of Euclid (circa 300 B.C.), any ass knows this. Put a haystack at one corner of a triangle and an ass at the other. The ass will certainly not go along the sides of the triangle to get to his hay (Euclid 1956).

A_{TLi} = truckload cost per mile to location i

A_i = total cost per truckload shipment to location $i = A + A_{TLi}\delta_i$

A_s = cost for a stop-off at location 1 on the way to location 2

c_e = inventory holding cost per unit-period

$Q_{\max}$ = truckload capacity

Q_i = delivery quantity to location i

Formulas for Truckload Stop-Off Analysis

Two Separate Shipments to Locations 1 and 2 (i.e., no stop-off)

D_i/Q_i = average number of replenishment shipments per period to a location with demand rate D_i

Q_i/D_i = average time between replenishment shipments, or replenishment cycle time

$Q_i/2$ = average cycle stock

$C(Q_i)$ = cost per period; includes transportation cost, transaction cost (e.g., order processing), and inventory holding cost at the receiving location = $(A + A_{TLi}\delta_i)D_i/Q_i + (Q_i/2)c_e = A_iD_i/Q_i + (Q_i/2)c_e$

Q_i^* = economic shipment quantity = $\min\left\{Q_{\max}, \left(\dfrac{2A_iD_i}{c_e}\right)^{1/2}\right\}$

D_i/Q_i^* = economic delivery frequency = $\max\left\{\dfrac{D_i}{Q_{\max}}, \left(\dfrac{D_ic_e}{2A_i}\right)^{1/2}\right\}$

$y(D_i)$ = truck capacity as a fraction of the "natural" economic shipment quantity at demand rate D_i

$= Q_{\max}/[2A_i\delta_i)D_i/c_e]^{1/2}$

$C(Q_i^*)$ = optimal transportation and inventory cost per period

$= \begin{cases} [2A_iD_ic_e]^{1/2}, & \text{if}\,[2A_iD_ic_e]^{1/2} \leq Q_{\max} \\ 0.5[y(D_i)^{-1} + y(D_i)][2A_iD_ic_e]^{1/2}, & \text{otherwise} \end{cases}$

A Stop-Off at Location 1 to Unload Q_1 Units on the Way to Location 2 to Unload Q_2 Units

Q = total shipment quantity

Q_i = quantity unloaded at location $i = QD_i/(D_1 + D_2)$

D = combined demand rate of locations 1 and 2 = $D_1 + D_2$

D/Q = average number of replenishment shipments per period to locations 1 and 2 with demand rate D

Q/D = average time between replenishment shipments, or replenishment cycle time

$Q/2$ = average cycle stock

$C(Q)$ = cost per period; includes transportation cost, transaction cost (e.g., order processing), and inventory holding cost at receiving locations 1 and 2 = $(A_s + A + A_{TL2}\delta_2)D/Q + (Q/2)c_e = (A_s + A_2)D/Q + (Q/2)c_e$

Q^* = economic shipment quantity = $\min\left\{Q_{\max}, \left(\dfrac{2(A_s + A_2)D}{c_e}\right)^{1/2}\right\}$

D/Q^* = economic delivery frequency = $\max\left\{\dfrac{D}{Q_{\max}}, \left(\dfrac{Dc_e}{2(A_s + A_2)}\right)^{1/2}\right\}$

$y(D)$ = truck capacity as a fraction of the "natural" economic shipment quantity at demand rate $D = Q_{\max}/[2(A_s + A_2)D/c_e]^{1/2}$

$C(Q^*)$ = optimal transportation and inventory cost per period

$$= \begin{cases} [2(A_s + A_2)Dc_e]^{1/2}, & \text{if } [2(A_s + A_2)D/c_e]^{1/2} \le Q_{\max} \\ 0.5[y(D)^{-1} + y(D)][2(A_s + A_2)Dc_e]^{1/2}, & \text{otherwise} \end{cases}$$

Summary of Insights into When/Where Stop-Offs Are Likely to Add Value

We have considered two extreme cases, and we have seen how back-of-the-envelope analysis can be useful for developing a sense of the merits and trade-offs associated with the tactic of stop-offs. When truckload capacity is not an issue, then the use of a stop-off will likely save money. When trucks are already operating at capacity, then stop-offs are less likely to add value. In fact, the use of a stop-off will increase transportation cost, but this may be more than offset by a decrease in inventory holding cost. Between these extremes, stop-offs generally become less attractive as trucks operate closer to capacity.

3. STRATEGIC DECISIONS

This section examines the strategic question of distribution network design, and, in particular, the number of warehouses to operate. The design influences how transportation resources are deployed and managed over a relatively long time horizon (e.g., because changes are costly and require long lead times), and, for many firms, the network plays a meaningful role in the cost and service characteristics of getting product to market.

Firms must weigh various considerations when deciding the number of warehouses for their products. At a fundamental level, the design of a distribution network represents a balance between competing pressures. As the number of warehouses increases and the market area that each warehouse serves gets smaller, outbound transportation cost decreases. In addition, the average distance between a customer and the closest warehouse gets smaller, and this may boost market share. These factors create incentives for a distribution network with many warehouses. On the other hand, the fixed overhead cost of operating a warehouse and the lower inventory investment associated with serving many customers from few warehouses (i.e., due to the law of large numbers) create incentives for a distribution network with few warehouses.

We will look at trade-offs and patterns associated with distribution network design decisions. Tactical considerations such as delivery frequency and use of stop-offs will be ignored, with the assumption that tactics appropriate to a particular design will be deployed. We'll begin in Section 3.1 by considering ways to estimate how delivery distance depends on the market area served by a warehouse. These distance formulas are a stepping-stone to estimating transportation cost, which, in combination with an estimate for warehouse operating cost, will be used to investigate characteristics of an effective design in Section 3.2. We'll look at the case where inbound transportation cost is largely unaffected by the number and location of warehouses. We'll also consider the roles of a warehouse, and how the choice of role affects the cost structure. Along the way, we'll consider alternatives to traditional warehousing, including cross-docking and drop-shipping, and we'll look at the effects of inbound transportation cost on network design.

3.1. Estimating Delivery Distance and Cost

This section reviews expressions that describe how delivery distance and cost are affected by the size of the warehouse market area. The main conclusions are **(1) average delivery distance is approximately proportional to the square root of the market area, (2) outbound transportation cost per unit is approximately proportional to the square root of the market area raised to a fractional power that depends on the economies of**

distance in transportation pricing, and (3) changes in the market area have little effect on outbound transportation cost per unit in small markets with deliveries via milk runs. The analysis relies on several assumptions.

A1. The demand rate is constant and customers are uniformly distributed throughout the market area.

A2. The warehouse is centrally located in the market area that it serves.

A3. Unit transportation cost as a function of miles traveled, δ, is $c_2\delta^\alpha$ where $0 < \alpha \leq 1$.

Economies of distance in transportation cost exist when $\alpha < 1$. If $\alpha = 1$, for example, then unit transportation cost is proportional to distance and c_2 is the cost per unit-mile.

Notation

D = annual demand per square mile

δ = shipping distance in miles

c_2 = outbound transportation cost coefficient

α = outbound transportation cost exponent

x = market area served by a warehouse in square miles

While expressions for transportation cost as a function of market area are necessary for exploring the cost trade-offs in network design, there are other types of questions where estimates of delivery distance may be useful (e.g., effect of market area on average transit time). Expressions for average distance to customers as a function of market area are available for a number of distance norms and market area shapes.[24] Table 10.7 lists distance formulas for various market area shapes according to straight-line distance, or the so-called Euclidean norm. For contrast, the rectilinear norm is based on rectangular movement (e.g., as in travel through a city with a rectangular grid of streets); for the rectilinear norm and a diamond-shaped market area,[25] the average distance between warehouse and customer is $0.471x^{1/2}$.

TABLE 10.7

Average Distance Formulas for the Euclidean Norm[26]

In developed countries, the average travel distance on road networks is about 25 percent more than Euclidean distance.

Market Shape	Average Euclidean Distance between Warehouse and Customer Given a Market Area of x Square Miles
Circle	$0.376x^{1/2}$
Hexagon	$0.377x^{1/2}$
Square	$0.382x^{1/2}$
Triangle	$0.403x^{1/2}$

Source: Newell 1973.

[24] The distance between two specific locations can be obtained from mileage tables (available on Internet sites such as MapQuest, among other sources). Alternatively, distance could be computed using the longitude and latitude of the two locations. Since the earth's circumference is about 24,902 miles, there are about 69 miles (= 24,902/360) per degree latitude and per degree longitude, and an estimate for straight-line distance is $69 \times [(\text{latitude}_1 - \text{latitude}_2)^2 + (\text{longitude}_1 - \text{longitude}_2)^2]^{1/2}$. (This formula is an approximation because it doesn't account for the curvature of the earth or the fact that the distance per degree longitude gets smaller as one gets closer to the poles.)

[25] Diamond-shaped market areas are most efficient for the rectilinear norm.

[26] The formulas in the table are based on the following general expression for average distance:

$$\int_{s_m}^{s_M} \int_{t_m(s)}^{t_M(s)} \delta(s,t) f(s,t)\, dt\, ds,$$ where $\delta(s,t)$ = distance from the warehouse to point (s, t), $f(s, t)$ = probability of a customer at point (s, t), s_m = smallest value of s in the market area, s_M = largest value of s in the market area, $t_m(s)$ = smallest value of t at point s in the market, $t_M(s)$ = largest value of t at point s in the market area.

Table 10.7 is based on one-way distance to each customer. The expressions would be doubled to estimate round-trip distance. In the case of milk runs, the distance of a tour with stop-offs at multiple customers can be divided into two components: (1) line-haul distance, which is the distance to and from the region where deliveries take place, and (2) local delivery distance. The literature provides guidelines on how to efficiently partition a market area into local delivery regions and how to identify efficient tours with stop-offs in each region, which we will not cover here.[27] However, average distance expressions have been developed under the assumption that efficient routes and delivery regions are used. There are two cases: (1) the number of customers per tour is much smaller than the number of local delivery regions and (2) the number of customers per tour is much larger than the number of local delivery regions. For the first case, the average line-haul distance per tour is approximately equal to the average distance to each customer and the local delivery distance is approximately proportional to the average distance between adjacent customers; that is, the average tour distance with deliveries to n customers is approximately

$2 \times$ (average distance from warehouse to customer) $+ n \times k_1 \times$ (average distance between adjacent customers)

Expressions from Table 10.7 can be used to estimate the average distance from warehouse to customer.

For the second case with few regions, there effectively is no line-haul distance (e.g., local delivery regions are adjacent to the warehouse, like slices of a pie with the warehouse at the center); that is, the average tour distance with deliveries to n customers is approximately

$n \times k_2 \times$ (average distance between adjacent customers)

The values of k_1 and k_2 depend on the distance norm; for example, for the Euclidean norm, $k_1 \approx 0.57$ and $k_2 \approx 0.75$ (Daganzo 1999).

There are **two main lessons** that follow from the above discussion. First, in many cases, the **average transport distance per customer is approximately proportional to the square root of the market area.** This structural relationship holds over a variety of distance norms, market area shapes, and delivery tactics. Second, **an exception to the preceding point can occur in small markets served by milk runs.** Average transport distance per customer is relatively unaffected by changes in market area when there are a few local delivery regions with many stop-offs per tour.

As noted in Section 2, transportation cost is approximately proportional to distance. However, economies of distance are usually present to some degree in transport rates in order to account for *terminal costs* incurred by the carrier (e.g., time/costs associated with loading and unloading). Economies of distance in freight rates, which is known as tapering, are illustrated in Figure 10.2.

The formula $c_2\delta^\alpha$ (see assumption A3 above) is used to approximate the transportation cost curves like those in Figure 10.2. The greater the economies of distance, the smaller the value of α. Straight lines, or curves that exhibit no economies of distance, correspond to $\alpha = 1$. In settings where economies of distance are not significant, expressions for unit transportation cost as a function of market area follow directly from the distance expressions; distance is multiplied by the cost per unit-mile to yield transportation cost as a function of market area. More generally, unit outbound transportation cost as a function of market area x is

$$C_T(x) = c_2\tau x^{\alpha/2}$$

---

[27] For example, see Daganzo (1999) and Simchi-Levi, Chen, and Bramel (2005).

FIGURE 10.2
Illustration of the Economies of Distance, Known as Tapering, in Freight Rates

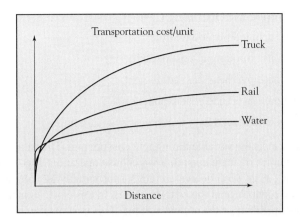

The value of τ depends on the distance norm and market shape.[28] For example, for the Euclidean norm and circular market shape, $\tau = 2/[(2 + \alpha)\pi^{\alpha/2}]$, and for the rectilinear norm and diamond market shape, $\tau = (2^{1-\alpha/2})/(2 + \alpha)$ (Erlenkotter 1989).[29]

3.2. Network Design

We will use the unit outbound transportation cost formula above (i.e., $C_T(x) = c_2\tau x^{\alpha/2}$) as we consider the issue of network design in this section. But first, a few words on the values of α and c_2. The values should reflect the approximate cost associated with the delivery tactics likely to be used over a range of possible sizes for warehouse market area. However, the purpose of the analysis in this section is to illuminate the nature of trade-offs in network design and expose basic indicators of an effective design. It is probably not worth spending a lot of time to develop refined estimates. In addition, as we will see below, the value of c_2 is irrelevant for some of the results.

General Optimal Market Area Model

Market area models concisely capture factors that influence the size of a facility in terms of the area that it serves. Early versions of these models can be traced to the early 1900s and central-place theory—a theory stemming from the work of economist August Lösch (1954) and geographer Walter Christaller (1966) that characterizes the geography of retail and service businesses. A variety of market area models have been used in a variety of application areas. Erlenkotter (1989) consolidates this work in the form of a general optimal market area (GOMA) model.

The GOMA model draws on assumptions A1 through A3 above, as well as an assumption on warehouse operating costs:

A4. The unit warehousing cost given annual volume Dx is $w_1 + w_2/(Dx)^{1-\beta}$, where $0 \le \beta < 1$.

---

[28] The formula for $C_T(x)$ and the formulas for τ are based on the general formula

$$C_T(x) = \int_{s_m}^{s_M} \int_{t_m(s)}^{t_M(s)} c_2\delta(s,t)^\alpha \, f(s,t)dtds.$$

[29] If $\alpha = 1$ (no economies of distance), then $\tau = 2/[(2 + \alpha)\pi^{\alpha/2}] \approx 0.376$ and $\tau = (2^{1-\alpha/2})/(2 + \alpha) \approx 0.471$, which are the coefficients in the corresponding distance formulas above.

Notation for Warehouse Operating Cost

D = annual demand per square mile

w_1 = warehouse throughput cost per unit

w_2 = warehouse overhead cost coefficient

β = warehouse overhead cost exponent

x = market area served by a warehouse in square miles

The value of w_1 is the variable throughput cost per unit. The value of β reflects the degree to which economies of scale exist in a warehouse operation. If $\beta = 0$, then the unit warehousing cost $w_1 + w_2/(Dx)$ decreases rather substantially as volume increases (e.g., high degree of scale economies in the cost structure). In this case, w_2 is the annual warehousing cost that is independent of the annual volume. This cost may include, for example, inventory carrying cost and other fixed overhead costs such as management salaries and warehouse management software and hardware. For values of β close to one, warehousing cost is approximately proportional to volume and economies of scale are nearly nonexistent.

As is the case for transportation cost, the values of w_1, w_2, and β should reflect the approximate cost associated with warehousing operation over a range of market area sizes, and, again, it is probably not worth spending a lot of time to develop refined estimates. This is especially true for w_1, which does not affect the optimal market area.

From Section 3.1, the unit outbound transportation cost as a function of the market area is

$$C_T(x) = c_2 \tau x^{\alpha/2}$$

which increases as the market area gets larger. We'll use $C_W(x)$ to represent the unit warehousing "overhead" cost as a function of the market area, that is,

$$C_W(x) = w_2/(Dx)^{1-\beta} = w_2 D^{\beta-1} x^{\beta-1}$$

which decreases as the market area gets larger. The optimal market area is the value of x that balances this trade-off and minimizes

$$C(x) = C_T(x) + C_W(x) = c_2 \tau x^{\alpha/2} + w_2 D^{\beta-1} x^{\beta-1}$$

The optimal market area and other GOMA formulas are summarized below.

Formulas for the General Optimal Market Area Model

$C_T(x)$ = unit outbound transportation cost as a function of market area

$\quad x = c_2 \tau x^{\alpha/2}$

$C_W(x)$ = unit warehousing overhead cost as a function of the market area

$\quad x = w_2 D^{\beta-1} x^{\beta-1}$

$C(x)$ = unit outbound transportation and warehousing overhead cost

$\quad = C_T(x) + C_W(x) = c_2 \tau x^{\alpha/2} + w_2 D^{\beta-1} x^{\beta-1}$

x^* = optimal market area = $\left(\dfrac{w_2 D^{\beta-1}(1-\beta)}{c_2 \tau \left(\frac{\alpha}{2} \right)} \right)^{\frac{1}{\alpha/2+1-\beta}}$

$C(x^*)$ = optimal unit outbound transportation and warehousing overhead cost

$\quad = (\alpha/2 + 1 - \beta) \left[\dfrac{c_2 \tau w_2 D^{\beta-1}}{(\alpha/2)(1-\beta)} \right]^{\frac{1}{\alpha/2+1-\beta}}$

$C_W(x^*)/C_T(x^*)$ = ratio of optimal warehousing overhead cost to transportation cost

$\quad = \dfrac{\alpha/2}{1-\beta}$

$C(yx^*)/C(x^*) - 1 =$ percentage increase in cost if market area is $x = yx^*$ instead of x^*

$$= y^{\beta - 1}\left(\frac{\alpha/2}{\alpha/2 + 1 - \beta}\right) + y^{\alpha/2}\left(\frac{1 - \beta}{\alpha/2 + 1 - \beta}\right) - 1$$

One notable result is that the last two formulas only depend on the degree to which economies of distance (α) and scale (β) are present in the cost structure. The other cost parameters, the market area shape, and the distance norm have no impact. The lack of dependence on these parameters and assumptions indicates that the two formulas are expressions of rather fundamental properties of the network design problem.

Example

It was during the Inditex board meeting that you decided your firm's distribution network will undergo a review when you return to Boston. Having satisfied your curiosity about decisions relating to delivery frequency and stop-offs, you turn your attention to network design. Through some quick analysis on the flight home, you hope to be in a position to influence, understand, and critically evaluate the analyses and recommendations coming out of the network design study. You focus first on the U.S. market and then on India.

1. *Is the number of warehouses in the United States reasonable?* Your firm operates one DC and 30 warehouses in the United States. The Boston DC directly serves about 10 percent of U.S. customer demand with a market area of about 150,000 square miles. With the 30 warehouses serving the balance of the continental United States, or about 2,850,000 square miles, the current average market area per warehouse is $x = 2,850,000/30 = 95,000$ mi^2.

   As a quick diagnostic, the ratio of current warehousing overhead to outbound transportation cost can be compared with the benchmark value that holds when the market area is optimal, that is, $C_W(x^*)/C_T(x^*) = (\alpha/2)/(1 - \beta)$. **A ratio based on current warehousing and outbound transportation costs that is significantly different from $(\alpha/2)/(1 - \beta)$ is an indicator that the current network is poorly designed.**

   For your firm, economies of distance in freight rates are minimal (i.e., $\alpha \approx 1$). In addition, the annual overhead expense to operate a warehouse cost is relatively unaffected by volume (i.e., $\beta \approx 0$), so the benchmark ratio is $C_W(x^*)/C_T(x^*) = (\alpha/2)/(1 - \beta) = 1/2$. In the recent past, outbound transportation cost for the 30 warehouses has been averaging $0.90 per cwt. The fixed overhead cost to operate a warehouse is $w_2 = \$100,000$ per year. The 30 warehouses shipped 8,550,000 cwt last year, which corresponds to a demand rate of $D = 8,550,000/2,850,000 = 3$ cwt per mi^2-year and a unit overhead cost of $30 \times 100,000/8,550,000 = \$0.35$ per cwt-year. Comparing the two ratios:

   Ratio based on current operations $= 0.35/0.90 \approx 0.4$

versus

   $0.5 =$ benchmark ratio

   The difference in ratios signals a potential opportunity to save money, and raises questions on the optimal network design and the magnitude of savings potential. The GOMA model can be used to get a quick sense of the answers to these questions.

   The optimal market area for a warehouse depends on the demand rate (D), the freight rate (c_2), the configuration factor (τ), warehouse overhead (w_2), and parameters for economies of distance and scale (α and β). As noted above, $D = 3$ cwt per mi^2-year, $w_2 = \$100,000$ per year, $\alpha = 1$, and $\beta = 0$. The freight rate is $c_2 = \$0.006$ per cwt-mi. What remains is to select a value for τ. One approach is to increase the configuration factor for a circular market area and Euclidean distance by 25 percent to account for added distance due to the road network and irregularities in the market shape, that is, $\tau = 0.376 \times 1.25 \approx 0.47$ (the term 1.25 is known as the *circuitry factor*). In addition, the actual unit outbound transportation cost could be used as a reasonability check on the formula, and for refining the value to be used for τ. Plugging the market area of $x = 95,000$ mi^2, $c_2 = \$0.006$ per cwt-mi, and $\tau = 0.47$ into the unit outbound transportation cost formula $C_T(x) = c_2 \tau x^{\alpha/2}$ yields $C_T(95,000) = (0.006)(0.47)(95,000)^{1/2} \approx \$0.87$ per cwt. In this case, a circuitry factor of 1.3 leads to a slightly closer match with actual cost of \$0.90 per cwt; that is, $\tau = 0.376 \times 1.3 \approx 0.49$ and $C_T(95,000) = (0.006)(0.49)(95,000)^{1/2} \approx \$0.91$ per cwt.

Based on the parameter estimates, the optimal market area is

$$x^* = \left[\frac{w_2 D^{\beta-1}(1-\beta)}{c_2 \tau \left(\frac{\alpha}{2}\right)} \right]^{\frac{1}{\alpha/2+1-\beta}} = \left[\frac{100,000 \times 3^{-1}}{.006 \times .49 \times 0.5} \right]^{\frac{1}{1/2+1}} \approx 80,114 \, \text{mi}^2$$

The current market area of 95,000 mi^2 is about 19 percent larger than x^*.

Example Summary

Optimal market area:
D = demand rate = 3 cwt per mi^2
w_2 = warehouse overhead cost = \$100,000 per yr (not affected by changes in volume, i.e., $\beta = 0$).
c_2 = outbound transportation cost = \$0.006 per cwt-mi (with no economies of distance, i.e., $\alpha = 1$)
At τ = configuration factor = 0.49,
x^* = optimal market area (given $\alpha = 1$ and $\beta = 0$) = $[2w_2/(c_2 D\tau)]^{2/3} \approx 80,114$ mi^2

For an alternative comparison, the optimal number of warehouses for the total area of 2,850,000 mi^2 is 2,850,000/80,114 = 35.6, or about 36 warehouses. This compares with the 30 warehouses in use today. These differences may seem large, but one of the insights from the analysis is that **cost is relatively insensitive to moderate deviations from the optimal market area.** For example, Table 10.8 reports the percentage cost premium for different values of the ratio of the actual market area to the optimal market area ($y = x/x^*$).

Table 10.8 shows that the cost premium of the current market area $x = 95,000$ mi^2, which is about 19 percent larger than x^*, is less than 0.8 percent (i.e., $C(1.2x^*)/C(x^*) - 1 = 0.8$ percent). In summary, the analysis suggests that the distribution network in the United States would be more efficient with additional warehouses, but any cost savings would be minimal.

2. *How should the distribution network in India differ from that in the United States?* Your firm is currently selling Kalina product in India through select outlets, and the market has responded well. Full-scale distribution will begin next year. A DC in the seaport of Madras will play a role similar to the Boston DC in the United States; the Madras DC will receive container loads and will ship direct to customers as well as resupply warehouses. The number and location of warehouses in India have yet to be determined.

The India market potential in the foreseeable future is projected at 1 percent of the U.S. market, as measured by annual demand per square mile. It may be clear that regions with low demand are served by warehouses with large market areas (e.g., there are fewer Wendy's restaurants per square mile in North Dakota than in New York City). But the degree

---

TABLE 10.8 **Percentage Increase in Cost If the Market Area Is $x = yx^*$ instead of the Optimal Market Area x^* over a Range of Possible Values of y**

The table is based on no economies of distance ($\alpha = 1$) and extreme economies of scale ($\beta = 0$). The percentages in the table would be smaller if $\alpha < 1$ and/or $\beta > 0$.

y	0.5	0.6	0.7	0.8	0.9	1.0	1.1	1.2	1.3	1.4	1.5
$C(yx^*)/C(x^*) - 1$	13.8%	7.2%	3.4%	1.3%	0.3%	0%	0.2%	0.8%	1.7%	2.7%	3.9%

of increase in the warehouse market area when demand is reduced by 99 percent may be less clear. In addition, there is the complicating factor of cost rate differences. Transportation rates in India are expected to be more expensive relative to warehousing overhead cost due to the road network and lower transport volumes. The GOMA model can be used to get a quick sense of the impact. If the ratio $w_2/c_2\tau$ in India is 90 percent of the U.S. ratio, then letting D, c_2, τ, and w_2 stand for the U.S. values,

$$\text{India } x^* = \left[\left(0.9 \times \frac{w_2}{c_2\tau}\right)(0.01 \times D)^{-1}\left(\frac{1}{1/2}\right)\right]^{\frac{1}{1/2+1}} = [0.9 \div 0.01]^{\frac{2}{3}}\left[\frac{w_2 D^{-1}}{c_2\tau/2}\right]^{\frac{2}{3}} \approx 20(\text{U.S. } x^*)$$

The calculation suggests that a warehouse in India should serve an area about 20 times larger than a warehouse in the United States.

Up to this point in the example, we have considered all of the GOMA formulas except for $C(x^*)$. The **expression for $C(x^*)$ contains lessons for cost savings due to volume increases and lower-cost rates.** For example, if $\alpha = 1$ and $\beta = 0$, then $C(x^*) = 1.5(2c_2\tau w_2/D)^{2/3}$. Accordingly, an increase in demand by a factor of three translates into a $1 - (1/3)^{2/3} \approx 50$ percent reduction in the unit outbound transportation and warehouse overhead cost.[30] In the case of India, insight into the volume–cost relationship could play a role in the formulation of a plan for particularly aggressive pricing and advertising during roll-out.

Example Summary

Optimal market area in India versus the United States:
Estimated demand rate per mi^2 in India = 1 percent of U.S. demand rate
Estimated ratio of warehousing overhead cost to outbound transportation rate in India = 90 percent of U.S. ratio
Optimal market area per warehouse in India = $(0.9/0.01)^{2/3} \approx 20$ times the optimal market area per warehouse in the United States

---

Applicability and Limits of the GOMA Model, and Cantalupo's Theorem   As noted above, the GOMA model, as well as other forms of back-of-the-envelope analysis, attempts to capture the essential elements of a question with minimal data. A main purpose is to gain insight and strengthen one's intuition into the most important trade-offs influencing a decision. A well-developed intuition is a powerful asset—it is the foundation for sensing areas of opportunity and for making quick and educated decisions in response to changing business conditions. The coarseness of back-of-the-envelope analysis means that it is generally not sufficient as sole support for large investment decisions. An example from McDonald's helps illustrate this point.

James Cantalupo was a successful executive at McDonald's. During his 16-month tenure as CEO beginning in 2003, stock price more than doubled and he was credited with leading the firm's turnaround. Earlier, in his role as CEO of McDonald's International during the 1990s, the number of non-U.S. McDonald's restaurants increased from 2,000 in 40 countries to 15,000 in 120 countries. It was also during this time that he coined Cantalupo's theorem (Serwer 1994). The theorem is a formula for estimating the number of McDonald's restaurants that should be opened in a country, or, equivalently, the average market area

---

[30] While it is true that a distribution network will not be continually adjusted to maximize efficiency (e.g., market area is not always x^* as demand and cost rates change), it is also true that the cost of moderate deviations from the optimal distribution network is minimal.

per restaurant. In brief, the number of restaurants is equal to the population of the country divided by the number of people per restaurant in the United States with an adjustment for differences in per capita income. Cantalupo's Theorem captures the economics of restaurant operation with minimal data. It reflects years of business experience as a concise distillation of factors underlying the viability of a restaurant. It is useful as a general guide, but not for locating and opening a specific restaurant. McDonald's is known for careful and detailed analysis of area demographics and traffic patterns prior to opening a restaurant and employs a group dedicated to this activity.

Impact of Inbound Freight

In settings where there are many geographically dispersed sources of supply, the location of a warehouse within its market area has little bearing on inbound transportation cost. A shift of a warehouse toward one source also moves the warehouse farther away from another source. Consequently, the decision on location hinges largely on outbound transportation considerations, and warehouses tend to be centrally located within their market areas. This is the setting of the previous section.

At the other extreme is a single source that replenishes all warehouses. In this case, inbound transportation considerations are a factor in network design decisions because total cost often can be reduced by shifting each warehouse toward the source of supply. In this section, we'll look at some simple analysis of this extreme. The objective is to provide a sense of when and how inbound transportation costs affect the warehouse market area.

Relative to a design that ignores inbound transportation cost, the main conclusions are **(1) there are fewer warehouses serving larger market areas, (2) the amount of increase in market area depends on the ratio of the inbound-to-outbound transportation rates, and (3) there is little increase in market area unless the ratio of inbound-to-outbound transportation rates is 50 percent or more.** Before we proceed, it is worth reinforcing that these conclusions are based on the case of a single source of supply. The effect of inbound transportation cost diminishes as the number and geographical dispersion of sources increases.

Envision a two-dimensional representation of the territory to be served by the distribution network that is compressed into a single dimension, or a line that is L miles long (see Figure 10.3). This provides a basis for specifying how inbound, outbound, and warehousing costs depend on the size of the market served by a warehouse.[31] The assumptions and notation are listed below.

A1. The demand rate is constant and customers are uniformly distributed along a line with the source of supply at one end.[32]

A2. Unit outbound transportation cost as a function of miles traveled, δ, is $c_2\delta$.

A3. Unit inbound transportation cost as a function of miles traveled, δ, is $c_1\delta$ where $c_1 < c_2$.[33]

A4. The unit warehousing cost given annual volume Dx is $w_1 + w_2/(Dx)$.

---

[31] Expanded discussion of this approach can be found in Geoffrion (1976).

[32] The case where the source of supply is not at an endpoint can be split into two separate cases consistent with the assumption—one for the line to the left of the source and another for the line to the right of the source.

[33] If $c_1 \geq c_2$, then there is no opportunity to save transportation cost by opening warehouses (e.g., product can be shipped directly to the customer from the source at the cheaper outbound rate of c_2).

FIGURE 10.3 The Distribution Area Compressed onto a Line of Length L

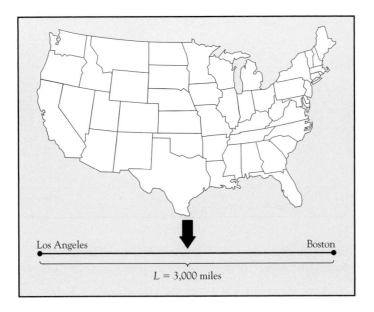

Los Angeles   Boston

$L = 3,000$ miles

Notation

L = length of the territory served by the distribution network

D = annual demand per linear mile

δ = shipping distance in miles

c_1 = inbound transportation cost per unit-mile

c_2 = outbound transportation cost per unit-mile

w_1 = warehouse throughput cost per unit

w_2 = warehouse fixed cost per year (e.g., overhead)

x = market length served by a warehouse in miles

The warehouse throughput cost is unaffected by the market length. $C_W(x)$ represents the unit warehousing overhead cost as a function of the market length, that is,

$$C_W(x) = w_2/(Dx)$$

which decreases as the market length gets larger.

Transportation cost is more complicated. We'll first look at the simple case where inbound costs are ignored. Each warehouse is centrally located within its market length x because this minimizes the average outbound distance. Figure 10.4 illustrates a distribution network with three centrally located warehouses. Due to uniform demand, the average outbound distance is half the distance from the center to the edge of the market, or $x/4$. The average inbound distance is $L/2$. Similar diagrams could be sketched for networks with more or fewer warehouses, but there would be no change in average distance formulas; that is, average outbound distance = $x/4$ and average inbound distance = $L/2$. One notable result is that inbound distance is unaffected by the market length x. In summary, the unit inbound and outbound transportation cost is

$$C_T(x) = c_1L/2 + c_2x/4$$

FIGURE 10.4

A distribution network with three warehouses, each centrally located in a market of length $x = L/3$. The average outbound distance is $x/4$. The average inbound distance is $1/3(L/6) + 1/3(3L/6) + 1/3(5L/6) = L/2$.

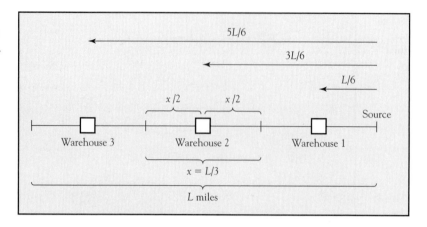

which increases as the market length gets larger. The optimal market length is the value of x that balances this transportation/warehousing cost trade-off and minimizes

$$C(x) = C_T(x) + C_W(x) = c_1L/2 + c_2x/4 + w_2/(Dx)$$

The optimal market length and other formulas are summarized below.

Formulas for the Optimal Market Length When Warehouses Are Centrally Located

$C_T(x) =$ unit inbound outbound transportation cost as a function of market length $x = c_1L/2 + c_2x/4$

$C_W(x) =$ unit warehousing overhead cost as a function of the market length $x = w_2/(Dx)$

$C(x) =$ unit transportation and warehousing overhead cost $= C_T(x) + C_W(x) = c_1L/2 + c_2x/4 + w_2/(Dx)$

$x^* =$ optimal market length $= 2\left(\dfrac{w_2}{c_2D}\right)^{1/2}$

Unit transportation cost can be reduced if the warehouses are shifted toward the source of supply instead of centrally located. Suppose that each warehouse serves a market of length x and is located y miles from its eastern boundary (with the source of supply at the eastern end of the territory). The challenge is to specify how average inbound and outbound distance depend on x and y. Figure 10.5 illustrates a distribution network with three warehouses. Since the fraction of demand to the west of a warehouse is $(x - y)/x$ and the fraction of demand to the east of a warehouse is y/x, the average outbound distance is $[(x - y)/x]$ $[(x - y)/2] + [y/x][y/2] = x/2 - y - y^2/x$.

It is helpful to divide inbound distance into two parts: (1) average distance from the source to the eastern boundaries of warehouse markets and (2) average distance from the eastern boundary to the warehouse. The first part is $(L - x)/2$. One way to see this is to think of each eastern boundary as a customer. Since the "customers" are evenly distributed along a line of length $L - x$, the average distance is one-half the length, or $(L - x)/2$. The second part is simply y, so the average inbound distance is $(L - x)/2 + y$.[34] In summary, the unit inbound and outbound transportation cost is

$$C_T(x, y) = c_1[(L - x)/2 + y] + c_2[x/2 - y - y^2/x]$$

---

[34] If the warehouse is centrally located, then $y = x/2$ and $(L - x)/2 + y = (L - x)/2 + x/2 = L/2$, as we saw earlier.

FIGURE 10.5

A distribution network with three warehouses, each in a market of length $x = L/3$ located y miles from the east market boundary and $x - y$ miles from the west market boundary. The average outbound distance is $[(x - y)/x][(x - y)/2] + [y/x][y/2] = x/2 - y - y^2/x$. The average inbound distance is $(L - x)/2 + y$.

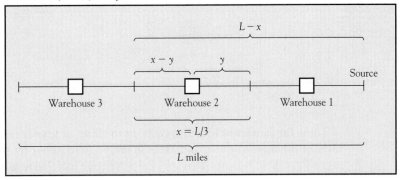

The optimal values of market length x and warehouse location y minimize the average unit cost

$$C(x, y) = C_T(x, y) + C_W(x) = c_1[(L - x)/2 + y] + c_2[x/2 - y - y^2/x] + w_2/(Dx)$$

The optimal expressions and other formulas are summarized below.

Formulas for the Optimal Market Length When Warehouses Are Optimally Located

$C_T(x, y) =$ unit inbound and outbound transportation cost as a function of market length x and location $y = c_1[(L - x)/2 + y] + c_2[x/2 - y - y^2/x]$

$C_W(x) =$ unit warehousing overhead cost as a function of the market length $x = w_2/(Dx)$

$C(x, y) =$ unit transportation and warehousing overhead cost $= C_T(x, y) + C_W(x) = c_1[(L - x)/2 + y] + c_2[x/2 - y - y^2/x] + w_2/(Dx)$

$x^* =$ optimal market length $= 2\left(\dfrac{w_2}{c_2 D}\right)^{1/2} \left(\dfrac{1}{1 - (c_1/c_2)^2}\right)^{1/2}$

$y^* =$ optimal distance from the market boundary $= \dfrac{x^*}{2}\left(1 - \dfrac{c_1}{c_2}\right)$

The expressions for x^* and y^* shed some light on the impact of inbound transportation costs on a network design. First, the relative values of inbound and outbound transportation rates influence the degree to which a warehouse is shifted toward a single source of supply. In fact, the formula for y^* shows that shift is proportional to c_1/c_2. At the extreme of $c_1/c_2 \approx 1$, the warehouse is located at its market boundary (i.e., $y^* \approx 0$) because the economic incentive to open warehouses vanishes. This effect also is seen in the formula for x^*; when $c_1/c_2 \approx 1$, the optimal market length is very large, effectively spanning the entire distribution territory (e.g., a single warehouse located at the source of supply).

Second, **market areas tend to increase when inbound costs from a single source are considered, and the rate of increase depends on c_1/c_2.** This can be seen by comparing the optimal market area $x^* = 2(w_2/c_2 D)^{1/2}$ that applies when inbound costs are ignored with the optimal market area

$$x^* = 2\left(\frac{w_2}{c_2 D}\right)^{1/2}\left(\frac{1}{1 - (c_1/c_2)^2}\right)^{1/2}$$

TABLE 10.9 **Percentage Increase in Optimal Market Area Due to Consideration of Inbound Costs over a Range of Values for Inbound-to-Outbound Freight Rates c_1/c_2**

c_1/c_2	0.0	0.1	0.2	0.3	0.4	0.5	0.6	0.7	0.8	0.9
Percent increase in x^*	0%	0.5%	2.1%	4.8%	9.1%	15.5%	25.0%	40.0%	66.7%	129.4%

that applies when inbound costs are considered. The only difference is the factor $\left(\dfrac{1}{1 - (c_1/c_2)^2}\right)^{1/2}$, which gets larger as c_1/c_2 gets larger.

Third, **the impact of inbound costs on the market area is relatively small unless the ratio of inbound-to-outbound rates is larger than about 50 percent.** This point is illustrated in Table 10.9, which shows the percentage increase in market area due to inbound cost considerations (i.e., $\left(\dfrac{1}{1 - (c_1/c_2)^2}\right)^{1/2} - 1$) for various values of c_1/c_2.

Cross-Docking and Drop-Shipping

Two nontraditional warehousing alternatives that may influence the design of a distribution network are briefly discussed in this section. Among other roles, warehouses are used to reduce transportation cost through one or more of three basic functions:

1. Break-bulk; for example, products from a few distant suppliers are shipped in truckload quantities to a warehouse, and the warehouse ships in LTL quantities to many nearby customers.

2. Mixing; for example, truckloads containing a single type of product coming from different sources arrive at a warehouse, and the warehouse ships truckloads of mixed product to customers.

3. Consolidation; for example, products from many nearby suppliers are shipped in LTL quantities to a warehouse, and the warehouse ships in truckload quantities to a few distant plants.

If inbound and outbound shipments are tightly coordinated so that incoming product leaves the warehouse within about 24 hours, then little space for product storage is required. **Product can move directly from the inbound loading docks to the outbound loading docks without being placed in storage. This activity is known as *cross-docking*.**

Cross-docking offers the potential to significantly reduce the overhead cost of warehouse operation. However, due to challenges and costs associated with synchronizing inbound and outbound shipments, cross-docking tends to be limited to firms with high volumes and relatively stable demand. Some firms that use cross-docking include Heineken, Kodak, Wal-Mart, and Whirlpool.

While cross-docking eliminates the storage function of a warehouse, *drop-shipping* eliminates the warehouse altogether, at least for the firm selling the product. **Drop-shipping refers to the process where product is shipped directly from a supplier to a customer. The firm taking the customer order doesn't handle or store the product.** The tactic reduces the selling firm's control of distribution, but also removes the task of warehousing. Drop-shipping is most common among e-commerce and mail-order firms selling consumer products shipped via small package carriers such as UPS.

4. SUMMARY AND MANAGERIAL INSIGHTS

This chapter covered the topic of transportation management in two parts. The first part dealt with the elements of transportation. Here we learned about the various resources and alternatives for getting product to market, including transportation modes, services, and service providers. We also learned a little about factors that influence transportation pricing, and the importance of knowledge of these factors when negotiating with carriers.

The second part dealt with tactical and strategic decisions associated with getting product to market in a cost-effective manner. The emphasis was on the mechanics and implications of approximate analysis—analysis suited to quickly gaining a meaningful sense of the underlying trade-offs as well as indicators of effective distribution. Accordingly, this part of the chapter served two roles. One role was to reinforce and enhance skills with back-of-the-envelope analysis. These skills are useful when facing new situations or questions, which leads to the second role: to use the analysis to bring out insights and strengthen intuition into complex settings related to transportation, without the benefit of years of experience. Key managerial insights from the chapter are summarized below.

4.1 Delivery Frequency to a Warehouse: Indicators That a Warehouse Should Receive Frequent Replenishment Deliveries Are High Volume, Close Proximity to Source of Supply, and High Inventory Holding Cost Rate; the Increase in Cost Due to Moderate Deviations from the Optimal Frequency Is Minor

If the cycle stock holding cost per period is higher than the shipping cost per period, then increasing the delivery frequency will probably save money. When the supply source is not far and/or the inventory cost rate is high, the relative dominance of inventory on total cost amplifies the benefit of frequent and small replenishment shipments.

Example 1   Baked goods and other perishable products that have high inventory cost rates tend to have high delivery frequencies (e.g., weekly).

Example 2   Higher-capacity carriers and modes that offer lower transport cost per unit-mile tend to be used more often for replenishing distant warehouses; for example, a Boston DC replenishes a Chicago warehouse about once every 10 days by truck, but a West Coast warehouse with similar volume is replenished about once every 30 days by railcar.

Example 3   Much time and effort gathering data, precisely estimating cost rates, and computing delivery frequencies are probably better spent elsewhere. Delivery frequencies in the neighborhood of the "optimal" frequency are a worthy target, but fine-tuning the frequencies offers relatively little return.

4.2. Use of Stop-Offs for Warehouse Replenishment: Look for Stop-Off Locations That Are Nearly on the Way and in Close Proximity to the More Distant Location

Trucks that are not being filled to capacity for replenishment shipments are a strong signal of a money-saving opportunity through stop-offs, if available. In addition, there may be money-saving opportunities through stop-offs when trucks are currently filled to capacity, and this is where insight 4.2 is relevant. However, a total-cost perspective is especially important when trucks are currently filled to capacity—transportation cost will likely increase as stop-offs are used while savings accrue through lower inventory cost.

4.3. Transportation Distance, Cost, and the Market Area Served by a Warehouse: Average Distance to Customers and Outbound Transportation Cost Are Approximately Proportional to the Square Root of the Market Area

If economies of distance in transportation rates are significant, then transportation cost is approximately proportional to the square root of the market area raised to a fractional power, that is, $(\sqrt{\text{market area}})^{\alpha}$. The fractional power α gets smaller as economies of distance become more significant.

Example

You purchased a Domino's restaurant about three years ago. Things are finally running smoothly and you've been profitable for the last year. You offer delivery over a 10-square-mile area. Due to the franchise contract, you are not able to expand your service territory, but you've begun to mull over the possibility of opening a second restaurant so that each serves a five-square-mile area. One of the things you're wondering about is the impact that this change will have on the average delivery time and distance. At first glance, it may be natural to expect that average delivery time and distance will be cut in half since the service territory area per restaurant will be cut in half. However, the reduction will likely not be this large, but will probably be closer to 30 percent (e.g., percentage reduction = $1 - 1/2^{1/2} \approx 30$ percent).

4.4. Network Design Diagnostic and Robustness: If the Number of Warehouses Is Cost-Effective, Then Annual Warehousing Overhead Cost Is About One-half of the Annual Outbound Transportation Cost; the Increase in Cost Due to Moderate Deviations from the Optimal Number of Warehouses Is Minor

The benchmark ratio could be larger or smaller when there are significant economies of distance in freight rates (as measured by α) and warehouse overhead expense is affected by volume (as measured by β). The more general benchmark ratio is $(\alpha/2)/(1 - \beta)$.

A significant difference between the benchmark ratio and a firm's actual ratio is an indicator of a potential money-saving opportunity through the addition or elimination of warehouses. A ratio that is smaller than the benchmark ratio indicates that efficiency can be improved by adding warehouses. A ratio that is larger than the benchmark ratio indicates that efficiency can be improved by eliminating warehouses.[35] However, savings will likely be minor (e.g., less than 1 percent of cost) unless the optimal number of warehouses differs from current by more than about 15 percent.

Example

As the new VP of logistics, you are reviewing financial statements and notice that annual outbound transportation costs are running about 10 times higher than annual warehouse overhead expense (i.e., inventory carrying cost, management salaries and benefits, warehouse management software and hardware, building lease). Over the next several weeks as opportunities arise, you begin asking questions on the rationale for the current distribution network design. As a result of this preliminary investigation, you launch a project to redesign the network. Three years later, the new design is up and running, distribution costs are down, customer service is up, and you've just been promoted to CEO.

---

[35] In growing markets, a ratio that is larger than the benchmark is less of a concern; that is, as demand increases over time, the network becomes better suited to the market and the cost ratio decreases, or, in other words, the optimal market area gets smaller as demand increases.

5. EXERCISES

1. Write a brief answer to each of the chapter keys in your own words. After writing down your answers, review the chapter with a focus on the content in bold to check and clarify your interpretations.

2. A DC in Boston replenishes warehouses in Las Vegas, Los Angeles, and San Diego. The capacity of a truck is $Q_{max} = 45,000$ pounds. Data on the warehouses are listed below.

	Las Vegas	Los Angeles	San Diego
Demand rate	500 pounds per day	1,500 pounds per day	1,500 pounds per day
Fixed cost/shipment	$3,000	$5,200	$5,600
Inventory cost rate	$0.0036 per pound-day	$0.0036 per pound-day	$0.0036 per pound-day

   a. Determine the economic shipment quantity and the length of the replenishment cycle for Las Vegas, Los Angeles, and San Diego.
   b. Determine the transportation and inventory cost per day for each warehouse.
   c. The cost to stop off in Los Angeles on the way to San Diego is $200. What is the cost per day with a stop-off in Los Angeles along the way to San Diego? How many units are dropped off in Los Angeles with each replenishment shipment? What is the savings or loss by stopping off in Los Angeles instead of independent shipments to Los Angeles and San Diego?
   d. The cost to stop off in Las Vegas on the way to Los Angeles (or San Diego) is $600. What is the cost per day with a stop-off in Las Vegas along the way to Los Angeles? How many units are dropped off in Las Vegas with each replenishment shipment? What is the savings or loss by stopping off in Las Vegas instead of independent shipments to Las Vegas and Los Angeles?
   e. Evaluate the option of stopping off in Las Vegas and Los Angeles on the way to San Diego. Which option for replenishment do you recommend?

3. A DC in Boston replenishes warehouses in Indianapolis and Chicago. The capacity of a truck is $Q_{max} = 45,000$ pounds. Data on the warehouses are listed below.

	Indianapolis	Chicago
Demand rate	300 pounds per day	700 pounds per day
Fixed cost/shipment	$1,500	$1,800
Inventory cost rate	$0.0030 per pound-day	$0.0036 per pound-day

   a. Determine the economic shipment quantity and the length of the replenishment cycle for Indianapolis and Chicago. (Note that the inventory holding cost rates differ; for example, the Indy warehouse is located in a zone that is exempt from taxes on inventory investment.)
   b. Determine the transportation and inventory cost per day for each warehouse.
   c. The cost to stop off in Indy on the way to Chicago is $1,000. What is the cost per day with a stop-off in Indy along the way to Chicago? How many units are dropped off in Indy with each replenishment shipment? What is the savings relative to independent shipments to Indy and Chicago?
   d. One of the results from analysis in Section 2.2 is that "with few exceptions, the use of a stop-off [when capacity is not binding] will save money over two independent

shipments." Suppose the stop-off fee is $1,400 instead of $1,000. The stop-off is less than the $1,500 cost of a separate truck to Indy, yet a stop-off increases cost over two independent shipments. Compute the cost of a stop-off in Indy and compare with the cost found in part (b). Why is it that, even though truckload capacity is not binding, a stop-off does not save money? (*Hint*: What is the possible "economic downside" of using a stop-off?)

4. Section 2.1 notes a relationship among holding and shipping cost. If truckload capacity is not binding, then the average cycle stock holding cost per period is equal to the shipping cost per period (i.e., $(Q^*/2)c_e = (A + A_{TL}\delta)D/Q^*$). If truckload capacity is binding, then the average cycle stock holding cost per period is less than the shipping cost per period (i.e., $(Q^*/2)c_e < (A + A_{TL}\delta)D/Q^*$). Verify these relationships.

5. You're planning for a large field study that will take place in Antarctica. A number of testing centers will be established over a 500,000-square-mile area. Each center will be manned by scientists who will be collecting and analyzing samples from their assigned territory. Naturally, the larger the market area, the more expensive it will be to gather samples. On the other hand, each center requires an investment in specialized testing equipment. You expect to be gathering one sample per square mile. A vehicle with sample storage equipment can hold only one sample. Operating cost for the vehicle (including a factor for the scientists' time en route) is estimated at $2.20 per mile. A portion of a center's operating cost is independent of volume; this fixed operating cost is estimated at $225,000 per year.

   a. What is the optimal market area per center, and how many centers should be opened?

   b. Suppose vehicles can be outfitted to store two samples. This will result in an additional amortized vehicle cost estimated to be in the range of $5,000,000 to $10,000,000 per year. Is this alternative worthwhile?

   c. Consider the data corresponding to part (a) and assess the impact of sending processed samples back to a home base. This means that, in addition to the costs of the testing centers and the transportation to pick up samples, there is also the transportation cost associated with periodically transferring samples from each testing center to the home base. Assume that 100 processed samples can fit in a vehicle that travels from a testing center back to the home base. The cost per mile for the vehicle is estimated at $2.00. How would this change your recommendation in part (a)?

6. This and the following exercise are variations of questions prepared by Linus Schrage. You are designing a system for the distribution in the United States of a new product. Somewhat detailed analysis has suggested that, if a single plant is centrally located in the United States, then the yearly transportation costs outbound from the plant will be approximately $1.4 million. Give an estimate of the yearly transportation costs if two plants are judiciously located in the United States.

7. A government agency is examining the number of service offices it should have in a certain metropolitan area. The fixed cost per year of having each office is $12,000. The metropolitan area to be served has an area of 400 square miles. It is estimated that citizens in the area would pay about 80,000 visits to these offices in a year. The agency assigns a cost of 20 cents per mile to the distance a citizen travels to and from an office. The agency director is suggesting that nine offices be installed in the area. Evaluate this recommendation.

8. Your firm has just acquired a competitor and has become the leading cheese producer in your region. One question is whether there may be opportunities to expand or

reduce the number of dairy farms. Three million residents are evenly distributed over the 150,000 square miles of territory. Each resident consumes an average of 27 pounds of cheese per year. Every farm requires $275,000 per year to cover fixed costs. One-way transportation of cargo costs $6.50 per pound-mile (i.e., you use a contract carrier, so you pay only the one-way distance).

   a. How many farms will you operate?

   b. If buyers want to visit one of your farms, how far, on average, will they travel?

   c. Suppose that demand doubles and fixed cost per farm-year increases to $400,000. Will you be better off?

9. Your firm sells electronic components to other companies located throughout Canada. Many of these companies pay by check through the mail, and these checks are currently sent to corporate headquarters in Ottawa. The possibility of opening up collection centers in various parts of the country is being considered. Each company will send payments to the closest collection center, one of which will continue to be in Ottawa. The idea is to get access to money faster by reducing the time that a check is in the mail. The annual cost of a collection center is about $1,000. Customers are located throughout a 1,000,000-square-mile area. Studies indicate that a check spends an average of 4.2 days in the mail. The annual opportunity cost of capital is 20 percent and revenues received through the mail are about $8,000,000 per year.

   a. What is the annual opportunity cost of checks in the mail?

   b. What is the savings or loss if, in addition to Ottawa, two more collection centers are opened (e.g., one west of Ottawa and one to the east)? You may assume that mail delivery time is proportional to distance.

   c. How many centers would you recommend, and why?

10. As a successful owner of a Las Vegas pharmacy, you are thinking of expanding due to expected growth in the area. The demand tends to be concentrated along a highway from Las Vegas to Tucson; the two cities are about 400 miles apart. You project a population of 10 million along this stretch of highway. On the basis of experience and intuition, you feel that you should have about one store per million people, or about 10 stores between Phoenix and Tucson. On the other hand, you've been burned by your intuition in the past, so you'd like to work through some analysis as a double check. You need to move quickly—if you don't come up with a plan and begin implementing, someone else will pick up on this opportunity.

   a. As a starting point, focus only on the delivery aspect of your business. Find the number of pharmacies that will effectively balance transportation costs with operation economies of scale. On the basis of total anticipated demand and a market share target, you believe demand for your delivered prescriptions should be about 40,000 per year. It costs you $0.20 per prescription-mile to supply your pharmacies from your storage facility in Phoenix and $0.55 per prescription-mile to deliver prescriptions to your customers. You project the annual fixed costs of running the delivery side of your business to be $10,000 per pharmacy.

   b. How would the number of pharmacies change if inbound costs were ignored?

11. The education committee for the state of New York is looking into major changes to be implemented in a region of the state (i.e., a test market for a new way of operating). The region is 150,000 square miles. Schools will house grades K–12. There are about 500,000 households throughout the region and each household averages two children between the ages of 6 and 18. It will cost about $0.25 per mile to transport the children to and from their respective homes busing is required only for students that live more than a mile from the school, and there are 200 school days per year. Consider an

alternative with an average school size of 1,000 students and an annual school operation budget (excluding busing costs) of $1,000,000 per year. Work through back-of-the-envelope analysis to estimate the annual cost to operate a school (including busing costs). In addition, estimate the average travel distance between students and their school. (This is an unstructured problem. There are many reasonable ways to attack and many reasonable answers.)

12. A district manager wants to open warehouses over a 500,000-square-mile territory. Managers in other territories have found that the warehouses have a fixed cost of $100,000 per year. Inbound product delivery is virtually zero because of special purchasing agreements with his suppliers. Annual demand for the entire region is 100,000 units. Average shipping cost is $0.05 per pound-mile with an average shipping weight of two pounds.

13. Section 2.1 contains an expression for the cost per period for the economic shipment quantity Q^* given that truckload capacity is a binding constraint, that is, $Q_{max} < [2(A + A_{TL}\delta)D/c_e]^{1/2}$. The cost per period is

$$C(Q^*) = 0.5[y(D)^{-1} + y(D)][2(A + A_{TL}\delta)Dc_e]^{1/2}$$

where $y(D) = Q_{max}/[2(A + A_{TL}\delta)D/c_e]^{1/2}$ is truckload capacity as a fraction of the natural economic shipment quantity. Verify that this expression is valid. (*Hint:* You may wish to use the fact from Chapter 6 that "transaction cost" is equal to inventory holding cost at the economic order quantity; that is, if truckload capacity is not binding, then $(A + A_{TL}\delta)(D/Q^*) = (Q^*/2)c_e$.)

14. The analysis of the one-dimensional network design model from this chapter is similar to the EOQ model in Chapter 6. In fact, when inbound costs are ignored, the one-dimensional network design model is identical to the EOQ model with planned backorders and a shortage cost rate that is identical to the excess cost rate. Explain and verify this equivalence.

15. The general formula for the average distance from warehouse to customer is $\int_{s_m}^{s_M} \int_{t_m(s)}^{t_M(s)} \delta(s, t)$

$f(s, t)\,dt\,ds$ where $\delta(s, t)$ = distance from the warehouse to point (s, t) in the market area, $f(s, t)$ = probability of a customer at point (s, t), s_m = smallest value of s in the market area, s_M = largest value of s in the market area, $t_m(s)$ = smallest value of t at point s in the market, and $t_M(s)$ = largest value of t at point s in the market area.

a. Verify that $\int_{s_m}^{s_M} \int_{t_m(s)}^{t_M(s)} \delta(s, t)\,f(s, t)\,dt\,ds = 0.376x^{1/2}$ when the market area shape is a circle, customers are uniformly distributed throughout the market area, the area of the market is x square miles, the warehouse is located in the center of the market area, and the Euclidean distance norm applies. *Hints:* In the case of a centrally located warehouse at point $(0, 0)$ in a circular market area, the expression for average distance can be alternatively expressed in terms of the radius. This alternative expression simplifies the analysis. In particular, for a given market area x with radius r (i.e., $x = \pi r^2$), the percentage of customers located $y \in [0, r]$ miles from the warehouse is the ratio of the circumference of a circle of radius y to the total area πr^2; that is, $f(y)$ = probability of a customer located y miles from the warehouse = $(2\pi y)/(\pi r^2) = 2y/r^2$. Accordingly, the average distance from warehouse to customer can be expressed as $\int_0^r yf(y)\,dy = \int_0^r y(2y/r^2)\,dy$.

b. Generalize part (a) to account for transportation cost by showing that $C_T(x) =$
$$\int_{s_m}^{s_M} \int_{t_m(s)}^{t_M(s)} c_2 \delta(s,t)^\alpha f(s,t)\,dt\,ds = c_2 \tau x^{\alpha/2} \text{ with } \tau = 2/[(2+\alpha)\pi^{\alpha/2}]$$ when the market area shape is a circle, customers are uniformly distributed throughout the market area, the area of the market is x square miles, the warehouse is located in the center of the market area, and the Euclidean distance norm applies.

16 For some industries, customer demand can be sensitive to the distance from a warehouse, where the larger the distance, the lower the demand. This can be due to convenience (e.g., customers can easily drive to the warehouse to pick up product when close by) and response time (e.g., short delivery lead times with short distances). The GOMA model is based on an assumption that demand is uniform over the market area. The objective of this exercise is to take a step toward understanding the impact that distance-sensitive demand can have on market area decisions, costs, and profits.

David Huff developed a widely applied model, known as the Huff gravity model, for describing how retail demand decreases with distance (Huff 1962). A version of the Huff gravity model will be used in this exercise to approximate how warehouse demand decreases with distance.

Suppose that the annual demand rate per square mile at distance δ from the warehouse is

$$d(\delta) = \begin{cases} D \text{ if } \delta \leq 1 \\ D\left(\dfrac{1}{\delta}\right)^\gamma \text{ if } \delta \geq 1 \end{cases}$$

where $\gamma \geq 0$. The value of D can be interpreted as the number of potential customers per square mile (e.g., population) and $\delta^{-\gamma}$ can be interpreted as the probability that a customer $\delta \geq 1$ miles from the warehouse will purchase a unit in a period. If $\gamma = 0$, then demand is unaffected by distance. The larger the value of γ, the more sensitive demand is to distance.

a. Develop expressions for the transportation cost per period and for total warehouse demand as a function of market area x. Assume that the warehouse is located at the center of a circular market area, the Euclidean distance norm applies, and there are no economies of distance in the freight rates (i.e., $\alpha = 1$).

b. Develop an expression for the profit (i.e., sales revenue less outbound transportation and warehousing cost) per mi^2-period given that the warehouse throughput cost rate is w_1 and the fixed warehousing cost per period is w_2. Each unit sells at price p.

17. According to the GOMA model, the annual warehousing overhead cost is 50 percent of the annual outbound transportation cost when the network is optimal (assuming "fixed" overhead cost per warehouse and no economies of distance in freight rates). A ratio that is significantly different from 0.50 signals a potential money-saving opportunity. At your firm, the ratio is about 0.95, yet results of analysis show that the network is optimal.

What differences in assumptions can explain an optimal ratio more than 0.50 (assuming "fixed" overhead cost per warehouse and no economies of distance in freight rates)? In order to answer this question, first identify the main assumptions of the GOMA model. Then identify a change in at least one of the assumptions that would lead to an optimal ratio more than 0.50.

Case Exercise: *GL Electric*[36]

Founded in 1900 in Syracuse, New York, GL Electric made its reputation manufacturing a premier line of heavy-duty and explosion-proof electrical products. By 2000, GL Electric was the world's largest manufacturer of industrial electrical products for hazardous environments with sales of nearly $800 million. Products include a range of industrial lighting products, conduits, heavy-duty circuit breaker and electrical control stations, outlet boxes, fittings, and even heavy-duty flashlights costing as much as $300 apiece. All products are designed for use in industries where the probability of an explosion is high or where conditions, either man-made or natural, are adverse. The primary customer base for GL Electric includes the oil and gas industry, the chemical industry, mining operations, airports, and government.

In the United States, GL Electric operates manufacturing facilities in Syracuse, New York; Pittsburgh, Pennsylvania; Windsor, Connecticut; Brunswick, Maine; LaGrange, North Carolina; Amarillo, Texas; and Montebello, California (an eastern suburb of Los Angeles). Virtually all of the products manufactured at their U.S. manufacturing facilities are shipped to their national distribution center (DC) located in Roanoke, Virginia. From Roanoke, finished products and parts are shipped either directly to large corporate customers or to smaller, privately owned distributors. International manufacturing facilities are located in Canada, Mexico, England, Germany, Spain, and India.

OUTBOUND TRANSPORTATION

Since the products manufactured by GL Electric are heavy duty, the products tend to be particularly dense. Paul Tharp had been the transportation manager for GL Electric for over 30 years and was very experienced. The nature of products being shipped (i.e., dense and durable) as well as the high volume provided Tharp significant leverage to negotiate the lowest outbound transportation rates possible. Since GL Electric sold their product *F.O.B. origin, freight prepaid*,[37] Tharp saw to it that all GL Electric outbound freight moved on the least expensive carrier.

Management attention focused mainly on the outbound side of transportation for two reasons. First, expenditures in outbound transportation are more visible because GL Electric pays for all the freight expense. Second, inbound transportation expense is viewed as a necessary by-product of purchasing. The majority of the items purchased are purchased F.O.B. destination, freight prepaid, so the true inbound transportation cost is never readily apparent (i.e., embedded in the purchase price). As such, inbound freight is part of the materials budget.

Outbound transportation expense as a percent of sales averages about 2 percent, well below the national average of 4 percent. With the exception of some emergency orders and some very large products, such as the large control stations that required a flatbed truck, all customer orders are filled out of the Roanoke DC. Most of the orders are shipped to customers via LTL. LTL pricing is particularly aggressive, so much so that an LTL shipment weighing as much as 750 pounds is rated as a minimum charge up to a distance of a few hundred miles.[38] There are some truckload shipments, but they are primarily intercompany shipments or to a few very large customers (i.e., about 10 percent of sales are shipped direct).

Regional LTL carriers are used extensively for distributing product to customers, primarily because regional carriers offer better pricing and service than the national LTL carriers such as Yellow Freight. For the most part, regional LTL carriers could pick up and deliver freight anywhere in "their system" within one to two days.[39] This is about half the transit time of a national LTL carrier. For example, it is common to see a national LTL carrier provide transit times of six or seven days to go from coast

---

[36] Adapted with permission from a case written by Gary LaPoint and Frances Gaither Tucker in 2004.

[37] *F.O.B. origin, freight prepaid* means that ownership (and responsibility for freight claims associated with damages in-transit) is transferred to the consignee at the origin when it is loaded on the truck, and that the supplier (i.e., GL Electric in this case) is responsible for paying the transportation costs. There are a number of possible freight terms that can be negotiated between buyer and seller. In general, freight terms answer two basic questions: when does the title to the product pass from seller to buyer (which also determines responsibility for freight claims) and who pays the transportation cost. F.O.B. origin means that the title transfers at the origin, and F.O.B. destination means that the title transfers at the destination. Freight prepaid means that the seller pays the transportation cost. Alternatively, freight collect means that the buyer pays the transportation cost. The various combinations of the preceding phrases lead to four possible freight terms: (1) F.O.B. origin, freight prepaid; (2) F.O.B. origin, freight collect; (3) F.O.B. destination, freight prepaid; and (4) F.O.B. destination, freight collect. Other freight terms exist, but the preceding four are representative of common possibilities for title transfer and cost responsibility (e.g., freight collect and allowed means that the buyer pays the transportation cost but deducts the cost from the invoice; freight prepaid and added means that the seller prepays the transportation cost and bills the buyer for the freight charges).

[38] The average minimum charge per delivery is $75 per shipment. Within 200 to 300 miles of the origin, the carrier charges GL Electric $75 to deliver any shipment up to 750 pounds.

[39] The "system" for a regional LTL carrier, which is the region in which the carrier can operate, varies by carrier but most do not extend more than 500 miles in any direction.

to coast or three to four days for a regional shipment. National LTL carriers are used, however, on longer hauls.[40] This avoids interline shipments that would be required if regional LTL carriers are used.[41] For GL Electric, regional LTL carriers are used almost exclusively in the eastern half of the United States.

ORDER PROCESSING

The Roanoke DC is approximately 350,000 square feet. About half of the facility is dedicated to warehousing and order fulfillment while the other half is dedicated to light assembly. The DC employed a warehouse management system to direct workers to pick customer orders. Actual customer orders are entered by customer service in Syracuse and are fed nightly to the warehouse management system. This nightly feed is referred to as "the drop." The warehouse management system receives the dropped orders each night and plans the workload for the upcoming day. Orders that are dropped overnight are picked beginning at 7 a.m. and shipped later that same day.

GL Electric sells the majority of their product through a large distributor network that, in turn, sells to the ultimate user. Each distributor is assigned a ship day that remains constant from week to week. Some large distributors are assigned two ship days per week.

The Marketing Department at GL Electric had determined that, from a customer-service standpoint, a customer order should not be split but shipped in its entirety from the Roanoke DC. The five largest states in shipments to customers are listed in Table 1.

TABLE 1 Recent Annual Shipment Volumes and Costs for the Five Largest States in Terms of Volume

Destination State	Number of Shipments	Total Weight (pounds)	Total Freight Cost
Texas	2,500	2,647,500	$536,500
California	2,000	1,500,000	555,000
Georgia	1,600	1,280,000	471,750
Louisiana	1,200	780,000	397,750
Virginia	600	630,000	231,250

INTER-COMPANY TRANSPORTATION

GL Electric's U.S. manufacturing locations ship via a truckload carrier to the DC in Roanoke.[42] Most of these are one-way shipments and the company was able to negotiate a truckload rate of $2.17 per mile for a single driver.[43] There is one round-trip movement between Syracuse and Roanoke, however. Due to the steady back-and-forth volume between these two facilities, the company was able to negotiate a better round-trip rate of $2.08 per mile. The approximate travel distance for a single driver is 500 miles per day. Normally, a driver team is more costly than a single driver, but when a round-trip move can be created, a lower rate can be negotiated similar to the scenario between Syracuse and Roanoke. The one-way rate for a driver team is $2.30 per mile. On long-haul trips, such as coast to coast, driver teams are used to reduce transit time (i.e., a pair of drivers will share the driving). A good driver team averages 1,000 miles per day instead of 500 miles per day for a single driver. Consequently, the transportation time on long-haul shipments for a driver team is about one-half the time of a single driver. Full truckload carriers prefer longer hauls, and they typically have a minimum charge for any shipment of about $550. Table 2 shows the average weekly volume and distances between GL Electric's U.S. manufacturing facilities and the Roanoke DC.

TABLE 2 Weekly Volume and Distance from GL Electric Plants to the Roanoke DC (Computed as annual volume divided by 50 weeks per year[44])

Manufacturing Location	Average Weekly Volume (pounds)	Mileage
Syracuse, New York	380,000	519
Pittsburgh, Pennsylvania	350,000	300
Montebello, California	17,000	2,430
Amarillo, Texas	40,000	1,353
Windsor, Connecticut	20,000	564
LaGrange, North Carolina	20,000	231
Brunswick, Maine	25,000	787

[40] GL Electric generally uses a national carrier if freight travels distances greater than 500 miles or if a destination is out of the operating authority of a regional carrier.

[41] Interlining is when a shipment needs to travel beyond the operating authority of a regional LTL carrier and the LTL carrier must transfer the freight to another carrier for delivery.

[42] A truck can carry up to about 40,000 pounds of GL Electric products.

[43] The truckload rate does not include any additional fees such as fuel surcharges or stop-off fees. A typical stop-off fee is $100 per stop.

[44] The Roanoke DC typically operates five days per week and 50 weeks per year (i.e., closed for about two weeks per year due to holidays).

PURCHASING AND INVENTORY

The Materials Group at GL Electric serves two main functions. First, the Materials Group is responsible for purchasing. Commodity buyers working in the Materials Group perform all the purchasing for the company. As noted above, most raw materials and components are purchased F.O.B. destination, freight prepaid. Since the inbound transportation cost is buried in the price of the product, not a lot of attention is devoted to inbound transportation. The materials manager estimates that inbound freight expense is approximately 5 percent of the total purchase price.

The dollars associated with vendor purchases are rolled into cost of goods sold and are managed through the purchased price variance (PPV) reports.[45] As the world's largest manufacturer of heavy-duty electrical products, GL Electric is able to apply a significant amount of leverage with its suppliers in obtaining the best pricing in the industry.

Second, the Materials Group plans material usage and is responsible for overall inventory. In the past, GL Electric had experienced transportation delays and at times material quality had not been acceptable. As a result, an average of six weeks of safety stock is kept on hand at Roanoke to cover fluctuations in replenishment deliveries, demand, and quality.

A MEETING WITH A MAJOR SUPPLIER

Belinda Adams is the new logistics manager for GL Electric. Belinda replaced Paul Tharp, who had retired earlier in the year. Belinda is very experienced in virtually all aspects of logistics, not just outbound transportation. As the logistics manager, Belinda's responsibilities extend beyond those of her predecessor. Among other things, part of Belinda's responsibility includes inbound transportation as well as outbound.

Belinda reports to Brian Bittner, the director of sourcing and logistics. The Materials Group also reports to Brian. Not long after Belinda had started working for GL Electric, she was invited to attend a meeting involving a supplier and buyers from the Materials Group. Belinda's manager, Brian, felt it would be a good opportunity for her to become familiar with the organization and how the front half of the supply chain functioned. Based on Belinda's background, Brian also wanted Belinda to see if there might be any improvement opportunities, even though it appeared as if there was nothing left to get out of the purchase price or the transportation rate.

At the meeting, Belinda was introduced to Paul Torrey, the materials manager; George Brindak, the commodity buyer; and Mark Garrett, the sales representative for M. Stevens, Inc. M. Stevens is located in East Los Angeles, only a few miles from GL Electric's Montebello plant, and supplies a variety of electrical steel boxes and box covers to GL Electric. The items supplied by M. Stevens are finished products requiring no further work; once the items are received at GL Electric's Roanoke DC, they go directly into finished goods inventory. These finished items are then sold by GL Electric to their customers and distributors.

M. Stevens was a fairly new supplier to GL Electric, but, after just one year, the annual spending with M. Stevens was $3.2 million, placing M. Stevens on GL Electric's top 10 list of supplier expenditures. This expenditure is expected to grow by 20 percent next year.

Torrey and Brindak had negotiated very favorable pricing with M. Stevens. They were already showing a very favorable PPV for the year. In the meeting, Belinda learned that GL Electric was purchasing M. Stevens products F.O.B. destination, freight prepaid. She also learned that to keep inventories in Roanoke to a minimum, GL Electric requested that M. Stevens ship orders daily. The average size order is about 3,000 pounds. As with other products, the Materials Group maintains a safety stock of M. Stevens product at the Roanoke DC equal to an average of six weeks of supply. The Materials Group estimates the annual cost of holding inventory to be 30 percent of product value.

Put yourself in Belinda's shoes. Identify a key problem/opportunity in the case. Analyze the problem and prepare a proposal. Your proposal should contain the following elements:

1. Problem statement (i.e., one or two sentences that succinctly state the key problem or opportunity; the statement should be free of causes or solutions).

2. Justification that the problem you identified is significant and worthy of management attention.

3. Recommended course of action (or actions) with an associated timeline.

4. Assessment of the impact of your recommendation as supported by your analysis (e.g., investment in time and money, improvement in profit, and any other relevant measures of performance).

5. Identification of significant risks associated with your recommendation, implementation strategies that can help mitigate these risks, and measures that will be used to evaluate the success of your recommendation.

---

[45] PPV reports show the difference between planned purchase cost per unit and actual purchase cost per unit for each month and year-to-date.

Supplement A

Diagnostic Analysis Illustration

This chapter supplement presents a case study in the form of a series of memos.[1] It illustrates how analysis outlined in Section 3 of Chapter 10 is used in practice. A newly appointed VP of logistics is interested in assessing the current distribution system. The study spans initial diagnostic analysis through the development of a recommended course of action.

TO: Director, Supply Chain Analysis Group
FROM: Vice President of Logistics
DATE: June 1

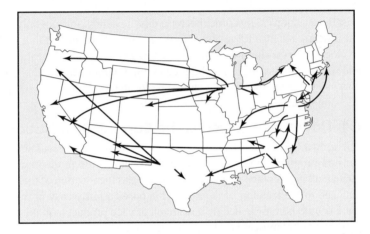

As a newly appointed Vice President with responsibility for our network of distribution centers, I would like to seek your advice concerning the suitability of this network in the current business environment.

We've had the same 13 DC locations for several years now, although the volume of business has been growing and freight rates, especially on the outbound side, have been increasing with alarming rapidity. In the most recent 12-month period, our costs have been as follows:

Distribution center fixed	$ 6,150,000
Distribution center variable	18,500,000
Inbound transportation	42,850,000
Outbound transportation	29,100,000
	$96,600,000

Total volume was 25 million cwt.

Do you think it would be worthwhile to build a model of our distribution system in order to help us reduce costs? I know that you could lead such an effort, but I would need some assurances concerning the potential for cost savings and where those savings might come from.

[1] Adapted with permission from A. M. Geoffrion, J. G. Morris, and S. T. Webster, "Distribution System Design," in *Facility Location: A Survey of Applications and Methods,* ed. Z. Drezner (New York: Springer-Verlag, 1995), pp. 185–202.

TO: **Vice President of Logistics**
FROM: **Director, Supply Chain Analysis Group**
DATE: **June 10**

Thank you for your inquiry concerning the possibility of a distribution network modeling study. It is always difficult to predict in advance what the cost savings will be for a major modeling effort, but I will do the best I can.

An evaluation of the merits of our current distribution network breaks down into three fundamental questions:

Q1. How well are we using our current distribution network? That is, how well are we loading plants, allocating production to the DCs, and assigning customers to DCs?

Q2. How good are our current 13 DC locations?

Q3. Do we have too many or too few DCs?

I list the questions in this order because it is the natural one not only for diagnosis, our present concern, but also for redesign of the network. We cannot think usefully about changing DC locations (Q2) until we understand how any given set of locations should be used (Q1), and we cannot think usefully about changing the number of DCs (Q3) until we understand how any given number of DCs should be located (Q2) and used (Q1). I shall consider each question in turn.

Q1. How Well Utilized Is the Current Distribution Network?

The growth of demand has, as you know, been putting a real strain on our capacity expansion program. For most product lines, nationwide production capacity is only about 10 percent greater than nationwide demand and the location of this capacity is quite poorly matched to the location of demand. This poses a fairly easy problem of plant loading, as there is little latitude to decide how much of each product to make at each plant, but it does present a rather intricate problem of allocating production to DCs.

For a given set of customer-to-DC assignments, the DCs look like demand points to the plants. It is possible to calculate the plant loadings and plant-to-DC allocations for each product so as to minimize the sum of production and inbound transportation costs while honoring plant capacities and DC demands. This could be done easily using an optimization technique you have no doubt encountered before called *linear programming*. But what if the customer-to-DC assignments are changed? That would require resolving the loading/allocation problems and also would change the outbound transportation costs. Simultaneous cost minimization for loading, allocation, and customer assignment presents a very difficult optimization problem owing to the gigantic number of possible ways to assign customers to DCs. The only good news is that our DCs have sufficient unused equipment and space so that customers probably do not have to compete significantly for limited DC capacity, but, even so, the problem is well beyond the reach of the general-purpose optimization software presently available.

The bottom line is this: if the joint plant loading/product allocation/customer assignment problem is so difficult for present-day computers and generally available software, we should not expect that our company is solving it particularly well. Indeed, we have never taken a systemwide look at this problem. We have only nibbled at it in manual studies of limited scope. A thorough analysis would not only capture the previously inaccessible savings, but it also would capture now the accessible savings that might otherwise escape notice for a year or two or even more. There is always a lag between the constant creation of savings opportunities by the turbulent business environment and our discovery of these opportunities in the normal course of running our business. A thorough analysis would eliminate this lag.

I would offer a conservative guess that, if we were to acquire the special-purpose computer software to solve this problem properly, transportation costs would drop by about 2 percent.

This savings factor seems modest enough and is in keeping, so I am told by consultants who specialize in this line of work, with the experience of other firms that have solved the joint plant loading/product allocation/customer assignment problem with tightly constrained supply on an integrated, systemwide basis for the first time. Thus, I estimate that our cost breakdown would have been as follows had we utilized our current 13 DCs optimally:

DC fixed costs	$ 6,150,000
DC variable costs	18,450,000
Inbound transportation	42,000,000
Outbound transportation	28,500,000
	$95,100,000

Additional savings would probably accrue for production costs, but I will omit consideration of that for the sake of simplicity.

Q2. How Good Are the Current 13 DC Locations?

A small random sample of outbound freight rates shows that delivery costs average $0.0075 per cwt-mile. Total annual delivered volume is 25 million cwt, of which about one-fourth is in the very cities in which our DCs are located. Suppose we assume an average delivery distance of 10 miles for the demand that is collocated with our DCs. That comes to

$$1/4 \times 25{,}000{,}000 \text{ cwt} \times 10 \text{ miles} \times \$0.0075/(\text{cwt-mi}) = \$468{,}750$$

For the noncollocated demand, assume an average delivery distance of 156 miles. That comes to

$$3/4 \times 25{,}000{,}000 \text{ cwt} \times 156 \text{ miles} \times \$0.0075/(\text{cwt-mi}) = \$21{,}937{,}500$$

Total predicted outbound transportation cost is the sum of these two numbers, or $22,406,250. This prediction is $6,093,750 below the adjusted figure of $28,500,000 given at the conclusion of the discussion of Ql. This suggests that the average delivery distance must actually be considerably greater than 156 miles, perhaps as much as 200 miles, which in turn suggests that our current DCs are not well situated with respect to current concentrations of demand.

To be conservative, I will assume that improved DC locations could achieve half of the savings potential indicated above, namely $3 million. This may, however, be gained at the price of increased inbound freight cost. Inbound costs should rise much less than outbound costs will fall. One reason is that our plants are scattered all over the country, so any DC move *away* from one plant will tend to be *toward* another plant. Cost changes thus will tend to cancel out. Another reason is that empirical studies with simplified one-plant models show that inbound transportation cost tends to change very little with the number and location of DCs provided there are at least 10 of them. Thus, I believe that no more than half of the outbound cost savings would be lost in increased inbound costs. This leads to the following revision of the cost breakdown given at the conclusion of the discussion of Q1:

DC fixed costs	$ 6,150,000
DC variable costs	18,450,000
Inbound transportation	43,500,000
Outbound transportation	25,500,000
	$93,600,000

Q3. Do We Have Too Many or Too Few DCs?

I believe that we have too few DCs. My reasons are several. First of all, demand growth implies that new DCs should be added over time because there is greater volume over which to spread the DC fixed costs. Second, more DCs are needed when outbound freight rates inflate faster than inbound freight rates because more DCs reduce the amount of outbound shipping. We are behind the times on both counts, as we have had 13 DCs for four years. Another tip-off that we have too few DCs is the fact that total outbound freight cost is more than four times total DC fixed cost, even after the adjustments made in my discussion of Q1 and Q2. An idealized analysis suggests that this ratio should be more like two than four, and hence that we need to increase the number of DCs (to decrease the numerator and increase the denominator of this ratio). The idealized analysis I have in mind is as follows:

If a DC has fixed cost w_2 \$/year, lies in a part of the country having demand evenly distributed with density D cwt/(mi^2-yr), can deliver for c_2 \$/(cwt-mi), and has a circular service area of x square miles, then it is an elementary exercise to show that the total associated annual cost is

$$0.376c_2x^{1/2}(Dx) + w_2$$

Total annual cost per cwt throughput (divide by Dx) is minimized when

$$x^* = 3.05[w_2/(Dc_2)]^{2/3}$$

Note that the outbound transportation cost at x^* is

$$0.376Dc_2\{3.05[w_2/(Dc_2)^{2/3}\}^{3/2}$$

which reduces to $2w_2$. This analysis can be applied to our problem with these numbers:

$w_2 = \$6,150,000/13 = \$473,077$

$D = 25,000,000$ cwt/2,000,000 mi$^2 = 12.5$ cwt/mi^2 (2 million square miles is actually two-thirds of the land area of the continental United States, to account for the absence of any significant population in much of the western central part of the country)

$c_2 = \$0.0075/$(cwt-mi)

The result is $x^* = 89,730$ square miles. To cover 2 million square miles, this requires **22 DCs.**

This estimate of 22 for the optimal number of DCs, besides being based on extremely simplified assumptions, does not consider the influence of inbound transportation costs or the fact that DCs tend to coincide with major demand concentrations. These considerations introduce cost trade-offs that tend to both increase and decrease the optimal number of DCs. I will not pursue such refinements here.

Suppose, for the sake of argument, that 22 is the best number of DCs for us. Let's examine the cost consequences. Total fixed cost should go up by about \$473,077 $\times$ (22 − 13) = \$4,257,693. Total DC variable cost should not change significantly, as the variation between individual DC variable cost rates is not great. Total inbound cost should not change much, for reasons described under Q2. I'll assume a generous \$1 million increase. Total outbound cost should decrease significantly. The idealized analysis discussed above predicts that total outbound cost varies as one over the square root of the number of DCs. It follows that total outbound cost will go down to a fraction of

$$\frac{1/\sqrt{22}}{1/\sqrt{13}} = 0.7686$$

of the former level. But this neglects the fact that many of the nine new DCs will fall on major demand concentrations, thereby reducing outbound freight even more. Suppose that the 9 new DCs are collocated even half as well as the current 13. Then an additional $1/2 \times 9/13 \times 0.25$ = 8.654 percent of all demand will be collocated, which will reduce the 0.7686 factor to $(1 - 0.08654) \times 0.7686 = 0.7021$. Applying this to the $25,500,000 figure given at the end of the discussion on Q2, we obtain a savings of $7,600,000. This is enough to overcome the increases in fixed and inbound costs, with a net annual savings of $2,350,000.

With these assumptions, the cost breakdown given at the end of the discussion of Q2 becomes:

DC fixed costs	$10,400,000
DC variable costs	18,450,000
Inbound transportation	44,500,000
Outbound transportation	17,900,000
	$91,250,000

SUMMARY

I have argued that possible improvements in our current distribution system can be viewed as occurring in three phases corresponding to the three questions stated at the outset. The cost breakdown is summarized as follows (costs in millions):

	Current	(Q1) Better Utilization	(Q2) Relocate Current DCs	(Q3) Add More DCs
DC fixed costs	$ 6.150	$ 6.150	$ 6.150	$10.400
DC variable costs	18.500	18.450	18.450	18.450
Inbound transportation	42.850	42.000	43.500	44.500
Outbound transportation	29.100	28.500	25.500	17.900
Total	$96.600	$95.100	$93.600	$91.250
Savings over previous system		$ 1.500	$ 1.500	$ 2.350

Adding more DCs (about nine of them) will make marketing happy, as each new DC would increase our "market presence" in a new area and probably lead to improved market penetration. Notice also that adding DCs should greatly reduce outbound shipments, which tends to reduce our vulnerability to continued rapid increases in motor carrier rates owing to the combined effects of deregulation and the energy situation.

The total potential savings of about 5½ percent—an estimate that I view as quite conservative—falls within the 5–15 percent range that distribution consultants claim is typical for a full-scale modeling study.

I hope that these "back-of-the-envelope" arguments will suffice to help you decide whether to sponsor a modeling effort. Comparable studies at other firms suggests that the costs of such a study would be under $100,000 and take about six months to complete. It looks to me like a high payoff venture.

TO: Director, Supply Chain Analysis Group
FROM: Vice President of Logistics
DATE: July 1

Your response to my June 1 memo makes a good case for undertaking a thorough analysis. With it, I can justify making a substantial commitment in labor and resources. Let's go ahead with the project.

The main target issues I would like to address are

- How many DCs should we have?
- Where should the DCs be located?
- What size should each DC be?
- How should our seven plants be loaded, and how should their output be allocated to the DCs?
- Which customers should be assigned to each DC?

Although cost minimization is the basic objective, customer service also should be considered. The physical proximity of DCs to their markets is an important factor there.

Please conduct the analysis so as to continue our present policy of assigning each customer to a single private full-line DC.

One more thing. My last employer had a real disaster with a computer-based model for inventory management. Finished goods inventory went up and up and up some more instead of down as promised. That experience taught me that it is important for executives to keep in close touch with their fancy models. Consequently, I will ask that you explain to me in nonmathematical terms the model as it evolves, and whatever results come out of the model after it is built. I want you to help me discover not only *what* to do, but also *why* to do it.

> **TO:** **VP of Logistics**
> **FROM:** **Director, Supply Chain Analysis Group**
> **DATE:** **October 1**
> **RE:** **Distribution Planning Model Synopsis**

The data development stage of the project is virtually complete now. Soon we will be commencing verification and validation. You mentioned in your July 1 memo your desire to "keep in close touch" with the model and to understand why, as well as merely know what it is trying to tell us. I'm glad that you feel this way, as it coincides exactly with my own philosophy.

An important step in this regard is for you to have at your fingertips a clear and concise synopsis of the model. Such a synopsis is attached. After scrutinizing it for possible errors, you can keep it at hand for ready reference as we move into the formal analysis stage of the project.

THUMBNAIL MODEL SKETCH AND DATA ELEMENT CHECKLIST

7 Plants $\Rightarrow$	35 Candidate DCs $\Rightarrow$	150 Customer Zones
(1) List of product groups (10)	(5) List of candidate sites for DCs (35); all private and stock the full line	(9) List of customer zones (150 most populous metropolitan markets)
(2) List of plants (7)	(6) Lower limit on each DC throughput is 100,000 cwt per year	(10) Annual customer demand in cwt per year (by product and customer zone)
(3) Plant capacities in cwt per year (by plant and product)	(7) Fixed cost for each DC in $/year	(11) Single-sourcing rule: each customer served by one DC
(4) Unit production cost in $/cwt (by plant and product)	(8) Variable cost in $/cwt by DC (same for all products)	(12) Net selling price (by product and customer zone); omitted
(13) List of permissible inbound links and freight rates in $/cwt (rates are the same for all products, mode is nearly all rail)	(14) All possible outbound links up to 1,500 miles long included (a total of 3,278 DC/customer pairs); freight charge is $0.0075 per cwt-mile for any product (mode is nearly all truck)	

TO: VP of Logistics
FROM: Director, Supply Chain Analysis Group
DATE: December 10
RE: Formal Analysis: Summary of Key Findings

Since completing the verification and validation exercises about a month ago, we have, as you know, been busy using the model as a tool to study how our distribution system can be improved. Your active participation in these studies has been invaluable. Although you have seen most of the results already in raw form, we are now in a position to summarize the key findings in a coherent way.

I want to stress that nothing in this memo is intended as a recommendation. We are, however, at the point where the findings and insights summarized here must be interpreted in light of various considerations outside the scope of the formal analysis. The result of that exercise will be specific, prioritized recommendations for action.

This memo makes three passes at summarizing the key findings. The first establishes that current annual distribution costs (according to the model) can be reduced from $96,600,000 to $88,810,000. This represents a projected savings of $7,790,000. The second pass establishes that the projected savings can be attributed to three distinct types of improvement carried out sequentially:

Types of Improvement	Savings
1. Improve plant loading, product allocation to DCs, and customer assignments (keeping the current DCs)	$2,269,000
2. Improve DC locations (keeping the number at 13)	2,412,000
3. Move to a network with 21 DCs	3,109,000
	$7,790,000

The third pass attempts to achieve a deeper understanding of each of the three types of improvement.

The figures mentioned above are exclusive of production costs. You will recall that we included no unit production costs at all in the model for product groups 4–10, owing to the severe limitations of our cost accounting systems. It turns out that the unit production costs we did include for products 1–3 exert only a negligible influence on the target issues of interest. Hence, this memo intentionally disregards the role of production costs.

FIRST PASS: THE BOTTOM LINE

The bottom line is that projected annual savings amount to $7,790,000.

Here is a comparison of current annual costs (in millions) with what is projected under the least-cost distribution network, which has eight more DCs:

	Current	Least-Cost Network	Savings (Loss)	Percent of Current
DC fixed costs	$ 6.150	$ 9.737	$(3.587)	58
DC variable costs	18.500	18.727	(0.227)	1
Inbound transportation	42.850	43.428	(0.578)	1
Outbound transportation	29.100	16.918	12.182	42
Total	$96.600	$88.810	$ 7.790	8

Considering our corporate challenge to reduce logistics costs, I think you will be pleased to see that massive savings in outbound trucking materialized as predicted. These more than offset increases in other cost categories caused (mainly) by the addition of new DCs. Profits may well go up *more* than $7,790,000 because our analysis assumed demand to be fixed, whereas it should actually increase somewhat owing to the addition of eight DCs. Marketing claims that each new DC improves local market share through improved "market presence." One measure of market presence is average delivery distance, which decreases from about 150 miles with the current network to about 90 miles with the least-cost network.

The answers to all of the target issues listed in your July 1 memo are available in a detailed set of reports describing the least-cost network.

SECOND PASS: THREE STEPS TO A LEAST-COST NETWORK

The cost comparison given above shows how the projected $7,790,000 savings is distributed by cost category but does not tell us *why* the cost categories change as they do in going from the current to the least-cost network. My aim now is to identify the major reasons why the costs change as they do.

The explanation has to do with the different kinds of changes that might be made in our current distribution network. There are five possible kinds of changes:

A. Change plant loadings (how much of each product is made at each plant).
B. Change product allocations (the shipping pattern from plants to DCs).
C. Change the assignment of customer zones to DCs.
D. Change the DC locations (keeping the number the same).
E. Change the number of DCs.

If we allow no changes at all, the Distribution Planning Model, of course, will simply mimic (simulate) our current distribution network and will therefore yield a total cost of $96,600,000. As more and more freedom is allowed to make changes, the model will be able to drive the total cost closer and closer to the $88,810,000 floor.

It is instructive to examine what happens when the model is given only partial freedom to make changes. In this way, we can better understand where the ultimate total savings come from. We have examined two such cases. These, along with the current and "full freedom to change" cases, can be portrayed as follows:

```
                A               B              C              D              E
"Current"===================fixed====================
"Step 1" ***************optimize****************======fixed======
"Step 2" *******************optimize***********************fixed=====
"Step 3" **************************optimize***************************
```

The model also lends itself to the case where optimization occurs only over A and B, but we did not pursue this one. The managerial interpretation of these cases is clear. Step 1 asks, "How much improvement is possible by better utilization of the current 13 DC locations?" Step 2 asks, "What is the least-cost distribution network having 13 DCs?" Step 3 asks, "What is the least-cost distribution network?"

The *differences* are particularly revealing, as they enable the total $7,790,000 savings to be decomposed into components associated with utilization alone, locational choice, and a change in the number of DCs. These differences and the cases themselves are summarized below. You may wish to make a comparison with a similar summary at the end of my June 10 memo.

This summary reveals that improved utilization of the current 13 DCs could save $2,269,000, improved locations of the 13 DCs could save another $2,412,000, and going to a 21-DC network could save $3,109,000 more.

THREE STEPS TO THE LEAST-COST DISTRIBUTION NETWORK

Cost Element	Step 1				Step 2			Step 3		
	Current Network	Optimal Utilization	Savings (Loss)	%△	Optimal Locations	Savings (Loss)	%△	Optimal Number	Savings (Loss)	%△
DC fixed costs	$ 6.150	6.139	0.011	−0.2	6.000	0.139	−2.3	9.737	(3.737)	62.3
DC variable costs	18.500	18.462	0.038	−0.2	18.716	(0.254)	1.4	18.727	(0.011)	0.1
Inbound transportation	41.777	41.777	0.000	0.0	42.693	(0.916)	2.2	43.428	(0.735)	−1.7
Outbound transporation	29.100	27.953	1.147	−3.9	24.510	3.443	−12.3	16.918	7.592	−31.0
Total	$96.600	94.331	2.269	−2.3	91.919	2.412	−2.6	88.810	3.109	−3.4

Legend:

[1] All costs in millions.

[2] Savings (loss) and % are with reference to the preceding step.

Supplement B

International Transportation *Services and Legal Requirements*

Supplement Outline

1. International Service Providers
    1.1. *Customs Brokers*
    1.2. *Freight Forwarders*
    1.3. *Carriers*
    1.4. *Banks*
2. International Commercial Terms
3. Foreign Trade Zones
4. U.S. Export Laws and Requirements
    4.1. *Documentation*
    4.2. *Other Considerations*
5. U.S. Import Laws and Requirements
    5.1. *Import Bonds*
    5.2. *Elements of Compliance*
    5.3. *Assists*
    5.4. *Security*
6. Concluding Comments
7. Glossary

Supplement Keys

1. What roles do customs brokers, freight forwarders, common carriers, contract carriers, and banks play in international trade?

2. What are INCOTERMS, and why is a good understanding of INCOTERMS important?

3. What is a free trade zone (FTZ), and what is the difference between general purpose FTZs and special purpose subzones?

4. Three documents accompany every U.S. import and export shipment (bill of lading, commercial invoice, packing list), and an SED must accompany most U.S. export shipments. What is the role of each of these documents?

5. What is the purpose of an import bond?

6. What is an entry form, and what requirement is placed on U.S. importers under the Customs Modernization Act?

7. How is an assist relevant for duties paid on imports to the United States?

8. What are the requirements of the Container Security Initiative, and how are these requirements affeçcted by participation in C-PAT?

This chapter supplement covers aspects of transportation management that are unique to moving materials across international borders (see Figure SB10.1). It is a primer on the terminology, laws, and specialized service providers associated with international transportation—a topic that is becoming increasingly important for a number of reasons.

The volume of material, information, and money flowing across international borders is significant and expanding. In the United States, for example, import and export trade has been growing faster than the U.S. economy, with this trend expected to continue over the foreseeable future. A growing number of components and subassemblies that were once produced in-house in the United States and other highly industrialized countries are now being sourced from low-cost regions such as Latin America, the Far East, and Eastern Europe. Off-shore sourcing is no longer limited to low-value and labor-intense items. The capabilities to design and produce sophisticated products requiring skilled labor and complex processes are rapidly advancing in low-cost regions of the world. This trend is especially evident in the developing high-tech industrial sectors in the Far East.

New trading blocs have emerged throughout the world during the last decade. Trading blocs are countries that have established trade agreements among one another for the purpose of increasing trade (e.g., via reduced tariffs and regulations). There are six different trading blocs in the Western hemisphere alone. Of these six, the North American Free Trade Agreement (NAFTA) is the largest in terms of trade. Other large trading blocs include the European Union (EU) and Asia-Pacific Economic Cooperation (APEC). There are many

FIGURE SB10.1

A supply chain with emphasis on transportation management links.

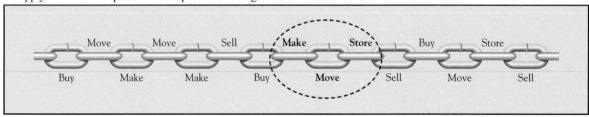

[1] The supplement draws on content, with permission, in G. LaPoint and S. Webster, "International Supply Chain Management," *The Internet Encyclopedia*, ed. H. Bidgoli (Hoboken, NJ: John Wiley & Sons, 2004), pp. 233–43.

smaller trade agreements throughout the world as well, all designed to ease tariffs and increase trade between selected trading partners.

Trade barriers are lowering, Internet-based communications technologies are advancing, and these technologies are becoming more widely available throughout the world. These factors are behind a trend toward increased international trade, and, in particular, supply chains that span an increasing number of countries. A firm's ability to effectively identify, establish, and manage relationships among multinational supply chain members has become a strategic core competency. Excellence in this area (1) provides cost, quality, and agility advantages through effective sourcing; (2) increases revenues as a firm is able to move quickly into high-growth foreign markets; and (3) is not easily duplicated by others. The objective of this supplement is to outline the rudiments of what every manager should know about moving product across international borders.

We'll begin in Section 1 by examining the various types of service providers that help with international shipments. Section 2 covers international commercial terms (INCOTERMS). The section describes the role and importance of INCOTERMS and identifies sources for additional detail. Section 3 discusses foreign trade zones. Sections 4 and 5 review import/export laws and customs requirements. Details on laws and requirements are presented from a U.S. perspective, but many of the basic features are common to other countries. Section 6 offers concluding comments, and, due to the extensive terminology specific to international transportation, a glossary is provided in Section 7.

1. INTERNATIONAL SERVICE PROVIDERS

International trading has many more variables than domestic trading, and these added variables increase the chances that orders or shipments can be delayed or assessed fines. Aside from the obvious complications such as distance, time, and language, other notable differences include government restrictions, different currencies, additional handling, intermodal transportation, additional paperwork, customs requirements, and trade terms. There are four commonly used international service providers: (1) customs brokers, (2) international freight forwarders, (3) international carriers, and (4) international banks.

1.1. Customs Brokers

While firms are allowed to clear their own freight through customs, the services of a customs broker are commonly used when importing. The complexity and periodic changes in customs requirements dictate a high level of specialized expertise, and improperly importing merchandise can be costly in terms of delays and fines. In the United States, customs brokers are licensed through U.S. Customs; the license affirms that the broker meets a certain level of competence to make entry of merchandise into the United States and permits the broker to clear freight on behalf of others.

The party responsible for an import is referred to as the importer of record. Generally the importer of record is the buyer of foreign merchandise. **Customs brokers operate on behalf of the importer of record,** though the importer of record is ultimately accountable for the import. U.S. customs brokers **provide preentry services such as providing preadvance clearing, filing formal entries, classifying material, paying duty, and performing postentry services** (e.g., filing protests on behalf of the importer, filing for partial tariff relief[2]). Brokers are responsible for maintaining their own records, but, contrary to belief among some importers, brokers are not responsible for maintaining records for the importer of record. Federal law requires that the importer of record maintain for five years all documentation used in the importation of material.

---

[2] More formally, filing for *duty drawback*.

1.2. Freight Forwarders

International freight forwarders act as a middleman between the carrier and the firm requiring international transport. Freight forwarders can work on behalf of either the exporter or the importer.

A freight forwarder's business is to **move freight as quickly as possible at prices lower than what their client could generally receive on their own.** Few exporters or importers ship enough volume to deal directly with an international carrier. **Freight forwarders contract for space on these carriers by committing a certain level of business based on the total shipping volume of their customer base.**

Although freight forwarders make international trade viable for the smaller to medium-size company, even the largest of shippers use them. Having a presence and contacts at the ports of entry can be critical when moving freight internationally. When imported merchandise reaches the port of entry, the slightest discrepancy or question places the merchandise on hold until the question is resolved. Many times the issue is easily resolved if someone is at the port of entry working on behalf of the importer. Few companies can afford to maintain this presence with their own staff.

Some international air freight forwarders are certified by the International Air Transport Association (IATA). The air freight industry is not regulated, and, as such, air freight forwarders do not have to be certified. Air freight forwarders certified by IATA, however, are issued an IATA number. Many commercial airlines will ask for an IATA number before they will accept any freight from an air freight forwarder.

In 1998 the Ocean Shipping Reform Act deregulated ocean shipping. Part of the act consolidated ocean freight forwarders with non-vessel-operating common carriers (NVOCCs; a.k.a. NVOs). The consolidated group is now known as *ocean transportation intermediaries*. Both ocean freight forwarders and NVOCCs are required to have a bond demonstrating financial stability, but only the ocean freight forwarder is required to be licensed by the Federal Maritime Association. Another difference relates to documentation. The paperwork prepared by the forwarder is in the name of the forwarder, not the carrier, whereas the paperwork prepared by the NVOCC is in the name of the carrier. In essence, an NVOCC is like a carrier except they do not operate a vessel. Freight forwarders are sometimes the largest customers of NVOCCs.

1.3. Carriers

Truck, rail, air, and water are all used for international freight, and multiple modes and carriers are often employed between origin and destination. This even occurs between contiguous countries due to restricted access to foreign carriers. In these cases, cargo must be transferred at the border to a carrier based in the country.

Carriers, whether domestic or international, may act as a common carrier or contract carrier. By law, **common carriers must accept business from anyone who tenders them business** (although there are ways carriers can discourage certain types of business and customers). **A contract carrier, on the other hand, has a formal relationship with a shipper, the terms of which are spelled out in a negotiated contract.** For situations in which there is a specific need (e.g., critical time frame, cargo requiring special handing) or significant ongoing volume, a shipper may be able to achieve better service and/or pricing through a contract carrier than a common carrier.

Shippers can work directly with international steamship lines and air carriers. Most international carriers presell their cargo space to freight forwarders, however, and, with the exception of firms with significant volume on a continual basis, it is generally difficult for a shipper to book space. Most shippers do not deal directly with international carriers, other than small-package international carriers such as DHL, FedEx, and UPS.

1.4. Banks

Financial risks are present in nearly every international transaction (e.g., buyer credit risk, political uncertainty, documentation errors, currency fluctuations, interest rate fluctuations). **International banks play a role in reducing financial risk by providing a letter of credit, more commonly known as an LC. An LC provides assurance of the buyer's ability to pay for a shipment, and a shipper may require an LC prior to shipment.** This means that a shipper requires the buyer to deposit an amount equal to the value of the commercial invoice in the buyer's bank. When the material arrives, shipping documents are presented to the buyer's bank, which in turn transfers the funds to the shipper's bank to collect funds on behalf of the shipper. LCs also can be used to protect against fluctuating currency and interest rates by setting a value for each and holding those values for a specific period of time. As a word of caution, an exporter should always verify that an LC is in accordance with UCP 500. UCP 500, which stands for Uniform Customs and Practice, is the international convention that governs the actions and obligations of a bank involved in an LC transaction.

2. INTERNATIONAL COMMERCIAL TERMS

International commercial terms, known as **INCOTERMS, were created by the International Chamber of Commerce to standardize the terms used for international trade.** The terms **specify such issues as the point where ownership and responsibility for insurance transfer from seller to buyer, as well as obligations for clearance of goods for export or import.** INCOTERMS were originally introduced in 1936 and have been revised and amended six times, most recently in 2000.

A basic awareness of the meaning and role of INCOTERMS is important for buyers and sellers, in part because of a notable difference in liability for in-transit loss or damage between a cargo ship and other modes. With truck and rail, the carrier is liable for the value of the freight in-transit,[3] with a few exceptions:

- Acts of God; for example, if Nike had a shipment of golf clubs and equipment destroyed by a hurricane, the carrier is not liable.
- Acts of public enemy; for example, if a terrorist blows up a roadway and ruins IBM's truckload of computers, the carrier is not liable.
- Acts of public authority; for example, if U.S. Customs stops a truck because they have reason to suspect the driver is smuggling contraband, and the fruit in the truck subsequently spoils because of the holdup, the carrier is not liable.
- Inherent defect; for example, if Century Foods ships aerosol cans of cheese spread to Mexico and all the cheese explodes as the cargo overheats in the 124-degree Texas sun, the carrier is not liable.
- Shipper fault; for example, if Nike stuffs 650 golf bags into a space that can only fit 550 and the doors subsequently pop open in transit, the carrier is not liable.

Liability limits for air carriers are normally set according to the product valuations in the airway bill, though cargo claims on international shipments are covered under the Warsaw Convention, which sets a liability limit of \$9.07 per pound (the Montreal Protocol No. 4, ratified by the United States in 1999, sets a slightly higher limit; Cutler 2006).[4]

---

[3] The bill of lading will normally include a line for the *released value* of the freight, which sets the upper limit of the carrier's liability. In some cases, the released value may be set (via negotiation) at a level below the true value of the freight in order to qualify for a lower freight rate. Cargo claims in the United States against rail and motor carriers are governed by the Carmack Amendment.

[4] Small package carriers such as DHL, FedEx, and UPS specify liability limits in their service guides and contracts. A shipper will want to carefully review these materials to determine if the limits are acceptable.

The liability limits for a cargo ship are much different. Specifically, the Carriage of Goods by Sea Act (COGSA) limits carrier liability to $500 per package. This means, for example, that if a Sealand Maersk ship hits rough waters and loses your container with $500,000 of inventory, Sealand's only obligation is to reimburse you $500 for the loss.[5]

There are a few things a shipper should be aware of with respect to the $500 limit. First, if cargo in containers is stored in separate packages, make sure that the number of packages in each container is identified in the bill of lading, as opposed to only identifying the number of containers. The carrier is liable up to $500 for each package identified in the bill of lading. Second, it may be possible to set higher liability limits through negotiations with the carrier, though the viability of this option is clearly affected by the shipper's negotiating leverage. Third, there are efforts under way by the United Nations Commission on International Trade Law to modernize the COGSA liability laws. However, any changes are likely years away. Fourth, a shipper can purchase insurance. Of course, this raises the question of how much insurance is warranted, and this is where INCOTERMS come into play. Among other impacts, INCOTERMS delineate the responsibility for freight claims between buyer and seller.

There are 13 INCOTERMS divided into four groups corresponding to the first letter of the term (i.e., C, D, E, and F). The goal of this section is to describe the basic differences between the four groups of INCOTERMS.[6] In brief, E and F INCOTERMS minimize a seller's risk and cost, and are least favorable to the buyer. C terms introduce more risk and cost for the seller and less for the buyer. D terms create the most risk and cost for the seller, and the least for the buyer. We'll briefly consider each INCOTERM group in order of increasing risk/cost for the seller and decreasing risk/cost for the buyer.

Group E—EXW named place. The letter "E" stands for the word "ex," which means "out of" in Latin. The three-character code is shorthand for <u>ex</u> <u>w</u>orks, which literally means that ownership and responsibility moves from seller to buyer at the point where goods move *out of* the place of *work* of the seller. More formally, the seller only has to make goods available to the buyer at his/her own premises. The buyer is responsible for arranging and paying the transportation, and, since the buyer takes ownership at the point of origin, the buyer assumes all risk (e.g., costs of loss or damage in transit) between origin and destination. As noted above, INCOTERMS are periodically revised and amended. Consequently, it is standard practice to explicitly identify the applicable version in the shipping documentation (i.e., normally the most recent). For example, "EXW Chicago USA—INCOTERMS 2000" means that the title and responsibility for the shipment transfers from seller to buyer at the seller's premises in Chicago, as dictated by the rules given in the INCOTERMS from year 2000.

Group F—FCA named place, FAS named port of shipment, FOB named port of shipment. The letter "F" stands for "free." The seller is responsible for export customs clearance and, depending on the particular INCOTERM, for costs and risks associated with getting the goods to the export port in the country of origin (known as precarriage), but is free of responsibility thereafter. For example, FOB stands for <u>f</u>ree <u>o</u>n <u>b</u>oard; "FOB Hong Kong—INCOTERMS 2000" means that the title and responsibility for the shipment transfers from seller to buyer when the goods pass the ship's rail at the Hong Kong port.

Group C—CFR named port of destination, CIF named port of destination, CPT named place of destination, CIP named place of destination. The letter "C" stands for either "cost" or "carriage," depending on the INCOTERM. In addition to precarriage, the

---

[5] As an aside, abandoned cargo in the ocean is known as *jetsam* if it is discarded (i.e., jettisoned) on purpose (e.g., to lighten the ship in an emergency) and *flotsam* if it is a consequence of an accident (e.g., shipwreck).

[6] See Stapleton and Saulnier (1999) for detailed coverage of INCOTERMS. In addition, a listing and description of each INCOTERM can be found at www.incoterms.org.

seller is responsible for arranging and paying for the main carriage (i.e., movement between a terminal in the country of origin to a terminal in another country). However, the seller does not assume the risk of the main carriage. For example, CFR stands for <u>c</u>ost and <u>f</u>reight; "CFR Singapore—INCOTERMS 2000" means that the seller arranges and pays for the costs of getting the goods to the Singapore port of entry, but the buyer assumes ownership at the export port in the country of origin and thus bears the risk of loss or damage from this point forward.

Group D—DAF named place, DES named port of destination, DEQ named port of destination, DDU named place of destination, DDP named place of destination. The letter "D" stands for "delivered." The seller assumes all costs and risks associated with getting the goods to the port or place of destination. For example, DES stands for <u>d</u>elivered <u>ex</u> <u>s</u>hip; "DES Hamburg Germany—INCOTERMS 2000" means the buyer takes ownership and responsibility for costs once the ship arrives at the Hamburg port, including import customs clearance. In contrast, DDP, which stands for <u>d</u>elivered <u>d</u>uty <u>p</u>aid, is the most expensive and risky of all INCOTERMS from the seller's perspective. "DDP Frankfort Germany—INCOTERMS 2000," for example, means that the seller's responsibility ends once the goods arrive in Frankfort. In effect, the seller becomes a nonresident importer of the country to which it is exporting. Accordingly, the seller is responsible for all transportation, customs clearance, duties, taxes, and any other fees between the point of origin and the buyer's loading dock in Frankfort.

While INCOTERMS are written to be specific and precise, their meaning can be subject to interpretation. To minimize the possibility of dispute, buyers and sellers may include a clause in the sales or purchase contract that clearly defines who has insurable interest and where the insurable interest is assumed. This is especially important when the shipment is consigned to a third party, such as a third-party logistics firm or a bank. A shipper or consignee may think the other party has insurable interest in a shipment only to find out after a loss that they did as well.

In summary, **international trade requires a thorough understanding of INCOTERMS. Ignorance can be costly;** it is not uncommon for those unfamiliar with INCOTERMS to be taken advantage of by those who do.

3. FOREIGN TRADE ZONES

Foreign trade zones (FTZs), also known as free trade zones, are specific areas within a country that have been designated as duty free. For customs purposes, these zones are considered to be outside the country, and, thus, no duties are paid when merchandise enters an FTZ. Merchandise leaving an FTZ for domestic use must go through customs and duties must be paid. FTZs offer a number of advantages for importers and exporters (Ballou 1999), for example:

- Duties may be deferred until the point in time when product is needed within the host country.

- Imported goods may be temporarily stored or modified and assembled in an FTZ, then shipped to another country with no duties or customs processing.
- Errors in documentation can be corrected in an FTZ prior to going through customs, thereby avoiding fines.
- Product subject to spoilage, damage, and loss does not incur duties on the amount lost.

There are two types of FTZs in the United States—general purpose FTZs and special purpose subzones—both of which fall under the supervision of the U.S. Customs Service and the Foreign Trade Zone Board.[7] **A general purpose FTZ is typically licensed to a municipality, public agency, port authority, or industrial park to operate on behalf of the general public.** A subzone, on the other hand, is a site authorized by the Foreign Trade Zone Board to operate as an FTZ but is not located within a general purpose FTZ. **Subzones are usually licensed to specific firms, frequently as a manufacturing site or distribution center.** They are designed to **permit companies to receive the benefits of an FTZ without being physically located in a general purpose FTZ.**

4. U.S. EXPORT LAWS AND REQUIREMENTS

A shipment is considered an export if the destination of the shipment is outside the country of origin. Specific documents are required to export material from the United States. The particular documents required depend to some degree on the nature of the product being shipped, the value of the shipment, the type of service required, and the destination. Documents required for all U.S. exports, along with other relatively common documents, are reviewed below.

4.1. Documentation

Bill of Lading

Every shipment must travel with some form of manifest. **The manifest for ground and ocean shipments is called a *bill of lading*, and for air shipments, an *airway bill*.** The bill of lading and the airway bill **serve as a contract between the shipper and the carrier.** Most international shipments use both a domestic and an ocean (or airway) bill of lading. **These documents are typically nonnegotiable, which means that they do not convey title.** As such, the carrier can deliver the order without the consignee presenting an original copy of the bill of lading. An *order* **bill of lading, however, is negotiable** and is often used in international transportation. If the **shipment includes an order bill of lading, then the consignee must pay the value of the invoice in order to receive the original bill of lading from the shipper. The carrier will not tender delivery unless the consignee can present the original bill of lading to the carrier. Only then does title of the merchandise pass from seller to buyer.**

Shipper's Export Declaration (SED)

Unless specifically identified as an exception in the export administration regulations, an SED is required for every export shipment in which any individual line item is valued at $2,500 or more. An **SED is used for compiling official U.S. export statistics and for export control.**

The shipper or its designated agent prepares the SED. The person who signs the SED, whether exporter or agent, must be in the United States at the time of signing and is held responsible for the truth, accuracy, and completeness of the SED, except insofar as that person can demonstrate that he or she reasonably relied on information furnished by others.

---

[7] There are 256 general purpose FTZs and 438 single-company subzones operating within the United States.

Furthermore, SEDs must be filed electronically with U.S. Customs. If the shipping location is not capable of electronic filing, then a forwarder, agent, or the carrier must file the SED. The forwarder, agent, or carrier's authority to sign the SED must be executed by a formal power of attorney.

Commercial Invoice

A commercial invoice is required for every export shipment. Unlike SEDs, there are no exceptions. **Foreign customs offices use the commercial invoice to determine the duty rates for imported merchandise. The commercial invoice contains (1) country of origin for each item, (2) seller's name and address, (3) buyer's name and address, (4) description of the items being shipped, (5) schedule B number (this number is a code that is used to determine the duty rate), and (6) extended value of each individual line item in U.S. dollars.**

For customer orders, the value used on the commercial invoice must reflect the transaction value for the merchandise. If a U.S. company conducts business with its foreign subsidiaries, then the prices charged to its foreign subsidiaries are to reflect the competitive conditions in the market and be comparable to prices charged to large unrelated customers.

Packing List

A packing list must accompany every export shipment. **The packing list contains the (1) description of the material being shipped, (2) quantity, (3) shipper's reference number, and (4) customer purchase order number.**

Certificate of Origin

Some export shipments require a certificate of origin. This is not a requirement of U.S. export law but a request on the part of the buyer or a requirement of foreign customs. The certificate of origin is a document, usually signed by an officer in the company, attesting to the country of origin of merchandise described on the commercial invoice.

Export License

Export licenses are required if a shipment is consigned to anyone or any country identified on restricted trade lists maintained by the U.S. government. These lists are discussed in Section 4.2.

Fumigation Certificates or Declaration

Some countries require U.S. shippers to produce a fumigation certificate or a declaration stating that the packaging or crating material is made from nonconiferous wood. If the packaging or crating is made of coniferous wood, then the wood must be either fumigated or heat treated to kill any insects that may inhabit the wood. These requirements are country specific. If crating, packaging, or fumigation is performed by an outside service, the service will be required to complete and sign the fumigation certificate or declaration.

Inspection Certificates

Some customers require inspection by a certified inspector prior to shipment. Upon inspection, the inspector will complete an inspection certificate that is typically sent to the buyer before the shipment takes place. The certificate states that the shipment meets the requirements of the importer or the importer's country.

Hazmat Documents

In the event that a shipment contains hazardous material, a hazmat bill of lading or hazardous airway bill is required. Many air carriers will not accept international shipments of hazardous material, so any such shipments may require investigation to locate a willing carrier.

Consularization

Some Middle Eastern and Latin American countries require export documents to be consularized, or stamped, by their foreign consulate prior to export. Consularization certifies the shipment to be exported to that foreign country. A certificate of origin and a commercial invoice must be presented to the foreign consulate. Some consulates will stamp the documents with an official stamp, whereas others will issue a consular invoice. If a consular invoice is generated, then the original document must travel with the shipment and be presented to the foreign customs.

Destination Control Statement

A destination control statement (DCS) is required for all exports from the United States for items that are restricted for export by the U.S. government. Lists of restricted persons and countries are discussed in the next section. The DCS informs the consignee that shipment cannot be forwarded to another party without the permission of the shipper.

ATA Carnet

One little-known document that can be useful for equipment or material that needs to temporarily move around a foreign country is the ATA carnet.[8] An ATA carnet is like a passport for merchandise that allows temporary importation free from duties, taxes, and security deposits. The material can move freely within a foreign country for the duration of the carnet. The ATA carnet is particularly useful for trade show or exhibition materials. Carnets are not universal. They are currently accepted in 58 countries and 27 territories (see www.uscib.org).

4.2. Other Considerations

During the 1990s, and particularly since September 11, 2001, the U.S. government has intensified its scrutiny of export shipments. Prior to releasing an export order, a firm must review several government lists to ensure that the countries, individuals, or organizations receiving these materials either directly or indirectly are not restricted by the U.S. government.

These lists with sources are briefly described below.

Denied Persons List (DPL). The DPL is maintained and updated by the Bureau of Industry and Security, formerly known as the Bureau of Export Administration. U.S. law prohibits exports to individuals and businesses on the DPL (available at www.bxa.doc.gov/dpl).

Commerce Control List and Economic Control Commodity Number (CCL/ECCN). The CCL is maintained and updated by the Bureau of Industry and Security. The list identifies all commodities that are restricted for export by the U.S. government. Every item on the CCL is assigned an economic control commodity number (ECCN). If an item is listed on the CCL, then proper authorization must be received from the U.S. Department of Commerce prior to export. Authorization is typically in the form of an export license. The CCL is available at www.access.gpo.gov/bis/ear/ear_data.html.

Embargoed Nations List. The U.S. government has identified nations with which it strictly forbids conducting business, either directly or indirectly. This list is maintained and updated by the U.S. Treasury Department, Office of Foreign Asset and Control (see www.treas.gov/ofac).

Special Designated Nationals and Blocked Persons (SDNB). The SDNB is maintained and updated by the U.S. Treasury, Office of Foreign Asset and Control (OFAC). The SDNB contains the names of individuals, organizations, and business concerns whose

---

[8] ATA stands for admissions temporary admissions.

assets have been frozen by the U.S. government. Conducting business with those who appear on the SDNB is prohibited unless approval in the form of a license is received from OFAC. The SDNB list is available at www.treas.gov/ofac.

In addition to the preceding lists, the export manager must be familiar with the International Trade on Arms Regulations (ITAR) and antiboycott regulations. ITAR defines the regulations associated with the exportation of products that can be used as a weapon or in conjunction with a weapon. Items of concern are identified on the U.S. Munitions List in part 121.1 of ITAR (see www.pmdtc.org/reference.htm#itar). Antiboycott regulations prohibit U.S. citizens and U.S. firms and their subsidiaries from participating in foreign embargoes that the U.S. government does not sanction. The effect is to prevent U.S. firms from being used to implement foreign policies of other nations that run counter to U.S. policy. For example, it is a violation of antiboycott regulations for a customer in a foreign country to require that airlines of a specific foreign country not be used to ship their order. Antiboycott regulations are maintained by the Bureau of Industry and Security (see www.bxa.doc.gov/antiboycottcompliance).

Foreign subsidiaries of U.S.-based companies are required to comply with the same U.S. export laws. The penalties for violating these restrictions can be harsh. Criminal and civil penalties can be assessed against violating companies, including revoking a company's export privileges. Additionally, individuals associated with the violation can be held personally responsible and can be subject to personal fines or imprisonment, depending on the severity of the offense.

5. U.S. IMPORT LAWS AND REQUIREMENTS

A shipment is considered an import if the origin of the shipment is outside the country of destination. For imports into the United States, **the importer of record is responsible for U.S. Customs clearance, and duties and taxes associated with the import.**

With the **exception of the shippers export declaration, the documents required for importing are the same as for exporting.** Mandatory items include a **commercial invoice, packing list, and either a bill of lading or airway bill.** Many of the other documents discussed in Section 4.1 also can be found in importing. Issues specific to importing are discussed in the following sections.

5.1. Import Bonds

An importer generally requires an import bond.[9] **The bond ensures that U.S. Customs gets paid the duty it is owed.** Bonds can be purchased individually as imports arrive or a company can purchase a continuous bond, which is also known as a surety bond. A continuous bond releases a large importer from having to purchase a bond each time it receives an import.

Another form of bond is the temporary import bond (TIB). A TIB allows an item to enter the United States duty free on a temporary basis with the requirement that the item will be exported out of the United States within one year. During that year, the item cannot be sold or transferred. If, at the end of a year, the material is not ready to be exported, the importer can apply for a TIB extension. If the item fails to be exported during the term of the TIB or if the item is sold, then U.S. Customs can, and generally will, levy fines and penalties on the importer.

5.2. Elements of Compliance

There are two key elements of U.S. import compliance. The first is known as the *entry*. When **an import arrives at a U.S. gateway, it must be cleared to enter the United States**

---

[9] An exception is for a low-value shipment (e.g., an import bond is not needed for a shipment valued at $200 or less).

with the preparation of an entry form. This form is **necessary for U.S. Customs to process the shipment and allow it to enter the country.**[10]

The entry form contains **four main pieces of information: (1) origin, (2) tariff classification, (3) value, and (4) buyer/seller relationship.** First, the entry form identifies the origin of the shipment to ensure the material is not originating from an embargoed nation or a specially designated national and blocked person. Second, the entry form identifies the harmonized tariff schedule (HTS) classification number used to describe the item(s). The HTS classification determines the duty rate of an item and whether the item is subject to countervailing or antidumping duties. Third, the entry form identifies the value of the shipment so a duty can be calculated. Fourth, the entry form identifies whether or not the two parties involved in the transaction are related. It is unlawful for an importer to take advantage of a related party by having it assign a value to a product that is unreasonably low for the purposes of lowering the duty (e.g., duty is based on the value of a good, so a lower value would result in a lower duty assessment).

The second key element of U.S. import compliance is record keeping. In 1993, the 103rd Congress passed the Customs Modernization Act (Mod Act). **The Mod Act shifts the legal burden to exercise "reasonable care" in conducting international trade from U.S. Customs to the trade community. Importers are required to maintain records of their import activities, and these may be audited by U.S. Customs at any time.** The North American Free Trade Agreement also permits the Canadian government to audit the records of a U.S. company that has shipped goods from the United States to Canada under NAFTA.

5.3. Assists

An *assist* is when a U.S. firm provides assistance to a foreign supplier to produce or provide merchandise that will eventually be sold and exported back to the U.S. firm. An assist can take many forms, including financial assistance, manufacturing equipment, tools, dies, molds, technical drawings, intellectual property, and technical advice. **The U.S. firm,** which in this case is also the importer of record, **is accountable for the duty on the value of the assistance at the duty rate applicable to the finished product being imported.** For example, suppose a U.S. firm provides $100,000 in start-up capital to a foreign concern to make a product that the U.S. firm, in turn, will purchase and import back into the United States. Additionally, suppose the U.S. firm provides tools and dies totaling $250,000 in value, and the finished product, when imported into the United States, will be subject to a 5 percent duty rate. This means that the U.S. firm, in addition to the normal duty on the finished product, will have to pay $17,500 ($350,000 × 5%) on the value of the assist.

5.4. Security

In the wake of September 11, 2001, security has been tightened, and international shipments are more heavily scrutinized. Customs agents in many countries are placing an even greater emphasis on compliance to import-export laws. Even the slightest of errors in paperwork can delay shipments at ports of entry.

In January 2002, U.S. Customs initiated the **Container Security Initiative as a means to ensure the integrity of container shipments entering the United States. The initiative requires inspection of ocean container contents, either through direct physical**

---

[10] Depending on the value of an item, an entry may be either *formal* or *informal*. A formal entry is required if the value exceeds $2,500, which means that the so-called *long form* must be completed. Informal entries do not require the long form, and entry is much faster and easier (e.g., small package carriers such as DHL, FedEx, and UPS are able to move freight through customs very quickly because the vast majority of their freight qualifies for informal entry).

examination or via noninvasive methods, at the foreign port of embarkation. In addition, all ocean carriers and NVOCCs are now required to send an electronic manifest 24 hours prior to the loading of the vessel at a foreign seaport. Depending on where a shipment is originating, it has been estimated that this new requirement will delay a shipment from two to four business days. As a result, shippers need to have material at the seaport at least one week earlier. Increased security by U.S. Customs at U.S. ports of entry also is causing delays.

Companies can reduce delays due to heightened security by participating in the Customs Trade Partnership Against Terrorism (C-PAT). By participating in C-PAT, a company agrees to conduct a comprehensive self-examination of its supply chain security using guidelines established by U.S. Customs and by the trade community. C-PAT participants are subject to less scrutiny by U.S. Customs on inbound shipments, which translates to lower processing times at ports of entry and border crossings.

6. CONCLUDING COMMENTS

This supplement has provided an introduction to the terminology, laws, and specialized service providers that are unique to international transportation. We learned that advancing technologies in combination with new trade agreements are driving growth in international trade and that this growth is likely to continue for years to come. We also learned that expertise in international transportation draws on an extensive array of detailed regulations, and that the area can be challenging to master.

While the tone of this supplement is different from that of other chapters due to the regulatory nature, the main lesson is similar to what we have seen before. A basic understanding of the area—international transportation in this case—is becoming increasingly important for a firm's survival, and mastery of the area holds promise for competitive advantage.

7. GLOSSARY

assist   A relationship in which a U.S. company provides assistance to a foreign supplier to produce or provide merchandise that eventually will be sold and exported to the U.S. company in the United States. Duties are paid on the value of the assist. Carriers provide transportation services to shippers.

commercial invoice   A document required for every export and import shipment. It contains such information as country of origin, buyer and seller names and addresses, descriptions of products being shipped, harmonized tariff schedule codes, and product values.

consignee   The receiver of a shipment.

duty drawback   The recovery of duty paid on an import when the item is later exported out of the United States.

foreign trade zones (FTZs)   Specific areas within a country that have been designated as a duty-free zone.

free-on-board (FOB) terms   U.S. domestic shipping terms that determine when title and risk pass between the seller and buyer.

freight forwarders   Entities that provide domestic and international shipping services. Most do not operate their own vehicles. They obtain lower rates by acting as a consolidator and contracting with common and contract carriers.

harmonized tariff schedule (HTS)   Used by governments to classify material and determine duties. The schedule contains classification numbers for products. For U.S.

imports, these numbers are called HTS numbers. For U.S. exports, these numbers are called schedule B numbers. The first six digits of the HTS number are universal. The remaining digits are country specific.

import bond   A certificate insuring that U.S. Customs gets paid the duty it is owed. Import bonds are required for imports to the United States. An import bond is also known as a surety bond.

importer of record   Generally the buyer of foreign merchandise that has the merchandise imported into its country.

international commercial terms (INCOTERMS)   Trade terms used in international commerce (i.e., international equivalent of FOB terms noted above). They define the costs, risks, and obligations of buyers and sellers in international transactions.

international freight forwarders   Entities that act as middlemen between the exporter and importer and the carrier.

non-vessel-operating common carriers (NVOCCs)   Found in ocean shipping only, these are considered common carriers, but they do not own or operate a vessel. NVOCCs and freight forwarders are similar in function and process except a freight forwarder cannot sign paperwork on behalf of the carrier whereas an NVOCC can.

packing list   A document that must accompany every export and import shipment. It identifies what is being shipped, the quantity, the shipper's reference number, and the customer purchase order number.

shipper   A term used in transport documentation to denote the seller of the merchandise.

third-party logistics firms   Entities that provide comprehensive logistics services (e.g., transportation, warehousing, order processing), thus representing a significant third party complementing the parties of buyer and seller.

trading bloc   A group of countries that have established trading agreements for the purpose of increasing trade among the participating countries. A trading bloc is also known as a regional trading agreement.

U.S. Customs brokers   Brokers licensed to clear imports into the United States that ensure all the necessary paperwork for entry is in order.

Chapter **Eleven**

Quality Management: Tools for Process Improvement

Chapter Outline

1. Diagnosis
   1.1. Pareto Analysis
   1.2. Cause-and-Effect Diagram
2. Control and Capability
   2.1. Statistical Process Control Charts
   2.2. Measures of Process Capability
3. Summary and Managerial Insights
   3.1. The Sum of Many Independent Random Elements Is Approximately Normally Distributed
   3.2. Put Improvement Tools and Authority in the Hands of Those Close to the Action
   3.3. Quick Feedback Is Often Critical for Effective and Continual Improvement
4. Exercises
   Case Exercise: RR Logistics

Chapter Keys

1. Why are process diagrams important?
2. How do the two process diagnosis tools work (i.e., Pareto analysis, cause-and-effect diagrams)?
3. What is the main purpose of statistical process control?
4. Control charts help detect changes in a process, and all control charts do this by taking advantage of two ideas. What are these two ideas?
5. What rule of thumb is used to determine when to stop a process when using a control chart, and what trade-off is considered when determining how tight to set control limits?
6. What types of process changes are $\bar{X}$, R, S, and P charts designed to detect?
7. What do process capability indices measure, how should an index value greater than 1.0 be interpreted, and what is the meaning of six sigma?
8. What are the Pareto phenomenon, central limit theorem, and law of large numbers, and how are these principles relevant for process improvement?
9. What are the managerial insights from the chapter?

FIGURE 11.1
A supply chain emphasizing that quality management is relevant for all links—buy, make, move, store, and sell.

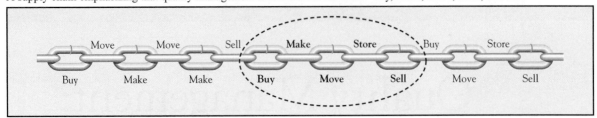

Chapters 4 through 10 in Part Two of this book have each concentrated on one of five basic supply chain activities: buy, make, move, store, and sell. This chapter, and its chapter supplement, take a broader view by considering a topic that is relevant for all five activities—quality management (see Figure 11.1).

At a basic level, any supply chain can be viewed as a network of processes that govern the movement, storage, usage, and transformation of resources (e.g., money, material, information) between producers, consumers, disposers, and recyclers/remanufacturers. Section 1 reviews two tools that are useful for identifying where to focus attention when working to improve a process. The tools are generic in the sense that they can be applied to any type of process, whether associated with buy, make, move, store, sell, or combinations of these activities. One of these tools is Pareto analysis, which also has appeared in earlier chapters and is based on a principle of nature called the Pareto phenomenon. Our consideration of Pareto analysis in this chapter not only illustrates its applicability to a wide range of settings, but also reinforces the fundamental and practical role of principles of nature in general.

Section 2 largely focuses on statistical process control, a set of tools that are used in both manufacturing and service settings. Statistical process control tools provide a means to detect when a process is, and is not, behaving as designed. Consequently, these tools shed light on key factors that affect the output of a process, and can play an important role in process improvement.[1] We'll examine several types of statistical process control tools, and we'll see how these tools take advantage of two principles of nature: the law of large numbers and the central limit theorem. Finally, since measures of performance often drive improvement efforts, we'll look at ways to measure the capability of a process.

1. DIAGNOSIS

The subtitle of this chapter is *tools for process improvement*. Processes add value through the conversion of inputs into outputs. We can think of very narrow and specific processes (e.g., filling out a customer order form) and more extensive processes involving multiple interconnected activities (e.g., activities between order entry and shipment). With the exception of simple, single-activity processes, it may not be obvious where to focus improvement efforts. This section outlines two simple tools that are useful for identifying high-priority elements of a process for attention, or, in other words, for process diagnosis. However, before introducing these tools, it is worth emphasizing that **process improvement begins with a sound understanding of the**

---

[1] For example, the case exercise at the end of this chapter requires you to apply these tools to address a supply chain problem in the coffee industry.

FIGURE 11.2   The Planning Process for Procuring Intel Product at Fujitsu Siemens Computers (FSC)
The shaded blocks are Intel activities and the clear blocks are FSC activities.

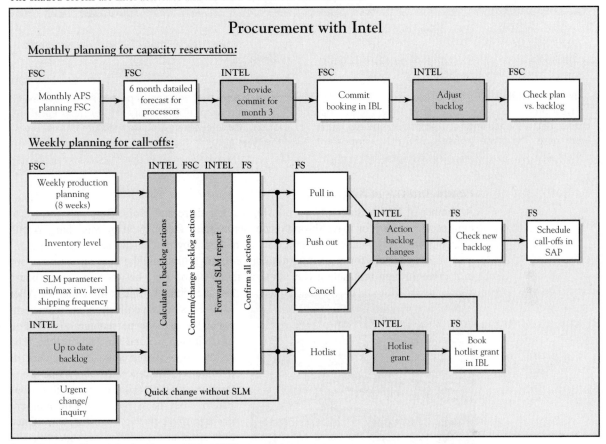

Source: Reprinted with permission from Brown and Heinzel (2001).

current process. At the very least, the **step-by-step execution of the process should be well documented, and diagrams known as process maps are often useful for this purpose.** Figure 11.2, for example, illustrates a process at Fujitsu Siemens Computers for planning the procurement of Intel products.[2]

1.1 Pareto Analysis

An aggregate measure, by definition, is the composite of many parts. The Pareto phenomenon is disparity of contribution among the parts; that is, all parts do not contribute equally to the whole. The phenomenon is present in almost all aggregate measures, and it points to a commonsense early step when attempting to improve a process—Pareto analysis. **Pareto analysis refers to separating the trivial many from the important few, where importance is defined according to degree of impact on a relevant aggregate measure.** Let's look at an example.

---

[2] More examples illustrating the use of diagrams to document business processes can be found in Jacka and Keller (2002) and Joiner Associates Staff (1995).

Principle of Nature: Pareto Phenomenon

DEFINITION
The lion's share of an aggregate measure is determined by relatively few factors.

IMPLICATION
Invest time and energy to identify a few factors that drive performance and focus attention and resources on these. The process of separating the "important

few" from the "trivial many" is known as *Pareto analysis.*

EXAMPLE
The extra time that you spend preparing for a heavily weighted exam is essentially the result of Pareto analysis. The relevant aggregate measure in this case is the final grade in the course.

Pareto Analysis at KFC[3]

A number of KFC restaurants were losing market share and profit. Research pointed to long service times for drive-through sales as a major factor. A team was charged with reducing drive-through service time. The team began by purchasing and installing automatic timing devices for measuring total drive-through time and the time for various steps in a drive-through transaction (i.e., time at menu board, time between the menu board

and the window, time at the window). After two weeks of data collection, the team computed the average percentage contribution of each step to total transaction time. The results showed that almost 60 percent of total transaction time was spent at the drive-through window. This example illustrates Pareto analysis of the aggregate measure *average drive-through service time.* Once time spent at the window was identified as a high-priority area for attention, the team began to focus on this element of the process with the help of a tool outlined in the next section.

1.2 Cause-and-Effect Diagram

A **cause-and-effect diagram[4] helps to organize thinking when brainstorming on root causes of an effect.** The diagram shows the effect linked to branches for major categories of possible causes (e.g., equipment, methods, material, people, reward system). Specific causes are added to the diagram under the appropriate category, which in turn may be identified as a symptom of more elementary causes. Over the duration of a brainstorming session, the diagram expands in density and depth with the lowest levels corresponding to "root causes" (see Figure 11.3).

Cause-and-Effect Diagram at KFC[5]

Recall from the previous section that KFC conducted Pareto analysis of service time data. The analysis identified time at the drive-through window (DTW) as a prime target for

---

[3] See Apte and Reynolds (1995).
[4] Also known as a fishbone chart.
[5] See Apte and Reynolds (1995).

FIGURE 11.3 A
Cause-and-Effect
Diagram Showing
Five Major Categories
of Causes Leading to
an Effect (e.g., high
defect rate)
The equipment category
branch illustrates how
the diagram expands
in density and depth
as ideas on possible
causes of an effect are
identified.

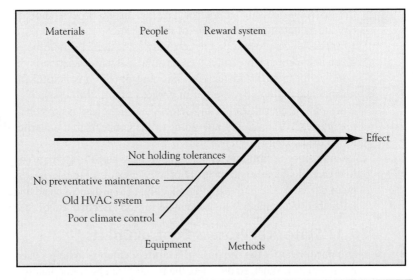

FIGURE 11.4 A
Cause-and-Effect
Diagram for Delays at
KFC's Drive-Through
Window (DTW)

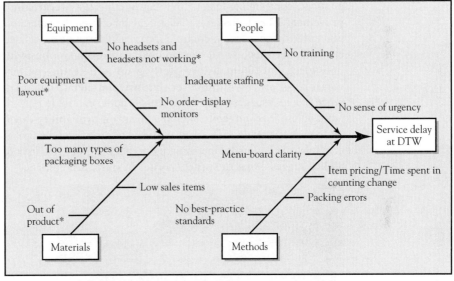

Source: Reprinted with permission from Apte and Reynolds (1995).

reduction. The team then set about collecting data on DTW delays. Employees maintained a log with the cause(s) of a delay whenever DTW time for a customer was beyond a target. Figure 11.4 shows one of the cause-and-effect diagrams created during a team meeting. Pareto analysis of the log data identified three critical root causes that are indicated by asterisks in the figure. *Epilogue*: KFC's process improvement efforts cut average drive-through service time by about 30 percent, market share and productivity increased, and the changes instituted at the pilot locations were rolled out nationally.

2. CONTROL AND CAPABILITY

The previous section described two tools that can help identify elements of a process most opportune for improvement. The next question is how to improve a process. This section is based on the idea that two important steps toward process improvement are (1) getting the current process under control (i.e., the current process should behave as designed) and (2) understanding the capability of the process.

Intuitively, a process that is behaving as designed should be consistent over time. But, given a fine enough measure, there is almost always variation in process output. In this section, we'll see how statistical process control (SPC) is helpful for distinguishing between normal and abnormal variation in process output. More specifically, we examine several types of SPC charts designed to detect when a process is not behaving as designed (i.e., not *in control*). We'll also see how some of the concepts that underlie SPC are used to characterize the capability of a process.

In practice, a firm may choose to purchase an SPC system. These systems make it easy to create SPC charts and measure process capability (e.g., via software linked to measurement devices). The purpose of this section is to provide a basic understanding of the underlying theory and methods—a requisite for the effective use of these systems.

2.1. Statistical Process Control Charts

In a narrow sense, **the purpose of a control chart** is to help a user detect when a process is not in control. When so detected, the process can be immediately examined to identify and eliminate contributing factors, thus **supporting the overarching purpose of process improvement.** The challenge is to distinguish between the naturally occurring random variation in the output of an in-control process and variation associated with some fundamental change in the process. **All control charts draw on two basic ideas** to make this distinction. **First, since humans are pretty good at detecting patterns in images, summary measures of process output over time are plotted** on a chart. The presence of a pattern in process output suggests that the process is not in control (e.g., variation in process output is not random). **Second, control charts draw on probability theory** and, more specifically, **on hypothesis testing.** The theory is used to determine the probability of observed values on a control chart under the assumption that the process is in control. **A very small probability suggests that the process is not in statistical control.**

The challenge of detecting fundamental change amid random variation, and the role of charts and hypothesis testing of process output in responding to this challenge, can be illustrated through fantasy baseball. Imagine that you are the successful manager of a fantasy baseball team. The rules are simple. Each team has a roster of major league players obtained through a draft and interteam trades. After each day's games, all teams in your league are ranked from first to last in a number of statistical categories, and points are awarded according to the order of finish. The team with the most points at the end of the season wins the league. Your success stems from (1) a statistic you created (and called MLB) that has proved quite accurate for quantifying the value of each big league player and (2) control chart techniques to detect when the value of a player is significantly changing. You've written a computer program that accesses a database of player statistics and displays a control chart for each player;

that is, a plot of MLB over time where each data point is the player's MLB over a 10-game stretch. The control charts have been useful for detecting fundamental shifts in a player's value before your competition. A few years ago, for example, you drafted Wayne Trientas, a promising rookie with the Dodgers. He started the season on a tear, but about one-third of the way through the season, your control chart picked up a drop in performance that, based on your estimates, would have less than a 1 percent chance of occurring without some fundamental change taking place. You promptly traded him for another player and a future draft pick. You later learned that shortly before you traded him, a pitcher discovered a pitch he couldn't hit. College pitchers didn't have the control to effectively exploit this weakness, but most major league pitchers did, and Trientas left major league baseball before the end of the season.

As illustrated in the example, control charts are essentially a commonsense response to the challenge of detecting change amid random variation. But the example leaves the details of implementation unanswered. Some of these details depend on the type of statistic being plotted on a control chart, and we will consider several types below. There are, however, three basic implementation features common to all statistical process control charts. First, control charts plot the value of a sample statistic over time. Samples of process output are periodically collected, the sample is measured, and a summary statistic is computed and plotted. Second, control charts have upper and lower control limits. An observed value outside the control limits is highly unlikely without a fundamental change in the process, and thus is a signal that the process is not in control. Third, control charts are based on a probability distribution of process output when the process is in control, which is used to set control limits. There is no exact approach to determine the probability distribution of process output. Most commonly, theory is used to identify the type of probability distribution that is likely to apply, and large samples of the process output are analyzed to estimate its parameter values. This approach is described for various types of control charts below.

Control charts can be classified into two categories according to the way in which the output of a process is measured: variable or attribute. A *variable* control chart is used for a measure of process output that is (at least approximately) continuous (e.g., size or weight of a part). An *attribute* control chart is used for a measure of process output that is based on a count or frequency of a particular attribute (e.g., defect rate). Each category is considered in turn in the next two sections.

Control Charts for Variable Data

Imagine a machine that compresses powdered metal to produce a cylindrical part. One meaningful measure of the part's usability is its diameter. We'll begin this section by looking at how an $\overline{X}$-chart is constructed and used to detect changes in the process that affect the mean part diameter.

An $\overline{X}$-chart is a plot of sample means; a sample of parts is periodically collected and the mean part diameter is computed and plotted on the $\overline{X}$-chart. **A pattern in the chart** (e.g., sample means are consistently increasing over time) or a **sample mean outside the control limits signals a change in the process** that is affecting the mean part diameter. In response, **the standard policy is to stop the process, try to identify what has caused the process to change, and eliminate the cause** (see Figure 11.5).

Figure 11.5 shows a center line (CL), an upper control limit (UCL), and a lower control limit (LCL). The value of the center line corresponds to the mean of the process output, which can be estimated from historical data. The control limits require information on the probability distribution of the process output, which leads to the question of how this can be estimated. A principle of nature known as the central limit theorem provides some guidance. The **central limit theorem** states that **the distribution of a sample mean will tend**

FIGURE 11.5 A Plot of Sample Means over Time on an $\overline{X}$-Chart

The two normal curves, which do not normally appear on an $\overline{X}$-chart, are included to illustrate the probability distribution of the sample means when the process is in control. The figure illustrates how control charts support a cycle of process improvement: The control chart helps identify fundamental change amid the randomness in process output so that the causes of change can be corrected. As corrections take place, the process eventually becomes consistently in control and well understood. Once under control, the process may be modified to gain further improvements, and the cycle begins anew.

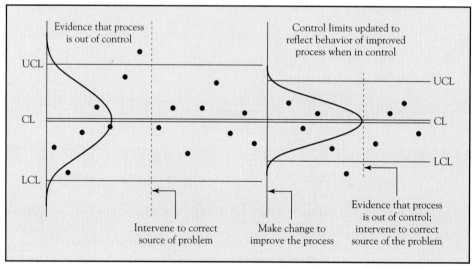

toward normal as the sample size increases. Consequently, even if little can be said about the probability distribution of individual values, the central limit theorem provides a basis for viewing sample means as approximately normally distributed.

There is, however, another reason why control charts plot a sample statistic rather than individual values, and it has to do with another principle of nature. Analysis of a sample statistic, instead of individual values, results in a more powerful statistical test. This means that one is more likely to detect changes in the process. The reason for this power is due to the **law of large numbers,** the principle of nature that **relative variability decreases as volume increases,** or, equivalently, the **variance of a sample mean decreases as the sample size increases** (e.g., notice the impact of sample size n on the standard deviation of the sample mean in the formula below).

The formulas for computing the values of CL, UCL, and LCL for an $\overline{X}$-chart are listed below.

The Center Line and Control Limits for an $\overline{X}$-Chart

X = random variable for the measure of interest when process is in control

μ_X = mean of X

σ_X = standard deviation of X

n = sample size

$\overline{X}$ = random variable for the mean of a sample (i.e., average of n random variables)

$\mu_{\overline{X}}$ = mean of $\overline{X} = \mu_X$

$\sigma_{\overline{X}}$ = standard deviation of the sample mean = $\frac{\sigma_X}{\sqrt{n}}$

Principle of Nature: Central Limit Theorem

DEFINITION

As the number of independent random variables increases, the probability distribution of the sum approaches the normal distribution.

IMPLICATION

Random measures of interest are often comprised of many approximately independent random components. In such cases, analysis of uncertainty based on the normal distribution is a good approximation.

EXAMPLE

If you take a large sample of people, ask them their height, and plot the distribution, you'll see that it looks like a graph of the normal distribution—it has a bell curve shape. There could be several factors that contribute to this result, but one likely factor is the effect of many "random" elements that come together to determine the height of a human. Roughly speaking, the central limit theorem tells us that a measure that is a combination of many random components will tend to be approximately normally distributed.

Principle of Nature: Law of Large Numbers

DEFINITION

As volume increases, relative variability decreases.

IMPLICATION

Look for ways to change operations so that planning can be done at a more aggregate unit.

EXAMPLE

The World Series just ended and your challenge is to predict your favorite player's batting average after the first five games of the upcoming season and at the end of the season. Which prediction do you think is likely to be more accurate? If you guessed your end-of-season forecast, you have an intuitive feel for the law of large numbers.

$$CL = \text{center line} = \mu_{\bar{X}}$$

$$UCL = \text{upper control limit} = \mu_{\bar{X}} + z\sigma_{\bar{X}} = \mu_X + z\frac{\sigma_X}{\sqrt{n}}$$

$$LCL = \text{lower control limit} = \mu_{\bar{X}} - z\sigma_{\bar{X}} = \mu_X - z\frac{\sigma_X}{\sqrt{n}}; \quad \text{if } LCL < 0, \text{ then set } LCL = 0$$

Note: The value of z is typically set to three (i.e., three-sigma control limits).

Estimating μ_X and σ_X from Historical Data for an $\bar{X}$-Chart

Collect N samples of process output (e.g., $N \geq 10$); the size of each sample is n

$x_i = $ measure of the ith part in a sample

$$\bar{x}_j = \text{mean of the } j\text{th sample} = \frac{1}{n}\sum_{i=1}^{n} x_i$$

$$\bar{\bar{x}} = \text{grand mean} = \frac{1}{N}\sum_{j=1}^{N} \bar{x}_j = \text{estimate of } \mu_{\bar{X}}$$

$$s_j = \text{sample standard deviation of the } j\text{th sample} = \left[\frac{\sum_{i=1}^{n}(x_i - \bar{x}_j)^2}{n-1}\right]^{1/2} {}^{6}$$

---

[6] The formula for s_j can be implemented in Excel as STDEV($x_1, x_2, \ldots, x_n$).

$$\bar{s} = \text{grand standard deviation} = \frac{1}{N}\sum_{j=1}^{N} s_j$$

$$\bar{s}/c_4 = \text{estimate of } \sigma_X, \text{ where } c_4 = \left(\frac{2}{n-1}\right)^{1/2} \frac{\Gamma(n/2)}{\Gamma((n-1)/2)}.^7 \text{ Selected values of } c_4 \text{ are}$$

n	3	4	5	6	7	8	9	10	11	12	13	14
c_4	0.886	0.921	0.940	0.952	0.959	0.965	0.969	0.973	0.975	0.978	0.979	0.981

Based on the above estimates,

$$\text{CL} = \text{center line} = \mu_{\bar{X}} = \bar{\bar{x}}$$

$$\text{UCL} = \text{upper control limit} = \mu_{\bar{X}} + z\sigma_{\bar{X}} = \mu_X + z\frac{\sigma_X}{\sqrt{n}} = \bar{\bar{x}} + z\frac{\bar{s}}{c_4\sqrt{n}}$$

$$\text{LCL} = \text{lower control limit} = \max\{\mu_{\bar{X}} - z\sigma_{\bar{X}}, 0\} = \max\left\{\mu_X - z\frac{\sigma_X}{\sqrt{n}}, 0\right\}$$

$$= \max\left\{\bar{\bar{x}} - z\frac{\bar{s}}{c_4\sqrt{n}}, 0\right\}$$

A Center Line and Control Limit Calculation Example

Suppose we would like to set up an $\bar{X}$-chart for the machine that compresses powdered metal to produce a cylindrical part. The sample size is nine ($n = 9$) and we are given estimates for the mean and standard deviation of part diameter when the process is in control: $\mu_X = 3.00$ and $\sigma_X = 0.01$. Control limits are to be set at the three-sigma level ($z = 3$). Then CL = $\mu_X =$ 3.00, UCL = $\mu_X + z\frac{\sigma_X}{\sqrt{n}} = 3.00 + (3)(0.01)/(9)^{1/2} = 3.01$, and LCL = $\max\{\mu_X - z\frac{\sigma_X}{\sqrt{n}}, 0\} =$ $\max\{3.00 - (3)(0.01)/(9)^{1/2}, 0\} = 2.99$

Example Summary

μ_X = mean part diameter when the process is in control = 3.00
σ_X = standard deviation of part diameter when the process is in control = 0.01
n = sample size = 9
The three-sigma control limits are
UCL = $\mu_X + 3\sigma_X/n^{1/2} = 3.01$
LCL = $\max\{\mu_X - 3\sigma_X/n^{1/2}, 0\} = 2.99$

How Can the Control Limits Be Interpreted? With control limits at the three-sigma level, we can expect that there is a 99.7 percent chance that a sample mean will be within the control limits when the process is in control.[8] In other words, we can expect the sample mean to fall outside the limits in about 3 out of 1,000 times when the process is in control. Therefore, if a sample mean lies outside the control limits, then there is a fair chance that the process is no longer in control and it is worthwhile to stop and check what's going on.

The example illustrated the calculation of control limits at the three-sigma level. Technically, there is no reason why z could not be set to some other value. At $z = 2$, for example, there is a 95.5 percent chance that a sample mean will be within the limits when the process is in control, or the sample mean will fall outside the limits about 1 out of 20 times when the process is in control. The tighter the control limits, the more frequently the process is

---

[7] The statistic $\bar{s}$ is a biased estimate of σ_X, and is divided by c_4 to remove the bias. The formula for c_4 can be implemented in Excel as $((2/(n-1))^0.5)*(\text{EXP(GAMMALN}(n/2)))/(\text{EXP(GAMMALN}((n-1)/2)))$.

[8] The value of 99.7 percent comes from the normal probability distribution where there is a 99.7 percent probability that a normal random variable will fall within plus or minus three standard deviations from the mean.

stopped. Thus, the decision on a **value of z can be viewed as a balance between the cost of stopping the process unnecessarily** (i.e., when in control) **and the cost of not stopping the process when the process is not behaving as designed** (i.e., out of control). It is customary in practice, however, to use control limits at the three-sigma level.

Detecting Process Changes That Affect the Variation in Output   An $\overline{X}$-chart is designed **to detect changes in the process that affect the process mean,** and it is typically used in conjunction with a chart designed to detect changes that affect the variation in process output. There are two common **alternatives for detecting changes in variation: an *R*-chart and an *S*-chart.** An *R*-chart is a plot of sample ranges and an *S*-chart is a plot of sample standard deviations. The range of a sample is the smallest value in the sample subtracted from the largest value in the sample, that is, $r_j = \max\{x_i\} - \min\{x_i\}$. For example, the range of 3.01, 2.97, 3.02, 3.03, 3.00, 2.99 is $3.03 - 2.97 = 0.06$. As noted above, the formula for the sample standard deviation is

$$s_j = \left[\frac{\sum_{i=1}^{n}(x_i - \overline{x}_j)^2}{n-1} \right]^{1/2}$$

What Factors Play a Role When Selecting between an R-Chart and an S-Chart?   The range of a sample is easier to calculate than a standard deviation, and this could favor the use of an *R*-chart when an operator is manually computing values for control charts. One drawback of a sample range statistic is that some information is ignored (i.e., the values between the largest and smallest value). Consequently, an *R*-chart is less effective than an *S*-chart for detecting change, though the difference is small when n is small,[9] and an *R*-chart is quite satisfactory up to sample sizes of about 10.

In contrast with an $\overline{X}$-chart, the control limits for the *R*-chart and the *S*-chart are based on the assumption that each value in the sample is normally distributed. In practice, the normal distribution is generally a reasonable approximation due to the central limit theorem; for example, the diameter of a part can be viewed as the composite of multiple elementary factors that are each susceptible to some randomness. As with the $\overline{X}$-chart, the control limits for the *R*-chart and *S*-chart are typically set at the three-sigma level.[10] The formulas for computing the values of CL, UCL, and LCL for an *R*-chart and an *S*-chart are listed below.

The Center Line and Control Limits for an *R*-Chart

R = random variable for difference between the largest and smallest value in a sample of size n

μ_R = mean of R

σ_R = standard deviation of R

CL = center line = μ_R

UCL = upper control limit = $\mu_R + z\sigma_R$

LCL = lower control limit = $\mu_R - z\sigma_R$;   if LCL < 0, then set LCL = 0

Note: The value of z is typically set to three (i.e., three-sigma control limits)

[9] The efficiency of the *R* statistic relative to the *S* statistic is 1.000, 0.975, 0.930, and 0.850 for samples sizes of 2, 4, 6, and 10, respectively. See www.itl.nist.gov/div898/handbook/index.htm for more detail on *R* versus *S*.

[10] The convention in the United States is to set control limits as *z* standard deviations above and below the center line where *z* is typically three (three-sigma control limits). In the United Kingdom it is more common to set control limits according to a probability target (e.g., 99.7 percent), which can lead to slightly different control limits for *R* and *S* charts. This is because, even when individual values are normally distributed, the *R* statistic and the *S* statistic are not normally distributed; that is, the three-sigma control limits do not necessarily match the 99.7 percent probability associated with a normal distribution.

Computing μ_R and σ_R from Historical Data

Collect N samples of process output (e.g., $N \geq 10$); the size of each sample is n

x_i = measure of the ith part in a sample

r_j = range of the jth sample = $\max\{x_i\} - \min\{x_i\}$

$\bar{r}$ = average range = $\dfrac{1}{N}\displaystyle\sum_{j=1}^{N} r_j$ = estimate of μ_R

$\bar{r} \times (d_3/d_2)$ = estimate of σ_R, where the values of d_3/d_2 for various sample sizes are[11]

n	2	3	4	5	6	7	8	9	10
d_3/d_2	0.756	0.525	0.427	0.372	0.335	0.308	0.288	0.272	0.259

Based on the above estimates,

$\quad$ CL = center line = $\mu_R = \bar{r}$

$\quad$ UCL = upper control limit = $\mu_R + z\sigma_R = \bar{r} + z\bar{r}(d_3/d_2)$

$\quad$ LCL = lower control limit = $\max\{\mu_R - z\sigma_R, 0\} = \max\{\bar{r} - z\bar{r}(d_3/d_2), 0\}$

A Center Line and Control Limit Calculation Example for an R-Chart Suppose we would like to set up an R-chart for the machine that compresses powdered metal to produce a cylindrical part. The sample size is nine ($n = 9$) and we are given an estimate for the mean sample range of part diameter when the process is in control: $\mu_R = \bar{r} = 0.029$. Control limits are to be set at the three-sigma level ($z = 3$). Then CL = $\bar{r}$ = 0.029, UCL = $\bar{r}$ + $z\bar{r}(d_3/d_2)$ = 0.029 + 3(0.029)(0.272) = 0.053, and LCL = $\max\{\bar{r} - z\bar{r}(d_3/d_2), 0\}$ = $\max\{0.005, 0\}$ = 0.005.

Example Summary

$\mu_R = \bar{r}$ = mean sample range when the process is in control = 0.029
n = sample size = 9
The three-sigma control limits are
UCL = $\bar{r} + z\bar{r}(d_3/d_2)$ = 0.053
LCL = $\max\{\bar{r} - z\bar{r}(d_3/d_2), 0\}$ = 0.005

The Center Line and Control Limits for an S-Chart

$\quad$ S = random variable for the sample standard deviation of a sample of size n

$\quad$ μ_S = mean of S

$\quad$ σ_S = standard deviation of S

$\quad$ CL = center line = μ_S

$\quad$ UCL = upper control limit = $\mu_S + z\sigma_S$

$\quad$ LCL = lower control limit = $\mu_S - z\sigma_S$; if LCL < 0, then set LCL = 0

Note: The value of z is typically set to three (i.e., three-sigma control limits).

---

[11] The cumulative distribution function of a range of a sample n normal random variables with CDF F and PDF f is $P[R < x] = n \int_{-\infty}^{\infty} [F(t + x) - F(t)]^{n-1} f(t)dt$, which can be numerically evaluated to obtain the values in the table (i.e., to determine σ_R as a function of μ_R and n).

Computing μ_S and σ_S from Historical Data

Collect N samples of process output (e.g., $N \geq 10$); the size of each sample is n

Compute $\bar{s}$ and c_4 as shown in the calculations for an $\bar{X}$-chart.

$$\bar{s} = \text{estimate of } \mu_S$$

$$\frac{\bar{s}}{c_4}[1 - c_4^2]^{1/2} = \text{estimate of } \sigma_S$$

$$\text{CL} = \text{center line} = \mu_S = \bar{s}$$

$$\text{UCL} = \text{upper control limit} = \mu_S + z\sigma_S = \bar{s} + z\frac{\bar{s}}{c_4}[1 - c_4^2]^{1/2}$$

$$\text{LCL} = \text{lower control limit} = \max\{\mu_S - z\sigma_S, 0\} = \max\left\{\bar{s} - z\frac{\bar{s}}{c_4}[1 - c_4^2]^{1/2}, 0\right\}$$

A Center Line and Control Limit Calculation Example for an S-Chart Suppose we would like to set up an S-chart for the machine that compresses powdered metal to produce a cylindrical part. The sample size is nine ($n = 9$) and we are given an estimate for the mean sample standard deviation of part diameter when the process is in control: $\mu_S = \bar{s} = 0.0097$. Control limits are to be set at the three-sigma level ($z = 3$). From the table, $c_4 = 0.969$.

Then $\text{CL} = \bar{s} = 0.0097$, $\text{UCL} = \bar{s} + z\frac{\bar{s}}{c_4}[1 - c_4^2]^{1/2} = 0.0097 + 3(0.0097/0.969)(1 - 0.969^2)^{1/2} = 0.017$, and $\text{LCL} = \max\{\bar{s} - z\frac{\bar{s}}{c_4}[1 - c_4^2]^{1/2}, 0\} = \max\{0.002, 0\} = 0.002$.[12]

Example Summary

$\mu_S = \bar{s}$ = mean sample standard deviation when the process is in control and the sample size is 9 = 0.0097
The three-sigma control limits are
$\text{UCL} = \bar{s} + 3(\bar{s}/c_4)[1 - c_4^2]^{1/2} = 0.017$
$\text{LCL} = \max\{\bar{s} - 3(\bar{s}/c_4)[1 - c_4^2]^{1/2}, 0\} = 0.002$

Control Charts for Attribute Data

As noted above, an attribute control chart is used when one is interested in the occurrence of a particular attribute. Rosenbluth Travel, for example, has used control charts to help improve the process of booking and delivering tickets (Rosenbluth 1991). In this case, a relevant measure of process output is not a continuous variable such as part diameter, but the rate at which defects occur (e.g., ticketing error or late delivery). The defect rate is based on an attribute of the process output; each unit is either defective or not defective.

This section covers a type of attribute control chart known as a P-chart. **A P-chart plots the proportion of a particular attribute in each sample and is designed to detect changes that affect the frequency of the attribute.**[13] P-charts are often used for plotting the proportion of defective units, and the underlying assumption is that each unit has the same probability of being defective when the process is in control. This assumption is the basis for using the binomial probability distribution to compute control limits on a P-chart.

---

[12] A sample outside the control limits is a signal that the process is not in control, but this could be a positive sign when below the lower control limit on an R-chart or S-chart; that is, variation in process output has reduced.

[13] An alternative to a P-chart is a C-chart, which is a plot of a "count" rather than a proportion; for example, the number of defects in a sample. The underlying theory for these two charts is similar (i.e., both are based on a binomial distribution for occurrences of the attribute), and we won't take the space to cover C-chart control limit formulas (available at www.itl.nist.gov/div898/handbook/index.htm).

Imagine that a weapons factory is being built along a river in your community. Water will be used, filtered, and returned to the river. A community group is concerned about the risk of an inadequate filtration system at the factory, particularly with respect to strontium 90. Strontium 90 is a radioactive isotope that will be one by-product in the factory. It is detected in about 1 out of 20 river samples today (e.g., a consequence of fallout from atmospheric nuclear testing), so the challenge is to assess whether there is any fundamental shift after the factory becomes operational. A *P*-chart is one possible alternative for detecting change amid apparent randomness in this setting. The formulas for computing the values of CL, UCL, and LCL for a *P*-chart are listed below.

The Center Line and Control Limits for a *P*-Chart

P = random variable for the proportion of a sample of size n with the attribute

μ_P = mean of P (e.g., expected proportion with the attribute when process is in control)

σ_P = standard deviation of $P = \left[\dfrac{\mu_P(1 - \mu_P)}{n}\right]^{1/2}$

CL = center line = μ_P

UCL = upper control limit = $\mu_P + z\sigma_P$; if UCL > 1, then set UCL = 1

LCL = lower control limit = $\mu_P - z\sigma_P$; if LCL < 0, then set LCL = 0

Note: The value of z is typically set to three (i.e., three-sigma control limits).

Computing μ_P and σ_P from Historical Data

Collect N samples of process output (e.g., $N \geq 10$); the size of each sample is n

p_j = proportion of units with the attribute in the jth sample

$\bar{p}$ = average proportion = $\dfrac{1}{N}\sum_{j=1}^{N} p_j$ = estimate of μ_P

$\left[\dfrac{\bar{p}(1 - \bar{p})}{n}\right]^{1/2}$ = estimate of σ_P

CL = center line = $\mu_p = \bar{p}$

UCL = upper control limit = $\min\{\mu_P + z\sigma_P, 1\} = \min\{\bar{p} + z\left[\dfrac{\bar{p}(1 - \bar{p})}{n}\right]^{1/2}, 1\}$

LCL = lower control limit = $\max\{\mu_P - z\sigma_P, 0\} = \max\{\bar{p} - z\left[\dfrac{\bar{p}(1 - \bar{p})}{n}\right]^{1/2}, 0\}$

A Center Line and Control Limit Calculation Example   A *P*-chart can be created for the weapons factory outflow, which will soon be operational. Samples of 100 vials of water from the river have been collected every Friday for the past 15 weeks. Strontium 90 has been detected in 5 percent of these samples. The plan is to collect and plot the strontium 90 detection rate each week after the factory becomes operational. A point lying outside the control limits would be a strong signal of fundamental change in strontium 90 levels. In this example, the sample size is $n = 100$ and an estimate for the mean detection rate when the process is in control is $\mu_P = \bar{p} = 0.05$. Control limits are to be set at the three-sigma level ($z = 3$). Then CL = $\bar{p} = 0.05$, UCL = $\min\{\bar{p} + z\left[\dfrac{\bar{p}(1 - \bar{p})}{n}\right]^{1/2}, 1\}$

$= 0.05 + 3[(0.05)(0.95)/100]^{1/2} = 0.115$, and LCL = $\max\{\bar{p} - z\left[\dfrac{\bar{p}(1 - \bar{p})}{n}\right]^{1/2}, 0\} =$ $\max\{0.05 - 3[(0.05)(0.95)/100]^{1/2}, 0\} = \max\{-0.015, 0\} = 0$.

Example Summary

$\mu_p = \bar{p}$ = mean proportion of samples with strontium 90 when the process is in control = 5 percent
n = sample size = 100
The three-sigma control limits are
UCL = min$\{\bar{p} + 3[\bar{p}(1-\bar{p})/n]^{1/2}, 1\} = 0.115$
LCL = max$\{\bar{p} - 3[\bar{p}(1-\bar{p})/n]^{1/2}, 0\} = 0$

2.2. Measures of Process Capability

From the previous section, we know that control charts facilitate a cycle of improvement: the charts are useful for detecting when a process is not in control so that intervention can immediately take place, the process eventually becomes better understood and consistently under control, and a well-understood process is the foundation for new ideas on how to change the process to achieve an even higher level of capability.

This section presents two related ways in which the capability of a process can be measured. Both measures use probability concepts from the previous section to relate the output of a process with the required specifications. Specifications are limits on variation that are acceptable to the customer. For instance, consider the example from the previous section of a machine that compresses powdered metal to produce a cylindrical part. For a part to be acceptable, its diameter must be between 2.97 mm and 3.03 mm. In other words, the *lower specification limit* (LSL) for part diameter is 2.97 mm and the *upper specification limit* (USL) for part diameter is 3.03 mm. The standard deviation of part diameter when the process is in control is $\sigma_X = 0.01$ mm. The formula for the C_p process capability index is

$$C_p = \frac{\text{USL} - \text{LSL}}{6\sigma_X}$$

FIGURE 11.6   The Probability Distribution of Part Diameter and the Lower and Upper Specification Limits

Given that the process output is normally distributed with mean $\mu_X = 3.00$ and standard deviation $\sigma_X = 0.01$, approximately 99.7 percent of parts will be within specifications. The value of the C_p process capability index is 1.0.

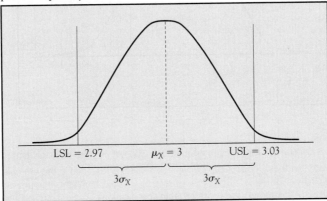

which, for this example, works out to

$$C_p = \frac{\text{USL} - \text{LSL}}{6\sigma_X} = \frac{(3.03 - 2.97)}{6(0.01)} = 1.0$$

(see Figure 11.6).[14]

As illustrated in Figure 11.6, a process with $C_p = 1.0$ corresponds to a process capable of producing within specifications 99.7 percent of the time. If $C_p < 1$, then the process is capable of producing within specifications *less* than 99.7 percent of the time. If **$C_p > 1$, then the process is capable of producing within specifications *more* than 99.7 percent of the time.** Typically, $C_p = 1$ is viewed as the benchmark for the minimum level of acceptable process capability.

The C_p process capability index is a reasonable measure of process capability when the process mean is centered within the specifications. The C_{pk} process capability index is more meaningful when the process mean is not centered within the specifications. As an example, suppose that LSL = 2.98 and USL = 3.04, but the mean and standard deviation of part diameter when the process is in control are $\mu_X = 3.00$ and $\sigma_X = 0.01$. The formula for the C_{pk} process capability index is

$$C_{pk} = \min\left\{\frac{\text{USL} - \mu_X}{3\sigma_X}, \frac{\mu_X - \text{LSL}}{3\sigma_X}\right\}$$

which, for this example, works out to

$$C_{pk} = \min\left\{\frac{\text{USL} - \mu_X}{3\sigma_X}, \frac{\mu_X - \text{LSL}}{3\sigma_X}\right\} = \min\left\{\frac{3.04 - 3}{3(0.01)}, \frac{3 - 2.98}{3(0.01)}\right\} = 0.67$$

(see Figure 11.7).[15] A value of **$C_{pk} > 1$ indicates that more than 99.7 percent of the parts are within the specifications.**

FIGURE 11.7 The Probability Distribution of Part Diameter and the Lower and Upper Specification Limits

Given that the process output is normally distributed with mean $\mu_X = 3.00$ and standard deviation $\sigma_X = 0.01$, fewer than 99.7 percent of parts will be within specifications. The value of the C_{pk} process capability index is 0.67.

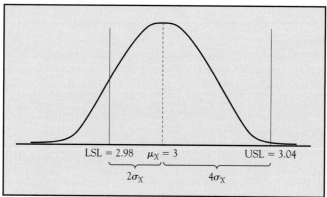

[15] Note that the C_p process capability index remains unchanged in this example; that is, $C_p = (3.04 - 2.98)/[6(0.01)] = 1.0$. The fact that $C_p = 1.0$ and $C_{pk} = 0.67$ highlights an opportunity to improve process capability by "centering" the process within specifications; that is, so that $C_p = C_{pk} = 1.0$.

In summary, C_p and C_{pk} **are measures for how effectively the outputs of a process satisfy market requirements.** In fact, some customers require that C_p or C_{pk} reports be included with shipments of product. The values of C_p and C_{pk} are identical when the process output is centered within the specifications; C_{pk} is a more meaningful indicator of capability when process output is not centered within the specifications.

Examples of Process Capability in Practice, and the Meaning of Six-Sigma Quality

As noted above, process capability indices essentially express the rate of defect-free output in terms of a number of standard deviations. A process operating at the three-sigma level (e.g., $C_{pk} = 1$), for example, means that approximately 99.7 percent of the process output is defect-free, or about 3 out of 1,000 units are defective. **A six-sigma process, on the other hand, corresponds to 3.4 defects per million.**[16] The meaning of various sigma levels of quality can be illustrated with a few processes that you may encounter in day-to-day life. For example, IRS tax advice is somewhere around 2.25-sigma (2.4 errors per 100), restaurant bills are about 3-sigma (3 errors per 1,000), payroll processing is around 3.5-sigma (4.7 errors per 10,000), and baggage handling is around 4-sigma (6.3 errors per 100,000).[17] Finally, and most important, airline safety is greater than 6-sigma, with accidents occurring in less than 3 out of 1,000,000 flights.

Beyond **a measure of quality, six-sigma is a quality improvement initiative pioneered by Motorola in the 1980s** and adopted by such firms as Bank of America, General Electric, Merrill Lynch, Microsoft, and 3M, among others. **It draws heavily on the principles and tenets of TQM (see Chapter 3) and includes the tools described in this chapter as a means to process improvement.** When executed well, six-sigma thinking pervades the entire organization, instilling an attitude and expertise for reducing variability and waste and increasing consistency in outputs via a focus on processes and inputs.

3. SUMMARY AND MANAGERIAL INSIGHTS

This chapter introduced several tools for process improvement. We began by considering tools that support diagnosis of a complex process in order to determine the most opportune areas for attention. A process diagram is a useful documentation tool to promote a high-level understanding of a complex process. Once the basic steps of the process are understood, Pareto analysis and cause-and-effect diagrams are useful to help identify where to concentrate improvement efforts.

We then considered statistical process control tools for day-to-day control and measurement that support a cycle of improvement. Statistical process control charts rely on pattern detection and probability theory to help distinguish between randomness and real change in process output. Process capability indices compare the output of a stable process with specifications to yield a measure of how well the process meets market requirements. Key managerial insights from the chapter are summarized below.

3.1. The Sum of Many Independent Random Elements Is Approximately Normally Distributed

This insight comes from the central limit theorem, which helps explain why many measures in real life appear to be normally distributed. There are occasions in business and

---

[16] The rate of 3.4 defects per million comes from upper and lower specifications that are 12 standard deviations apart, but with a process mean that is off-center (relative to specifications) by 1.5 standard deviations (e.g., $P[\mu - 7.5\sigma \le X \le \mu + 4.5\sigma] = 99.99966$ percent where X is a normal random variable).

[17] You may verify the rates in parentheses using the normal probability table in Appendix 4.

life where it is useful to have insight into the probability distribution of some measure. In some cases, there may be extensive historical data available for this purpose. In other cases, knowledge of the central limit theorem allows one to assess whether the normal probability distribution is a reasonable approximation.

3.2. Put Improvement Tools and Authority in the Hands of Those Close to the Action

Statistical process control is a tool that helps those who are actually working with a process, who, after all, are the ones who are likely in the best position to make improvements. In this sense, SPC reflects the importance of giving people the latitude they need to accomplish the tasks at hand—a notion that was not apparent to the coach in the following story.[18]

> A college football team was playing its number 1 rival. The score was tied and the first-string quarterback was benched with an injury. In the fourth quarter with less than two minutes to play and no time outs, the second-string quarterback was injured and had to leave the game. With the team deep inside its own territory, the coach sent in an inexperienced third stringer. The coach instructed the quarterback to call three simple plays and then punt the ball. As the quarterback went into the game, the coach yelled: "Don't call any other plays." The first play, a slant to the right, gained 30 yards. The second play, a slant left, gained 40. The third play, a run up the middle pushed the team to the opponent's two-yard line, for an opportunity to win the game. Then, according to instructions, the quarterback dropped back and punted the ball out of the stadium. After the game, the coach called the quarterback aside. He said: "Son, just what in the world were you thinking out there when you punted the ball?" The quarterback replied, "I was thinking I must have the stupidest coach in the world."

3.3. Quick Feedback Is Often Critical for Effective and Continual Improvement

Statistical process control is based on the insight that quick feedback is essential for process improvement. An operator using SPC has a sense of whether a process is out of control within minutes of examining the sample output of a process.

The importance of quick feedback is evident in an epiphany of a process improvement team member at Motorola. This person enjoyed bowling, and one evening at the alley, he was struck by how much the mechanics of bowling were similar to his job in the warehouse (i.e., lifting and moving objects). After thinking about why he found work to be tedious and bowling to be great fun, he concluded that a key for him was quick feedback—he saw exactly how he did moments after releasing the ball. This inspired him and his team to look for ways to provide very fast feedback at work, and his team became known as the "See the Pins" group.

4. EXERCISES

1. Write a brief answer to each of the chapter keys in your own words. After writing down your answers, review the chapter with a focus on the content in bold to check and clarify your interpretations.

2. A filling machine is used to fill one-liter bottles with soda. The output is approximately normal with a mean of 1 liter and a standard deviation of 0.01 liter. Output is monitored using a sample size of 25.

---

[18] Unknown source.

   a. Determine the center line and the upper and lower control limits for an $\overline{X}$-chart at the three-sigma level.

   b. Parameter estimates of the probability distribution of sample standard deviation are $\mu_S = 0.0099$ and $\sigma_S = 0.0014$. Determine the center line and the upper and lower control limits for an S-chart at the three-sigma level.

   c. The upper and lower specification limits are USL $= 1.02$ and LSL $= 0.98$. Compute the values of the process capability indices C_p and C_{pk}. Is the process capable?

   d. Using the values of $\mu_X = 1.00$ and $\sigma_X = 0.01$, determine the upper and lower control limits for a P-chart for the defect rate at the three-sigma level. The output from the filling machine is considered defective if the quantity of soda in a bottle is outside specifications. *Hint:* Since the output is approximately normally distributed, you can estimate the value of μ_P when the process is in control.

3. The following measurements have been taken: 4.5, 4.6, 4.5, 4.7, 4.2, 4.5, 4.6, 4.6, 4.2, 4.4, 4.4, 4.8, 4.3, 4.7, 4.4.

   a. Given that the process was in control, provide estimates of the mean and standard deviation of the process. Provide an estimate of the mean sample range (μ_R) given a sample size of five.

   b. Determine the center line and control limits for an $\overline{X}$-chart and an R-chart at the three-sigma level. The sample size is five.

4. A sample of 50 parts has a mean of 25.3. The standard deviation is estimated at 1.02. Calculate the two-sigma control limits on an $\overline{X}$-chart. The sample size is 10. What percent of the sample means should fall within the control limits when the process is in control?

5. What factors might one consider when deciding between the use of two-sigma and three-sigma control limits?

6. What is the range of the following sample: 45.8, 32.7, 45.0, 42.8, 43.6? What is the smallest possible value for a lower control limit on a range chart? What are the upper and lower control limits at the three-sigma level given $\bar{r} = 3.02$ and $n = 5$?

7. If a process is "in control," is it producing product that is within specifications?

8. Besides the benefits relating to early detection of potential quality problems, can you identify other benefits of control charts? What are some disadvantages?

9. Why are sample means plotted on an $\overline{X}$ control chart (i.e., why not set up a control chart for individual values instead of sample means)?

10. This and the following exercise are variations of questions prepared by Linus Schrage. The Vollman Manufacturing Company produces ball bearings over a wide range of sizes. At the moment, Vollman is having informal discussions with a space agency contractor regarding a potential order for high-precision bearings. It seems clear that Vollman's performance in meeting tolerances must be improved in order to win and make a profit on this possible order. A question is whether this can be accomplished by doing a better job using its current technology, or whether it has to switch to new technology. In particular, Vollman is concerned about whether it should do a careful study of its current production methods to see if there is some systematic variability that is a candidate for eradication. The crucial tolerances are on the outer raceway of the bearing. Below are listed measurements taken from the last sequence of outer raceways produced. The ordering is from left to right and then down. For simplicity, the numbers have already been normalized by subtracting off the smallest value and are scaled by 100.

Sample 1	32	48	03	00	20
Sample 2	28	38	48	20	37
Sample 3	57	58	68	10	49
Sample 4	68	78	82	94	86
Sample 5	48	55	52	78	59
Sample 6	10	96	06	09	49
Sample 7	26	69	44	60	69
Sample 8	63	54	62	47	68
Sample 9	62	67	51	25	16
Sample 10	66	55	60	10	47

a. The lower and upper specifications are 0 and 80. Use the first 15 observations as a basis for computing C_{pk}. Why would C_p be a less-accurate measure of process capability in this example?

b. Use $\overline{X}$-chart and R-chart analysis to decide if there is potential for improving performance simply by doing a better job of managing the current technology. Use the first 15 observations to determine the three-sigma control limits for the control charts.

11. At the Tivoli Gardens amusement park in Copenhagen, you may find the following little game of chance. Nine balls are dropped at once into a container, the bottom of which is partitioned into six compartments labeled 1, 2, . . . , 6. Five minutes of observation support the hypothesis that the compartments are equally likely. Each compartment can easily accommodate nine balls. Your score is the sum over compartments of the number of balls in the compartment times the label of the compartment. Thus, your score ranges from 9 to 54. An interesting feature of the game is that the lady who operates it can compute the score in under two seconds. You win if and only if your score is less than 23 or more than 40. What is the probability of winning? (*Hint:* If X is a random variable that has an equal chance of taking on values 1, 2, . . . , m, then $\mu_X = (m + 1)/2$ and $\sigma_X^2 = (m^2 - 1)/12$.)

12. You have invented a gasoline pump that fills up the tank without the driver's getting out of the car. In order to evaluate consistency, you run some tests on cars requiring 10 gallons. Your machine output is approximately normal with a mean of 10 gallons and a standard deviation of 0.1 gallon. Use a sample size of 16 cars.

a. What are the two-sigma control limits on an $\overline{X}$-chart ?

b. What are the three-sigma control limits on an $\overline{X}$-chart?

13. You receive a strange memo. The numbers 8.1, 8.2, 7.8, 6.9, 7.4, 7.7, 8.2, 8.4, 7.9, 8.0, 7.1, 7.9, 8.2, 7.5, 8.2, 7.0 are written on it . . . nothing else. Determine the sample range, the sample mean, and the sample standard deviation.

14. For a particular measurement, you know the standard deviation is 2.14, the two-sigma upper control limit is 33.07, and the sample size is 16. Would you bet $100 that you could find the mean when the process is in control? If so, what is the mean? If not, why?

15. You are the operator of a machine that produces baseball caps. All hats are a single size, 7¾". When the process is under control, the standard deviation of hat sizes is   ". Furthermore, one cap is produced about every four minutes. Machine capacity is 20 caps per hour, the arrival process is Poisson, and machine output is normally distributed. If you were to sample one hour's worth of output (i.e., sample size is set to the average production per hour), what would be the three-sigma control limits on an $\overline{X}$-chart?

16. A gravel loading process provides a truck with about one-half ton of product per hopper. Over the past several days, data have been captured about this stable process. On the basis of the following observations, determine the control limits for an $\overline{X}$-chart, an R-chart, and an S-chart, each at the three-sigma level.

	Observations			
Sample	**1**	**2**	**3**	**4**
1	1,010	991	985	986
2	995	996	1,009	994
3	990	1,003	1,015	1,008
4	1,015	1,020	1,009	998
5	1,013	1,019	1,005	993
6	994	1,001	994	1,005
7	989	992	982	1,020
8	1,001	986	996	996
9	1,006	989	1,005	1,007
10	992	1,007	1,006	979
11	996	1,006	997	989
12	1,019	996	991	1,011
13	981	991	989	1,003
14	999	993	988	984
15	1,013	1,002	1,005	992

Case Exercise: *RR Logistics*

In hindsight, it is clear that significant change affecting supply chain processes occurred in late fall 2004 at Sanchez Coffee. However, it wasn't until two major accounts switched to a competitor in February 2005 that the seriousness of the problem was fully recognized by management.

BACKGROUND ON THE BUSINESS

Sanchez Coffee is the largest and oldest provider of coffee to commercial customers in the southwestern United States, with over 10,000 accounts. The business is divided into standard and full-service accounts. Standard accounts include restaurants, hotels, and other food service institutions that purchase ground coffee. Full-service accounts, which make up about 20 percent of total revenue, are typically convenience stores and cafés. For these accounts, Sanchez provides and maintains equipment for brewing and dispensing coffee at the location, assumes responsibility for coffee inventory, and is paid according to coffee consumption.

THE SUPPLY CHAIN

The supply chain and associated processes at Sanchez are relatively simple. There is a single facility located in Tucson, Arizona, for blending, roasting, grinding, packaging, and storage. The primary purchased items are green coffee beans and materials used for packaging. Coffee buyers purchase green beans directly from growers in Central America, Africa, and Indonesia. Packaging material is supplied by two vendors, one located in Maine and the other in Ontario. Sanchez uses

truck, and primarily LTL, for delivery to standard accounts. Sanchez relies on an outside firm for deliveries and other responsibilities associated with the full-service accounts.

A HISTORY OF CUSTOMER FOCUS AND FEEDBACK

The founder, Paul Sanchez, emphasized close relationships with customers from the firm's beginning in 1936. He traveled to each customer at least once per month, and he knew each one on a personal basis. He listened to complaints and suggestions, and discussed ideas for improving the value of Sanchez's offerings. Sanchez had his hand on the pulse of the market.[19] Over time, the company grew and this time-intensive approach became less practical, but the culture of customer focus remained. In 1995, Sanchez implemented a formal process for collecting customer feedback. Each week, 20 random customers complete a brief survey on the value of Sanchez's product and service. Comments are recorded, and a composite score, called a *customer satisfaction index,* is computed for each survey. Survey results are widely distributed throughout the company.

A CHALLENGE INTERPRETING SURVEY RESULTS

Table 1 contains survey results over the last three years (the data are available in the Excel file "RR Logistics.xls"). The high degree of variation in the scores within and between weeks makes it challenging to interpret the results. In fact, the "randomness"

---

[19] In fact, Sanchez Coffee is an example of a firm that embodied elements of total quality management (i.e., customer focus and a view that quality is measured relative to customer expectations) before the ideas of TQM were first described in the literature in the 1950s.

TABLE 1   Customer Satisfaction Indices from 2002 to 2005

Twenty random customers are surveyed each week.

Week Starting	Customer Satisfaction Indices by Random Customer in a Week																			
	1	2	3	4	5	6	7	8	9	10	11	12	13	14	15	16	17	18	19	20
1/6/02	55.0	51.8	97.1	72.5	81.5	74.0	72.8	100.0	74.8	76.4	70.8	73.1	76.9	86.0	74.0	79.3	70.3	72.8	80.1	72.8
1/13/02	69.4	74.1	63.4	69.7	63.0	68.9	80.7	61.9	69.6	69.4	69.1	67.8	69.4	57.8	64.5	76.3	69.4	72.2	51.2	97.2
1/20/02	65.0	65.3	70.5	65.3	48.6	55.9	65.3	60.6	72.6	65.3	65.3	53.3	65.3	65.3	51.4	65.3	65.3	66.7	59.1	50.6
1/27/02	56.6	75.7	60.8	36.8	56.5	71.2	58.7	61.8	60.3	61.0	64.9	67.1	71.8	56.2	61.0	66.6	56.4	69.2	71.8	61.0
2/3/02	79.2	57.7	56.0	67.1	75.5	68.2	67.1	68.1	58.0	87.8	67.1	69.4	70.3	66.0	59.0	63.1	72.5	63.7	64.0	79.4
2/10/02	69.2	94.4	63.6	69.2	69.2	69.2	78.5	52.7	67.2	60.9	72.6	91.1	53.6	49.9	81.5	73.3	56.2	83.3	69.2	57.5
2/17/02	66.0	53.2	63.1	64.3	71.6	85.3	63.7	53.4	63.7	60.4	63.7	71.7	85.6	64.6	52.5	63.7	63.7	69.7	40.1	69.7
2/24/02	83.6	90.6	84.1	59.2	76.6	80.9	78.0	79.5	83.9	81.5	82.2	92.0	72.3	74.6	76.6	76.6	73.8	86.8	84.4	59.7
3/3/02	89.0	75.5	76.6	60.4	76.7	78.1	86.4	76.6	62.5	72.0	91.1	70.8	81.1	59.1	100.0	73.2	68.7	59.8	69.5	79.8
3/10/02	70.4	84.7	78.2	69.9	65.0	65.0	66.7	63.1	65.0	49.9	63.7	65.0	66.5	63.4	81.7	65.0	79.6	65.0	79.0	63.7
3/17/02	52.6	65.3	63.0	67.0	60.1	64.0	82.6	35.9	48.7	64.2	57.2	63.1	64.0	54.7	80.2	41.9	77.2	64.0	65.3	69.2
3/24/02	64.0	64.0	68.6	72.8	56.2	79.2	83.7	70.1	50.9	67.2	59.6	59.6	61.9	62.1	53.2	60.1	66.3	51.2	51.0	76.9
3/31/02	85.1	88.0	79.4	69.2	100.0	86.7	82.2	80.0	88.0	80.0	86.0	78.6	77.8	86.2	89.9	67.8	65.8	70.8	69.9	61.4
4/7/02	70.0	55.9	70.0	68.1	42.9	63.2	71.4	72.5	71.3	63.1	70.0	73.1	74.5	65.8	83.4	70.3	71.6	70.0	73.5	70.0
4/14/02	84.7	88.5	88.4	77.5	74.1	77.5	83.0	91.0	74.8	92.6	77.5	75.2	72.5	74.2	82.2	69.6	73.3	76.0	67.1	83.7
4/21/02	90.6	75.4	72.4	73.9	68.3	73.9	59.3	51.3	80.3	78.6	73.9	60.7	93.1	78.1	84.0	87.3	73.9	73.9	73.9	73.9
4/28/02	95.2	75.6	96.3	78.8	83.9	64.9	63.8	70.1	75.4	75.5	78.5	70.3	78.8	85.9	96.2	82.9	89.2	80.7	83.4	56.8
5/5/02	57.4	73.9	64.0	86.3	62.9	68.9	71.6	59.1	78.2	85.2	75.3	80.6	89.6	70.2	80.6	85.7	80.9	52.8	71.5	64.7
5/12/02	60.9	56.9	64.0	86.9	61.5	64.9	66.7	89.6	57.9	53.4	64.0	77.7	64.0	64.0	40.6	41.4	64.0	51.7	86.0	62.6
5/19/02	75.4	69.8	69.4	83.6	75.4	64.9	92.7	64.9	73.9	79.4	88.8	75.2	80.3	59.0	78.4	81.0	79.0	65.7	75.4	73.6
5/26/02	80.9	79.3	84.0	68.7	88.7	83.2	63.3	72.2	63.5	60.2	82.5	68.8	66.7	74.4	60.8	76.4	60.1	75.6	71.3	66.1
6/2/02	73.7	82.4	82.4	69.3	72.9	91.6	88.6	57.5	73.9	77.0	84.5	67.9	91.9	68.4	90.3	82.4	100.0	82.4	100.0	100.0
6/9/02	45.1	56.9	73.0	78.9	53.8	85.0	74.3	82.9	65.9	56.5	60.6	72.8	67.5	76.1	60.1	58.9	64.9	77.1	59.6	71.8
6/16/02	88.8	84.1	73.5	85.2	95.0	83.6	83.6	54.5	83.6	83.6	83.6	76.6	92.4	81.2	90.1	79.7	67.1	94.7	100.0	83.6
6/23/02	77.0	68.8	77.9	69.9	67.6	82.7	71.5	63.2	60.1	63.2	60.7	80.5	74.3	69.4	72.5	67.6	67.6	74.2	67.6	60.9
6/30/02	67.6	67.6	67.6	63.2	67.6	59.3	95.0	67.6	67.6	60.3	56.0	67.6	55.5	66.4	64.9	67.6	68.5	62.0	79.1	54.9
7/7/02	84.4	93.4	84.3	86.4	87.0	80.9	80.4	86.3	71.4	96.0	88.5	84.2	83.0	82.1	85.3	74.8	90.3	93.0	83.9	84.4
7/14/02	71.9	69.9	69.9	57.8	69.9	53.6	60.6	56.9	78.2	69.9	69.9	66.1	68.5	72.2	69.9	71.3	70.6	62.9	67.3	63.6
7/21/02	74.0	62.5	69.5	75.5	77.0	77.4	77.0	100.0	71.0	71.0	83.0	61.5	69.7	77.0	78.4	77.0	79.3	83.4	58.0	78.6
7/28/02	69.9	73.2	68.1	73.2	69.9	68.4	76.7	74.4	59.8	75.5	75.6	62.6	74.1	63.6	66.0	67.1	79.2	84.2	77.0	67.4
8/4/02	94.4	80.1	87.8	77.3	70.6	79.1	88.3	89.9	97.3	80.1	61.9	80.1	73.2	91.4	95.5	57.9	80.1	80.1	74.0	97.7
8/11/02	66.4	74.3	79.7	80.6	62.5	89.8	92.4	62.5	63.5	58.5	64.7	84.5	61.7	72.5	61.7	81.6	69.7	74.3	83.0	85.3
8/18/02	80.5	74.7	73.8	77.3	82.3	74.6	78.6	82.2	80.5	100.0	91.9	65.3	80.5	81.6	76.2	66.6	80.5	89.6	72.3	58.9
8/25/02	82.2	70.4	84.4	93.3	81.8	88.9	67.4	80.6	89.3	80.0	74.9	82.5	71.4	63.7	75.6	64.1	63.1	84.9	78.3	89.2
9/1/02	80.9	83.7	66.1	71.3	77.5	88.9	88.9	92.7	79.6	83.9	80.6	76.6	84.9	97.4	100.0	80.8	81.1	98.8	82.8	82.6
9/8/02	96.9	79.7	86.3	71.3	72.3	71.3	73.9	71.2	81.3	68.5	61.9	72.3	86.8	69.9	73.6	71.7	58.5	77.6	71.3	60.9
9/15/02	80.7	81.8	77.9	80.0	82.9	78.7	74.6	82.9	74.5	82.9	96.6	84.3	95.5	82.9	88.0	82.9	64.5	84.7	86.4	78.1
9/22/02	75.6	73.2	70.7	70.7	92.7	73.2	81.9	78.7	81.0	74.6	79.5	74.4	87.3	89.6	45.8	64.1	67.7	84.9	63.6	59.0
9/29/02	73.1	76.4	73.1	73.1	60.3	75.8	73.1	79.0	69.6	61.8	80.5	73.1	66.3	60.9	66.1	67.0	54.9	78.5	69.1	76.1
10/6/02	58.8	70.1	71.3	81.8	75.4	70.1	51.4	69.3	81.9	88.0	73.4	84.6	70.4	74.1	74.0	64.1	88.6	71.5	50.9	67.3
10/13/02	92.2	90.7	100.0	93.2	86.5	89.1	86.5	91.3	75.4	78.0	86.5	94.3	90.2	67.8	86.5	99.8	71.1	86.5	81.4	67.4
10/20/02	67.2	61.8	81.3	54.1	85.0	68.6	68.6	62.0	57.0	67.3	78.1	68.6	68.6	68.6	80.4	66.1	68.6	68.9	68.6	58.0
10/27/02	74.3	63.5	74.3	85.4	88.3	85.6	73.1	74.6	74.3	85.1	83.7	74.3	72.0	61.0	74.3	60.3	79.2	69.8	74.3	74.3
11/3/02	79.2	60.4	79.1	88.8	76.4	83.2	72.4	76.4	89.1	76.4	76.1	61.9	76.4	89.8	76.4	86.5	67.2	89.9	73.9	76.4
11/10/02	83.3	99.6	87.3	100.0	64.9	68.4	83.3	67.8	100.0	75.2	83.1	79.6	69.4	80.5	78.8	87.5	83.3	72.7	77.2	83.3
11/17/02	78.3	87.2	71.1	77.7	81.6	79.7	60.3	67.6	72.6	80.5	100.0	76.1	74.1	79.7	77.5	72.6	78.6	64.6	61.9	69.6
11/24/02	71.1	78.6	40.6	56.7	66.8	71.2	80.8	72.9	84.5	89.2	69.7	64.3	76.2	82.5	64.5	65.3	52.4	66.8	79.9	70.4
12/1/02	72.1	72.1	65.6	84.0	63.4	90.2	81.2	76.3	64.7	72.1	73.9	75.4	72.1	70.7	79.3	65.2	62.0	73.5	77.7	79.8
12/8/02	73.3	72.6	73.3	64.1	73.3	73.3	73.3	84.0	73.3	82.8	65.0	65.4	75.6	70.0	86.3	73.3	73.3	68.2	83.6
12/15/02	75.4	70.1	71.3	52.4	73.3	63.3	51.5	71.3	76.1	81.5	75.9	71.3	85.0	71.3	76.7	71.6	71.3	62.5	68.7	71.3
12/22/02	76.9	73.1	90.7	72.1	74.7	65.9	74.4	72.1	79.4	75.4	63.0	65.7	80.9	72.1	65.4	76.8	51.6	71.2	75.7	60.0
12/29/02	79.7	76.7	84.3	66.2	81.9	62.0	73.6	72.0	56.4	80.6	91.3	88.6	72.0	72.0	72.5	72.0	67.3	72.0	71.2	81.0
1/5/03	57.3	46.7	64.5	81.9	70.7	56.5	74.5	62.4	67.2	70.7	70.7	70.7	77.2	70.7	70.7	81.2	67.9	71.6	70.7	67.6
1/12/03	85.7	90.2	78.0	83.0	99.7	78.6	100.0	76.9	83.0	86.2	64.7	83.0	81.2	83.0	83.0	83.8	93.2	82.9	80.6	96.2
1/19/03	76.1	75.0	75.2	83.8	50.7	76.1	78.8	76.1	81.9	75.5	76.5	66.5	92.7	75.0	77.7	86.1	70.1	87.6	76.1	76.1
1/26/03	74.2	68.6	83.8	67.9	79.0	62.2	68.1	82.6	72.1	78.3	78.0	81.1	56.1	68.9	53.6	74.2	74.2	63.5	74.0	65.8
2/2/03	85.0	76.5	74.5	89.3	84.3	84.6	76.2	73.8	94.3	81.3	71.7	81.3	92.6	85.5	82.6	81.3	81.3	60.5	89.3	78.2

Week Starting	1	2	3	4	5	6	7	8	9	10	11	12	13	14	15	16	17	18	19	20

Customer Satisfaction Indices by Random Customer in a Week

Week Starting	1	2	3	4	5	6	7	8	9	10	11	12	13	14	15	16	17	18	19	20
2/9/03	93.0	67.3	89.9	100.0	93.9	86.6	96.5	86.6	86.6	86.6	86.6	79.7	95.4	98.5	89.9	85.5	98.4	95.5	86.6	86.6
2/16/03	80.0	87.3	91.9	78.9	88.4	87.3	81.9	93.0	87.3	100.0	80.9	87.3	100.0	87.3	69.2	87.3	89.6	86.4	85.9	88.4
2/23/03	79.0	55.9	68.0	64.6	69.9	72.1	82.2	77.8	72.1	81.7	80.4	55.9	61.6	54.9	66.2	58.2	81.2	72.8	77.8	83.2
3/2/03	74.9	74.9	74.9	65.9	76.5	92.1	74.9	74.9	100.0	57.4	74.9	83.0	90.4	93.4	78.7	89.2	65.4	74.9	85.8	79.0
3/9/03	65.7	75.0	81.9	100.0	100.0	65.7	88.6	77.9	92.7	79.7	80.6	89.6	88.3	95.2	88.3	71.2	83.4	88.3	88.3	100.0
3/16/03	76.8	88.8	88.8	85.9	88.8	78.5	78.6	88.8	91.8	98.4	75.3	88.8	92.7	100.0	93.8	88.8	88.8	79.3	91.6	100.0
3/23/03	93.6	97.4	80.8	67.7	80.8	75.8	80.8	80.8	82.9	80.8	64.1	80.8	87.2	100.0	87.2	89.5	78.9	71.9	86.2	87.5
3/30/03	100.0	92.5	75.9	84.3	68.8	63.1	82.7	81.1	79.8	78.1	100.0	72.1	73.7	64.2	87.0	51.6	100.0	74.6	88.6	76.1
4/6/03	95.7	69.5	81.2	81.2	81.2	74.7	68.2	79.5	62.0	81.2	81.2	74.0	74.3	81.2	90.1	79.6	81.2	75.1	81.2	100.0
4/13/03	72.8	67.8	77.2	80.2	100.0	79.6	82.7	82.7	91.7	81.7	97.3	91.8	86.9	82.7	77.2	88.7	82.7	82.7	82.7	100.0
4/20/03	100.0	100.0	86.2	75.0	89.2	77.6	87.8	76.2	76.8	100.0	87.8	84.2	88.6	76.7	70.9	83.9	87.2	78.8	89.1	87.8
4/27/03	78.2	87.7	84.3	78.0	84.9	84.3	88.8	84.3	84.3	87.9	75.2	74.3	78.3	100.0	96.3	80.0	86.6	87.1	75.7	88.6
5/4/03	79.4	60.8	77.6	72.1	87.4	77.2	68.3	81.2	74.5	76.7	77.6	77.6	85.8	52.5	91.7	80.9	76.0	79.7	73.7	68.0
5/11/03	75.6	78.6	89.2	82.8	82.8	83.0	81.2	75.4	73.5	70.6	77.2	70.4	93.6	74.4	89.6	73.6	76.5	82.8	69.1	67.6
5/18/03	76.7	76.7	76.7	88.3	76.7	87.7	90.1	82.7	76.7	76.7	86.9	76.7	73.1	75.8	76.7	76.7	74.6	76.7	79.1	81.4
5/25/03	63.6	80.7	71.7	79.4	87.8	73.1	79.4	91.9	79.4	62.5	66.3	91.2	79.5	76.1	71.0	83.9	82.6	79.4	74.8	75.9
6/1/03	82.8	85.0	72.9	87.6	86.5	74.6	61.6	100.0	82.8	95.7	52.2	82.8	82.8	82.8	89.0	84.6	99.4	72.8	82.8	82.8
6/8/03	83.2	75.9	89.3	96.5	83.2	82.0	77.8	79.3	81.9	83.2	89.4	81.9	83.2	77.2	83.2	100.0	87.8	90.7	83.2	86.0
6/15/03	86.6	87.0	81.3	79.0	80.7	81.3	89.7	82.9	81.3	86.1	92.1	81.3	81.3	82.0	76.3	78.9	81.3	93.7	68.1	81.3
6/22/03	87.2	74.0	100.0	83.5	51.9	73.7	82.7	74.0	83.5	62.2	91.5	88.0	81.6	71.8	87.8	74.0	93.6	59.6	74.0	87.4
6/29/03	69.2	72.1	61.5	72.0	95.3	74.0	64.5	63.1	72.1	77.3	66.1	67.5	72.1	70.5	67.8	72.1	68.9	68.5	72.1	73.2
7/6/03	86.0	83.5	86.0	69.8	86.0	86.0	84.8	90.1	82.2	79.0	77.5	100.0	76.6	75.5	98.1	86.0	100.0	57.1	77.2	90.9
7/13/03	65.3	97.0	77.9	79.7	79.7	79.3	79.7	64.4	65.0	61.0	79.7	79.7	70.1	69.6	79.7	57.8	80.2	78.6	72.4	77.8
7/20/03	78.5	71.4	78.2	71.2	80.7	73.0	78.5	81.6	90.8	71.7	73.3	89.3	67.2	79.6	80.7	70.1	75.5	83.9	67.0	95.9
7/27/03	88.9	86.8	93.3	79.9	98.8	86.0	69.9	89.8	82.4	93.9	81.0	70.8	89.6	100.0	88.8	81.7	73.7	82.4	83.4	80.9
8/3/03	85.6	89.5	87.2	92.0	85.6	78.2	92.3	85.6	85.6	84.8	100.0	79.2	70.7	75.6	84.5	74.5	85.6	97.5	78.7	82.5
8/10/03	55.9	71.9	76.4	74.1	73.9	74.1	74.1	83.6	70.6	73.2	73.3	74.1	66.7	80.5	76.7	77.7	75.7	68.1	69.1	74.1
8/17/03	69.9	78.8	80.8	80.8	78.3	73.7	89.1	82.1	96.1	80.8	80.8	80.8	94.8	71.9	85.2	67.0	88.3	80.8	75.1	85.5
8/24/03	89.7	76.8	66.0	70.5	76.8	64.2	66.5	79.9	67.9	67.9	76.8	68.0	88.9	80.6	83.6	81.2	72.7	76.8	63.3	67.9
8/31/03	75.3	87.1	74.2	81.3	53.9	75.3	75.2	86.7	72.6	83.7	85.3	58.1	91.2	75.0	72.9	75.3	75.3	64.1	88.9	66.0
9/7/03	72.0	81.3	73.6	69.8	78.4	62.1	78.4	84.8	94.7	78.4	99.5	73.8	78.4	89.1	100.0	78.4	81.8	100.0	71.1	75.3
9/14/03	85.7	96.4	83.2	69.9	85.7	85.7	64.2	65.6	99.1	86.3	75.5	87.9	92.1	91.6	87.8	91.0	97.8	97.5	73.0	85.7
9/21/03	74.1	81.5	85.6	76.5	88.5	86.5	93.6	90.3	81.5	81.5	97.8	81.5	68.8	82.5	81.5	72.9	85.2	71.2	90.5	84.9
9/28/03	95.7	74.4	83.0	76.4	83.7	83.8	95.2	91.2	100.0	88.9	83.8	73.5	83.8	86.1	74.2	79.4	83.8	62.1	94.4	83.8
10/5/03	71.7	73.5	62.8	71.2	49.6	57.9	84.7	77.9	84.2	79.9	77.9	77.9	73.8	70.3	77.9	82.4	84.6	76.0	97.2	92.3
10/12/03	81.9	84.3	79.5	84.3	87.9	90.2	81.1	84.3	85.7	73.0	84.3	79.7	85.1	72.1	74.8	84.9	93.8	84.3	70.8	69.6
10/19/03	64.4	65.9	74.9	57.7	58.1	72.4	78.9	65.1	64.7	71.2	63.5	88.3	73.9	78.6	71.2	75.1	79.2	70.8	67.9	63.4
10/26/03	78.8	64.2	82.5	72.2	72.5	82.1	72.5	80.1	88.5	67.7	72.6	83.6	72.5	61.9	72.5	64.0	64.8	72.5	75.0	72.5
11/2/03	57.4	78.7	61.5	78.0	100.0	49.9	74.7	74.8	100.0	56.9	85.2	79.3	64.8	84.9	59.3	82.6	94.6	75.6	56.6	62.5
11/9/03	75.4	63.7	75.4	75.4	75.4	72.4	75.4	75.4	93.5	88.8	75.4	69.1	62.9	99.8	63.1	82.6	100.0	76.0	83.8	79.1
11/16/03	88.3	75.5	64.9	75.5	75.5	55.1	84.7	73.4	75.5	96.4	64.3	75.5	72.8	80.9	53.8	67.8	55.3	74.0	86.1	71.6
11/23/03	59.9	72.7	77.4	87.2	83.1	80.2	68.9	57.8	70.7	88.3	57.9	91.3	77.4	100.0	83.6	77.4	77.4	61.7	68.3	57.3
11/30/03	62.8	65.4	79.8	64.0	85.8	63.6	79.0	66.9	79.0	81.9	77.2	79.0	91.9	67.2	82.5	81.5	74.9	97.7	76.6	79.1
12/7/03	74.3	55.0	56.5	66.9	53.4	84.5	83.9	70.8	70.8	61.3	70.8	96.5	81.3	67.1	69.0	76.0	67.9	83.4	75.7	65.0
12/14/03	77.1	79.5	83.4	59.0	81.5	70.8	76.1	67.0	58.1	70.8	72.1	75.0	68.8	69.3	79.4	80.6	76.3	89.9	70.8	65.8
12/21/03	53.1	73.1	74.4	55.8	74.4	45.5	83.5	71.4	89.9	65.2	62.4	76.4	78.3	64.6	75.7	77.3	77.8	79.2	54.5	68.5
12/28/03	84.1	82.4	85.5	77.9	98.7	81.3	72.4	81.3	84.2	81.9	100.0	55.8	86.5	81.3	93.3	67.5	96.9	81.3	48.0	86.6
1/4/04	93.3	88.4	94.1	86.8	83.8	72.9	83.8	83.8	83.8	81.3	90.6	92.9	88.9	88.9	83.8	83.8	85.3	77.0	71.6	78.7
1/11/04	87.6	89.9	72.3	87.0	78.9	89.8	97.0	75.5	83.5	100.0	84.1	77.6	96.9	87.0	82.2	96.9	84.3	87.0	100.0	92.9
1/18/04	69.3	70.7	70.7	72.0	60.8	59.6	66.3	70.7	70.7	70.7	63.5	74.2	70.7	68.1	70.7	69.7	60.8	63.0	57.5	73.2
1/25/04	79.3	73.3	82.2	77.4	81.2	67.5	76.7	71.4	75.0	80.2	65.3	84.0	52.4	75.0	76.1	73.6	64.2	91.3	74.1	74.2
2/1/04	73.9	91.8	83.4	77.6	73.1	83.3	77.6	77.6	75.5	77.6	77.6	80.7	77.6	77.6	69.4	77.6	71.3	77.6	82.3	71.3
2/8/04	83.8	84.4	87.6	82.6	82.6	80.1	78.6	82.6	80.8	72.8	81.2	73.3	85.2	62.2	82.6	85.0	85.8	82.6	92.5	71.3
2/15/04	92.2	81.9	92.3	95.9	80.3	81.9	74.9	98.4	78.7	96.7	57.3	81.9	86.2	81.8	84.2	81.9	91.2	73.3	69.5	82.9
2/22/04	89.6	86.2	81.7	86.0	82.8	100.0	85.4	97.7	89.6	79.2	80.7	78.8	92.7	91.3	85.3	90.6	89.6	80.0	96.1	92.3
2/29/04	75.8	56.2	73.0	71.0	67.3	72.1	71.0	71.0	81.0	66.4	71.0	67.0	71.0	63.9	71.0	67.8	72.8	86.5	67.1	72.2
3/7/04	75.0	65.7	72.4	63.3	62.8	84.2	78.4	75.8	72.4	75.4	72.5	80.4	49.4	59.0	65.1	72.4	61.6	64.4	73.7	78.7
3/14/04	56.7	77.5	66.7	77.5	67.6	81.3	59.5	79.4	63.4	72.0	67.6	53.9	70.9	76.2	52.3	100.0	96.5	76.1	73.2	66.9
3/21/04	72.2	48.2	100.0	70.1	85.0	85.2	59.2	59.5	72.2	89.0	72.2	72.2	72.2	72.2	71.9	75.4	60.5	79.7	55.9	57.3
3/28/04	68.6	72.5	72.5	79.6	78.9	88.1	79.0	72.5	77.2	62.8	82.8	72.5	64.5	74.1	82.2	72.5	56.6	66.5	68.8	72.5

(Continued)

TABLE 1   (*Continued*)

Week Starting	Customer Satisfaction Indices by Random Customer in a Week																			
	1	2	3	4	5	6	7	8	9	10	11	12	13	14	15	16	17	18	19	20
4/4/04	82.0	100.0	83.2	75.9	84.6	75.9	75.9	76.4	65.1	81.1	69.1	78.1	75.9	76.0	100.0	87.1	75.9	75.9	80.0	86.8
4/11/04	82.9	73.9	82.4	81.8	82.9	84.7	71.8	69.0	66.0	82.9	83.0	80.8	82.9	71.4	85.4	90.9	79.3	69.9	90.3	82.9
4/18/04	81.2	61.3	79.6	78.7	78.7	75.3	65.0	84.9	81.6	69.8	78.7	67.4	78.7	88.8	79.9	70.4	75.3	77.6	79.2	81.5
4/25/04	79.7	74.8	87.4	95.3	74.9	93.4	79.7	81.5	97.0	89.4	61.5	97.4	79.7	79.7	81.7	83.1	92.6	70.6	67.3	73.5
5/2/04	74.7	90.2	87.5	78.4	79.0	92.4	73.2	78.1	80.0	89.8	78.4	78.4	70.0	63.9	78.4	81.0	85.5	81.1	78.4	75.3
5/9/04	76.6	92.1	83.3	83.9	94.4	83.2	84.7	87.1	67.1	80.7	82.3	84.5	86.5	84.9	85.2	83.8	84.6	83.2	93.6	89.0
5/16/04	78.3	78.3	80.9	67.4	88.1	80.0	80.3	71.3	99.1	78.3	72.5	85.5	69.2	63.2	87.2	78.3	82.5	69.5	78.3	75.8
5/23/04	69.6	71.3	71.9	63.3	71.3	71.3	71.3	62.1	70.7	79.0	63.0	79.5	74.1	70.3	73.2	75.4	61.7	70.6	82.6	71.3
5/30/04	76.0	71.3	81.4	59.7	78.5	92.4	85.6	73.5	77.0	74.8	77.6	81.2	81.2	85.7	82.0	98.6	78.3	65.3	80.7	83.7
6/6/04	87.6	77.1	72.7	77.8	93.9	77.8	82.9	77.8	68.8	96.1	77.6	84.0	78.2	60.9	76.5	87.2	83.3	66.9	58.6	89.6
6/13/04	73.1	78.8	78.7	79.4	72.9	88.1	79.4	78.2	78.4	69.6	79.4	79.4	83.7	99.6	96.5	98.4	79.3	82.4	79.4	86.6
6/20/04	81.1	83.0	63.2	71.4	47.6	73.1	70.9	71.4	55.4	59.5	71.1	73.1	60.2	73.1	70.4	87.6	66.8	65.0	73.1	68.0
6/27/04	93.7	86.7	80.1	80.1	80.1	81.8	91.5	80.1	80.1	80.1	84.7	80.1	81.2	77.4	80.1	87.5	93.4	86.2	80.1	83.7
7/4/04	72.9	64.4	95.7	72.3	74.1	74.1	74.1	80.4	68.7	74.1	66.2	70.7	58.9	73.2	78.1	66.1	68.7	77.0	62.5	83.9
7/11/04	82.3	76.5	52.2	68.8	74.0	91.4	81.1	76.5	68.7	76.5	76.5	76.5	76.5	65.0	55.8	76.5	65.3	70.0	85.7	76.4
7/18/04	91.6	100.0	74.0	70.5	66.6	86.6	77.2	94.5	92.4	87.7	97.5	53.2	100.0	81.7	86.6	100.0	87.7	100.0	92.7	71.7
7/25/04	70.9	65.5	73.6	60.8	65.2	83.6	80.5	81.6	75.7	70.5	68.9	61.7	72.5	78.8	56.0	70.9	77.9	64.0	74.9	73.2
8/1/04	92.3	86.6	86.6	72.1	86.6	86.6	97.9	86.6	80.6	69.4	93.8	84.6	88.8	72.9	86.3	78.7	77.9	87.4	80.2	84.8
8/8/04	76.8	77.0	76.8	90.8	68.4	84.3	70.5	96.6	85.1	72.9	65.4	76.8	81.3	76.0	69.0	81.9	95.6	75.1	77.3	80.8
8/15/04	85.8	80.8	83.7	80.6	80.6	80.7	73.1	80.6	89.6	80.6	71.3	80.6	100.0	62.5	68.1	59.4	67.3	74.2	82.3	79.7
8/22/04	78.3	80.3	86.0	89.4	66.2	76.9	99.6	82.3	83.0	87.7	89.6	60.8	85.9	76.9	90.8	76.9	76.9	76.9	60.9	71.6
8/29/04	85.6	65.4	69.8	71.2	71.2	75.9	71.2	60.1	68.7	68.2	65.3	65.2	80.8	50.9	60.0	68.6	62.6	71.2	59.4	79.3
9/5/04	100.0	88.2	88.7	78.9	93.2	81.3	81.3	88.2	81.3	51.9	86.3	91.1	69.9	85.2	76.4	89.3	96.7	85.3	87.6	78.3
9/12/04	82.5	85.3	69.1	72.2	85.5	79.6	91.4	79.3	82.5	67.6	81.5	64.1	77.3	82.5	70.9	99.8	89.0	67.5	70.9	82.4
9/19/04	81.5	80.8	80.4	92.3	82.3	91.5	79.4	79.4	86.0	91.1	70.1	79.2	79.4	79.8	84.4	66.1	89.0	76.1	89.7	79.4
9/26/04	84.3	83.5	88.9	88.9	89.5	82.5	100.0	96.7	82.1	88.9	100.0	96.4	81.1	100.0	74.6	88.9	98.6	81.1	86.8	100.0
10/3/04	75.2	73.6	81.0	85.2	74.5	55.1	76.2	61.5	77.9	51.3	59.3	74.5	65.8	100.0	89.5	68.8	74.5	64.0	67.3	63.1
10/10/04	84.4	78.6	78.6	78.6	78.6	78.6	75.4	66.0	91.1	79.4	73.8	78.6	78.6	59.8	91.1	70.6	78.6	89.3	78.6	83.9
10/17/04	73.6	70.3	75.4	91.3	86.7	82.0	100.0	97.8	92.8	90.8	82.0	75.1	100.0	57.6	100.0	89.7	100.0	90.0	71.9	52.6
10/24/04	69.9	43.9	68.5	55.4	79.8	69.9	61.2	69.9	69.9	64.8	90.3	58.7	64.3	72.6	87.7	57.1	72.6	69.9	58.1	89.5
10/31/04	17.4	67.5	90.8	67.5	65.8	38.9	76.6	67.5	88.2	75.4	67.5	67.5	50.4	52.8	64.1	43.6	77.7	99.8	67.5	51.8
11/7/04	64.2	94.9	77.7	70.5	85.5	26.9	70.5	63.8	84.2	30.9	70.5	70.5	61.3	87.6	53.6	70.5	68.8	70.5	70.5	59.6
11/14/04	92.3	60.2	55.5	14.0	38.8	83.3	79.7	88.9	94.8	31.3	16.5	33.1	30.1	51.4	74.2	60.1	79.3	71.1	37.1	86.5
11/21/04	73.8	90.6	42.8	58.6	58.6	56.3	58.6	38.0	37.2	58.6	96.9	54.1	23.4	48.6	62.0	39.8	58.6	44.9	58.6	82.4
11/28/04	52.3	93.8	48.8	100.0	48.9	73.6	73.6	73.6	73.6	72.0	77.5	76.1	73.6	73.6	80.1	73.6	76.0	75.0	49.5	88.0
12/5/04	72.2	88.7	77.8	57.6	93.5	62.2	71.3	100.0	65.2	60.0	100.0	73.6	67.7	71.3	57.7	54.9	37.1	56.8	84.2	61.7
12/12/04	62.2	67.6	67.6	67.6	92.9	59.5	65.4	82.2	59.7	85.8	67.2	45.1	92.2	67.6	85.5	67.6	100.0	86.5	90.7	95.2
12/19/04	88.0	40.0	81.9	35.3	62.1	45.4	73.9	56.0	55.7	76.5	66.5	73.1	63.2	60.0	87.0	50.0	61.9	75.6	81.3	63.2
12/26/04	47.4	64.3	17.9	39.0	50.6	75.3	53.8	48.5	56.8	16.3	57.4	52.7	68.3	44.0	66.8	47.4	35.4	74.0	47.4	47.4
1/2/05	46.4	75.8	26.5	45.9	61.4	71.1	46.4	54.4	46.4	38.9	46.4	44.8	49.7	36.2	46.4	47.0	52.9	46.4	47.6	46.4
1/9/05	82.8	62.9	100.0	39.4	57.6	51.8	57.6	41.6	59.1	77.6	57.6	57.6	57.6	42.5	53.0	47.4	53.2	57.6	33.1	57.6
1/16/05	89.8	28.3	51.9	71.7	53.7	60.1	60.1	60.1	48.4	73.3	48.1	79.6	33.8	48.9	60.1	60.1	60.1	60.1	68.2	60.1
1/23/05	69.9	48.3	48.1	45.5	65.7	56.2	61.9	46.4	43.9	55.4	49.2	43.6	46.1	62.4	59.6	51.6	33.3	51.8	48.3	61.2
1/30/05	55.7	70.1	64.0	67.8	50.4	57.2	57.2	57.2	48.9	57.2	52.5	70.1	52.4	56.9	43.8	56.6	51.2	57.2	57.2	48.0
2/6/05	46.4	55.5	60.4	80.3	67.0	60.4	60.9	71.5	60.4	44.5	59.4	69.6	83.6	60.4	54.2	58.2	81.9	58.7	66.0	
2/13/05	75.6	55.7	44.3	55.7	53.8	66.3	57.7	57.3	48.4	54.2	55.1	35.2	54.5	54.5	55.7	60.1	48.6	70.0	42.6	47.0
2/20/05	49.9	81.0	71.2	37.9	41.9	70.1	60.9	58.7	62.0	53.6	44.9	56.4	81.2	63.2	59.3	47.4	60.3	49.4	60.6	60.9
2/27/05	61.5	64.4	25.3	78.7	58.3	57.7	66.1	55.8	50.2	57.9	43.7	52.2	34.5	41.4	60.9	56.8	43.2	78.0	52.2	52.2
3/6/05	40.0	56.0	58.2	60.3	50.2	62.6	49.2	52.8	50.1	49.2	60.2	49.2	41.5	39.3	50.0	49.2	59.8	33.1	49.2	49.2
3/13/05	65.0	63.6	45.4	42.4	61.1	64.6	57.2	60.5	70.3	66.4	58.7	50.6	50.8	55.7	58.7	54.6	50.5	45.0	61.6	54.7
3/20/05	63.1	67.1	62.3	59.1	60.0	67.4	68.5	64.3	62.3	67.4	63.5	61.0	53.8	59.5	63.5	61.8	64.4	58.5	60.8	62.0
3/27/05	59.4	59.4	53.8	50.1	49.6	59.4	69.6	65.0	64.4	51.4	53.2	85.5	63.7	63.0	59.4	68.4	48.7	83.7	54.2	47.5
4/3/05	79.6	66.3	64.6	68.1	69.7	72.9	77.3	68.4	70.3	69.1	70.0	68.4	69.8	80.2	71.5	70.0	72.1	71.9	74.7	70.0
4/10/05	69.9	57.0	64.5	64.5	67.2	66.0	66.3	67.6	55.7	64.5	62.9	61.3	70.8	64.5	63.8	64.5	64.9	64.5	57.3	64.5
4/17/05	71.1	72.2	72.2	75.5	74.5	79.1	83.6	79.2	81.8	75.0	67.7	59.8	67.5	85.5	83.2	72.2	78.7	72.2	69.2	72.2
4/24/05	78.6	78.5	68.6	67.8	81.6	71.2	64.9	65.2	72.0	74.7	72.0	76.4	76.5	71.9	68.7	72.0	74.1	74.2	81.1	74.7
5/1/05	67.4	67.4	65.6	71.7	65.9	71.8	50.4	69.1	72.1	78.2	81.3	67.4	66.4	67.4	71.7	64.6	65.2	76.3	53.6	72.4
5/8/05	58.1	54.4	61.1	57.7	64.9	63.5	59.3	61.1	61.1	62.9	68.8	58.4	57.4	62.9	57.1	56.4	61.1	57.6	72.8	62.3
5/15/05	87.7	72.3	92.4	81.7	76.5	83.1	79.2	86.5	62.2	81.7	66.1	81.7	75.3	87.8	81.7	83.4	81.7	83.0	71.7	81.7

Week Starting	Customer Satisfaction Indices by Random Customer in a Week																			
	1	2	3	4	5	6	7	8	9	10	11	12	13	14	15	16	17	18	19	20
5/22/05	67.3	67.3	72.8	60.0	70.2	51.2	72.7	67.3	66.8	66.0	58.8	67.3	67.3	64.6	60.3	80.6	64.8	67.3	61.0	67.3
5/29/05	91.2	79.2	89.4	86.5	90.9	84.7	86.5	85.7	86.5	85.2	78.0	77.5	90.5	87.0	95.1	80.3	86.5	80.3	89.9	86.5
6/5/05	82.5	81.0	80.3	89.3	84.0	90.8	81.1	80.3	79.0	81.7	80.3	70.8	80.2	80.2	82.4	79.7	67.1	79.7	78.3	80.3
6/12/05	80.4	88.8	86.7	89.3	80.4	80.8	78.6	74.2	86.1	54.4	82.3	71.4	81.1	71.1	81.3	90.4	76.7	92.5	85.4	75.7
6/19/05	85.0	85.1	86.2	80.6	89.7	77.2	89.3	73.5	77.9	69.4	73.9	77.7	80.6	88.3	80.6	76.7	80.6	77.3	78.9	85.3
6/26/05	79.8	73.0	78.8	75.9	89.3	77.3	86.3	74.1	81.9	83.6	79.5	79.7	81.8	85.2	83.6	77.9	81.3	87.4	85.3	79.7
7/3/05	86.2	84.0	91.2	88.9	82.2	83.8	84.8	84.8	92.2	84.5	89.2	84.8	86.5	84.4	89.6	84.6	84.8	87.3	84.8	87.7
7/10/05	76.8	80.7	78.1	78.1	74.6	79.2	76.8	89.8	70.9	67.3	64.8	68.0	74.6	67.9	65.3	74.6	83.2	74.6	53.5	78.3
7/17/05	76.2	87.5	84.5	76.0	86.2	82.4	81.3	85.8	82.4	82.4	76.4	70.4	78.7	82.4	84.7	82.4	83.3	82.4	88.7	80.3
7/24/05	79.9	77.3	78.0	92.7	79.9	68.2	86.3	79.9	80.6	89.0	73.6	74.6	84.8	81.5	95.2	75.6	79.9	80.7	75.8	79.9
7/31/05	86.4	82.5	79.8	81.6	81.8	79.9	76.1	68.3	75.1	72.9	82.9	88.3	66.3	80.4	74.2	64.4	82.9	73.9	81.9	76.8
8/7/05	84.5	73.8	79.0	81.7	73.1	78.7	77.0	79.1	81.0	72.6	66.5	79.1	78.5	87.6	79.1	69.3	82.9	68.6	67.0	78.9
8/14/05	80.3	73.9	81.7	78.4	75.9	74.7	80.7	78.8	74.5	75.6	78.5	72.9	77.0	72.9	76.3	72.7	77.0	75.6	83.3	83.0
8/21/05	89.4	90.7	94.9	98.9	94.9	90.2	91.4	94.9	89.7	100.0	90.0	89.4	100.0	93.0	98.6	94.9	98.2	100.0	98.8	95.9
8/28/05	75.8	74.2	80.7	82.7	73.4	86.0	80.7	80.5	78.0	69.6	83.5	74.9	79.7	80.7	84.0	73.9	80.7	88.3	80.7	88.6
9/4/05	92.3	85.4	98.7	88.5	87.0	89.0	92.0	76.7	89.2	88.3	88.1	89.2	88.9	93.4	100.0	96.4	86.8	94.5	91.6	84.1
9/11/05	83.8	83.5	88.7	80.3	89.7	87.9	86.3	87.3	87.8	89.9	87.3	79.2	89.4	83.7	89.0	79.7	87.3	87.3	87.3	90.0
9/18/05	92.6	87.1	100.0	100.0	92.4	94.4	94.7	94.4	97.5	100.0	96.1	79.0	100.0	85.1	88.1	100.0	94.4	89.6	95.4	100.0
9/25/05	81.5	100.0	95.8	96.8	90.6	93.9	99.4	90.1	92.9	100.0	90.4	100.0	79.3	94.0	92.9	88.1	97.6	90.5	88.3	81.4
10/2/05	94.9	95.1	98.1	98.4	94.9	94.3	94.5	94.9	93.6	100.0	100.0	91.7	94.9	94.8	94.9	85.4	94.9	100.0	100.0	100.0
10/9/05	96.7	80.2	82.9	98.6	90.6	88.9	97.7	93.4	93.4	100.0	93.4	100.0	93.4	93.4	93.4	96.2	95.1	95.6	96.1	82.1
10/16/05	100.0	100.0	99.3	91.3	94.2	100.0	100.0	87.8	100.0	94.2	100.0	85.4	94.2	91.3	96.3	94.2	100.0	78.8	86.4	100.0
10/23/05	78.5	94.8	87.2	92.3	87.2	84.7	87.2	96.9	89.9	86.7	90.5	87.2	76.6	87.2	88.1	100.0	82.7	75.7	87.2	95.5
10/30/05	91.7	91.7	92.4	100.0	95.3	91.7	96.6	79.6	97.5	92.6	89.6	98.7	82.4	90.5	91.7	90.4	94.6	95.1	87.9	91.7
11/6/05	85.2	85.2	86.3	85.2	85.2	81.8	85.2	84.8	80.9	72.5	85.0	83.5	91.2	79.3	85.2	85.2	85.2	82.8	85.5	81.5
11/13/05	82.1	81.9	94.5	84.3	88.7	82.4	79.9	81.9	78.4	81.5	81.2	84.1	81.9	79.2	87.6	81.9	85.3	82.9	83.8	81.9
11/20/05	78.0	73.1	85.6	68.6	78.0	82.5	75.9	85.0	77.1	73.8	78.0	81.2	78.3	68.5	85.0	84.4	78.0	75.1	81.5	72.0
11/27/05	86.2	86.9	85.1	83.4	86.9	84.9	86.9	87.4	86.9	80.6	86.9	100.0	85.6	86.9	84.5	100.0	86.9	86.9	97.4	86.7
12/4/05	83.6	83.6	92.3	78.2	82.1	82.2	77.5	83.2	83.4	79.8	83.6	85.7	90.7	78.2	83.0	83.0	83.6	86.0	84.6	80.4
12/11/05	92.7	85.8	85.8	85.0	86.8	79.6	80.8	84.9	87.2	82.0	89.8	81.6	83.9	90.8	85.8	85.8	89.9	83.5	79.2	85.8
12/18/05	92.9	84.7	82.6	90.0	84.7	84.7	81.2	84.6	88.7	81.4	95.3	79.8	80.5	84.9	87.9	76.7	80.0	88.9	83.3	78.0
12/25/05	99.7	100.0	96.1	98.3	94.6	88.7	91.7	89.6	81.9	97.3	100.0	97.5	100.0	82.2	99.4	90.2	97.2	90.3	92.3	100.0

in the results helped hide the presence and significance of a problem that began to emerge in late fall 2004. The problem, which was largely due to a change made by a packaging supplier that affected product freshness, has since been corrected. As a result of this experience, management has identified sense and response capability as a key area for improvement, and has retained your firm to help with this initiative.

THE ROLE OF RR LOGISTICS

For a variety of reasons, firms are increasingly concerned about the resiliency of their supply chains.[20] In addition to proactive actions (e.g., establishment of secondary and geographically diverse suppliers, scenario planning and formulation of contingency plans, and so forth), resiliency is enhanced by investment and attention in reactive capabilities. Your consulting firm, RR Logistics, has gained a reputation for innovative and effective approaches for improving reactive capabilities. The first step is to do a better job taking advantage of existing information, and customer survey data provide a rich information source for this purpose.

Questions

1. Explain how control charts can be useful for analyzing customer satisfaction index data. What type of control chart(s) would you recommend, and why?

2. Implement the control chart(s) that you recommended in Excel and plot the year 2006 data (i.e., compute the center line and control limits using data in Table 1, and display the year 2006 control chart(s) using the data in Table 2). Clearly explain how you computed control chart parameters (i.e., center line, upper and lower control limits).

3. Suppose that the number of surveys collected each week is not constant (e.g., customers don't always complete the survey). Develop and implement a control chart approach in Excel that accounts for the possibility of sample sizes that are not the same over time.

[20] Supply chains are increasing in length and complexity with the reduction of trade barriers (e.g., market globalization) and advances in communication technologies (e.g., Internet and related technologies). At the same time, threats of terrorism, natural disasters, and pandemics have increased. See Sheffi (2005) for more on this issue.

TABLE 2   Customer Satisfaction Indices during Year 2006
Twenty random customers are surveyed each week.

Week Starting	Customer Satisfaction Indices by Random Customer in a Week																			
	1	2	3	4	5	6	7	8	9	10	11	12	13	14	15	16	17	18	19	20
1/1/06	93.3	79.4	86.4	89.7	89.7	92.2	89.7	85.3	86.6	89.7	100.0	89.7	100.0	88.0	86.5	92.4	90.7	85.5	84.6	91.3
1/8/06	85.6	86.1	82.4	80.9	86.1	84.8	86.1	86.1	84.9	87.6	88.1	86.1	80.4	82.4	82.8	81.0	86.1	86.1	84.3	86.5
1/15/06	93.7	86.3	86.0	84.1	83.9	93.2	86.8	99.3	79.8	86.0	82.9	86.0	92.8	86.0	92.8	86.0	73.1	97.5	91.4	83.1
1/22/06	89.7	93.9	87.7	92.5	91.9	87.5	84.9	87.7	74.6	87.7	87.7	87.7	88.9	85.9	91.7	99.0	95.2	87.9	94.4	75.7
1/29/06	85.0	85.4	85.4	87.1	77.4	85.1	89.6	73.6	80.5	88.1	78.0	85.4	91.2	98.6	84.0	80.6	87.2	92.6	85.4	85.4
2/5/06	89.7	87.6	93.2	93.5	90.2	82.9	83.3	86.8	96.1	100.0	100.0	93.5	82.4	95.4	93.8	93.5	100.0	91.0	93.5	100.0
2/12/06	89.7	87.7	90.7	93.8	92.1	77.3	85.2	87.7	87.7	90.9	93.9	83.0	88.2	96.8	82.1	87.2	90.5	69.2	90.3	92.5
2/19/06	91.9	97.1	96.8	86.3	90.2	92.0	89.3	91.9	100.0	91.9	100.0	91.9	89.2	87.3	94.5	91.9	95.1	89.7	95.3	91.9
2/26/06	94.1	95.6	96.1	98.6	100.0	96.3	94.9	95.6	93.2	92.0	97.6	100.0	95.0	95.8	94.0	99.3	96.8	96.1	95.8	100.0
3/5/06	94.9	95.8	98.5	94.6	100.0	91.6	94.6	90.0	92.0	94.6	94.2	93.9	90.6	85.7	94.6	94.6	94.6	89.9	97.0	100.0
3/12/06	82.7	76.4	78.7	79.3	79.2	83.7	75.3	81.5	79.9	72.9	81.5	76.9	81.7	80.4	81.5	85.1	82.3	80.4	78.8	82.6
3/19/06	84.4	82.2	89.6	82.2	82.2	89.4	75.9	83.6	88.6	82.2	86.9	71.8	93.0	82.2	90.8	82.2	81.2	83.7	80.7	84.1
3/26/06	89.2	75.9	77.0	75.3	79.4	78.8	77.0	76.6	64.2	75.8	89.6	77.0	83.8	68.9	82.7	61.4	73.4	70.1	82.2	73.9
4/2/06	86.7	85.0	91.8	87.7	82.2	73.0	81.8	87.7	87.7	87.7	79.8	87.7	97.4	84.4	87.7	81.6	85.0	96.4	87.3	81.1
4/9/06	99.1	76.8	88.9	89.4	89.1	82.9	85.8	84.0	80.1	86.8	89.0	87.2	93.2	83.7	83.4	74.4	69.1	85.7	85.0	97.6
4/16/06	86.1	87.0	86.8	85.9	83.9	88.4	86.1	87.6	89.2	87.6	85.9	92.1	91.1	86.1	91.5	90.5	87.9	85.9	79.3	88.0
4/23/06	71.7	79.2	79.3	72.9	85.4	80.5	84.9	79.2	79.2	79.1	83.7	79.3	82.7	75.6	79.3	76.1	72.5	85.4	73.9	83.8
4/30/06	80.3	90.7	85.1	85.7	85.1	89.1	84.7	86.8	91.5	87.9	85.8	86.2	82.7	87.1	84.7	84.7	88.0	86.8	84.7	84.3
5/7/06	81.0	85.2	90.0	86.0	85.4	86.7	90.9	86.7	90.9	83.0	86.7	79.3	81.4	79.2	86.6	88.3	92.6	89.3	87.5	85.7
5/14/06	88.0	89.8	86.3	83.4	91.4	85.8	84.2	88.1	84.6	89.0	90.3	91.9	92.2	90.3	92.2	94.9	82.2	97.1	83.5	94.9
5/21/06	83.2	67.5	76.4	75.5	77.0	75.5	67.0	65.3	72.9	78.4	75.6	75.5	75.5	72.0	75.5	73.1	75.5	75.5	82.3	78.9
5/28/06	75.5	84.0	86.3	84.0	90.4	71.8	95.9	88.6	80.0	75.6	86.6	75.4	84.0	89.6	78.3	86.6	84.5	85.9	91.0	87.0
6/4/06	91.2	97.0	91.2	93.3	91.2	99.7	83.6	89.7	89.1	100.0	87.9	91.2	90.7	88.8	88.6	91.7	90.2	99.1	94.1	91.2
6/11/06	81.3	89.7	80.6	66.6	81.3	74.1	81.8	80.2	81.3	83.8	83.6	63.8	98.1	83.4	81.3	67.9	81.3	89.4	88.1	81.3
6/18/06	77.2	76.8	84.1	72.6	72.4	77.2	77.2	82.4	85.3	77.2	86.4	83.2	79.3	78.6	84.8	74.5	73.2	82.8	76.7	76.5
6/25/06	94.6	87.9	75.4	88.0	83.8	78.7	81.8	97.7	81.4	51.4	76.0	69.5	85.3	60.5	92.9	96.5	81.0	83.9	100.0	85.3
7/2/06	70.9	70.9	64.5	70.9	70.9	58.8	70.9	89.5	88.0	61.9	62.1	77.6	70.9	58.5	80.5	51.5	70.9	100.0	68.7	57.3
7/9/06	69.2	59.1	87.0	72.6	67.7	91.5	69.9	60.2	61.3	72.6	76.1	69.9	72.6	72.6	69.2	72.6	45.6	61.5	49.6	67.5
7/16/06	78.5	75.5	75.3	70.4	65.7	70.4	79.4	79.4	71.1	75.5	47.3	70.4	81.3	61.4	54.7	62.2	62.2	45.1	70.4	44.1
7/23/06	39.3	69.8	86.4	69.8	70.0	71.0	83.6	48.6	69.7	91.3	60.0	67.7	82.1	69.8	52.0	88.8	69.8	64.9	69.8	84.9
7/30/06	90.3	87.9	91.6	60.6	65.0	80.7	80.7	80.8	67.2	88.5	75.8	100.0	80.7	100.0	96.5	91.6	79.1	81.0	85.9	80.7
8/6/06	69.7	59.1	67.5	76.1	76.1	76.1	67.9	58.8	68.4	76.2	51.6	76.1	76.1	87.9	76.4	61.3	63.1	76.1	66.7	76.1
8/13/06	95.7	75.7	100.0	79.0	79.0	81.1	92.3	98.8	74.7	88.0	74.2	65.4	83.8	70.5	79.0	80.6	60.4	89.2	79.0	55.3
8/20/06	93.2	100.0	100.0	84.9	81.1	86.7	94.8	94.1	90.7	86.7	86.6	79.7	78.5	99.6	80.3	86.7	86.7	100.0	90.9	80.1
8/27/06	74.4	52.3	68.1	67.5	87.7	69.6	52.0	69.3	64.7	68.1	60.7	68.1	81.3	73.4	70.8	51.1	67.3	69.0	64.6	72.3
9/3/06	78.8	85.9	89.1	83.0	84.8	90.0	78.8	76.4	89.1	63.4	83.1	61.1	91.3	74.9	93.3	74.7	78.8	74.8	91.8	89.7
9/10/06	75.0	75.0	75.0	75.0	68.7	76.1	75.0	79.8	81.8	64.9	68.2	73.1	64.0	75.0	79.1	73.4	76.9	75.0	71.2	64.8
9/17/06	83.6	77.4	79.6	64.3	95.9	78.9	75.2	83.6	89.4	84.4	79.6	87.6	85.0	86.0	83.6	77.3	83.6	83.6	91.7	86.4
9/24/06	77.0	67.1	68.1	67.1	49.3	65.7	69.0	65.6	67.1	61.8	51.2	87.9	45.7	67.1	67.1	66.8	67.1	62.5	67.1	75.1
10/1/06	61.4	71.4	65.0	74.4	84.5	78.0	56.5	72.7	78.6	80.1	75.7	76.5	78.0	85.8	78.7	67.3	74.4	80.6	77.4	74.4
10/8/06	94.5	67.6	66.7	79.4	86.3	72.6	47.7	85.3	59.0	65.8	66.0	45.3	73.5	62.9	86.0	77.3	64.4	90.3	69.8	46.7
10/15/06	85.1	77.3	76.9	72.8	81.3	85.7	81.6	68.1	81.2	72.3	70.6	76.8	79.6	81.4	79.5	69.5	79.7	76.9	74.5	74.2
10/22/06	74.9	75.3	70.7	81.2	72.9	79.3	61.5	67.2	75.3	81.9	79.5	75.2	55.9	68.2	81.1	78.9	75.3	66.3	96.1	64.5
10/29/06	68.1	67.8	66.2	79.7	67.5	69.5	66.0	64.5	71.6	54.2	79.4	67.8	72.4	61.9	67.2	48.3	77.5	56.0	76.5	67.7
11/5/06	87.6	62.4	77.7	74.8	78.0	68.1	78.9	77.4	71.1	89.2	74.1	78.0	67.4	78.0	78.0	78.0	76.2	78.0	64.1	75.9
11/12/06	93.5	73.7	74.5	79.0	93.1	84.8	75.1	84.8	77.6	84.8	83.8	70.8	78.9	84.8	79.5	91.9	84.8	95.1	88.2	78.7
11/19/06	82.9	80.1	80.1	76.2	63.2	77.1	80.0	68.9	79.1	81.9	75.5	79.6	81.6	71.4	85.9	76.0	77.5	80.1	62.9	76.2
11/26/06	76.3	63.8	97.4	85.4	77.4	76.1	80.0	82.9	76.1	76.1	63.2	59.3	66.8	62.5	71.5	71.4	66.5	76.1	69.2	66.3
12/3/06	93.0	79.5	76.1	91.6	79.5	79.5	89.9	79.5	74.9	62.8	76.7	75.0	81.0	75.0	70.9	82.7	79.5	81.2	85.0	80.7
12/10/06	74.0	72.2	67.9	72.1	72.5	60.3	61.9	72.8	60.5	70.1	72.1	82.4	83.1	72.1	72.1	62.4	71.3	72.1	69.5	79.0
12/17/06	80.9	80.9	62.8	100.0	90.3	94.5	84.3	86.4	80.9	77.9	80.9	84.0	90.6	80.9	74.7	70.6	82.1	72.9	74.1	100.0
12/24/06	79.7	81.5	81.5	92.2	97.8	76.0	69.8	92.7	81.5	81.5	81.5	77.3	81.5	75.2	61.1	86.7	88.5	69.0	84.5	87.0

Supplement

Creative Problem Solving *Strategies and Pitfalls*

Supplement Outline

1. Carefully Consider the Problem Definition
2. Check for Artificial Constraints
3. Strive for Flexibility in Idea Generation
4. Develop Fluency in Idea Generation
5. Recognize the Need for Persistence
6. Beware of the Curse of Experience
7. Concluding Comments
8. Further Reading
9. Exercises

Supplement Keys

1. What is the definition of creativity?
2. Can creativity be enhanced through training?
3. What are six strategies for improving creativity, and how might they be applied?
4. What is the fat-head effect?

Creativity is one of those words (like quality) that means different things to different people. We will use the **definition of creativity** as simply **the ability to generate novel ideas.**

The question addressed in this chapter supplement is how to improve creativity, or ability to generate novel ideas; the question is relevant for all five supply chain activities (see Figure S11.1). In order to answer this question, we need to first make a distinction between organizational creativity and individual creativity. There are a variety of tactics for promoting a creative climate in an organization (e.g., openness to debate and unconventional ideas, reward risk taking, etc.),[1] but our focus will be on individual creativity.

So why study individual creativity? Two reasons: First, contrary to common belief, creativity is not something you either do or don't have. **Many studies have shown that one's ability to generate novel ideas is significantly enhanced through training.** Second, and this probably goes without saying, creativity is a desirable trait in business and, more specifically, problem solving. This chapter outlines **six strategies that can help you avoid**

FIGURE S11.1

A supply chain emphasizing that creative problem solving is relevant for all links—buy, make, move, store, and sell.

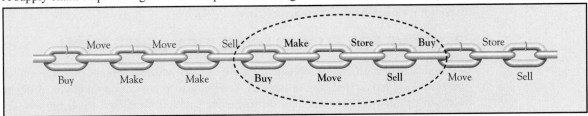

[1] For more on creating a creative corporate climate, see Robinson and Sterm (1997).

common problem-solving pitfalls and thereby improve your ability to generate novel ideas.

1. CAREFULLY CONSIDER THE PROBLEM DEFINITION

The way a problem is defined can have a large impact on the types of solutions generated. Albert Einstein touched on this point: "The formulation of a problem is far more often essential than its solution, which may be merely a matter of mathematical or experimental skill."

Time may be better spent on carefully defining a problem than in the search for solutions. As one example (also noted in Chapter 8, "Capacity Management"), an airline was receiving complaints about the delays in baggage claim. The complaints got so bad that they began to look into the problem. What sort of possible solutions come to mind? Perhaps some possibilities such as hiring more people to get luggage off the plane faster, more trucks to cart luggage to the claim area, training in methods to speed the transfer of luggage from the plane to the claim area. All of these solutions may be effective, but the solution the company came up with would not have been generated if they had defined the problem in perhaps a natural way. One might view the problem as how to reduce the time it takes to get luggage from the plane to the claim area. The airline, in this case, made arrangements to use a baggage claim area that was farther away from the terminal; it took passengers more time to walk to the baggage claim area, which gave the company time to get the luggage there shortly after the passengers arrived. Complaints reduced significantly (Evans 1991). This solution came about by viewing the problem as how to reduce complaints.

A common pitfall in problem solving is jumping too quickly into solution generation. Recognizing the importance of problem definition helps avoid this pitfall.

2. CHECK FOR ARTIFICIAL CONSTRAINTS

Be careful not to make unnecessary assumptions about a problem. Russell Ackoff relates a story of his grade school daughter who was having some difficulty with a homework assignment (Ackoff 1991). The problem was to connect nine dots arranged in a square with no more than four straight lines without picking up your pencil. Feel free to give a try below before reading on.

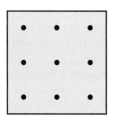

One possible unnecessary assumption is that you must stay in boundaries defined by straight lines connecting the outermost dots. When Ackoff considered the problem, the artificial constraint that came to mind first was that the paper could not be folded. He began to consider possible solutions that incorporated paper folding and thought of a way to connect the dots with three straight lines (can you see how?).

Wolpert (1992) shares a historical example of experts who neglected to question assumptions: "Charles II once invited Fellows of the Royal Society to explain why a dead fish weighs more than when it was alive. The fellows responded with ingenious explanations, until the King pointed out that what he had told them was not true." You may test your awareness of artificial constraints by trying to name a former president of the United States who is not buried in the United States (Rivett 1994).

3. STRIVE FOR FLEXIBILITY IN IDEA GENERATION

Flexibility in idea generation refers to the ability to generate a wide range of different (i.e., unrelated) solutions. One way to improve flexibility is to consider a variety of different ways of defining the problem, and then generate solution ideas for each definition. For example, imagine that your problem is to tie two strings together. The strings are attached to the ceiling. When you grab one string and walk toward the other string, you find that you cannot reach it without letting go of the string in your hand. As you think about this problem, you will likely find that there are many possible solutions, each associated with a different way of defining the problem (e.g., how to make the string longer, how to extend your reach, how to keep the string in place when you let go to grab the other one, etc.). Periodic shifting of the way you think about a problem can help you generate novel solutions.

Here is an example of flexible, even playful, thinking. It appeared in the Copenhagen newspaper *Berlingske Tidende* and it considers the question of how to catch elephants (Gullberg 1997, p. 375).[2]

> All you need is a blackboard, a piece of chalk, a mariner's telescope, a pair of tweezers and an empty jampot. You begin by writing $1 + 1 = 3$ on the blackboard and set it up in a place rich in elephants, and hide yourself in a nearby tree. Very soon an inquisitive little baby elephant will draw near to muse upon this remarkable statement and by and by several of her elders will join her. When there are enough of them, you just turn your telescope the wrong way around, so that the assembled elephants become quite small. Then you pick the small elephants up with your tweezers, one by one, and put them in the jampot.

4. DEVELOP FLUENCY IN IDEA GENERATION

Fluency in this context refers to the ability to generate lots of ideas in a short period of time. It is a skill that can be developed with practice (e.g., when faced with a problem, push yourself to write down as many ideas as possible within some time limit). The importance of fluency is evident in one of the two principles of problem solving that underlie brainstorming; namely, **quantity breeds quality** (for curiosity sake, the other principle is defer judgment). The really good (and often creative) ideas are usually few and far between. This last point also relates to the next strategy.

5. RECOGNIZE THE NEED FOR PERSISTENCE

One common characteristic of creative solutions is that they appear obvious in hindsight (for more on this point, read the story of *Obvious Adams* noted in Section 8, "Further Reading"). As a result, there is sometimes an impression that coming up with a creative solution should be easy. We know from the principle of nature, satisfaction = perception − expectation, that if expectations are high and a good solution doesn't quickly come to mind, we become frustrated and may give up. Most creative ideas are preceded by lots of hard work, or, in other words, the point of the strategy is to place expectations more in line with reality. Thomas Edison, for example, spent over two years searching and testing materials for a light bulb filament (he even had assistants searching Amazon rain forests and the Far East). Another example is Harold Black's 1927 invention of a negative feedback amplifier. He had been working hard on the problem of output distortion for several years and one day, while traveling to work, the "obvious" suddenly occurred to him. What was needed was to feed the amplifier output back to the input in reverse phase, thereby canceling out the distortion of the output (Black 1977).

6. BEWARE OF THE CURSE OF EXPERIENCE

Experience is great. It is one key to effective problem solving. It saves us a lot of time and allows us to be much more effective in our professional and personal lives. There is a downside, however. The **curse of experience** is that experience **(1) encourages short cuts and a lack of skepticism and (2) leads to habits**. Both elements of the "curse" can inhibit ability to generate novel ideas.

[2] From MATHEMATICS: FROM THE BIRTH OF NUMBERS by Jan Gullberg. Copyright © 1997 by Jan Gullberg. Used by permission of W.W. Norton & Company, Inc.

Principle of Nature: Fat-Head Effect

DEFINITION
People tend to be overconfident in their decision-making ability.

IMPLICATION
Identifying biases in your mental models that underlie your decisions is difficult. Maintain a critical eye and humility in your judgments, and seek honest input from others.

EXAMPLE
A group of nine physicians recorded their assessment of the probability of pneumonia for 1,531 patients who complained of a cough. The physicians were consistently overconfident in their assessments. For example, only 20 percent of the patients viewed by physicians as almost certain to have pneumonia (probability estimated at 88 percent) actually had pneumonia (Christensen-Szalanski and Bushyhead 1981).

Point one of the curse is related to the **fat-head effect; that is, people tend to be overconfident in their decision-making ability**. There is some evidence that the fat-head effect becomes worse with experience; that is, experience increases confidence more than decision-making accuracy (Oskamp 1965). *BusinessWeek* has used the term *CEO disease* for this type of phenomenon. CEOs and other successful executives are very talented, but they may begin to believe they have all the answers. CEO disease has led to the downfall of a number of CEOs and their companies. When looking for top executive talent, the CEO of a small freezer company in Michigan looks expressly for people who have "bloodied their nose"; by this he means successful people who also have had a major business failure in their lives. He believes that a good nosebleed will make a person less apt to catch CEO disease. The 1994 annual report for Berkshire Hathaway indicates that CEO Warren Buffet learned this lesson the hard way. He writes that sloppy analysis and hubris contributed to his money-losing investment in USAIR Inc. DaimlerChrysler went through one of the biggest losses of shareholder value in year 2000. Interviews with executives suggest that much of the responsibility lies with CEO Schrempp, a man of supreme self-confidence and ambition who fell victim to his own hubris (Andrews and Bradsher 2000).

In some settings, the recency effect may contribute to the fat-head effect. For example, Hilary and Menzly (2006) find that analysts who forecast earnings more accurately than the median analyst in the recent past are likely to forecast less accurately in the near future. The authors suggest that the experience of recent success contributes to a cognitive bias of overconfidence that leads to poor near-term future performance (i.e., success leads analysts to place too much weight on their private sense of the market and too little weight on public signals of market direction). The phenomenon tends to be cyclical, where negative feedback from poor performance reduces overconfidence, forecast accuracy improves, and overconfidence returns. In summary, extraordinary success breeds extraordinary confidence, which sometimes extends to overconfidence and poor decisions. The main lesson is that the fat-head effect can be costly, and that simply being aware of this trap can help avoid it; that is, by maintaining a healthy dose of humility in decision-making ability.

The second point of the curse of experience refers to the relationship between experience and habits. The risk of habits gained from experience is evident in the following business saying:

> If you do something the same way for one year, look it over carefully. If you do something the same way for three years, look at it with suspicion. If you do something the same way for five years, throw it out and start over.

John Diebold (1952) comments on how the inefficient operation of the New York Stock Exchange is a consequence of the curse of experience. "We often become so accustomed to doing things in a certain way that we no longer question the basic purposes of our actions.

This happens in all areas of human endeavor. As time goes on, we are likely to decorate obsolete processes with new gadgets and then deceive ourselves into thinking that we have made improvements. The world is rife with examples, but none is more typical than the New York Stock Exchange." It is interesting that the changes he suggested in 1952 are close to what was implemented several decades later in the 1980s.

7. CONCLUDING COMMENTS

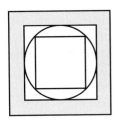

As we saw in many of the earlier chapters, mathematical skills are useful for developing managerial insight. While these skills are important, I think a playful approach to problem solving (complemented by deep understanding of a few key principles of nature) is even more useful. This is one reason why I like the following question—a question that can be answered with no mathematics at all. I leave it as a question to ponder (*hint:* think of how you might fold a napkin): The larger square in the accompanying diagram is 10 square inches. What is the area of the smaller square?[3]

8. FURTHER READING

Here are a few references if you'd like to explore individual creativity in more depth:

Ackoff, R. L. 1978. *The Art of Problem Solving.* New York: Wiley.

Couger, J. D. 1995. *Creative Problem Solving and Opportunity Finding.* New York: Boyd and Fraser.

Evans, J. R. 1991. *Creative Thinking in the Decision and Management Sciences.* Cincinnati, OH: South-Western.

Gause, D. C., and G. M. Weinberg. 1977. *Are Your Lights On?* Lincoln, NE: Ethnotech.

Osborn, A. 1953. *Applied Imagination.* New York: Charles Scribner's Sons.

Parnes, S. J., R. B. Noller, and A. M. Biondi (eds.). 1977. *Guide to Creative Action.* New York: Charles Scribner's Sons.

Updegraff, R. R. 1990. *Obvious Adams: The Story of a Successful Businessman.* Louisville, KY: Updegraff Press. (Originally published as a short story in the *Saturday Evening Post* in April 1916.)

An answer to the question on a former U.S. president not buried in the United States: Any ex-president who is still living.

9. EXERCISES

1. Write a brief answer to each of the supplement keys in your own words. After writing down your answers, review the supplement with a focus on the content in bold to check and clarify your interpretations.

2. You are building a house on wooden stilts. The ground is not perfectly level. How do you get all the stilts at a height so that the floor of the house is perfectly level?

3. A Ping-Pong ball falls down a four-foot tube with diameter slightly larger that the diameter of the ball. The tube is fastened securely to the ground. How do you retrieve the ball given that the tube can't be moved, cut, or broken?

4. You give a craftsman a one-pound block of gold that she is to fashion into an elegant plate. The plate, when finished, weighs about one pound. How can you check if the plate is unadulterated gold?

[3] From "Ask Marilyn," *Parade Magazine*, November 21, 1999.

5. You plant some phony documents in a cabinet. You will be leaving for a two-week vacation and would like to be able to know whether someone has looked at the documents during your absence.

6. An A-frame located on a wooded lot has a leaky roof. The leak is where the chimney meets the roof. This can potentially be repaired by applying a sealer (similar to a caulking compound) along the chimney flashing. The roof is far too steep for climbing (about a 60-degree angle with the ground) and there is no ladder of the right size in the neighborhood.

7. The state has recently purchased 500 acres that are to become a state park. Including the entrance gate, there are six places of interest in the park that must be connected by roadways. The problem is to determine the system of roads that minimizes the amount of land that must be cleared for laying down the road. The width of the road is not a variable, so the problem can be restated as minimizing the total length of the road network such that there is access to all six points of interest.

8. Prove that the shortest distance between two points is given by a straight line.

9. Why was Ben 20 years old in 1980 but only fifteen years old in 1985?

10. What is it that the person who makes does not want, the person who buys does not need, and the person who uses it does not know it?

11. Zor the knight is alone in the Great Hall, where two golden cords hang from rings one foot apart on the 100-foot ceiling. He wants to take as much cord as possible by climbing up it and cutting it with his dagger, but a fall from anywhere above 30 feet is fatal. How much cord can he take?[4]

12. A clerk in a butcher shop is six feet tall. What does he probably weigh?[5]

13. A mail-order company uses crumpled newspaper as packing material. The problem is that workers tend to read the papers from time to time instead of working (Evans 1991).

14. Your neighbors own chickens that spend time in your yard destroying your plants. Chasing the chickens and complaining to your neighbor have no effect (Parnes, Noller, and Biondi 1977).

15. You are babysitting and the baby develops a high fever. You are unable to contact the parents and the only doctor you know is out of town (Parnes, Noller, and Biondi 1977).

16. Your friend is on a cruiser passing through the Panama Canal, and you are watching with thousands of others from the shore. The problem is how to get his attention (Parnes, Noller, and Biondi 1977).

17. People are stealing light bulbs from subway cars. It is too expensive to use police or hire personnel to patrol the cars (Parnes, Noller, and Biondi 1977).

18. Try the following. (1) Enter the first three digits of your phone number into your calculator (excluding the area code). (2) Multiply that number by 80. (3) Add 1. (4) Multiply by 250. (5) Add the last four digits of your phone number. (6) Add the last four digits of your phone number again. (7) Subtract 250. (8) Divide by 2. (9) Do you recognize the number, and if so, why?

19. Consider your assumptions (i.e., beware of artificial constraints) as you answer the following four questions: (1) If you have only one match and walk into a room where there is an oil burner, a kerosene lamp, and a wood-burning stove, which would you light first? (2) Some months have 31 days. How many have 28? (3) Two men play five games of chess. There are no ties, but each wins the same number of games. How is this possible? (4) A man builds a house rectangular in shape. All sides have a southern exposure. A big bear walks by. What color is the bear?

[4] *Omni*, March 1993, p 96.

[5] From "Ask Marilyn," *Parade Magazine*, October 28, 2000.

Synthesis

Chapter **Twelve**

Supply Chain Strategy: Frameworks and Synthesis

Chapter Outline

Chapter Keys

1. What is the process–product matrix, and how is it relevant for aligning supply chain processes with the business strategy?
2. What is the supply chain–product matrix, and how is it relevant for aligning supply chain processes with the business strategy?
3. What is SCOR, and how may it be used to improve supply chain performance?
4. How does awareness of principles of nature help to understand and manage system slack?
5. How do insights from analysis and principles of nature contribute to supply chain intuition?

FIGURE 12.1

A supply chain emphasizing that supply chain design is relevant for all links—buy, make, move, store, and sell.

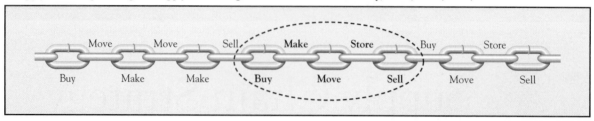

A supply chain is a system—a system of processes spanning multiple departments, firms, and countries that are linked by flows of resources. The field of supply chain management seeks to understand how individual processes should be designed and managed, and, more significantly, how processes can be effectively coordinated to maximize value from a systemwide perspective (see Figure 12.1). In this sense, supply chain management shares a common spirit with the field of strategic management.

We will examine two strategic management frameworks in Section 1 of this chapter. There is much written about business strategy, though our coverage here will be brief and

focused. The main point of this coverage is to highlight the importance of strategic fit—the behavior and decisions of units in a firm should be aligned with the overall business strategy and the business strategy should be consistent with external (e.g., market and competition) and internal (e.g., firm strengths) realities. While this point may seem obvious, continually changing conditions sometimes lead to increasing strategic misalignment that is undetected by management. The frameworks provide broad indicators of strategic fit and can be useful for detecting problems in this area.

The formulation and clear communication of a suitable business strategy are of paramount importance. The consequences of mistakes on this dimension are severe, to the point of driving a firm out of business in short order. Most firms recognize this point, and, while susceptible to missteps, the challenges, problems, and opportunities are generally greater at the level of design and execution. From a supply chain perspective, this translates into improving the supply chain systems and processes for allocating and deploying resources that support the business strategy. Most of the content in this chapter is contained in Sections 2 and 3 and is aimed at this level. Section 2 reviews the Supply Chain Operations Reference model (SCOR), and Section 3 recaps principles and insights from earlier chapters.

SCOR provides a step-by-step guide and a language for describing current and world-class processes with corresponding performance metrics, which in turn serve as a basis for supply chain improvement efforts. Imagine a supply chain or a firm as a novel—rich, complex, and nuanced. SCOR is analogous to a systematic approach for critical analysis of the novel. Through this analysis, and analysis of highly regarded other works, we seek to become better writers. But critical analysis alone (e.g., facilitated by SCOR) is not enough. Good writing also requires the ability to generate the core ideas that become the basis for a powerful story, and a gifted sense for weaving the story lines together to create a cohesive and compelling whole. This text is dedicated to two related ideas. First, talent for good "writing" rests to a large degree on well-developed business intuition. Second, while it is true that this intuition is often gained through years of hard-won lessons, two keys for speeding up this process are (1) a deep understanding of principles governing human and system behavior and (2) a capacity for deft back-of-the-envelope analysis. Section 3 reviews how principles of nature and insights from analysis are relevant for improving supply chain performance. More specifically, we will first review the causes of system slack discussed in Chapter 3. We'll then recap the role of principles, insights, and analysis in understanding and managing the causes of system slack.

1. OVERVIEW OF STRATEGIC FRAMEWORKS

The business strategy of a firm specifies the basis for its competitive advantage, or, in other words, what the firm should do especially well. For example, three generic business strategies are cost, differentiation, and focus (Porter 1998). A firm pursuing a cost strategy concentrates on low cost to support pricing below its competition (e.g., Wal-Mart). A differentiation strategy, on the other hand, stresses unique or innovative products/services as a means for competitive advantage (e.g., Harley-Davidson). A focus strategy is based on identifying a small market segment or market niche in which either low price or differentiation may be emphasized (e.g., custom-made bicycle frames).

Naturally, the business strategy must be regularly reviewed and periodically adjusted in order to maintain effectiveness under changing conditions (e.g., markets, competition). And, as the business strategy evolves, the supply chain performance metrics and processes should be scrutinized for consistency with the business strategy. It is not uncommon to find firms moving toward a differentiation strategy while adhering to efficiency-oriented performance metrics, and, as a consequence, overly rigid supply chain processes.[1] We'll consider two frameworks for detecting misalignment between the business strategy and the supply chain metrics/processes.

[1] See Ferdows, Lewis, and Machuca (2004); Lee (2004); and Sheffi (2005) for examples of supply chains that use agility and resiliency as a means to strategic competitive advantage.

1.1. Process–Product Matrix

The process–product matrix, which was developed by Hayes and Wheelwright (1979), specifies a logical relationship between process structure and product type (see Figure 12.2). The **horizontal axis classifies types of products produced by a process, from highly customized to highly standardized. The vertical axis categorizes processes according to material flow, from jumbled to continuous.** A job shop, where each job is potentially unique, typically exhibits a jumbled flow process. The flow of a particular job depends on its special requirements, which can be quite different from other jobs. A jumbled flow process is flexible, but is generally inefficient (e.g., high unit cost). At the other extreme is a continuous flow process, which relies on high capital investment to support continuous movement and processing of material. A continuous flow process is efficient but generally inflexible (e.g., capable of producing a limited number of different products).

A main point of the process–product matrix is that certain process structures are well suited to certain types of products, which is reflected in the diagonal of Figure 12.2. And it is not uncommon to see multiple process structures at a single firm; for example, products in the early stages of their life cycle tend to be positioned toward the upper left, whereas mature products tend to be positioned toward the lower right. Areas of mismatch, and therefore indicators of improvement opportunities via a change in product type and/or process, are located in the lower-left and upper-right corners. For example, a firm employing a rigid continuous flow process for low-volume, highly customized product is likely paying more than necessary in the form of high fixed costs and high setup times/costs due to frequent changeovers. Hayes and Wheelwright note that firms do not always operate along the diagonal. However, when this is the case, management should have well-thought-out reasons for doing so.

FIGURE 12.2 **The Process–Product Matrix**

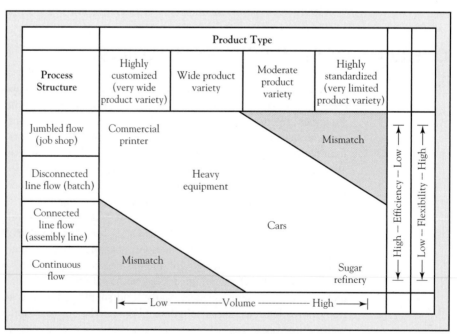

Source: Hayes and Wheelwright (1979).

1.2. Supply Chain–Product Matrix

The process–product matrix links product type to the material flow of the production process. The supply chain–product matrix is a framework for characterizing fitness between product type and supply chain design. However, the supply chain–product matrix differs from the process–product matrix in three ways. First, **products are classified according to the predictability of product demand instead of the degree of product standardization.** Second, the **processes are classified according to a performance attribute rather than the nature of material flow.** Third, the supply chain–product matrix is explicit in its indication that relevant processes often extend beyond the firm.

The supply chain–product matrix was proposed by Fisher (1997) and is illustrated in Figure 12.3. Products are classified along the horizontal axis according to their demand patterns. A product with predictable demand is labeled functional. Functional products include the staples that people buy to satisfy basic needs. Life cycles are long (e.g., more than one year), and demand is stable and predictable. The stability invites competition, and, as a consequence, functional products tend to have low contribution margins.

One approach to increase margins is to add new features or innovations with potential to command a higher price. Frequent innovations lead to short product life cycles (e.g., less than one year) and unpredictable demand. A product with unpredictable demand is labeled innovative. Innovative product carries more risk as the market may respond poorly to the new feature or flavor, but offers higher potential return through higher margins. Examples of industries offering innovative products include fashion clothing and personal computers. However, competitive pressures ensure that innovative products can be found in almost any industry.

The vertical axis in Figure 12.3 classifies the supply chain for a product as either responsive or efficient. Table 12.1 illustrates basic differences between responsive and efficient supply chains.

As with the process–product matrix, a **main point of the supply chain–product matrix is that certain processes are well suited to certain types of products.** Process priorities should shift from efficiency to responsiveness as product demand becomes less predictable. Firms selling historically functional product may fall into the trap of matching an efficient supply chain with innovative product. The result is a supply chain strategy stressing efficiency that is misaligned with a business strategy stressing an innovative product line. A good indicator of this problem is a declining fill rate while inventory is increasing (e.g., an overly rigid supply chain is breaking down under increasingly unpredictable demand). The trap is a consequence of the rapid growth in the rate of new product introductions as firms look for ways to increase margins; a historically functional product becomes increasingly

FIGURE 12.3 **The Supply Chain–Product Matrix**

	Product Type	
Supply Chain Performance	Innovative products (unpredictable demand)	Functional products (predictable demand)
Responsive supply chain		Mismatch
Efficient supply chain	Mismatch	

Source: Fisher (1997).

TABLE 12.1
Characteristics of Responsive and Efficient Supply Chain Processes

	Responsive Supply Chain	Efficient Supply Chain
Primary purpose	Respond quickly to unpredictable demand in order to minimize stockouts, forced markdowns, and obsolete inventory	Supply predictable demand at the lowest possible cost
Manufacturing	Deploy excess buffer capacity	Maintain high average utilization rate
Inventory	Deploy significant buffer stocks of parts or finished goods	Generate high turns and minimize inventory throughout the chain
Lead time	Invest aggressively in ways to reduce lead time	Shorten lead time as long as it doesn't increase cost
Supplier selection	Select primarily for speed, flexibility, and quality	Select primarily for cost and quality
Product design	Use modular design to postpone product differentiation as long as possible	Maximize performance and minimize cost

Source: Reprinted with permission from Fisher (1997).

innovative, but the change is gradual enough to be unrecognized, and, consequently, performance metrics and processes continue to emphasize efficiency.

Given that suitable strategic priorities for supply chain processes have been established, the next questions are (1) what metrics should be used to measure the performance of supply chain processes and (2) what changes and investments should be made to improve performance. These questions are considered in the next two sections.

2. SUPPLY CHAIN OPERATIONS REFERENCE MODEL

The Supply Chain Operations Reference model (SCOR) was developed and is maintained by the Supply-Chain Council (SCC), which is a nonprofit organization formed in 1996 by AMR Research and Pittiglio Rabin Todd & Rath with the support of 69 member companies. SCC now has approximately 1,000 members from around the globe, primarily firms from a broad spectrum of industries, but also includes universities and government agencies.

Supply chains span multiple interconnected processes. The complexity and scope have historically contributed to a lack of standard ways to measure supply chain performance and describe supply chain processes—two important elements for assessing and ultimately improving supply chain performance. The challenges have been particularly acute for software selection; firms have made large investments in supply chain software that failed to address their particular problems. SCOR was introduced to provide such a standard. In brief, **SCOR specifies a framework for describing supply chain processes with associated terminology, metrics, and best practices.** The framework integrates well-known concepts from business process reengineering, benchmarking, and best practice analysis. SCOR is regularly updated as technologies and best practices change. Version 7.0, for example, was introduced in January 2005, and SCC communicates developments via their Web site at www.supply-chain.org.[2]

---

[2] While most of the materials on the SCOR model are limited to members, a 21-page document presenting an overview of the model is available to the public on the SCC Web site.

Let's take a look at SCOR in more detail. We'll focus first on expanding the picture of what SCOR is and then on how it may be used to improve supply chain performance. The goal is not to gain mastery of the model, which can take years, but rather to gain enough of an understanding to gauge when and how SCOR may be useful in different settings.

What Is SCOR?

As you might imagine, there are many elementary ongoing processes associated with managing flows of resources in supply chains. Version 7.0 of SCOR defines 177 elementary supply chain processes called process elements. The process elements contribute to five basic tasks known as process types: (1) plan, (2) source, (3) make, (4) deliver, and (5) return. Planning process elements (type one) are further subdivided into supply chain planning, planning related to a particular supply chain function, and process elements that enable planning (e.g., processes to prepare and manage information needed for planning). Process types two through five delineate the functional range of SCOR—from procurement (source), through production (make), to warehousing and shipment (deliver) and processing of returns (return). For example, processes related to sales and marketing, product development, and research and development are not part of SCOR. The process elements associated with source, make, deliver, and return are either execution processes or enable processes. Execution processes are triggered by plans and events, whereas enable processes relate to infrastructure (e.g., processes to prepare and manage information needed for execution). The categorization of SCOR process elements is illustrated in Table 12.2.

A description of a process element in SCOR exhibits five basic characteristics (see Tables 12.3 and 12.4 for examples). First, the process element is defined. The definition is a statement of what the process does. Second, key performance indicators of the process are identified and associated with one of five process attributes—reliability, responsiveness, flexibility, cost, and assets. Version 7.0 of SCOR, for example, contains 143 standard metrics for measuring relevant attributes of process performance. Third, best practices of the process are identified through a brief description and a characterization of features (e.g., technology that can help achieve the best practice). Fourth, inputs and outputs are listed. This list indicates where the information and material associated with the process comes from (inputs) and goes to (outputs). The linkages in SCOR are based on a standard that may, or may not, match the linkages at a particular firm. Fifth, the terminology throughout the description of the process element is defined, which is clearly important if one wishes

TABLE 12.2   SCOR Process Elements

Process elements defined in SCOR version 7.0 are grouped into five process types: plan, source, make, deliver, and return. Supply chain planning processes span multiple processes, as opposed to source, make, deliver, and return processes, which are limited to a single process.

Plan			
Develop and enable supply chain plans, source plans, make plans, deliver plans, and return plans (29 process elements)			
Source	**Make**	**Deliver**	**Return**
Execute and enable source function (26 process elements)	Execute and enable make function (27 process elements)	Execute and enable deliver function (60 process elements)	Execute and enable return function (35 process elements)

TABLE 12.3
A Supply Chain Planning Process Element in SCOR Version 7.0

Process Element: Balance Supply Chain Resources with Supply Chain Requirements	Process Element Number: P1.3

Process Category Definition

The process of identifying and measuring the gaps and imbalances between demand and resources in order to determine how to best resolve the variances through marketing, pricing, packaging, warehousing, outsource plans or some other action that will optimize service, flexibility, costs, assets (or other supply chain inconsistencies) in an iterative and collaborative environment.

Performance Attributes	Metric
Reliability	Delivery Performance to Customer Commit Date Fill Rate
Responsiveness	None Identified
Flexibility	None Identified
Cost	None Identified
Assets	Inventory Days of Supply Asset Turns

Best Practices	Features
Demand Planning, Demand Flow Leadership	Software that provides multiple data models including the business rules and metrics for the entire supply chain planning process. Algorithms use the business rules and metrics as the drivers for the planning engine.
Collaborative Planning, Forecasting and Replenishment (CPFR)	Supply chain planning systems and communication technologies as well as newly defined standards that reflect the CPFR model and "participate" in the entire planning process.
Business Intelligence (BI)	A data warehouse/data mart is the source of all planning (master) data, business rules and transaction data. Analytical tools enable the ongoing maintenance and improvement of the business rules based on actual data.
Customer Relationship Management (CRM)	Software that provides customer input and keeps the customer informed about the planning of the production and delivery process by managing all contacts and communication with the customer through all channels including Internet and traditional sales and customer service channels.

Inputs	Plan	Source	Make	Deliver	Return
Planning Decision Policies	EP.1				
Supply Chain Performance Improvement Plan	EP.2				
Inventory Strategy	EP.4				

Outputs	Plan	Source	Make	Deliver	Return

Note: The codes listed under "Inputs" correspond to other process elements.
Source: Reprinted with permission from SCC.

TABLE 12.4
An Execution Process Element in SCOR Version 7.0 That Is Part of the Source Process

Process Element: Receive Product	Process Element Number: S1.2

Process Element Definition

The process and associated activities of receiving product to contract requirements.

Performance Attributes	Metric
Reliability	% Orders/lines received damage free
	% Orders/lines received complete
	% Orders/lines received on-time to demand requirement
	% Orders/lines received with correct shipping documents
Responsiveness	Receive Product Cycle Time
Flexibility	None Identified
Cost	Receiving Costs as a % of Product Acquisition Costs
Assets	None Identified

Best Practices	Features
Supplier certification programs are used to reduce (skip lot) or eliminate receiving inspection	Skip lot/sampling inspection logic
Bar coding is used to minimize handling time and maximize data accuracy	Bar code interface for data collection devices / Generate bar coded receiving documents
Deliveries are balanced throughout each working day and throughout the week	None Identified
Supplier delivers directly to point of use (dock to line or end destination)	Electronic Tag tracking to Point of Use (POU) destination
Supplier (Carrier) Agreements	See Glossary

Inputs	Plan	Source	Make	Deliver	Return
(Supplier) Sourced Products					
MRO Products					DR2.4

Outputs	Plan	Source	Make	Deliver	Return
Receipt Verification		ES.1, ES.2, ES.6, ES.8			

Note: The codes listed under "Inputs" and "Outputs" correspond to other process elements.
Source: Reprinted with permission from SCC.

to unambiguously describe and communicate supply chain processes (356 terms, metrics, and best practices are defined in the appendices of SCOR version 7.0).

How Can SCOR Be Used to Improve Supply Chain Performance?

SCOR is a three-level hierarchical framework. The **process elements** discussed above correspond to **level 3**, which is the lowest level in the hierarchy. Process elements are grouped into **process categories** (26 categories in version 7.0[3]), and these categories correspond to **level 2.** The categories are grouped into the five **process types** noted above (i.e., plan, source, make, deliver, and return), which correspond to **level 1.** The hierarchy helps to make the model easier to understand and, more important, facilitates its application. SCC outlines a **four-step approach for using SCOR to improve supply chain performance: (1) analyze the basis of competition; (2) configure the supply chain; (3) align performance levels, practices, and systems; (4) implement supply chain processes and systems.** The first three steps correspond to a progression through the three levels of the model. The fourth step concerning implementation is outside the scope of SCOR.

The first step—analyze the basis of competition—focuses on operations strategy. The main outcome is a determination of performance needs; for example, what performance metrics should be improved and by how much. Of course, the firm's strategy is highly relevant for this step. A firm that chooses to compete on reliability and responsiveness, for example, will pay close attention to reliability and responsiveness metrics. Data on the firm's level 1 performance metrics are collected and compared to best-in-class performance or desired targets. Examples of level 1 performance metrics include perfect order fulfillment rate, order fulfillment cycle time, upside supply chain flexibility,[4] upside supply chain adaptability,[5] supply chain management cost, and cash-to-cash cycle time.[6] Organizations can join SCC for a fee and gain access to SCOR resources, including the values of level 1 performance metrics in different industries. The targeted improvements in particular performance metrics identified in this step help to concentrate the analysis in step two.

The second step—configure the supply chain—focuses on documenting material flow for a particular business unit. The main outcomes are an understanding of current material flows in a supply chain with associated changes to achieve the desired performance improvements. Maps are created that show current and desired material flows between physical locations and between process categories (i.e., level 2 processes in SCOR). Those process categories identified as critical and warranting change are considered in more detail in step three.

The third step—align performance levels, practices, and systems—focuses on information and workflow. The main outcomes are a more detailed understanding of those processes identified as critical in step two and a specification of desired process changes. Current and proposed processes are described using SCOR process elements (level 3) and are linked to relevant performance metrics. The best practices, linkages, and metrics in SCOR may be used as a guide during redesign. However, each firm will need to adapt and extend SCOR process elements, linkages, and metrics in a manner appropriate for the organization. This is one area where sound intuition into behavior and trade-offs associated with supply chain processes is useful. We'll consider this point further in the next section by reviewing content from earlier chapters in the context of what it means for detecting areas of meaningful supply chain opportunity and for seeing novel paths to improvement; that is, for developing supply chain intuition.

---

[3] Five planning process categories (plan, source, make, deliver, return), 5 enable process categories (plan, source, make, deliver, return), 16 execution process categories (source make-to-stock, source make-to-order, source engineer-to-order, make make-to-stock, make make-to-order, make engineer-to-order, deliver make-to-stock, deliver make-to-order, deliver engineer-to-order, deliver retail, return defectives to source, return MROs to source, return excess to source, return defectives from customer, return MROs from customer, return excess from customer).

[4] Number of days required to achieve an unplanned sustainable 20 percent increase in quantities delivered.

[5] The maximum sustainable percentage increase in quantity delivered that can be achieved in 30 days.

[6] The time it takes for a dollar to flow back into the company after it's been spent on raw materials.

3. RECAP OF SYSTEM SLACK AND THE ROLE OF PRINCIPLES, INSIGHTS, AND ANALYSIS SKILL

Recall that system slack is idle, underutilized, or non-value-adding resources. Examples include inventory, underutilized funds, rework of defective product, and surplus or poorly deployed human capital, materials, building space, and equipment. System slack in supply chains is expensive but is necessary to be competitive in the market; the challenge is to effectively manage it, which begins with an understanding of why it exists. Chapter 3 covered **six basic causes of system slack over which management has some control: (1) quantity uncertainty—input, output, and demand; (2) time lags; (3) scale economies; (4) changing supply and demand; (5) conflicting objectives (and reward systems) across departments or firms; and (6) high market standards for quick response.**

Throughout Part Two of this text, we have seen that **causes of system slack are interrelated and tied to principles of nature. Scale economies** provide incentives to produce or order in excess of immediate need. Excess inventory due to batching is called cycle stock, and we know that high average inventories contribute to high flowtimes **(Little's law)** and consequently **time lags.** In some industries, **time lags** are exacerbated by the **seasonal (or changing) nature of supply and/or demand. Time lags** influence how far in advance certain decisions on resource acquisition and deployment must be made, and the longer the time lags, the greater the **uncertainty (trumpet of doom). Uncertainty in demand** on a system contributes to long flowtimes due to periods of high congestion **(curse of variability),** especially when capacity is highly utilized **(curse of utilization).** Of course, safety stock in combination with investments in excess and/or flexible capacity may be used to improve system responsiveness in the face of uncertainty, especially when **market standards for quick response are higher than processing and transit times.** However, the question of where and how much to invest in safety stock and excess/flexible capacity, as well as other forms of system slack, is influenced by **reward systems** that are specific to individual firms and to departments within a firm. The compartmentalization of **reward systems,** while sometimes a pragmatic reality, can **inhibit opportunities for benefits that come from a broader systemwide perspective.**

The preceding observations regarding the **causes of system slack with linkages to principles of nature represent one step toward developing intuition useful for managing system slack or, more generally, supply chains.** However, the implications of the principles and insights go beyond this (see Tables 12.5 and 12.6 for a summary of principles and insights). A manager is continually exposed to information, out of which the problems and opportunities with the highest payoff potential must be sorted out. The **Pareto phenomenon** is a principle of nature that highlights the importance of effective filtering; for example, the lion's share of an aggregate measure is influenced by relatively few factors. From our awareness of the **Pareto phenomenon** and a human tendency to be overconfident in decision-making abilities **(fat-head effect),** we know that careful attention to this filtering process is likely to be well spent.

TABLE 12.5 **Principles of Nature in the Text**

1. Benford's Law	8. It's Hard to Play Catch-Up Ball	15. Satisfaction = Perception – Expectation
2. Bullwhip Effect	9. Khintchine's Limit Theorem	
3. Central Limit Theorem	10. Law of Large Numbers	16. Time Distortion
4. Curse of Utilization	11. Little's Law	17. Trumpet of Doom
5. Curse of Variability	12. Obligation to Reciprocate	18. Winner's Curse
6. Fat-Head Effect	13. Pareto Phenomenon	
7. Hockey Stick Effect	14. Recency Effect	

TABLE 12.6 **Managerial Insights at the Ends of Chapters**

Chapter 4, "Demand Management"

1. Pay attention to order processing.
2. Consider operational changes as a means to improve forecast accuracy (e.g., early warning, part standardization, postponement, lead-time reduction, mitigation of the hockey stick effect, pricing that may amplify and dampen demand volatility, Pareto analysis of product line).
3. Use the Winters method, which is a simple and practical short-term forecasting tool.

Chapter 5, "Supply Management"

4. Keep an eye on XML developments.
6. Tame the bullwhip.
7. Use Pareto analysis, which is a widely applicable tool.
8. Look for opportunities to align behavior and decisions with the best interests of the entire supply chain.

Chapter 6, "Inventory Management I"

For systems with an EOQ-type cost structure,
9. Optimal operating cost increases with the square root of volume.
10. Transaction cost per period should equal cycle stock holding cost per period.
11. It is not worth spending a lot of time and money to accurately estimate parameter values.
12. One should focus on reducing the cost per transaction.
13. The time between transactions should be reduced when the holding cost rate increases and/or cost per transaction decreases.

Chapter 7, "Inventory Management II"

14. The optimal probability of not stocking out is equal to the shortage cost rate divided by the sum of the shortage and excess cost rates.
15. For a given level of service, the level of safety stock is approximately proportional to the level of uncertainty.
16. Incremental investments in safety stock yield diminishing improvements in fill rate.

Chapter 8, "Capacity Management"

17. Average inventory = throughput rate × average flowtime (Little's law)
18. Average flowtime skyrockets as utilization gets close to 100 percent (curse of utilization)
19. Average flowtime increases with variance in demand and variance in processing times (curse of variability).
20. Cross-training helps reduce flowtimes (law of large numbers).
21. Customer satisfaction depends on perception and expectation, both of which can be influenced by management (satisfaction = perception − expectation).
22. Customers tend to be more sensitive to losses than gains (it's hard to play catch-up ball).
23. Perceived wait time increases significantly when one is bored (time distortion).

Chapter 9, "Production Management"

24. Be skeptical of vendors who claim that a software system will generate optimal schedules.

For sequencing jobs for processing at a single resource,
25. Sequence in order of smallest to largest time-to-value ratios to minimize the average value of unprocessed jobs.
26. Sequence in due date order to determine if it is possible for everything to be done on time.

TABLE 12.6 *(Continued)*

Chapter 10, "Transportation Management"

27. Indicators of efficient high delivery frequency are high volume, close proximity to supply, and a high inventory cost rate.
28. Look for stop-off locations that are nearly on the way and in close proximity to the final location.
29. Transportation cost/distance is approximately proportional to the square root of the market area.
30. If the number of warehouses is cost-effective, then annual warehousing overhead cost is about one-half of the annual outbound transportation cost.

Chapter 11, "Quality Management"

31. The sum of many independent random elements is approximately normally distributed.
32. Improvement tools and authority should be put in the hands of those close to the action.
33. Quick feedback is often critical for effective and continual improvement.

Other principles and insights from Part Two of this text help to enhance filtering skills and provide a basis for generating and evaluating supply chain improvement ideas. The **law of large numbers** is a principle of nature that underlies many existing, and possibly yet undiscovered, tactics for managing quantity uncertainty. For example, part standardization reduces the variability in part requirements, cross-training reduces the variability in workload on individual employees, and postponement of form or place reduces the variability in demand. The **Pareto phenomenon** is prevalent in aggregate measures such as sales, and the periodic critical examination of the product line through a type of Pareto analysis called length of line analysis can be useful. Very-slow-moving products may be identified and eliminated with minimal or no decrease in total sales, resulting in higher average demand per product and, due to the **law of large numbers,** lower relative demand variability.

Policies and reward systems may contribute to increased volatility and uncertainty in demand. A severe manifestation of the **hockey stick effect** is a diagnostic indicator that critical examination of such policies is warranted. Reductions in the **hockey stick effect** can lead to better efficiency through better alignment of supply with demand as well as lower quantity uncertainty. Another diagnostic indicator that policies and reward systems may be contributing to poor performance is a severe **bullwhip effect** in a supply chain. We also have seen that proactive pricing and other market incentives can be used to dampen the natural imbalances that may exist between supply and demand, as well as encourage early commitment of future demand (**early warning**). Differing reward systems also may create incentives to violate trust. First-digit frequencies of numbers often conform to a counterintuitive pattern known as **Benford's law.** Frequencies that deviate from this pattern signal the possibility of concocted numbers, or fraud.

We have seen examples and emphasis throughout the text on time lag reduction as a means to reduce quantity uncertainty (**trumpet of doom**), excess inventory (**Little's law**), and, more generally, imbalances between supply and demand. Some of this has centered on applications of information technology to reduce communication delays, errors, and transaction costs. In cases where time lags correspond to customer wait times, we have seen examples of tactics that follow from an understanding of psychological principles (**satisfaction = perception − expectation, it's hard to play catch-up ball, time distortion**).

The **principles of nature recapped above represent one theme of this text. A second theme is development of analysis skills.** Within this theme, the **emphasis is on identifying and representing the most salient features of a particular issue for the purposes of gaining insight.** We developed and analyzed four fundamental supply chain issues that can be stated in question form: (1) How much time or distance is needed between "transactions"? (2) How much extra inventory is needed to protect against uncertainty? (3) How much extra capacity is needed to protect against uncertainty? (4) Which task should be done first, second, and so on?

How Much Time or Distance Is Needed between "Transactions"? We analyzed two different types of issues involving transaction costs. In one case, the fixed cost of placing an order or transporting product is balanced against the cost of carrying cycle stock. In another case, the fixed cost of operating a distribution center or warehouse is balanced against the cost of transporting product to market. In both cases, we discovered that the **cost structure is robust with respect to errors in parameter estimates;** for example, it doesn't make sense to spend a lot of time and money to develop precise estimates of cost rates. In the case of ordering, we discovered that optimal **operating cost is proportional to the square root of the demand rate and cost rates** and that the **transaction cost per period should equal the cycle stock holding cost per period.** We also derived a **rule of thumb for how much extra to order before an announced price increase.** In the case of distribution network design, we discovered that the **average distance to the market is approximately proportional to the square root of the market area** and that the **annual fixed warehouse cost should be about one-half the annual outbound transportation cost.** Large discrepancies from these relationships signal that the system may be "out of balance" (i.e., diagnostics for sensing potential opportunities to save money by making changes).

How Much Extra Inventory Is Needed to Protect against Uncertainty? We examined the **linkage between level of inventory, level of uncertainty, and level of service in sufficient detail to predict the value of any one given the values of the other two.** We discovered that, for a given level of uncertainty, the **relationship between level of inventory and level of service is highly nonlinear**—that larger and larger increases in inventory are required for each incremental improvement in service. We discovered a **mechanism for quickly approximating the return from efforts to reduce uncertainty and became aware of a simple diagnostic property of the optimal service level.** For example, we know that for a service level target of 80 percent to be optimal, it must be that the shortage cost rate is four times the excess cost rate. A shortage-to-excess-cost-rate ratio implied by a service level target that seems inconsistent with reality signals a potential opportunity to increase profit with minimal investment (e.g., through a slight policy change).

How Much Extra Capacity Is Needed to Protect against Uncertainty? We considered a few simple queueing models. We discovered a specific **relationship between level of capacity and throughput time for different degrees of uncertainty in demand and processing time.** In addition to a means for estimating the impact of changes in capacity on response time, our **analysis reinforced three principles of nature** that were noted above: **Little's law, curse of variability,** and **curse of utilization.**

Which Task Should Be Done First, Second, and so on? Sequencing decisions—what to do first, second, third, and so on—arise in production scheduling, as well as many other settings. We discovered that while most real-world scheduling problems are challenging, there are some rules of thumb that, in simple settings, lead to sequences with special properties. We saw how awareness of these **rules and properties may be useful for improving performance with minimal investment.** For example, there are about 10^{18} different sequences for processing 20 insurance claims, but there is a quick way to determine if there is a sequence where all can be completed on time (i.e., EDD rule). Similarly, a variant of the WSPT rule may be useful in reducing the cost of float for unprocessed checks in a bank.

In summary, we have seen how analysis skills are useful for conducting quick pay-off assessments to sort out ideas worthy of further consideration. More significantly, as we saw with many of the **principles of nature, back-of-the-envelope analysis is useful for developing intuition**—intuition for **sensing promising opportunities for improvement and for sensing the types of changes likely to effectively respond to a particular symptom, concern, or opportunity.**

4. CONCLUDING COMMENTS

The field of supply chain management is distinctive in its focus on the boundaries between autonomous and semiautonomous units (e.g., firms, departments, individuals) linked by flows of resources, and this is the source of its greatest value proposition. Overall performance relies on the sum of the parts, and the boundaries—where interests collide and information gets distorted, delayed, and withheld—will always be a rich source for creative and substantive improvements.

This text has covered many concepts, principles, and tools for supply chain management, but if forced to remember only one thing, remember this: *look to the links*. Seek to understand how relationships between distinct areas of accountability are contributing to, or inhibiting, the performance of the whole. Focus on the boundaries, look for misalignment of interests that limit performance, and look for information barriers that inhibit timely and effective action.

5. EXERCISES

1. Write a brief answer to each of the chapter keys in your own words. After writing down your answers, review the chapter with a focus on the content in bold to check and clarify your interpretations.

2. Both the process–product matrix and the supply chain–product matrix associate certain types of products with certain types of processes. Discuss the differences and similarities between the two frameworks.

3. Fisher (1997) observes that a sure sign that a firm should move a product line to the right in the supply chain–process matrix is when the product line has great variety, lots of new product introductions, and low margins. Why is this?

4. The following quote is from SCC's Web site (www.supply-chain.org, June 2004): "The SCOR-model has been developed to describe the business activities associated with all phases of satisfying a customer's demand. By describing supply chains using process building blocks, the model can be used to describe supply chains that are very simple or very complex using a common set of definitions. As a result, disparate industries can be linked to describe the depth and breadth of virtually any supply chain." Assess how the building blocks of SCOR can be used to describe supply chains by answering two basic questions: What exactly are the process building blocks and what information is provided in a SCOR description of a building block?

5. There is a truism in business that *you get what you measure*. Discuss how either or both of the strategic frameworks support this truism, and how SCOR supports this truism.

6. Sport Obermeyer makes skiwear. Most of the product lines of jackets and ski pants are redesigned each year, market demand during the selling season is highly unpredictable, and supply chain lead times are long. Fisher et al. (1994) describe a number of discoveries and changes made at Sport Obermeyer,[7] including that Sport Obermeyer

---

[7] See Fisher et al. (2000) for examples of similar tactics at other companies.

a. Observed that the distribution of demand for a product during the selling season followed a normal distribution—a result that was used in analysis underlying new and more effective approaches to decision making.

b. Started a program that encouraged large dealers to place orders several months in advance, thus improving the firm's ability to predict which products were likely to be hot and cold in the upcoming season.

c. Analyzed forecast accuracy across the product line, observed significant differences in accuracy, and found a way to predict forecast accuracy prior to the selling season. On the basis of this information, managers postponed production decisions on the most unpredictable items until early season sales results were available.

d. Redesigned its product line to reduce the number of different zippers by a factor of five (e.g., black in place of multiple colors).

e. Began booking aggregate production capacity during peak periods in advance but did not specify the specific styles to be produced until a later date.

f. Hedged against the shortage and excess cost due to demand uncertainty by using the optimal probability of not stocking out as a guide when determining production quantities.

All told, Sport Obermeyer estimates profits increased by between 50 and 100 percent as a result of the improvement efforts. Observation (a) is closely related to a principle of nature (see Table 12.5). Which one and why? Each of the remaining items [(b) through (f)] is closely related to at least one managerial insight listed in Table 12.6. In some cases, the managerial insight is based on a principle of nature. For each of (b) through (f), identify a closely related managerial insight (and principle of nature if applicable), and explain your reasoning.

7. Your group is considering the purchase of a software system that should cut average forecast error by about 20 percent. The up-front cost is $3 million plus an annual fee of $250,000. Based on some quick calculations that draw on Chapter 7 content, the improvement should increase fill rate from 60 percent to 90 percent with no increase in inventory, which in turn should increase market share by 20 percent and annual profit by more than $1 million. It looks like a potential go. However, there is significant risk: the system will take almost 12 months to implement and the estimated impact on forecasts and market share could be wrong. As you are reviewing the pros and cons in your mind, your thoughts drift to the law of large numbers. Your firm sells handheld multimedia digital players, ranging in capacity from 100 gigabytes to 2 terabytes. One characteristic is that the increase in cost for additional gigabytes is small compared to perceived value in the market, and consequently pricing. For example, the 150-gigabyte unit costs about 2 percent more than the 100-gigabyte unit to produce, yet the selling price is 8 percent higher. From this property, it occurs to you that you might be able to generate meaningful service and market share impact with lower cost by exploiting the law of large numbers. Your thought is to introduce an "up-substitution" policy; that is, if a customer places an order for an out-of-stock unit, then a higher-capacity in-stock unit is shipped with no change in price. Explain the role of the law of large numbers in the up-substitution policy, and discuss how you might estimate the impact on service and profit. How do the two approaches—new forecasting system and up-substitution policy—differ in terms of implementation risk?

8. Diagnostics for signaling profitable opportunities to modify existing policies or designs can be useful. But benchmarks are based on underlying assumptions. When you interpret the merits of a particular diagnostic, it is useful to assess the reasonability of the assumptions, as well as the likely impact of changes in assumptions. Critically evaluate the EOQ diagnostic ratio $TC(Q^*)/HC(Q^*) = 1$ by identifying how a specific change in an assumption would cause the benchmark ratio to either increase or decrease.

Case Exercise *Seagate Technologies: Operational Hedging*[8]

On July 10, 1997, Ron Verdoorn, Executive Vice President of Seagate Technologies and Chief Operating Officer of its Storage Products Group, was reading the capital appropriation request for the *Barracuda 9LP* and the *Cheetah 9LP*. The *Barracuda 9LP* and *Cheetah 9LP* were two of Seagate's new high-end disk-drive product families that were scheduled to go into volume production in the first calendar quarter of 1998. The capital appropriation request called for a $103 million capital investment in two final assembly facilities, one for the *Barracuda* and one for the *Cheetah*, and one joint test facility. The capacities of the new facilities would enable the execution of the master production plan, which was derived by the Material Division based on the sales forecast by the Marketing Division.

While the capital investment plan was definitely reasonable, Ron was wondering whether the plan would provide Seagate with a sufficient hedge against demand uncertainty, which was intrinsic to the sales forecast in the highly volatile disk drive industry.

COMPANY BACKGROUND

Seagate Technology, Inc. is a data technology company that provides products for storing, managing, and accessing digital information on the world's computer and data communications systems. At more than $8.9 billion in revenue for its fiscal year ended June 27, 1997, Seagate is the largest independent disc drive and related components

company in the world. (Selected financials are shown in Exhibit 1.) Founded in 1979, the Scotts Valley, California-based company had shipped more than 100 million disc drives by 1997.

Seagate designs, manufactures and markets disc drives for use in computer systems ranging from notebook computers and desktop personal computers to workstations and supercomputers, as well as in multimedia applications such as digital video and video-on-demand. Seagate leads the disc drive storage industry offering the broadest product line including disc drives with 2.5, 3.5 and 5.25-inch form factors and capacity points up to 23 gigabytes. The company sells its products to original equipment manufacturers ("OEMs") for inclusion in their computer systems or subsystems, and to distributors, resellers, dealers and retailers.

Seagate has pursued a strategy of vertical integration and accordingly designs and manufactures rigid disc drive components including recording heads, discs, disc substrates, motors and custom integrated circuits. It also assembles certain of the key subassemblies for use in its products including printed circuit board and head stack assemblies. Products are manufactured primarily in the Far East with limited production in the United States and the Republic of Ireland.

As of June 27, 1997, Seagate employed 111,000 persons worldwide, approximately 93,000 of whom were located in the company's Far East operations.

EXHIBIT 1
Selected Financial Statement Data (Data in thousands)

Fiscal Year Ended	June 27, 1997	June 28, 1996	June 30, 1995	July 1, 1994	July 2, 1993
Net sales	$8,940,022	$8,588,350	$7,256,209	$5,865,255	$5,195,276
Gross profit	2,022,255	1,581,001	1,373,385	1,170,821	909,872
Income (loss) from operations	857,585	286,969	459,301	473,097	−195,442
Income (loss) before extraordinary gain	658,038	213,261	312,548	329,685	−267,605
Net income (loss)	658,038	213,261	318,719	329,685	−267,605
Total assets	6,722,879	5,239,635	4,899,832	4,307,937	3,470,970
Long-term debt, less current portion	701,945	798,305	1,066,321	1,176,551	941,882
Stockholders' equity	$3,475,666	$2,466,088	$1,936,132	$1,634,700	$1,228,829

Source: Seagate Technologies 1997-10K.

[8] This case was prepared by Professor Jan A. Van Mieghem (Kellogg School of Management at Northwestern University) as a basis for class discussion rather than to illustrate either effective or ineffective handling of a managerial situation. © Jan A. Van Mieghem. This case is reprinted by permission for inclusion only in print versions of this entire book. Inquiries to VanMieghem@northwestern.edu.

DISK DRIVE TECHNOLOGY

Magnetic disc drives are used in computer systems to record, store and retrieve digital information. Most computer applications require access to a greater volume of data than can economically be stored in the random access memory of the computer's central processing unit (commonly known as "semiconductor" memory). This information can be stored on a variety of storage devices, including rigid disc drives, both fixed and removable, flexible disc drives, magnetic tape drives, optical disc drives and semiconductor memory. Rigid disc drives provide access to large volumes of information faster than optical disc drives, flexible disc drives or magnetic tape drives and at substantially lower cost than high-speed semiconductor memory.

Although products vary, all rigid disc drives incorporate the same basic technology (Exhibit 2). One or more rigid discs are attached to a spindle assembly that rotates the discs at a high constant speed around a hub. The discs (also known as media or disc media) are the components on which data is stored and from which it is retrieved. Each disc typically consists of a substrate of finely machined aluminum or glass with a magnetic layer of a "thin-film" metallic material.

Rigid disc drive performance is commonly measured by four key characteristics:

1. Average access time (expressed in milliseconds—"msec"), which is the time needed to position the heads over a selected track on the disc surface;

2. Media data transfer rate (expressed in megabits per second), which is the rate at which data is transferred to and from the disc;

3. Storage capacity (expressed in megabytes or gigabytes—"MB" or "GB"), which is the amount of data that can be stored on the disc; and

4. Spindle rotation speed (commonly expressed in revolutions per minute—"rpm"), which has an effect on speed of access to data.

Read/write heads, mounted on an arm assembly similar in concept to that of a record player, fly extremely close to each disc surface, and record data on and retrieve it from concentric tracks in the magnetic layers of the rotating discs.

Upon instructions from the drive's electronic circuitry, a head positioning mechanism (an "actuator") guides the heads to the selected track of a disc where the data will be recorded or retrieved. The disc drive communicates with the host computer through an internal controller. Disc drive manufacturers may use one or more of several industry standard interfaces, such as SCSI (Small Computer System Interface).

DISK DRIVE MARKET

Rigid disc drives are used in a broad range of computer systems as well as for multimedia applications such as digital video and video-on-demand. Users of computer systems are increasingly demanding additional data storage capacity with higher performance. They use more sophisticated applications software, including database management, CAD/CAM/CAE, desktop publishing, video editing and enhanced graphics applications, and increasingly operate in multi-user, multitasking and multimedia environments. Additionally, there is a sizable market for rigid disc drives in the existing installed base of computer systems, some of which require additional storage capacity.

The computer system market includes four segments: desktop personal computers, mobile computers, workstation systems and server/multi-user systems.

THE PERSONAL COMPUTERS (desktop and mobile) market in 1997 was characterized by a minimum storage requirements for entry-level personal computers of 810MB to 1.7GB of formatted capacity with seek times ranging from 12.5msec down to 10.5msec. The entry-level capacities continue to increase. In addition, users of personal computers have become increasingly price sensitive. Seagate's objective for the desktop and mobile personal computer market is to design drives for high-volume, low-cost manufacture.

EXHIBIT 2
Disc Drive
Technology

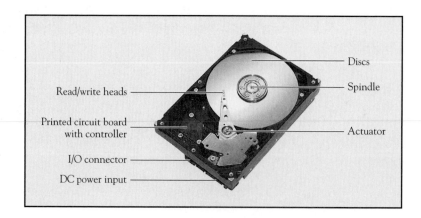

Smaller footprint systems, such as mobile, laptop, notebook and ultra-portable computers require rigid disc drives in form factors of less than 3.5 inches that emphasize durability and low power consumption in addition to capacity and performance characteristics found in their desktop functional equivalents. Personal digital assistants and hand-held pen-based computers may use 1.8-inch or 2.5-inch hard disc drives or flash memory such as a PCMCIA card for additional memory. These mobile applications also emphasize low power consumption as well as very high degrees of durability.

WORKSTATION SYSTEMS include high performance microcomputers, technical workstations, servers and minicomputers. Applications are compute-intensive and data-intensive so that workstation systems typically require rigid disc drive storage capacities of 2GB and greater per drive, average seek times of 8msec and rotation speeds of 7,200rpm to 10,000rpm. Due to the leading edge characteristics required by end-users of workstation systems, manufacturers of such systems emphasize performance as well as price as the key selling points.

SERVER/MULTI-USER SYSTEMS are large systems that include mainframes and supercomputers. Typical applications such as business management systems, transaction processing, parallel processing and other applications require intensive data manipulation. Also included in high-end applications are systems designed for video-on-demand and near-line storage. Users of these systems generally require capacities of 4GB and greater per drive with average seek times of 8msec and rotation speeds of 5,400rpm to 10,000rpm. End-users of large systems are less concerned than users of smaller systems with the size, weight, power consumption and absolute cost of the drive.

As with workstation systems, the OEM typically designs drive products into these systems with emphasis on performance, reliability and capacity. In this market segment, data storage subsystems are used containing large numbers of disc drives. Because data integrity is paramount, high device reliability and maintainability are key features. Mainframe, supercomputer and digital video systems also benefit from very high data transfer rates (up to ten times that in small computer systems).

With the proliferation of multimedia applications, the demand for increased drive capacities has and continues to increase at an accelerating rate since sound and moving pictures require many times the storage capacity of simple text.

DISK DRIVE PRODUCTS

Seagate's products include over 50 rigid disc drive models with form factors from 2.5 to 5.25 inches and capacities from 1GB to 23GB. Seagate believes it offers the broadest range of disc storage products available. It provides more than one product at some capacity points and differentiates products on a price/performance and form factor basis. Seagate typically devotes its resources to developing products with industry leading performance characteristics and to being among

the first to introduce such products to market. The company continuously seeks to enhance its market presence in emerging segments of the rigid disc drive market by drawing on its established capabilities in high-volume, low-cost production.

The *Marathon* and *Medalist* disk drive product lines are targeted for the personal mobile and desktop computing market, respectively, while the high-end workstation and server/multi-user systems market is served with the *Barracuda*, *Cheetah* and *Elite* product families.

The *Barracuda* family of 3.5-inch drives was first introduced in 1992. At 7,200rpm the Barracuda had the highest rotation speed of any drives produced at that time. In fiscal year 1997, Seagate introduced two new products in the Barracuda family, the Barracuda 4LP and the Barracuda 4XL, with 4GB and 4.5GB respectively. The Barracuda 4XL, which began volume production during the fourth quarter of fiscal 1997, was designed to provide a balance of price and performance for the workstation market as it matures.

In August 1996, the Company announced the 3.5-inch *Cheetah* family—the world's first disc drives to offer rotation speeds of 10,000rpm for increased data throughput and lower latency times. The *Cheetah* drive is focused at the very high performance segment of the market. Volume production of the Cheetah 4LP and the Cheetah 9 began in the third and fourth quarters of fiscal 1997, respectively. Seagate is going to announce the fifth generation *Barracuda 9LP* and the second generation *Cheetah 9LP* in early fall 1997, with volume production scheduled to begin in the first calendar quarter of 1998.

Finally, the Elite product line covers the high-end 5.25-inch market. In the third quarter of fiscal year 1997, production commenced on the Elite 23, a high performance, 5.25-inch disc drive with 23GB of formatted capacity, a rotation speed of 5,400rpm and mean-time-between-failures (MTBF) of 500,000 hours.

DISK DRIVE INDUSTRY AND COMPETITION

The rigid disc drive industry is intensely competitive, with manufacturers competing for a limited number of major customers. In addition to the product performance dimension described earlier, the principal competitive factors in the rigid disc drive market include product quality and reliability, form factor, price per unit, price per megabyte, production volume capability and responsiveness to customers. The relative importance of these factors varies with different customers and for different products.

Seagate experiences intense competition from a number of domestic and foreign companies, some of which have far greater resources. In addition to independent rigid disc drive manufacturers—Quantum and Western Digital Corporation being the two most important independent competitors with 1997 revenues of $5.3B and $4.1B, respectively—Seagate also faces competition from present and potential customers. The latter include IBM, Toshiba, NEC and Fujitsu Limited who continually evaluate whether to manufacture their own drives or

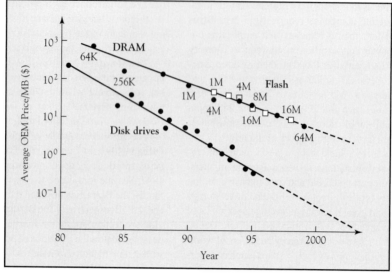

Source: Dataquest.

purchase them from outside sources. These manufacturers also sell drives to third parties, which results in direct competition with Seagate. IBM's Storage Division, for example, has successfully invested in mobile disk drive technology and has now captured a 40% share of the global mobile disk drive market.

The rigid disc drive industry is characterized by ongoing, rapid technological change, relatively short product life cycles and rapidly changing user needs. This, together with intense competition, has manifested in an industry with a history of declining prices. The price per megabyte of disk storage has dropped at a steady pace of about 40 percent per year from 1980 through 1995–even faster than the price drop for computer memory chips (Exhibit 3). In addition, the famous volatility of demand for computer products and peripherals translates into highly fluctuating demand for disk drives. Seagate often must accommodate changes in orders of up to 20% within only two weeks of production.

Competitors offer new and existing products at prices necessary to gain or retain market share and customers. To remain competitive, Seagate believes it will be necessary to continue to reduce its prices and aggressively enhance its product offerings. In addition, Seagate's ability to compete successfully will also depend on its ability to provide timely product introductions and to continue to reduce production costs. The company's establishment and ongoing expansion of production facilities in Singapore, Thailand, Malaysia, China and Ireland are directed toward such cost reductions.

PRODUCT AND PROCESS DEVELOPMENT

Seagate's strategy for new products emphasizes developing and introducing on a timely and cost effective basis products that offer functionality and performance equal to or better than competitive product offerings. Seagate believes that its future success will depend upon its ability to develop, manufacture and market products which meet changing user needs, and which successfully anticipate or respond to changes in technology and standards on a cost-effective and timely basis. Accordingly, the company is committed to the development of new component technologies, new products, and the continuing evaluation of alternative technologies.

The upcoming introduction of the two new products under discussion, the *Barracuda 9LP* and the *Cheetah 9LP*, were thus in line with Seagate's ongoing strategy. The *Cheetah* boasted the faster seek time (5.2 vs. 7.1msec) and higher throughput rate (21 vs. 15.3Mbytes/sec). The *Barracuda*, on the other hand, was 15% more energy-efficient and enjoyed the *Barracuda* family's reputation for a high level of reliability. While the primary market for the *Cheetah* is in enterprise servers, both drives appeal to high-end workstation users for graphics imaging applications. At about $1090 for a 9.1Gbyte drive, the pricing for the new Cheetah family would be approximately 15% above the industry-leading *Barracuda* series.

Seagate develops new disc drive products and the processes to produce them at six locations: Longmont, Colorado; Moorpark and San Jose, California; Oklahoma City, Oklahoma; Bloomington, Minnesota; and Singapore. Generally speaking, Longmont, Moorpark, and Singapore are responsible for development of 3.5-inch form factor drives intended for desktop personal computer systems. San Jose is responsible for development of 2.5-inch form factor drives intended for mobile personal computers. Oklahoma City is responsible for development of 3.5-inch disc drives with capacities and interfaces intended for use in minicomputers, super-microcomputers, workstations and file servers. Finally, Bloomington is responsible for 3.5-inch and 5.25-inch products principally intended for use in systems ranging from workstations and super-mini-computers to mainframe and supercomputers as well as new markets such as digital video and video-on-demand.

In addition to developing new products and components, the company devotes significant resources to product engineering aimed at improving manufacturing processes, lowering manufacturing costs and increasing volume production of new and existing products. Process engineering groups are located with the disc drive development groups and the reliability engineering groups in locations listed above. Most of Seagate's volume production, however, is done in locations remote from these groups and the development of the volume processes is completed at the volume manufacturing sites.

MANUFACTURING STRATEGY

Seagate's manufacturing managers face difficult challenges. Because of surging global demand, their facilities very frequently are running at full capacity. Changes in technology and short product life cycles force frequent equipment purchases. Long equipment acquisition lead-times often require that capacity decisions be made six months in advance of need. And establishing manufacturing capacity in anticipation of highly volatile market demand is critical to bottom line performance.

The key elements of the Seagate's manufacturing strategy are high-volume, low-cost assembly and test; vertical integration in the manufacture of selected components; and establishment and maintenance of key vendor relationships.

Because of the significant fixed costs associated with the production of its products and components and the industry's history of declining prices, the company must continue to produce and sell its disc drives in significant volume, continue to lower manufacturing costs and carefully monitor inventory levels. Toward these ends, Seagate continually evaluates its components and manufacturing processes. It is paramount that Seagate rapidly achieve high manufacturing yields in new production processes and obtain uninterrupted access to high-quality components in required volumes at competitive prices. Also, it often is desirable to transfer volume production of disc drives and related components between facilities, including transfer overseas to countries where labor costs and other manufacturing costs are significantly lower than in the U.S., principally Singapore, Thailand, Malaysia and China.

MANUFACTURING PROCESSES

Manufacturing of disc drives is a complex process, requiring a "clean room" environment, the assembly of precision components within narrow tolerances and extensive testing to ensure

reliability. The first step in the manufacturing of a rigid disc drive is the assembly of the actuator mechanism, heads, discs, and spindle motor in a housing to form the head-disc assembly (the "HDA"). The assembly of the HDA involves a combination of manual and semi-automated processes. After the HDA is assembled, a servo pattern is magnetically recorded on the disc surfaces. Upon completion, circuit boards are mated to the HDA during final assembly and the completed unit is thoroughly tested prior to packaging and shipment. Final assembly and test operations take place primarily at facilities located in Singapore, Thailand, Malaysia, China, Ireland, Minnesota and Oklahoma. Subassembly and component operations are performed at facilities in Singapore, Malaysia, Thailand, Minnesota, California, Northern Ireland, Indonesia, Mexico, China and Scotland. In addition, independent entities manufacture or assemble components for Seagate.

Volume production of the two new products, the *Barracuda 9LP* and the *Cheetah 9LP*, would require investment in new final assembly and test capacity. Given the different technology, each family's HDA and printed circuit board final assembly needed its own product-specific equipment. Both families, however, could be tested in one facility. Disk drive testing involves connecting the drive to intelligent drive testers (IDTs), fast computers that perform a set of read-write tests. IDTs can quickly switch over between testing a *Barracuda* and a *Cheetah* (both take approximately the same amount of tester time).

Product life cycles of disk drives were already short (high volume products introduced in 1995 were sold for about 6 to 7 quarters), but were expected to drop even further. The two new products were planned to be in volume production only for the four quarters of 1998. The capital investment to build production capacity was significant and had two components. First, there were significant fixed costs—estimated at about $40 million—associated with designing, commissioning, and starting up the three new facilities. The second component was that the capital expense (CapEx) of building new capacity increased with the amount of capacity: larger production capacity required larger space requirements and tooling costs, leading to an (approximately) linear increase in the capital expense. These linear components of the CapEx were expressed in terms of a capacity cost for an aggregate, *annual production rate* (APR) of one thousand units.[9]

Note that the capacity investment costs are incurred during construction and before production. To better understand this, imagine building a house: its construction costs have a fixed and variable component that increases with the square footage of the house. However, the construction costs are incurrent independent of the extent to which the house is later used. The challenge in capacity investment thus is to size facilities relative to expected subsequent usage or production: facilities

[9] While actual production was planned in terms of a *daily going rate*, capacity planning for investment purposes was done on an aggregate basis.

EXHIBIT 4
Demand Forecast

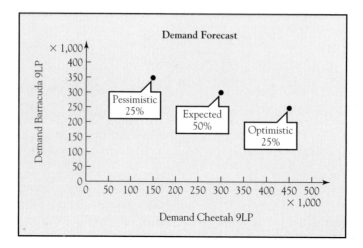

should be neither too small nor too big. A good estimate of required production rates for each product was thus paramount to a well-sized capacity investment plan. Given the frequency with which Seagate made such investments, an extensive *Capacity Requirements Planning* (CRP) process had been developed over time to assist capital investment planning.

CAPITAL INVESTMENTS AND "SALES-PLAN DRIVEN PLANNING"

To support its growth and frequent new product and technology introductions, Seagate made investments in property and equipment in fiscal 1997 totaling $920 million. This amount included $301 million for manufacturing facilities and equipment related to subassembly and disc drive final assembly and test (FA&T) facilities in the United States, Far East and Ireland.

Capital investments are the result of an extensive Capacity Requirement Planning (CRP) process, which intermeshes with the production planning process. (See Exhibit 5 for a representation of the production and capacity planning process.) Seagate's monthly "demand-planning" cycle begins with individual marketing and sales product managers using their specialized knowledge of local markets to estimate sales potential for the following twelve, or even twenty-four, months. These estimates capture both planned purchases by major OEMs as well as possible orders by distributors, resellers, dealers and retailers. Obviously, some of these estimates are more reliable than others and the accuracy of these forecasts degrades sharply beyond the immediate quarter so that significant uncertainty in total demand remained. The *demand forecast* represents the combined estimates of the monthly, worldwide demand for each individual product. Conceptually, the demand forecast captures demand uncertainty by a probability distribution over likely demand scenarios.

Total demand[10] for the two new products was forecasted to be most likely about 600,000 units, as shown in Exhibit 4. Given that the two products were (imperfect) substitutes, total demand was relatively reliable with about plus or minus 100,000 unit error estimate. There was however significant uncertainty regarding the adoption of the Cheetah and thus the ultimate mix: A pessimistic scenario (with likelihood estimated at 25%) would demand only 150,000 *Cheetah*'s and 350,000 *Barracuda*'s. The optimistic scenario (likelihood of 25%), however, called for 450,000 *Cheetah*'s and 250,000 *Barracuda*'s.

Through a process of aggregation and negotiation, the marketing and sales division summarizes the demand forecast in a *sales plan*. The sales plan may adjust the most likely or the average demand scenario to account for additional factors such as end-of-life-cycle effects of unannounced products on the sales of the products they supersede. Senior managers also may decide to curtail production of products whose margins have fallen below profitability hurdles or to adjust the mix of capacity or material constrained products.

The sales plan is then passed to the master production schedulers in the materials division who construct a preliminary Master Production Schedule (MPS). The MPS spells out monthly production quantities ("build proposal") for each product, based on the sales plan and current and future finished goods inventory status. The MPS is then "exploded" to subassembly production schedules for each individual factory location and forms the basis for their component manufacturing and materials acquisition decisions.

Before the MPS is finalized, each facility performs a feasibility check of the preliminary MPS. Usually within one day, vice presidents of the various manufacturing plants contact the MPS schedulers to suggest changes to the MPS if needed. After a few iterations, and all within three days, the final version of the MPS is set, signed off by Ron Verdoorn

[10] The following demand, margins and cost data are estimated.

EXHIBIT 5
Production &
Capacity Planning

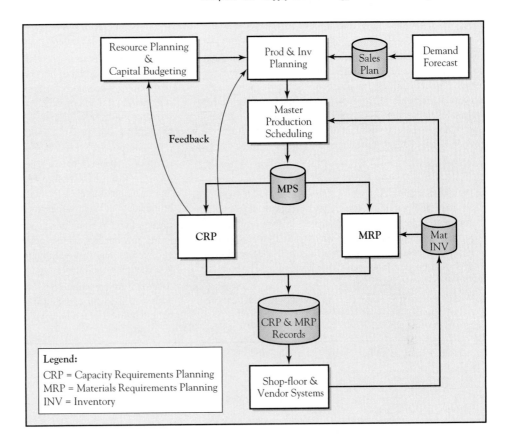

and the senior VPs of Components and Materials, and transmitted to each manufacturing facility. Each manufacturing facility thus receives an estimate of required production rates and plant managers can adjust capacity when needed. As such, the sales plan and MPS serve as an efficient coordination tool for corporate wide capacity planning.

It is rare for a production facility to fail to meet the output levels required by the final MPS, and a production facility has several options when a proposed MPS appears to be infeasible. If the infeasibility is detected early enough, the plant manager can inform the MPS schedulers and production can be shifted to other facilities. Alternatively, equipment may be flown from one facility to another, which occurs frequently when product lines are shifted among manufacturing locations. Senior managers, who can determine whether the cost of moving the equipment is justified by the profitability of the product, must approve these decisions. Sometimes, however, constraints on equipment and material availability caused some demand to remain unfilled. During 1995, a shortage of media forced Seagate to ration supply among its customers and market segments.

To make longer-term equipment purchases and install new capacity, plant managers submit a Capital Appropriation Request that must be approved by senior managers.

THE *BARRACUDA* AND *CHEETAH* CAPACITY INVESTMENT

The "sales-plan driven planning" process for the two new products thus *coordinates* capacity decisions to the single sales plan (and associated master production plan) that marketing, manufacturing and financial managers have approved. Consistent with cost incentives, the current Capital Appropriation Request on Ron Verdoorn's desk asked for the minimal cost capacity plan to enable the production plan: a *Cheetah* FA facility with an annual production capacity of 300,000 units, a *Barracuda* FA facility also with a 300,000 unit capacity and a testing facility with a corresponding 600,000 unit capacity. A capital appropriation of $103 million was requested. In addition to the fixed $40 million, the CapEx of $103 million included the linear capacity sizing costs of $30,000 per one thousand units of annual production rate (APR) in the *Cheetah* final assembly facility, whereas the more cost-efficient *Barracuda* FA facility would require a modest $20,000 per one thousand APR. The testing facility, however, would be more expensive at about $80,000 per thousand APR, reflecting the cost of many expensive IDT's.

New high-end drives such as the *Cheetah* and *Barracuda* are the "bread and butter" of Seagate. Such high-end drives are relatively immune from competition and were estimated to command average unit contribution margins of about $400 and $300 for the *Cheetah* and *Barracuda*, respectively, throughout the production cycle. Given the high demand uncertainty of the two product families, Ron was wondering whether the current capital appropriation request, which implemented the most likely sales forecast, should be approved or whether he should "adjust" the capacity investment to provide Seagate with a better operational hedge against uncertainty.

Questions:

1. What is Seagate's corporate strategy? Describe and evaluate how its operations strategy and processes support the corporate strategy. Critically evaluate Seagate's product and process development strategy, which calls for development in its respective product/process center in the U.S. and then exporting the developed process to a site in the Far-East for high-volume production.

2. What are Seagate's major risks? How does it manage those risks?

3. How would you describe the "capacity of the processing network" if the current CAR capacity proposal were implemented? What is the expected profit and ROI under this investment? (Given the short product life, assume the firm is making its decisions for a single time period of length one year, at the end of which manufacturing capacity will have zero salvage value.)

4. The case states that the true demand forecast contains uncertainty. Given this forecast, recommend a capacity portfolio that maximizes expected NPV. (Recall, capacity investment must be performed before you observe actual market demand.) Verify financial attractiveness of your recommendation: What is the expected profit and ROI now?

5. Interpret your recommended capacity portfolio in intuitive terms: in what sense does your capacity configuration prepare you to deal well with demand uncertainty? What are you "hedging" and why is your plan to be preferred?

6. In broad conceptual terms, what are the advantages of "sales-plan driven capacity planning?" What is "wrong" with that practice and how would you improve on it?

Appendix **One**

Principles of Nature: Insights into Human and System Behavior

This appendix covers 18 principles of nature. Principles of nature are phenomena that generally hold true in human or system behavior (see Table A1.1).

The principles of nature are presented and discussed at various points throughout the chapters of this book. The purpose of this appendix is to provide a single point of reference for all of the principles. For each principle, we'll begin with a definition and the managerial implications, and then we'll see examples of how these principles are applied in practice. The examples come from supply chain management applications and many other areas, which serves to reinforce the broad application and fundamental quality of the principles.

Read the material carefully, think about the examples, and begin to look for examples of these principles around you. Your goal should not be to memorize these principles, but to begin to develop an understanding of their meaning and implications.

1. BENFORD'S LAW

Definition
Numbers starting with 1 appear about six times more frequently than numbers starting with 9, or, more specifically, the predicted frequencies by starting digit are

First Digit	1	2	3	4	5	6	7	8	9
Frequency	30.1%	17.6%	12.5%	9.7%	7.9%	6.7%	5.8%	5.1%	4.6%

Implications
Humans commonly view the likelihood of each starting digit to be approximately equal, meaning that data with roughly equal starting digits may be concocted numbers, or potentially evidence of fraud.

Examples

Example 1   Frank Benford, a physicist at General Electric, proposed a frequency distribution for first digits and compared his predictions with results from a variety of datasets; for example, river basin areas, population figures, baseball statistics, and numbers appearing in *Reader's Digest* articles (see Table A1.2; Benford 1938).

TABLE A1.1   **18 Principles of Nature That Appear throughout the Text**

1. Benford's Law	7. Hockey Stick Effect	13. Pareto Phenomenon
2. Bullwhip Effect	8. It's Hard to Play Catch-Up Ball	14. Recency Effect
3. Central Limit Theorem	9. Khintchine's Limit Theorem	15. Satisfaction = Perception – Expectation
4. Curse of Utilization	10. Law of Large Numbers	16. Time Distortion
5. Curse of Variability	11. Little's Law	17. Trumpet of Doom
6. Fat-Head Effect	12. Obligation to Reciprocate	18. Winner's Curse

TABLE A1.2   **A Comparison of First Digit Frequencies Predicted by Benford's Law with Various Datasets**

First Digit	1	2	3	4	5	6	7	8	9
Benford's law	30.1%	17.6%	12.5%	9.7%	7.9%	6.7%	5.8%	5.1%	4.6%
River basin areas	31.0%	16.4%	10.7%	11.3%	7.2%	8.6%	5.5%	4.2%	5.1%
Population	33.9%	20.4%	14.2%	8.1%	7.2%	6.2%	4.1%	3.7%	2.2%
American League	32.7%	17.6%	12.6%	9.8%	7.4%	6.4%	4.9%	5.6%	3.0%
Reader's Digest	33.4%	18.5%	12.4%	7.5%	7.1%	6.5%	5.5%	4.9%	4.2%

Example 2   Benford's law has been used to detect fraudulent tax returns. For example, if the percentage of numbers on a tax return beginning with 1 is much less than 30 percent, then there is reason to suspect concocted figures (Hill 1998).

Example 3   About 30 percent of the constants in physics (gravitation, speed of light, Planck, Avogadro, etc.) begin with 1 (Knuth 1969), and, more generally, the first digit frequencies are approximated by the Benford frequencies. This result hints at a fundamental property that was shown to hold by Pinkham (1961) and Hill (1995): a random variable with sample space $(0, \infty)$ is scale invariant if and only if the probability distribution of first digits is the Benford distribution. Loosely speaking, scale invariance means that the unit of measure does not affect the probability distribution.[1] In light of this property, it is not surprising that the first-digit frequencies of constants in physics are close to Benford frequencies (i.e., the probability distribution of constants in physics, of which the current known constants represent a sample, is plausibly a scale invariant probability distribution over the positive real numbers).

Example 4   Randomly select a bunch of probability distributions, then randomly select samples from each of these distributions. The more distributions and samples you select, the closer your first-digit frequencies will be to Benford's law. This is a fairly deep limit theorem proved by Hill (1995). This theorem, along with the property noted in example 3, help explain why Benford first-digit frequencies are common in tables of collected data.

Example 5   Your firm has been helping a key supplier to reduce their costs for the past several years with the arrangement that any cost savings are split. As you're viewing the monthly unit cost reports from the supplier, a name suddenly pops into your head, "Benford." Thinking back to college days, you recall a couple of benchmarks for first-digit Benford frequencies: 30 percent for a first digit of 1 and 70 percent for the first digits of 1 through 4. The data in the reports don't match up, you become suspicious, and you do a

---

[1] More precisely, if X is a random variable, c is some fixed number, and $Y = cX$, then the probability distribution of X is scale invariant if $P[Y < y] = P[X < y/c]$.

little investigation. It's now six months later. Your firm just received a $250,000 check from the supplier due to an "accounting error" in costing, and your boss is still talking about your uncanny sense of something amiss in the supplier cost reports.

Example 6   Charlie, one of the stars in the TV show *Numb3rs,* uses Benford's law to identify a fabricated set of data (in episode 28 entitled "The Running Man," first aired on February 2, 2006).

Comments

What is the intuition behind Benford's law? Some intuition may come from thinking about numbers and percentage changes, especially for numbers that tend to grow over time (e.g., population, stock price). Since a much larger percentage change is required to change the first digit of smaller numbers than for larger numbers (e.g., $+100$ percent to go from 10 to 20 versus $+50$ percent to go from 20 to 30), a small first digit should be more common than a large first digit. This notion is captured in the following rough approximation for the predicted frequency of first digit i: $(1/i)/[1/1 + 1/2 + \cdots + 1/9]^2$ (the precise formula for Benford's law is $\log_{10}(1 + 1/i)$).

Benford was not the first to notice this phenomenon. Simon Newcomb conjectured the first-digit frequency formula $\log_{10}(1 + 1/i)$ in 1881 (Newcomb 1881). He came to this observation by wondering why the beginning of a book of logarithms was much more worn than the end (Peterson1998). Additional background on this principle of nature can be found in Raimi (1969).

2. BULLWHIP EFFECT

Definition

Variability in observed demand increases with higher stages in a supply chain; for example, consumer demand on a retailer is less volatile than factory orders.

Implication

The bullwhip effect contributes to high cost and poor service in supply chains. Understand the causes of the bullwhip effect and look for ways to limit the effect by controlling the causes.

Examples

Example 1   Management at Procter & Gamble was struck by the wide variability in orders to the P&G factory for Pampers disposable diapers. Management reckoned that consumer demand for Pampers should be fairly stable, and, upon investigation, they found this to be the case. They also noticed that the orders they placed with their suppliers for diaper raw materials fluctuated even more than the demand they observed. They coined this phenomenon the *bullwhip effect,* and they set about reducing the causes by making the supplier–wholesaler–retailer–consumer more like a continuous loop while reducing price fluctuation. Today, when a P&G product is scanned at the checkout register, the information is sent directly to P&G and is used to automatically plan where and when to send

---

[2] The idea underlying the formula is that $1/i$ is the percentage increase required to change the first digit from i to $i + 1$, so $(1/i)/[1/1 + 1/2 + \cdots + 1/9]$ is the percentage increase required to change first digit i as the percent of the total. The result is a rough approximation of the relative size of the bucket containing numbers with first digit i given that period-to-period percentage increases in all of the numbers, while possibly random, have a fairly stable mean.

replenishment shipments. The paperless system not only reduces mistakes, but reduces lead times and inventory while improving service and cash flow. P&G also reduced the number of price changes in a day from 55 to 1 and reduced the number of price brackets by 80 percent. The efforts helped reduce the bullwhip effect and improve performance; that is, a 60 percent reduction in inventory and a companywide improvement in efficiency from 55 percent to over 80 percent (Saporito 1994).

Example 2 Robert Grove, a regional marketing director for Viewlocity, has experience with the bullwhip effect. He observes how business reactions to a change in the market get more exaggerated as the firm gets further away from the source of the change. Information becomes more distorted, which contributes to poor forecasting, poor customer service, and higher costs (Ng 2001).

Example 3 Figure A1.1 illustrates the bullwhip effect by comparing customer demand history for Hewlett-Packard printers at a reseller with replenishment orders shipped to the reseller.

FIGURE A1.1 HP printer demand at the warehouse (orders) is more volatile than customer demand (sales).

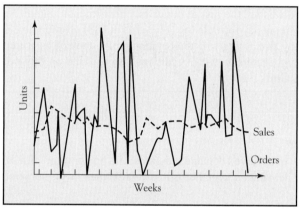

Source: Used with permission from Callioni and Billington (2001).

Example 4 The beer game is a simulated beer supply chain that developed at MIT in the 1960s. Players take on the role of manufacturer, distributor, wholesaler, or retailer. The retailer observes demand each week and places orders with the wholesaler. The wholesaler in turn orders from the distributor, the distributor orders from the manufacturer, and the manufacturer decides how much beer to brew. With the exception of the retailer, the other companies in the supply chain do not have a good idea of consumer demand, and this uncertainty contributes to overreaction. A small change in consumer demand tends to create large changes in the ordering patterns further up the supply chain (Surowiecki 2003).

Comments on the Causes of the Bullwhip Effect

The bullwhip effect is present in many supply chains. The causes include (1) demand forecast updating, (2) order batching, (3) price fluctuation, and (4) an attempt to beat the system during shortage periods (Lee, Padmanabhan, and Whang 1997a, 1997b).

1. Demand forecast updating refers to how an increase or decrease in a demand forecast by a firm tends to get amplified in an order to a supplier. Two reasons for this are time lags and quantity uncertainty. A small change in the demand forecast gets translated into a large change in the next replenishment order as pipeline and safety stock inventory

targets are updated to account for the updated forecast. As time lags and quantity uncertainty increases, the sensitivity of pipeline and safety stock inventory targets (and ultimately the replenishment order quantity) to changes in the demand forecast increases. In addition, adjustments in the demand forecast are susceptible to overreaction due to the recency effect.

2. Order batching refers to the practice of placing periodic large orders. A retailer may save transportation costs, for example, by ordering in full truckload quantities. A consequence is that a steady consumer demand pattern is transformed into an irregular retailer demand pattern of periodic larger orders.[3]

3. Changes in price contribute to the bullwhip effect because large orders tend to appear before price increases go into effect, or in response to promotions. This surge in demand may be interpreted at higher levels in the supply chain as an increase in true consumer demand. The result is that orders increase, and then drop off when the demand is not sustained.

4. Finally, the last cause of the bullwhip effect refers to gaming. It has been common practice to allocate supply to customers in proportion to order quantities during periods of shortages. This means that if I'm a retailer selling a hot product and the supplier can't satisfy all demand, I may place an order for 400 cases even if I expect that I can sell no more than 100 cases. I'm betting that the supplier will try to satisfy around 25 percent of demand right away, and I can always cancel a portion of my order later on.

Investigation of the bullwhip effect, or, more generally, oscillations in supply chains, goes back to the 1950s with the work of Jay Forrester on industrial dynamics (Forrester 1961). At the most basic level, industrial dynamics seeks to understand the causes of boom-bust cycles in the economy. Forrester observed how a small jump in consumer sales would lead to larger increases in orders further up the supply chain, which would lead to overproduction (the boom) and a presage to significant cutbacks (the bust). Industrial dynamics has helped clarify the role of organizational structure, operating policies, and time delays on the success of an enterprise.

3. CENTRAL LIMIT THEOREM

Definition
As the number of independent random variables increases, the probability distribution of the sum approaches the normal distribution.

Implication
Random measures of interest are often comprised of many approximately independent random components. In such cases, analysis of uncertainty based on the normal distribution is a good approximation.

---

[3] As an aside, the effect of order batching on demand volatility tends to shrink as the number of customers increases. This is due to another principle of nature—the law of large numbers. For example, consider a grocery store selling Coke. The store may have a customer base of, say, 500 Coke buyers. On average, an individual customer may buy a case or two of Coke about once every three weeks. However, the composite demand from all 500 buyers is relatively steady on a day-to-day basis. Similarly, if a wholesaler supplies 500 outlets and each outlet places an order about once every three weeks, then the composite daily demand is relatively steady.

Examples

Example 1 Statistical process control is a tool for process improvement (see Chapter 11). The tool is based on estimating probabilities that a system has changed from observations. The central limit theorem is the basis for a common way of estimating these probabilities.

Example 2 If you take a large sample of people, ask them their height, and plot the distribution, you'll see that it looks like a graph of the normal distribution—it has a bell curve shape. There could be several factors that contribute to this result, but one likely factor is the effect of many "random" elements that come together to determine the height of a human. Roughly speaking, the central limit theorem tells us that a measure that is a combination of many random components will tend to be approximately normally distributed.

Example 3 American Airlines finds that demand for any given route (e.g., the 10 a.m. flight from Detroit to Dallas) tends to be approximately normally distributed. AA uses knowledge of the demand distribution as input to their revenue management system. This system supports decisions on prices to charge for various tickets (first class, super saver, Saturday night layover, 21-day advance, etc.) and the degree to which a flight may be over-booked. AA estimates that their revenue management system generates almost $1 billion in annual incremental revenue. To put this in perspective, 1997 was the only year in its history that AA has had operating earnings approaching $1 billion (Cook 1998).

Example 4 Cineval LLC is a media-consulting firm that develops valuations of film investments. Their data on profits from 28 live-action films show a wide range of performance with a sizable percentage of the films incurring losses or miniscule profits, and a random scattering of increasingly profitable films up to a single extraordinarily successful film. But a different picture, in the shape of a bell curve, appears when the distribution of average profit from multiple randomly selected films is plotted. As predicted by the central limit theorem, the distribution of profit approaches normal as one diversifies across additional films, and this phenomenon is incorporated into Cineval's valuation methods. Interestingly, Cineval also finds evidence of another principle of nature. Their data suggest that "the chance of losing your shirt drops from about 20% with a single film to about 1% with four films" (Savage 2003). Why is this? It's because of the law of large numbers; the uncertainty in the valuation per film is lower with a group of four films than for a single film. According to the president of Cineval, it requires decades of experience for some people to learn that.

Comments

The fundamental nature of the normal probability distribution is also apparent in information theory and the notion of entropy (Shannon 1948). The entropy of a probability distribution measures the amount of uncertainty (or information content) associated with the distribution.[4] Among all continuous probability distributions with known mean and standard deviation, the normal probability distribution has the maximum entropy. Therefore, if all you know about a distribution is its mean and standard deviation, it is reasonable to assume that the distribution is normal (e.g., any other distribution assumes knowledge of additional information). As an aside, if all you know about a distribution is the minimum and maximum possible values of the random variable, then it is reasonable to assume that the distribution is uniform (i.e., the uniform probability distribution has the maximum entropy among all distributions with known finite range).

---

[4] For a continuous probability distribution $f(x)$, the measure of entropy is $-\int f(x)\log f(x)dx$.

4. CURSE OF UTILIZATION

Definition

Average flowtime skyrockets as resource utilization gets close to 100 percent.

Implication

Utilization of a system or resource is the percent of time that the system or resource is busy. Unless there is very little variability in a process, resources will have to be underutilized to provide responsive service.

Examples

Example 1   Ananth is registered for 9 credit hours in the fall semester while Vernon has an 18-hour credit load and is also a member of the football team. Vernon, whose utilization with respect to scholastic and athletic time commitments is very high, will probably have more difficulty completing assignments on time.

Example 2   Helkama Bica Oy is a Finnish company that manufactures communication cables and bicycles. In the early 1990s, the company looked at different ways to improve response time. After analysis, they identified a bottleneck resource and invested in a system that reduced the run time on this machine, and hence its utilization (de Treville 1992). The notion of planned excess capacity is sometimes difficult to accept because it runs counter to a historical view that a well-run factory was one where labor and equipment were 100 percent utilized—a view that does not mesh with firms that compete on short lead times in volatile markets.

Example 3   A study by the New Jersey Institute of Technology was commissioned to examine problems with traffic jams and delays on New Jersey highways. The researchers found that the highway system had very little excess capacity, which meant that any small increase in volume creates a disproportionate increase in delay (Stile 2000).

5. CURSE OF VARIABILITY

Definition

Variability causes congestion. In other words, as variance in interarrival times and/or processing times increases, average flowtime increases.

Implications

Look for ways to reduce variance in processes.

Examples

Example 1   Carnegie Mellon University has worked on a system that essentially allows cars to drive themselves using sensors. Imagine, it's 15 years from now; you hop in your car, specify your route, say "go," then take a nap or surf the Net until you get there. In addition to safety benefits, the researchers expect the road network to be able to handle much more volume with less congestion. One reason: reduced variance in vehicle speeds— vehicles on the highway appear a little like railcars in a train.

Example 2   A common way to reduce variance in service time, as well as service time, is to simplify the process of providing the service. Next time you go to McDonald's, look behind the cash register. In some markets, McDonald's is testing registers that have pictures of food items rather than numbers on the buttons. One advantage of this design is that it helps reduce variance in checkout time by making it harder to make a mistake when pricing an order.

Comments

Variance in the time to provide a service or the time between when customers arrive will not be much of a problem when resource utilization is low. For example, high or low variance will not have much impact on the time it takes to get a Big Mac if there are 300 cashiers. Variance really starts to cause problems as resource utilization increases. For you as a manager, this means that efforts to reduce variance are more likely to pay off if resources are highly utilized in your business.

6. FAT-HEAD EFFECT

Definition

People tend to be overconfident in their decision-making ability.

Implication

Identifying biases in your mental models that underlie your decisions is difficult. Maintain a critical eye and humility in your judgments, and seek honest input from others.

Examples

Example 1[5]   Suppose you fold a piece of paper in half 50 times. Take a moment to think about how thick the folded up paper will be. Now estimate a high number and a low number such that you think there is a 95 percent chance that the actual thickness will be within the range. If you are similar to most, the correct answer will fall outside your 95 percent confidence bounds, or, in other words, most are overconfident in their judgment.[6]

Example 2   A group of nine physicians recorded their assessment of the probability of pneumonia for 1,531 patients who complained of a cough. The physicians were consistently overconfident in their assessments. For example, only 20 percent of the patients viewed by physicians as almost certain to have pneumonia (probability estimated at 88 percent) actually had pneumonia (Christensen-Szalanski and Bushyhead 1981).

Example 3   Compare your sense of how you performed on an exam versus actual performance. The fat-head effect suggests that you generally have a sense that you did better than actual performance.

Example 4   Hilary and Menzly (2006) find that analysts who forecast earnings more accurately than the median analyst in the recent past are likely to forecast less accurately in the near future. The authors suggest that the experience of recent success contributes to a cognitive bias of overconfidence that leads to poor near-term future performance (i.e., success leads analysts to place too much weight on their private sense of the market and too little weight on public signals of market direction). The phenomenon tends to be cyclical, where negative feedback from poor performance reduces overconfidence, forecast accuracy improves, and overconfidence returns.

Comments

Judgmental bias toward overconfidence can be a significant handicap, especially for those who are unaware of the phenomenon. In the view of Plous (1993), "no problem in judgment and decision-making is more prevalent and more potentially catastrophic than overconfidence." That said, some qualifications are in order. First, there are exceptions. Weather

---

[5] From Sterman (2000, p. 272).

[6] For curiosity sake, a piece of paper 0.1 mm thick folded 50 times will be $2^{50} \times 10^{-1}$ mm $\times$ 10^{-7} km/mm $\approx$ 113 million km thick, or nearly the distance between the earth and sun (approx 149 million km)—you'll need a really, really big piece of paper.

forecasters and bookies, for example, seem fairly resistant to the fat-head effect—perhaps in part due to extensive practice and feedback (Lichtenstein, Fischhoff, and Phillips 1992). Second, the strength of the fat-head effect appears to be somewhat dependent on difficulty. For example, there is evidence that overconfidence is reduced as tasks or judgments get easier, sometimes to the point of underconfidence (Lichtenstein and Fischhoff 1977).

7. HOCKEY STICK EFFECT

Definition

On October 6, 2000, Boston Bruins defenseman Marty McSorley was found guilty of assault for slashing Vancouver Canuck Donald Brashear in the head with a hockey stick (Jourard 2000). I suppose this is one interpretation of the hockey stick effect, but the one we are concerned with is the phenomenon: volume and activity increase near the end of a reporting period.

Implication

Be aware and plan for the effect and, since the periods of mad rush are usually relatively inefficient, look for ways to reduce the magnitude of the effect.

Examples

Example 1 If you graph the number of hours spent studying for this class each week, you'll probably see an upward spike (i.e., the blade of the hockey stick) near exam time. This example highlights a major cause of the hockey stick effect—procrastination. (Professors sometimes give frequent quizzes/exams to help reduce the hockey stick effect.)

Example 2 Many companies get caught in a cycle where more than half of their quarterly sales are booked in the last two weeks of the quarter. Over the years, customers learn to hold off on ordering until near the end of the quarter when salespeople are forced to offer deals to hit their sales targets (*Sales Manager's Bulletin* 1996).

Example 3 One company reports performance so frequently and exhaustively that there is little opportunity for much of a hockey stick effect. C.R. England is a family-owned, long-haul refrigerated trucking company in Salt Lake City. A computer system continually monitors about 500 different performance measures, and feedback is given weekly (Fierman 1995).

Example 4 You may have heard the admonition "Beware of speeding, especially near the end of a month." Police squads sometimes have monthly quotas or targets for speeding tickets, and due to the hockey stick effect, there tends to be a rash of tickets issued near the end of the month.

Example 5 Compaq has used channel stuffing to hit revenue targets and has suffered the consequences. First quarter 1998 was particularly disastrous. After shoving excess product into its distribution channels to hit 1997 revenue targets, IBM announced steep price cuts in February. Compaq sales plummeted and the firm was stuck with 8 to 10 weeks of inventory—a very expensive proposition when PC component prices are dropping by about 1 to 2 percent per week (Schonfeld 1998).

Example 6 Enterprise software companies are particularly susceptible to the hockey stick effect. The percentage of total quarterly revenue by month can be as distorted as 10 percent, 10 percent, 80 percent. Contracts are large—deals worth $1 million or more are not uncommon. Quarterly sales reports in the fast-paced software market have a large impact on stock price and a software company's ability to raise funds. There is great pressure to hit sales targets, and customers are known to wait until the very last day of the quarter before signing (Gurley 2001).

Example 7 Coors ran a promotion for their salespeople. Whoever had highest sales in the quarter would receive a free vacation. The person who won was a good friend of some of his buyers—as a favor, very large orders were placed that filled the backroom space of grocery stores with Coors beer.

Example 8 When is the best time to buy a new car in the United States? According to Charles Givens in his book entitled *Financial Self Defense,* at the end of the year, end of the quarter, or end of the month—in that order. Most dealers submit sales reports to the manufacturer at these times, and if sales have been slow, there is extra pressure to increase sales before the end of the reporting period. Fleet managers know that if sales are in decline, manufacturers may reduce the dealer's allocation (e.g., the number of top-selling cars shipped to the dealer). In addition, by January 3 of each year, auto dealers must pay $1,200 to $3,000 in taxes on each vehicle in the dealer's lot. The end of December or just after the New Year is a great time to buy.

Comments

You may hear the phrase "end of period push," which is the same thing as the hockey stick effect. You also may hear the term "channel stuffing" or "trade loading," which is an activity that contributes to the hockey stick effect. Channel stuffing (a.k.a. trade loading) occurs when a company encourages their customers to load up on inventory, usually by offering a limited term discount. It occurs at the end of a key financial reporting period (e.g., at the end of a quarter or a year) to boost sales, perhaps to hit a sales target (e.g., see examples 2 and 5–7). The practice borders on being bookkeeping sleight of hand—future sales suffer because high levels of inventory in the distribution channel must be sold off. A variation on the hockey stick effect also appears in financial markets, where it is known as *window dressing* (Chen 2000). Stocks that have done well in a quarter tend to do even better near the end of the quarter (similarly, poor-performing stocks tend to do worse near the end of the quarter). One explanation is that fund managers tend to sell laggards and buy winners near the end of a quarter in order to boost quarterly performance.

8. IT'S HARD TO PLAY CATCH-UP BALL

Definition

Once you're behind in the eyes of your customer, it's difficult to turn the situation around (Maister 1984). In other words, people tend to be more sensitive to losses than gains.

Implication

Invest extra attention and resources in the front end of a service to avoid getting behind.

Examples

Example 1 Restaurants sometimes have a policy of overestimating the time it will take to get a table. If you're willing to wait, and you get seated earlier than the estimate, the experience begins on a positive note. On the other hand, if you're told a table should be ready in 15 minutes and you end up waiting 30 minutes, it may be difficult for the restaurant to turn your attitude around so that you walk away feeling good about the experience.

Example 2 Getting a good job is probably a concern for many. This principle is one reason why it's especially important to avoid a negative first impression during the interview.

Example 3 Richard Thaler, an economist at the University of Chicago, has conducted many experiments with students and executives that center on how people value gains and losses (e.g., see Thaler 1994). For example, suppose you have the opportunity to play a game where the outcome is determined by a flip of a coin. If the toss returns heads, then you have to pay $500. How much would you have to win in the event of tails in order to want to play the game? For most people, the answer is at least $1,000. Thaler's research suggests that losing money feels twice as bad as making money feels good (O'Reilly 1998).

Example 4   Awareness of the insight can be traced back at least 2,000 years to an observation in the writings of Plutarch, who observed that "bad news travels fast."

Comments

A managerial implication of this principle is "invest extra attention and resources in the front end of a service to avoid getting behind." This deserves some qualification in light of another principle of nature, that is, satisfaction = perception – expectation. Getting behind in the eyes of a customer may not be so bad as long as you can recover very quickly relative to expectations. For example, a global hotel chain discovered that guests who experienced a problem that was quickly resolved rated the hotel service higher than those guests who experienced no problems (Schrage 2001). In this case, investments in recovery management may be more profitable than investments in problem prevention. Of course, a key to the success of this tactic is the continued preponderance of poor service with minimal resolution in everyday life; customers are so surprised by the rapid and polite resolution of their problem that the experience stands out in a positive way, or, in other words, satisfaction = perception – expectation.

9. KHINTCHINE'S[7] LIMIT THEOREM

Definition

As the number of independent random arrival processes increases, the probability distribution of the time between arrivals of the aggregate process is more closely approximated by an exponential distribution. To make this more concrete, think of one arrival process as your arrivals at a particular grocery store. Your friend also shops at the same store, so a second arrival process is her arrivals at the store. There are thousands of other customers, and, consequently, thousands of other arrival processes. The probability distributions governing the time between arrivals may be different for each process. However, in rough terms, (1) if these processes are independent of one another and (2) successive arrivals for any one process are independent of one another, then the time between arrivals of customers at the store is approximately exponentially distributed.[8]

Note on Terminology

If the time between successive events (e.g., arrivals) is exponentially distributed, then the number of events per period follows a Poisson probability distribution, and the process of events is known as a *Poisson process*.

Implication

If a random process is an aggregation of many independent processes, then it is likely to be well approximated by a Poisson process. This is meaningful because there are insights and simple predictive formulas that hold for models with Poisson processes. The Khintchine limit theorem supports the validity and use of these insights and formulas in a range of practical settings.

---

[7] Pronounced "hinchin."

[8] More formally, under fairly general conditions, the superposition of a large number of independent renewal processes is close to a Poisson process (see Khintchine 1960 or Feller 1965).

Examples

Example 1   Poisson processes are observed in a diverse range of phenomena, including radioactive decay (Kendall 1943), the number of raisins in a slice of raisin bread (Feller 1965), the number of new wars in the world during a year (Richardson 1956), the number of tornado touchdowns, and the number of Web server hits (Hayes 2002).

Example 2   A Poisson arrival process has a feast-or-famine character. For example, David Kelton of Penn State noted that, in the context of a Poisson distribution, the rash of shark attacks along Florida's coast during summer 2001 is not unusual. If any event is plotted on a timeline (e.g., airline crash, shark attack, a customer entering a fast food restaurant), then a pattern will emerge—there will be periods where not much happens followed by a rash of events (*ORMS Today* 2001).

Comments

Hints of the fundamental nature of the exponential distribution can be seen elsewhere in the world around us. For example, imagine gravity acting upon a gas at constant pressure and temperature. The height of a random molecule can be viewed as a random variable, say X. The potential energy, which is proportional to the expected value of X (i.e., average height of a molecule), remains fixed. However, over time, the system will tend toward maximum entropy due to the second law of thermodynamics. At maximum entropy, the probability distribution of X is the exponential distribution.

The concept of entropy, and the connection to the exponential distribution, extends to information theory (Shannon 1948). The value of a randomly selected piece of information transmitted over a communication channel can be viewed as a random variable. Entropy in information theory is a measure of uncertainty in the communication system. If only the mean value of information is known, then entropy is maximized when the probability distribution of X is exponentially distributed.

The name of the principle comes from Aleksandr Khintchine (Khintchine 1960).

10. LAW OF LARGE NUMBERS

Definition[9]

As volume increases, relative variability decreases.

Implication

Look for ways to change operations so that planning can be done at a more aggregate unit.

Examples

Example 1   Benetton used to forecast demand for each color of a particular sweater. They have since invested in equipment that allows them to dye sweaters very quickly (Camuffo, Romano, and Vinelli 2001). As a result, they now forecast demand for all colors of a sweater and, based on this forecast, produce a bunch of white sweaters. Then, as customer orders are received, they color accordingly. By postponing the coloring of sweaters until there are more reliable indicators of demand, forecast errors have reduced.

Example 2   The World Series just ended and your challenge is to predict your favorite player's batting average after the first five games of the upcoming season and at the end of that season. Which prediction do you think is likely to be more accurate? If you guessed your end-of-season forecast, you have an intuitive feel for the law of large numbers.

---

[9] There are more precise ways to state the law of large numbers (e.g., see Ross 1988). This definition is most convenient for our purposes.

Example 3 The order processing department at a small company had two people: one person was responsible for order entry and the other person was responsible for credit checking. The company decided to train both workers to perform both tasks. They found that the workload on each person became much smoother.

Example 4 Hewlett-Packard used to customize printers for foreign markets at the factory, which is cheaper than customizing in the field. But there were significant mismatches between demand and supply; for example, there were not enough printers configured for the British market and too many for the French market. HP changed operations so that generic printers were shipped to a European warehouse and configured in response to customer orders (Feitzinger and Lee 1997). This change increased production costs, but, by more effectively matching supply and demand, HP saved more than $3 million per month (Coy 1999).

Example 5 A canning company sold fish under various private labels and their own company label. There was no difference in the product; only the labels were different. After canning, product was shipped to warehouses, where it was later sent to customers. Forecasting was difficult, and product had to periodically be sold for a loss as the expiration date approached. The company decided to install labeling equipment in the warehouses and cans were labeled as orders were received. Accordingly, product was shipped to warehouses based on a total demand forecast for a type of fish rather than forecasts for each label. The cost of the labeling equipment was more than offset by inventory savings (Stolle 1967).

Example 6 The law of large numbers is largely the basis for the emergence of an industry. Costs and capabilities of telecommunications switching equipment have steadily improved over the years. By the early 1990s, this technology reached a point where centralized answering service companies began to form. For example, Communications Centers Midwest contracts with organizations such as AAA (American Automobile Association) and S.C. Johnson, among others. If a customer calls one of about 300 AAA offices in Wisconsin and the line is busy, then the call is automatically routed to CCM. Operators either provide information to the customer or take a message. The average call volume at CCM is much larger than the average call volume at any of the individual AAA locations, and, consequently, the relative variability in call volume is less; CCM is able to staff more efficiently. What we see in this example is an industry where the source of customer value is largely due to a principle of nature—the law of large numbers.

Example 7 Paul Molitor was traded from the Milwaukee Brewers to the Toronto Blue Jays in 1993. Molitor, who was a very good hitter, was placed in the batting order immediately after John Olerud. There was a time during the season that Olerud was batting over .400, and the consensus among analysts was that the trade should increase Olerud's chances of a .400 season. The reason: pitchers would be less able to pitch around Olerud with Molitor on deck. The analysts may have been right, but it was interesting that a sportswriter named Andy Cohen argued just the opposite; he said the trade should reduce the chance of Olerud hitting over .400 for the season. His argument was based on the law of large numbers. Since pitchers would be less likely to pitch around Olerud, he would get more official "at bats" (i.e., fewer walks), which would cause his season-ending batting average to be closer to his true batting average, and, since he's mortal, his true batting average is probably less than .400. For the curious, Olerud's batting average for the 1993 season was .363 and the Blue Jays won the World Series.

Example 8 Years ago I worked on a project related to new product introductions. We had demand rate projections but no information on demand volatility, which, among other uses, is important for planning inventory buildup prior to market introduction. In the end, we used the projected demand rate to estimate demand volatility. From regression analysis, we found that the standard deviation of demand per week was proportional to the demand rate raised to the 0.63 power. This means, for example, that a 100 percent increase in the demand rate is associated with only a 55 percent increase in the standard deviation, or, in other words, as volume increases, relative variability decreases.[10]

Example 9 Sherwin-Williams used to stock different colors of paints in their stores. Today, stores basically carry only white paint and an inventory of dyes. The company has installed precise mixing machines. A customer selects the color of paint from a template of options, and the dyes are mixed with white paint to create the desired color. Customized colors are also possible; a customer can bring in a sample of a desired color and paint is mixed to match it. The result is a wide array of color choices, high availability of colors "in stock," and relatively low inventory investment.

Example 10 Next time you place an order in the McDonald's drive-though line, pay careful attention to the voice in order to assess whether it matches the person at the pick-up window. The person taking your order may be located many miles away. McDonald's operates a drive-through call center in Santa Maria, California, that provides drive-through order-taking service to restaurants throughout the country (Richtel 2006). Other order-takers work out of their homes in rural North Dakota. After your order is taken, it is transmitted instantaneously over the Internet to the restaurant. The benefits of such an approach are not due to lower wages of order-takers, which are comparable to other McDonald's employees. Rather, a key advantage stems from the law of large numbers. With the high order volume, the workload of incoming orders to the group of remote order-takers is relatively steady—there are few gaps in time between taking orders. The result is higher productivity with each worker taking up to 95 orders per hour.

Comments

This is one of the more powerful principles. It underlies such tactics as postponement of form (a.k.a. delayed differentiation; illustrated in examples 1, 4, 5, and 9), cross-training (illustrated in example 3), and postponement of place through centralization of inventory (e.g., Amazon.com). It also underlies tactics you may have seen in other classes such as diversification of financial portfolios, methods for determining sample sizes in market research studies, and geographical diversification in insurance. For those interested in insurance and the tactic of geographical diversification, the law of large numbers is why you wouldn't want all of your homeowner policyholders to be concentrated in the Los Angeles area (e.g., the big one hits and you're out of business).

11. LITTLE'S LAW

Definition

Average inventory = throughput rate × average flowtime.

Implication

If you can find ways to reduce flowtime, you will benefit from reduced inventory investment, and vice versa.

---

[10] This type of relationship between volume and volatility is also discussed in Brown (1963); see also Brown (1967).

Examples

Example 1　Many of you are probably familiar with the financial ratio *inventory turnover*. One way to express inventory turnover is $T = C/I$ where T = turns per year, C = cost of goods sold for the year, and I = average inventory investment during the year. We can rewrite this formula as $I = C(1/T)$, or, in other words, average inventory = throughput rate $\times$ average flowtime.

Example 2　On average, two gallons of milk will last twice as long in your refrigerator as one gallon of milk.

Example 3　Little's law also can be written as average inventory $\div$ throughput rate = average flowtime. Suppose, for example, that the average demand rate is 20 units per day and average inventory is 100 units. With these numbers, it makes sense that inventory can cover an average of five days' worth of demand (i.e., five days of supply) and so the average length of time a unit is in inventory is five days (i.e., average flowtime is five days). In terms of the numbers in the example, 100 units $\div$ 20 units/day = 5 days, or, more generally, average inventory $\div$ throughput rate = average flowtime.

Comment

The name of the law comes from John Little (Little 1961).

12. OBLIGATION TO RECIPROCATE

Definition

Individuals feel some obligation to repay in kind.

Implication

Reciprocity can be a basis for tactics to persuade others, or for others to persuade you.

Examples

Example 1[11]　Random pedestrians were asked if they would be willing to chaperone juvenile detention center inmates for a day trip to the zoo; 17 percent said yes. In another trial, pedestrians were asked if they would be willing to serve as an unpaid counselor at the center for two hours per week for the next two years. Everyone said no. They were then asked, "if you can't do that, would you chaperone a group of juvenile detention center inmates on a day trip to the zoo?" The percentage of those who agreed nearly tripled to 50 percent. In this example, the requester offered a concession from a two-year request to a few hours, which in turn created some pressure on the person to repay with a concession of her own.

Example 2　Free labels with your postal address will sometimes accompany requests in the mail for donations.

Comments

There is a branch of social psychology that attempts to understand why and how people are influenced to say yes. In addition to reciprocation, Cialdini (2001) describes five other principles: consistency, social validation, liking, authority, and scarcity.

The principle of consistency is that individuals feel some obligation to be consistent with earlier public behavior. For example, researchers found that contributions for the disabled doubled when they got residents to sign a petition supporting the cause two weeks before returning to ask for a contribution.

[11] From Cialdini (2001).

The principle of social validation is that individuals are more open to widely accepted ideas and behaviors. Evidence of the principle is widespread in advertising with phrases such as "best seller" or "fastest growing." Cialdini (2001) recounts an experiment in the late 1960s. A man stood on a New York sidewalk and stared at the sky. About 4 percent of pedestrians stopped to look up. The experiment was repeated, but with five men starring at the sky; 18 percent of pedestrians stopped to look up.

The principle of liking is that individuals are more open to those they like. Notice, for example, how a car salesperson freely dispenses compliments and probes for something that you both have in common. Reingen and Kernan (1993) found that attractive fundraisers received nearly twice as many donations as others and that attractive salespeople were more effective.

The principle of authority is that authority influences trust. For example, much of the early success of Crest is commonly credited to being the only toothpaste with a seal of approval from the American Dental Association. Cialdini (2001) reports a 1995 study on the willingness of pedestrians to follow someone's lead of crossing a street against the crosswalk light. The rate increased by 350 percent when the leader wore a suit and tie (i.e., markers of authority) rather than casual dress.

The principle of scarcity is that perceived value increases with perceived scarcity. This is a reason for the phrase "limited time offer" that appears in advertisements. Researchers in Florida found that impressions of cafeteria food increased significantly with no other change than an announcement that meals would not be available for several weeks due to a fire (Cialdini 2001).

13. PARETO PHENOMENON

Definition

The *lion's share*[12] of an aggregate measure is determined by relatively few factors, or, in other words, the important are few and the trivial are many.

Implication

Invest time and energy to identify a few factors that drive performance and focus attention and resources on these. The process of separating the "important few" from the "trivial many" is known as *Pareto analysis*.

Examples

Example 1   Amana, an appliance maker, has used a tactic they call ABC scheduling that works like this. First, the product line is stratified according to importance. A items are the high-volume products; they tend to be the most popular models at each price point (e.g., around 15 percent of the product line that makes up about 80 percent of the volume). B items are of moderate volume and C items are the dogs. A items are produced every month, B items are produced about once per quarter, and C items are produced once every six months. A items are critical for the business and thus warrant close synchronization

---

[12] One of Aesop's fables concerns a lion, fox, and ass who must divide the kill after a joint hunt. The ass divides the kill into three equal parts and invites the others to choose. The lion is incensed and eats the ass, and, afterwards, asks the fox to make the division. The fox divides into one huge heap and one tiny morsel. "Who has taught you, my excellent fellow, the art of division," says the lion. The fox replies, "I learned it from the ass, by witnessing his fate," proving once again that the party with the power gets the "lion's share."

with the market. For the less important items, it makes more economic sense to produce large batches infrequently.

Example 2   Sunbeam changed their approach to developing demand forecasts a while back. One major element of their approach was the use of customer input, though they first conducted Pareto analysis to rank their customers by volume, and then focused on a small set of customers that contributed most of the volume. Each month, their 200 largest customers would provide demand estimates for Sunbeam products in their market. Sunbeam found demand forecast accuracy improved significantly, which allowed them to reduce their inventory by nearly 50 percent. The impact of this change was significant.[13]

Example 3   Dataram produces computer memory devices. The company went from $3 million to $10 million in annual revenues over a period of four years. Rapid growth is a red flag that inventories may be out of control, and this is what was happening at Dataram—they had way too much of some purchased parts and not enough of others. As a result, the company went through Pareto analysis of their raw material inventories. A items were defined as those parts where they were spending an average of $40 per week or more in purchase cost. The firm changed operations to maintain tight control of these parts through manual material requirements planning (i.e., a proactive, but time-consuming, approach). The remaining parts were managed using a simple bin reserve system (i.e., a reactive approach where, for example, four bins' worth of a part are ordered whenever inventory drops below two bins).

Example 4   I know of someone who worked in an insurance agency. He always meant well and he worked hard, but his mode of operation was the antithesis of Pareto analysis. He would come up with an idea and run with it without thinking it through or even seeing it to completion, and then repeat the process. The office gave him a book that captured his approach—*Ready, Fire, Aim.*

Example 5   There are thousands of magazine titles sold through nearly a quarter of million retail outlets in the United States, but the top 100 titles account for over 80 percent of all unit sales.

Comments

This is another principle that underlies a wide variety of tactics in practice. The name comes from the person who formally recognized the phenomenon, though it was no doubt known before this time. Vilfredo Pareto was a 19th-century Italian economist who studied the distribution of wealth. He found, for example, that 15 percent of the population controlled 85 percent of the wealth in Milan, Italy. At a more fundamental level, the phenomenon stems from diversity in the environment.

14. RECENCY EFFECT

Definition
People tend to overreact to recent events.

Implication
Consider recent events when filtering human judgment.

---

[13] For the purposes of illustration, I'll estimate earnings before taxes at 5 percent of sales and inventory investment expense at 2 percent prior to the new forecasting approach. If inventory investment expense drops to 1 percent of sales, then earnings before taxes increase by 20 percent. We get even more leverage if we look at the impact on return on assets: if inventory is, say, 20 percent of assets and profit increases by 20 percent, return on assets increases by 50 percent.

Examples

Example 1   Aggregate planning (AP) is the process of planning output and employment levels, usually by month over a period of one year or more. In 1963, E. H. Bowman proposed a tool for AP that is based on an insight into human behavior. He observed that planners would respond to negative feedback by overcompensating in the next plan (e.g., a plan with insufficient inventory is followed by a plan with excessive inventory). Bowman's idea was to collect data on past demand levels, relevant costs, and AP decisions, then perform statistical analysis (i.e., regression analysis) of the data. The analysis results in guidelines that provide more consistency in future decisions.

Example 2   Hughes Electronics Corp. developed an artificial intelligence–based financial trading system. The developers did this by encoding the wisdom of Christine Downton, a successful portfolio manager. One motivation for creating the system is that it is immune to the recency effect; that is, humans tend to get overly fixated on the most recent information (Davidson 1996).

Example 3   Your East Coast sales force has put together a string of extraordinarily high sales figures for the last several months. Part of your job as sales manager is to develop quarterly sales forecasts by region, and, naturally, sales force input plays a large role. In recognition of the recency effect, your final East Coast forecast is a little lower than the sales force estimate.

Example 4   Historically, the U.S. stock market has exhibited sustained periods of growth and sustained periods of stagnation. For example, we have witnessed three long-term bull markets where the Dow has gained a total of approximately 11,000 points. There also have been two long-term bear markets where the Dow lost almost 300 points. The curious thing about the bear markets is that they occurred during periods of economic growth. This raises the question of how the stock market could be stagnant when the economy as a whole is growing. Economists attribute the cause to human psychology, and, more specifically, the recency effect—investors are overly influenced by the recent past (Loomis 2001).

Example 5   In the late 1990s and early 21st century, the Oakland A's won more games than almost every other professional baseball team with a payroll among the lowest in the league. In 2002, for example, the New York Yankees had a payroll of $126 million, or more than three times the Oakland A's payroll of about $40 million. Michael Lewis writes about their success in his 2003 best seller *Moneyball.* In essence, Lewis argues that that A's management team recognized the existence of biases and human irrationalities that come into play when assessing talent, including the recency effect: "There was also a tendency to be overly influenced by a guy's most recent performance: what he did last was not necessarily what he would do next." The A's mitigated these biases and human irrationalities by using careful analysis of data to identify high-value players that others missed. Their success has changed the way talent is evaluated in professional baseball.

15. SATISFACTION = PERCEPTION − EXPECTATION

Definition

How good you feel about an experience depends on the gap between what you experienced and what you expected (Maister 1984).

Implications

Look for opportunities to influence both customer expectations and customer perceptions.

Examples

Example 1   A company that owned a high-rise office building began to receive complaints about the long wait times at the elevators. They ignored these complaints until one of the major tenants threatened to leave unless something was done. At this point, an engineering company was invited to analyze the situation and provide recommendations. In order of increasing cost and effectiveness, the options were (1) allow different elevators to stop only at a limited number of floors rather than all floors, (2) install a new propulsion system to speed ascent and descent rates, or (3) install new elevators. All the options would affect wait times but were expensive. The company held a brainstorming session to discuss options. During the session, a new hire with a psychology background suggested installing mirrors next to the elevators. The rationale was that mirrors might influence the *perception* of waiting time (even though actual waiting time would not change)—people like looking at themselves. The cost of the mirror idea was minimal so they gave it a try. Complaints decreased by approximately 80 percent. (Next time you go to a high-rise office building or hotel, look at the elevators; there's a fair chance you'll see mirrors.)

Example 2   Football coaches sometimes downplay the strength of their team, even when they are clear favorites. This is an example of managing expectations to relieve pressure.

Example 3   If you go to Disney World, you'll see all sorts of tactics to entertain you while you're waiting in line (e.g., you can play video games while you're waiting for a tour of Nickelodeon Studios). These tactics don't change the length of time that you wait, but they do influence your perception of the wait.

Example 4   A tactic in the hospitality and restaurant industry that is based on this principle of nature is the "unexpected extra." The idea is to try to surprise your customer with something extra that he or she didn't expect. For example, I went to a restaurant for breakfast in Chicago. The place is well known, but not fancy at all—just a simple breakfast place. As we were standing in a line about 15 people deep, the owner did two things: he visited with waiting customers and he passed out Milk Duds and bananas. After breakfast, we were served a small scoop of ice cream. These two unexpected extras, which cost relatively little, stood out in my mind; I was impressed.

Example 5   Of course, the power of the unexpected extra is not limited to the hospitality and restaurant industry. Hans Brondmo, who is a loyal customer of eBags, relates how he received a colorful camera in the mail as a thank-you for his luggage purchases; he felt appreciated from this unexpected and thoughtful gesture (Brondmo 2000, p. 244).

Example 6[14]   "After you've sewn up the tears and holes, we'll launder and press them. Mrs. Hilda Macy isn't expecting that. This way you'll soon be quite in demand. Something extra, you see. You must offer something extra to be noticed."

Example 7   When the team expected to win ends up losing, the team is "upset."

16. TIME DISTORTION

Definition

Perceived time increases approximately with the square of actual time when there is something else you'd much rather be doing. More to the point, time slows down with boredom.

---

[14] From *Ahab's Wife,* a novel by Sena Jeter Naslund (2000).

Implication

There is a tendency to underestimate the negative effect of making a customer wait, especially when the customer is bored (e.g., if the average customer waiting time doubles, it can feel four times longer in the eyes of the customer). Be aware of this principle when considering investments either that result in reduced wait time or that make wait time more tolerable.

Examples

Example 1[15]   An oil company was finding that a number of their newly opened gas stations were losing money due to a lack of customers. After many months of market analysis directed at identifying key determinants of demand (e.g., their price, competitors' price, location of competitors, appearance of the station, layout of the station, etc.), they found the most important factor to be time. This insight came about from studying the rate at which cars stopped for gas according to the 16 ways to get in and out of an intersection (the company almost always located gas stations on a street corner). They observed that the highest stop rate was for cars turning right at an intersection where the station was located at the near-right corner (on average, this pattern also takes the least amount of time to get in and out of the station). They also found that the rate at which cars stopped decreased roughly in proportion with the square of the time to get in and out of the station (e.g., a route that took twice as much time had one-fourth of the stop rate). They used this insight to their advantage in two ways: selecting the corner at which to locate a new station and investing in ways to speed up the service time.

Example 2   "A watched pot never boils."

17. TRUMPET OF DOOM

Definition

As the forecast horizon increases, forecast accuracy decreases.

Implication

Look for ways to reduce flowtimes in a production and delivery system. This offers the dual benefits of improved customer satisfaction through increased responsiveness (perhaps the more obvious benefit), but also makes it easier to accurately forecast future requirements (the trumpet of doom benefit). The other side of this is to reduce the age of the information that is used for forecasting and decision making. The staleness of information can be significant, and thus a potential opportunity area. For example, traditionally managers make decisions using data that are 20 to 30 days old, whereas newer information technologies are allowing some firms to base decisions on data that are only 24 hours old (Slywotzky 2001).

Examples

Example 1   The primary compressor supplier for a U.S. manufacturer was located in Italy. The time between placing an order and receiving the goods was six weeks. The manufacturer switched to a compressor supplier in Michigan that is able to provide delivery within

---

[15] From Ackoff (1991).

one week of the order. As a result, the company needs to forecast its compressor needs for one week into the future instead of six weeks.

Example 2   Wal-Mart electronically sends their sales data of P&G product to P&G every evening. P&G uses this information to adjust their expectations of demand. Prior to this new way of doing business, P&G may have updated demand forecasts on a monthly basis, potentially using sales information at least a week out of date. Forecast accuracy improved through more up-to-date information.

Example 3   Your friend challenges you to forecast Amazon.com's stock price within plus or minus 10 percent, but she gives you two choices. You may forecast stock price either one week from today or one year from today. Which option would you select? If you go for one week, then you have an intuitive feel for the trumpet of doom.

Example 4   General Electric has been successful in making their processes more responsive, with the result being a shorter forecast horizon and big savings. After investing heavily in methods to reduce setup times and costs, GE now produces every model every day in many of its plants, and has eliminated its long-term forecasting process. Lead times have been cut by more than 80 percent and inventory investment has been reduced by about $400 million (Tully 1994).

Example 5   The November–December 2001 issue of *The Futurist* contained several predictions:

1. Get ready for 1 billion people aged 60 or older by 2020.
2. Fish farming will overtake cattle ranching as a food source by 2010.
3. Researchers will find ways to genetically modify foods with viral proteins to fight diseases.
4. Fifty percent of coastal wetlands could disappear by 2080.

Which two predictions would you select as mostly likely to come true? The first two might be a good choice. For item (1), we currently know the population that will qualify as 60 or older by 2020, so it's a matter of predicting the number that will die before 2020. The fish farming prediction is not many years away, so there are probably current trends that give strong support for this prediction.

Example 6   A New York surgical needle manufacturer uses two raw materials: stainless steel wire and silicone. The steel is produced overseas on a make-to-order basis with a lead time of 8 to 12 months. Silicone is available from a supplier in Illinois with a lead time of five days. Consequently, the director of purchasing has a high degree of confidence in the timing and quantity of silicone orders while he is much more nervous about ordering steel based on projected requirements 12 months from now.

Comments

Figure A1.2 shows how this principle of nature gets its name.[16] The trumpet, or error range curve, expands with the forecast horizon. Many ongoing improvement activities in industry are directly related to the trumpet of doom. This is due to (1) advances in information technology that are making it easier and less expensive to reduce lead times and (2) product variety that is increasing and life cycles that are shortening, which in turn increase the pressure to improve responsiveness.

---

[16] Computer Associates, a software company, has used the term "trumpet of doom" when describing the phenomenon. I don't know if CA originated the term.

FIGURE A1.2 The **"Trumpet of Doom"** Forecast accuracy gets worse when forecasting farther into the future.

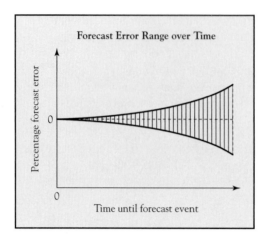

18. WINNER'S CURSE

Definition

The probability of unfavorable bidding error in an auction is highest for the winner. In other words, the winner of a reverse auction is likely to lose money.

Implication

Cost uncertainty makes the winner's curse more pronounced. A seller should (1) consider investments to reduce cost estimation errors prior to quoting and (2) bear in mind that it is not necessarily a good thing to win every auction.[17] A buyer may consider the potential significance of the winner's curse when considering whether to set up a reverse auction.

Examples

Example 1 The phenomenon of the winner's curse was originally proposed by three petroleum engineers who wondered why oil companies experienced consistent and unexpectedly low rates of return on oil leases (Capen, Clapp, and Campbell 1971). They suggested that the cause was the winner's curse: the winning bidder of a mineral rights lease tended to overpay. Evidence of the winner's curse has since been seen in a wide range of settings including professional baseball's free agency market (Cassing and Douglas 1980) and corporate takeover battles (Roll 1986).

Example 2 An early experiment demonstrating the winner's curse was conducted by Bazerman and Samuelson (1983). MBA students placed sealed bids on jars of pennies, nickels, and paper clips. The winner would receive the jar and the right to sell it for its true value, which, unknown to the subjects, was $8.00. Students also submitted their estimate of the value of each jar with the closest estimate worth a $2.00 reward. The average value estimate was $5.13, or $2.87 below the true value, while the average winning bid was $10.01, resulting in an average loss $2.01. The winner lost money in over half of the auctions.

Example 3 Initial public offerings (IPOs) of a stock are generally underpriced, and many have questioned why this is so. One explanation is based on the winner's curse (Rock 1986). IPO valuation is characterized by a great deal of uncertainty. Nevertheless, there

---

[17] There are also bidding strategies that one can employ to mitigate the winner's curse (see, e.g., Kagel and Levin 2002).

are some investors who are much more informed than others and who naturally do a better job at picking the most underpriced IPOs. The uninformed investors are subject to the winner's curse and thus experience lower returns. An underpricing tendency helps offset the winner's curse so that the average return to the uninformed investor is sufficient to remain in the market.

19. CONCLUDING COMMENTS

Read the principles carefully, look for evidence of them around you, try to see how they apply in different settings, and try to apply them yourself in creative ways. There are good reasons for this, one of which has to do with *horse sense.*

Many leaders in government and industry owe part of their success to a well-developed horse sense. By horse sense, I mean common sense in general, but with especially strong understanding and insight into human nature. One of my bosses had very good horse sense . . . he was able to get a good read on one's character after talking with the person for a short while and he was adept at seeing past false pretenses and detecting the true underlying motivations of a statement or action. Another example of horse sense is King Solomon's solution to a baby problem. Two women claimed to be the mother of a baby. King Solomon settled the dispute by decreeing that the baby would be divided in two and thereby split between the two women. Upon the pronouncement, the true mother became apparent when she offered the baby to the other mother.

If you think back on the principles in this appendix, you'll see that many describe phenomena relating to human nature. In other words, this appendix is in part a primer to help you develop your horse sense.

20. FURTHER READING

The following are worthwhile if you'd like to explore human nature, or horse sense, in more depth:

Cialdini, R. B. 2001. *Influence: Science and Practice.* 4th ed. Needham Heights, MA: Allyn & Bacon.

Gracian, B. 1992. *The Art of Worldly Wisdom.* Translated by C. Maurer. New York: Doubleday.

Machiavelli, N. 1997. *The Prince.* Translated and edited by A. M. Codevilla. New Haven, CT: Yale University Press.

Sun-Tzu. 1963. *The Art of War.* Translated by S. B. Griffith. Oxford: Clarendon Press. (See also www.belisarius.com/ for military strategy and tactics applied to business.)

Appendix Two

Linchpin of Electronic Commerce: Basics of Encryption and Digital Signatures

Appendix Outline

1. Private and Public Key Cryptosystems
2. Complexity Theory
3. The Knapsack Public Key Cryptosystem
4. The RSA Public Key Cryptosystem
5. Digital Signatures and Digital Certificates
6. Concluding Comments
7. Further Reading

Appendix Keys

1. What is cryptology?
2. Why is cryptosystem software the linchpin of e-commerce?
3. What are the differences between private and public key cryptosystems?
4. What is the purpose and essential result of complexity theory, and how is the result relevant to cryptography?
5. What are the mechanics of the knapsack public key cryptosystem?
6. What are the mechanics of the RSA public key cryptosystem?
7. What is the role of digital certificates and how are digital signatures created?

Why Bother Studying This Topic?

This appendix is about *cryptology*—a topic that can trigger imagination with thoughts of secret agents and inspire our curiosity in the world around us.[1] Of course, one of the nice

---

[1] Cryptology is a relatively little-understood area that may appeal to the curiosity of many. Part of my motivation for including this appendix comes from the spirit of a traditional liberal arts education—learning just for the fun of it.

side benefits is that, especially at this point in time with Internet-based electronic commerce, a basic knowledge of cryptology is highly practical.

What Is Cryptology?

Cryptology is the study of secret codes, or, more specifically, the study of devising and cracking *cryptosystems*. The devising part is known as *cryptography,* whereas the cracking part is known as *cryptanalysis.* As an example, one of the earlier-known cryptosystems is the *Caesar shift.* It was used by Caesar himself during the Roman Empire and it works by shifting each letter in a message a given number of letters forward in the alphabet. Some people think HAL—the name for the devious computer system in *2001: A Space Odyssey*—is actually a Caesar shift code for the name of a well-known computer company (*hint:* the first letter is I).

A Linchpin?

Cryptosystem software is the linchpin of Internet-based electronic commerce. Traditional electronic commerce is characterized by specialized and private networks between a firm and a limited number of trading partners.[2] In contrast, Internet-based electronic commerce is wide open with a worldwide playing field, spontaneous business transactions, and unlimited trading partners—a business environment full of opportunity, but also ripe for fraud.[3] **So we have this well-developed, sophisticated, and expensive infrastructure that, for the purposes of supporting high-volume commerce, is dependent on this relatively small and inexpensive linchpin—cryptosystem software.**

What Will We Cover?

We won't go through a comprehensive treatment of cryptology, but we will get a basic understanding of those elements that are not only the most critical for electronic commerce but are inspiring in their simplicity and elegance. By the end of the appendix, you should understand

- The differences between private and public key cryptosystems.
- The purpose and essential result of complexity theory, and its relevance to cryptography.
- The mechanics of the knapsack public key cryptosystem.
- The mechanics of the RSA public key cryptosystem.
- The role of digital certificates and how digital signatures are created.

This is a full plate, but we'll take a bite at a time beginning with . . .

1. PRIVATE AND PUBLIC KEY CRYPTOSYSTEMS

First, it is important to know that **the *key* in a cryptosystem is what is used to "lock" and "unlock" a message.** For example, the key used to transform the word "cryptology" into "dszq upmp hz" using the Caesar shift cryptosystem with four-letter blocks is $k = (+1)$ (i.e., c becomes d, r becomes s, and so on). The standard assumption in cryptology is that the "enemy" has a copy of the *ciphertext* and knows the cryptosystem in use ("dszq upmp hz" and Caesar shift in this case) . . . all that is missing is the key. The idea is that if a given

---

[2] These networks support computer-to-computer exchange of information, or, in other words, electronic data interchange (EDI). A well-known example is the daily transmission of P&G product sales from Wal-Mart to P&G. P&G uses this information to replenish Wal-Mart's inventory of P&G product and to schedule production.

[3] The difference in the level of privacy between traditional and unencrypted Internet-based electronic commerce is somewhat like the difference between sending mail via letter versus postcard.

cryptosystem is secure in the face of this assumption, the method should be fairly safe. By this reasoning, we can see that the Caesar shift cryptosystem is in trouble; there are only 25 possible keys: $k = (+1)$, $k = (+2)$, . . ., $k = (+25)$. The enemy could try all 25 keys and odds are that only one of the 25 unscrambled messages will make sense.

The Private Option

A *private key* cryptosystem is probably what naturally comes to mind when thinking about secret codes. **It's a cryptosystem where the same key is used for encoding and decoding a message.** This is why private key cryptosystems are also known as *symmetric* key cryptosystems. Caesar shift is a private key cryptosystem. In the example above, it's as if I locked the word "cryptology" by turning the key one notch to the right; to unlock, I merely turn the key one notch to the left. The main limitation of a private key cryptosystem is the key must be in the hands of both the sender and the receiver. If Anwer sends Beth an encoded message, Beth can only decode the message if she has the key that Anwer used. This means that Anwer must somehow get the key to Beth over a secure channel. In short, arrangements must be made ahead of time before the private key cryptosystem can be used for communication.

Example The best known and most widely used private key cryptosystem is *Data Encryption Standard* (DES). The U.S. government solicited proposals for a standard encryption system in the 1970s. IBM's proposal, which described the cryptosystem that became known as DES, was adopted by the U.S. government in 1976 with encouragement for use in the private sector. DES is only used in certain government branches; in fact, the National Security Agency stopped certifying it for government security in 1988. DES has a *fixed key length,* which means there is a fixed upper limit on the number of possible keys. In the case of DES, there are about 7×10^{16} different keys.[4] This was thought to be more than sufficient at the time of its inception, but rapid advances in computing power have changed this view. Just to give you an idea of what is involved in cracking DES, in 1977 it was projected that all 7×10^{16} possible keys could be checked in one day using a specially designed computer that would cost about $20 million. In 1993, the cost estimate was reduced to $1 million. Then, in 1997, the theory was tested by the Electronic Frontier Foundation (EFF). EFF cracked a DES message in less than a week using a special purpose massively parallel machine that cost less than $250,000. Nevertheless, DES is very fast and generally viewed to be sufficiently secure for all but very sensitive communications. The Department of Commerce, for example, uses DES for electronic funds transfer and HBO uses DES to scramble cable TV signals.[5]

The Public Option

A *public key* **cryptosystem is made up of two keys: one that is kept private and another that is publicly available. The public key is used for encoding a message, which can only be decoded with the corresponding private key.** This means that Anwer doesn't need to give Beth a key prior to sending her a secret message. He scrambles his message using Beth's public key and sends it over an unsecured channel (e.g., the Internet) with the assurance that his message cannot be decoded by anyone but Beth (unless someone else has Beth's private key). One example of a public key cryptosystem is RSA (more on this later).

---

[4] The DES key length is 56 bits. Each bit can be 0 or 1, so there are $2^{56} - 1$ possible keys; $7 \times 10^{16} \approx 2^{56} - 1$.

[5] The National Institute of Standards and Technology solicited designs for *Advanced Encryption Standard* to replace DES (Schwartz 2000). AES will use a key size of 128, 192, or 256 bits (Zimmermann 1998). In October of 2000, the winner of a worldwide competition for the AES design was announced; NIST selected an encryption technique called Rijndael (named for the two Danish inventors).

RSA is the most widely used cryptosystem;[6] it is arguably the de facto standard among public key cryptosystems and it is the cornerstone of secure communication in Internet-based electronic commerce.

Getting around a Weak Link

The concept of a public key cryptosystem, which was originally proposed in 1976 by Diffie and Hellman, introduces a potential weak link—the "enemy" has access to the key used for encoding a message and can try to take advantage of this information to crack the code. This means that a necessary characteristic of any public key cryptosystem is that the problem of encoding a message with the public key be very easy, while the problem of decoding the message with the public key be very hard. In other words, the encoding function needs to be easy to calculate but nearly impossible to invert without the private key. A function with this characteristic is known as a *trap-door one-way function,* and the discovery and design of such functions borrows from the subtle and powerful theory of problem complexity.

2. COMPLEXITY THEORY

Some Problems Are Harder Than Others

Computational complexity theory provides a basis for classifying problem complexity where, loosely speaking, complexity refers to how long it can take to get an "answer" to a given problem. The origins of complexity theory stem from the work of Alan Turing in the 1930s and 1940s. There are entire books on this topic, but our focus will be narrow; we will limit consideration to properties essential for a meaningful understanding of a one-way function.

A Path to a One-Way Function

The problem of cracking a code is an example of a *number problem.* Other examples of number problems include calculating the value of a stock option and developing an airline schedule that maximizes profit subject to relevant constraints. The main point is that many problems in business, and in life, qualify as number problems.[7] Number problems can be classified into sets. Just about any number problem that one might imagine belongs to the set NP and the most difficult of these problems belong to the subset NP-complete. So what does all this mean? In short, something amazing. In 1971, **Steven Cook of the University of Toronto showed that every problem in NP can be efficiently solved if one could devise an efficient method to solve the *satisfiability* problem.**[8] Consequently, the satisfiability problem was said to be NP-complete—a solution method for the satisfiability problem will lead to solution methods for solving the *complete* set of problems in NP. Since 1971,

---

[6] As of year 2006, the estimated installed base of RSA encryption engines is more than one billion.

[7] For contrast, the problem of determining whether Fermat's last theorem is true is an example that does not qualify as a number problem. Pierre de Fermat, a 17th-century French mathematician, wrote in the margin of one of his books: "If n is a number greater than two, there are no whole numbers, a, b, c such that $a^n + b^n = c^n$. I have found a truly wonderful proof which this margin is too small to contain." Proving this proposed theorem has been one of the most studied mathematical questions over the past 350 years. In 1993, Andrew Wiles of Princeton University announced a proof. After initial necessary corrections (the proof is over 150 pages long), most experts now believe the proof is correct.

[8] For curiosity sake, a simple example of the satisfiability problem is the question of whether there exist binary values for x_1, x_2, and x_3 that can make the following statement true: $(x_1$ or not $x_2)$ and $(x_2$ and $x_3)$. Solving this particular instance is fairly easy; setting $x_1 = 1$, $x_2 = 1$, and $x_3 = 1$ tells us that the answer is *yes.*

many other problems have been shown to be NP-complete, with the implication being: find an efficient method for any one of these problems and you'll have an efficient method for all problems in NP. Also, and very important, **no one has found an efficient method for solving any NP-complete problem, and many computer scientists believe that no one ever will.**[9] In other words, **NP-complete problems seem to exhibit inherent intractability that makes them very difficult to solve**—naturally a desirable characteristic for the problem of cracking a code. **The bottom line: NP-complete problems are attractive candidates for one-way functions.** In the next section, we'll look at one NP-complete problem that is the basis for the *knapsack public key cryptosystem.*

3. THE KNAPSACK PUBLIC KEY CRYPTOSYSTEM

Packing for a Trip

Imagine that you are about to go on a trip carrying one knapsack that can hold a specific weight, say, B pounds. You are in the middle of packing and in front of you lie a bunch of goodies with weights denoted $a_1, a_2, \ldots, a_n$. Your task is to determine if there is a collection of goodies that weighs exactly B pounds. This is known as the knapsack problem, a problem that is NP-complete. So the knapsack problem is hard to solve, which satisfies one criterion of a trap-door one-way function, but it also must be easy to solve given information contained in a private key. In other words, the function needs to have a *trap door* that can only be opened with the private key.

It turns out that the knapsack problem is easy to solve when the weights satisfy a special condition known as the *super-increasing* property. The super-increasing property holds if, when the weights are indexed in order of smallest to largest, $a_j > \Sigma_{i<j} a_i$. For example, the super-increasing property holds for $A = \{1, 3, 7, 13, 26, 65, 119, 267\}$.

Into the Guts

Now let's look at the mechanics, then illustrate the method with a simple example. The key is made up of two parts, $k = (k_s, k_p)$, where k_s stands for the "secret " or private part of the key and k_p stands for the public part of the key.

Forming the Private Key $k_s = (A, p, m, m^{-1})$

- Select some knapsack set $A = \{a_1, a_2, \ldots, a_n\}$ that satisfies the super-increasing property.
- Select some prime number p that satisfies $p > \Sigma_j a_j$.
- Randomly select a value m in the interval $[1, p - 1]$.
- Calculate m^{-1}, the multiplicative inverse of m with respect to modulus p (i.e., find m^{-1} satisfying $m^{-1} m \bmod p = 1$).

Forming the Public Key $k_p = (A')$ Given k_s

- Calculate $a'_j = m a_j \bmod p$ for all j and set $A' = \{a', a'_2, \ldots, a'_n\}$.[10]

Encoding the Plaintext $x_1 x_2 \ldots x_n$ That Is in Binary Format (i.e., each $x_j = 0$ or 1)

- $c = \Sigma_j x_j a'_j$ (i.e., a number c is calculated for each block of n binary digits in the message).

---

[9] The question of whether an efficient solution method can be found for an NP-complete problem is one of the seven Millennium Prize problems. These seven problems are widely considered the most important outstanding problems in mathematics, and there is a $7 million prize fund, with the solution to each problem worth $1 million (www.claymath.org/millennium).

[10] The function $x \bmod y$ returns the remainder of x divided by y; for example, $10 \bmod 3 = 1$ and $20 \bmod 3 = 2$.

Decoding the Ciphertext c

- Calculate $B = m^{-1}c \bmod p$.
- Find the weights in A that add up to B; the selected weights define nonzero values in the binary message.

Example Suppose Beth goes through the first two steps and comes up with $A = \{1, 3, 7, 13, 26, 65, 119, 267\}$, $p = 523$, and $m = 467$. The inverse of $m = 467$ is $m^{-1} = 28$ (i.e., $28(467) \bmod 523 = 1$). This completes the private key. Based on this private key, the corresponding public key is calculated: $a'_1 = 467(1) \bmod 523$, $a'_2 = 467(3) \bmod 523$, and so on, yielding $A' = \{467, 355, 131, 318, 113, 21, 135, 215\}$. Notice that A' does not satisfy the super-increasing property (a good thing). Now, Anwer wants to send Beth a secret message (a Visa number perhaps?) so he first gets Beth's public key. Beth may send this to Anwer by e-mail, or it may be posted in a public place. In binary form, let's suppose Anwer's message is $m = 01001011$. The *plaintext* is encoded into *ciphertext* as $c = \Sigma_j x_j a'_j = 0(467) + 1(355) + 0(131) + 0(318) + 1(113) + 0(21) + 1(135) + 1(215) = 818$. Anwer sends 818 to Beth, who first calculates $B = 28(818) \bmod 523 = 415$. Now all Beth has to do is find the goodies in $A = \{1, 3, 7, 13, 26, 65, 119, 267\}$ that add up to 415. This is easy to do because A has the super-increasing property. In this case, she finds $415 = 0(1) + 1(3) + 0(7) + 0(13) + 1(26) + 0(65) + 1(119) + 1(267)$, meaning that Anwer sent her the message 01001011.

Cracking the Code

How could we decode Anwer's message if we didn't have Beth's private key? We'd simply have to find the goodies with weights in $A' = \{467, 355, 131, 318, 113, 21, 135, 215\}$ that add up to 818. It may not take long to find an answer here because $n = 8$. However, due to the inherent intractability of the knapsack problem, searching for a solution becomes impractical when n is large.

The knapsack method is useful for illustrating the relationship between complexity theory and cryptography. The method is not widely used in practice because cryptanalysis has exposed some weaknesses. The method in the next section, at least so far, has been largely free of such criticisms.

4. THE RSA PUBLIC KEY CRYPTOSYSTEM

The Challenge

In 1977, a curious challenge appeared in the pages of *Scientific American*. Three MIT professors—Ron Rivest, Adi Shamir, and Leonard Adleman—presented ciphertext, described the encoding method along with the public key, and offered $100 to anyone who could crack it. They also predicted that they might not lose their money for 40 quadrillion years. On the surface, it may seem to be an easy buck; all one would have to do is factor a 129-digit number into the product of two primes—perhaps a few nights of lost sleep, but nothing more. However, factoring appears to be one of those inherently intractable problems. It may be easy to factor 21 into 3×7, but factoring large numbers takes an exceedingly long time.[11] As it turns out, the reward was paid out ahead of schedule in 1994. Six hundred volunteers running 2,000 workstations were able to crack the code in eight months.[12]

---

[11] Interestingly, no one yet knows whether factoring is an NP-complete problem. However, most suspect that factoring *is* inherently intractable.

[12] The secret encrypted message: "The magic words are squeamish ossifrage."

The method proposed by Rivest, Shamir, and Adleman is known as the *RSA public key cryptosystem*. RSA Data Security was founded in 1982 to develop and market cryptographic software, and the spirit evident in the *Scientific American* challenge lives on . . . RSA maintains a list of factoring challenges and has paid out over $100,000 in rewards. The catch is that to collect the reward, you will have to provide information on your factoring method, information that RSA can potentially use to improve the security of their software.

Really Old Stuff

In order to outline the mechanics of RSA we need to step back in time and introduce two properties from number theory. The properties, which were discovered in the 18th century by the famed Swiss mathematician Leonhard Euler, concern the *Euler totient function*. The totient of *n*—denoted $\phi(n)$—is the number of integers between 1 and *n* that are *relatively prime* to *n*. Two numbers are relatively prime if their greatest common divisor (GCD) is one. As an example, $\phi(15) = 8$ because 1, 2, 4, 7, 8, 11, 13, and 14 are the only integers between 1 and 15 that are relatively prime to 15 (e.g., the GCD of 3 and 15 is 3 while the GCD of 4 and 15 is 1).

- *Property 1.* If $n = pq$ where *p* and *q* are primes, then $\phi(n) = (p - 1)(q - 1)$. For example, $\phi(15) = \phi(3 \times 5) = (3 - 1)(5 - 1) = 8$.
- *Property 2.*[13] $m^{k\phi(n)+1} \bmod n = m$ for any positive integers *m*, *k*, and *n* as long as *n* is the product of two distinct primes. For example, if $m = 3$, $k = 2$, and $n = 6$, then $\phi(6) = 2$ and $m^{k\phi(n)+1} \bmod n = 3^5 \bmod 6 = 243 \bmod 6 = 3 = m$; alternatively, if $k = 1$ with no other changes, then $m^{k\phi(n)+1} \bmod n = 3^3 \bmod 6 = 27 \bmod 6 = 3 = m$.

Into the Guts

As an aside, I think these properties illustrate the difficulty of assessing the value of theoretical research. On the surface, it may appear—as it probably did to many at the time—that these properties have absolutely no practical value to society. Yet over 200 years after their discovery, they have become the basis for the most widely used cryptosystem in the world. Let's see how.

Forming the Private Key $k_s = (p, q, d)$

- Select *p* and *q* as primes.
- Set $n = pq$.
- Select random $d \in [\max\{p,q\} + 1, \phi(n) - 1]$ with *d* relatively prime to *n*.

Forming the Public Key $k_p = (n, e)$ Given k_s

- Calculate *e*, the multiplicative inverse of *d* with respect to modulus $\phi(n)$ (i.e., find *e* satisfying $ed \bmod \phi(n) = 1$).

Encoding the Plaintext *m* That Is in Numeric Format

- $c = m^e \bmod n$

Decoding the ciphertext *c*

- $m = c^d \bmod n$

---

[13] This is actually a slight extension of Euler's original property, which said $m^{\phi(n)} \bmod n = 1$ if *m* and *n* are relatively prime.

For the skeptics, I'll use a little theory to prove that $c^d \bmod n$ actually is m . . .

$$c^d \bmod n = (m^e)^d \bmod n \quad \text{(because } c = m^e \bmod n\text{)}$$
$$= m^{k\phi(n)+1} \bmod n \quad \text{(because } ed \bmod \phi(n) = 1, \text{ or, in other words,}$$
$$ed = k\phi(n)+1) = m \quad \text{(because of Property 2)}$$

Example First, Beth creates her private and public keys by selecting primes $p = 41$ and $q = 53$. This means $n = (41)(53) = 2{,}173$ and $\phi(2{,}173) = (41 - 1)(53 - 1) = 2{,}080$. She randomly selects $d = 623$, a number that is between 54 and 2,079 and that is relatively prime to 2,080. Finally, she calculates the inverse of d to find $e = 207$ (i.e., $207(623) \bmod 2{,}080 = 1$) so that $k_s = (p, q, d) = (41, 53, 623)$ and $k_p = (n, e) = (2{,}173, 207)$.

Suppose Anwer wants to send the message "SupplyChain" to Beth. Plaintext and ciphertext eventually will be encoded as integers between 0 and $n - 1$, but the first steps are to express the message in binary notation and select a *block length*. For example, in binary notation S = **01010011** and u = **011**10101. Each letter requires eight bits, so the entire message is 88 bits (11 letters $\times$ 8 bits per letter). This string of 0's and 1's will be transformed into blocks of the same length where each block will be interpreted as an integer. Because the integers can be no more than 2,172 (recall that $n = 2{,}173$ and the integers must be between 0 and $n - 1$), the block length must be 11 or less. This is because a number expressed as 11 bits could be as large as $2^{11} - 1 = 2{,}047$ while a number expressed as 12 bits could be as large as $2^{12} - 1 = 4{,}095 > 2{,}172$. Suppose the block length is 11 bits. The first 11 bits in the 88-bit message are 01010011011 (indicated in **boldface** above). This corresponds to the number $m_1 = 667$ (i.e., $0 \times 2^{10} + 1 \times 2^9 + 0 \times 2^8 + 1 \times 2^7 + \cdots + 1 \times 2^1 + 1 \times 2^0 = 667$). This same process yields $m_2 = 1{,}372$, $m_3 = 224$, $m_4 = 1{,}735$, $m_5 = 1{,}185$, $m_6 = 1{,}441$, $m_7 = 1{,}069$, and $m_8 = 366$ for the remaining seven numbers of plaintext. At this point, Anwer is ready to encode his message. He retrieves Beth's public key $k_p = (2{,}173, 207)$ and calculates $c_1 = m_1{}^e \bmod n = 667^{207} \bmod 2{,}173 = 976$, and so on for the other seven numbers. He sends $c_1, \ldots, c_8$ and Beth decodes using information in her private key $k_s = (41, 53, 623)$ by calculating $m = c^d \bmod n$. In the case of c_1, this works out to $m_1 = c_1{}^d \bmod n = 976^{623} \bmod 2{,}173 = 667$.

Cracking the Code

In order to decode $c_1 = 976$ without knowledge of Beth's private key, we would have to invert the function $m_1{}^{207} \bmod 2{,}173 = 976$. There is common belief that the problem of inverting this function is equivalent to factoring 2,173. If the factors—41 and 53—of 2,173 are known, then it is a simple matter to calculate d, the multiplicative inverse of e with respect to modulus $\phi(2{,}173)$ and then use d to crack the code.

Thus, the security of RSA depends in part on the difficulty of factoring a number that is the product of two primes, or a *composite number.* Factoring "small" composite numbers such as 2,173 will take no time using a computer. The largest composite number factored to date is 167 digits long.[14] Some composite numbers are easier to factor than others, and this 167-digit number is not among the most difficult. RSA attempts to select the most difficult composites for use in their software. The largest RSA composite factored to date is 140 digits long and RSA Data Security estimates that factoring a 200-digit RSA composite would take 70 million years on a computer capable of a million instructions per second.

One advantage of RSA, and many other public key cryptosystems, is that they can be used to verify the presumed identity of a sender without making special arrangements ahead of time. This is the idea behind digital signatures, the topic of the next section.

---

[14] The task was coordinated by a team of researchers from Purdue University and required approximately 100,000 hours of computing time (Peterson 1997).

5. DIGITAL SIGNATURES AND DIGITAL CERTIFICATES

A Problem

Here I am watching the half-time show of the Super Bowl and I see this ad for a combination microwave/computer from Amana Corporation. Since I need a new microwave and a new computer, I decide to buy it. I connect to the Internet, type www.amana.com, and get connected to their Web site. I begin to enter information for my order, including my MasterCard number, and it occurs to me that I don't know if I'm really interacting with Amana's Web site or some scammer out to collect credit card numbers. This is an example of a problem that *digital signatures* address. **Digital signatures play the role of a driver's license when cashing a check; that is, used to verify you are who you say you are.**

Digital Signature Solution

An RSA-based digital signature works by running the RSA cryptosystem *backwards.* For the example above, Amana would send me a message that they encoded with their **private** key. I use Amana's **public** key to decode the message. If the message makes sense, it must be from Amana (or from someone who stole Amana's private key). Why is this? Because if $c = m^d \bmod n$ where d is part of Amana's private key, then $c^e \bmod n$ will return the original m (this can be verified by examining the RSA proof above but by interchanging d and e).

Another Problem

If we think about this example for a while, we may begin to see another potential problem. How do we know that the public key we used to decode the message is actually Amana's public key? This is where digital certificates come in. In the case of a driver's license being used to verify the identity of a person cashing a check, the government is the certification authority. With the issue of a driver's license, the government essentially certifies that the name and the face on the license really do go together. In the same vein, there are various **certification authorities who certify that a public key really belongs to the organization or person listed on the key** (e.g., VeriSign, GTE CyberTrust).

Digital Certificate Solution

Let's look at a simplified **example of how digital certificates and digital signatures can be used to verify the identity of a business partner.** This time I want to order a book. I connect to Amazon's Web site and indicate I want to place an order. A window pops up and informs me that information will be transmitted over a secure channel. As I click the OK button, two things happen. First, the picture of a padlock in the lower-right-hand corner of my browser goes from an unlocked position to a locked position, and, second, the Web site address goes from http://. . . to https://. . . This tells me that information I transmit from this point on will be encoded. If I double-click on the padlock in the lower-right-hand corner, a window pops up. Included in this window is information on the name of the company that "owns" the site and the name of the certification authority that has validated the owner. This is what is going on at the surface; now let's see what's going on underneath. When I clicked the OK button to switch to a secure channel, Amazon sent their public key that includes a digital certificate.[15] The digital certificate is a message encoded with the

---

[15] In order to receive a digital certificate, the certifying authority has to authenticate Amazon's identity. After collecting relevant information and verifying that Amazon's credentials are valid, a digital certificate is issued confirming that the public key associated with the certificate does indeed belong to Amazon. Amazon can now use this certificate for all their secure transactions.

certification authority's public key. When I double-click on the padlock, the public key from the certification authority[16] is used to decode the certificate. The result is a message along the lines of "The official owner of this site is Amazon Books as certified by VeriSign." Remember that since I decoded the digital certificate using VeriSign's public key, the message can only make sense if VeriSign encoded it. This tells me that the digital certificate is really from VeriSign, and I can be assured that the public key actually belongs to Amazon. Furthermore, I can safely assume that I am communicating with Amazon's Web site rather than some scammer. Feeling confident, I enter all my order information. As I push the Send button, the information is encoded using Amazon's public key. The ciphertext is sent over the Internet and can only be decoded using Amazon's private key.

6. CONCLUDING COMMENTS

Combining the Best of Both Worlds

We've now completed our coverage of the basics of cryptology with an emphasis on those elements most relevant to Internet-based electronic commerce. One of the main points is that public key cryptosystems allow you to get around the problem of having to exchange a key over a secure channel prior to engaging in confidential business transactions. This is achieved through easily accessible public information—information that can be used to both encode messages and verify the identity of a sender. There is a downside, however, and that is speed.[17] Compared to symmetric key cryptosystems, the time to encode and decode is generally much longer. This is the motivation for a concept known as a *digital envelope* that combines the advantages of public and symmetric key cryptosystems. The basic idea of a digital envelope is to encode the key for a symmetric key cryptosystem using a public key cryptosystem and send it over the Internet. The time to encode and decode the symmetric key is minimal because the amount of data to specify a symmetric key is minimal. The symmetric key cryptosystem can then be used as the "workhorse" for encoding and decoding long messages.

Ah-Ha!

Here is a final point to ponder. As computing power increases through advances in technology, the problem of factoring takes less time, with the apparent result that the RSA cryptosystem becomes less secure. Oddly enough, the opposite is true; advances in computing power actually help make many public key cryptosystems more secure. In the case of RSA, this is because there are efficient methods for searching and finding large prime numbers—numbers that can be used to create very large keys. There are no publicly known efficient methods for factoring. Consequently, the problem of searching for large prime numbers is better able to take advantage of the increased computing power, thus increasing the gap between the problem of creating a strong key and the problem of cracking the key.

---

[16] Public keys from certification authorities are typically embedded in Web browsers.

[17] One way that the process is streamlined (especially for digital signatures) is through the use of *hash algorithms*. In brief, hash algorithms compress a message into a fixed length called a *digest*. It is highly unlikely that two messages compressed by a hash algorithm will yield the same digest. A shorter message takes less time to encode and decode.

7. FURTHER READING

Brassard, G. 1988. *Modern Cryptology: A Tutorial.* New York: Springer-Verlag.

Diffie, W., and M. E. Hellman. 1976. "New Directions in Cryptography." *IEEE Transactions on Information Theory,* IT-22, pp. 644–54.

Gardner, M. 1977. "A New Kind of Cipher That Would Take Millions of Years to Break." *Scientific American* 237 (August), pp. 120–24.

Kippenhahn, R. 1999. *Code Breaking: A History and Exploration.* Woodstock, NY: Overlook Press.

Levy, S. 2000. *Crypto: When the Code Rebels Beat the Government—Saving Privacy in the Digital Age.* New York: Viking.

Patterson, W. 1987. *Mathematical Cryptology.* Savage, MD: Rowman & Littlefield.

Schneier, B. 2000. *Secrets & Lies: Digital Security in a Networked World.* New York: John Wiley and Sons.

Simmons, G. J. (ed.). 1992. *Contemporary Cryptology.* New York: IEEE Press.

Singh, S. 1999. *The Code Book: The Evolution of Secrecy from Mary, Queen of Scots to Quantum Cryptography.* New York: Doubleday.

Van Tilborg, H. C. A. 1988. *An Introduction to Cryptology.* Boston: Kluwer Academic Publishers.

Zimmermann, P. R. 1998. "Cryptology for the Internet." *Scientific American* 279 (October), pp. 110–15.

Web Sites

csrc.nist.gov/encryption

www.epic.org

www.pgp.com/phil

www.rsa.com

Appendix **Three**

Summary of Notation and Formulas

CHAPTER 4

Demand Management

Notation

x_t = actual in period t (could be demand, sales, interest rate, etc.)

ma_t = moving average calculated at the end of period t

m = number of periods used in the average calculation

s_t = smoothed estimate of the mean demand in period t, calculated at the end of period t

α = smoothing parameter for s_t, $\alpha \in [0, 1]$

b_t = smoothed estimate of the trend component in period t, calculated at the end of period t; the value of b_t is an estimate for the amount of increase or decrease per period after seasonality effects are removed.

β = smoothing parameter for b_t, $\beta \in [0, 1]$

M_t = smoothed estimate of the seasonal index for the season of period t, calculated at the end of period t; the seasonal index for a particular season is a measure of (mean demand in the season) ÷ (mean demand over all seasons). For example, if the seasonal index for the month of January is 1.20, then we expect demand in January to be 20 percent higher than the average monthly demand.

γ = smoothing parameter for M_t, $\gamma \in [0, 1]$

L = number of seasons in a cycle

$F_{t,j}$ = forecast calculated at the end of period t for period $t + j$

Moving Average

$$ma_t = \frac{\sum\limits_{i=1}^{m} x_{t-m+i}}{m} = (x_{t-m+1} + \cdots + x_{t-1} + x_t)/m$$

$$F_{t,j} = ma_t$$

Basic Exponential Smoothing

$$s_t = \alpha x_t + (1 - \alpha)s_{t-1} = s_{t-1} + \alpha(x_t - s_{t-1}) = \text{old estimate} + \alpha(\text{error})$$

$$F_{t,j} = s_t$$

Exponential Smoothing with Trend

$$s_t = \alpha x_t + (1 - \alpha)(s_{t-1} + b_{t-1}) = s_{t-1} + b_{t-1} + \alpha[x_t - (s_{t-1} + b_{t-1})] = \text{old estimate} + \alpha(\text{error})$$

$$b_t = \beta(s_t - s_{t-1}) + (1 - \beta)b_{t-1} = b_{t-1} + \beta[(s_t s_{t-1}) - b_{t-1}] = \text{old estimate} + \beta(\text{error})$$

$$F_{t,j} = s_t + jb_t$$

Exponential Smoothing with Seasonality

$$s_t = \alpha(x_t/M_{t-L}) + (1 - \alpha)s_{t-1} = s_{t-1} + \alpha[(x_t/M_{t-L}) - s_{t-1}] = \text{old estimate} + \alpha(\text{error})$$

$$M_t = \gamma(x_t/s_t) + (1 - \gamma)M_{t-L} = M_{t-L} + \gamma[(x_t/s_t) - M_{t-L}] = \text{old estimate} + \gamma(\text{error})$$

$$F_{t,j} = \begin{cases} s_t M_{t-L+j \bmod L} & \text{if } j \bmod L > 0 \\ s_t M_t & \text{if } j \bmod L = 0 \end{cases}$$

Exponential Smoothing with Trend and Seasonality (Winters method)

$$s_t = \alpha(x_t/M_{t-L}) + (1 - \alpha)(s_{t-1} + b_{t-1}) = s_{t-1} + b_{t-1} + \alpha[(x_t/M_{t-L}) - (s_{t-1} + b_{t-1})] = \text{old estimate} + \alpha(\text{error})$$

$$b_t = \beta(s_t - s_{t-1}) + (1 - \beta)b_{t-1} = b_{t-1} + \beta[(s_t - s_{t-1}) - b_{t-1}] = \text{old estimate} + \beta(\text{error})$$

$$M_t = \gamma(x_t/s_t) + (1 - \gamma)M_{t-L} = M_{t-L} + \gamma[(x_t/s_t) - M_{t-L}] = \text{old estimate} + \gamma(\text{error})$$

$$F_{t,j} = \begin{cases} (s_t + jb_t) M_{t-L+j \bmod L} & \text{if } j \bmod L > 0 \\ (s_t + jb_t) M_t & \text{if } j \bmod L = 0 \end{cases}$$

Measures of Forecast Accuracy

MAD = mean absolute deviation over most recent n periods

$$= \frac{\sum_{i=1}^{n} |x_{t-n+i} - F_{t-1-n+i,1}|}{n}$$

MFE = mean forecast error (e.g., bias) over most recent n periods

$$= \frac{\sum_{i=1}^{n} (x_{t-n+i} - F_{t-1-n+i,1})}{n}$$

CFE = cumulative forecast error over most recent n periods = $n \times$ MFE

TS = tracking signal over most recent n periods = CFE/MAD

MSE = mean squared error over most recent n periods

$$= \frac{\sum_{i=1}^{n} (x_{t-n+i} - F_{t-1-n+i,1})^2}{n}$$

MAPE = mean absolute percentage error over most recent n periods

$$= \frac{1}{n} \left[\sum_{i=1}^{n} \frac{|x_{t-n+i} - F_{t-1-n+i,1}|}{x_{t-n+i}} \right] \times 100$$

CHAPTER 6

Inventory Management I

Notation

D = demand rate in units per period

P = production capacity in units per period

c = purchase (or production) cost per unit

h = inventory holding cost per \$-period

c_e = inventory holding cost per unit-period (excess cost rate); for example, $c_e = h \times c$

c_s = backorder cost per unit-period (shortage cost rate)

A = cost per transaction (cost to place order or begin production)

Q = amount to order (or produce) at a time, or units per transaction

b = number of units on backorder when replenishment order arrives (or production begins)

Economic Order Quantity

D/Q = average number of orders per period = (demand per period)/(quantity per order)

Q/D = number of periods between placement of orders = 1/(number of orders per period)

$Q/2$ = average cycle stock

$TC(Q)$ = average transaction cost per period = (cost per transaction)(transactions per period) = AD/Q

$HC(Q)$ = average inventory holding cost per period = (average inventory)c_e = $(Q/2)c_e$

$C(Q)$ = average transaction and holding cost per period
= $AD/Q + (Q/2)c_e$

Q^* = economic order quantity (order size with lowest average transaction plus inventory holding cost) = $(2AD/c_e)^{1/2}$

$TC(Q^*)$ = average transaction cost per period if the order quantity is $Q^* = AD/Q^* = (ADc_e/2)^{1/2}$

$HC(Q^*)$ = average inventory holding cost per period if the order quantity is Q^*
= $(Q^*/2)c_e = (ADc_e/2)^{1/2}$

$C(Q^*)$ = average transaction and holding cost per period if the order quantity is Q^*
= $(2ADc_e)^{1/2}$

Economic Order Quantity with Planned Backorders

D/Q = average number of orders per period

Q/D = number of periods between placement of orders

$(Q - b)^2/2Q$ = average cycle stock

$b^2/2Q$ = average number of units backordered

$TC(Q)$ = average transaction cost per period = AD/Q

$HC(Q, b)$ = average inventory holding cost per period = $[(Q - b)^2/2Q]c_e$

$SC(Q, b)$ = average backorder cost per period = $[b^2/2Q]c_s$

$C(Q, b)$ = average transaction, holding, and backorder cost per period
$$= AD/Q + [(Q - b)^2/2Q]c_e + [b^2/2Q]c_s$$

Q^* = economic order quantity = $[2AD/c_e]^{1/2}[(c_e + c_s)/c_s]^{1/2}$

b^* = optimal backorder quantity when order arrives = $Q^*c_e/(c_e + c_s)$

$TC(Q^*)$ = average transaction cost per period if the order quantity is $Q^* = AD/Q^*$
$$= (ADc_e/2)^{1/2}[c_s/(c_e + c_s)]^{1/2}$$

$HC(Q^*, b^*)$ = average inventory holding cost per period if the order quantity is Q^* and b^* units are backordered when the order arrives = $[(Q^* - b^*)^2/2Q^*]c_e = (ADc_e/2)^{1/2}[c_s/(c_e + c_s)]^{1/2}[c_s/(c_e + c_s)]$

$SC(Q^*, b^*)$ = average backorder cost per period if the order quantity is Q^* and b^* units are backordered when the order arrives = $[b^{*2}/2Q^*]c_s = (ADc_e/2)^{1/2}[c_s/(c_e + c_s)]^{1/2}[c_e/(c_e + c_s)]$

$C(Q^*, b^*)$ = average transaction, holding, and backorder cost per period if the order quantity Q^* and b^* units are backordered when the order arrives = $(2ADc_e)^{1/2}[c_s/(c_e + c_s)]^{1/2}$

Economic Production Quantity

D/Q = average number of production setups per period

Q/D = number of periods between production setups

Q/P = number of periods to produce Q units

$I_{max}(Q)$ = maximum inventory level given production quantity $Q = Q(P - D)/P$

$I_{max}(Q)/2$ = average cycle stock

$TC(Q)$ = average transaction cost per period = AD/Q

$HC(Q)$ = average inventory holding cost per period = $c_eQ(P - D)/2P$

$C(Q)$ = average transaction and holding cost per period
$$= AD/Q + [Q(P - D)/2P]c_e$$

Q^* = economic production quantity = $[2AD/c_e)]^{1/2}[P/(P - D)]^{1/2}$

$TC(Q^*)$ = average transaction cost per period if the production quantity is $Q^* = AD/Q^* = (ADc_e/2)^{1/2}[(P - D)/P]^{1/2}$

$HC(Q^*)$ = average inventory holding cost per period if the production quantity is $Q^* = c_eQ^*(P - D)/2P = (ADc_e/2)^{1/2}[(P - D)/P]^{1/2}$

$C(Q^*)$ = average transaction and holding cost per period if the production quantity is $Q^* = (2ADc_e)^{1/2}[(P - D)/P]^{1/2}$

Economic Order Quantity with Quantity Discounts

$c(Q)$ = average unit price as a function of the order quantity Q (provided by the vendor)

h = inventory holding cost per $-period

c_e = inventory holding cost per unit-period = $hc(Q)$

$TC(Q)$ = average transaction cost per period = (cost per transaction)(average # of transactions per period) = $(A)(D/Q)$

$HC(Q)$ = average inventory holding cost per period
= (average inventory)c_e = $(Q/2)hc(Q)$

$PC(Q)$ = average purchase cost per period = (demand per period)(average purchase cost per unit) = $Dc(Q)$

$C(Q)$ = average transaction, holding, and purchase cost per period
= $TC(Q) + HC(Q) + PC(Q)$

Economic Order Quantity prior to a price Increase

h = inventory holding cost per \$-period

c = current price per unit

c_{new} = higher price per unit to go into effect in the near future

Q^* = current optimal order quantity (at price c)

Q_{new}^* = optimal order quantity at price c_{new}

$TC(Q_{new}^*)$ = average transaction cost per period at price c_{new} if the order quantity is Q_{new}^*

$HC(Q_{new}^*)$ = average holding cost per period at price c_{new} if the order quantity is Q_{new}^*

Δ^* = optimal number of extra units in the last order before a price increase =
$(c_{new} - c)D/(hc) + [TC(Q_{new}^*) + HC(Q_{new}^*) - Q^*hc]/(hc)$

If Q^* and Q_{new}^* are set according to the basic EOQ formula (e.g., no quantity discounts), then

$$Q^* = [2AD/hc]^{1/2}$$
$$TC(Q_{new}^*) = [ADhc_{new}/2]^{1/2}$$
$$HC(Q_{new}^*) = [ADhc_{new}/2]^{1/2}$$
$$\Delta^* = \{(c_{new} - c)D + (c_{new}^{1/2} - c^{1/2}) \times [2ADh]^{1/2}\}/hc \approx (c_{new} - c)D/hc$$

CHAPTER 7

Inventory Management II

Notation for the Single-Period Model

D = demand during the period, which is uncertain (i.e., D is a random variable)

p = selling price per unit

c = cost per unit

s = salvage value per unit (i.e., selling price per unit for units left over at the end of the period)

g = goodwill cost per unit (e.g., lost future profit due to unsatisfied demand or, alternatively, cost to reimburse a customer for inconvenience due to unsatisfied demand)

c_e = cost per unit excess (e.g., purchase cost less salvage value, or $c - s$)

c_s = cost per unit short (e.g., lost profit plus goodwill cost, or $p - c + g$)

Q = order quantity

$P[D \le x]$ = probability that demand during the period is x units or less; $P[D \le x]$ defines the probability distribution of demand in the period as a function of possible realized demand x, and $P[D \le Q]$ is the anticipated "service level" (SL) during the period if Q units are ordered

$E[D]$ = expected (or mean) value of D

Single-Period Model

Q^* = optimal order quantity

SL^* = optimal service level = $c_s/(c_s + c_e)$

Finding the value of Q^* in general: select the quantity Q^* that satisfies

$$P[D \le Q^*] = SL^*$$

If there is no quantity satisfying $P[D \le Q^*] = SL^*$, then Q^* is the smallest value satisfying

$$P[D \le Q^*] > SL^*$$

Finding the value of Q^* if unknown demand is approximated by a uniform distribution between a and b; that is, $D \sim U(a, b)$ and $E[D] = (a + b)/2$:

$$Q^* = a + SL^*(b - a)$$

(because $P[D \le Q] = (Q - a)/(b - a)$ for the uniform distribution)

Finding the value of Q^* if unknown demand is approximated by a normal distribution with mean μ_D and variance σ_D^2; that is, $D \sim N(\mu_D, \sigma_D^2)$:

$$Q^* = \mu_D + z_{SL}^*\sigma_D$$

(because $P[D \le Q = \mu_D + z_{SL}\sigma_D] = SL$ for the normal distribution)

Notation for When and How Much to Order

LD = demand during the replenishment lead time, which is uncertain (i.e., LD is a random variable)

ILD = demand during the order interval plus replenishment lead time, which is uncertain (i.e., ILD is a random variable)

$P[X \le x]$ = probability that random variable X is x units or less; for example, $P[LD \le x]$ defines the probability distribution of LD and $P[ILD \le x]$ defines the probability distribution of ILD

$E[X]$ = expected (or mean) value of X; for example, $E[LD]$ is the mean of LD and $E[ILD]$ is the mean of ILD

c = cost per unit (e.g., purchase cost)

h = inventory holding cost per \$-period

c_e = inventory holding cost per unit-period (excess cost rate), for example, $c_e = h \times c$

c_s = backorder cost per unit-period (shortage cost rate)

Q = order quantity

S = base stock level

R = reorder point

SL = service level = probability of no backorders during some period of time

FR = fill rate = proportion of demand shipped from inventory (e.g., proportion shipped on time)

Base Stock Policy

S = base stock level

$E[LD]$ = expected (or mean) demand during the replenishment lead time

$S - E[LD]$ = safety stock inventory

S^* = optimal base stock level

SL^* = optimal service level = $c_s/(c_s + c_e)$

Finding the value of S^* in general: select the quantity S^* that satisfies

$$P[LD \leq S^*] = SL^*$$

If there is no quantity satisfying $P[LD \leq S^*] = SL^*$, then S^* is the smallest value satisfying

$$P[LD \leq S^*] > SL^*$$

Finding the value of S^* if unknown demand is approximated by a uniform distribution between a and b; that is, $LD \sim U(a, b)$ and $E[LD] = (a + b)/2$:

$$S^* = a + SL^*(b - a)$$

(because $P[LD \leq S] = (S - a)/(b - a)$ for the uniform distribution)

Finding the value of S^* if unknown demand is approximated by a normal distribution with mean μ_{LD} and variance σ_{LD}^2; that is, $LD \sim N(\mu_{LD}, \sigma_{LD}^2)$:

$$S^* = \mu_{LD} + z_{SL}^*\sigma_{LD}$$

(because $P[LD \leq S = \mu_{LD} + z_{SL}\sigma_{LD}] = SL$ for the normal distribution)

(Q, R) Policy Based on Service Level

Q = order quantity

R = reorder point

$E[LD]$ = expected (or mean) demand during the replenishment lead time

$Q/2$ = average cycle stock inventory

$R - E[LD]$ = safety stock inventory

SL^* = optimal service level = $c_s/(c_s + c_e)$

Finding the value of R in general: select the quantity R that satisfies

$$P[LD \leq R] = SL^*$$

If there is no quantity satisfying $P[LD \leq R] = SL^*$, then R is the smallest value satisfying

$$P[LD \leq R] > SL^*$$

Finding the value of R if unknown demand is approximated by a uniform distribution between a and b; that is, $LD \sim U(a, b)$ and $E[LD] = (a + b)/2$:

$$R = a + SL^*(b-a)$$

(because $P[LD \leq R] = (R - a)/(b - a)$ for the uniform distribution)

Finding the value of R if unknown demand is approximated by a normal distribution with mean μ_{LD} and variance σ_{LD}^2; that is, $LD \sim N(\mu_{LD}, \sigma_{LD}^2)$:

$$R = \mu_{LD} + z_{SL}{}^*\sigma_{LD}$$

(because $P[LD \leq R = \mu_{LD} + z_{SL}\sigma_{LD}] = SL$ for the normal distribution)

(Q, R) Policy Based on Fill Rate

Q = order quantity = expected demand between receipt of orders

R = reorder point

FR = fill rate

$E[LD]$ = expected (or mean) demand during the replenishment lead time

$Q/2$ = average cycle stock inventory

$R - E[LD]$ = safety stock inventory

$E[(LD - R)^+]$ = expected number of units backordered when a replenishment order arrives

$E[(LD - (R + Q))^+]$ = expected number of units left over on backorder from the previous replenishment cycle

$E[(LD - R)^+] - E[(LD - (R + Q))^+]$ = expected number of units backordered from demand during the current replenishment cycle when a replenishment order arrives

Finding the value of FR in general:

$$FR = 1 - \{E[(LD - R)^+] - E[(LD - (R + Q))^+]\}/Q$$

Finding the value of FR if unknown demand is approximated by a uniform distribution between a and b; that is, $LD \sim U(a, b)$ and $E[LD] = (a + b)/2$:

$$FR = P[LD \leq R + Q/2] = (R + Q/2 - a)/(b - a) \quad \text{if } R + Q \leq b$$

$$FR = 1 - P[LD > R](b - R)/2Q = 1 - (b - R)^2/[2Q(b - a)] \quad \text{if } R + Q \geq b$$

(because $E[(LD - x)^+] = 1/2(b - x)^2/(b - a)$ for the uniform distribution)

Finding the value of FR if unknown demand is approximated by a normal distribution with mean μ_{LD} and variance σ_{LD}^2; that is, $LD \sim N(\mu_{LD}, \sigma_{LD}^2)$:

$$FR = 1 - [G(z_1) - G(z_2)]\sigma_{LD}/Q$$

where

G = unit normal loss function

$z_1 = (R - \mu_{LD})/\sigma_{LD}$

$z_2 = (R + Q - \mu_{LD})/\sigma_{LD}$

(because $E[(LD - x)^+] = \sigma_{LD}G[(x - \mu_{LD})/\sigma_{LD}]$ for the normal distribution)

(I, S) Policy Based on Service Level

I = order interval

S = order-up-to quantity

$E[ILD]$ = expected (or mean) demand during the replenishment lead time plus order interval

$Q/2$ = average cycle stock inventory

$S - E[ILD]$ = safety stock inventory

SL^* = optimal service level = $c_s/(c_s + c_e)$

Finding the value of S in general: select the quantity S that satisfies

$$P[ILD \leq S] = SL^*$$

If there is no quantity satisfying $P[ILD \leq S] = SL^*$, then S is the smallest value satisfying

$$P[ILD \leq S] > SL^*$$

Finding the value of S if unknown demand is approximated by a uniform distribution between a and b; that is, $ILD \sim U(a, b)$ and $E[ILD] = (a + b)/2$:

$$S = a + SL^*(b - a)$$

(because $P[ILD \leq S] = (S - a)/(b - a)$ for the uniform distribution)

Finding the value of S if unknown demand is approximated by a normal distribution with mean μ_{ILD} and variance σ_{ILD}^2; that is, $ILD \sim N(\mu_{ILD}, \sigma_{ILD}^2)$:

$$S = \mu_{ILD} + z_{SL^*}\sigma_{ILD}$$

(because $P[ILD \leq S = \mu_{ILD} + z_{SL}\sigma_{ILD}] = SL$ for the normal distribution)

(I, S) Policy Based on Fill Rate

I = order interval

S = order-up-to quantity

μ_D = mean demand per period

$I \times \mu_D$ = average order quantity

FR = fill rate

$E[LD]$ = expected (or mean) demand during the replenishment lead time

$E[ILD]$ = expected (or mean) demand during the replenishment lead time plus order nterval

$I \times \mu_D/2$ = average cycle stock inventory

$S - E[ILD]$ = safety stock inventory

$E[(ILD - S)^+]$ = expected number of units backordered when a replenishment order arrives

$E[(LD - S)^+]$ = expected number of units left over on backorder from the previous replenishment cycle

$E[(ILD - S)^+] - E[(LD - S)^+]$ = expected number of units backordered from demand during the current replenishment cycle when a replenishment order arrives

Finding the value of FR in general:

$$FR = 1 - \{E[(ILD - S)^+] - E[(LD - S)^+]\}/(I \times \mu_D)$$

Finding the value of FR if unknown demand is approximated by normal distributions; that is, $ILD \sim N(\mu_{ILD}, \sigma_{ILD}{}^2)$ and $LD \sim N(\mu_{LD}, \sigma_{LD}{}^2)$:

$$FR = 1 - [G(z_1) - G(z_2)]\sigma_{ILD}/(I \times \mu_D)$$

. where

G = unit normal loss function

$z_1 = (S - \mu_{ILD})/\sigma_{ILD}$

$z_2 = (S - \mu_{LD})/\sigma_{LD}$

Impact of Reducing Demand Uncertainty

D = demand during a period (e.g., one day), which is uncertain (i.e., D is a random variable)

L = replenishment lead time

LD = demand during the replenishment lead time

ILD = demand during the order interval plus replenishment lead time

$D \sim N(\mu_D, \sigma_D)$

$L \sim N(\mu_L, \sigma_L)$

$LD \sim N(\mu_{LD}, \sigma_{LD})$ where $\mu_{LD} = \mu_L\mu_D$ and $\sigma_{LD} = [\mu_L\sigma_D^2 + \mu_D^2\sigma_L^2]^{1/2}$

$I + L \sim N(\mu_{IL}, \sigma_{IL})$ where $\mu_{IL} = I + \mu_L$ and $\sigma_{IL} = \sigma_L$

$ILD \sim N(\mu_{ILD}, \sigma_{ILD})$ where $\mu_{ILD} = (I + \mu_L)\mu_D$ and $\sigma_{ILD} = [(I + \mu_L)\sigma_D^2 + \mu_D^2\sigma_L^2]^{1/2}$

For a (Q, R) policy:

safety stock $= z_1\sigma_{LD}$

backorder rate $= [G(z_1) - G(z_2)]\sigma_{LD}/Q$

$\approx G(z_1)\sigma_{LD}/Q$ where G = unit normal loss function, $z_1 = (R - \mu_{LD})/\sigma_{LD}$,   and $z_2 = (R + Q - \mu_{LD})/\sigma_{LD}$

$FR = 1 -$ backorder rate

For an (I, S) policy:

safety stock $= z_1\sigma_{ILD}$

backorder rate $= [G(z_1) - G(z_2)]\sigma_{ILD}/(I \times \mu_D)$

$\approx G(z_1)\sigma_{ILD}/(I \times \mu_D)$ where G = unit normal loss function, $z_1 = (S - \mu_{ILD})/\sigma_{ILD}$, and $z_2 = (S - \mu_{LD})/\sigma_{LD}$

$FR = 1 -$ backorder rate

CHAPTER 8

Capacity Management

Notation

Parameters:

λ = mean arrival rate = average number of units arriving at the system per period

$1/\lambda$ = mean interarrival time, or time between arrivals (i.e., the inverse of a *rate* is *time*, and vice versa)

μ = mean service rate per server = average number of units that a server can process per period

$1/\mu$ = mean service time (i.e., the inverse of a *rate* is *time*, and vice-versa)

m = number of servers

Performance Measures:

ρ = system utilization = proportion of the time that a server is busy

W_s = mean time that a unit spends in the system (i.e., in queue or in service)

W_q = mean time that a unit spends waiting for service (i.e., in queue)

L_s = mean number of units in the system (i.e., in queue or in service)

L_q = mean number of units in line for service (i.e., in queue)

p_n = probability of n units in the system (i.e., in queue or in service)

Performance Relationships in Steady State

$m\mu$ = total service rate = number of servers $\times$ service rate of each server

ρ = system utilization = arrival rate $\div$ total service rate = $\lambda/(m\mu)$

W_s = average time in system = average time in queue + average service time = $W_q + 1/\mu$

L_s = average number in system = average number in queue + average number in service = $L_q + m\rho$

L_s = average number in system = arrival rate $\times$ average time in system = λW_s (and $W_s = L_s/\lambda$)

L_q = average number in queue = arrival rate $\times$ average time in queue = λW_q (and $W_q = L_q/\lambda$)

M/M/1 Model

ρ = system utilization = λ/μ

L_q = average number in queue = $\rho^2/(1 - \rho)$

L_s = average number in system = $\rho/(1 - \rho)$

W_q = average time in queue = L_q/λ

W_s = average time in system = L_s/λ

p_0 = probability of 0 in system = $1 - \rho$

p_n = probability of n in system = $p_0\rho^n = (1 - \rho)\rho^n$

M/D/1 Model

ρ = system utilization = λ/μ

L_q = average number in queue = $1/2\rho^2/(1 - \rho)$

L_s = average number in system = $\rho/(1 - \rho) - 1/2\rho^2/(1 - \rho)$

W_q = average time in queue = L_q/λ

W_s = average time in system = L_s/λ

p_0 = probability of 0 in system = $1 - \rho$

CHAPTER 10

Transportation Management

Notation for Shipment Quantity Analysis

D = demand rate in units per period

A = fixed cost per shipment transaction; for example, order processing and other costs that are independent of distance and shipment quantity

δ = shipping distance in miles

A_{TL} = truckload cost per mile

c_e = inventory holding cost per unit-period

Q_{max} = truckload capacity

Q = shipment quantity

Economic Shipment Quantity

D/Q = average number of replenishment shipments per period to a location with demand rate D

Q/D = average time between replenishment shipments, or replenishment cycle time

$Q/2$ = average cycle stock

$C(Q)$ = cost per period; includes transportation cost, transaction cost (e.g., order processing), and inventory holding cost at the receiving location = $(A + A_{TL}\delta)D/Q + (Q/2)c_e$

Q^* = economic shipment quantity = $\min\left\{ Q_{max}, \left(\dfrac{2(A + A_{TL}\delta)D}{c_e} \right)^{1/2} \right\}$

D/Q^* = economic delivery frequency = $\max\left\{ \dfrac{D}{Q_{max}}, \left(\dfrac{Dc_e}{2(A + A_{TL}\delta)} \right)^{1/2} \right\}$

$y(D)$ = truck capacity as a fraction of the "natural" economic shipment quantity at demand rate D = $Q_{max}/[2(A + A_{TL}\delta)D/c_e]^{1/2}$

$C(Q^*)$ = optimal transportation and inventory cost per period

$= [2(A + A_{TL}\delta)Dc_e]^{1/2}$ if $[2(A + A_{TL}\delta)D/c_e]^{1/2} \le Q_{max}$

$= 0.5[y(D)^{-1} + y(D)][2(A + A_{TL}\delta)Dc_e]^{1/2}$ otherwise

Notation for Stop-Off Analysis

D_i = demand rate in units per period at location i

A = fixed cost per shipment transaction; for example, order processing and other costs that are independent of distance and shipment quantity

δ_i = shipping distance in miles to location i

A_{TLi} = truckload cost per mile to location i

A_i = total cost per truckload shipment to location i = $A + A_{TLi}\delta_i$

A_s = cost for a stop-off at location 1 on the way to location 2

c_e = inventory holding cost per unit-period

Q_{max} = truckload capacity

Q_i = delivery quantity to location i

Formulas for Stop-Off Analysis

A stop-off at location 1 to unload Q_1 units on the way to location 2 to unload Q_2 units

Q = total shipment quantity

Q_i = quantity unloaded at location i = $QD_i/(D_1 + D_2)$

D = combined demand rate of locations 1 and 2 = $D_1 + D_2$

D/Q = average number of replenishment shipments per period to locations 1 and 2 with demand rate D

Q/D = average time between replenishment shipments, or replenishment cycle time

$Q/2$ = average cycle stock

$C(Q)$ = cost per period; includes transportation cost, transaction cost (e.g., order processing), and inventory holding cost at receiving locations 1 and 2 = $(As + A + A_{TL2}\delta_2)D/Q + (Q/2)c_e = (A_s + A_2)D/Q + (Q/2)c_e$

Q^* = economic shipment quantity = $\min \left\{ Q_{\max}, \left(\dfrac{2(A_s + A_2)D}{c_e} \right)^{1/2} \right\}$

D/Q^* = economic delivery frequency = $\max \left\{ \dfrac{D}{Q_{\max}}, \left(\dfrac{Dc_e}{2(A_s + A_2)} \right)^{1/2} \right\}$

$y(D)$ = truck capacity as a fraction of the "natural" economic shipment quantity at demand rate D = $Q_{\max}/[2(A_s + A_2)D/c_e]^{1/2}$

$C(Q^*)$ = optimal transportation and inventory cost per period

$\qquad = [2(A_s + A_2)Dc_e]^{1/2} \qquad$ if $[2(A_s + A_2)Dc_e]^{1/2} \le Q_{\max}$

$\qquad = 0.5[y(D)^{-1} + y(D)][2(A_s + A_2)Dc_e]^{1/2} \qquad$ otherwise

Notation for the GOMA Model

D = annual demand per square mile

τ = configuration factor (the value of τ depends on the shape of the market area and the road network)

c_2 = outbound transportation cost coefficient

w_1 = warehouse throughput cost per unit

w_2 = warehouse overhead cost coefficient

α = outbound transportation cost exponent

β = warehouse overhead cost exponent

x = market area served by a warehouse in square miles

GOMA Model

$C_T(x)$ = unit outbound transportation cost as a function of market area x = $c_2\tau x^{\alpha/2}$

$C_W(x)$ = unit warehousing overhead cost as a function of the market area x = $w_2 D^{\beta-1}x^{\beta-1}$

$C(x)$ = unit outbound transportation and warehousing overhead cost = $C_T(x) + C_W(x) = c_2\tau x^{\alpha/2} + w_2 D^{\beta-1}x^{\beta-1}$

x^* = optimal market area = $\left(\dfrac{w_2 D^{\beta-1}(1-\beta)}{c_2\tau\left(\frac{\alpha}{2}\right)} \right)^{1/(\alpha/2 + 1 - \beta)}$

$C(x^*)$ = optimal unit outbound transportation and warehousing overhead

$$\text{cost} = (\alpha/2 + 1 - \beta)\left[\frac{c_2 \tau w_2 D^{\beta-1}}{(\alpha/2)(1-\beta)}\right]^{1/\alpha/2 + 1 - \beta}$$

$C_W(x^*)/C_T(x^*)$ = ratio of optimal warehousing overhead cost to transportation cost

$$= \frac{\alpha/2}{1-\beta}$$

$C(yx^*)/C(x^*) - 1$ = percentage increase in cost if market area is $x = yx^*$ instead of x^*

$$= y^{\beta-1}\left(\frac{\alpha/2}{\alpha/2 + 1 - \beta}\right) + y^{\alpha/2}\left(\frac{1-\beta}{\alpha/2 + 1 - \beta}\right) - 1$$

Notation for Model with Inbound Freight

L = length of the territory served by the distribution network

D = annual demand per linear mile

c_1 = inbound transportation cost per unit-mile

c_2 = outbound transportation cost per unit-mile

w_1 = warehouse throughput cost per unit

w_2 = warehouse fixed cost per year (e.g., overhead)

x = market length served by a warehouse in miles

Optimal Market Length When Warehouses Are Centrally Located

$C_T(x)$ = unit inbound outbound transportation cost as a function of market length x =
$c_1 L/2 + c_2 x/4$

$C_W(x)$ = unit warehousing overhead cost as a function of the market length $x = w_2/(Dx)$

$C(x)$ = unit transportation and warehousing overhead cost = $C_T(x) + C_W(x)$ =
$c_1 L/2 + c_2 x/4 + w_2/(Dx)$

x^* = optimal market length = $2\left(\frac{w_2}{c_2 D}\right)^{1/2}$

Optimal Market Length When Warehouses Are Optimally Located

$C_T(x, y)$ = unit inbound and outbound transportation cost as a function of market
length x and location $y = c_1[(L - x)/2 + y] + c_2[x/2 - y - y^2/x]$

$C_W(x)$ = unit warehousing overhead cost as a function of the market length $x = w_2/(Dx)$

$C(x, y)$ = unit transportation and warehousing overhead cost = $C_T(x, y) + C_W(x)$ =
$c_1[(L - x)/2 + y] + c_2[x/2 - y - y^2/x] + w_2/(Dx)$

x^* = optimal market length = $2\left(\frac{w_2}{c_2 D}\right)^{1/2}\left(\frac{1}{1 - (c_1/c_2)^2}\right)^{1/2}$

y^* = optimal distance from the market boundary = $\frac{x^*}{2}\left(1 - \frac{c_1}{c_2}\right)$

CHAPTER 11

Quality Management

$\overline{X}$ -Chart

X = random variable for the measure of interest when process is in control

μ_X = mean of X

σ_X = standard deviation of X

n = sample size

$\bar{X}$ = random variable for the mean of a sample (i.e., average of n random variables)

$\mu_{\bar{X}}$ = mean of $\bar{X} = \mu_X$

$\sigma_{\bar{X}}$ = standard deviation of the sample mean $= \frac{\sigma_X}{\sqrt{n}}$

CL = center line $= \mu_{\bar{X}}$

UCL = upper control limit $= \mu_{\bar{X}} + z\sigma_{\bar{X}} = \mu_X + z\frac{\sigma_X}{\sqrt{n}}$

LCL = lower control limit $= \mu_{\bar{X}} - z\sigma_{\bar{X}} = \mu_X - z\frac{\sigma_X}{\sqrt{n}}$;   if LCL < 0, then set LCL $= 0$

Note: The value of z is typically set to three (i.e., three-sigma control limits).

Estimating μ_X and σ_X from historical data: collect N samples of process output (e.g., $N \geq 10$); the size of each sample is n

x_i = measure of the ith part in a sample

$\bar{x}_j$ = mean of the jth sample $= \frac{1}{n}\sum_{i=1}^{n} x_i$

$\bar{\bar{x}}$ = grand mean $= \frac{1}{N}\sum_{j=1}^{N} x_i$ = estimate of $\mu_{\bar{X}}$

s_j = sample standard deviation of the jth sample $= \left[\dfrac{\sum_{i=1}^{n}(x_i - \bar{x}_j)^2}{n-1}\right]^{1/2}$

$\bar{s}$ = grand standard deviation $= \frac{1}{N}\sum_{j=1}^{N} s_j$

$\bar{s}/c_4$ = estimate of σ_X, where $c_4 = \left(\dfrac{2}{n-1}\right)^{1/2}\dfrac{\Gamma(n/2)}{\Gamma((n-1)/2)}$ (see Chapter 11 for a table of c_4 values)

CL = center line $= \mu_{\bar{X}} = \bar{\bar{x}}$

UCL = upper control limit $= \mu_{\bar{X}} + z\sigma_{\bar{X}} = \mu_X + z\frac{\sigma_X}{\sqrt{n}} = \bar{\bar{x}} + z\frac{\bar{s}}{c_4\sqrt{n}}$

LCL = lower control limit $= \max\{\mu_{\bar{X}} - z\sigma_{\bar{X}}, 0\} =$

$\max\{\mu_{\bar{X}} - z\frac{\sigma_X}{\sqrt{n}}, 0\} = \max\{\bar{\bar{x}} - z\frac{\bar{s}}{c_4\sqrt{n}}, 0\}$

R-Chart

R = random variable for difference between the largest and smallest value in a sample of size n

μ_R = mean of R

σ_R = standard deviation of R

CL = center line $= \mu_R$

UCL = upper control limit $= \mu_R + z\sigma_R$

LCL = lower control limit $= \mu_R - z\sigma_R$; if LCL < 0, then set LCL $= 0$

Note: The value of z is typically set to three (i.e., three-sigma control limits).

Computing μ_R and σ_R from historical data: collect N samples of process output (e.g., $N \geq 10$); the size of each sample is n

x_i = measure of the ith part in a sample

r_j = range of the jth sample = $\max\{x_i\} - \min\{x_i\}$

$\bar{r}$ = average range = $\dfrac{1}{N}\displaystyle\sum_{j=1}^{N} r_j$ = estimate of μ_R

$\bar{r} \times (d_3/d_2)$ = estimate of σ_R, where the values of d_3/d_2 for various sample sizes are

n	2	3	4	5	6	7	8	9	10
d_3/d_2	0.756	0.525	0.427	0.372	0.335	0.308	0.288	0.272	0.259

CL = center line = $\mu_R = \bar{r}$

UCL = upper control limit = $\mu_R + z\sigma_R = \bar{r} + z\bar{r}(d_3/d_2)$

LCL = lower control limit = $\max\{\mu_R - z\sigma_R, 0\} = \max\{\bar{r} - z\bar{r}(d_3/d_2), 0\}$

S-Chart

S = random variable for the sample standard deviation of a sample of size n

μ_S = mean of S

σ_S = standard deviation of S

CL = center line = μ_S

UCL = upper control limit = $\mu_S + z\sigma_S$

LCL = lower control limit = $\mu_S - z\sigma_S$; if LCL < 0, then set LCL = 0

Note: The value of z is typically set to three (i.e., three-sigma control limits).

Computing μ_S and σ_S from historical data: collect N samples of process output (e.g., $N \geq 10$); the size of each sample is n

$$s_j = \text{sample standard deviation of the } j\text{th sample} = \left[\frac{\displaystyle\sum_{i=1}^{n} (x_i - \bar{x}_j)^2}{n-1}\right]^{1/2}$$

$$\bar{s} = \text{estimate of } \mu_S = \text{grand standard deviation} = \frac{1}{N}\sum_{j=1}^{N} s_j$$

$\dfrac{\bar{s}}{c_4}[1 - c_4^2]^{1/2}$ = estimate of σ_s

CL = center line = $\mu_S = \bar{s}$

UCL = upper control limit = $\mu_S + z\sigma_S = \bar{s} + z\dfrac{\bar{s}}{c_4}[1 - c_4^2]^{1/2}$

LCL = lower control limit = $\max\{\mu_S - z\sigma_S, 0\}$ =
$\max\{\bar{s} - z\dfrac{\bar{s}}{c_4}[1 - c_4^2]^{1/2}, 0\}$

P-Chart

P = random variable for the proportion of a sample of size n with the attribute

μ_P = mean of P (e.g., expected proportion with the attribute when process is in control)

σ_P = standard deviation of P = $\left[\dfrac{\mu_P(1-\mu_P)}{n}\right]^{1/2}$

CL = center line = μ_P

UCL = upper control limit = $\mu_P + z\sigma_P$;   if UCL > 1, then set UCL = 1

LCL = lower control limit = $\mu_P - z\sigma_P$;   if LCL < 0, then set LCL = 0

Note: The value of z is typically set to three (i.e., three-sigma control limits).

Computing μ_P and σ_P from historical data: collect N samples of process output (e.g., $N \geq 10$); the size of each sample is n

$$p_j = \text{proportion of units with the attribute in the } j\text{th sample}$$

$$\bar{p} = \text{average proportion} = \frac{1}{N}\sum_{j=1}^{N}p_j = \text{estimate of } \mu_P$$

$$\left[\frac{\bar{p}(1-\bar{p})}{n}\right]^{1/2} = \text{estimate of } \sigma_P$$

$$CL = \text{center line} = \mu_p = \bar{p}$$

$$UCL = \text{upper control limit} = \min\{\mu_P + z\sigma_P, 1\} = \min\left\{\bar{p} + z\left[\frac{\bar{p}(1-\bar{p})}{n}\right]^{1/2}, 1\right\}$$

$$LCL = \text{lower control limit} = \max\{\mu_P - z\sigma_P, 0\} = \max\left\{\bar{p} - z\left[\frac{\bar{p}(1-\bar{p})}{n}\right]^{1/2}, 0\right\}$$

Process Capability

$$LSL = \text{lower specification limit}$$

$$USL = \text{upper specification limit}$$

$$C_p = \text{process capability index} = \frac{USL - LSL}{6\sigma_X}$$

$$C_{pk} = \text{process capability index when process is not centered}$$

$$= \min\left\{\frac{USL - \mu_X}{3\sigma_X}, \frac{\mu_X - LSL}{3\sigma_X}\right\}$$

Appendix **Four**

Standard Normal Probability and Unit Normal Loss Table

z	$P[X \leq z]$	$P[X \leq -z]$	$P[-z \leq X \leq z]$	$G(z)$	$G(-z)$
0.00	0.50000	0.50000	0.00000	0.39894	0.39894
0.01	0.50399	0.49601	0.00798	0.39396	0.40396
0.02	0.50798	0.49202	0.01596	0.38902	0.40902
0.03	0.51197	0.48803	0.02393	0.38412	0.41412
0.04	0.51595	0.48405	0.03191	0.37926	0.41926
0.05	0.51994	0.48006	0.03988	0.37444	0.42444
0.06	0.52392	0.47608	0.04784	0.36966	0.42966
0.07	0.52790	0.47210	0.05581	0.36492	0.43492
0.08	0.53188	0.46812	0.06376	0.36022	0.44022
0.09	0.53586	0.46414	0.07171	0.35556	0.44556
0.10	0.53983	0.46017	0.07966	0.35094	0.45094
0.11	0.54380	0.45620	0.08759	0.34635	0.45635
0.12	0.54776	0.45224	0.09552	0.34181	0.46181
0.13	0.55172	0.44828	0.10343	0.33731	0.46731
0.14	0.55567	0.44433	0.11134	0.33285	0.47285
0.15	0.55962	0.44038	0.11924	0.32842	0.47842
0.16	0.56356	0.43644	0.12712	0.32404	0.48404
0.17	0.56749	0.43251	0.13499	0.31969	0.48969
0.18	0.57142	0.42858	0.14285	0.31539	0.49539
0.19	0.57535	0.42465	0.15069	0.31112	0.50112
0.20	0.57926	0.42074	0.15852	0.30689	0.50689
0.21	0.58317	0.41683	0.16633	0.30271	0.51271
0.22	0.58706	0.41294	0.17413	0.29856	0.51856
0.23	0.59095	0.40905	0.18191	0.29445	0.52445
0.24	0.59483	0.40517	0.18967	0.29038	0.53038
0.25	0.59871	0.40129	0.19741	0.28634	0.53634
0.26	0.60257	0.39743	0.20514	0.28235	0.54235
0.27	0.60642	0.39358	0.21284	0.27840	0.54840
0.28	0.61026	0.38974	0.22052	0.27448	0.55448
0.29	0.61409	0.38591	0.22818	0.27060	0.56060
0.30	0.61791	0.38209	0.23582	0.26676	0.56676
0.31	0.62172	0.37828	0.24344	0.26296	0.57296
0.32	0.62552	0.37448	0.25103	0.25920	0.57920

z	P[X ≤ z]	P[X ≤ −z]	P[−z ≤ X ≤ z]	G(z)	G(−z)
0.33	0.62930	0.37070	0.25860	0.25547	0.58547
0.34	0.63307	0.36693	0.26614	0.25178	0.59178
0.35	0.63683	0.36317	0.27366	0.24813	0.59813
0.36	0.64058	0.35942	0.28115	0.24452	0.60452
0.37	0.64431	0.35569	0.28862	0.24094	0.61094
0.38	0.64803	0.35197	0.29605	0.23740	0.61740
0.39	0.65173	0.34827	0.30346	0.23390	0.62390
0.40	0.65542	0.34458	0.31084	0.23044	0.63044
0.41	0.65910	0.34090	0.31819	0.22701	0.63701
0.42	0.66276	0.33724	0.32551	0.22362	0.64362
0.43	0.66640	0.33360	0.33280	0.22027	0.65027
0.44	0.67003	0.32997	0.34006	0.21695	0.65695
0.45	0.67364	0.32636	0.34729	0.21367	0.66367
0.46	0.67724	0.32276	0.35448	0.21042	0.67042
0.47	0.68082	0.31918	0.36164	0.20721	0.67721
0.48	0.68439	0.31561	0.36877	0.20404	0.68404
0.49	0.68793	0.31207	0.37587	0.20090	0.69090
0.50	0.69146	0.30854	0.38292	0.19780	0.69780
0.51	0.69497	0.30503	0.38995	0.19473	0.70473
0.52	0.69847	0.30153	0.39694	0.19170	0.71170
0.53	0.70194	0.29806	0.40389	0.18870	0.71870
0.54	0.70540	0.29460	0.41080	0.18573	0.72573
0.55	0.70884	0.29116	0.41768	0.18281	0.73281
0.56	0.71226	0.28774	0.42452	0.17991	0.73991
0.57	0.71566	0.28434	0.43132	0.17705	0.74705
0.58	0.71904	0.28096	0.43809	0.17422	0.75422
0.59	0.72240	0.27760	0.44481	0.17143	0.76143
0.60	0.72575	0.27425	0.45149	0.16867	0.76867
0.61	0.72907	0.27093	0.45814	0.16595	0.77595
0.62	0.73237	0.26763	0.46474	0.16325	0.78325
0.63	0.73565	0.26435	0.47131	0.16059	0.79059
0.64	0.73891	0.26109	0.47783	0.15797	0.79797
0.65	0.74215	0.25785	0.48431	0.15537	0.80537
0.66	0.74537	0.25463	0.49075	0.15281	0.81281
0.67	0.74857	0.25143	0.49714	0.15028	0.82028
0.68	0.75175	0.24825	0.50350	0.14778	0.82778
0.69	0.75490	0.24510	0.50981	0.14531	0.83531
0.70	0.75804	0.24196	0.51607	0.14288	0.84288
0.71	0.76115	0.23885	0.52230	0.14048	0.85048
0.72	0.76424	0.23576	0.52848	0.13810	0.85810
0.73	0.76730	0.23270	0.53461	0.13576	0.86576
0.74	0.77035	0.22965	0.54070	0.13345	0.87345
0.75	0.77337	0.22663	0.54675	0.13117	0.88117
0.76	0.77637	0.22363	0.55275	0.12892	0.88892
0.77	0.77935	0.22065	0.55870	0.12669	0.89669
0.78	0.78230	0.21770	0.56461	0.12450	0.90450
0.79	0.78524	0.21476	0.57047	0.12234	0.91234
0.80	0.78814	0.21186	0.57629	0.12021	0.92021
0.81	0.79103	0.20897	0.58206	0.11810	0.92810
0.82	0.79389	0.20611	0.58778	0.11603	0.93603
0.83	0.79673	0.20327	0.59346	0.11398	0.94398
0.84	0.79955	0.20045	0.59909	0.11196	0.95196

z	P[X ≤ z]	P[X ≤ −z]	P[−z ≤ X ≤ z]	G(z)	G(−z)
0.85	0.80234	0.19766	0.60468	0.10997	0.95997
0.86	0.80511	0.19489	0.61021	0.10801	0.96801
0.87	0.80785	0.19215	0.61570	0.10607	0.97607
0.88	0.81057	0.18943	0.62114	0.10417	0.98417
0.89	0.81327	0.18673	0.62653	0.10229	0.99229
0.90	0.81594	0.18406	0.63188	0.10043	1.00043
0.91	0.81859	0.18141	0.63718	0.09860	1.00860
0.92	0.82121	0.17879	0.64243	0.09680	1.01680
0.93	0.82381	0.17619	0.64763	0.09503	1.02503
0.94	0.82639	0.17361	0.65278	0.09328	1.03328
0.95	0.82894	0.17106	0.65789	0.09156	1.04156
0.96	0.83147	0.16853	0.66294	0.08986	1.04986
0.97	0.83398	0.16602	0.66795	0.08819	1.05819
0.98	0.83646	0.16354	0.67291	0.08654	1.06654
0.99	0.83891	0.16109	0.67783	0.08491	1.07491
1.00	0.84134	0.15866	0.68269	0.08332	1.08332
1.01	0.84375	0.15625	0.68750	0.08174	1.09174
1.02	0.84614	0.15386	0.69227	0.08019	1.10019
1.03	0.84849	0.15151	0.69699	0.07866	1.10866
1.04	0.85083	0.14917	0.70166	0.07716	1.11716
1.05	0.85314	0.14686	0.70628	0.07568	1.12568
1.06	0.85543	0.14457	0.71086	0.07422	1.13422
1.07	0.85769	0.14231	0.71538	0.07279	1.14279
1.08	0.85993	0.14007	0.71986	0.07138	1.15138
1.09	0.86214	0.13786	0.72429	0.06999	1.15999
1.10	0.86433	0.13567	0.72867	0.06862	1.16862
1.11	0.86650	0.13350	0.73300	0.06727	1.17727
1.12	0.86864	0.13136	0.73729	0.06595	1.18595
1.13	0.87076	0.12924	0.74152	0.06465	1.19465
1.14	0.87286	0.12714	0.74571	0.06336	1.20336
1.15	0.87493	0.12507	0.74986	0.06210	1.21210
1.16	0.87698	0.12302	0.75395	0.06086	1.22086
1.17	0.87900	0.12100	0.75800	0.05964	1.22964
1.18	0.88100	0.11900	0.76200	0.05844	1.23844
1.19	0.88298	0.11702	0.76595	0.05726	1.24726
1.20	0.88493	0.11507	0.76986	0.05610	1.25610
1.21	0.88686	0.11314	0.77372	0.05496	1.26496
1.22	0.88877	0.11123	0.77753	0.05384	1.27384
1.23	0.89065	0.10935	0.78130	0.05274	1.28274
1.24	0.89251	0.10749	0.78502	0.05165	1.29165
1.25	0.89435	0.10565	0.78870	0.05059	1.30059
1.26	0.89617	0.10383	0.79233	0.04954	1.30954
1.27	0.89796	0.10204	0.79592	0.04851	1.31851
1.28	0.89973	0.10027	0.79945	0.04750	1.32750
1.29	0.90147	0.09853	0.80295	0.04650	1.33650
1.30	0.90320	0.09680	0.80640	0.04553	1.34553
1.31	0.90490	0.09510	0.80980	0.04457	1.35457
1.32	0.90658	0.09342	0.81316	0.04363	1.36363
1.33	0.90824	0.09176	0.81648	0.04270	1.37270
1.34	0.90988	0.09012	0.81975	0.04179	1.38179
1.35	0.91149	0.08851	0.82298	0.04090	1.39090
1.36	0.91308	0.08692	0.82617	0.04002	1.40002
1.37	0.91466	0.08534	0.82931	0.03916	1.40916

z	P[X ≤ z]	P[X ≤ −z]	P[−z ≤ X ≤ z]	G(z)	G(−z)
1.38	0.91621	0.08379	0.83241	0.03831	1.41831
1.39	0.91774	0.08226	0.83547	0.03748	1.42748
1.40	0.91924	0.08076	0.83849	0.03667	1.43667
1.41	0.92073	0.07927	0.84146	0.03587	1.44587
1.42	0.92220	0.07780	0.84439	0.03508	1.45508
1.43	0.92364	0.07636	0.84728	0.03431	1.46431
1.44	0.92507	0.07493	0.85013	0.03356	1.47356
1.45	0.92647	0.07353	0.85294	0.03281	1.48281
1.46	0.92785	0.07215	0.85571	0.03208	1.49208
1.47	0.92922	0.07078	0.85844	0.03137	1.50137
1.48	0.93056	0.06944	0.86113	0.03067	1.51067
1.49	0.93189	0.06811	0.86378	0.02998	1.51998
1.50	0.93319	0.06681	0.86639	0.02931	1.52931
1.51	0.93448	0.06552	0.86896	0.02865	1.53865
1.52	0.93574	0.06426	0.87149	0.02800	1.54800
1.53	0.93699	0.06301	0.87398	0.02736	1.55736
1.54	0.93822	0.06178	0.87644	0.02674	1.56674
1.55	0.93943	0.06057	0.87886	0.02612	1.57612
1.56	0.94062	0.05938	0.88124	0.02552	1.58552
1.57	0.94179	0.05821	0.88358	0.02494	1.59494
1.58	0.94295	0.05705	0.88589	0.02436	1.60436
1.59	0.94408	0.05592	0.88817	0.02380	1.61380
1.60	0.94520	0.05480	0.89040	0.02324	1.62324
1.61	0.94630	0.05370	0.89260	0.02270	1.63270
1.62	0.94738	0.05262	0.89477	0.02217	1.64217
1.63	0.94845	0.05155	0.89690	0.02165	1.65165
1.64	0.94950	0.05050	0.89899	0.02114	1.66114
1.65	0.95053	0.04947	0.90106	0.02064	1.67064
1.66	0.95154	0.04846	0.90309	0.02015	1.68015
1.67	0.95254	0.04746	0.90508	0.01967	1.68967
1.68	0.95352	0.04648	0.90704	0.01920	1.69920
1.69	0.95449	0.04551	0.90897	0.01874	1.70874
1.70	0.95543	0.04457	0.91087	0.01829	1.71829
1.71	0.95637	0.04363	0.91273	0.01785	1.72785
1.72	0.95728	0.04272	0.91457	0.01742	1.73742
1.73	0.95818	0.04182	0.91637	0.01699	1.74699
1.74	0.95907	0.04093	0.91814	0.01658	1.75658
1.75	0.95994	0.04006	0.91988	0.01617	1.76617
1.76	0.96080	0.03920	0.92159	0.01578	1.77578
1.77	0.96164	0.03836	0.92327	0.01539	1.78539
1.78	0.96246	0.03754	0.92492	0.01501	1.79501
1.79	0.96327	0.03673	0.92655	0.01464	1.80464
1.80	0.96407	0.03593	0.92814	0.01428	1.81428
1.81	0.96485	0.03515	0.92970	0.01392	1.82392
1.82	0.96562	0.03438	0.93124	0.01357	1.83357
1.83	0.96638	0.03362	0.93275	0.01323	1.84323
1.84	0.96712	0.03288	0.93423	0.01290	1.85290
1.85	0.96784	0.03216	0.93569	0.01257	1.86257
1.86	0.96856	0.03144	0.93711	0.01226	1.87226
1.87	0.96926	0.03074	0.93852	0.01195	1.88195
1.88	0.96995	0.03005	0.93989	0.01164	1.89164
1.89	0.97062	0.02938	0.94124	0.01134	1.90134
1.90	0.97128	0.02872	0.94257	0.01105	1.91105

z	P[X ≤ z]	P[X ≤ −z]	P[−z ≤ X ≤ z]	G(z)	G(−z)
1.91	0.97193	0.02807	0.94387	0.01077	1.92077
1.92	0.97257	0.02743	0.94514	0.01049	1.93049
1.93	0.97320	0.02680	0.94639	0.01022	1.94022
1.94	0.97381	0.02619	0.94762	0.00996	1.94996
1.95	0.97441	0.02559	0.94882	0.00970	1.95970
1.96	0.97500	0.02500	0.95000	0.00945	1.96945
1.97	0.97558	0.02442	0.95116	0.00920	1.97920
1.98	0.97615	0.02385	0.95230	0.00896	1.98896
1.99	0.97670	0.02330	0.95341	0.00872	1.99872
2.00	0.97725	0.02275	0.95450	0.00849	2.00849
2.01	0.97778	0.02222	0.95557	0.00827	2.01827
2.02	0.97831	0.02169	0.95662	0.00805	2.02805
2.03	0.97882	0.02118	0.95764	0.00783	2.03783
2.04	0.97932	0.02068	0.95865	0.00762	2.04762
2.05	0.97982	0.02018	0.95964	0.00742	2.05742
2.06	0.98030	0.01970	0.96060	0.00722	2.06722
2.07	0.98077	0.01923	0.96155	0.00702	2.07702
2.08	0.98124	0.01876	0.96247	0.00683	2.08683
2.09	0.98169	0.01831	0.96338	0.00665	2.09665
2.10	0.98214	0.01786	0.96427	0.00647	2.10647
2.11	0.98257	0.01743	0.96514	0.00629	2.11629
2.12	0.98300	0.01700	0.96599	0.00612	2.12612
2.13	0.98341	0.01659	0.96683	0.00595	2.13595
2.14	0.98382	0.01618	0.96765	0.00579	2.14579
2.15	0.98422	0.01578	0.96844	0.00563	2.15563
2.16	0.98461	0.01539	0.96923	0.00547	2.16547
2.17	0.98500	0.01500	0.96999	0.00532	2.17532
2.18	0.98537	0.01463	0.97074	0.00517	2.18517
2.19	0.98574	0.01426	0.97148	0.00503	2.19503
2.20	0.98610	0.01390	0.97219	0.00489	2.20489
2.21	0.98645	0.01355	0.97289	0.00475	2.21475
2.22	0.98679	0.01321	0.97358	0.00462	2.22462
2.23	0.98713	0.01287	0.97425	0.00449	2.23449
2.24	0.98745	0.01255	0.97491	0.00436	2.24436
2.25	0.98778	0.01222	0.97555	0.00423	2.25423
2.26	0.98809	0.01191	0.97618	0.00411	2.26411
2.27	0.98840	0.01160	0.97679	0.00400	2.27400
2.28	0.98870	0.01130	0.97739	0.00388	2.28388
2.29	0.98899	0.01101	0.97798	0.00377	2.29377
2.30	0.98928	0.01072	0.97855	0.00366	2.30366
2.31	0.98956	0.01044	0.97911	0.00356	2.31356
2.32	0.98983	0.01017	0.97966	0.00345	2.32345
2.33	0.99010	0.00990	0.98019	0.00335	2.33335
2.34	0.99036	0.00964	0.98072	0.00325	2.34325
2.35	0.99061	0.00939	0.98123	0.00316	2.35316
2.36	0.99086	0.00914	0.98173	0.00307	2.36307
2.37	0.99111	0.00889	0.98221	0.00298	2.37298
2.38	0.99134	0.00866	0.98269	0.00289	2.38289
2.39	0.99158	0.00842	0.98315	0.00280	2.39280
2.40	0.99180	0.00820	0.98360	0.00272	2.40272
2.41	0.99202	0.00798	0.98405	0.00264	2.41264
2.42	0.99224	0.00776	0.98448	0.00256	2.42256
2.43	0.99245	0.00755	0.98490	0.00248	2.43248

z	$P[X \leq z]$	$P[X \leq -z]$	$P[-z \leq X \leq z]$	$G(z)$	$G(-z)$
2.44	0.99266	0.00734	0.98531	0.00241	2.44241
2.45	0.99286	0.00714	0.98571	0.00234	2.45234
2.46	0.99305	0.00695	0.98611	0.00227	2.46227
2.47	0.99324	0.00676	0.98649	0.00220	2.47220
2.48	0.99343	0.00657	0.98686	0.00213	2.48213
2.49	0.99361	0.00639	0.98723	0.00207	2.49207
2.50	0.99379	0.00621	0.98758	0.00200	2.50200
2.51	0.99396	0.00604	0.98793	0.00194	2.51194
2.52	0.99413	0.00587	0.98826	0.00188	2.52188
2.53	0.99430	0.00570	0.98859	0.00183	2.53183
2.54	0.99446	0.00554	0.98891	0.00177	2.54177
2.55	0.99461	0.00539	0.98923	0.00171	2.55171
2.56	0.99477	0.00523	0.98953	0.00166	2.56166
2.57	0.99492	0.00508	0.98983	0.00161	2.57161
2.58	0.99506	0.00494	0.99012	0.00156	2.58156
2.59	0.99520	0.00480	0.99040	0.00151	2.59151
2.60	0.99534	0.00466	0.99068	0.00146	2.60146
2.61	0.99547	0.00453	0.99095	0.00142	2.61142
2.62	0.99560	0.00440	0.99121	0.00137	2.62137
2.63	0.99573	0.00427	0.99146	0.00133	2.63133
2.64	0.99585	0.00415	0.99171	0.00129	2.64129
2.65	0.99598	0.00402	0.99195	0.00125	2.65125
2.66	0.99609	0.00391	0.99219	0.00121	2.66121
2.67	0.99621	0.00379	0.99241	0.00117	2.67117
2.68	0.99632	0.00368	0.99264	0.00113	2.68113
2.69	0.99643	0.00357	0.99285	0.00110	2.69110
2.70	0.99653	0.00347	0.99307	0.00106	2.70106
2.71	0.99664	0.00336	0.99327	0.00103	2.71103
2.72	0.99674	0.00326	0.99347	0.00099	2.72099
2.73	0.99683	0.00317	0.99367	0.00096	2.73096
2.74	0.99693	0.00307	0.99386	0.00093	2.74093
2.75	0.99702	0.00298	0.99404	0.00090	2.75090
2.76	0.99711	0.00289	0.99422	0.00087	2.76087
2.77	0.99720	0.00280	0.99439	0.00084	2.77084
2.78	0.99728	0.00272	0.99456	0.00081	2.78081
2.79	0.99736	0.00264	0.99473	0.00079	2.79079
2.80	0.99744	0.00256	0.99489	0.00076	2.80076
2.81	0.99752	0.00248	0.99505	0.00074	2.81074
2.82	0.99760	0.00240	0.99520	0.00071	2.82071
2.83	0.99767	0.00233	0.99535	0.00069	2.83069
2.84	0.99774	0.00226	0.99549	0.00066	2.84066
2.85	0.99781	0.00219	0.99563	0.00064	2.85064
2.86	0.99788	0.00212	0.99576	0.00062	2.86062
2.87	0.99795	0.00205	0.99590	0.00060	2.87060
2.88	0.99801	0.00199	0.99602	0.00058	2.88058
2.89	0.99807	0.00193	0.99615	0.00056	2.89056
2.90	0.99813	0.00187	0.99627	0.00054	2.90054
2.91	0.99819	0.00181	0.99639	0.00052	2.91052
2.92	0.99825	0.00175	0.99650	0.00051	2.92051
2.93	0.99831	0.00169	0.99661	0.00049	2.93049
2.94	0.99836	0.00164	0.99672	0.00047	2.94047
2.95	0.99841	0.00159	0.99682	0.00046	2.95046
2.96	0.99846	0.00154	0.99692	0.00044	2.96044

z	$P[X \le z]$	$P[X \le -z]$	$P[-z \le X \le z]$	G(z)	G(-z)
2.97	0.99851	0.00149	0.99702	0.00042	2.97042
2.98	0.99856	0.00144	0.99712	0.00041	2.98041
2.99	0.99861	0.00139	0.99721	0.00040	2.99040
3.00	0.99865	0.00135	0.99730	0.00038	3.00038
3.01	0.99869	0.00131	0.99739	0.00037	3.01037
3.02	0.99874	0.00126	0.99747	0.00036	3.02036
3.03	0.99878	0.00122	0.99755	0.00034	3.03034
3.04	0.99882	0.00118	0.99763	0.00033	3.04033
3.05	0.99886	0.00114	0.99771	0.00032	3.05032
3.06	0.99889	0.00111	0.99779	0.00031	3.06031
3.07	0.99893	0.00107	0.99786	0.00030	3.07030
3.08	0.99896	0.00104	0.99793	0.00029	3.08029
3.09	0.99900	0.00100	0.99800	0.00028	3.09028
3.10	0.99903	0.00097	0.99806	0.00027	3.10027
3.11	0.99906	0.00094	0.99813	0.00026	3.11026
3.12	0.99910	0.00090	0.99819	0.00025	3.12025
3.13	0.99913	0.00087	0.99825	0.00024	3.13024
3.14	0.99916	0.00084	0.99831	0.00023	3.14023
3.15	0.99918	0.00082	0.99837	0.00022	3.15022
3.16	0.99921	0.00079	0.99842	0.00021	3.16021
3.17	0.99924	0.00076	0.99848	0.00021	3.17021
3.18	0.99926	0.00074	0.99853	0.00020	3.18020
3.19	0.99929	0.00071	0.99858	0.00019	3.19019
3.20	0.99931	0.00069	0.99863	0.00019	3.20019
3.21	0.99934	0.00066	0.99867	0.00018	3.21018
3.22	0.99936	0.00064	0.99872	0.00017	3.22017
3.23	0.99938	0.00062	0.99876	0.00017	3.23017
3.24	0.99940	0.00060	0.99880	0.00016	3.24016
3.25	0.99942	0.00058	0.99885	0.00015	3.25015
3.26	0.99944	0.00056	0.99889	0.00015	3.26015
3.27	0.99946	0.00054	0.99892	0.00014	3.27014
3.28	0.99948	0.00052	0.99896	0.00014	3.28014
3.29	0.99950	0.00050	0.99900	0.00013	3.29013
3.30	0.99952	0.00048	0.99903	0.00013	3.30013
3.31	0.99953	0.00047	0.99907	0.00012	3.31012
3.32	0.99955	0.00045	0.99910	0.00012	3.32012
3.33	0.99957	0.00043	0.99913	0.00011	3.33011
3.34	0.99958	0.00042	0.99916	0.00011	3.34011
3.35	0.99960	0.00040	0.99919	0.00010	3.35010
3.36	0.99961	0.00039	0.99922	0.00010	3.36010
3.37	0.99962	0.00038	0.99925	0.00010	3.37010
3.38	0.99964	0.00036	0.99928	0.00009	3.38009
3.39	0.99965	0.00035	0.99930	0.00009	3.39009
3.40	0.99966	0.00034	0.99933	0.00009	3.40009
3.41	0.99968	0.00032	0.99935	0.00008	3.41008
3.42	0.99969	0.00031	0.99937	0.00008	3.42008
3.43	0.99970	0.00030	0.99940	0.00008	3.43008
3.44	0.99971	0.00029	0.99942	0.00007	3.44007
3.45	0.99972	0.00028	0.99944	0.00007	3.45007
3.46	0.99973	0.00027	0.99946	0.00007	3.46007
3.47	0.99974	0.00026	0.99948	0.00007	3.47007
3.48	0.99975	0.00025	0.99950	0.00006	3.48006

z	$P[X \leq z]$	$P[X \leq -z]$	$P[-z \leq X \leq z]$	G(z)	G(-z)
3.49	0.99976	0.00024	0.99952	0.00006	3.49006
3.50	0.99977	0.00023	0.99953	0.00006	3.50006
3.51	0.99978	0.00022	0.99955	0.00006	3.51006
3.52	0.99978	0.00022	0.99957	0.00005	3.52005
3.53	0.99979	0.00021	0.99958	0.00005	3.53005
3.54	0.99980	0.00020	0.99960	0.00005	3.54005
3.55	0.99981	0.00019	0.99961	0.00005	3.55005
3.56	0.99981	0.00019	0.99963	0.00005	3.56005
3.57	0.99982	0.00018	0.99964	0.00004	3.57004
3.58	0.99983	0.00017	0.99966	0.00004	3.58004
3.59	0.99983	0.00017	0.99967	0.00004	3.59004
3.60	0.99984	0.00016	0.99968	0.00004	3.60004
3.61	0.99985	0.00015	0.99969	0.00004	3.61004
3.62	0.99985	0.00015	0.99971	0.00004	3.62004
3.63	0.99986	0.00014	0.99972	0.00003	3.63003
3.64	0.99986	0.00014	0.99973	0.00003	3.64003
3.65	0.99987	0.00013	0.99974	0.00003	3.65003
3.66	0.99987	0.00013	0.99975	0.00003	3.66003
3.67	0.99988	0.00012	0.99976	0.00003	3.67003
3.68	0.99988	0.00012	0.99977	0.00003	3.68003
3.69	0.99989	0.00011	0.99978	0.00003	3.69003
3.70	0.99989	0.00011	0.99978	0.00003	3.70003
3.71	0.99990	0.00010	0.99979	0.00002	3.71002
3.72	0.99990	0.00010	0.99980	0.00002	3.72002
3.73	0.99990	0.00010	0.99981	0.00002	3.73002
3.74	0.99991	0.00009	0.99982	0.00002	3.74002
3.75	0.99991	0.00009	0.99982	0.00002	3.75002
3.76	0.99992	0.00008	0.99983	0.00002	3.76002
3.77	0.99992	0.00008	0.99984	0.00002	3.77002
3.78	0.99992	0.00008	0.99984	0.00002	3.78002
3.79	0.99992	0.00008	0.99985	0.00002	3.79002
3.80	0.99993	0.00007	0.99986	0.00002	3.80002
3.81	0.99993	0.00007	0.99986	0.00002	3.81002
3.82	0.99993	0.00007	0.99987	0.00002	3.82002
3.83	0.99994	0.00006	0.99987	0.00001	3.83001
3.84	0.99994	0.00006	0.99988	0.00001	3.84001
3.85	0.99994	0.00006	0.99988	0.00001	3.85001
3.86	0.99994	0.00006	0.99989	0.00001	3.86001
3.87	0.99995	0.00005	0.99989	0.00001	3.87001
3.88	0.99995	0.00005	0.99990	0.00001	3.88001
3.89	0.99995	0.00005	0.99990	0.00001	3.89001
3.90	0.99995	0.00005	0.99990	0.00001	3.90001
3.91	0.99995	0.00005	0.99991	0.00001	3.91001
3.92	0.99996	0.00004	0.99991	0.00001	3.92001
3.93	0.99996	0.00004	0.99992	0.00001	3.93001
3.94	0.99996	0.00004	0.99992	0.00001	3.94001
3.95	0.99996	0.00004	0.99992	0.00001	3.95001
3.96	0.99996	0.00004	0.99993	0.00001	3.96001
3.97	0.99996	0.00004	0.99993	0.00001	3.97001
3.98	0.99997	0.00003	0.99993	0.00001	3.98001
3.99	0.99997	0.00003	0.99993	0.00001	3.99001
4.00	0.99997	0.00003	0.99994	0.00001	4.00001

References

A

Ackoff, R. L. 1991. *Ackoff's Fables: Irreverent Reflections on Business and Bureaucracy.* New York: Wiley.

Aldeman, L. 1998. "Computing with DNA." *Scientific American,* August, pp. 54–61.

Andrews, E. L., and K. Bradsher. 2000. "DaimlerChrysler: New Model Looks Like Lemon." *New York Times,* December 2.

Ansberry, C. 2002. "A New Hazard for Recovery: Last-Minute Pace of Orders." *The Wall Street Journal,* June 25, pp. A1, A12.

Ante, S. E. 2000. "The Second Coming of Software." *BusinessWeek,* June 19, pp. 88–90.

APICS—The Performance Advantage. 1999. "Managing the Supply Chain: Important but Difficult." July, p. 4.

Apte, U. M., and C. C. Reynolds. 1995. "Quality Management at Kentucky Fried Chicken." *Interfaces* 25, no. 3, pp. 6–21.

Aviv, Y., and A. Federgruen. 2001. "Capacitated Multi-Item Inventory Systems with Random and Seasonally Fluctuating Demands: Implications for Postponement Strategies." *Management Science* 47, no. 4, pp. 512–31.

B

Baker, K. R. 2005. *Elements of Sequencing and Scheduling.* Hanover, NH: Dartmouth College.

Bakos, Y., and E. Brynjolfsson. 1999. "Bundling Information Goods: Pricing, Profits, and Efficiency." *Management Science* 45, pp. 1613–30.

Baldwin, C. Y., and K. B. Clark. 1997. "Managing in an Age of Modularity." *Harvard Business Review,* September/October, pp. 84–93.

Ballou, R. H. 1999. *Business Logistics Management.* Upper Saddle River, NJ: Prentice Hall.

Ballou, R. H., S. M. Gilbert, and A. Mukherjee. 1999. "Managing in the New Era of Multi-Enterprise Supply Chains." *Proceedings of the 28th Annual Transportation and Logistics Educators Conference.* Toronto, Ontario, October 17, pp. 23–38.

Bazerman, M. H., and W. F. Samuelson. 1983. "I Won the Auction but Don't Want the Prize." *Journal of Conflict Resolution* 27, pp. 618–34.

Benford, F. 1938. "The Law of Anomalous Numbers." *Proceedings of the American Philosophical Society* 78, p. 551.

Black, H. S. 1977. "Inventing the Negative Feedback Amplifier." *IEEE Spectrum,* pp. 55–60.

Bosak, J., and T. Bray. 1999. "XML and the Second-Generation Web." *Scientific American,* May, pp. 89–93.

Bowersox, D. J. 1974. *Logistical Management.* New York: Macmillan Publishing.

Boyer, K. D. 1997. *Principles of Transportation Economics.* Reading, MA: Addison-Wesley.

Brondmo, H. P. 2000. *The Eng@ged Customer: The New Rules of Internet Direct Marketing.* New York: Harper Business.

Bronson, P. 1999. *The Nudist on the Late Shift.* New York: Random House.

Brooker, K. 2002. "Jim Kilts Is an Old-School Curmudgeon." *Fortune,* December 30, pp. 95–102.

Brown, G., and H. Heinzel. 2001. "Intel-Siemens Project: Chandler Workshop." SCOR Research Study, February, www.supply-chain.org/(accessed November 10, 2004).

Brown, R. G. 1963. *Smoothing, Forecasting and Prediction of Discrete Time Series.* Englewood Cliffs, NJ: Prentice Hall.

———. 1967. *Decision Rules for Inventory Management.* New York: Holt, Rinehart and Winston.

Burchett, C. 2000. "Mobile Virtual Enterprises—The Future of Electronic Business and Consumer Services." *Proceedings from the Academia/Industry Working Conference on Research Challenges.* Buffalo, NY, April 27–29.

Burt, D. N., D. W. Dobler, and S. L. Starling. 2003. *World Class Supply Management.* New York: McGraw-Hill/Irwin.

BusinessWeek. 2001. "Web Smart for a Changed World." October 29, pp. EB18–20.

Bylinsky, G. 2001. "The E-Factory Catches On: Huge Increases in Productivity Result When Customers Can Design the Products They Want and Send Orders Straight to the Plant Floor via the Internet." *Fortune* 144, no. 2 (July 23), p. 200.

Byrne, J. A. 2000. "Management by Web." *BusinessWeek,* August 28, pp. 84–96.

C

Cachon, G. P., and M. A. Lariviere. 2001. "Turning the Supply Chain into a Revenue Chain." *Harvard Business Review,* March, pp. 20–21.

———. 2005. "Supply Chain Coordination with Revenue-Sharing Contracts: Strengths and Limitations." *Management Science* 51, no. 1, pp. 30–44.

Callioni, G., and C. Billington. 2001. "Effective Collaboration." *OR/MS Today,* October, pp. 34–39.

Camuffo, A., P. Romano, and A. Vinelli. 2001. "Back to the Future: Benetton Transforms Its Global Network." *Sloan Management Review,* Fall, pp. 46–52.

Capen, E. C., R. V. Clapp, and W. M. Campbell. 1971. "Competitive Bidding in High-Risk Situations." *Journal of Petroleum Technology* 23, pp. 641–53.

Carley, W. M. 1997. "To Keep GE's Profits Rising, Welch Pushes Quality-Control Plan." *The Wall Street Journal,* January 13, pp. A1, A8.

Carlton, J. 1995. "Fading Shine: What's Eating Apple?" *The Wall Street Journal,* September 21, p. A1.

Caroll, P., J. Carlton, and J. Rigdon. 1996. "Next Task at Apple: First Order, Then Orders." *The Wall Street Journal,* February 5, p. A3.

Cassing, J., and R. W. Douglas. 1980. "Implications of the Auction Mechanism in Baseball's Free Agent Draft." *Southern Economic Journal* 47, pp. 110–21.

Cayirli, T., and E. Veral. 2003. "Outpatient Scheduling in Health Care: A Review of the Literature." *Production and Operations Management* 12, no. 4, pp. 519–49.

Chabrow, E. 2002. "Survey: Internet Key to Collaboration." *Information Week,* February 6.

Charny, B. 2002. "Is Wi-Fi Ready to Roam?" *ZDNet News,* September 11, http://netscape.com.com/2100-1105-957411.html?type=pt.

Chen, F. 2000. "Sales-Force Incentives and Inventory Management." *Manufacturing & Service Operations Management* 2, pp. 186–202.

Chopra, S., and P. Meindl. 2004. *Supply Chain Management: Strategy, Planning, and Operation.* 2nd ed. Upper Saddle River, NJ: Pearson/Prentice Hall.

Christaller, W. 1966. *Central Places in Southern Germany: The Pioneer Work in Theoretical Economic Geography.* Translated by C. Baskin. Englewood Cliffs, NJ: Prentice Hall.

Christensen-Szalanski, J. J. J., and J. B. Bushyhead. 1981. "Physicians' Use of Probabilistic Information in a Real Clinical Setting." *Journal of Experimental Psychology: Human Perception and Performance* 7, pp. 928–35.

Cialdini, R. B. 2001. "The Science of Persuasion." *Scientific American,* February, pp. 76–81.

Colvin, G. 1999. "A Century of Business." *Fortune* 139, no. 8 (April 26), pp. 499–500.

Cook, T. M. 1998. "Sabre Soars." *OR/MS Today,* June.

Copacino, W. 1999. "Keynote Address." *Proceedings of the 28th Annual Transportation and Logistics Educators Conference.* Toronto, Ontario, October 17, pp. 1–22.

Corbett, C. J., and G. A. DeCroix. 2001. "Materials in Supply Chains: Channel Profits and Environmental Impacts." *Management Science* 47, no. 7, pp. 881–93.

Coy, P. 1999. "Exploiting Uncertainty." *BusinessWeek,* June 7, pp. 120–25.

Coyle, J. J., E. J. Bardi, and R. A. Novak. 2006. *Transportation.* 6th ed. Cincinnati, OH: South-Western College Pub.

Croson, R., and K. Donohue. 2003. "Impact of POS Data Sharing on Supply Chain Management: An Experimental Study." *Production and Operations Management* 12, no. 1, pp. 1–11.

Cutler, J. M., Jr. 2006. *Rules of the Game: Legal and Regulatory Issues Facing the Supply Chain Manager.* Oak Brook, IL: Council of Supply Chain Management Professionals.

D

Daganzo, C. F. 1999. *Logistics Systems Analysis.* 3rd ed. New York: Springer.

Davidson, C. 1996. "Christine Downton's Brain." *Wired,* December.

de Treville, S. 1992. "Time Is Money." *OR/MS Today,* October, pp. 30–34.

Deming, W. E. 1950. *Some Theory of Sampling.* New York: Wiley.

———. 1960. *Sample Design in Business Research.* New York: Wiley.

———. 1982. *Quality Productivity and Competitive Position.* Cambridge, MA: MIT, Center for Advanced Engineering Study.

———. 1986. *Out of Crisis.* Cambridge, MA: MIT Press.

Diebold, J. 1952. *Automation: The Advent of the Automatic Factory.* Princeton, NJ: D. Van Nostrand Company.

Downes, L., and M. Chunka. 1998. *Unleashing the Killer App: Digital Strategies for Market Dominance.* Boston: Harvard Business School Press.

Drucker, P. 1962. "The Economy's Dark Continent." *Fortune* 103, no. 4, pp. 265, 268, 270.

E

Edgeworth, F. 1888. "The Mathematical Theory of Banking." *Journal of the Royal Statistical Society* 51, pp. 113–27.

Edmondson, G., and S. Baker. 1997. "Silicon Valley on the Rhine." *BusinessWeek,* November 3, pp. 162–67.

Elmaghraby, W. J. 2000. "Supply Contract Competition and Sourcing Policies." *Manufacturing & Service Operations Management* 2, pp. 350–71.

Eppen, G. D. 1979. "Effects of Centralization on Expected Costs in a Multi-Location Newsboy Problem." *Management Science* 25, no. 5, pp. 498–501.

Eppen, G. D., and A. V. Iyer. 1997. "Improved Fashion Buying Using Bayesian Updates." *Operations Research* 45, no. 6, pp. 805–19.

Erlenkotter, D. 1989. "The General Optimal Market Area Model." *Annals of Operations Research* 18, pp. 45–70.

Euclid. 1956. *The Thirteen Books of Euclid's Elements.* Vol. 1. Edited by Sir Thomas Heath. New York: Dover.

Evans, J. R. 1991. *Creative Thinking in the Decision and Management Sciences.* Cincinnati, OH: South-Western.

F

Feigenbaum, A. V. 1956. "Total Quality Control." *Harvard Business Review,* November/December, pp. 93–101.

———. 1961. *Total Quality Control: Engineering and Management.* New York: McGraw-Hill.

Feitzinger, E., and H. L. Lee. 1997. "Mass-Customization at Hewlett-Packard: The Power of Postponement." *Harvard Business Review,* January/February, pp. 116–21.

Feller, W. 1965. *An Introduction to Probability Theory and Its Applications.* Vol. II. New York: Wiley.

Ferdows, K., M. A. Lewis, and J. A. D. Machuca. 2004. "Rapid-Fire Fulfillment." *Harvard Business Review,* November, pp. 104–11.

Ferguson, M. E. 2003. "When to Commit in a Serial Supply Chain with Forecast Updating." *Naval Research Logistics* 50, no. 8, pp. 917–36.

Fichman, R. G., and S. A. Moses. 1999. "An Incremental Process for Software Implementation." *Sloan Management Review,* Winter, pp. 39–52.

Fierman, J. 1995. "Winning Ideas from Maverick Managers." *Fortune* 131, no. 2 (February 6), pp. 66–71.

Fisher, M. L. 1997. "What Is the Right Supply Chain for Your Product?" *Harvard Business Review,* March/April, pp. 105–16.

Fisher, M. L., J. H. Hammond, W. R. Obermeyer, and A. Raman. 1994. "Making Supply Meet Demand in an Uncertain World." *Harvard Business Review,* May/June, pp. 83–93.

Fisher, M. L., A. Raman, and A. S. McClelland. 2000. "Rocket Science Retailing Is Almost Here: Are You Ready?" *Harvard Business Review,* July/August, pp. 115–24.

Fonstad, J. 2000. "From the Ground Floor: Where's the Beef?" *Red Herring,* July, pp. 122–24.

Forrester, J. W. 1961. *Industrial Dynamics.* Boston: MIT Press.

Fortune. 2002a. "500 Largest U.S. Corporations." Vol. 145, no. 8 (April 15), pp. F1–F71.

Fortune. 2002b. "The World's Largest Corporations." Vol. 146, no. 2 (July 22), p. F1.

Friedman, T. L. 2006. *The World Is Flat: A Brief History of the Twenty-First Century.* Expanded and updated ed. New York: Farrar, Straus and Giroux.

Fries, B. E., and V. P. Marathe. 1981. "Determination of

Optimal Variable-Sized Multiple-Block Appointment Systems." *Operations Research* 29, no. 2, pp. 324–45.

Fuller, G. 1991. *The Negotiator's Handbook.* Englewood Cliffs, NJ: Prentice Hall.

G

Gans, N., G. Koole, and A. Mandelbaum. 2003. "Telephone Call Centers: Tutorial, Review, and Research Prospects." *Manufacturing & Service Operations Management* 5, no. 2, pp. 79–141.

Geoffrion, A. M. 1976. "The Purpose of Mathematical Programming Is Insight, Not Numbers." *Interfaces* 7, no. 1, pp. 81–92.

Gershenfeld, N., and I. L. Chuang. 1998. "Quantum Computing with Molecules." *Scientific American,* June, pp. 66–71.

Gilliland, M. 2002. "Is Forecasting a Waste of Time?" *Supply Chain Management Review,* July.

Goldstein, L. 1998. "Clever Calvin Sells Suits Like Socks." *Fortune,* November 23, p. 62.

Greising, D. 1994. "Quality: How to Make It Pay?" *BusinessWeek,* August 8, pp. 54–57.

Gross, D., and C. M. Harris. 1998. *Fundamentals of Queueing Theory.* 3rd ed. New York: John Wiley & Sons.

Gullberg, J. 1997. *Mathematics: From the Birth of Numbers.* New York: W.W. Norton.

Gurley, B. 2001. "When It Comes to Pricing Software, the Greener Grass Is Hard to Find." *Fortune,* November 13.

H

Hall, R. W. 1997. *Queueing Methods.* Upper Saddle River, NJ: Prentice Hall.

Hamm, S. 2001. "The Tech Challenge." *BusinessWeek,* August 27, pp. 140–44.

Harmon, R. L., and L. D. Peterson. 1990. *Reinventing the Factory.* New York: Free Press.

Hart, B. 2005. "The Next Stage in Integrating Trade Finance with the Global Supply Chain." *World Trade* 18, no. 11 (November), pp. 26–28.

Harvard Business Review. 2004. "HBR Spotlight: The 21st Century Supply Chain." October, p. 100.

Hayes, B. 2002. "The Killing by the Numbers." *Wired,* September, pp. 81–82.

Hayes, R. H., and S. C. Wheelwright. 1979. "Link Manufacturing Process and Product Life Cycles." *Harvard Business Review,* January/February, pp. 133–40.

Hendricks, K. B., and V. R. Singhal. 2003. "The Effect of Supply Chain Glitches on Shareholder Wealth." *Journal of Operations Management* 21, no. 5, pp. 501–22.

Henig, P. D. 2000. "Revenge of the Bricks." *Red Herring,* August, pp. 121–34.

Hilary, G., and L. Menzly. 2006. "Does Past Success Lead Analysts to Become Overconfident." *Management Science* 52, no. 4, pp. 489–500.

Hill , T. P. 1995. "A Statistical Derivation of the Significant-Digit Law." *Statistical Science* 10, pp. 354–63.

———. 1998. "The First-Digit Phenomenon." *American Scientist,* July/August.

Holstein, W. J. 2001. "Old Dogs, New Tricks: Using the Internet . . . and, Yes, Getting Their Groove Back." *US News & World Report,* February 26, pp. 38–40.

Hopp, W. J., and M. L. Spearman. 2001. *Factory Physics.* 2nd ed. New York: McGraw-Hill/Irwin.

Hopp, W. J., E. Tekin, and M. P. Van Oyen. 2004. "Benefits of Skill Chaining in Serial Production Lines with Cross-Trained Workers." *Management Science* 50, no. 1, pp. 83–98.

Houlihan, J. B. 1985. "International Supply Chain Management." *International Journal of Physical Distribution & Materials Management* 15, no. 1, pp. 22–38.

Huff, D. L. 1962. "A Probabilistic Analysis of Consumer Spatial Behavior." In *Emerging Concepts in Marketing,* ed. W. S. Decker. Chicago: American Marketing Association.

J

Jacka, J. M., and P. J. Keller. 2002. *Business Process Mapping.* New York: John Wiley & Sons.

Jackson, D. 2006. "Dependable Software by Design." *Scientific American* 294, no. 6 (June), pp. 68–75.

Jackson, P. 1957. "Networks of Waiting Lines." *Operations Research* 5, pp. 518–21.

Jeuland, A. P., and S. M. Shugan. 1983. "Managing Channel Profits." *Marketing Science* 2, no. 3, pp. 239–72.

Johnson, D. S. 1973. *Near-Optimal Bin Packing Algorithms.* Doctoral thesis, Department of Mathematics, MIT, Cambridge, MA.

Johnson, M. E., and S. Whang. 2002. "E-Business and Supply Chain Management: An Overview and Framework." *Production and Operations Management* 11, no. 4, pp. 413–23.

Joiner Associates Staff. 1995. *Flowcharts: Plain and Simple.* Madison, WI: Joiner Associates Inc.

Jourard, R. 2000. "McSorley Found Guilty of Assault with Weapon." *Criminal Lawyer,* October 17, www.criminal-lawyer.on.ca/hockey-assault.html.

Juran, J. M. 1964. *Managerial Breakthrough.* New York: McGraw-Hill.

———. 1989. *Juran on Leadership for Quality: An Executive Handbook.* New York: Free Press.

———. 1992. *Juran on Quality by Design: The New Steps for Planning Quality into Goods and Services.* New York: Free Press.

Juran, J. M. (ed.), and F. M. Gryna (assoc. ed.). 1988. *Juran's Quality Control Handbook.* 4th ed. New York: McGraw-Hill.

K

Kagel, J. H., and D. Levin. 2002. *Common Value Auctions and the Winner's Curse.* Princeton, NJ: Princeton University Press.

Kahneman, D., P. Slovic, and A. Tversky (eds.). 1982. *Judgment under Uncertainty: Heuristics and Biases.* Cambridge: Cambridge University Press.

Kahneman, D., and A. Tversky. 1979. "Prospect Theory: An Analysis of Decision under Risk." *Econometrica* 4, pp. 263–91.

Kaihla, P. 2002. "Inside Cisco's $2 Billion Blunder." *Business 2.0,* March.

Keenan, F. 2001. "The Marines Learn New Tactics—From Wal-Mart: To Fix Its Supply Chains, the Corps Studied the Private Sector." *BusinessWeek,* December 24, p. 74.

Kendall, M. G. 1943. *The Advanced Theory of Statistics.* London: Charles Griffin & Co.

Kephart, J. O., and A. R. Greenwald. 2000. "When Bots Collide." *Harvard Business Review,* July/August, pp. 17–18.

Kerstetter, J. 2001. "When Machines Chat." *BusinessWeek,* July 23, pp. 76–77.

Kerwin, K., M. Stepanek, and D. Welch. 2000. "At Ford, E-Commerce Is Job 1." *BusinessWeek,* February 28, pp. 74–78.

Khintchine, A. Y. 1960. *Mathematical Methods in the Theory of Queueing.* Translated by D. M. Andrews and M. H. Quenouille. London: Charles Griffin & Co.

Knoeppel, C. E. 1911. "Maximum Production in Machine-Shop and Foundry." *Engineering Magazine* (New York).

Knüsel, L. 2005. "On the Accuracy of Statistical Distributions in Microsoft Excel 2003." *Computational Statistics & Data Analysis* 48, pp. 445–49.

Knuth, D. 1969. *The Art of Computer Programming.* Vol. 2. Reading, MA: Addison-Wesley.

Kratz, E. F. 2005. "Marked Down." *Fortune* 152, no. 4 (August 22), pp. 103–7.

L

LaGesse, D. 2006. "Makeover Artist." *U.S. News & World Report,* June 19, pp. EE2–EE4.

Lambert, D. M. 1975. *The Development of an Inventory Costing Methodology: A Study of the Costs Associated with Holding Inventory.* Chicago: National Council of Physical Distribution Management.

Lambert, D. M., and A. M. Knemeyer. 2004. "We're in This Together." *Harvard Business Review,* December, pp. 114–23.

Laseter, T., and K. Oliver. 2003. "When Will Supply Chain Management Grow Up?" *Strategy + Business,* no. 32 (Fall), pp. 1–5.

Lee, H. L. 2004. "The Triple-A Supply Chain." *Harvard Business Review,* October, pp. 102–13.

Lee, H. L., V. Padmanabhan, and S. Whang. 1997a. "The Bullwhip Effect in Supply Chains." *Sloan Management Review* 38, no. 3, pp. 93–103.

———. 1997b. "Information Distortion in a Supply Chain: The Bullwhip Effect." *Management Science* 43, no. 4, pp. 546–58.

Leibs, S. 2001. "Shipment Fever." *CFO Magazine,* September 1.

Lewis, M. 2003. *Moneyball.* New York: W.W. Norton.

Lichtenstein, S., and B. Fischhoff. 1977. "Do Those Who Know More Also Know More about How Much They Know? The Calibration of Probability Judgments." *Organizational Behavior and Human Performance* 20, pp. 159–83.

Lichtenstein, S., B. Fischhoff, and L. D. Phillips. 1992. "Calibration of Probabilities: The State of the Art to 1980." In *Judgment under Uncertainty: Heuristics and Biases,* ed. D. Kahneman, P. Slovic, and A. Tversky. Cambridge: Cambridge University Press, pp. 306–34.

Liker, J. K., and T. Y. Choi. 2004. "Building Deep Supplier Relationships." *Harvard Business Review,* December, pp. 104–14.

Lipin, S. 1993. "A New Vision: Citicorp's Reed, Once a Big Thinker, Gets Down to Basics." *The Wall Street Journal,* June 25, pp. A1, A4.

Little, D. 2000. "3M: Glued to the Web." *BusinessWeek,* November 20, pp. EB64–66.

Little, J. D. C. 1961. "A Proof for the Queueing Formula: $L = \lambda W$." *Operations Research* 9, pp. 383–87.

Loomis, C. 2001. "Warren Buffet on the Stock Market." *Fortune* 144, no. 12 (December 10), pp. 80–94.

Lösch, A. 1954. *The Economics of Location.* Translated by W. H. Woglom. New Haven, CT: Yale University Press.

Lynch, R. P. 1998. *Negotiations Guide.* Providence, RI: The Warren Company.

M

Maister, D. 1984. "The Psychology of Waiting Lines." Harvard Business School Publication 9-684-064.

McAuley, J. 2001. "Big Picture: Goodbye to Just-in-Time Inventories?" *The Wall Street Journal,* October 10.

McKay, K. N. 2003. "Historical Survey of Production Control Practices." *International Journal of Production Research* 41, no. 3, pp. 411–26.

McManus, N. 2002. "Why Telemarketing Is Evil." *Wired,* November, p. 38.

Mentzer, J. T., and M. A. Moon. 2004. "Understanding Demand." *Supply Chain Management Review,* May/June, pp. 38–45.

N

Nadel, B. 2006. "Tag, You're It!" *Fortune* 153, no. 10 (May 29), pp. s1–s5.

Narayanan, V. G., and A. Raman. 2004. "Aligning Incentives in Supply Chains." *Harvard Business Review,* November, pp. 94–103.

Naslund, S. J. 2000. *Ahab's Wife.* New York: Perennial.

Nelson, E., and A. Zimmerman. 2000. "Kimberly-Clark Keeps Costco in Diapers, Absorbing Costs Itself." *The Wall Street Journal,* September 7, pp. A1, A12.

Netessine, S., G. Dobson, and R. A. Shumsky. 2002. "Flexible Service Capacity: Optimal Investment and the Impact of Demand Correlation." *Operations Research* 50, no. 2, pp. 375–88.

Newcomb, S. 1881. "Note on the Frequency of the Use of Digits in Natural Numbers." *American Journal of Mathematics* 4, p. 39.

Newell, G. F. 1973. "Scheduling, Location, Transportation, and Continuum Mechanics; Some Simple Approximations to Optimization Problems." *SIAM Journal of Applied Mathematics* 25, no. 3, pp. 346–60.

Ng, E. W. 2001. "The Visibility Factor." *Computerworld Singapore,* July 20–26.

O

Ohno, T. 1988. *Toyota Production System: Beyond Large-Scale Production.* Cambridge, MA: Productivity Press. (Japanese ed. 1978.)

Ohno, T., and S. Mito. 1988. *Just-in-Time for Today and Tomorrow.* Cambridge, MA: Productivity Press. (Japanese ed. 1986.)

O'Reilly, B. 1998. "Why Johnny Can't Invest." *Fortune,* November 9, pp. 173–78.

ORMS Today. 2001. "Poisson Theory May Explain Sharks' Fishy Behavior." October, p. 25.

Oskamp, S. 1965. "Overconfidence in Case Study Judgments." *Journal of Consulting Psychology* 29, pp. 261–65.

P

Padmanabhan, V., and I. P. L. Png. 1995. *Sloan Management Review,* Fall, pp. 65–72.

Park, A., and P. Burrows. 2001. "Dell, the Conqueror." *BusinessWeek,* September 24, pp. 92–102.

Parnes, S. J., R. B. Noller, and A. M. Biondi (eds.). 1977. *Guide to Creative Action.* New York: Charles Scribner's Sons.

Perakis, G., and G. Roels. 2006. "Regret in the Newsvendor Model with Partial Information." MIT working paper.

Perkins, M. C. and A. B. Perkins. 1999. "The Economy's New Clothes." *Red Herring,* December, pp. 239–50.

Peterson, I. 1997. "Cracking a Record Number." *Science News* 151, no. 2 (May 31), p. 340.

———. 1998. "First Digits." *Science News Online,* July 27, www.sciencenews.org/sn_arc98/6_27_98/mathland.htm.

Petruzzi, N. C., and M. Dada. 1999. "Pricing and the Newsvendor Problem: A Review with Extensions." *Operations Research* 47, no. 2, pp. 183–94.

Petruzzi, N. C., and G. E. Monahan. 2003. "Managing Fashion Goods Inventories: Dynamic Recourse for Retailers with Outlet Stores." *IIE Transactions* 35, no. 11, pp. 1033–47.

Pinedo, M. 2001. *Scheduling: Theory, Algorithms, and Systems.* 2nd ed. Upper Saddle River, NJ: Prentice Hall.

Pinkham, R. S. 1961. "On the Distribution of First Significant Digits." *Annals of Mathematical Statistics* 32, pp. 1223–30.

Plous, S. 1993. *The Psychology of Judgment and Decision Making.* New York: McGraw-Hill.

Porter, M. E. 1998. Competitive Advantage: Creating and Sustaining Superior Performance. New York: Free Press.

PricewaterhouseCoopers. 1999. "Global Study Finds Business Process Outsourcing Is Driving Organizational Change at the Nation's Largest Companies." April 1, www.pwcglobal.com (accessed November 24, 2002).

R

Raimi, R. A. 1969. "The Peculiar Distribution of First Digits." *Scientific American,* December, pp. 109–19.

Raman, A., and B. Kim. 2002. "Quantifying the Impact of Inventory Holding Cost and Reactive Capacity on an Apparel Manufacturer's Profitability." *Production and Operations Management* 11, no. 3, pp. 358–73.

Randolph, W. A., and B.Z. Posner. 1992. *Getting the Job Done! Managing Project Teams and Task Forces for Success.* Englewood Cliffs, NJ: Prentice Hall.

Rao, C. R. 1989. *Statistics and Truth.* New Delhi: Council of Scientific & Industrial Research.

Regis, E. 2000. "Greetings from the Info Mesa." *Wired,* June, pp. 337–45.

Rehring, E. 2005. "Wal-Mart Tags RFID Benefits." *Traffic World,* October 31, p. 1.

Reingen, P. H., and J. B. Kernan. 1993. "Social Perception and Interpersonal Influence: Some Consequences of the Physical Attractiveness Stereotype in a Personal Selling Setting." *Journal of Consumer Psychology* 2, pp. 25–38.

Reinhardt, A. 2001. "Fisher Scientific UK." *BusinessWeek,* October 29, pp. EB22–24.

Richardson, L. F. 1956. "Mathematics of War and Foreign Politics." In *The World of Mathematics.* Vol. 2. New York: Simon & Schuster, pp. 1240–63.

Richtel, M. 2006. "The Long-Distance Journey of a Fast-Food Order." *New York Times,* April 11.

Rivett, P. 1994. *The Craft of Decision Modeling.* New York: Wiley.

Robinson, A. G., and S. Sterm. 1997. *Corporate Creativity: How Innovation and Improvement Actually Happen.* San Francisco, CA: Berrett-Koehler.

Roche, E. 2000. "Explaining XML." *Harvard Business Review,* July/August, p. 18.

Rock, K. 1986. "Why New Issues Are Underpriced." *Journal of Financial Economics* 15, pp. 187–212.

Rocks, D. 2000. "Dell's Second Web Revolution." *BusinessWeek,* September 18, pp. EB62–63.

Rocks, D., A. M. Pascual, D. Little, and J. Brown. 2001. "The Net as a Lifeline." *BusinessWeek,* October 29, pp. EB16–23.

Roll, R. 1986. "The Hubris Hypothesis of Corporate Takeovers." *Journal of Business* 59, pp. 197–216.

Rosato, D. 1998. "Giving Up Jet Seat Can Be Ticket to Free Ride." *USA Today,* April 28, p. 5B.

Rosenbluth, H. 1991. "Tales from a Nonconformist Company." *Harvard Business Review,* July/August, pp. 26–35.

Ross, S. 1988. *A First Course in Probability.* 3rd ed. New York: Macmillan Publishing.

Roundy, R. 1985. "98%-Effective Integer-Ratio Lot-Sizing for One-Warehouse Multi-Retailer Systems." *Management Science* 31, pp. 1416–30.

S

Sahin, F., and E. P. Robinson. 2002. "Flow Coordination and Information Sharing in Supply Chains: Review, Implications, and Directions for Future Research." *Production and Operations Management* 33, no. 4, pp. 505–36.

Sales Manager's Bulletin. 1996. Sales Process Systems, Cupertino, CA.

Samuelson, D. A. 1999. "Predictive Dialing for Outbound Telephone Call Centers." *Interfaces* 29, no. 5, pp. 66–81.

Saporito, B. 1994. "Behind the Tumult at P&G." *Fortune* 129, no. 5 (March 7), pp. 74–80.

Savage, S. 2003. "Weapons of Mass Instruction." *ORMS Today* 30, no. 4 (August), pp. 36–40.

Schonfeld, E. 1998. "The Squeeze Is On for PC Makers." *Fortune* 137, no. 7 (April 13), pp. 182–86.

Schrage, M. 2001. "Make No Mistake?" *Fortune,* December 24, p. 184.

Schiller, Z., G. Burns, and K. L. Miller. 1996. "Make It Simple." *BusinessWeek,* September 9, pp. 96–104.

Schwartz, B. 2004. "The Tyranny of Choice." *Scientific American,* April, pp. 70–75.

Schwartz, J. 2000. "U.S. Selects New Encryption Technique," *New York Times,* October 3.

Sebenius, J. K. 2001. "Six Habits of Merely Effective Negotiators." *Harvard Business Review,* March/April, pp. 87–95.

Serwer, A. E. 1994. "McDonald's Conquers the World." *Fortune* 130, no. 8 (October 17), pp. 103–9.

Shannon, C. E. 1948. "A Mathematical Theory of Communication." *Bell System Technical Journal* 27 (July and October), pp. 379–423, 623–56.

Sheffi, Y. 2004. "Combinatorial Auctions in the Procurement of Transportation Services." *Interfaces* 34, no. 4, pp. 245–52.

———. 2005. *The Resilient Enterprise.* Cambridge, MA: MIT Press.

Shingo, S. 1985. *A Revolution in Manufacturing: The SMED System.* Cambridge, MA: Productivity Press.

Simchi-Levi, D., X. Chen, and J. Bramel. 2005. *The Logic of Logistics: Theory, Algorithms, and Applications for Logistics and Supply Chain Management.* 2nd ed. New York: Springer Science + Business Media.

Slone, R. E. 2004. "Leading a Supply Chain Turnaround." *Harvard Business Review,* October, pp. 114–22.

Slywotzky, A. 2001. "Standing Tall in the Tech Slump." *Fortune,* February 5, pp. 176–78.

Spengler, J. J. 1950. "Vertical Integration and Antitrust Policy." *Journal of Political Economy* 58, no. 4, pp. 347–52.

Stapleton, D. M., and V. Saulnier. 1999. "Defining Dyadic Cost and Risk in International Trade: A Review of INCOTERMS 2000 with Strategic Implications." *Journal of Transportation Management* 11, no. 2 (Fall), pp. 25–44.

Sterman, J. D. 2000. *Business Dynamics.* New York: Irwin McGraw-Hill.

Stewart, T. A. 1999. "Larry Bossidy's New Role Model: Michael Dell: Fear and Anxiety in the Old Economy." *Fortune* 139, no. 7 (April 12), p. 166.

Stile, C. 2000. "Traffic Carries a Price Tag." *Bergen Record,* March 21.

Stolle, J. F. 1967. "How to Manage Physical Distribution." *Harvard Business Review.* July/August, pp. 95–102.

Stuart, F. I., and D. M. McCutcheon. 2000. "The Manager's Guide to Supply Chain Management." *Business Horizons,* March/April, pp. 35–44.

Suri, R. 1998. Quick Response Manufacturing: A Companywide Approach to Reducing Lead Times. Portland, OR: Productivity Press.

———. 2003. "QRM and POLCA: A Winning Combination for Manufacturing Enterprises in the 21st Century." Technical Report, Center for Quick Response Manufacturing, University of Wisconsin–Madison, May, www.qrmcenter.org.

Suri, R., and A. Krishnamurthy. 2003. "How to Plan and Implement POLCA: A Material Control System for High-Variety or Custom-Engineered Products." Technical Report, Center for Quick Response Manufacturing, University of Wisconsin–Madison, May, www.qrmcenter.org. Surowiecki, J. 2003. "EZ Does It." *New Yorker,* September 8, p. 36.

Suzaki, K. 1987. *The New Manufacturing Challenge.* New York: Free Press.

T

Talluri, K. T., and G. J. van Ryzin. 2004. *The Theory and Practice of Revenue Management.* Berlin, Germany: Springer Science + Business Media.

Thaler, R. H. 1994. *The Winner's Curse: Paradoxes and Anomalies of Economic Life.* Princeton, NJ: Princeton University Press.

Thompson, L. 2001. *The Mind and Heart of the Negotiator.* Upper Saddle River, NJ: Prentice Hall.

Tilin, A. 2001. "Slick as Teflon! Tough as Kevlar! Limber as Lycra!" *Wired,* October, pp. 159–63.

Tsay, A. A. 1999. "The Quantity Flexibility Contract and Supplier-Customer Incentives." *Management Science* 45, no. 10, pp. 1339–58.

———. 2001. "Managing Retail Channel Overstock: Markdown Money and Return Policies." *Journal of Retailing* 77, pp. 457–92.

Tsay, A. A, S. Nahmias, and N. Agrawal. 1999. "Modeling Supply Chain Contracts: A Review." In *Quantitative Models for Supply Chain Management,* ed. S. Tayur, R. Ganeshan, and M. Magazine, pp. 299–336. Boston: Kluwer Academic Publishers.

Tully, S. 1994. "Raiding a Company's Hidden Cash." *Fortune,* August 24.

Tversky, A., and D. Kahneman. 1992. "Advances in Prospect Theory: Cumulative Representation of Uncertainty." *Journal of Risk and Uncertainty* 5, pp. 297–323.

U

U.S. Department of Commerce. 2003. "Digital Economy 2003." December, www.esa.doc.gov/.

V

Van Mieghem, J. A. 2003. "Capacity Management, Investment, and Hedging: Review and Recent Developments." *Manufacturing & Service Operations Management* 5, no. 4, pp. 269–302.

W

The Wall Street Journal. 1989. "McClean Makes Containers Shipshape, 1956." September 29, p. B1.

Want, R. 2004. "RFID: A Key to Automating Everything." *Scientific American,* January, pp. 56–65.

Weimer, D. 1998. "A New Cat on the Hot Seat." *Business-Week,* March 9, pp. 56–58.

Whyte, C. 2001. "Collaboration Equals Domination." *iSource,* October, pp. 40–42.

Williams, P. B. 1996. *Getting a Project Done on Time: Managing People, Time, and Results.* New York: American Management Association.

Wilson, R. A. 2002. *Transportation in America.* 19th ed. Lansdowne, VA: ENO Transportation Foundation.

Wilson, R. 2005. *16th Annual State of Logistics Report.* Sponsored by the Council of Supply Chain Management Professionals and presented at the National Press Club, Washington, D.C., June 27.

Winters, P. 1960. "Forecasting Sales by Exponentially Weighted Moving Averages." *Management Science* 6, no. 3, pp. 324–42.

Wolpert, L. 1992. *The Unnatural Nature of Science.* London: Faber.

Womack, J. P., and D. T. Jones. 1994. "From Lean Production to the Lean Enterprise." *Harvard Business Review,* March/April, pp. 93–103.

———. 2003. *Lean Thinking: Banish Waste and Create Wealth in Your Corporation.* 2nd ed. New York: Free Press.

———. 2005. *Lean Solutions: How Companies and Customers Can Create Value and Wealth Together.* 2nd ed. New York: Free Press.

Womack, J. P., D. T. Jones, and D. Roos. 1991. *The Machine That Changed the World.* New York: Harper Perennial.

Y

Young, E. 2002. "Web Marketplaces That Really Work." *Fortune,* Winter, pp. 78–86.

Z

Zheng, Z., and B. Padmanabhan. 2006. "Selectively Acquiring Customer Information: A New Data Acquisition Problem and an Active Learning-Based Solution." *Management Science* 52, no. 5, pp. 697–712.

Zimmermann, P. R. 1998. "Cryptology for the Internet." *Scientific American,* October, pp. 110–15.

Zipkin, P. H. 2000. *Foundations of Inventory Management.* New York: McGraw-Hill.

Photo Credits

Index